D1634652

HANDFUL OF LEAVES

Volume Two

Handful of Leaves

VOLUME TWO:

AN ANTHOLOGY FROM THE MAJJHIMA NIKĀYA

TRANSLATED BY

Ṭhānissaro Bhikkhu
(Geoffrey DeGraff)

FOR FREE DISTRIBUTION

INQUIRIES CONCERNING THIS BOOK
MAY BE SENT TO :

Metta Forest Monastery
PO Box 1409
Valley Center, CA 92082 USA

ELECTRONIC VERSIONS OF THIS BOOK
MAY BE FOUND AT :

dhammatalks.org

PRINTED IN THE UNITED STATES OF AMERICA

Once the Blessed One was staying at Kosambī in the siṁsapā forest. Then, picking up a few siṁsapā leaves with his hand, he asked the monks, "What do you think, monks? Which are more numerous, the few siṁsapā leaves in my hand or those overhead in the siṁsapā forest?"

"The leaves in the hand of the Blessed One are few in number, lord. Those overhead in the forest are far more numerous."

"In the same way, monks, those things that I have known with direct knowledge but haven't taught are far more numerous [than what I have taught]. And why haven't I taught them? Because they aren't connected with the goal, don't relate to the rudiments of the holy life, and don't lead to disenchantment, to dispassion, to cessation, to stilling, to direct knowledge, to self-awakening, to unbinding. That's why I haven't taught them.

"And what have I taught? 'This is stress ... This is the origination of stress ... This is the cessation of stress ... This is the path of practice leading to the cessation of stress': This is what I have taught. And why have I taught these things? Because they are connected with the goal, relate to the rudiments of the holy life, and lead to disenchantment, to dispassion, to cessation, to stilling, to direct knowledge, to self-awakening, to unbinding. This is why I have taught them."

—SN 56:31

Contents

Abbreviations

AN	*Aṅguttara Nikāya*
Cv	*Cullavagga*
Dhp	*Dhammapada*
DN	*Dīgha Nikāya*
Iti	*Itivuttaka*
Khp	*Khuddakapāṭha*
MLDB	*The Middle Length Discourses of the Buddha*
MLS	*The Collection of the Middle Length Sayings*
MN	*Majjhima Nikāya*
Mv	*Mahāvagga*
SN	*Saṁyutta Nikāya*
Sn	*Sutta Nipāta*
Thag	*Theragāthā*
Thig	*Therīgāthā*
Ud	*Udāna*

References to DN, Iti, and MN are to discourse (sutta). Those to Dhp are to verse. Those to Cv and Mv are to chapter, section, and sub-section. References to other texts are to section (saṁyutta, nipāta, or vagga) and discourse.

All translations are based on the Royal Thai Edition of the Pali Canon (Bangkok: Mahāmakut Rājavidyālaya, 1982).

*The Majjhima Nikāya—
the Middle Collection—is the
second collection in the Sutta
Piṭaka. It takes its name from
the length of the discourses it
contains: shorter than those in
the Long Collection, longer than
those in the Connected and
Numerical Collections. There are
152 suttas in all. This anthology
offers complete translations of 76
of these suttas, and excerpts
from five.*

1 The Root Sequence

Mūlapariyāya Sutta

INTRODUCTION

The Buddha listed clinging to views as one of the four forms of clinging that tie the mind to the processes of suffering. He thus recommended that his followers relinquish their clinging, not only to views in their full-blown form as specific positions, but also in their rudimentary form as the categories & relationships that the mind reads into experience. This is a point he makes in the following discourse, which is apparently his response to a particular school of Brahmanical thought that was developing in his time—the Sāṅkhya, or classification school.

This school had its beginnings in the thought of Uddālaka, a ninth-century B.C. philosopher who posited a "root": an abstract principle out of which all things emanate and which remains immanent in all things. Philosophers who carried on this line of thinking offered a variety of theories, based on logic and meditative experience, about the nature of the ultimate root and about the hierarchy of the emanation. Many of their theories were recorded in the Upaniṣads and eventually developed into the classical Sāṅkhya system around the time of the Buddha.

Although the present discourse says nothing about the background of the monks listening to it, the Commentary states that before their ordination they were brahmans, and that even after their ordination they continued to interpret the Buddha's teachings in light of their previous training, which may well have been proto-Sāṅkhya. If this is so, then the Buddha's opening lines—"I will teach you the sequence of the root of all phenomena"—would have them prepared to hear his contribution to their line of thinking. And, in fact, the list of topics he covers reads like a Buddhist Sāṅkhya. Paralleling the classical Sāṅkhya, it contains 24 items, begins with the physical world (here, the four physical properties), and leads back through ever more refined & inclusive levels of being & experience, culminating with the ultimate Buddhist concept: unbinding (nibbāna). In the pattern of Sāṅkhya thought, unbinding would thus be the ultimate "root" or ground of being immanent in all things and out of which they all emanate.

However, instead of following this pattern of thinking, the Buddha attacks it at its very root: the notion of a principle in the abstract, the "in" (immanence) & "out of" (emanation) superimposed on experience. Only an uninstructed run of the mill person, he says, would read experience in this way. In contrast, a person in training should look for a different kind of "root"—the root of suffering experienced in the present—and find it in the act of delight. Developing dispassion for that delight, the trainee can then comprehend the process of coming-into-being for what it is, drop all participation in it, and thus achieve true awakening.

If the listeners present at this discourse were indeed interested in fitting Buddhist teachings into a Sāṅkhyan mold, then it's small wonder that they were displeased—one of the few places where we read of a negative reaction to the Buddha's words. They had hoped to hear his contribution to their project, but instead they hear their whole pattern of thinking & theorizing attacked as ignorant & ill-informed. The Commentary tells us, though, they were later able to overcome their displeasure and eventually attain awakening on listening to the discourse reported in AN 3:126.

Although at present we rarely think in the same terms as the Sāṅkhya philosophers, there has long been—and still is—a common tendency to create a "Buddhist" metaphysics in which the experience of emptiness, the Unconditioned, the Dharma-body, Buddha-nature, rigpa, etc., is said to function as the ground of being from which the "All"—the entirety of our sensory & mental experience—is said to spring and to which we return when we meditate. Some people think that these theories are the inventions of scholars without any direct meditative experience, but actually they have most often originated among meditators, who label (or in the words of the discourse, "perceive") a particular meditative experience as the ultimate goal, identify with it in a subtle way (as when we are told that "we are the knowing"), and then suppose that level of experience to be the ground of being out of which all other experience comes.

Any teaching that follows these lines would be subject to the same criticism that the Buddha directed against the monks who first heard this discourse.

* * *

I have heard that on one occasion the Blessed One was staying near Ukkaṭṭhā, in the shade of a royal Sal tree in the Very Blessed Forest. There he addressed the monks, "Monks!"

"Yes, lord," the monks responded to him.

The Blessed One said, "Monks, I will teach you the sequence of the root of all phenomena [or: the root sequence of all phenomena]. Listen & pay close attention. I will speak."

"As you say, lord," they responded to him.

The Blessed One said: "There is the case, monks, where an uninstructed run-of-the-mill person—who has no regard for noble ones, is not well-versed or disciplined in their Dhamma; who has no regard for people of integrity, is not well-versed or disciplined in their Dhamma—perceives earth as earth. Perceiving earth as earth, he supposes (things) about earth, he supposes (things) in earth, he supposes (things) coming out of earth, he supposes earth as 'mine,' he delights in earth. Why is that? Because he has not comprehended it, I tell you.

"He perceives water as water… fire as fire… wind as wind[1]… beings as beings… devas as devas… Pajāpati as Pajāpati… Brahmā as Brahmā… the Radiant devas as Radiant devas… the Beautiful Black devas as Beautiful Black devas… the Sky-fruit devas as Sky-fruit devas… the Conqueror as the Conqueror[2]… the dimension of the infinitude of space as the dimension of the infinitude of space… the dimension of the infinitude of consciousness as the dimension of the infinitude of consciousness… the dimension of nothingness as the dimension of nothingness… the dimension of neither perception nor non-perception as the dimension of neither perception nor non-perception[3]… the seen as the seen… the heard as the heard… the sensed as the sensed… the cognized as the cognized[4]… singleness as singleness… multiplicity as multiplicity[5]… the All as the All[6]…

"He perceives unbinding as unbinding.[7] Perceiving unbinding as unbinding, he supposes things about unbinding, he supposes things in unbinding, he supposes things coming out of unbinding, he supposes unbinding as 'mine,' he delights in unbinding. Why is that? Because he has not comprehended it, I tell you.

THE TRAINEE

"A monk who is a trainee—yearning for the unexcelled relief from bondage, his aspirations as yet unfulfilled—directly knows earth as earth. Directly knowing earth as earth, let him not suppose things about earth, let him not suppose things in earth, let him not suppose things coming out of earth, let him not suppose earth as 'mine,' let him not delight in earth. Why is that? So that he may comprehend it, I tell you.

"He directly knows water as water… fire as fire… wind as wind… beings as beings… devas as devas… Pajāpati as Pajāpati… Brahmā as Brahmā… the Radiant devas as Radiant devas… the Beautiful Black devas as Beautiful Black devas… the Sky-fruit devas as Sky-fruit devas… the Conqueror as the Conqueror… the dimension of the infinitude of space as the dimension of the infinitude of space… the dimension of the infinitude of consciousness as the dimension of the infinitude of consciousness… the dimension of nothingness as the dimension of nothingness… the dimension of neither perception nor non-perception as the dimension of neither perception nor non-perception… the seen as the seen… the heard as the heard… the sensed as the sensed… the cognized as the cognized… singleness as singleness… multiplicity as multiplicity… the All as the All…

"He directly knows unbinding as unbinding. Directly knowing unbinding as unbinding, let him not suppose things about unbinding, let him not suppose things in unbinding, let him not suppose things coming out of unbinding, let him not suppose unbinding as 'mine,' let him not delight in unbinding. Why is that? So that he may comprehend it, I tell you.

THE ARAHANT

"A monk who is a Worthy One, devoid of effluents—who has attained completion, finished the task, laid down the burden, attained the true goal, destroyed the fetters of becoming, and is released through right knowledge—directly knows earth as earth. Directly knowing earth as earth, he doesn't suppose things about earth, doesn't suppose things in earth, doesn't suppose things coming out of earth, doesn't suppose earth as 'mine,' doesn't delight in earth. Why is that? Because he has comprehended it, I tell you.

"He directly knows water as water… fire as fire… wind as wind… beings as beings… devas as devas… Pajāpati as Pajāpati… Brahmā as Brahmā… the Radiant devas as Radiant devas… the Beautiful Black devas as Beautiful Black devas… the Sky-fruit devas as Sky-fruit devas… the Conqueror as the Conqueror… the dimension of the infinitude of space as the dimension of the infinitude of space… the dimension of the infinitude of consciousness as the dimension of the infinitude of consciousness… the dimension of nothingness as the dimension of nothingness… the dimension of neither perception nor non-perception as the dimension of neither perception nor non-perception… the seen as the seen… the heard as the heard… the sensed as the sensed… the cognized as the cognized… singleness as singleness… multiplicity as multiplicity… the All as the All…

"He directly knows unbinding as unbinding. Directly knowing unbinding as unbinding, he doesn't suppose things about unbinding, doesn't suppose things in unbinding, doesn't suppose things coming out of unbinding, doesn't suppose unbinding as 'mine,' doesn't delight in unbinding. Why is that? Because he has comprehended it, I tell you.

"A monk who is a Worthy One, devoid of effluents... directly knows earth as earth. Directly knowing earth as earth, he doesn't suppose things about earth, doesn't suppose things in earth, doesn't suppose things coming out of earth, doesn't suppose earth as 'mine,' doesn't delight in earth. Why is that? Because, with the ending of passion, he is devoid of passion, I tell you.

"He directly knows water as water... the All as the All...

"He directly knows unbinding as unbinding. Directly knowing unbinding as unbinding, he doesn't suppose things about unbinding, doesn't suppose things in unbinding, doesn't suppose things coming out of unbinding, doesn't suppose unbinding as 'mine,' doesn't delight in unbinding. Why is that? Because, with the ending of passion, he is devoid of passion, I tell you.

"A monk who is a Worthy One, devoid of effluents... directly knows earth as earth. Directly knowing earth as earth, he doesn't suppose things about earth, doesn't suppose things in earth, doesn't suppose things coming out of earth, doesn't suppose earth as 'mine,' doesn't delight in earth. Why is that? Because, with the ending of aversion, he is devoid of aversion, I tell you.

"He directly knows water as water... the All as the All...

"He directly knows unbinding as unbinding. Directly knowing unbinding as unbinding, he doesn't suppose things about unbinding, doesn't suppose things in unbinding, doesn't suppose things coming out of unbinding, doesn't suppose unbinding as 'mine,' doesn't delight in unbinding. Why is that? Because, with the ending of aversion, he is devoid of aversion, I tell you.

"A monk who is a Worthy One, devoid of mental effluents... directly knows earth as earth. Directly knowing earth as earth, he doesn't suppose things about earth, doesn't suppose things in earth, doesn't suppose things coming out of earth, doesn't suppose earth as 'mine,' doesn't delight in earth. Why is that? Because, with the ending of delusion, he is devoid of delusion, I tell you.

"He directly knows water as water... the All as the All...

"He directly knows unbinding as unbinding. Directly knowing unbinding as unbinding, he doesn't suppose things about unbinding, doesn't suppose things in unbinding, doesn't suppose things coming out of unbinding, doesn't suppose unbinding as 'mine,' doesn't delight in unbinding. Why is that? Because, with the ending of delusion, he is devoid of delusion, I tell you.

THE TATHĀGATA

"The Tathāgata—a worthy one, rightly self-awakened—directly knows earth as earth. Directly knowing earth as earth, he doesn't suppose things about earth, doesn't suppose things in earth, doesn't suppose things coming out of earth, doesn't suppose earth as 'mine,' doesn't delight in earth. Why is that? Because the Tathāgata has comprehended it to the end, I tell you.

"He directly knows water as water... fire as fire... wind as wind... beings as beings... devas as devas... Pajāpati as Pajāpati... Brahmā as Brahmā... the Radiant devas as Radiant devas... the Beautiful Black devas as Beautiful Black devas... the Sky-fruit devas as Sky-fruit devas... the Conqueror as the Conqueror... the dimension of the infinitude of space as the dimension of the infinitude of space... the dimension of the infinitude of consciousness as the dimension of the infinitude of consciousness... the dimension of nothingness as the dimension of nothingness... the dimension of neither perception nor non-perception as the dimension of neither perception nor non-perception... the seen as the seen... the heard as the heard... the sensed as the sensed... the cognized as the cognized... singleness as singleness... multiplicity as multiplicity... the All as the All...

"He directly knows unbinding as unbinding. Directly knowing unbinding as unbinding, he doesn't suppose things about unbinding, doesn't suppose things in unbinding, doesn't suppose things coming out of unbinding, doesn't suppose unbinding as 'mine,' doesn't delight in unbinding. Why is that? Because the Tathāgata has comprehended it to the end, I tell you.

"The Tathāgata—a worthy one, rightly self-awakened—directly knows earth as earth. Directly knowing earth as earth, he doesn't suppose things about earth, doesn't suppose things in earth, doesn't suppose things coming out of earth, doesn't suppose earth as 'mine,' doesn't delight in earth. Why is that? Because he has known that delight is the root of suffering & stress, that from coming-into-being there is birth, and that for what has come into being there is aging & death. Therefore, with the total ending, fading away, cessation, letting go, relinquishment of craving, the Tathāgata has totally awakened to the unexcelled right self-awakening, I tell you.

"He directly knows water as water... the All as the All...

"He directly knows unbinding as unbinding. Directly knowing unbinding as unbinding, he doesn't suppose things about unbinding, doesn't suppose things in unbinding, doesn't suppose things coming out of unbinding, doesn't suppose unbinding as 'mine,' doesn't delight in unbinding. Why is that? Because he has known that delight is the root of suffering & stress, that from coming-into-being there is birth, and that for what has come into being there is aging & death. Therefore, with the total ending, fading away, cessation, letting go, relinquishment of craving, the Tathāgata has totally awakened to the unexcelled right self-awakening, I tell you."

That is what the Blessed One said. Displeased, the monks did not delight in the Blessed One's words.

NOTES

1. Earth, water, fire, and wind are the four properties that comprise the experience of physical form.

2. In this section of the list, "beings" denotes all living beings below the level of the gods. "Devas" denotes the beings in the sensual heavens. The remaining terms— Pajāpati, Brahmā, the Radiant devas, the Beautiful Black devas, the Sky-fruit devas, & the Conqueror—denote devas in the heavens of form & formlessness.

3. The dimension of the infinitude of space, the dimension of the infinitude of consciousness, the dimension of nothingness, & the dimension of neither perception nor non-perception are four formless states that can be attained in concentration.

4. "The seen, the heard, the sensed, & the cognized" is a set of terms to cover all things experienced through the six senses.

5. Singleness = experience in states of intense concentration (jhāna). Multiplicity = experience via the six senses. See MN 137.

6. "What is the All? Simply the eye & forms, ear & sounds, nose & aromas, tongue & flavors, body & tactile sensations, intellect & ideas. This is termed the All. Anyone who would say, 'Repudiating this All, I will describe another,' if questioned on what exactly might be the grounds for his assertion, would be unable to explain and, furthermore, would be put to grief. Why is that? Because it lies beyond range." — SN 35:23

For more on this topic, see *The Mind Like Fire Unbound,* Chapter 1.

7. Unbinding = nibbāna (nirvāṇa).

See also: MN 49; MN 72; MN 140; SN 12:23; AN 4:24; AN 4:199; AN 4:200; AN 9:36; AN 10:81; Ud 1:10

2 *All the Effluents*

Sabbāsava Sutta

I have heard that on one occasion the Blessed One was staying near Sāvatthī in Jeta's Grove, Anāthapiṇḍika's monastery. There he addressed the monks: "Monks!"

"Yes, lord," the monks responded to him.

The Blessed One said, "Monks, the ending of the effluents is for one who knows & sees, I tell you, not for one who doesn't know & doesn't see. For one who knows what & sees what? Appropriate attention & inappropriate attention. When a monk attends inappropriately, unarisen effluents arise, and arisen effluents increase. When a monk attends appropriately, unarisen effluents do not arise, and arisen effluents are abandoned. There are effluents to be abandoned by seeing, those to be abandoned by restraining, those to be abandoned by using, those to be abandoned by tolerating, those to be abandoned by avoiding, those to be abandoned by destroying, and those to be abandoned by developing.

"[1] And what are the effluents to be abandoned by seeing? There is the case where an uninstructed run-of-the-mill person—who has no regard for noble ones, is not well-versed or disciplined in their Dhamma; who has no regard for people of integrity, is not well-versed or disciplined in their Dhamma—doesn't discern what ideas are fit for attention or what ideas are unfit for attention. This being so, he doesn't attend to ideas fit for attention and attends (instead) to ideas unfit for attention.

"And what are the ideas unfit for attention that he attends to? Whatever ideas such that, when he attends to them, the unarisen effluent of sensuality arises in him, and the arisen effluent of sensuality increases; the unarisen effluent of becoming arises in him, and the arisen effluent of becoming increases; the unarisen effluent of ignorance arises in him, and the arisen effluent of ignorance increases. These are the ideas unfit for attention that he attends to.

"And what are the ideas fit for attention that he doesn't attend to? Whatever ideas such that, when he attends to them, the unarisen effluent of sensuality doesn't arise in him, and the arisen effluent of sensuality is abandoned; the unarisen effluent of becoming doesn't arise in him, and the arisen effluent of becoming is abandoned; the unarisen effluent of ignorance doesn't arise in him, and the arisen effluent of ignorance is abandoned. These are the ideas fit for attention that he doesn't attend to. Through his attending to ideas unfit for attention and through his not attending to ideas fit for attention, both unarisen effluents arise in him, and arisen effluents increase.

"This is how he attends inappropriately: 'Was I in the past? Was I not in the past? What was I in the past? How was I in the past? Having been what, what was I in the past? Shall I be in the future? Shall I not be in the future? What shall I be in the future? How shall I be in the future? Having been what, what shall I be in the future?' Or else he is inwardly perplexed about the immediate present: 'Am I? Am I not? What am I? How am I? Where has this being come from? Where is it bound?'

"As he attends inappropriately in this way, one of six kinds of view arises in him: The view *I have a self* arises in him as true & established, or the view *I have no self* ... or the view *It is precisely by means of self that I perceive self* ... or the view *It is precisely by means of self that I perceive not-self* ... or the view *It is precisely by means of not-self that I perceive self* arises in him as true & established, or else he has a view like this: *This very self of mine—the knower that is sensitive here & there to the ripening of good & bad actions—is the self of mine that is constant, everlasting, eternal, not subject to change, and will endure as long as eternity.* This is called a thicket of views, a wilderness of views, a contortion of views, a writhing of views, a fetter of views. Bound by a fetter of views, the uninstructed run-of-the-mill person is not freed from birth, aging, & death, from sorrow, lamentation, pain, distress, & despair. He is not freed, I tell you, from suffering & stress.

"The well-instructed disciple of the noble ones—who has regard for noble ones, is well-versed & disciplined in their Dhamma; who has regard for people of integrity, is well-versed & disciplined in their Dhamma—discerns what ideas are fit for attention and what ideas are unfit for attention. This being so, he doesn't attend to ideas unfit for attention and attends (instead) to ideas fit for attention.

"And what are the ideas unfit for attention that he doesn't attend to? Whatever ideas such that, when he attends to them, the unarisen effluent of sensuality arises in him, and the arisen effluent of sensuality increases; the unarisen effluent of becoming arises in him, and the arisen effluent of becoming increases; the unarisen effluent of ignorance arises in him, and the arisen effluent of ignorance increases. These are the ideas unfit for attention that he doesn't attend to.

"And what are the ideas fit for attention that he does attend to? Whatever ideas such that, when he attends to them, the unarisen effluent of sensuality doesn't arise in him, and the arisen effluent of sensuality is abandoned; the unarisen effluent of becoming doesn't arise in him, and the arisen effluent of becoming is abandoned; the unarisen effluent of ignorance doesn't arise in him, and the arisen effluent of ignorance is abandoned. These are the ideas fit for attention that he does attend to. Through his not attending to ideas unfit for attention and through his attending to ideas fit for attention, unarisen effluents do not arise in him, and arisen effluents are abandoned.

"He attends appropriately, *This is stress ... This is the origination of stress ... This is the cessation of stress ... This is the way leading to the cessation of stress.* As he attends appropriately in this way, three fetters are abandoned in him: self-identification view, doubt, and grasping at habits & practices. These are called the effluents to be abandoned by seeing.

"[2] And what are the effluents to be abandoned by restraining? There is the case where a monk, reflecting appropriately, dwells restrained with the restraint of the eye-faculty. The effluents, vexation, or fever that would arise if he were to dwell unrestrained with the restraint of the eye-faculty do not arise for him when he dwells restrained with the restraint of the eye-faculty.

"Reflecting appropriately, he dwells restrained with the restraint of the ear-faculty...

"Reflecting appropriately, he dwells restrained with the restraint of the nose-faculty...

"Reflecting appropriately, he dwells restrained with the restraint of the tongue-faculty...
Reflecting appropriately, he dwells restrained with the restraint of the body-faculty ....

"Reflecting appropriately, he dwells restrained with the restraint of the intellect-faculty. The effluents, vexation, or fever that would arise if he were to dwell unrestrained with the restraint of the intellect-faculty do not arise for him when he dwells restrained with the restraint of the intellect-faculty. These are called the effluents to be abandoned by restraining.

"[3] And what are the effluents to be abandoned by using? There is the case where a monk, reflecting appropriately, uses the robe simply to counteract cold, to counteract heat, to counteract the touch of flies, mosquitoes, wind, sun, & reptiles; simply for the purpose of covering the parts of the body that cause shame.

"Reflecting appropriately, he uses alms food, not playfully, nor for intoxication, nor for putting on bulk, nor for beautification; but simply for the survival & continuance of this body, for ending its afflictions, for the support of the holy life, thinking, 'Thus will I destroy old feelings (of hunger) and not create new feelings (from overeating). I will maintain myself, be blameless, & live in comfort.'

"Reflecting appropriately, he uses lodging simply to counteract cold, to counteract heat, to counteract the touch of flies, mosquitoes, wind, sun, & reptiles; simply for protection from the inclemencies of weather and for the enjoyment of seclusion.

"Reflecting appropriately, he uses medicinal requisites that are used for curing the sick simply to counteract any pains of illness that have arisen and for maximum freedom from disease.

"The effluents, vexation, or fever that would arise if he were not to use these things (in this way) do not arise for him when he uses them (in this way). These are called the effluents to be abandoned by using.

"[4] And what are the effluents to be abandoned by tolerating? There is the case where a monk, reflecting appropriately, endures. He tolerates cold, heat, hunger, & thirst; the touch of flies, mosquitoes, wind, sun, & reptiles; ill-spoken, unwelcome words & bodily feelings that, when they arise, are painful, racking, sharp, piercing, disagreeable, displeasing, & menacing to life. The effluents, vexation, or fever that would arise if he were not to tolerate these things do not arise for him when he tolerates them. These are called the effluents to be abandoned by tolerating.

"[5] And what are the effluents to be abandoned by avoiding? There is the case where a monk, reflecting appropriately, avoids a wild elephant, a wild horse, a wild bull, a wild dog, a snake, a stump, a bramble patch, a chasm, a cliff, a cesspool, an open sewer. Reflecting appropriately, he avoids sitting in the sorts of unsuitable seats, wandering to the sorts of unsuitable habitats, and associating with the sorts of bad friends that would make his observant companions in the holy life suspect him of evil conduct. The effluents, vexation, or fever that would arise if he were not to avoid these things do not arise for him when he avoids them. These are called the effluents to be abandoned by avoiding.

"[6] And what are the effluents to be abandoned by destroying? There is the case where a monk, reflecting appropriately, doesn't tolerate an arisen thought of sensuality. He abandons it, destroys it, dispels it, & wipes it out of existence.

"Reflecting appropriately, he doesn't tolerate an arisen thought of ill will…

"Reflecting appropriately, he doesn't tolerate an arisen thought of cruelty…

"Reflecting appropriately, he doesn't tolerate arisen evil, unskillful qualities. He abandons them, destroys them, dispels them, & wipes them out of existence. The effluents, vexation, or fever that would arise if he were not to destroy these things do not arise for him when he destroys them. These are called the effluents to be abandoned by destroying.

"[7] And what are the effluents to be abandoned by developing? There is the case where a monk, reflecting appropriately, develops *mindfulness* as a factor for awakening dependent on seclusion… dispassion… cessation, resulting in letting go. He develops *analysis of qualities* as a factor for awakening… *persistence* as a factor for awakening… *rapture* as a factor for awakening… *calm* as a factor for awakening… *concentration* as a factor for awakening… *equanimity* as a factor for awakening dependent on seclusion… dispassion… cessation, resulting in letting go. The effluents, vexation, or fever that would arise if he were not to develop these qualities do not arise for him when he develops them. These are called the effluents to be abandoned by developing.

"When a monk's effluents that should be abandoned by seeing have been abandoned by seeing, his effluents that should be abandoned by restraining have been abandoned by restraining, his effluents that should be abandoned by using have been abandoned by using, his effluents that should be abandoned by tolerating have been abandoned by tolerating, his effluents that should be abandoned by avoiding have been abandoned by avoiding, his effluents that should be abandoned by destroying have been abandoned by destroying, his effluents that should be abandoned by developing have been abandoned by developing, then he is called a monk who dwells restrained with the restraint of all the effluents. He has severed craving, thrown off the fetters, and—through the right penetration of conceit—has made an end of suffering & stress."

That is what the Blessed One said. Gratified, the monks delighted in the Blessed One's words.

See also: MN 63; MN 72; SN 12:20; SN 22:122; SN 44:10; AN 4:42; AN 4:200; AN 10:93

4 *Fear & Terror*

Bhaya-bherava Sutta

I have heard that on one occasion the Blessed One was staying near Sāvatthī in Jeta's Grove, Anāthapiṇḍika's monastery. Then Jāṇussoṇin the brahman went to the Blessed One and, on arrival, exchanged courteous greetings with him. After an exchange of friendly greetings & courtesies, he sat to one side. As he was sitting there, he said to the Blessed One, "Master Gotama, the sons of good families who have gone forth from the home life into homelessness out of conviction in Master Gotama: Is Master Gotama their leader? Is Master Gotama their helper? Is Master Gotama their inspirer? Do they take Master Gotama as their example?"

"Yes, brahman, so it is. The sons of good families who have gone forth from the home life into homelessness out of conviction in me: I am their leader. I am their helper. I am their inspirer. They take me as their example."

"But, Master Gotama, it's not easy to endure isolated forest or wilderness dwellings. It's not easy to maintain seclusion, not easy to enjoy being alone. The forests, as it were, plunder the mind of a monk who has not gained concentration."

"Yes, brahman, so it is. It's not easy to endure isolated forest or wilderness dwellings. It's not easy to maintain seclusion, not easy to enjoy being alone. The forests, as it were, plunder the mind of a monk who has not gained concentration. Before my self-awakening, when I was still just an unawakened Bodhisatta, the thought occurred to me as well: 'It's not easy to endure isolated forest or wilderness dwellings. It's not easy to maintain seclusion, not easy to enjoy being alone. The forests, as it were, plunder the mind of a monk who has not gained concentration.'

"The thought occurred to me: 'When contemplatives or brahmans who are unpurified in their bodily activities resort to isolated forest or wilderness dwellings, it's the fault of their unpurified bodily activities that they give rise to unskillful fear & terror. But it's not the case that I am unpurified in my bodily activities when I resort to isolated forest or wilderness dwellings. I am purified in my bodily activities. I am one of those noble ones who are purified in their bodily activities when they resort to isolated forest or wilderness dwellings.' Seeing in myself this purity of bodily activities, I felt even more undaunted about staying in the wilderness.

"The thought occurred to me: 'When contemplatives or brahmans who are unpurified in their verbal activities… unpurified in their mental activities… unpurified in their livelihood resort to isolated forest or wilderness dwellings, it's the fault of their unpurified livelihood that they give rise to unskillful fear & terror. But it's not the case that I am unpurified in my livelihood when I resort to isolated forest or wilderness dwellings. I am purified in my livelihood. I am one of those noble ones who are purified in their livelihood when they resort to isolated forest or wilderness dwellings.' Seeing in myself this purity of livelihood, I felt even more undaunted about staying in the wilderness.

"The thought occurred to me: 'When contemplatives or brahmans who are covetous & fiercely passionate for sensual pleasures… I am not covetous… ' ….

" … 'When contemplatives or brahmans who have minds of ill will, with destructive attitudes… I have a mind of goodwill… ' ….

" … 'When contemplatives or brahmans who are overcome by sloth & drowsiness… I am devoid of sloth & drowsiness… ' ….

" … 'When contemplatives or brahmans who are restless & with an unstilled mind… I have a stilled mind… ' ….

" … 'When contemplatives or brahmans who are uncertain & doubting… I have gone beyond uncertainty… ' ….

" … 'When contemplatives or brahmans who tend to praise themselves & disparage others… I do not praise myself or disparage others… ' ….

" … 'When contemplatives or brahmans who tend toward panic & dread… I have gone beyond horripilation… ' ….

" … 'When contemplatives or brahmans who are desirous of gains, offerings, & fame… I am modest… ' ….

" … 'When contemplatives or brahmans who are lazy & lacking in persistence… My persistence is aroused… ' ….

" … 'When contemplatives or brahmans who are muddled in their mindfulness & unalert… I have mindfulness established…' ….

" … 'When contemplatives or brahmans who are unconcentrated, with straying minds… I am consummate in concentration…' ….

"The thought occurred to me: 'When contemplatives or brahmans who are drooling idiots resort to isolated forest or wilderness dwellings, it's the fault of their drooling idiocy that they give rise to unskillful fear & terror. But it's not the case that I am a drooling idiot when I resort to isolated forest or wilderness dwellings. I am consummate in discernment. I am one of those noble ones who are consummate in discernment when they resort to isolated forest or wilderness dwellings.' Seeing in myself this consummate discernment, I felt even more undaunted about staying in the wilderness.

"The thought occurred to me: 'What if—on recognized, designated nights such as the eighth, fourteenth, & fifteenth of the lunar fortnight—I were to stay in the sort of places that are awe-inspiring and make your hair stand on end, such as park-shrines, forest-shrines, & tree-shrines? Perhaps I would get to see that fear & terror.' So at a later time—on recognized, designated nights such as the eighth, fourteenth, & fifteenth of the lunar fortnight—I stayed in the sort of places that are awe-inspiring and make your hair stand on end, such as park-shrines, forest-shrines, & tree-shrines. And while I was staying there a wild animal would come, or a bird would drop a twig, or wind would rustle the fallen leaves. The thought would occur to me: 'Is this that fear & terror coming?' Then the thought occurred to me: 'Why do I just keep waiting for fear? What if I were to subdue fear & terror in whatever state they come?'

"So when fear & terror came while I was walking back & forth, I would not stand or sit or lie down. I would keep walking back & forth until I had subdued that fear & terror. When fear & terror came while I was standing, I would not walk or sit or lie down. I would keep standing until I had subdued that fear & terror. When fear & terror came while I was sitting, I would not lie down or stand up or walk. I would keep sitting until I had subdued that fear & terror. When fear & terror came while I was lying down, I would not sit up or stand or walk. I would keep lying down until I had subdued that fear & terror.

"There are some contemplatives & brahmans, brahman, who have the perception of 'day' when it is night, and of 'night' when it is day. This, I tell you, is their being in a dwelling of delusion. As for me, I have the perception of 'day' when it is day, and of 'night' when it is night. If anyone, when speaking rightly, were to say, 'A being not subject to delusion has appeared in the world for the benefit & happiness of many, out of sympathy for the world, for the welfare, benefit, & happiness of human & divine beings,' he would rightly be speaking of me.

"Unflagging persistence was aroused in me, and unmuddled mindfulness established. My body was calm & unaroused, my mind concentrated & single. Quite secluded from sensuality, secluded from unskillful qualities, I entered & remained in the first jhāna: rapture & pleasure born of seclusion, accompanied by directed thought & evaluation. With the stilling of directed thoughts & evaluations, I entered & remained in the second jhāna: rapture & pleasure born of concentration, unification of awareness free from directed thought &

evaluation—internal assurance. With the fading of rapture, I remained equanimous, mindful, & alert, and sensed pleasure with the body. I entered & remained in the third jhāna, of which the noble ones declare, 'Equanimous & mindful, he has a pleasant abiding.' With the abandoning of pleasure & pain—as with the earlier disappearance of elation & distress—I entered & remained in the fourth jhāna: purity of equanimity & mindfulness, neither pleasure nor pain.

"When the mind was thus concentrated, purified, bright, unblemished, rid of defilement, pliant, malleable, steady, & attained to imperturbability, I directed it to the *knowledge of recollecting my past lives.* I recollected my manifold past lives, i.e., one birth, two… five, ten… fifty, a hundred, a thousand, a hundred thousand, many eons of cosmic contraction, many eons of cosmic expansion, many eons of cosmic contraction & expansion: 'There I had such a name, belonged to such a clan, had such an appearance. Such was my food, such my experience of pleasure & pain, such the end of my life. Passing away from that state, I re-arose there. There too I had such a name, belonged to such a clan, had such an appearance. Such was my food, such my experience of pleasure & pain, such the end of my life. Passing away from that state, I re-arose here.' Thus I recollected my manifold past lives in their modes & details.

"This was the first knowledge I attained in the first watch of the night. Ignorance was destroyed; knowledge arose; darkness was destroyed; light arose—as happens in one who is heedful, ardent, & resolute.

"When the mind was thus concentrated, purified, bright, unblemished, rid of defilement, pliant, malleable, steady, & attained to imperturbability, I directed it to the *knowledge of the passing away & reappearance of beings.* I saw—by means of the divine eye, purified & surpassing the human—beings passing away & re-appearing, and I discerned how they are inferior & superior, beautiful & ugly, fortunate & unfortunate in accordance with their kamma: 'These beings—who were endowed with bad conduct of body, speech & mind, who reviled noble ones, held wrong views and undertook actions under the influence of wrong views—with the breakup of the body, after death, have reappeared in a plane of deprivation, a bad destination, a lower realm, hell. But these beings—who were endowed with good conduct of body, speech, & mind, who did not revile noble ones, who held right views and undertook actions under the influence of right views—with the break-up of the body, after death, have re-appeared in a good destination, a heavenly world.' Thus—by means of the divine eye, purified & surpassing the human—I saw beings passing away & re-appearing, and I discerned how they are inferior & superior, beautiful & ugly, fortunate & unfortunate in accordance with their kamma.

"This was the second knowledge I attained in the second watch of the night. Ignorance was destroyed; knowledge arose; darkness was destroyed; light arose—as happens in one who is heedful, ardent, & resolute.

"When the mind was thus concentrated, purified, bright, unblemished, rid of defilement, pliant, malleable, steady, & attained to imperturbability, I directed it to the *knowledge of the ending of effluents.* I discerned, as it had come to be, that 'This is stress... This is the origination of stress... This is the cessation of stress... This is the way leading to the cessation of stress... These are effluents... This is the origination of effluents... This is the cessation of effluents... This is the way leading to the cessation of effluents.' My heart, thus knowing, thus seeing, was released from the effluent of sensuality, released from the effluent of becoming, released from the effluent of ignorance. With release, there was the knowledge, 'Released.' I discerned that 'Birth is ended, the holy life fulfilled, the task done. There is nothing further for this world.'

"This was the third knowledge I attained in the third watch of the night. Ignorance was destroyed; knowledge arose; darkness was destroyed; light arose—as happens in one who is heedful, ardent, & resolute.

"Now, brahman, if the thought should occur to you, 'Perhaps Gotama the contemplative is even today not free of passion, not free of aversion, not free of delusion, which is why he resorts to isolated forest & wilderness dwellings,' it should not be seen in that way. It's through seeing two compelling reasons that I resort to isolated forest & wilderness dwellings: seeing a pleasant abiding for myself in the present, and feeling sympathy for future generations."

"How truly future generations have been shown sympathy by Master Gotama, as by one who is worthy & rightly self-awakened! Magnificent, Master Gotama! Magnificent! Just as if he were to place upright what was overturned, to reveal what was hidden, to show the way to one who was lost, or to carry a lamp into the dark so that those with eyes could see forms, in the same way has Master Gotama—through many lines of reasoning—made the Dhamma clear. I go to Master Gotama for refuge, to the Dhamma, and to the Saṅgha of monks. May Master Gotama remember me as a lay follower who has gone to him for refuge, from this day forward, for life."

See also: MN 36; SN 5:1–10; SN 11:3; AN 4:184; AN 4:263; AN 10:99; Thag 161; Thig 14

5 Unblemished

Anaṅgaṇa Sutta

I have heard that on one occasion the Blessed One was staying near Sāvatthī in Jeta's Grove, Anāthapiṇḍika's monastery. There Ven. Sāriputta addressed the monks: "Friend monks!"

"Yes, friend," the monks responded to him.

Ven. Sāriputta said, "There are these four individuals to be found existing in the world. Which four?

"There is the case where a certain individual, being blemished, does not discern as it has come to be that 'I have an inner blemish.' Then there is the case where a certain individual, being blemished, discerns as it has come to be that 'I have an inner blemish.' Then there is the case where a certain individual, being unblemished, does not discern as it has come to be that 'I have no inner blemish.' Then there is the case where a certain individual, being unblemished, discerns as it has come to be that 'I have no inner blemish.'

"With regard to that, the individual who, being blemished, doesn't discern as it has come to be that 'I have an inner blemish' is called the inferior man of the two individuals who are blemished. The individual who, being blemished, discerns as it has come to be that 'I have an inner blemish' is called the superior man of the two individuals who are blemished.

"Then again, the individual who, being unblemished, doesn't discern as it has come to be that 'I have no inner blemish' is called the inferior man of the two individuals who are unblemished. The individual who, being unblemished, discerns as it has come to be that 'I have no inner blemish' is called the superior man of the two individuals who are unblemished."

When this was said, Ven. Mahā Moggallāna said to Ven. Sāriputta, "Friend, what is the reason, what is the cause, that of the two individuals who are blemished, one is called the inferior man and one is called the superior man? And what is the reason, what is the cause, that of the two individuals who are unblemished, one is called the inferior man and one is called the superior man?"

[Ven. Sāriputta:] "With regard to that, my friend, when an individual, being blemished, doesn't discern that 'I have an inner blemish,' it can be expected of him that he will not generate desire, endeavor, or arouse persistence for the abandoning of that blemish. He will die with passion, with aversion, with delusion—blemished & with a mind defiled.

"Just like a bronze bowl brought back from a shop or a family of smiths all covered with dust & dirt, that the owners would neither use nor clean, but would throw away in a dusty place: Wouldn't that bronze bowl eventually become even more dirty & defiled with time?"

[Ven. Mahā Moggallāna:] "Yes, my friend."

[Ven. Sāriputta:] "In the same way, friend, when an individual, being blemished, doesn't discern as it has come to be that 'I have an inner blemish,' it can be expected of him that he will not generate desire, endeavor, or arouse persistence for the abandoning of that blemish. He will die with passion, with aversion, with delusion—blemished & with a mind defiled.

"Then again, when an individual, being blemished, discerns as it has come to be that 'I have an inner blemish,' it can be expected of him that he will generate desire, endeavor, & arouse persistence for the abandoning of that blemish. He will die without passion, without aversion, without delusion—unblemished & with a mind undefiled.

"Just like a bronze bowl brought back from a shop or a family of smiths all covered with dust & dirt, that the owners would both use & clean, and would not throw away in a dusty place: Wouldn't that bronze bowl eventually become clean & pure with time?"

[Ven. Mahā Moggallāna:] "Yes, my friend."

[Ven. Sāriputta:] "In the same way, friend, when an individual, being blemished, discerns as it has come to be that 'I have an inner blemish,' it can be expected of him that he will generate desire, endeavor, & arouse persistence for the abandoning of that blemish. He will die without passion, without aversion, without delusion—unblemished & with a mind undefiled.

"Then again, when an individual, being unblemished, doesn't discern as it has come to be that 'I have no inner blemish,' it can be expected of him that he will attend to the theme of beauty. As he attends to the theme of beauty, passion will assault his mind. He will die with passion, with aversion, with delusion—blemished & with a mind defiled.

"Just like a bronze bowl brought back from a shop or a family of smiths clean & pure, that the owners would neither use nor clean, but would throw away in a dusty place. Wouldn't that bronze bowl eventually become dirty & defiled with time?"

[Ven. Mahā Moggallāna:] "Yes, my friend."

[Ven. Sāriputta:] "In the same way, when an individual, being unblemished, doesn't discern as it has come to be that 'I have no inner blemish,' it can be expected of him that he will attend to the theme of beauty. As he attends to the theme of beauty, passion will assault his mind. He will die with passion, with aversion, with delusion—blemished & with a mind defiled.

"Then again, when an individual, being unblemished, discerns as it has come to be that 'I have no inner blemish,' it can be expected of him that he will not attend to the theme of beauty. As he doesn't attend to the theme of beauty, passion won't assault his mind. He will die without passion, without aversion, without delusion—unblemished & with a mind undefiled.

"Just like a bronze bowl brought back from a shop or a family of smiths clean & pure, that the owners would both use & clean, and would not throw away in a dusty place: Wouldn't that bronze bowl eventually become even more clean & pure with time?"

[Ven. Mahā Moggallāna:] "Yes, my friend."

[Ven. Sāriputta:] "In the same way, friend, when an individual, being unblemished, discerns as it has come to be that 'I have no inner blemish,' it can be expected of him that he will not attend to the theme of beauty. As he doesn't attend to the theme of beauty, passion won't assault his mind. He will die without passion, without aversion, without delusion—unblemished & with a mind undefiled.

"This, friend Moggallāna, is the reason, this is the cause why, of the two individuals who are blemished, one is called the inferior man and one is called the superior man. This is the reason, this is the cause why, of the two individuals who are unblemished, one is called the inferior man and one is called the superior man."

[Ven. Mahā Moggallāna:] "'Blemish, blemish' it's said. What does 'blemish' stand for?"

[Ven. Sāriputta:] "The influences of evil, unskillful wishes: That's what 'blemish' stands for.

"It's possible, friend, that there's the case where this sort of wish might arise in a certain monk: 'O, should I have fallen into an offense, may the monks not know about me, that I have fallen into an offense.' But it's possible that the monks would know about that monk that he had fallen into an offense. (Thinking,) 'The monks know about me that I have fallen into an offense,' he is angry & disgruntled. Anger & disgruntlement are both a blemish.

"It's possible, friend, that there's the case where this sort of wish might arise in a certain monk: 'O, should I have fallen into an offense, may the monks accuse me in private, and not in the middle of the Saṅgha.' But it's possible that the monks would accuse him in the middle of the Saṅgha, not in private. (Thinking,) 'It's in the middle of the Saṅgha that the monks accuse me, and not in private,' he is angry & disgruntled. Anger & disgruntlement are both a blemish.

"It's possible, friend, that there's the case where this sort of wish might arise in a certain monk: 'O, should I have fallen into an offense, may a friend accuse me, and not an enemy.' But it's possible that an enemy would accuse him, and not a friend. (Thinking,) 'An enemy accuses me, and not a friend,' he is angry & disgruntled. Anger & disgruntlement are both a blemish.

"It's possible, friend, that there's the case where this sort of wish might arise in a certain monk: 'O, may the Teacher instruct the monks, cross-questioning just me again & again, and not cross-questioning another monk again & again.' But it's possible that the Teacher would instruct the monks, cross-questioning another monk again & again, and not cross-questioning that monk again & again. (Thinking,) 'The Teacher instructs the monks, cross-questioning another monk again & again, and not cross-questioning me again & again,' he is angry & disgruntled. Anger & disgruntlement are both a blemish.

"It's possible, friend, that there's the case where this sort of wish might arise in a certain monk: 'O, may the monks enter the village for alms following just me, and not following another monk.' But it's possible that the monks would enter the village for alms following another monk, and not following that monk. (Thinking,) 'It's following another monk, and not me, that the monks enter the village for alms,' he is angry & disgruntled. Anger & disgruntlement are both a blemish.

"It's possible, friend, that there's the case where this sort of wish might arise in a certain monk: 'O, may I alone receive the foremost meals, the foremost seat, the foremost water, the foremost alms, and not another monk.' But it's possible that another monk would receive the foremost meals, the foremost seat, the foremost water, the foremost alms. (Thinking,) 'It's another monk who receives the foremost meals, the foremost seat, the foremost water, the foremost alms, and not me' he is angry & disgruntled. Anger & disgruntlement are both a blemish.

"It's possible, friend, that there's the case where this sort of wish might arise in a certain monk: 'O, may I alone give the blessing in the dining hall after the meal, and not another monk.' But it's possible that another monk would give the blessing in the dining hall after the meal. (Thinking,) 'It's another monk who gives the blessing in the dining hall after the meal, and not me' he is angry & disgruntled. Anger & disgruntlement are both a blemish.

"It's possible, friend, that there's the case where this sort of wish might arise in a certain monk: 'O, may I alone, and not another monk, teach the Dhamma to monks… nuns… men lay followers… women lay followers who have come to the monastery.' But it's possible that another monk would teach the Dhamma, and not that monk…

"It's possible, friend, that there's the case where this sort of wish might arise in a certain monk: 'O, may the monks… nuns… men lay followers… women lay followers pay honor, respect, reverence, & veneration to me alone, and not to another monk.' But it's possible that the monks… nuns… men lay followers… women lay followers would pay honor, respect, reverence, & veneration to another monk, and not to that monk…

"It's possible, friend, that there's the case where this sort of wish might arise in a certain monk: 'O, may I alone, and not another monk, be the one who receives exquisite robes… exquisite alms… exquisite lodgings… exquisite medicinal requisites for curing the ill. But it's possible that another monk, and not that monk, is the one who receives exquisite medicinal requisites for curing the ill. (Thinking,) 'It's another monk who receives exquisite medicinal requisites for curing the ill, and not me,' he is angry & disgruntled. Anger & disgruntlement are both a blemish.

"Now friend, if these influences of evil, unskillful wishes are seen or heard to be unabandoned in any monk, then even though he's a wilderness dweller, a dweller in isolated lodgings, an alms-goer, a house-to-house alms-goer, a refuse-rag wearer, a wearer of coarse robes, still his companions in the holy life don't pay him honor, respect, reverence, or veneration. Why is that? Because these influences of evil, unskillful wishes are seen or heard to be unabandoned in him.

"Just like a bronze bowl brought back from a shop or a family of smiths clean & pure, into which the owners would arrange the carcass of a snake, a dog, or a human being and—covering it with another bronze bowl—would carry back into the market: A person, seeing them, would say, ' Well, what's this, being carried around as if it were so splendid?' He, raising & opening the lid, would look in. As soon as he saw, he would be inspired with displeasure, with loathing, with disgust, so that even if he were hungry, he would not want to eat—to say nothing of if he were full.

"In the same way, if these influences of evil, unskillful wishes are seen or heard to be unabandoned in any monk, then even though he's a wilderness dweller, a dweller in isolated lodgings, an alms-goer, a house-to-house alms-goer, a refuse-rag wearer, a wearer of coarse robes, still his companions in the holy life don't pay him honor, respect, reverence, or veneration. Why is that? Because these influences of evil, unskillful wishes are seen or heard to be unabandoned in him.

"But, friend, if these influences of evil, unskillful wishes are seen or heard to be abandoned in any monk, then even though he's a village dweller, a receiver of meal invitations, a wearer of robes given by lay people, still his companions in the holy life pay him honor, respect, reverence, or veneration. Why is that? Because these influences of evil, unskillful wishes are seen or heard to be abandoned in him.

"Just like a bronze bowl brought back from a shop or a family of smiths clean & pure, into which the owners would arrange boiled white rice with various sauces and curries and—covering it with another bronze bowl—would carry back into the market: A person, seeing them, would say, 'Well, what's this, being carried around as if it were so splendid?' He, raising & opening the lid, would look in. As soon as he saw, he would be inspired with enticement, with non-loathing, & with non-disgust, so that even if he were full, he would want to eat—to say nothing of if he were hungry.

"In the same way, if these influences of evil, unskillful wishes are seen or heard to be abandoned in any monk, then even though he's a village dweller, a receiver of meal invitations, a wearer of robes given by lay people, still his companions in the holy life pay him honor, respect, reverence, or veneration. Why is that? Because these influences of evil, unskillful wishes are seen or heard to be abandoned in him."

When this was said, Ven. Moggallāna said to Ven. Sāriputta, "A simile occurs to me, friend Sāriputta."

"Let it occur to you, friend Moggallāna."

"On one occasion I was staying near Rājagaha, at the Hill Fort. Then, early in the morning, I adjusted my under robe and—carrying my bowl & outer robe—went into Rājagaha for alms. And on that occasion Samīti the cartwright was planing the rim of a chariot wheel, and the Ājīvaka Paṇḍuputta, a former cartwright, was standing by. Then this line of thinking arose in the awareness of Ājīvaka Paṇḍuputta, the former cartwright: 'O, may Samīti the cartwright plane away this bend, this twist, this fault in this rim, so that this rim would be clean—its bends, twists, and faults removed—standing in heartwood.' And just as the line of thinking occurred to Ājīvaka Paṇḍuputta, the former cartwright, in just the same way did Samīti the cartwright plane away that bend, that twist, that fault in the rim. So Ājīvaka Paṇḍuputta, the former cartwright, gratified, uttered words of gratification: 'He planes, knowing my heart with his heart, as it were!'

"In the same way, any individuals without conviction, who—for the sake of a livelihood and not out of conviction—have gone forth from the home life into homelessness; who are fraudulent, deceitful, wily, restless, rowdy, flighty, talkative, of loose words; who leave their faculties unguarded; who know no moderation in food, are undevoted to wakefulness, unconcerned with the qualities of a contemplative, with no respect for the training; who are luxurious, lethargic, foremost in falling back; who shirk the duties of solitude; who are lazy, lowly in their persistence, of muddled mindfulness, unalert, unconcentrated, their minds scattered, undiscerning, drivelers: Ven. Sāriputta, with this Dhamma discourse, planes away their (faults), knowing my heart with his heart, as it were!

"But as for those sons of good families who, out of conviction, have gone forth from the home life into homelessness; who are unfraudulent, undeceitful, not wily, not restless, not rowdy, not flighty, not talkative or of loose words; who guard their faculties, know moderation in food, are devoted to wakefulness, are concerned with the qualities of a contemplative, have fierce respect for the training; who are not luxurious, not lethargic, not foremost in falling back; who observe the duties of solitude; who are not lazy; who are aroused in their effort, of unmuddled mindfulness, alert, concentrated, their minds unified, discerning, not drivelers: They, hearing this Dhamma discourse from Ven. Sāriputta, drink it up & devour it, as it were, both by word & by mind: 'How good it is that, having made his companions in the holy life rise up from what's unskillful, he establishes them in what's skillful!'[1]

"Just as a young & youthful woman or man—fond of adornment, with head bathed—on receiving a garland of blue lotuses, jasmine, or camellias, would take it with both hands and place it on top of his or her head; in the same way, those sons of good families who, out of conviction, have gone forth from the home life into homelessness; who are unfraudulent, undeceitful, not wily, not restless, not rowdy, not flighty, not talkative or of loose words; who guard their faculties, know moderation in food, are devoted to wakefulness, are concerned with the qualities of a contemplative, have fierce respect for the training; who are not luxurious, not lethargic, not foremost in falling back; who observe the duties of solitude; who are not lazy; who are aroused in their effort, of unmuddled mindfulness, alert, concentrated, their minds unified, discerning, not drivelers: They, hearing this Dhamma discourse from Ven. Sāriputta, drink it up & devour it, as it were, both by word & by mind: 'How good it is that, having made his companions in the holy life rise up from what's unskillful, he establishes them in what's skillful!'"

Thus did those two great beings *[nāgas]* rejoice in each other's well-spoken words.

NOTE: 1. Both MLS and MLDB miss the fact that Ven. Moggallāna is here quoting the words of the good monks.

6 *If One Would Wish*

Ākaṅkheyya Sutta

I have heard that on one occasion the Blessed One was staying near Sāvatthī in Jeta's Grove, Anāthapiṇḍika's monastery. There he addressed the monks, "Monks!"

"Yes, lord," the monks responded to him.

The Blessed One said: "Monks, dwell consummate in virtue, consummate in terms of the Pāṭimokkha. Dwell restrained in accordance with the Pāṭimokkha, consummate in your behavior & sphere of activity. Train yourselves, having undertaken the training rules, seeing danger in the slightest faults.

"If a monk would wish, 'May I be dear & pleasing to my companions in the holy life, respected by & inspiring to them,' then he should be one who brings the precepts to perfection, who is committed to inner tranquility of awareness, who doesn't neglect jhāna, who is endowed with insight, and who frequents empty dwellings.

"If a monk would wish, 'May I be someone who receives robes, alms food, lodgings, & medicinal requisites for curing the sick,' then he should be one who brings the precepts to perfection, who is committed to inner tranquility of awareness, who doesn't neglect jhāna, who is endowed with insight, and who frequents empty dwellings.

"If a monk would wish, 'Whatever I use or consume in terms of robes, alms food, lodgings, & medical requisites for curing the sick, may that be of great fruit, of great benefit to those who provided them,' then he should be one who brings the precepts to perfection, who is committed to inner tranquility of awareness, who doesn't neglect jhāna, who is endowed with insight, and who frequents empty dwellings.

"If a monk would wish, 'When my kinsmen & relatives who have died & passed away recollect me with brightened minds, may it be of great fruit, of great benefit,' then he should be one who brings the precepts to perfection, who is committed to inner tranquility of awareness, who doesn't neglect jhāna, who is endowed with insight, and who frequents empty dwellings.

"If a monk would wish, 'May I overcome displeasure & delight, and not be overcome by displeasure & delight. May I dwell conquering again & again any displeasure & delight that has arisen,' then he should be one who brings the precepts to perfection, who is committed to inner tranquility of awareness, who doesn't neglect jhāna, who is endowed with insight, and who frequents empty dwellings.

"If a monk would wish, 'May I overcome fear & dread, and not be overcome by fear & dread. May I dwell conquering again & again any fear & dread that have arisen,' then he should be one who brings the precepts to perfection, who is committed to inner tranquility of awareness, who doesn't neglect jhāna, who is endowed with insight, and who frequents empty dwellings.

"If a monk would wish, 'May I attain—whenever I want, without strain, without difficulty—the four jhānas that are heightened mental states, pleasant abidings in the here-&-now,' then he should be one who brings the precepts to perfection, who is committed to inner tranquility of awareness, who doesn't neglect jhāna, who is endowed with insight, and who frequents empty dwellings.

"If a monk would wish, 'May I dwell touching with the body those liberations that are peaceful, formless, transcending forms,'[1] then he should be one who brings the precepts to perfection, who is committed to inner tranquility of awareness, who doesn't neglect jhāna, who is endowed with insight, and who frequents empty dwellings.

"If a monk would wish, 'May I—with the ending of (the first) three fetters—be a stream-winner, certain, never again destined for the lower realms, headed for self-awakening,' then he should be one who brings the precepts to perfection, who is committed to inner tranquility of awareness, who doesn't neglect jhāna, who is endowed with insight, and who frequents empty dwellings.

"If a monk would wish, 'May I—with the ending of (the first) three fetters, and with the attenuation of passion, aversion, & delusion—be a once-returner, who, on returning only once more to this world, would make an ending to stress,' then he should be one who brings the precepts to perfection, who is committed to inner tranquility of awareness, who doesn't neglect jhāna, who is endowed with insight, and who frequents empty dwellings.

"If a monk would wish, 'May I—with the ending of the five lower fetters, be one who is due to arise spontaneously (in the Pure Abodes), there to be totally unbound, destined never again to return from that world,' then he should be one who brings the precepts to perfection, who is committed to inner tranquility of awareness, who doesn't neglect jhāna, who is endowed with insight, and who frequents empty dwellings.

"If a monk would wish, 'May I wield manifold supranormal powers. Having been one, may I become many; having been many, may I become one. May I appear & vanish. May I go unimpeded through walls, ramparts, & mountains as if through space. May I dive in & out of the earth as if it were water. May I walk on water without sinking as if it were dry land. Sitting cross-legged, may I fly through the air like a winged bird. With my hand may I touch & stroke even the sun and moon, so mighty and powerful. May I influence with my body even as far as the Brahmā worlds,' then he should be one who brings the precepts to perfection, who is committed to inner tranquility of awareness, who doesn't neglect jhāna, who is endowed with insight, and who frequents empty dwellings.

"If a monk would wish, 'May I hear—by means of the divine ear-element, purified and surpassing the human—both kinds of sounds: divine and human, whether near or far,' then he should be one who brings the precepts to perfection, who is committed to inner tranquility of awareness, who doesn't neglect jhāna, who is endowed with insight, and who frequents empty dwellings.

"If a monk would wish, 'May I know the awareness of other beings, other individuals, having encompassed it with my own awareness. May I discern a mind with passion as "a mind with passion," and a mind without passion as "a mind without passion." May I discern a mind with aversion as "a mind with aversion," and a mind without aversion as "a mind without aversion." May I discern a mind with delusion as "a mind with delusion," and a mind without delusion as "a mind without delusion." May I discern a restricted mind as "a restricted mind," and a scattered mind as "a scattered mind." May I discern an enlarged mind as "an enlarged mind," and an unenlarged mind as "an unenlarged mind." May I discern an excelled mind [one that is not at the most excellent level] as "an excelled mind," and an unexcelled mind as "an unexcelled mind." May I discern a concentrated mind as "a concentrated mind," and an unconcentrated mind as "an unconcentrated mind." May I discern a released mind as "a released mind," and an unreleased mind as "an unreleased mind,"' then he should be one who brings the precepts to perfection, who is committed to inner tranquility of awareness, who doesn't neglect jhāna, who is endowed with insight, and who frequents empty dwellings.

"If a monk would wish, 'May I recollect my manifold past lives, i.e., one birth, two births, three births, four, five, ten, twenty, thirty, forty, fifty, one hundred, one thousand, one hundred thousand, many eons of cosmic contraction, many eons of cosmic expansion, many eons of cosmic contraction & expansion, (recollecting,) 'There I had such a name, belonged to such a clan, had such an appearance. Such was my food, such my experience of pleasure & pain, such the end of my life. Passing away from that state, I re-arose there. There too I had such a name, belonged to such a clan, had such an appearance. Such was my food, such my experience of pleasure & pain, such the end of my life. Passing away from that state, I re-arose here.' Thus may I recollect my manifold past lives in their modes & details,' then he should be one who brings the precepts to perfection, who is committed to inner tranquility of awareness, who doesn't neglect jhāna, who is endowed with insight, and who frequents empty dwellings.

"If a monk would wish, 'May I see—by means of the divine eye, purified and surpassing the human—beings passing away and re-appearing, and may I discern how they are inferior and superior, beautiful and ugly, fortunate and unfortunate in accordance with their kamma: 'These beings—who were endowed with bad conduct of body, speech, and mind, who reviled the noble ones, held wrong views and undertook actions under the influence of wrong views—with the break-up of the body, after death, have re-appeared in a plane of deprivation, a bad destination, a lower realm, hell. But these beings—who were endowed with good conduct of body, speech, and mind, who did not revile the noble ones, who held right views and undertook actions under the influence of right views—with the break-up of the body, after death, have re-appeared in a good destination, a heavenly world.' Thus—by means of the divine eye, purified and surpassing the human—may I see beings passing away and re-appearing, and may I discern how they are inferior and superior, beautiful and ugly, fortunate and unfortunate in accordance with their kamma,' then he should be one who brings the precepts to perfection, who is committed to inner tranquility of awareness, who doesn't neglect jhāna, who is endowed with insight, and who frequents empty dwellings.

"If a monk would wish, 'May I—with the ending of effluents—remain in the effluent-free awareness-release & discernment-release, having directly known & realized them for myself right in the here-&-now,' then he should be one who brings the precepts to perfection, who is committed to inner tranquility of awareness, who doesn't neglect jhāna, who is endowed with insight, and who frequents empty dwellings.

"'Monks, dwell consummate in virtue, consummate in terms of the Pāṭimokkha. Dwell restrained in accordance with the Pāṭimokkha, consummate in your behavior & sphere of activity. Train yourselves, having undertaken the training rules, seeing danger in the slightest faults.' Thus was it said. And in reference to this was it said."

That is what the Blessed One said. Gratified, the monks delighted in the Blessed One's words.

NOTE: 1. See AN 9:45 and AN 9:47.

See also: AN 3:85–86; AN 4:128; AN 8:70; AN 9:43; AN 10:13; AN 10:71

9 *Right View*

Sammādiṭṭhi Sutta

INTRODUCTION

Right view is normally explained in terms of the four noble truths. In this discourse, Ven. Sāriputta expands the discussion in several directions.

He begins by focusing on two concepts that underlie the structure of the four noble truths: the dichotomy of skillful and unskillful action, and the concept of nutriment.

Focusing on the dichotomy of skillful and unskillful action draws attention to a general principle of cause and effect—the fact that actions give results—and to the particular role of action in determining one's experience of pleasure and pain: Unskillful actions lead to pain, skillful actions to pleasure. The search for the root of skillful and unskillful actions leads ultimately to the mind, because the presence or lack of skill in any action is determined by the mental state motivating it. Thus the issue of skillful and unskillful action provides in a nutshell some of the basic principles of the four noble truths in terms of causality, wise and unwise uses of causality, and the dominant role of the mind in the causal chain leading to happiness or pain.

The image of "root" carries further implications. Because the function of roots is to draw nourishment from the soil, the natural question is: Where do the roots of skillful and unskillful behavior draw their nourishment? This is why the next topic in the sutta is nutriment, which is of two sorts, physical and mental. And implicit in the idea of nutriment is the possibility for a strategy to use nutriment skillfully: If the mental state being nourished is unskillful, it can be overcome by depriving it of nutriment; if it's skillful, it can be fostered by feeding it more (see, for example, SN 46:51). This points to the possibility of training the mind through a strategy of selective feeding and starving, while the analysis of mental nutriment shows precisely which events are most basic in the mental food chain: contact, intellectual intention, and consciousness.

Ven. Sāriputta combines the issues of skillfulness and nutriment by approaching the topic of nutriment with a fourfold framework: nutriment, its origination (nutriment, in turn, has its own food), its cessation (the possibility of starving it of that food), and the path of practice leading to its cessation (the way to starve it). This line of thinking leads naturally to the next topic, in which this same framework is applied to the focal issue of the Buddha's teaching—suffering and stress—yielding the four noble truths. In this way, Ven. Sāriputta shows how the four noble truths derive from the two topics of skillful/unskillful and nutriment.

It's interesting to note that both these topics figure prominently in discourses directed at young people. The Buddha's instruction to Rāhula in MN 61 focuses on skillful and unskillful behavior; the first of the Novice's Questions (Khp 4), on nutriment. Seeing how basic these concepts are to understanding the role of causality in putting an end to suffering, the Buddha taught them to young people as an entry into the Dhamma. In this sutta, Ven. Sāriputta shows how these topics can perform the same function for adults. And perhaps he is also showing us the line of reasoning through which his own first glimpse of the deathless followed upon a simple statement of a causal principle:

> *Whatever phenomena arise from cause:*
> *their cause*
> *and their cessation.*
> *Such is the teaching of the Tathāgata,*
> *the Great Contemplative. (Mv.I.23.5)*

The remainder of this sutta expands on the four noble truths with a reverse-order analysis of dependent co-arising. Two features of this section stand out. To begin with, Ven. Sāriputta points out that understanding the relationship between any two adjacent factors in the pattern of dependent co-arising provides enough discernment to abandon unskillful obsessions and put an end to suffering. There is no need to comprehend the entire pattern, for the whole is implicit in each paired relationship. This is a point with important practical implications. Sn 3:12 makes the same point, but pairs the objects for contemplation in a different way: Every factor in dependent co-arising is paired directly with stress. A comparison between these two suttas provides much practical food for thought, showing how the ability to see and comprehend dualities is essential to the Buddha's strategy for discernment and release.

Second, Ven. Sāriputta here continues the pattern of dependent co-arising past ignorance—the usual endpoint—to look for its origination, which is the effluents (āsava). Because these effluents in turn depend on ignorance, the discussion shows how ignorance tends to prompt more ignorance. But, as Ven. Sāriputta has demonstrated throughout his discussion, ignorance needn't keep propagating forever. Because it is simply a lack of knowledge in terms of the four noble truths, it can be replaced by knowledge that does look at things in terms of the four noble truths—the framework derived from the topics of skillful/unskillful and nutriment. When knowledge in terms of this framework is applied at any point in the causal framework, the entire framework dependent on ignorance can be brought to an end.

In this way Ven. Sāriputta fills in a blank contained in the stock Canonical description of awakening. The central part of that description states, "He discerns, as it has come to be, that 'This is stress... This is the origination of stress... This is the cessation of stress... This is the way leading to the cessation of stress... These are effluents... This is the origination of effluents... This is the cessation of effluents... This is the way leading to the cessation of effluents." This description, however, does not explain these last four insights into effluents, nor does it explain how they relate to the four insights into stress. In the last section of this discourse, Ven. Sāriputta explains the first of these issues, while in the overall structure of the discourse he explains the second.

Ven. Sāriputta offers further explanations of right view in two other suttas in the Majjhima Nikāya. In MN 141 he offers a word-by-word analysis of the four noble truths. In MN 28 he analyzes the first noble truth—in particular, the form clinging-aggregate—showing how the comprehension of that one aggregate encompasses the comprehension of all five aggregates, all four noble truths, and the principle of dependent co-arising.

* * *

I have heard that on one occasion the Blessed One was staying near Sāvatthī in Jeta's Grove, Anāthapiṇḍika's monastery. Then Ven. Sāriputta addressed the monks, "Friend monks!"

"Yes, friend," the monks responded to him.

Ven. Sāriputta said, "'Right view, right view' it is said.[1] To what extent is a disciple of the noble ones a person of right view, one whose view is made straight, who is endowed with verified confidence in the Dhamma, and who has arrived at this true Dhamma?"

"We would come from a long distance, friend, to learn the meaning of these words in Ven. Sāriputta's presence. It would be good if Ven. Sāriputta himself would enlighten us as to their meaning. Having listened to him, the monks will bear it in mind."

"Then in that case, friends, listen & pay close attention. I will speak."

"As you say, friend," the monks responded to him.

SKILLFUL & UNSKILLFUL

Ven. Sāriputta said, "When a disciple of the noble ones discerns what is unskillful, discerns the root of what is unskillful, discerns what is skillful, and discerns the root of what is skillful, it is to that extent that he is a person of right view, one whose view is made straight, who is endowed with verified confidence in the Dhamma, and who has arrived at this true Dhamma.

"And what is unskillful? Taking life is unskillful, taking what is not given… sexual misconduct… lying… divisive speech… harsh speech… idle chatter is unskillful. Covetousness… ill will… wrong views are unskillful. These things are called unskillful.

"And what are the roots of what is unskillful? Greed is a root of what is unskillful, aversion is a root of what is unskillful, delusion is a root of what is unskillful. These are called the roots of what is unskillful.

"And what is skillful? Abstaining from taking life is skillful, abstaining from taking what is not given… from sexual misconduct… from lying… from divisive speech… from harsh speech… abstaining from idle chatter is skillful. Lack of covetousness… lack of ill will… right views are skillful. These things are called skillful.

"And what are the roots of what is skillful? Lack of greed is a root of what is skillful, lack of aversion… lack of delusion is a root of what is skillful. These are called the roots of what is skillful.

"When a disciple of the noble ones discerns what is unskillful in this way, discerns the root of what is unskillful in this way, discerns what is skillful in this way, and discerns the root of what is skillful in this way, when—having entirely abandoned passion-obsession, having abolished aversion-obsession, having uprooted the view-&-conceit obsession 'I am'; having abandoned ignorance & given rise to clear knowing—he has put an end to suffering & stress right in the here-&-now, it is to this extent that a disciple of the noble ones is a person of right view, one whose view is made straight, who is endowed with verified confidence in the Dhamma, and who has arrived at this true Dhamma."

NUTRIMENT

Saying "Good, friend," having delighted in and approved of Ven. Sāriputta's words, the monks asked him a further question: "Would there be another line of reasoning by which a disciple of the noble ones is a person of right view… who has arrived at this true Dhamma?"

"There would. When a disciple of the noble ones discerns nutriment, the origination of nutriment, the cessation of nutriment, and the way of practice leading to the cessation of nutriment, then he is a person of right view… who has arrived at this true Dhamma.

"And what is nutriment? What is the origination of nutriment? What is the cessation of nutriment? What is the way of practice leading to the cessation of nutriment?

"There are these four nutriments for the maintenance of beings who have come into being or for the support of those in search of a place to be born. Which four? Physical food, gross or refined; contact as the second, intellectual intention the third, and consciousness the fourth. From the origination of craving comes the origination of nutriment. From the cessation of craving comes the cessation of nutriment. And the way of practice leading to the cessation of nutriment is just this very noble eightfold path: right view, right resolve, right speech, right action, right livelihood, right effort, right mindfulness, right concentration.

"Now, when a disciple of the noble ones discerns nutriment, the origination of nutriment, the cessation of nutriment, and the way of practice leading to the cessation of nutriment in this way, when—having entirely abandoned passion-obsession, having abolished aversion-obsession, having uprooted the view-&-conceit obsession 'I am'; having abandoned ignorance & given rise to clear knowing—he has put an end to suffering & stress right in the here-&-now, it is to this extent, too, that a disciple of the noble ones is a person of right view… who has arrived at this true Dhamma."

STRESS

Saying "Good, friend," having delighted in and approved of Ven. Sāriputta's words, the monks asked him a further question: "Would there be another line of reasoning by which a disciple of the noble ones is a person of right view… who has arrived at this true Dhamma?"

"There would. When a disciple of the noble ones discerns stress, the origination of stress, the cessation of stress, and the way of practice leading to the cessation of stress, then he is a person of right view… who has arrived at this true Dhamma.

"And what is stress? Birth is stressful, aging is stressful, death is stressful; sorrow, lamentation, pain, distress, & despair are stressful; not getting what one wants is stressful.[2] In short, the five clinging-aggregates are stressful. This is called stress.

"What is the origination of stress? The craving that makes for further becoming — accompanied by passion & delight, relishing now here & now there — i.e., craving for sensuality, craving for becoming, craving for non-becoming. This is called the origination of stress.

"And what is the cessation of stress? The remainderless fading & cessation, renunciation, relinquishment, release, & letting go of that very craving. This is called the cessation of stress.

"And what is the way of practice leading to the cessation of stress? Just this very noble eightfold path: right view, right resolve, right speech, right action, right livelihood, right effort, right mindfulness, right concentration. This is called the way of practice leading to the cessation of stress.

"Now, when a disciple of the noble ones discerns stress, the origination of stress, the cessation of stress, and the way of practice leading to the cessation of stress in this way, when—having entirely abandoned passion-obsession, having abolished aversion-obsession, having uprooted the view-&-conceit obsession 'I am'; having abandoned ignorance & given rise to clear knowing—he has put an end to suffering & stress right in the here-&-now, it is to this extent, too, that a disciple of the noble ones is a person of right view... who has arrived at this true Dhamma."

AGING & DEATH

Saying "Good, friend," having delighted in and approved of Ven. Sāriputta's words, the monks asked him a further question: "Would there be another line of reasoning by which a disciple of the noble ones is a person of right view... who has arrived at this true Dhamma?"

"There would. When a disciple of the noble ones discerns aging & death, the origination of aging & death, the cessation of aging & death, and the way of practice leading to the cessation of aging & death, then he is a person of right view... who has arrived at this true Dhamma.

"And what is aging & death? What is the origination of aging & death? What is the cessation of aging & death? What is the way of practice leading to the cessation of aging & death?

"Whatever aging, decrepitude, brokenness, graying, wrinkling, decline of life-force, weakening of the faculties of the various beings in this or that group of beings, that is called aging. Whatever deceasing, passing away, breaking up, disappearance, dying, death, completion of time, break up of the aggregates, casting off of the body, interruption in the life faculty of the various beings in this or that group of beings, that is called death. This aging & this death are called aging & death.

From the origination of birth comes the origination of aging & death. From the cessation of birth comes the cessation of aging & death. And the way of practice leading to the cessation of aging &

death is just this very noble eightfold path: right view, right resolve, right speech, right action, right livelihood, right effort, right mindfulness, right concentration.

"Now, when a disciple of the noble ones discerns aging & death, the origination of aging & death, the cessation of aging & death, and the way of practice leading to the cessation of aging & death in this way, when—having entirely abandoned passion-obsession, having abolished aversion-obsession, having uprooted the view-&-conceit obsession 'I am'; having abandoned ignorance & given rise to clear knowing—he has put an end to suffering & stress right in the here-&-now, it is to this extent, too, that a disciple of the noble ones is a person of right view... who has arrived at this true Dhamma."

BIRTH

Saying "Good, friend," having delighted in and approved of Ven. Sāriputta's words, the monks asked him a further question: "Would there be another line of reasoning by which a disciple of the noble ones is a person of right view... who has arrived at this true Dhamma?"

"There would. When a disciple of the noble ones discerns birth, the origination of birth, the cessation of birth, and the way of practice leading to the cessation of birth, then he is a person of right view... who has arrived at this true Dhamma.

"And what is birth? What is the origination of birth? What is the cessation of birth? What is the way of practice leading to the cessation of birth?

"Whatever birth, taking birth, descent, coming-to-be, coming-forth, appearance of aggregates, & acquisition of (sense) spheres of the various beings in this or that group of beings, that is called birth.

"From the origination of becoming comes the origination of birth. From the cessation of becoming comes the cessation of birth. And the way of practice leading to the cessation of birth is just this very noble eightfold path: right view, right resolve, right speech, right action, right livelihood, right effort, right mindfulness, right concentration.

"Now, when a disciple of the noble ones discerns birth, the origination of birth, the cessation of birth, and the way of practice leading to the cessation of birth in this way, when—having entirely abandoned passion-obsession, having abolished aversion-obsession, having uprooted the view-&-conceit obsession 'I am'; having abandoned ignorance & given rise to clear knowing—he has put an end to suffering & stress right in the here-&-now, it is to this extent, too, that a disciple of the noble ones is a person of right view… who has arrived at this true Dhamma."

BECOMING

Saying "Good, friend," having delighted in and approved of Ven. Sāriputta's words, the monks asked him a further question: "Would there be another line of reasoning by which a disciple of the noble ones is a person of right view… who has arrived at this true Dhamma?"

"There would. When a disciple of the noble ones discerns becoming, the origination of becoming, the cessation of becoming, and the way of practice leading to the cessation of becoming, then he is a person of right view… who has arrived at this true Dhamma.

"And what is becoming? What is the origination of becoming? What is the cessation of becoming? What is the way of practice leading to the cessation of becoming?

"There are these three becomings: sensual becoming, form becoming, & formless becoming. This is called becoming.

"From the origination of clinging comes the origination of becoming. From the cessation of clinging comes the cessation of becoming. And the way of practice leading to the cessation of becoming is just this very noble eightfold path: right view, right resolve, right speech, right action, right livelihood, right effort, right mindfulness, right concentration.

"Now, when a disciple of the noble ones discerns becoming, the origination of becoming, the cessation of becoming, and the way of practice leading to the cessation of becoming in this way, when—having entirely abandoned passion-obsession, having abolished aversion-obsession, having uprooted the view-&-conceit obsession 'I am'; having abandoned ignorance & given rise to clear knowing—he has put an end to suffering & stress right in the here-&-now, it is to this extent, too, that a disciple of the noble ones is a person of right view… who has arrived at this true Dhamma."

CLINGING

Saying "Good, friend," having delighted in and approved of Ven. Sāriputta's words, the monks asked him a further question: "Would there be another line of reasoning by which a disciple of the noble ones is a person of right view… who has arrived at this true Dhamma?"

"There would. When a disciple of the noble ones discerns clinging, the origination of clinging, the cessation of clinging, and the way of practice leading to the cessation of clinging, then he is a person of right view… who has arrived at this true Dhamma.

"And what is clinging? What is the origination of clinging? What is the cessation of clinging? What is the way of practice leading to the cessation of clinging?

"There are these four clingings: sensuality clinging, view clinging, habit & practice clinging, and doctrine of self clinging. This is called clinging.

"From the origination of craving comes the origination of clinging. From the cessation of craving comes the cessation of clinging. And the way of practice leading to the cessation of clinging is just this very noble eightfold path: right view, right resolve, right speech, right action, right livelihood, right effort, right mindfulness, right concentration.

"Now, when a disciple of the noble ones discerns clinging, the origination of clinging, the cessation of clinging, and the way of practice leading to the cessation of clinging in this way, when—having entirely abandoned passion-obsession, having abolished aversion-obsession, having uprooted the view-&-conceit obsession 'I am'; having abandoned ignorance & given rise to clear knowing—he has put an end to suffering & stress right in the here-&-now, it is to this extent, too, that a disciple of the noble ones is a person of right view… who has arrived at this true Dhamma."

CRAVING

Saying "Good, friend," having delighted in and approved of Ven. Sāriputta's words, the monks asked him a further question: "Would there be another line of reasoning by which a disciple of the noble ones is a person of right view… who has arrived at this true Dhamma?"

"There would. When a disciple of the noble ones discerns craving, the origination of craving, the cessation of craving, and the way of practice leading to the cessation of craving, then he is a person of right view… who has arrived at this true Dhamma.

"And what is craving? What is the origination of craving? What is the cessation of craving? What is the way of practice leading to the cessation of craving?

"There are these six cravings: craving for forms, craving for sounds, craving for smells, craving for tastes, craving for tactile sensations, craving for ideas. This is called craving.

"From the origination of feeling comes the origination of craving. From the cessation of feeling comes the cessation of craving. And the way of practice leading to the cessation of craving is just this very noble eightfold path: right view, right resolve, right speech, right action, right livelihood, right effort, right mindfulness, right concentration.

"Now, when a disciple of the noble ones discerns craving, the origination of craving, the cessation of craving, and the way of practice leading to the cessation of craving in this way, when—having entirely abandoned passion-obsession, having abolished aversion-obsession, having uprooted the view-&-conceit obsession 'I am'; having abandoned ignorance & given rise to clear knowing—he has put an end to suffering & stress right in the here-&-now, it is to this extent, too, that a disciple of the noble ones is a person of right view… who has arrived at this true Dhamma."

FEELING

Saying "Good, friend," having delighted in and approved of Ven. Sāriputta's words, the monks asked him a further question: "Would there be another line of reasoning by which a disciple of the noble ones is a person of right view… who has arrived at this true Dhamma?"

"There would. When a disciple of the noble ones discerns feeling, the origination of feeling, the cessation of feeling, and the way of practice leading to the cessation of feeling, then he is a person of right view… who has arrived at this true Dhamma.

"And what is feeling? What is the origination of feeling? What is the cessation of feeling? What is the way of practice leading to the cessation of feeling?

"There are these six feelings: feeling born from eye-contact, feeling born from ear-contact, feeling born from nose-contact, feeling born from tongue-contact, feeling born from body-contact, feeling born from intellect-contact. This is called feeling.

"From the origination of contact comes the origination of feeling. From the cessation of contact comes the cessation of feeling. And the way of practice leading to the cessation of feeling is just this very noble eightfold path: right view, right resolve, right speech, right action, right livelihood, right effort, right mindfulness, right concentration.

"Now, when a disciple of the noble ones discerns feeling, the origination of feeling, the cessation of feeling, and the way of practice leading to the cessation of feeling in this way, when—having entirely abandoned passion-obsession, having abolished aversion-obsession, having uprooted the view-&-conceit obsession 'I am'; having abandoned ignorance & given rise to clear knowing—he has put an end to suffering & stress right in the here-&-now, it is to this extent, too, that a disciple of the noble ones is a person of right view... who has arrived at this true Dhamma."

CONTACT

Saying "Good, friend," having delighted in and approved of Ven. Sāriputta's words, the monks asked him a further question: "Would there be another line of reasoning by which a disciple of the noble ones is a person of right view... who has arrived at this true Dhamma?"

"There would. When a disciple of the noble ones discerns contact, the origination of contact, the cessation of contact, and the way of practice leading to the cessation of contact, then he is a person of right view... who has arrived at this true Dhamma.

"And what is contact? What is the origination of contact? What is the cessation of contact? What is the way of practice leading to the cessation of contact?

"There are these six classes of contact: eye-contact, ear-contact, nose-contact, tongue-contact, body-contact, intellect-contact: This is called contact.

"From the origination of the six sense media comes the origination of contact. From the cessation of the six sense media comes the cessation of contact. And the way of practice leading to the cessation of contact is just this very noble eightfold path: right view, right resolve, right speech, right action, right livelihood, right effort, right mindfulness, right concentration.

"Now, when a disciple of the noble ones discerns contact, the origination of contact, the cessation of contact, and the way of practice leading to the cessation of contact in this way, when—having entirely abandoned passion-obsession, having abolished aversion-obsession, having uprooted the view-&-conceit obsession 'I am'; having abandoned ignorance & given rise to clear knowing—he has put an end to suffering & stress right in the here-&-now, it is to this extent, too, that a disciple of the noble ones is a person of right view... who has arrived at this true Dhamma."

SIX SENSE MEDIA

Saying "Good, friend," having delighted in and approved of Ven. Sāriputta's words, the monks asked him a further question: "Would there be another line of reasoning by which a disciple of the noble ones is a person of right view... who has arrived at this true Dhamma?"

"There would. When a disciple of the noble ones discerns the six sense media, the origination of the six sense media, the cessation of the six sense media, and the way of practice leading to the cessation of the six sense media, then he is a person of right view... who has arrived at this true Dhamma.

"And what are the six sense media? What is the origination of the six sense media? What is the cessation of the six sense media? What is the way of practice leading to the cessation of the six sense media?

"There are these six sense media: the eye-medium, the ear-medium, the nose-medium, the tongue-medium, the body-medium, the intellect-medium: These are called the six sense media.

"From the origination of name-&-form comes the origination of the six sense media. From the cessation of name-&-form comes the cessation of the six sense media. And the way of practice leading to the cessation of the six sense media is just this very noble eightfold path: right view, right resolve, right speech, right action, right livelihood, right effort, right mindfulness, right concentration.

"Now, when a disciple of the noble ones discerns the six sense media, the origination of the six sense media, the cessation of the six sense media, and the way of practice leading to the cessation of the six sense media in this way, when—having entirely abandoned passion-obsession, having abolished aversion-obsession, having uprooted the view-&-conceit obsession 'I am'; having abandoned ignorance & given rise to clear knowing—he has put an end to suffering & stress right in the here-&-now, it is to this extent, too, that a disciple of the noble ones is a person of right view... who has arrived at this true Dhamma."

NAME-&-FORM

Saying "Good, friend," having delighted in and approved of Ven. Sāriputta's words, the monks asked him a further question: "Would there be another line of reasoning by which a disciple of the noble ones is a person of right view... who has arrived at this true Dhamma?"

"There would. When a disciple of the noble ones discerns name-&-form, the origination of name-&-form, the cessation of name-&-form, and the way of practice leading to the cessation of name-&-form, then he is a person of right view... who has arrived at this true Dhamma.

"And what is name-&-form? What is the origination of name-&-form? What is the cessation of name-&-form? What is the way of practice leading to the cessation of name-&-form?

"Feeling, perception, intention, contact, & attention: This is called name. The four great elements, and the form dependent on the four great elements: This is called form. This name & this form are called name-&-form.

"From the origination of consciousness comes the origination of name-&-form. From the cessation of consciousness comes the cessation of name-&-form. And the way of practice leading to the cessation of name-&-form is just this very noble eightfold path: right view, right resolve, right speech, right action, right livelihood, right effort, right mindfulness, right concentration.

"Now, when a disciple of the noble ones discerns name-&-form, the origination of name-&-form, the cessation of name-&-form, and the way of practice leading to the cessation of name-&-form in this way, when—having entirely abandoned passion-obsession, having abolished aversion-obsession, having uprooted the view-&-conceit obsession 'I am'; having abandoned ignorance & given rise to clear knowing—he has put an end to suffering & stress right in the here-&-now, it is to this extent, too, that a disciple of the noble ones is a person of right view… who has arrived at this true Dhamma."

CONSCIOUSNESS

Saying "Good, friend," having delighted in and approved of Ven. Sāriputta's words, the monks asked him a further question: "Would there be another line of reasoning by which a disciple of the noble ones is a person of right view… who has arrived at this true Dhamma?"

"There would. When a disciple of the noble ones discerns consciousness, the origination of consciousness, the cessation of consciousness, and the way of practice leading to the cessation of consciousness, then he is a person of right view… who has arrived at this true Dhamma.

"And what is consciousness? What is the origination of consciousness? What is the cessation of consciousness? What is the way of practice leading to the cessation of consciousness?

"There are these six classes of consciousness: eye-consciousness, ear-consciousness, nose-consciousness, tongue-consciousness, body-consciousness, intellect-consciousness. This is called consciousness.

"From the origination of fabrication comes the origination of consciousness. From the cessation of fabrication comes the cessation of consciousness. And the way of practice leading to the cessation of consciousness is just this very noble eightfold path: right view, right resolve, right speech, right action, right livelihood, right effort, right mindfulness, right concentration.

"Now, when a disciple of the noble ones discerns consciousness, the origination of consciousness, the cessation of consciousness, and the way of practice leading to the cessation of consciousness in this way, when—having entirely abandoned passion-obsession, having abolished aversion-obsession, having uprooted the view-&-conceit obsession 'I am'; having abandoned ignorance & given rise to clear knowing—he has put an end to suffering & stress right in the here-&-now, it is to this extent, too, that a disciple of the noble ones is a person of right view… who has arrived at this true Dhamma."

FABRICATION

Saying "Good, friend," having delighted in and approved of Ven. Sāriputta's words, the monks asked him a further question: "Would there be another line of reasoning by which a disciple of the noble ones is a person of right view… who has arrived at this true Dhamma?"

"There would. When a disciple of the noble ones discerns fabrication, the origination of fabrication, the cessation of fabrication, and the way of practice leading to the cessation of fabrication, then he is a person of right view… who has arrived at this true Dhamma.

"And what is fabrication? What is the origination of fabrication? What is the cessation of fabrication? What is the way of practice leading to the cessation of fabrication?

"There are these three fabrications: bodily fabrication, verbal fabrication, mental fabrication. These are called fabrication.

"From the origination of ignorance comes the origination of fabrication. From the cessation of ignorance comes the cessation of fabrication. And the way of practice leading to the cessation of fabrication is just this very noble eightfold path: right view, right resolve, right speech, right action, right livelihood, right effort, right mindfulness, right concentration.

"Now, when a disciple of the noble ones discerns fabrication, the origination of fabrication, the cessation of fabrication, and the way of practice leading to the cessation of fabrication in this way, when—having entirely abandoned passion-obsession, having abolished aversion-obsession, having uprooted the view-&-conceit obsession 'I am'; having abandoned ignorance & given rise to clear knowing—he has put an end to suffering & stress right in the here-&-now, it is to this extent, too, that a disciple of the noble ones is a person of right view… who has arrived at this true Dhamma."

IGNORANCE

Saying "Good, friend," having delighted in and approved of Ven. Sāriputta's words, the monks asked him a further question: "Would there be another line of reasoning by which a disciple of the noble ones is a person of right view... who has arrived at this true Dhamma?"

"There would. When a disciple of the noble ones discerns ignorance, the origination of ignorance, the cessation of ignorance, and the way of practice leading to the cessation of ignorance, then he is a person of right view... who has arrived at this true Dhamma.

"And what is ignorance? What is the origination of ignorance? What is the cessation of ignorance? What is the way of practice leading to the cessation of ignorance?

"Any lack of knowledge with reference to stress, any lack of knowledge with reference to the origination of stress, any lack of knowledge with reference to the cessation of stress, any lack of knowledge with reference to the way of practice leading to the cessation of stress: This is called ignorance.

"From the origination of effluents comes the origination of ignorance. From the cessation of effluents comes the cessation of ignorance. And the way of practice leading to the cessation of ignorance is just this very noble eightfold path: right view, right resolve, right speech, right action, right livelihood, right effort, right mindfulness, right concentration.

"Now, when a disciple of the noble ones discerns ignorance, the origination of ignorance, the cessation of ignorance, and the way of practice leading to the cessation of ignorance in this way, when—having entirely abandoned passion-obsession, having abolished aversion-obsession, having uprooted the view-&-conceit obsession 'I am'; having abandoned ignorance & given rise to clear knowing—he has put an end to suffering & stress right in the here-&-now, it is to this extent, too, that a disciple of the noble ones is a person of right view... who has arrived at this true Dhamma."

EFFLUENTS

Saying "Good, friend," having delighted in and approved of Ven. Sāriputta's words, the monks asked him a further question: "Would there be another line of reasoning by which a disciple of the noble ones is a person of right view... who has arrived at this true Dhamma?"

"There would. When a disciple of the noble ones discerns effluents, the origination of effluents, the cessation of effluents, and the way of practice leading to the cessation of effluents, then he is a person of right view... who has arrived at this true Dhamma.

"And what are effluents? What is the origination of effluents? What is the cessation of effluents? What is the way of practice leading to the cessation of effluents?

"There are these three effluents: the effluent of sensuality, the effluent of becoming, the effluent of ignorance. These are called effluents.

"From the origination of ignorance comes the origination of effluents. From the cessation of ignorance comes the cessation of effluents. And the way of practice leading to the cessation of effluents is just this very noble eightfold path: right view, right resolve, right speech, right action, right livelihood, right effort, right mindfulness, right concentration.

"Now, when a disciple of the noble ones discerns effluents, the origination of effluents, the cessation of effluents, and the way of practice leading to the cessation of effluents in this way, when—having entirely abandoned passion-obsession, having abolished aversion-obsession, having uprooted the view-&-conceit obsession 'I am'; having abandoned ignorance & given rise to clear knowing—he has put an end to suffering & stress right in the here-&-now, it is to this extent, too, that a disciple of the noble ones is a person of right view, one whose view is made straight, who is endowed with verified confidence in the Dhamma, and who has arrived at this true Dhamma."

That is what Ven. Sāriputta said. Gratified, the monks delighted in Ven. Sāriputta's words.

NOTES

1. This reading follows the Thai edition. The Burmese and PTS editions say, "'A person of right view, a person of right view' it is said."

2. In passages where the Buddha defines stress, (e.g., SN 56:11, DN 22), he includes the statements, "association with the unbeloved is stressful; separation from the loved is stressful," prior to "not getting what one wants is stressful." For some reason, in passages where Ven. Sāriputta defines stress (here and at MN 28 and MN 141), he drops these statements from the definition.

See also: MN 28; MN 61; MN 117; MN 141; SN 12:11-12; SN 12:15; SN 12:63-64; AN 10:94; Sn 3:12

13 *The Great Mass of Stress*

Mahā Dukkhakkhandha Sutta

I have heard that on one occasion the Blessed One was staying near Sāvatthī in Jeta's Grove, Anāthapiṇḍika's monastery. Then, early in the morning, several monks adjusted their under robes and, carrying their bowls & outer robes, went into Sāvatthī for alms. The thought occurred to them, "It's still too early to go into Sāvatthī for alms. What if we were to visit the park of the wanderers of other persuasions?"

So they headed to the park of the wanderers of other persuasions. On arrival, they exchanged courteous greetings with the wanderers of other persuasions. After an exchange of friendly greetings & courtesies, they sat to one side. As they were sitting there, the wanderers of other persuasions said to them, "Friends, Gotama the contemplative describes the comprehension of sensuality. We, too, describe the comprehension of sensuality. He describes the comprehension of forms. We, too, describe the comprehension of forms. He describes the comprehension of feelings. We, too, describe the comprehension of feelings. So what is the difference, what the distinction, what the distinguishing factor between him and us in terms of his teaching and ours, his message and ours?"

The monks, neither delighting nor disapproving of the words of the wanderers of other persuasions, got up from their seats, (thinking,) "We will learn the meaning of these words in the Blessed One's presence."

Then, having gone for alms in Sāvatthī, after their meal, returning from their alms round, the monks went to the Blessed One and, on arrival, having bowed down to him, sat to one side. As they were sitting there, they [told him what had happened].

"Monks, when the wanderers of other persuasions say this, they are to be told, 'What, friends, with regard to sensuality, is the allure, what the drawback, what the escape? What, with regard to forms, is the allure, what the drawback, what the escape? What, with regard to feelings, is the allure, what the drawback, what the escape?' When asked this, they will not manage an answer and, what is more, will get themselves into trouble. Why is that? Because it lies outside their range. Monks, in this world with its devas, Māras, and Brahmās, in this people with its contemplatives & brahmans, its royalty & commonfolk, I do not see anyone who can satisfy the mind with an answer to these questions, aside from a Tathāgata, a Tathāgata's disciples, or someone who has heard it from them.

SENSUALITY

"Now what, monks, is the allure of sensuality? These five strings of sensuality. Which five? Forms cognizable via the eye—agreeable, pleasing, charming, endearing, enticing, linked with sensual desire. Sounds cognizable via the ear… Aromas cognizable via the nose… Flavors cognizable via the tongue… Tactile sensations cognizable via the body—agreeable, pleasing, charming, endearing, enticing, linked with sensual desire. Now whatever pleasure or happiness arises in dependence on these five strands of sensuality, that is the allure of sensuality.

"And what is the drawback of sensuality? There is the case where, on account of the occupation by which a clansman makes a living—whether checking or accounting or calculating or plowing or trading or cattle-tending or archery or as a king's man, or whatever the occupation may be—he faces cold, he faces heat, being harassed by mosquitoes & flies, wind & sun & creeping things, dying from hunger & thirst.

"Now this drawback in the case of sensuality, this mass of stress visible here & now, has sensuality for its reason, sensuality for its source, sensuality for its cause, the reason being simply sensuality.

"If the clansman gains no wealth while thus working & striving & making effort, he sorrows, grieves, & laments, beats his breast, becomes distraught: 'My work is in vain, my efforts are fruitless!' Now this drawback too in the case of sensuality, this mass of stress visible here & now, has sensuality for its reason, sensuality for its source, sensuality for its cause, the reason being simply sensuality.

"If the clansman gains wealth while thus working & striving & making effort, he experiences pain & distress in protecting it: 'How will neither kings nor thieves make off with my property, nor fire burn it, nor water sweep it away, nor hateful heirs make off with it?' And as he thus guards and watches over his property, kings or thieves make off with it, or fire burns it, or water sweeps it away, or hateful heirs make off with it. And he sorrows, grieves, & laments, beats his breast, becomes distraught: 'What was mine is no more!' Now this drawback too in the case of sensuality, this mass of stress visible here & now, has sensuality for its reason, sensuality for its source, sensuality for its cause, the reason being simply sensuality.

"Again, it is with sensuality for the reason, sensuality for the source, sensuality for the cause, the reason being simply sensuality, that kings quarrel with kings, nobles with nobles, brahmans with brahmans, householders with householders, mother with child, child with mother, father with child, child with father, brother with brother, sister with sister, brother with sister, sister with brother, friend with friend. And then in their quarrels, brawls, & disputes, they attack one another with fists or with clods or with sticks or with knives, so that they incur death or deadly pain. Now this drawback too in the case of sensuality, this mass of stress visible here & now, has sensuality for its reason, sensuality for its source, sensuality for its cause, the reason being simply sensuality.

"Again, it is with sensuality for the reason, sensuality for the source… that (men), taking swords & shields and buckling on bows & quivers, charge into battle massed in double array while arrows & spears are flying and swords are flashing; and there they are wounded by arrows & spears, and their heads are cut off by swords, so that they incur death or deadly pain. Now this drawback too in the case of sensuality, this mass of stress visible here & now, has sensuality for its reason, sensuality for its source, sensuality for its cause, the reason being simply sensuality.

"Again, it is with sensuality for the reason, sensuality for the source… that (men), taking swords & shields and buckling on bows & quivers, charge slippery bastions while arrows & spears are flying and swords are flashing; and there they are splashed with boiling cow dung and crushed under heavy weights, and their heads are cut off by swords, so that they incur death or deadly pain. Now this drawback too in the case of sensuality, this mass of stress visible here & now, has sensuality for its reason, sensuality for its source, sensuality for its cause, the reason being simply sensuality.

"Again, it is with sensuality for the reason, sensuality for the source… that (men) break into windows, seize plunder, commit burglary, ambush highways, commit adultery, and when they are captured, kings have them tortured in many ways. They flog them with whips, beat them with canes, beat them with clubs; they cut off their hands, cut off their feet, cut off their hands & feet; they cut off their ears, cut off their noses, cut off their ears & noses; they subject them to the 'porridge pot,' the 'polished-shell shave,' the 'Rāhu's mouth,' the 'flaming garland,' the 'blazing hand,' the 'grass-duty (ascetic),' the 'bark-dress (ascetic),' the 'burning antelope,' the 'meat hooks,' the 'coin-gouging,' the 'lye pickling,' the 'pivot on a stake,' the 'rolled-up bed'; they have them splashed with boiling oil, devoured by dogs, impaled alive on stakes; they have their heads cut off with swords, so that they incur death or deadly pain. Now this drawback too in the case of sensuality, this mass of stress visible here

& now, has sensuality for its reason, sensuality for its source, sensuality for its cause, the reason being simply sensuality.

"Again, it is with sensuality for the reason, sensuality for the source… that (people) engage in bodily misconduct, verbal misconduct, mental misconduct. Having engaged in bodily, verbal, and mental misconduct, they—on the break-up of the body, after death—re-appear in the plane of deprivation, the bad destination, the lower realms, in hell. Now this drawback too in the case of sensuality, this mass of stress in the future life, has sensuality for its reason, sensuality for its source, sensuality for its cause, the reason being simply sensuality.

"And what, monks, is the escape from sensuality? The subduing of desire-passion for sensuality, the abandoning of desire-passion for sensuality: That is the escape from sensuality.

"That any contemplatives or brahmans who do not discern, as it has come to be, the allure of sensuality as allure, the drawback of sensuality as drawback, the escape from sensuality as escape, would themselves comprehend sensuality or would rouse another with the truth so that, in line with what he has practiced, he would comprehend sensuality: That is impossible. But that any contemplatives or brahmans who discern, as it has come to be, the allure of sensuality as allure, the drawback of sensuality as drawback, the escape from sensuality as escape, would themselves comprehend sensuality or would rouse another with the truth so that, in line with what he has practiced, he would comprehend sensuality: That is possible.

FORM

"Now what, monks, is the allure of forms? Suppose there were a maiden of the noble caste, the brahman caste, or the householder class, fifteen or sixteen years old, neither too tall nor too short, neither too thin nor too plump, neither too dark nor too pale. Is her beauty & charm at that time at its height?"

"Yes, lord."

"Whatever pleasure & happiness arise in dependence on that beauty & charm: That is the allure of forms."

"And what is the drawback of form? There is the case where one might see that very same woman at a later time, when she's eighty, ninety, one hundred years old: aged, roof-rafter crooked, bent-over, supported by a cane, palsied, miserable, broken-toothed, gray-haired, scanty-haired, bald, wrinkled, her body all blotchy. What do you think? Has her earlier beauty & charm vanished, and the drawback appeared?"

"Yes, lord."

"This, monks, is the drawback of forms.

"Again, one might see that very same woman sick, in pain, & seriously ill, lying soiled with her own urine & excrement, lifted up by others, laid down by others. What do you think? Has her earlier beauty & charm vanished, and the drawback appeared?"

"Yes, lord."

"This too, monks, is the drawback of forms.

"Again, one might see that very same woman as a corpse cast away in a charnel ground—one day, two days, three days dead, bloated, livid, & oozing. What do you think? Has her earlier beauty & charm vanished, and the drawback appeared?"

"Yes, lord."

"This too, monks, is the drawback of forms.

"Again, one might see that very same woman as a corpse cast away in a charnel ground picked at by crows, vultures, & hawks, by dogs, hyenas, & various other creatures… a skeleton smeared with flesh & blood, connected with tendons… a fleshless skeleton smeared with blood, connected with tendons… a skeleton without flesh or blood, connected with tendons… bones detached from their tendons, scattered in all directions—here a hand bone, there a foot bone, here a shin bone, there a thigh bone, here a hip bone, there a back bone, here a rib, there a breast bone, here a shoulder bone, there a neck bone, here a jaw bone, there a tooth, here a skull… the bones whitened, somewhat like the color of shells…piled up, more than a year old… decomposed into a powder. What do you think? Has her earlier beauty & charm vanished, and the drawback appeared?"

"Yes, lord."

"This too, monks, is the drawback of forms.

"And what, monks, is the escape from forms? The subduing of desire-passion for forms, the abandoning of desire-passion for forms: That is the escape from form.

"That any contemplatives or brahmans who do not discern, as it has come to be, the allure of forms as allure, the drawback of forms as drawback, the escape from forms as escape, would themselves comprehend form or would rouse another with the truth so that, in line with what he has practiced, he would comprehend form: That is impossible. But that any contemplatives or brahmans who discern, as it has come to be, the allure of forms as allure, the drawback of forms as drawback, the escape from forms as escape, would themselves comprehend form or would rouse another with the truth so that, in line with what he has practiced, he would comprehend form: That is possible.

FEELING

"Now what, monks, is the allure of feelings? There is the case where a monk—quite secluded from sensuality, secluded from unskillful (mental) qualities—enters & remains in the first jhāna: rapture & pleasure born from seclusion, accompanied by directed thought & evaluation. At that time he does not intend his own affliction, the affliction of others, or the affliction of both. He feels a feeling totally unafflicted. The unafflicted, I tell you, is the highest allure of feelings.

"Again the monk, with the stilling of directed thoughts & evaluations, enters & remains in the second jhāna: rapture & pleasure born of concentration, unification of awareness free from directed thought & evaluation—internal assurance… With the fading of rapture he remains equanimous, mindful & alert, and senses pleasure with the body. He enters & remains in the third jhāna, of which the noble ones declare, 'Equanimous & mindful, he has a pleasant abiding'… With the abandoning of pleasure & pain—as with the earlier disappearance of elation & distress—he enters & remains in the fourth jhāna: purity of equanimity & mindfulness, neither pleasure nor pain. At that time he does not intend his own affliction, the affliction of others, or the affliction of both. He feels a feeling totally unafflicted. The unafflicted, I tell you, is the highest allure of feelings.

"And what is the drawback of feelings? That feeling is inconstant, stressful, subject to change: This is the drawback of feelings.

"And what is the escape from feelings? The subduing of desire-passion for feelings, the abandoning of desire-passion for feelings: That is the escape from feelings.

"That any contemplatives or brahmans who do not discern, as it has come to be, the allure of feelings as allure, the drawback of feelings as drawback, the escape from feelings as escape, would themselves comprehend feeling or would rouse another with the truth so that, in line with what he has practiced, he would comprehend feeling: That is impossible. But that any contemplatives or brahmans who discern, as it has come to be, the allure of feelings as allure, the drawback of feelings as drawback, the escape from feelings as escape, would themselves comprehend feeling or would rouse another with the truth so that, in line with what he has practiced, he would comprehend feeling: That is possible."

That is what the Blessed One said. Gratified, the monks delighted in the Blessed One's words.

See also: MN 54; SN 35:63; SN 35:115; SN 35:189; AN 6:63; AN 9:34; AN 9:36; Thig 13:1

14 *The Lesser Mass of Stress*

Cūḷa Dukkhakkhandha Sutta

I have heard that on one occasion the Blessed One was staying among the Sakyans at Kapilavatthu in the Banyan Park. Then Mahānāma the Sakyan[1] went to the Blessed One and, on arrival, having bowed down to him, sat to one side. As he was sitting there he said to the Blessed One, "For a long time now, lord, I have understood the Dhamma taught by the Blessed One thus: 'Greed is a defilement of the mind; aversion is a defilement of the mind; delusion is a defilement of the mind.' Yet even though I understand the Dhamma taught by the Blessed One that greed is a defilement of the mind, aversion is a defilement of the mind, delusion is a defilement of the mind, there are still times when the quality of greed invades my mind and remains, when the quality of aversion… the quality of delusion invades my mind and remains. The thought occurs to me: What quality is unabandoned within me so that there are times when the quality of greed invades my mind and remains, when the quality of aversion… the quality of delusion invades my mind and remains?"

"Mahānāma, that very quality [i.e., greed, aversion, or delusion] is what is unabandoned within you so that there are times when the quality of greed… the quality of aversion… the quality of delusion invades your mind and remains.[2] For if that quality were abandoned in you, you would not live the household life and would not partake of sensuality. It's because that quality is not abandoned in you that you live the household life and partake of sensuality.

"Even though a disciple of the noble ones has clearly seen as it has come to be with right discernment that sensuality is of much stress, much despair, & greater drawbacks, still—if he has not attained a rapture & pleasure apart from sensuality, apart from unskillful qualities, or something more peaceful than that[3]—he can be tempted by sensuality. But when he has clearly seen as it has come to be with right discernment that sensuality is of much stress, much despair, & greater drawbacks, and he has attained a rapture & pleasure apart from sensuality, apart from unskillful qualities, or something more peaceful than that, he cannot be tempted by sensuality.

"I myself, before my self-awakening, when I was still just an unawakened Bodhisatta, saw as it had come to be with right discernment that sensuality is of much stress, much despair, & greater drawbacks, but as long as I had not attained a rapture & pleasure apart from sensuality, apart from unskillful qualities, or something more peaceful than that, I did not claim that I could not be tempted by sensuality. But when I saw as it had come to be with right discernment that sensuality is of much stress, much despair, & greater drawbacks, and I had attained a rapture & pleasure apart from sensuality, apart from unskillful qualities, or something more peaceful than that, that was when I claimed that I could not be tempted by sensuality.

"Now what, Mahānāma, is the allure of sensuality? These five strings of sensuality. Which five? Forms cognizable via the eye—agreeable, pleasing, charming, endearing, enticing, linked with sensual desire. Sounds cognizable via the ear... Aromas cognizable via the nose... Flavors cognizable via the tongue... Tactile sensations cognizable via the body—agreeable, pleasing, charming, endearing, enticing, linked with sensual desire. Now whatever pleasure or happiness arises in dependence on these five strands of sensuality, that is the allure of sensuality.

"And what is the drawback of sensuality? There is the case where, on account of the occupation by which a clansman makes a living—whether checking or accounting or calculating or plowing or trading or cattle-tending or archery or as a king's man, or whatever the occupation may be—he faces cold, he faces heat, being harassed by mosquitoes & flies, wind & sun & creeping things, dying from hunger & thirst.

"Now this drawback in the case of sensuality, this mass of stress visible here & now, has sensuality for its reason, sensuality for its source, sensuality for its cause, the reason being simply sensuality.

"If the clansman gains no wealth while thus working & striving & making effort, he sorrows, grieves, & laments, beats his breast, becomes distraught: 'My work is in vain, my efforts are fruitless!' Now this drawback too in the case of sensuality, this mass of stress visible here & now, has sensuality for its reason, sensuality for its source, sensuality for its cause, the reason being simply sensuality.

"If the clansman gains wealth while thus working & striving & making effort, he experiences pain & distress in protecting it: 'How will neither kings nor thieves make off with my property, nor fire burn it, nor water sweep it away, nor hateful heirs make off with it?' And as he thus guards and watches over his property, kings or thieves make off with it, or fire burns it, or water sweeps it away, or hateful heirs make off with it. And he sorrows, grieves, & laments, beats his breast, becomes distraught: 'What was mine is no more!' Now this drawback too in the case of sensuality, this mass of stress visible here & now, has sensuality for its reason, sensuality for its source, sensuality for its cause, the reason being simply sensuality.

"Again, it is with sensuality for the reason, sensuality for the source, sensuality for the cause, the reason being simply sensuality, that kings quarrel with kings, nobles with nobles, brahmans with brahmans, householders with householders, mother with child, child with mother, father with child, child with father, brother with brother, sister with sister, brother with sister, sister with brother, friend with friend. And then in their quarrels, brawls, & disputes, they attack one another with fists or with clods or with sticks or with knives, so that they incur death or deadly pain. Now this drawback too in the case of sensuality, this mass of stress visible here & now, has sensuality for its reason, sensuality for its source, sensuality for its cause, the reason being simply sensuality.

"Again, it is with sensuality for the reason, sensuality for the source… that (men), taking swords & shields and buckling on bows & quivers, charge into battle massed in double array while arrows & spears are flying and swords are flashing; and there they are wounded by arrows & spears, and their heads are cut off by swords, so that they incur death or deadly pain. Now this drawback too in the case of sensuality, this mass of stress visible here & now, has sensuality for its reason, sensuality for its source, sensuality for its cause, the reason being simply sensuality.

"Again, it is with sensuality for the reason, sensuality for the source… that (men), taking swords & shields and buckling on bows & quivers, charge slippery bastions while arrows & spears are flying and swords are flashing; and there they are splashed with boiling cow dung and crushed under heavy weights, and their heads are cut off by swords, so that they incur death or deadly pain. Now this drawback too in the case of sensuality, this mass of stress visible here & now, has sensuality for its reason, sensuality for its source, sensuality for its cause, the reason being simply sensuality.

"Again, it is with sensuality for the reason, sensuality for the source… that (men) break into windows, seize plunder, commit burglary, ambush highways, commit adultery, and when they are captured, kings have them tortured in many ways. They flog them with whips, beat them with canes, beat them with clubs; they cut off their hands, cut off their feet, cut off their hands & feet; they cut off their ears, cut off their noses, cut off their ears & noses; they subject them to the 'porridge pot,' the 'polished-shell shave,' the 'Rāhu's mouth,' the 'flaming garland,' the 'blazing hand,' the 'grass-duty (ascetic),' the 'bark-dress (ascetic),' the 'burning antelope,' the 'meat hooks,' the 'coin-gouging,' the 'lye pickling,' the 'pivot on a stake,' the 'rolled-up bed'; they have them splashed with boiling oil, devoured by dogs, impaled alive on stakes; they have their heads cut off with swords, so that they incur death or deadly pain. Now this drawback too in the case of sensuality, this mass of stress visible here & now, has sensuality for its reason, sensuality for its source, sensuality for its cause, the reason being simply sensuality.

"Again, it is with sensuality for the reason, sensuality for the source… that (people) engage in bodily misconduct, verbal misconduct, mental misconduct. Having engaged in bodily, verbal, and mental misconduct, they—on the break-up of the body, after death—re-appear in the plane of deprivation, the bad destination, the lower realms, in hell. Now this drawback too in the case of sensuality, this mass of stress in the future life, has sensuality for its reason, sensuality for its source, sensuality for its cause, the reason being simply sensuality.

"Once, Mahānāma, when I was staying near Rājagaha on Vulture Peak Mountain, a number of Niganṭhas were at Black Rock on the slopes of Isigili, practicing continuous standing: rejecting seats, experiencing fierce, sharp, racking pains due to exertion. So, emerging from my seclusion in the late afternoon, I went to the Niganṭhas at Black Rock on the slopes of Isigili and on arrival asked them, 'Why are you practicing continuous standing: rejecting seats, experiencing fierce, sharp, racking pains due to exertion?' When this was said, the Niganṭhas said to me, 'Friend, the Niganṭha Nāṭaputta[4] is all-knowing, all-seeing, and claims total knowledge & vision thus: "Whether I am walking or standing, sleeping or awake, knowledge & vision are continuously & continually established in me." He has told us, "Niganṭhas, there are evil actions that you have done in the past. Exhaust them with these painful austerities. When in the present you are restrained in body, restrained in speech, and restrained in mind, that is the non-doing of evil action for the future. Thus, with the destruction of old actions through asceticism, and with the non-doing of new actions, there will be no flow into the future. With no flow into the future, there is the ending of action. With the ending of action, the ending of stress. With the ending of stress, the ending of feeling. With the ending of feeling, all suffering & stress will be exhausted."[5] We approve of that (teaching), prefer it, and are gratified by it.'

"When this was said, I asked them, 'But friends, do you know that you existed in the past, and that you did not not exist?'

"'No, friend.'

"'And do you know that you did evil actions in the past, and that you did not not do them?'

"'No, friend.'

"'And do you know that you did such-and-such evil actions in the past?'

"'No, friend.'

"'And do you know that so-and-so much stress has been exhausted, or that so-and-so much stress remains to be exhausted, or that with the exhaustion of so-and-so much stress all stress will be exhausted?'

"'No, friend.'

"'But do you know what is the abandoning of unskillful qualities and the attainment of skillful qualities in the here-&-now?'

"'No, friend.'

"'So, friends, it seems that you don't know that you existed in the past, and that you did not not exist; you don't know that you did evil actions in the past, and that you did not not do them; you don't know that you did such-and-such evil actions in the past; you don't know that so-and-so much stress has been exhausted, or that so-and-so much stress remains to be exhausted, or that with the exhaustion of so-and-so much stress all stress will be exhausted; you don't know what is the abandoning of unskillful qualities and the attainment of skillful qualities in the here-&-now. That being the case, those in the world who are murderers, bloody-handed doers of what is cruel, when they are later reborn among human beings, go forth with the Nigaṇṭhas.'

"'But, friend Gotama, it's not the case that pleasure is to be attained through pleasure. Pleasure is to be attained through pain. For if pleasure were to be attained through pleasure, then King Seniya Bimbisāra of Magadha would attain pleasure, for he lives in greater pleasure than you, friend Gotama.'

"'Surely the venerable Nigaṇṭhas said that rashly and without reflecting... for instead, I should be asked, "Who lives in greater pleasure: King Seniya Bimbisāra of Magadha or master Gotama?"'

"'Yes, friend Gotama, we said that rashly and without reflecting... but let that be. We now ask you, master Gotama: Who lives in greater pleasure: King Seniya Bimbisāra of Magadha or master Gotama?'

"'In that case, Nigaṇṭhas, I will question you in return. Answer as you like. What do you think? Can King Seniya Bimbisāra of Magadha—without moving his body, without uttering a word—dwell sensitive to unalloyed pleasure for seven days & nights?'

"'No, friend."

"'... for six days & nights.... for five days & nights... for a day & a night?'

"'No, friend."

"'Now, I—without moving my body, without uttering a word—can dwell sensitive to unalloyed pleasure for a day and a night... for two days & nights... for three... four... five... six... seven days & nights.[6] So what do you think? That being the case, who dwells in greater pleasure: King Seniya Bimbisāra of Magadha or me?'

"'That being the case, master Gotama dwells in greater pleasure than King Seniya Bimbisāra of Magadha.'"

That is what the Blessed One said. Gratified, Mahānāma the Sakyan delighted in the Blessed One's words.

NOTES

1. A cousin of the Buddha. The Commentary claims that he was already a once-returner when this discourse took place, but there is nothing in the Canon to indicate that this is so.

2. This sentence is mistranslated in both MLS and MLDB. Its point is that the qualities that invade Mahānāma's mind are precisely the ones he has not yet abandoned. In practical terms, this means that he does not have to look for another quality lurking behind them, but instead can focus his attention on abandoning these qualities directly as they arise. The remainder of the sutta gives a lesson in how greed, aversion, and delusion can be abandoned by understanding the object on which they most frequently focus: sensuality.

3. The rapture & pleasure apart from sensuality, apart from unskillful qualities, is a factor of the first or second jhāna. "Something more peaceful than that" would be any attainments higher than the second jhāna.

4. See DN 2.

5. One of the great ironies in the history of Buddhism is the extent to which teachings that the Buddha clearly disapproved of, such as this one, have later been taught as quintessentially Buddhist. In some circles, a teaching similar to this one—that non-reactivity to pain burns away the impurity of past kamma and creates no new kamma for the future—is still taught as Buddhist to this day.

6. The Buddha here is apparently referring to the concentration attainment called the cessation of perception and feeling. As to how the cessation of feeling could be called unalloyed pleasure, MN 59 says this: "Now it's possible, Ānanda, that some wanderers of other sects might say, 'Gotama the contemplative speaks of the cessation of per-

ception & feeling, and yet describes it as pleasure. What is this? How is this?' When they say that, they are to be told, 'It's not the case, friends, that the Blessed One describes only pleasant feeling as included under pleasure. Wherever pleasure is found, in whatever terms, the Blessed One describes it as pleasure.'"

This is one of several passages in the Canon indicating that not all experience is limited to the aggregates. Others include DN 15, MN 49, and SN 35:117.

See also: MN 36; MN 54; MN 59; MN 101; SN 35:63; SN 35:115; SN 35:189; SN 36:6; AN 2:30; AN 3:35; AN 6:63; AN 9:13; AN 9:34; AN 9:40

18 The Ball of Honey

Madhupiṇḍika Sutta

INTRODUCTION

This discourse plays a central role in the early Buddhist analysis of conflict. As might be expected, the blame for conflict lies within, in the unskillful habits of the mind, rather than without. The culprit in this case is a habit called papañca. Unfortunately, none of the early texts give a clear definition of what the word papañca means, so it's hard to find a precise English equivalent for the term. However, they do give a clear analysis of how papañca arises, how it leads to conflict, and how it can be ended. In the final analysis, these are the questions that matter—more than the precise definition of terms—so we will deal with them first before proposing a few possible translation equivalents for the word.

Three passages in the discourses—DN 21, MN 18, and Sn 4:11—map the causal processes that give rise to papañca and lead from papañca to conflict. Because the Buddhist analysis of causality is generally non-linear, with plenty of room for feedback loops, the maps vary in some of their details. In DN 21, the map reads like this:

the perceptions & categories of papañca > thinking > desire > dear-&-not-dear > envy & stinginess > rivalry & hostility

In Sn 4:11, the map is less linear and can be diagrammed like this:

perception > the categories of papañca

perception > name & form > contact > appealing & unappealing > desire > dear-&-not-dear > stinginess/divisiveness/quarrels/disputes

In MN 18, the map is this:

contact > feeling > perception > thinking > the perceptions & categories of papañca

In this last case, however, the bare outline misses some of the important implications of the way this process is phrased. In the full passage, the analysis starts out in an impersonal tone:

> *"Dependent on eye & forms, eye-consciousness arises [similarly with the rest of the six senses]. The meeting of the three is contact. With contact as a requisite condition, there is feeling."*

Starting with feeling, the notion of an "agent"—in this case, the feeler—acting on "objects," is introduced:

> *"What one feels, one perceives [labels in the mind]. What one perceives, one thinks about. What one thinks about, one 'papañcizes.'"*

Through the process of papañca, the agent then becomes a victim of his/her own patterns of thinking:

> *"Based on what a person papañcizes, the perceptions & categories of papañca assail him/her with regard to past, present, & future forms cognizable via the eye [as with the remaining senses]."*

What are these perceptions & categories that assail the person who papañcizes? Sn 4:14 states that the root of the categories of papañca is the perception, "I am the thinker." From this self-reflexive thought—in which one objectifies a "self," a thing corresponding to the concept of "I"— a number of categories can be derived: being/not-being, me/not-me, mine/not-mine, doer/done-to, signifier/signified. Once one's self becomes a thing under the rubric of these categories, it's impossible not to be assailed by the perceptions & categories derived from these basic distinctions. When there's the sense of identification as a being that needs to feed (see Khp 4), then based on the feelings arising from sensory contact, some feelings will seem appealing—worth feeding on—and others will seem worth pushing away. From this there grows desire, which comes into conflict with the desires of others who are also feeding because they, too, engage in papañca. This is how inner objectification breeds external contention.

How can this process be ended? Through a shift in perception, caused by the way one attends to feelings, using the categories of appropriate attention (see MN 2). As the Buddha states in DN 21, rather than viewing a feeling as an appealing or unappealing thing, one should look at it as part of a causal process: When a particular feeling is pursued, do skillful or unskillful qualities increase in the mind? If skillful qualities increase, the feeling may be pursued. If unskillful qualities increase, it shouldn't. When comparing feelings that lead to skillful qualities, notice that those endowed with thinking (directed thought) and evaluation are less refined than those free of thinking and evaluation, as in the higher stages of mental absorption, or jhāna. When seeing this, there is a tendency to opt for the more refined feelings, and this cuts through the act of thinking that, according to MN 18, provides the basis for papañca.

In following this program, the notion of agent and victim is avoided, as is self-reflexive thinking in general. There is simply the analysis of cause-effect processes. One is still making use of dualities—distinguishing between unskillful and skillful (and affliction/lack of affliction, the results of unskillful and skillful qualities)—but the distinction is between processes, not things. Thus one's analysis avoids the type of thinking that, according to DN 21, depends on the perceptions and categories of papañca, and in this way the vicious cycle by which thinking and papañca keep feeding each other is cut.

Ultimately, by following this program to greater and greater levels of refinement through the higher levels of mental absorption, one finds less and less to relish and enjoy in the six senses and the mental processes based on them. With this sense of disenchantment, the processes of feeling and thought are stilled, and there is a breakthrough to the cessation of the six sense spheres. When these spheres cease, is there anything else left? Ven. Sāriputta, in AN 4:173 warns us not to ask, for to ask if there is, isn't, both-is-and-isn't, neither-is-nor-isn't anything left in that dimension is to papañcize what is free from papañca. However, this dimension is not a total annihilation of experience. It's a type of experience that DN 11 calls consciousness without surface, luminous all around, where water, earth, fire, & wind have no footing, where long/short, coarse/fine, fair/foul, name/form are all brought to an end. This is the fruit of the path of arahantship—a path that makes use of dualities but leads to a fruit beyond them.

It may come as cold comfort to realize that conflict can be totally overcome only with the realization of arahantship, but it's important to note that by following the path recommended in DN 21—learning to avoid references to any notion of "self" and learning to view feelings not as things but as parts of a causal process affecting the qualities in the mind—the basis for papañca is gradually undercut, and there are fewer and fewer occasions for conflict. In following this path, one reaps its increasing benefits all along the way.

Translating papañca: *As one writer has noted, the word papañca has had a wide variety of meanings in Indian thought, with only one constant: In Buddhist philosophical discourse it always carries negative connotations, usually of falsification and distortion. The Pali Commentaries define papañca as covering three types of thought: craving, conceit, and views. They also note that it functions to slow the mind down in its escape from saṁsāra. Because its categories begin with the objectifying thought, "I am the thinker," I have chosen to render the word as "objectification," although some of the following alternatives might be acceptable as well: self-reflexive thinking, reification, proliferation, complication, elaboration, distortion. The word offers some interesting parallels to the postmodern notion of logocentric thinking, but it's important to note that the Buddha's program of deconstructing this process differs sharply from that of postmodern thought.*

* * *

I have heard that on one occasion the Blessed One was staying among the Sakyans near Kapilavatthu in the Banyan Park. Then in the early morning, having adjusted his under robe and carrying his bowl & outer robe, he went into Kapilavatthu for alms. Having gone for alms in Kapilavatthu, after the meal, returning from his alms round, he went to the Great Wood for the day's abiding. Plunging into the Great Wood, he sat down at the root of a young clump of bamboo for the day's abiding.

Daṇḍapāṇin ["Stick-in-hand"] the Sakyan, out roaming & rambling for exercise, also went to the Great Wood. Plunging into the Great Wood, he went to the Blessed One under the young clump of bamboo. On arrival, he exchanged courteous greetings with him. After an exchange of friendly greetings & courtesies, he stood to one side. As he was standing there, he said to the Blessed One, "What is the contemplative's doctrine? What does he proclaim?"

"The sort of doctrine, friend, where one does not keep quarreling with anyone in the cosmos with its devas, Māras, & Brahmās, with its contemplatives & brahmans, its royalty & commonfolk; the sort (of doctrine) where perceptions no longer obsess the brahman who remains dissociated from sensuality, free from perplexity, his uncertainty cut away, devoid of craving for becoming & non-. Such is my doctrine; such is what I proclaim."

When this was said, Daṇḍapāṇin the Sakyan—shaking his head, wagging his tongue, raising his eyebrows so that his forehead was wrinkled in three furrows—left, leaning on his stick.

Then the Blessed One, emerging from his seclusion in the late afternoon, went to the Banyan Park and, on arrival, sat down on a seat made ready. Having sat down, he [told the monks what had happened]. When this was said, a certain monk said to the Blessed One, "Lord, what sort of doctrine is it where one does not keep quarreling with anyone in the cosmos with its devas, Māras, & Brahmās, with its contemplatives & brahmans, its royalty & commonfolk; where perceptions no longer obsess the brahman who remains dissociated from sensuality, free from perplexity, his uncertainty cut away, devoid of craving for becoming & non-?"

"If, monk, with regard to the cause whereby the perceptions & categories of objectification assail a person, there is nothing there to relish, welcome, or remain fastened to, then that is the end of the obsessions of passion, the obsessions of resistance, the obsessions of views, the obsessions of uncertainty, the obsessions of conceit, the obsessions of passion for becoming, & the obsessions of ignorance. That is the end of taking up rods & bladed weapons, of arguments, quarrels, disputes, accusations, divisive speech, & lies. That is where these evil, unskillful things cease without remainder." That is what the Blessed One said. Having said it, he—the One Well-Gone—got up from his seat and went into his dwelling.

Then, not long after the Blessed One had left, this thought occurred to the monks: "This brief statement the Blessed One made, after which he went into his dwelling without analyzing the detailed meaning—i.e., 'If, with regard to the cause whereby the perceptions & categories of objectification assail a person, there is nothing to relish… that is where these evil, unskillful things cease without remainder': Now who might analyze the unanalyzed detailed meaning of this brief statement?" Then the thought occurred to them, "Ven. Mahā Kaccāna is praised by the Teacher and esteemed by his observant companions in the holy life. He is capable of analyzing the unanalyzed detailed meaning of this brief statement. Suppose we were to go to him and, on arrival, cross-question him about this matter."

So the monks went to Ven. Mahā Kaccāna and, on arrival, exchanged courteous greetings with him. After an exchange of friendly greetings & courtesies, they sat to one side. As they were sitting there, they [told him what had happened, and added,] "Analyze the meaning, Ven. Mahā Kaccāna!"

(He replied:) "Friends, it's as if a man needing heartwood, looking for heartwood, wandering in search of heartwood—passing over the root & trunk of a standing tree possessing heartwood—were to imagine that heartwood should be sought among its branches & leaves. So it is with you, who—having bypassed the Blessed One when you were face to face with him, the Teacher—imagine that I should be asked about this matter. For knowing, the Blessed One knows; seeing, he sees. He is the Eye, he is Knowledge, he is Dhamma, he is Brahmā. He is the speaker, the proclaimer, the elucidator of meaning, the giver of the deathless, the lord of the Dhamma, the Tathāgata. That was the time when you should have cross-questioned him about this matter. However he answered, that was how you should have remembered it."

"Yes, friend Kaccāna: Knowing, the Blessed One knows; seeing, he sees. He is the Eye, he is Knowledge, he is Dhamma, he is Brahmā. He is the speaker, the proclaimer, the elucidator of meaning, the giver of the deathless, the lord of the Dhamma, the Tathāgata. That was the time when we should have cross-questioned him about this matter. However he answered, that was how we should have remembered it. But you are praised by the Teacher and esteemed by your observant companions in the holy life. You are capable of analyzing the unanalyzed detailed meaning of this brief statement. Analyze the meaning, Ven. Mahā Kaccāna, without making it difficult!"

"In that case, my friends, listen & pay close attention. I will speak."

"As you say, friend," the monks responded to him.

Ven. Mahā Kaccāna said this: "Friends, concerning the brief statement the Blessed One made, after which he went into his dwelling without analyzing the detailed meaning—i.e., 'If, with regard to the cause whereby the perceptions & categories of objectification assail a person, there is nothing there to relish, welcome, or remain fastened to, then that is the end of the obsessions of passion, the obsessions of resistance, the obsessions of views, the obsessions of uncertainty, the obsessions of conceit, the obsessions of passion for becoming, & the obsessions of ignorance. That is the end of taking up rods & bladed weapons, of arguments, quarrels, disputes, accusations, divisive speech, & lies. That is where these evil, unskillful things cease without remainder'—I understand the detailed meaning to be this:

"Dependent on eye & forms, eye-consciousness arises. The meeting of the three is contact. With contact as a requisite condition, there is feeling. What one feels, one perceives [labels in the mind]. What one perceives, one thinks about. What one thinks about, one complicates. Based on what a person complicates, the perceptions & categories of objectification assail him/her with regard to past, present, & future forms cognizable via the eye.

"Dependent on ear & sounds, ear-consciousness arises....

"Dependent on nose & aromas, nose-consciousness arises....

"Dependent on tongue & flavors, tongue-consciousness arises....

"Dependent on body & tactile sensations, body-consciousness arises....

"Dependent on intellect & ideas, intellect-consciousness arises. The meeting of the three is contact. With contact as a requisite condition, there is feeling. What one feels, one perceives. What one perceives, one thinks about. What one thinks about, one complicates. Based on what a person complicates, the perceptions & categories of objectification assail him/her with regard to past, present, & future ideas cognizable via the intellect.

"Now, when there is the eye, when there are forms, when there is eye-consciousness, it is possible that one will delineate a delineation of contact.[1] When there is a delineation of contact, it is possible that one will delineate a delineation of feeling. When there is a delineation of feeling, it is possible that one will delineate a delineation of perception. When there is a delineation of perception, it is possible that one will delineate a delineation of thinking. When there is a delineation of thinking, it is possible that one will delineate a delineation of being assailed by the perceptions & categories of objectification.

"When there is the ear.... the nose.... the tongue.... the body....

"When there is the intellect, when there are ideas, when there is intellect-consciousness, it is possible that one will delineate a delineation of contact. When there is a delineation of contact, it is possible that one will delineate a delineation of feeling. When there is a delineation of feeling, it is possible that one will delineate a delineation of perception. When there is a delineation of perception, it is possible that one will delineate a delineation of thinking. When there is a delineation of thinking, it is possible that one will delineate a delineation of being assailed by the perceptions & categories of objectification.

"Now, when there is no eye, when there are no forms, when there is no eye-consciousness, it is impossible that one will delineate a delineation of contact. When there is no delineation of contact, it is impossible that one will delineate a delineation of feeling. When there is no delineation of feeling, it is impossible that one will delineate a delineation of perception. When there is no delineation of perception, it is impossible that one will delineate a delineation of thinking. When there is no delineation of thinking, it is impossible that one will delineate a delineation of being assailed by the perceptions & categories of objectification.

"When there is no ear.... no nose.... no tongue.... no body....

"When there is no intellect, when there are no ideas, when there is no intellect-consciousness, it is impossible that one will delineate a delineation of contact. When there is no delineation of contact, it is impossible that one will delineate a delineation of feeling. When there is no delineation of feeling, it is impossible that one will delineate a delineation of perception. When there is no delineation of perception, it is impossible that one will delineate a delineation of thinking. When there is no delineation of thinking, it is impossible that one will delineate a delineation of being assailed by the perceptions & categories of objectification.

"So, concerning the brief statement the Blessed One made, after which he entered his dwelling without analyzing the detailed meaning—i.e., 'If, with regard to the cause whereby the perceptions

& categories of objectification assail a person, there is nothing there to relish, welcome, or remain fastened to, then that is the end of the obsessions of passion, the obsessions of resistance, the obsessions of views, the obsessions of uncertainty, the obsessions of conceit, the obsessions of passion for becoming, & the obsessions of ignorance. That is the end of taking up rods & bladed weapons, of arguments, quarrels, disputes, accusations, divisive speech, & lies. That is where these evil, unskillful things cease without remainder'—this is how I understand the detailed meaning. Now, friends, if you wish, having gone to the Blessed One, cross-question him about this matter. However he answers is how you should remember it."

Then the monks, delighting in & approving of Ven. Mahā Kaccāna's words, got up from their seats and went to the Blessed One. On arrival, having bowed down to him, they sat to one side. As they were sitting there, they [told him what had happened after he had gone into his dwelling, and ended by saying,] "Then Ven. Mahā Kaccāna analyzed the meaning using these words, these statements, these phrases."

"Mahā Kaccāna is wise, monks. He is a person of great discernment. If you had asked me about this matter, I too would have answered in the same way he did. That is its meaning, and that is how you should remember it."

When this was said, Ven. Ānanda said to the Blessed One, "Lord, it's as if a man—overcome with hunger, weakness, & thirst—were to come across a ball of honey. Wherever he might taste it, he would experience a sweet, delectable flavor. In the same way, wherever a monk of capable awareness might investigate the meaning of this Dhamma discourse with his discernment, he would experience gratification, he would experience confidence. What is the name of this Dhamma discourse?"

"Then, Ānanda, you can remember this Dhamma discourse as the 'Ball of Honey Discourse.'"

That is what the Blessed One said. Gratified, Ven. Ānanda delighted in the Blessed One's words.

NOTE

1. The artificiality of this phrase—"delineate a delineation"—seems intentional. It underlines the artifice implicit in the process by which the mind, in singling out events, turns them into discrete things. See MN 109, note 2.

See also: DN 21; MN 138; SN 35:207; AN 3:73; AN 8:30; Sn 4:11

19 *Two Sorts of Thinking*

Dvedhāvitakka Sutta

I have heard that on one occasion the Blessed One was staying near Sāvatthī in Jeta's Grove, Anāthapiṇḍika's monastery. There he addressed the monks: "Monks!"

"Yes, lord," the monks responded to him.

The Blessed One said, "Monks, before my self-awakening, when I was still just an unawakened Bodhisatta, the thought occurred to me: 'Why don't I keep dividing my thinking into two sorts?' So I made thinking imbued with sensuality, thinking imbued with ill will, & thinking imbued with harmfulness one sort, and thinking imbued with renunciation, thinking imbued with non-ill will, & thinking imbued with harmlessness another sort.

"And as I remained thus heedful, ardent, & resolute, thinking imbued with sensuality arose in me. I discerned that 'Thinking imbued with sensuality has arisen in me; and that leads to my own affliction or to the affliction of others or to the affliction of both. It obstructs discernment, promotes vexation, & does not lead to unbinding.'

"As I noticed that it leads to my own affliction, it subsided. As I noticed that it leads to the affliction of others… to the affliction of both… it obstructs discernment, promotes vexation, & does not lead to unbinding, it subsided. Whenever thinking imbued with sensuality had arisen, I simply abandoned it, destroyed it, dispelled it, wiped it out of existence.

"And as I remained thus heedful, ardent, & resolute, thinking imbued with ill will arose in me. I discerned that 'Thinking imbued with ill will has arisen in me; and that leads to my own affliction or to the affliction of others or to the affliction of both. It obstructs discernment, promotes vexation, & does not lead to unbinding.'

"As I noticed that it leads to my own affliction, it subsided. As I noticed that it leads to the affliction of others… to the affliction of both… it obstructs discernment, promotes vexation, & does not lead to unbinding, it subsided. Whenever thinking imbued with ill will had arisen, I simply abandoned it, destroyed it, dispelled it, wiped it out of existence.

"And as I remained thus heedful, ardent, & resolute, thinking imbued with harmfulness arose in me. I discerned that 'Thinking imbued with harmfulness has arisen in me; and that leads to my own affliction or to the affliction of others or to the affliction of both. It obstructs discernment, promotes vexation, & does not lead to unbinding.'

"As I noticed that it leads to my own affliction, it subsided. As I noticed that it leads to the affliction of others… to the affliction of both… it obstructs discernment, promotes vexation, & does not lead to unbinding, it subsided. Whenever thinking imbued with harmfulness had arisen, I simply abandoned it, destroyed it, dispelled it, wiped it out of existence.

"Whatever a monk keeps pursuing with his thinking & pondering, that becomes the inclination of his awareness. If a monk keeps pursuing thinking imbued with sensuality, abandoning thinking imbued with renunciation, his mind is bent by that thinking imbued with sensuality. If a monk keeps pursuing thinking imbued with ill will, abandoning thinking imbued with non-ill will, his mind is bent by that thinking imbued with ill will. If a monk keeps pursuing thinking imbued with harmfulness, abandoning thinking imbued with harmlessness, his mind is bent by that thinking imbued with harmfulness.

"Just as in the last month of the Rains, in the autumn season when the crops are ripening, a cowherd would look after his cows: He would tap & poke & check & curb them with a stick on this side & that. Why is that? Because he foresees flogging or imprisonment or a fine or public censure arising from that [if he let his cows wander into the crops]. In the same way I foresaw in unskillful qualities drawbacks, degradation, & defilement, and I foresaw in skillful qualities rewards related to renunciation & promoting cleansing.

"And as I remained thus heedful, ardent, & resolute, thinking imbued with renunciation arose in me. I discerned that 'Thinking imbued with renunciation has arisen in me; and that leads neither to my own affliction, nor to the affliction of others, nor to the affliction of both. It fosters discernment, promotes lack of vexation, & leads to unbinding. If I were to think & ponder in line with that even for a night… even for a day… even for a day & night, I do not envision any danger that would come from it, except that thinking & pondering a long time would tire the body. When the body is tired, the mind is disturbed; and a disturbed mind is far from concentration.' So I steadied my mind right within, settled, unified, & concentrated it. Why is that? So that my mind would not be disturbed.

"And as I remained thus heedful, ardent, & resolute, thinking imbued with non-ill will arose in me. I discerned that 'Thinking imbued with non-ill will has arisen in me; and that leads neither to my own affliction, nor to the affliction of others, nor to the affliction of both. It fosters discernment, promotes lack of vexation, & leads to unbinding. If I were to think & ponder in line with that even for a night… even for a day… even for a day & night, I do not envision any danger that would come from it, except that thinking & pondering a long time would tire the body. When the body is tired, the mind is disturbed; and a disturbed mind is far from concentration.' So I steadied my mind right within, settled, unified, & concentrated it. Why is that? So that my mind would not be disturbed.

"And as I remained thus heedful, ardent, & resolute, thinking imbued with harmlessness arose in me. I discerned that 'Thinking imbued with harmlessness has arisen in me; and that leads neither to my own affliction, nor to the affliction of others, nor to the affliction of both. It fosters discernment, promotes lack of vexation, & leads to unbinding. If I were to think & ponder in line with that even for a night… even for a day… even for a day & night, I do not envision any danger that would come from it, except that thinking & pondering a long time would tire the body. When the body is tired, the mind is disturbed; and a disturbed mind is far from concentration.' So I steadied my mind right within, settled, unified, & concentrated it. Why is that? So that my mind would not be disturbed.

"Whatever a monk keeps pursuing with his thinking & pondering, that becomes the inclination of his awareness. If a monk keeps pursuing thinking imbued with renunciation, abandoning thinking imbued with sensuality, his mind is bent by that thinking imbued with renunciation. If a monk keeps pursuing thinking imbued with non-ill will, abandoning thinking imbued with ill will, his mind is bent by that thinking imbued with non-ill will. If a monk keeps pursuing thinking imbued with harmlessness, abandoning thinking imbued with harmfulness, his mind is bent by that thinking imbued with harmlessness.

"Just as in the last month of the hot season, when all the crops have been gathered into the village, a cowherd would look after his cows: While resting under the shade of a tree or out in the open, he simply keeps himself mindful of 'those cows.' In the same way, I simply kept myself mindful of 'those qualities.'

"Unflagging persistence was aroused in me, and unmuddled mindfulness established. My body was calm & unaroused, my mind concentrated & single. Quite secluded from sensuality, secluded from unskillful qualities, I entered & remained in the first jhāna: rapture & pleasure born of seclusion, accompanied by directed thought & evaluation. With the stilling of directed thoughts & evaluations, I entered & remained in the second jhāna: rapture & pleasure born of concentration, unification of awareness free from directed thought & evaluation—internal assurance. With the fading of rapture I remained equanimous, mindful, & alert, and sensed pleasure with the body. I entered & remained in the third jhāna, of which the noble ones declare, 'Equanimous & mindful, he has a pleasant abiding.' With the abandoning of pleasure & pain—as with the earlier disappearance of elation & distress—I entered & remained in the fourth jhāna: purity of equanimity & mindfulness, neither pleasure nor pain.

"When the mind was thus concentrated, purified, bright, unblemished, rid of defilement, pliant, malleable, steady, & attained to imperturbability, I directed it to the *knowledge of recollecting my past lives.* I recollected my manifold past lives, i.e., one birth, two… five, ten… fifty, a hundred, a thousand, a hundred thousand, many eons of cosmic contraction, many eons of cosmic expansion, many eons of cosmic contraction & expansion: 'There I had such a name, belonged to such a clan, had such an appearance. Such was my food, such my experience of pleasure & pain, such the end of my life. Passing away from that state, I re-arose there. There too I had such a name, belonged to such a clan, had such an appearance. Such was my food, such my experience of pleasure & pain, such the end of my life. Passing away from that state, I re-arose here.' Thus I recollected my manifold past lives in their modes & details.

"This was the first knowledge I attained in the first watch of the night. Ignorance was destroyed; knowledge arose; darkness was destroyed; light arose —as happens in one who is heedful, ardent, & resolute.

"When the mind was thus concentrated, purified, bright, unblemished, rid of defilement, pliant, malleable, steady, & attained to imperturbability, I directed it to the *knowledge of the passing away & reappearance of beings.* I saw—by means of the divine eye, purified & surpassing the human—beings passing away & re-appearing, and I discerned how they are inferior & superior, beautiful & ugly, fortunate & unfortunate in accordance with their kamma: 'These beings—who were endowed with bad conduct of body, speech & mind, who reviled the noble ones, held wrong views and undertook actions under the influence of wrong views—with the break-up of the body, after death, have re-appeared in a plane of deprivation, a bad destination, a lower realm, hell. But these beings—who were endowed with good conduct of body, speech, & mind, who did not revile the noble ones, who held right views and undertook actions under the influence of right views—with the break-up of the body, after death, have re-appeared in a good destination, a heavenly world.' Thus—by means of the divine eye, purified & surpassing the human—I saw beings passing away & re-appearing, and I discerned how they are inferior & superior, beautiful & ugly, fortunate & unfortunate in accordance with their kamma.

"This was the second knowledge I attained in the second watch of the night. Ignorance was destroyed; knowledge arose; darkness was destroyed; light arose—as happens in one who is heedful, ardent, & resolute.

"When the mind was thus concentrated, purified, bright, unblemished, rid of defilement, pliant, malleable, steady, & attained to imperturbability, I directed it to the *knowledge of the ending of effluents.* I discerned, as it had come to be, that 'This is stress... This is the origination of stress... This is the cessation of stress... This is the way leading to the cessation of stress... These are effluents... This is the origination of effluents... This is the cessation of effluents... This is the way leading to the cessation of effluents.' My heart, thus knowing, thus seeing, was released from the effluent of sensuality, released from the effluent of becoming, released from the effluent of ignorance. With release, there was the knowledge, 'Released.' I discerned that 'Birth is ended, the holy life fulfilled, the task done. There is nothing further for this world.'

"This was the third knowledge I attained in the third watch of the night. Ignorance was destroyed; knowledge arose; darkness was destroyed; light arose—as happens in one who is heedful, ardent, & resolute.

"Suppose, monks, that in a forested wilderness there were a large low-lying marsh, in dependence on which there lived a large herd of deer; and a certain man were to appear, not desiring their benefit, not desiring their welfare, not desiring their rest from bondage. He would close off the safe, restful path that led to their rapture, and would open up a false path, set out a male decoy, place a female decoy, and thus the large herd of deer, at a later time, would fall into ruin & disaster. Then suppose that a certain man were to appear to that same large herd of deer, desiring their benefit, desiring their welfare, desiring their rest from bondage. He would open up the safe, restful path that led to their rapture, would close off the false path, take away the male decoy, destroy the female decoy, and thus the large herd of deer, at a later time, would come into growth, increase, & abundance.

"I have given this simile in order to convey a meaning. The meaning is this: 'The large, low-lying marsh' is a term for sensual pleasures. 'The large herd of deer' is a term for beings. 'The man not desiring their benefit, not desiring their welfare, not desiring their rest from bondage' is a term for Māra, the Evil One. 'The false path' is a term for the eightfold wrong path, i.e., wrong view, wrong resolve, wrong speech, wrong action, wrong livelihood, wrong effort, wrong mindfulness, & wrong concentration. 'The male decoy' is a term for passion & delight. 'The female decoy' is a term for ignorance. 'The man desiring their benefit, desiring their welfare, desiring their rest from bondage' is a term for the Tathāgata, the Worthy One, the Rightly Self-awakened One. 'The safe, restful path that led to their rapture' is a term for the noble eightfold path, i.e., right view, right resolve, right speech, right action, right livelihood, right effort, right mindfulness, & right concentration.

"So, monks, I have opened up the safe, restful path, closed off the false path, removed the male decoy, destroyed the female. Whatever a teacher should do—seeking the welfare of his disciples, out of sympathy for them—that have I done for you. Over there are (places to sit at) the roots of trees; over there, empty dwellings. Practice jhāna, monks. Don't be heedless. Don't later fall into remorse. This is our message to you."

That is what the Blessed One said. Gratified, the monks delighted in the Blessed One's words.

See also: MN 61; AN 3:102; AN 9:41; AN 10:94; Ud 4:1

20 *The Relaxation of Thoughts*

Vitakkasaṇṭhāna Sutta

I have heard that on one occasion the Blessed One was staying near Sāvatthī in Jeta's Grove, Anāthapiṇḍika's monastery. There he addressed the monks, "Monks!"

"Yes, lord," the monks responded to him.

The Blessed One said: "When a monk is intent on the heightened mind, there are five themes he should attend to at the appropriate times. Which five?

"There is the case where evil, unskillful thoughts—connected with desire, aversion, or delusion—arise in a monk while he is referring to and attending to a particular theme. He should attend to another theme, apart from that one, connected with what is skillful. When he is attending to this other theme, apart from that one, connected with what is skillful, then those evil, unskillful thoughts—connected with desire, aversion, or delusion—are abandoned and subside. With their abandoning, he steadies his mind right within, settles it, unifies it, and concentrates it. Just as a dexterous carpenter or his apprentice would use a small peg to knock out, drive out, and pull out a large one; in the same way, if evil, unskillful thoughts—connected with desire, aversion, or delusion—arise in a monk while he is referring to and attending to a particular theme, he should attend to another theme, apart from that one, connected with what is skillful. When he is attending to this other theme, apart from that one, connected with what is skillful, then those evil, unskillful thoughts—connected with desire, aversion, or delusion—are abandoned and subside. With their abandoning, he steadies his mind right within, settles it, unifies it, and concentrates it.

"If evil, unskillful thoughts—connected with desire, aversion, or delusion—still arise in the monk while he is attending to this other theme, connected with what is skillful, he should scrutinize the drawbacks of those thoughts: 'Really, these thoughts of mine are unskillful, these thoughts of mine are blameworthy, these thoughts of mine result in stress.' As he is scrutinizing the drawbacks of those thoughts, those evil, unskillful thoughts—connected with desire, aversion, or delusion—are abandoned and subside. With their abandoning, he steadies his mind right within, settles it, unifies it, and concentrates it. Just as a young woman—or man—

fond of adornment, would be horrified, humiliated, and disgusted if the carcass of a snake or a dog or a human being were hung from her neck; in the same way, if evil, unskillful thoughts—connected with desire, aversion, or delusion—still arise in the monk while he is attending to this other theme, connected with what is skillful, he should scrutinize the drawbacks of those thoughts: 'Really, these thoughts of mine are unskillful, these thoughts of mine are blameworthy, these thoughts of mine result in stress.' As he is scrutinizing the drawbacks of those thoughts, those evil, unskillful thoughts—connected with desire, aversion, or delusion—are abandoned and subside. With their abandoning, he steadies his mind right within, settles it, unifies it, and concentrates it.

"If evil, unskillful thoughts—connected with desire, aversion or delusion—still arise in the monk while he is scrutinizing the drawbacks of those thoughts, he should pay no mind and pay no attention to those thoughts. As he is paying no mind and paying no attention to them, those evil, unskillful thoughts are abandoned and subside. With their abandoning, he steadies his mind right within, settles it, unifies it, and concentrates it. Just as a man with good eyes, not wanting to see forms that had come into range, would close his eyes or look away; in the same way, if evil, unskillful thoughts—connected with desire, aversion or delusion—still arise in the monk while he is scrutinizing the drawbacks of those thoughts, he should pay no mind and pay no attention to those thoughts. As he is paying no mind and paying no attention to them, those evil, unskillful thoughts are abandoned and subside. With their abandoning, he steadies his mind right within, settles it, unifies it, and concentrates it.

"If evil, unskillful thoughts—connected with desire, aversion or delusion—still arise in the monk while he is paying no mind and paying no attention to those thoughts, he should attend to the relaxing of thought-fabrication with regard to those thoughts. As he is attending to the relaxing of thought-fabrication with regard to those thoughts, those evil, unskillful thoughts are abandoned and subside. With their abandoning, he steadies his mind right within, settles it, unifies it, and concentrates it. Just as the thought would occur to a man walking quickly, 'Why am I walking quickly? Why don't I walk slowly?' So he walks slowly. The thought occurs to him, 'Why am I walking slowly? Why don't I stand?' So he stands. The thought occurs to him, 'Why am I standing? Why don't I sit down?' So he sits down. The thought occurs to him, 'Why am I sitting? Why don't I lie down?' So he lies down. In this way, giving up the grosser posture, he takes up the more refined one. In the same way, if evil, unskillful thoughts—connected with desire, aversion or delusion—still arise in the monk while he is paying no mind and paying no attention to those thoughts, he should attend to the relaxing of thought-fabrication with regard to those thoughts. As he is attending to the relaxing of thought-fabrication with regard to those thoughts, those evil, unskillful thoughts are abandoned and subside. With their abandoning, he steadies his mind right within, settles it, unifies it, and concentrates it.

"If evil, unskillful thoughts—connected with desire, aversion or delusion—still arise in the monk while he is attending to the relaxing of thought-fabrication with regard to those thoughts, then—with his teeth clenched and his tongue pressed against the roof of his mouth—he should beat down, constrain, and crush his mind with his awareness. As—with his teeth clenched and his tongue pressed against the roof of his mouth—he is beating down, constraining, and crushing his mind with his awareness, those evil, unskillful thoughts are abandoned and subside. With their abandoning, he steadies his mind right within, settles it, unifies it, and concentrates it. Just as a strong man, seizing a weaker man by the head or the throat or the shoulders, would beat him down, constrain, and crush him; in the same way, if evil, unskillful thoughts—connected with desire, aversion or delusion—still arise in the monk while he is attending to the relaxing of thought-fabrication with regard to those thoughts, then—with his teeth clenched and his tongue pressed against the roof of his mouth—he should beat down, constrain, and crush his mind with his awareness. As—with his teeth clenched and his tongue pressed against the roof of his mouth—he is beating down, constraining, and crushing his mind with his awareness, those evil, unskillful thoughts are abandoned and subside. With their abandoning, he steadies his mind right within, settles it, unifies it, and concentrates it.

"Now when a monk... attending to another theme... scrutinizing the drawbacks of those thoughts... paying no mind and paying no attention to those thoughts... attending to the relaxing of thought-fabrication with regard to those thoughts... beating down, constraining and crushing his mind with his awareness... steadies his mind right within, settles it, unifies it and concentrates it: He is then called a monk with mastery over the ways of thought sequences. He thinks whatever thought he wants to, and doesn't think whatever thought he doesn't. He has severed craving, thrown off the fetters, and—through the right penetration of conceit—has made an end of suffering & stress."

That is what the Blessed One said. Gratified, the monks delighted in the Blessed One's words.

See also: MN 54; MN 75; AN 3:103; AN 7:58; AN 10:80; Ud 4:1

21 *The Simile of the Saw (Excerpt)*

Kakacūpama Sutta

... "Once, monks, in this same Sāvatthī, there was a lady of a household named Vedehikā. This good report about Lady Vedehikā had circulated: 'Lady Vedehikā is gentle. Lady Vedehikā is mild-tempered. Lady Vedehikā is calm.' Now, Lady Vedehikā had a slave named Kālī who was diligent, deft, & neat in her work. The thought occurred to Kālī the slave, 'This good report about my Lady Vedehikā has circulated: "Lady Vedehikā is gentle. Lady Vedehikā is mild-tempered. Lady Vedehikā is calm." Now, is anger present in my lady without showing, or is it absent? Or is it just because I'm diligent, deft, & neat in my work that the anger present in my lady doesn't show? Why don't I test her?'

"So Kālī the slave got up after daybreak. Then Lady Vedehikā said to her: 'Hey, Kālī!'

"'Yes, madam?'

"'Why did you get up after daybreak?'

"'No reason, madam.'

"'No reason, you wicked slave, and yet you get up after daybreak?' Angered & displeased, she scowled.

Then the thought occurred to Kālī the slave: 'Anger *is* present in my lady without showing, and not absent. And it's just because I'm diligent, deft, & neat in my work that the anger present in my lady doesn't show. Why don't I test her some more?'

"So Kālī the slave got up later in the day. Then Lady Vedehikā said to her: 'Hey, Kālī!'

"'Yes, madam?'

"'Why did you get up later in the day?'

"'No reason, madam.'

"'No reason, you wicked slave, and yet you get up later in the day?' Angered & displeased, she grumbled.

Then the thought occurred to Kālī the slave: 'Anger *is* present in my lady without showing, and not absent. And it's just because I'm diligent, deft, & neat in my work that the anger present in my lady doesn't show. Why don't I test her some more?'

"So Kālī the slave got up even later in the day. Then Lady Vedehikā said to her: 'Hey, Kālī!'

"'Yes, madam?'

"'Why did you get up even later in the day?'

"'No reason, madam.'

"'No reason, you wicked slave, and yet you get up even later in the day?' Angered & displeased, she grabbed hold of a rolling pin and gave her a whack over the head, cutting it open.

Then Kālī the slave, with blood streaming from her cut-open head, went and denounced her mistress to the neighbors: 'See, ladies, the gentle one's handiwork? See the mild-tempered one's handiwork? See the calm one's handiwork? How could she, angered & displeased with her only slave for getting up after daybreak, grab hold of a rolling pin and give her a whack over the head, cutting it open?'

"After that this evil report about Lady Vedehikā circulated: 'Lady Vedehikā is vicious. Lady Vedehikā is foul-tempered. Lady Vedehikā is violent.'

"In the same way, monks, a monk may be ever so gentle, ever so even-tempered, ever so calm, as long as he is not touched by disagreeable aspects of speech. But it is only when disagreeable aspects of speech touch him that he can truly be known as gentle, even-tempered, & calm. I don't call a monk easy to admonish if he is easy to admonish and makes himself easy to admonish only by reason of robes, almsfood, lodging, & medicinal requisites for curing the sick. Why is that? Because if he doesn't get robes, almsfood, lodging, & medicinal requisites for curing the sick, then he isn't easy to admonish and doesn't make himself easy to admonish. But if a monk is easy to admonish and makes himself easy to admonish purely out of esteem for the Dhamma, respect for the Dhamma, reverence for the Dhamma, then I call him easy to admonish. Thus, monks, you should train yourselves: 'We will be easy to admonish and make ourselves easy to admonish purely out of esteem for the Dhamma, respect for the Dhamma, reverence for the Dhamma.' That's how you should train yourselves.

"Monks, there are these five aspects of speech by which others may address you: timely or untimely, true or false, affectionate or harsh, beneficial or unbeneficial, with a mind of goodwill or with inner hate. Others may address you in a timely way or an untimely way. They may address you with what is true or what is false. They may address you in an affectionate way or a harsh way. They may address you in a beneficial way or an unbeneficial way. They may address you with a mind of goodwill or with inner hate. In any event, you should train yourselves: 'Our minds will be unaffected and we will say no evil words. We will remain sympathetic to that person's welfare, with a mind of goodwill, and with no inner hate. We will keep pervading him with an awareness imbued with goodwill and, beginning with him, we will keep pervading the all-encompassing world with an awareness imbued with goodwill—abundant, enlarged, immeasurable, free from hostility, free from ill will.' That's how you should train yourselves.

"Suppose that a man were to come along carrying a hoe & a basket, saying, 'I will make this great earth be without earth.' He would dig here & there, scatter soil here & there, spit here & there, urinate here & there, saying, 'Be without earth. Be without earth.' Now, what do you think? Would he make this great earth be without earth?"

"No, lord. Why is that? Because this great earth is deep & enormous. It can't easily be made to be without earth. The man would reap only a share of weariness & disappointment."

"In the same way, monks, there are these five aspects of speech by which others may address you: timely or untimely, true or false, affectionate or harsh, beneficial or unbeneficial, with a mind of goodwill or with inner hate. Others may address you in a timely way or an untimely way. They may address you with what is true or what is false. They may address you in an affectionate way or a harsh way. They may address you in a beneficial way or an unbeneficial way. They may address you with a mind of goodwill or with inner hate. In any event, you should train yourselves: 'Our minds will be unaffected and we will say no evil words. We will remain sympathetic to that person's welfare, with a mind of goodwill, and with no inner hate. We will keep pervading him with an awareness imbued with goodwill and, beginning with him, we will keep pervading the all-encompassing world with an awareness imbued with goodwill equal to the great earth—abundant, enlarged, immeasurable, free from hostility, free from ill will.' That's how you should train yourselves.

"Suppose that a man were to come along carrying lac, yellow orpiment, indigo, or crimson, saying, 'I will draw pictures in space, I will make pictures appear.' Now, what do you think? Would he draw pictures in space & make pictures appear?"

"No, lord. Why is that? Because space is formless & without surface. It's not easy to draw pictures there and to make them appear. The man would reap only a share of weariness & disappointment."

"In the same way, monks, there are these five aspects of speech by which others may address you: timely or untimely, true or false, affectionate or harsh, beneficial or unbeneficial, with a mind of goodwill or with inner hate. Others may address you in a timely way or an untimely way. They may address you with what is true or what is false. They may address you in an affectionate way or a harsh way. They may address you in a beneficial way or an unbeneficial way. They may address you with a mind of goodwill or with inner hate.

In any event, you should train yourselves: 'Our minds will be unaffected and we will say no evil words. We will remain sympathetic to that person's welfare, with a mind of goodwill, and with no inner hate. We will keep pervading him with an awareness imbued with goodwill and, beginning with him, we will keep pervading the all-encompassing world with an awareness imbued with goodwill equal to space—abundant, enlarged, immeasurable, free from hostility, free from ill will.' That's how you should train yourselves.

"Suppose that a man were to come along carrying a burning grass torch and saying, 'With this burning grass torch I will heat up the river Ganges and make it boil.' Now, what do you think? Would he, with that burning grass torch, heat up the river Ganges and make it boil?"

"No, lord. Why is that? Because the river Ganges is deep & enormous. It's not easy to heat it up and make it boil with a burning grass torch. The man would reap only a share of weariness & disappointment."

"In the same way, monks, there are these five aspects of speech by which others may address you: timely or untimely, true or false, affectionate or harsh, beneficial or unbeneficial, with a mind of goodwill or with inner hate. Others may address you in a timely way or an untimely way. They may address you with what is true or what is false. They may address you in an affectionate way or a harsh way. They may address you in a beneficial way or an unbeneficial way. They may address you with a mind of goodwill or with inner hate. In any event, you should train yourselves: 'Our minds will be unaffected and we will say no evil words. We will remain sympathetic to that person's welfare, with a mind of goodwill, and with no inner hate. We will keep pervading him with an awareness imbued with goodwill and, beginning with him, we will keep pervading the all-encompassing world with an awareness imbued with goodwill equal to the river Ganges—abundant, enlarged, immeasurable, free from hostility, free from ill will.' That's how you should train yourselves.

"Suppose there were a catskin bag—beaten, well-beaten, beaten through & through, soft, silky, free of rustling & crackling—and a man were to come along carrying a stick or shard and saying, 'With this stick or shard I will take this catskin bag—beaten, well-beaten, beaten through & through, soft, silky, free of rustling & crackling—and I will make it rustle & crackle.' Now, what do you think? Would he, with that stick or shard, take that catskin bag—beaten, well-beaten, beaten through & through, soft, silky, free of rustling & crackling—and make it rustle & crackle?"

"No, lord. Why is that? Because the catskin bag is beaten, well-beaten, beaten through & through, soft, silky, free of rustling & crackling. It's not easy to make it rustle & crackle with a stick or shard. The man would reap only a share of weariness & disappointment."

"In the same way, monks, there are these five aspects of speech by which others may address you: timely or untimely, true or false, affectionate or harsh, beneficial or unbeneficial, with a mind of goodwill or with inner hate. Others may address you in a timely way or an untimely way. They may address you with what is true or what is false. They may address you in an affectionate way or a harsh way. They may address you in a beneficial way or an unbeneficial way. They may address you with a mind of goodwill or with inner hate. In any event, you should train yourselves: 'Our minds will be unaffected and we will say no evil words. We will remain sympathetic to that person's welfare, with a mind of goodwill, and with no inner hate. We will keep pervading him with an awareness imbued with goodwill and, beginning with him, we will keep pervading the all-encompassing world with an awareness imbued with goodwill equal to a catskin bag—abundant, enlarged, immeasurable, free from hostility, free from ill will.' That's how you should train yourselves.

"Monks, even if bandits were to carve you up savagely, limb by limb, with a two-handled saw, he among you who let his heart get angered even at that would not be doing my bidding. Even then you should train yourselves: 'Our minds will be unaffected and we will say no evil words. We will remain sympathetic, with a mind of goodwill, and with no inner hate. We will keep pervading these people with an awareness imbued with goodwill and, beginning with them, we will keep pervading the all-encompassing world with an awareness imbued with goodwill—abundant, enlarged, immeasurable, free from hostility, free from ill will.' That's how you should train yourselves.

"Monks, if you attend constantly to this admonition on the simile of the saw, do you see any aspects of speech, slight or gross, that you could not endure?"

"No, lord."

"Then attend constantly to this admonition on the simile of the saw. That will be for your long-term welfare & happiness."

That is what the Blessed One said. Gratified, the monks delighted in the Blessed One's words.

See also: MN 28; AN 5:161–162; AN 7:60; AN 10:80; SN 1:71; SN 6:2; SN 20:4–5; SN 35:88; SN 42:8; AN 7:60; Ud 2:4; Thag 6:2; Thag 16:1

22 The Water-Snake Simile

Alagaddūpama Sutta

INTRODUCTION

This is a discourse about clinging to views (diṭṭhi). Its central message is conveyed in two similes, among the most famous in the Canon: the simile of the water-snake and the simile of the raft. Taken together, these similes focus on the skill needed to grasp right view properly as a means of leading to the cessation of suffering, rather than an object of clinging, and then letting it go when it has done its job.

The first section of the discourse, leading up to the simile of the water-snake, focuses on the danger of misapprehending the Dhamma in general, and particularly the teachings on sensuality. The discourse doesn't explain how the offending monk, Ariṭṭha, formulated his misapprehension of the Dhamma, but the Commentary suggests a plausible scenario:

> *"Here the monk… having gone into seclusion, reasons as follows: 'There are people living the household life, enjoying the five pleasures of the senses, who are stream-winners, once-returners, and non-returners. As for monks, they see pleasurable forms cognizable via the eye, hear… smell… taste… feel (pleasurable) tactile sensations cognizable via the body. They use soft carpets and clothing. All this is proper. Then why shouldn't the sight, sound, smell, taste, and feel of a woman be proper? They too are proper!' Thus… comparing a mustard seed with Mount Sineru, he gives rise to the evil viewpoint, 'Why did the Blessed One—binding the ocean, as it were, with great effort—formulate the first pārājika training rule (against sexual intercourse)? There is nothing wrong with that act.'"*

Regardless of how Ariṭṭha actually arrived at his position, the Commentary's suggestion makes an important point: that just because an idea can be logically inferred from the Dhamma does not mean that the idea is valid or useful. The Buddha himself makes the same point in AN 2:24:

> *"Monks, these two slander the Tathāgata. Which two? He who explains a discourse whose meaning needs to be inferred as one whose meaning has already been fully drawn out. And he who*

explains a discourse whose meaning has already been fully drawn out as one whose meaning needs to be inferred."

Having established this point, the discourse illustrates it with the simile of the water-snake, which in turn is an introduction to the simile of the raft. It is important to underline the connection between these two similes, for it is often missed. Many a casual reader has concluded from the simile of the raft simply that the Dhamma is to be let-go. In fact, one major Mahāyāna text—the Diamond Sūtra—interprets the raft simile as meaning that one has to let go of the raft in order to cross the river. However, the simile of the water-snake makes the point that the Dhamma has to be grasped; the trick lies in grasping it properly. When this point is then applied to the raft simile, the implication is clear: One has to hold onto the raft properly in order to cross the river. Only when one has reached the safety of the further shore can one let go.

Taken together, these two similes set the stage for the remainder of the discourse, which focuses on the teaching of not-self. This is one of the most easily misapprehended teachings in the Canon largely because it is possible to draw the wrong inferences from it.

Two mistaken inferences are particularly relevant here. The first concerns the range of the not-self teaching. Some have argued that, because the Buddha usually limits his teachings on not-self to the five aggregates—form, feeling, perceptions, fabrications, and consciousness—he leaves open the possibility that something else may be regarded as self. Or, as the argument is often phrased, he denies the limited, temporal self as a means of pointing to one's identity with the larger, unlimited, cosmic self. However, in this discourse the Buddha explicitly phrases the not-self teaching in such a way as to refute any notion of cosmic self. Instead of centering his discussion of not-self on the five aggregates, he focuses on the first four aggregates plus two other possible objects of self-identification, both more explicitly cosmic in their range: (1) all that can be seen, heard, sensed, cognized, attained, sought after, pondered by the intellect; and (2) the cosmos as a whole, eternal and unchanging. In fact, the Buddha holds this last view up to particular ridicule, as the teaching of a fool, for two reasons that are developed at different points in this discourse: (1) If the cosmos were "me," then it must also be "mine," which is obviously not the case. (2) There is nothing in the experience of the cosmos that fits the bill of being eternal, unchanging, or that deserves to be clung to as "me" or "mine."

The second mistaken inference is that, given the thoroughness with which the Buddha teaches not-self, one should draw the inference that there is no self. This inference is treated less explicitly in this discourse, although it is touched upon briefly in terms of what *the Buddha teaches here and* how *he teaches.*

In terms of what: He explicitly states he cannot envision a doctrine of self that, if clung to, would not lead to sorrow, lamentation, pain, grief, & despair. He does not list all the possible doctrines of self included under this statement, but MN 2 provides at least a partial list:

> *I have a self ... I have no self ... It is precisely by means of self that I perceive self ... It is precisely by means of self that I perceive not-self ... It is precisely by means of not-self that I perceive self ... or ... This very self of mine—the knower that is sensitive here & there to the ripening of good & bad actions—is the self of mine that is constant, everlasting, eternal, not subject to change, and will endure as long as eternity. This is called a thicket of views, a wilderness of views, a contortion of views, a writhing of views, a fetter of views. Bound by a fetter of views, the uninstructed run-of-the-mill person is not freed from birth, aging, & death, from sorrow, lamentation, pain, distress, & despair. He is not freed, I tell you, from suffering & stress.*

Thus the view "I have no self" is just as much a doctrine of self as the view "I have a self." Because the act of clinging involves what the Buddha calls "I-making"—the creation of a sense of self—if one were to cling to the view that there is no self, one would be creating a very subtle sense of self around that view (see AN 4:24). But, as he says, the Dhamma is taught for "the elimination of all view-positions, determinations, biases, inclinations, & obsessions; for the pacification of all fabrications; for the relinquishing of all acquisitions; the ending of craving; dispassion; cessation; unbinding."

So it is important to focus on how the Dhamma is taught: Even in his most thoroughgoing teachings about not-self, the Buddha never recommends replacing the assumption that there is a self with the assumption that there is no self. Instead, he only goes so far as to point out the drawbacks of various ways of conceiving the self and then to recommend dropping them. For example, in his standard series of questions building on the logic of the inconstancy and stress of the aggregates, he does not say that because the aggregates are inconstant and stressful there is no self. He simply asks, When they are inconstant and stressful, is it proper to assume that they are "me, my self, what I am"? Now, because the sense of self is a product of "I-making," this question seeks to do nothing more than to induce disenchantment and dispassion for that process of I-making, so as to put a stop to it. Once that is accomplished, the teaching has fulfilled its purpose in putting an end to suffering and stress. That's the safety of the further shore. As the Buddha says in this discourse, "Both formerly and now, monks, I declare only stress and the cessation of stress." As he also says here, when views of self are finally dropped, one is free from agitation; and as MN 140 points out, when one is truly unagitated one is unbound. The raft has reached the shore, and one can leave it there—free to go where one likes, in a way that cannot be traced.

* * *

I have heard that on one occasion the Blessed One was staying near Sāvatthī in Jeta's Grove, Anāthapiṇḍika's monastery. Now on that occasion this evil viewpoint *[diṭṭhigata]* had arisen in the monk Ariṭṭha Formerly-of-the-Vulture-Killers: "As I understand the Dhamma taught by the Blessed One, those acts the Blessed One says are obstructive, when indulged in, are not genuine obstructions." A large number of monks heard, "They say that this evil viewpoint has arisen in the monk Ariṭṭha Formerly-of-the-Vulture-Killers: 'As I understand the Dhamma taught by the Blessed One, those acts the Blessed One says are obstructive, when indulged in, are not genuine obstructions.'" So they went to the monk Ariṭṭha Formerly-of-the-Vulture-Killers and on arrival said to him, "Is it true, friend Ariṭṭha, that this evil viewpoint has arisen in you—'As I understand the Dhamma taught by the Blessed One, those acts the Blessed One says are obstructive, when indulged in, are not genuine obstructions'?"

"Yes, indeed, friends. I understand the Dhamma taught by the Blessed One, and those acts the Blessed One says are obstructive, when indulged in are not genuine obstructions."

Then those monks, desiring to pry the monk Ariṭṭha Formerly-of-the-Vulture-Killers away from that evil viewpoint, quizzed him back and forth and rebuked him, saying, "Don't say that, friend Ariṭṭha. Don't misrepresent the Blessed One, for it is not good to misrepresent the Blessed One. The Blessed One would not say anything like that. In many ways, friend, the Blessed One has described obstructive acts, and when indulged in they are genuine obstructions. The Blessed One has said that sensual pleasures are of little satisfaction, much stress, much despair, & greater drawbacks. The Blessed One has compared sensual pleasures to a chain of bones: of much stress, much despair, & greater drawbacks. The Blessed One has compared sensual pleasures to a lump of flesh... a grass torch... a pit of glowing embers... a dream... borrowed goods... the fruits of a tree... a butcher's ax and chopping block... swords and spears... a snake's head: of much stress, much despair, & greater drawbacks."[1] And yet even though he was quizzed back & forth and rebuked by those monks, the monk Ariṭṭha Formerly-of-the-Vulture-Killers, through stubbornness and attachment to that very same evil viewpoint, continued to insist, "Yes, indeed, friends. I understand the Dhamma taught by the Blessed One, and those acts the Blessed One says are obstructive, when indulged in are not genuine obstructions."

So when the monks were unable to pry the monk Ariṭṭha Formerly-of-the-Vulture-Killers away from that evil viewpoint, they went to the Blessed One and on arrival, having bowed down to him, sat to one side. As they were sitting there, they [told him what had happened.]

So the Blessed One told a certain monk, "Come, monk. In my name, call the monk Ariṭṭha Formerly-of-the-Vulture-Killers, saying, 'The Teacher calls you, friend Ariṭṭha.'"

"As you say, lord," the monk responded and, having gone to the monk Ariṭṭha Formerly-of-the-Vulture-Killers, on arrival he said, "The Teacher calls you, friend Ariṭṭha."

"As you say, my friend," the monk Ariṭṭha Formerly-of-the-Vulture-Killers responded. Then he went to the Blessed One and, on arrival, having bowed down to him, sat to one side. As he was sitting there, the Blessed One said to him, "Is it true, Ariṭṭha, that this evil viewpoint has arisen in you—'As I understand the Dhamma taught by the Blessed One, those acts the Blessed One says are obstructive, when indulged in, are not genuine obstructions'?"

"Yes, indeed, lord. I understand the Dhamma taught by the Blessed One, and those acts the Blessed One says are obstructive, when indulged in are not genuine obstructions."

"Worthless man, from whom have you understood that Dhamma taught by me in such a way? Worthless man, haven't I in many ways described obstructive acts? And when indulged in they are genuine obstructions. I have said that sensual pleasures are of little satisfaction, much stress, much despair, & greater drawbacks. I have compared sensual pleasures to a chain of bones: of much stress, much despair, & greater drawbacks. I have compared sensual pleasures to a lump of flesh… a grass torch… a pit of glowing embers… a dream… borrowed goods… the fruits of a tree… a butcher's ax and chopping block… swords and spears… a snake' head: of much stress, much despair, & greater drawbacks. But you, worthless man, through your own wrong grasp (of the Dhamma), have both misrepresented us as well as injuring yourself and accumulating much demerit for yourself, for that will lead to your long-term harm & suffering."[2]

Then the Blessed One said to the monks, "What do you think, monks? Is this monk Ariṭṭha Formerly-of-the-Vulture-Killers even warm[3] in this Dhamma & Vinaya?"

"How could he be, lord? No, lord."

When this was said, the monk Ariṭṭha Formerly-of-the-Vulture-Killers sat silent, abashed, his shoulders drooping, his head down, brooding, at a loss for words.

Then the Blessed One, seeing that the monk Ariṭṭha Formerly-of-the-Vulture-Killers was sitting silent, abashed, his shoulders drooping, his head down, brooding, at a loss for words, said to him, "Worthless man, you will be recognized for your own evil viewpoint. I will cross-examine the monks on this matter."

Then the Blessed One addressed the monks, "Monks, do you, too, understand the Dhamma as taught by me in the same way that the monk Ariṭṭha Formerly-of-the-Vulture-Killers does when, through his own wrong grasp, both misrepresents us as well as injuring himself and accumulating much demerit for himself?"

"No, lord, for in many ways the Blessed One has described obstructive acts to us, and when indulged in they are genuine obstructions. The Blessed One has said that sensual pleasures are of little satisfaction, much stress, much despair, & greater drawbacks. The Blessed One has compared sensual pleasures to a chain of bones: of much stress, much despair, & greater drawbacks. The Blessed One has compared sensual pleasures to a lump of flesh… a grass torch… a pit of glowing embers… a dream… borrowed goods… the fruits of a tree… a butcher's ax and chopping block… swords and spears… a snake' head: of much stress, much despair, & greater drawbacks."

"It's good, monks, that you understand the Dhamma taught by me in this way, for in many ways I have described obstructive acts to you, and when indulged in they are genuine obstructions. I have said that sensual pleasures are of little satisfaction, much stress, much despair, & greater drawbacks. I have compared sensual pleasures to a chain of bones: of much stress, much despair, & greater drawbacks. I have compared sensual pleasures to a lump of flesh… a grass torch… a pit of glowing embers… a dream… borrowed goods… the fruits of a tree… a butcher's ax and chopping block… swords and spears… a snake' head: of much stress, much despair, & greater drawbacks. But this monk Ariṭṭha Formerly-of-the-Vulture-Killers, through his own wrong grasp (of the Dhamma), has both misrepresented us as well as injuring himself and accumulating much demerit for himself, and that will lead to this worthless man's long-term harm & suffering. For a person to indulge in sensual pleasures without sensual passion, without sensual perception, without sensual thinking: That isn't possible.[4]

THE WATER-SNAKE SIMILE

"Monks, there is the case where some worthless men study the Dhamma: dialogues, narratives of mixed prose and verse, explanations, verses, spontaneous exclamations, quotations, birth stories, amazing events, question & answer sessions [the earliest classifications of the Buddha's teachings]. Having studied the Dhamma, they don't ascertain the meaning [or: the purpose] of those Dhammas[5] with their discernment. Not having ascertained the meaning of those Dhammas with their discernment, they don't come to an agreement through pondering. They study the Dhamma both for attacking others and for defending themselves in debate. They don't reach the goal for which (people) study the Dhamma. Their wrong grasp of those Dhammas will lead to their long-term harm & suffering. Why is that? Because of the wrong-graspedness of the Dhammas.

"Suppose there were a man needing a water-snake, seeking a water-snake, wandering in search of a water-snake. He would see a large water-snake and grasp it by the coils or by the tail. The water-snake, turning around, would bite him on the hand, on the arm, or on one of his limbs, and from that cause he would suffer death or death-like suffering. Why is that? Because of the wrong-graspedness of the water-snake. In the same way, there is the case where some worthless men study the Dhamma.... Having studied the Dhamma, they don't ascertain the meaning of those Dhammas with their discernment. Not having ascertained the meaning of those Dhammas with their discernment, they don't come to an agreement through pondering. They study the Dhamma both for attacking others and for defending themselves in debate. They don't reach the goal for which (people) study the Dhamma. Their wrong grasp of those Dhammas will lead to their long-term harm & suffering. Why is that? Because of the wrong-graspedness of the Dhammas.

"But then there is the case where some clansmen study the Dhamma.... Having studied the Dhamma, they ascertain the meaning of those Dhammas with their discernment. Having ascertained the meaning of those Dhammas with their discernment, they come to an agreement through pondering. They don't study the Dhamma either for attacking others or for defending themselves in debate. They reach the goal for which people study the Dhamma. Their right grasp of those Dhammas will lead to their long-term welfare & happiness. Why is that? Because of the right-graspedness of the Dhammas.

"Suppose there were a man needing a water-snake, seeking a water-snake, wandering in search of a water-snake. He would see a large water-snake and pin it down firmly with a cleft stick. Having pinned it down firmly with a forked stick, he would grasp it firmly by the neck. Then no matter how much the water-snake might wrap its coils around his hand, his arm, or any of his limbs, he would not from that cause suffer death or death-like suffering. Why is that? Because of the right-graspedness of the water-snake. In the same way, there is the case where some clansmen study the Dhamma.... Having studied the Dhamma, they ascertain the meaning of those Dhammas with their discernment. Having ascertained the meaning of those Dhammas with their discernment, they come to an agreement through pondering. They don't study the Dhamma either for attacking others or for defending themselves in debate. They reach the goal for which people study the Dhamma. Their right grasp of those Dhammas will lead to their long-term welfare & happiness. Why is that? Because of the right-graspedness of the Dhammas.[6]

"Therefore, monks, when you understand the meaning of my statements, that is how you should remember them. But when you don't understand the meaning of my statements, then right there you should ask me or the experienced monks.

THE RAFT SIMILE

"Monks, I will teach you the Dhamma compared to a raft, for the purpose of crossing over, not for the purpose of holding onto. Listen & pay close attention. I will speak."

"As you say, lord," the monks responded to the Blessed One.

The Blessed One said: "Suppose a man were traveling along a path. He would see a great expanse of water, with the near shore dubious & risky, the further shore secure & free from risk, but with neither a ferryboat nor a bridge going from this shore to the other. The thought would occur to him, 'Here is this great expanse of water, with the near shore dubious & risky, the further shore secure & free from risk, but with neither a ferryboat nor a bridge going from this shore to the other. What if I were to gather grass, twigs, branches, & leaves and, having bound them together to make a raft, were to cross over to safety on the other shore in dependence on the raft, making an effort with my hands & feet?' Then the man, having gathered grass, twigs, branches, & leaves, having bound them together to make a raft, would cross over to safety on the other shore in dependence on the raft, making an effort with his hands &

feet.[7] Having crossed over to the further shore, he might think, 'How useful this raft has been to me! For it was in dependence on this raft that, making an effort with my hands & feet, I have crossed over to safety on the further shore. Why don't I, having hoisted it on my head or carrying it on my back, go wherever I like?' What do you think, monks? Would the man, in doing that, be doing what should be done with the raft?"

"No, lord."

"And what should the man do in order to be doing what should be done with the raft? There is the case where the man, having crossed over, would think, 'How useful this raft has been to me! For it was in dependence on this raft that, making an effort with my hands & feet, I have crossed over to safety on the further shore. Why don't I, having dragged it on dry land or sinking it in the water, go wherever I like?' In doing this, he would be doing what should be done with the raft. In the same way, monks, I have taught the Dhamma compared to a raft, for the purpose of crossing over, not for the purpose of holding onto. Understanding the Dhamma as taught compared to a raft, you should let go even of Dhammas, to say nothing of non-Dhammas."

SIX VIEW-POSITIONS

"Monks, there are these six view-positions *[diṭṭhiṭṭhāna]*. Which six? There is the case where an uninstructed run-of-the-mill person—who has no regard for noble ones, is not well-versed or disciplined in their Dhamma; who has no regard for people of integrity, is not well-versed or disciplined in their Dhamma—assumes about form: 'This is me, this is my self, this is what I am.'

"He assumes about feeling: 'This is me, this is my self, this is what I am.'

"He assumes about perception: 'This is me, this is my self, this is what I am.'

"He assumes about fabrications: 'This is me, this is my self, this is what I am.'

"He assumes about what is seen, heard, sensed, cognized, attained, sought after, pondered by the intellect: 'This is me, this is my self, this is what I am.'

"He assumes about the view-position—'This cosmos is the self.[8] After death this I will be constant, permanent, eternal, not subject to change. I will stay just like that for an eternity': 'This is me, this is my self, this is what I am.'

"Then there is the case where a well-instructed disciple of the noble ones—who has regard for noble ones, is well-versed & disciplined in their Dhamma; who has regard for people of integrity, is well-versed & disciplined in their Dhamma assumes about form: 'This is not me, this is not my self, this is not what I am.'

"He assumes about feeling: 'This is not me, this is not my self, this is not what I am.'

"He assumes about perception: 'This is not me, this is not my self, this is not what I am.'

"He assumes about fabrications: 'This is not me, this is not my self, this is not what I am.'

"He assumes about what is seen, heard, sensed, cognized, attained, sought after, pondered by the intellect: 'This is not me, this is not my self, this is not what I am.'

"He assumes about the view-position—'This cosmos is the self. After death this I will be constant, permanent, eternal, not subject to change. I will stay just like that for an eternity': 'This is not me, this is not my self, this is not what I am.'

"Seeing thus, he is not agitated over what is not present."[9]

When this was said, a certain monk said to the Blessed One, "Lord, might there be agitation over what is externally not present?"

"There might, monk," the Blessed One said. "There is the case where someone thinks, 'O, it was mine! O, what was mine is not! O, may it be mine! O, I don't obtain it!' He grieves & is tormented, weeps, beats his breast, & grows delirious. It's thus that there is agitation over what is externally not present."

"But, lord, might there be non-agitation over what is externally not present?"

"There might, monk," the Blessed One said. "There is the case where someone doesn't think, 'O, it was mine! O, what was mine is not! O, may it be mine! O, I don't obtain it!' He doesn't grieve, isn't tormented, doesn't weep, beat his breast, or grow delirious. It's thus that there is non-agitation over what is externally not present."

AGITATION & NON-AGITATION

"But, lord, might there be agitation over what is internally not present?"

"There might, monk," the Blessed One said. "There is the case where someone has this view: 'This cosmos is the self. After death this I will be constant, permanent, eternal, not subject to change. I will stay just like that for an eternity.' He hears a Tathāgata or a Tathāgata's disciple teaching the Dhamma for the elimination of all view-positions, determinations, biases, inclinations, & obsessions; for the pacification of all fabrications; for the relinquishing of all acquisitions; the ending of craving; dispassion; cessation; unbinding. The thought occurs to him, 'So it might be that I will be annihilated! So it might be that I will perish! So it might be that I will not exist!' He grieves & is tormented, weeps, beats his breast, & grows delirious. It's thus that there is agitation over what is internally not present."

"But, lord, might there be non-agitation over what is internally not present?"

"There might, monk," the Blessed One said. "There is the case where someone doesn't have this view: 'This cosmos is the self. After death this I will be constant, permanent, eternal, not subject to change. I will stay just like that for an eternity.' He hears a Tathāgata or a Tathāgata's disciple teaching the Dhamma for the elimination of all view-positions, determinations, biases, inclinations, & obsessions; for the pacification of all fabrications; for the relinquishing of all acquisitions; the ending of craving; dispassion; cessation; unbinding. The thought doesn't occur to him, 'So it might be that I will be annihilated! So it might be that I will perish! So it might be that I will not exist!' He doesn't grieve, isn't tormented, doesn't weep, beat his breast, or grow delirious. It's thus that there is non-agitation over what is internally not present."

"Monks, you would do well to possess that possession, the possession of which would be constant, permanent, eternal, not subject to change, that would stay just like that for an eternity. But do you see that possession, the possession of which would be constant, permanent, eternal, not subject to change, that would stay just like that for an eternity?"

"No, lord."

ABANDONING POSSESSIONS & VIEWS

"Very good, monks. I, too, do not envision a possession, the possession of which would be constant, permanent, eternal, not subject to change, that would stay just like that for an eternity.

"Monks, you would do well to cling to that clinging to a doctrine of self, clinging to which there would not arise sorrow, lamentation, pain, grief, & despair. But do you see a clinging to a doctrine of self, clinging to which there would not arise sorrow, lamentation, pain, grief, & despair?"

"No, lord."

"Very good, monks. I, too, do not envision a clinging to a doctrine of self, clinging to which there would not arise sorrow, lamentation, pain, grief, & despair.

"Monks, you would do well to depend on a view-dependency *[diṭṭhi-nissaya]*, depending on which there would not arise sorrow, lamentation, pain, grief, & despair. But do you see a view-dependency, depending on which there would not arise sorrow, lamentation, pain, grief, & despair?"

"No, lord."

"Very good, monks. I, too, do not envision a view-dependency, depending on which there would not arise sorrow, lamentation, pain, grief, & despair.

"Monks, where there is a self, would there be (the thought,) 'belonging to my self'?"

"Yes, lord."

"Or, monks, where there is what belongs to self, would there be (the thought,) 'my self'?"

"Yes, lord."

"Monks, where a self or what belongs to self are not pinned down as a truth or reality, then the view-position—'This cosmos is the self. After death this I will be constant, permanent, eternal, not subject to change. I will stay just like that for an eternity'—Isn't it utterly & completely a fool's teaching?"

"What else could it be, lord? It's utterly & completely a fool's teaching."

"What do you think, monks? Is form constant or inconstant?" "Inconstant, lord." "And is that which is inconstant easeful or stressful?" "Stressful, lord." "And is it fitting to regard what is inconstant, stressful, subject to change as: 'This is mine. This is my self. This is what I am'?"

"No, lord."

"... Is feeling constant or inconstant?" "Inconstant, lord." ...

"... Is perception constant or inconstant?" "Inconstant, lord." ...

"... Are fabrications constant or inconstant?" "Inconstant, lord." ...

"What do you think, monks? Is consciousness constant or inconstant?" "Inconstant, lord." "And is that which is inconstant easeful or stressful?" "Stressful, lord." "And is it fitting to regard what is inconstant, stressful, subject to change as: 'This is mine. This is my self. This is what I am'?"

"No, lord."

"Thus, monks, any form whatsoever that is past, future, or present; internal or external; blatant or subtle; common or sublime; far or near: Every[10] form is to be seen as it has come to be with right discernment as: 'This is not mine. This is not my self. This is not what I am.'

"Any feeling whatsoever....

"Any perception whatsoever....

"Any fabrications whatsoever....

"Any consciousness whatsoever that is past, future, or present; internal or external; blatant or subtle; common or sublime; far or near: Every consciousness is to be seen as it has come to be with right discernment as: 'This is not mine. This is not my self. This is not what I am.'

"Seeing thus, the instructed disciple of the noble ones grows disenchanted with form, disenchanted with feeling, disenchanted with perception, disenchanted with fabrications, disenchanted with consciousness. Disenchanted, he becomes dispassionate. Through dispassion, he is released. With release, there is the knowledge, 'Released.' He discerns that 'Birth is ended, the holy life fulfilled, the task done. There is nothing further for this world.'

"This, monks, is called a monk whose cross-bar is thrown off,[11] whose moat is filled in, whose pillar is pulled out, whose bolt is withdrawn, a noble one with banner lowered, burden placed down, unfettered.

"And how is a monk one whose cross-bar is thrown off? There is the case where a monk's ignorance is abandoned, its root destroyed, made like a palmyra stump, deprived of the conditions of development, not destined for future arising. This is how a monk is one whose cross-bar is thrown off.

"And how is a monk one whose moat is filled in? There is the case where a monk's wandering-on to birth, leading on to further-becoming, is abandoned, its root destroyed, made like a palmyra stump, deprived of the conditions of development, not destined for future arising. This is how a monk is one whose moat is filled in.

"And how is a monk one whose pillar is pulled out? There is the case where a monk's craving is abandoned, its root destroyed, made like a palmyra stump, deprived of the conditions of development, not destined for future arising. This is how a monk is one whose pillar is pulled out.

"And how is a monk one whose bolt is withdrawn? There is the case where a monk's five lower fetters are abandoned, their root destroyed, made like a palmyra stump, deprived of the conditions of development, not destined for future arising. This is how a monk is one whose bolt is withdrawn.

"And how is a monk a noble one with banner lowered, burden placed down, unfettered? There is the case where a monk's conceit 'I am' is abandoned, its root destroyed, made like a palmyra stump, deprived of the conditions of development, not destined for future arising. This is how a monk is a noble one with banner lowered, burden placed down, unfettered.

"And when the devas, together with Indra, the Brahmās, & Pajāpati, search for the monk whose mind is thus released, they cannot find that 'The consciousness of the one truly gone *[tathāgata]*[12] is dependent on this.' Why is that? The one truly gone is untraceable even in the here & now.[13]

"Speaking in this way, teaching in this way, I have been erroneously, vainly, falsely, unfactually misrepresented by some contemplatives & brahmans (who say), 'Gotama the contemplative is one who misleads. He declares the annihilation, destruction, extermination of the existing being.' But as I am not that, as I do not say that, so I have erroneously, vainly, falsely, unfactually misrepresented by those venerable contemplatives & brahmans (who say), 'Gotama the contemplative is one who misleads. He declares the annihilation, destruction, extermination of the existing being.'[14]

"Both formerly and now, monks, I declare only stress and the cessation of stress.[15] And if others insult, abuse, taunt, bother, & harass the Tathāgata for that, he feels no hatred, no resentment, no dissatisfaction of heart because of that. And if others honor, respect, revere, & venerate the Tathāgata for that, he feels no joy, no happiness, no elation of heart because of that. And if others honor, respect, revere, & venerate the Tathāgata for that, he thinks, 'They do me such service at this that has already been comprehended.'[16]

"Therefore, monks, if others insult, abuse, taunt, bother, & harass you as well, you should feel no hatred, no resentment, no dissatisfaction of heart because of that. And if others honor, respect, revere, & venerate you as well, you should feel no joy, no gladness, no elation of heart because of that. And if others honor, respect, revere, & venerate you, you should think, 'They do us[17] such service at this that has already been comprehended.'

"Therefore, monks, whatever isn't yours: Let go of it. Your letting go of it will be for your long-term welfare & happiness. And what isn't yours? Form isn't yours: Let go of it. Your letting go of it will be for your long-term welfare & happiness. Feeling isn't yours... Perception... Fabrications... Consciousness isn't yours:

Let go of it. Your letting go of it will be for your long-term welfare & happiness.

"What do you think, monks? If a person were to gather or burn or do as he likes with the grass, twigs, branches & leaves here in Jeta's Grove, would the thought occur to you, 'It's us that this person is gathering, burning, or doing with as he likes'?"

"No, lord. Why is that? Because those things are not our self, nor do they belong to our self."

"Even so, monks, whatever isn't yours: Let go of it. Your letting go of it will be for your long-term welfare & happiness. And what isn't yours? Form isn't yours... Feeling isn't yours... Perception... Fabrications... Consciousness isn't yours: Let go of it. Your letting go of it will be for your long-term welfare & happiness.

THE WELL-PROCLAIMED DHAMMA

"The Dhamma thus well-proclaimed by me is clear, open, evident, stripped of rags. In the Dhamma thus well-proclaimed by me—clear, open, evident, stripped of rags—there is for those monks who are arahants—whose effluents are ended, who have reached fulfillment, done the task, laid down the burden, attained the true goal, totally destroyed the fetter of becoming, and who are released through right gnosis—no (future) cycle for manifestation. This is how the Dhamma well-proclaimed by me is clear, open, evident, stripped of rags.[18]

"In the Dhamma thus well-proclaimed by me—clear, open, evident, stripped of rags—those monks who have abandoned the five lower fetters are all due to arise spontaneously (in the Pure Abodes), there to be totally unbound, never again to return from that world. This is how the Dhamma well-proclaimed by me is clear, open, evident, stripped of rags.

"In the Dhamma thus well-proclaimed by me—clear, open, evident, stripped of rags—those monks who have abandoned (the first) three fetters, with the attenuation of passion, aversion, & delusion, are all once-returners who, on returning only one more time to this world, will make an ending to stress. This is how the Dhamma well-proclaimed by me is clear, open, evident, stripped of rags.

"In the Dhamma thus well-proclaimed by me—clear, open, evident, stripped of rags—those monks who have abandoned (the first) three fetters, are all stream-winners, certain, never again destined for the lower realms, headed for self-awakening. This is how the Dhamma well-proclaimed by me is clear, open, evident, stripped of rags.

"In the Dhamma thus well-proclaimed by me—clear, open, evident, stripped of rags—those monks who are Dhamma-followers and conviction-followers[19] are all headed for self-awakening. This is how the Dhamma well-proclaimed by me is clear, open, evident, stripped of rags.

"In the Dhamma thus well-proclaimed by me—clear, open, evident, stripped of rags—those monks who have a (sufficient) measure of conviction in me, a (sufficient) measure of love for me, are all headed for heaven. This is how the Dhamma well-proclaimed by me is clear, open, evident, stripped of rags."

That is what the Blessed One said. Gratified, the monks delighted in the Blessed One's words.

NOTES

1. The first seven of these comparisons are treated in detail in MN 54. The simile of the butcher's ax and chopping block is mentioned in MN 23, the simile of swords and spears in SN 5:1, and the simile of the snake's head in Sn 4:1.

2. Apart from a few minor details, this story up to this point is identical with the origin story for Pācittiya 68 and the origin story for the rules concerning the act of suspension given in Cullavagga (CvI.32.1-3.) Ariṭṭha was the first monk to be suspended from the Saṅgha. Cv I.34 reports that, instead of making an effort to mend his ways so that the act of suspension might be rescinded, he simply disrobed.

3. The image here is apparently that of trying to start a fire with the friction of a fire stick. Ariṭṭha hasn't even been able to create any warmth, much less the spark of insight that would create light.

4. According to the Commentary, "indulge in sensual pleasures" here means indulging in sexual intercourse; the Sub-commentary adds that other acts expressing sexual desire—such as hugging and petting—should be included under this phrase as well.

5. The Pali switches from the singular (Dhamma) to the plural (Dhammas) here. This is one of the few discourses that use the plural form to mean "teachings" rather than "phenomena." This same use of "Dhammas" to mean "teachings" reoccurs in the raft simile, below.

6. These last two sentences are missing in MLDB but are present in MLS.

7. According to SN 35:197: "The great expanse of water stands for the fourfold flood: the flood of sensuality, the flood of becoming, the

flood of views, & the flood of ignorance. The near shore, dubious & risky, stands for self-identification. The further shore, secure and free from risk, stands for unbinding. The raft stands for just this noble eightfold path: right view... right concentration. Making an effort with hands & feet stands for the arousing of persistence."

8. The Pali here reads, *so loko so attā.* The translation given here follows the interpretation of Nyanaponika Thera in his translation of this discourse. Bhikkhu Bodhi, in his notes to the translation of this discourse in MLDB, calls this interpretation hypothetical, and instead suggests that this phrase indicates the Sāṅkhya theory of the changeless "person" as opposed to unchanging "nature." However, in his later translation of SN 22:81, which contains an identical passage, he adopts Nyanaponika's interpretation as well.

9. On non-agitation, see MN 138 and MN 140.

10. The word "every" here and in all parallel passages is *sabba,* which is the same as the word for "all." On the range of meaning covered by the word "all," see SN 35:23. DN 11, DN 15, MN 49, and AN 10:81 indicate that there is a type of consciousness that lies outside the range of "all," and so would not fall under the aggregate of consciousness. This apparently corresponds to the dimension mentioned in SN 35:117 and Ud 8:1.

11. See Dhp 398.

12. The term "Tathāgata" is often, but not always, reserved for the Buddha. Sometimes, as in the case here, it is used to refer to the arahant.

13. See SN 22:85 and SN 22:86. Compare Dhp 92–93.

14. Annihilationism is one of the two extremes of wrong view criticized most heavily by the Buddha (the other is eternalism, as represented by the sixth of the six view-positions). Some interpreters, citing this passage, have tried to limit the meaning of annihilationism simply to the idea of the annihilation of an existing being. The teaching that there is no self, they then argue, does not count as annihilationism because there is no self to be annihilated. This interpretation ignores SN 44:10, which counts the statement "there is no self" as siding with annihilationism.

As for the term, "existing being": SN 22:36 and SN 23:2 state that a being is defined by his/her/its objects of clinging. SN 5:10 indicates that one of the ways of overcoming clinging is to focus on how the concept of "being" arises, without assuming the truth of the concept. And as MN 72, SN 22:85, and SN 22:86 maintain, when clinging is gone, one is called not a being but a *Tathāgata*—who, freed from clinging, cannot be classified as or identified with anything at all.

15. Some have suggested, citing SN 12:15, that this passage means that there are only two things happening in reality: stress and the cessation of stress. However, in the context of SN 22:86, where this statement also occurs, it clearly means simply that the Buddha is selective in the topics he chooses to address. In that discourse, he is refusing to take a stand on questions regarding the ontological status of the Tathāgata after death. Here he is refusing to take a stand on the related question of the status of the "existing being" (see note 13). In every case, the Buddha chooses to take a stand only on questions where the process of answering would be conducive to awakening. On this point, see MN 63 and SN 56:31.

16. According to the Commentary, "this" here refers to the five aggregates. As SN 22:23 points out, "comprehension" means the ending of passion, aversion, and delusion with regard to the object comprehended. In other words, the Buddha sees that the honor and respect he receives is aimed at the five aggregates; because he has no passion, aversion, or delusion with regard to those aggregates, he is not overjoyed by any honor paid to them.

17. The Thai edition of the Pali Canon has the word "us" here, whereas the Burmese, Sinhalese, and PTS editions have "me."

18. This last sentence is missing from this paragraph and all the following paragraphs both in MLDB and in MLS.

19. Dhamma-followers and conviction-followers are apparently those who are following the path to stream entry but have yet to reach the fruit of stream entry. See MN 70.

See also: DN 9; DN 15; MN 2; MN 38; MN 70; SN 25:1–10; SN 35:99; SN 44:10; AN 3:87–88; Sn 4:9

24 *Relay Chariots*

Ratha-vinīta Sutta

I have heard that on one occasion the Blessed One was staying near Rājagaha in the Bamboo Grove, the Squirrels' Sanctuary. Then a number of monks from the (Blessed One's) native land, having completed the Rains Retreat in the native land, went to the Blessed One and, on arrival, having bowed down to him, sat to one side.

As they were sitting there, the Blessed One said to them, "Monks, whom in our native land do the native-land monks—his companions in the holy life—esteem in this way: 'Modest himself, he gives talks to the monks on modesty. Contented himself, he gives talks to the monks on contentment. Secluded himself, he gives talks to the monks on seclusion. Unentangled himself, he gives talks to the monks on non-entanglement. Having aroused persistence in himself, he gives talks to the monks on arousing persistence. Consummate in his own virtue, he gives talks to the monks on becoming consummate in virtue. Consummate in his own concentration, he gives talks to the monks on becoming consummate in concentration. Consummate in his own discernment, he gives talks to the monks on becoming consummate in discernment. Consummate in his own release, he gives talks to the monks on becoming consummate in release. Consummate in his own knowledge & vision of release, he gives talks to the monks on becoming consummate in the knowledge & vision of release.[1] He is one who exhorts, informs, instructs, urges, rouses, & encourages his companions in the holy life.'"

"Lord, the monk named Puṇṇa Mantāṇiputta [Mantāṇi's son] is esteemed by the native-land monks—his companions in the holy life—in this way: 'Modest himself, he gives talks to the monks on modesty. Contented himself, he gives talks to the monks on contentment. Secluded himself, he gives talks to the monks on seclusion. Unentangled himself, he gives talks to the monks on non-entanglement. Having aroused persistence in himself, he gives talks to the monks on arousing persistence. Consummate in his own virtue, he gives talks to the monks on becoming consummate in virtue. Consummate in his own concentration, he gives talks to the monks on becoming consummate in concentration. Consummate in his own discernment, he gives talks to the monks on becoming consummate in discernment. Consummate in his own release, he gives talks to the monks on becoming consummate in release. Consummate in his own knowledge & vision of release, he gives talks to the monks on becoming consummate in the knowledge & vision of release. He is one who exhorts, informs, instructs, urges, rouses, & encourages his companions in the holy life.'"

Now at that time Ven. Sāriputta was sitting not far from the Blessed One. The thought occurred to him: "It's a gain, a great gain for Ven. Puṇṇa Mantāṇiputta that his observant companions in the holy life speak his praise point by point in the presence of the Teacher, and that the Teacher seconds that praise. Maybe sometime or other I, too, will go to meet with Ven. Puṇṇa Mantāṇiputta; maybe I'll have some conversation with him."

Then the Blessed One, having stayed at Rājagaha as long as he liked, set out wandering to Sāvatthī. Wandering by stages, he arrived there and stayed in Jeta's Grove, Anāthapiṇḍika's monastery. Ven. Puṇṇa Mantāṇiputta heard, "The Blessed One has arrived at Sāvatthī and is staying near Sāvatthī in Jeta's Grove, Anāthapiṇḍika's monastery." Setting his lodgings in order and taking his robes & bowl, he set out wandering to Sāvatthī. Wandering by stages, he went to where the Blessed One was staying in Jeta's Grove, Anāthapiṇḍika's monastery. On arrival, having bowed down to the Blessed One, he sat to one side. As he was sitting there, the Blessed One instructed, urged, roused, & encouraged him with a Dhamma talk. Then Ven. Puṇṇa—instructed, urged, roused, & encouraged with the Blessed One's Dhamma talk; delighting & approving of the Blessed One's words—got up from his seat, bowed down to the Blessed One, circumambulated him, and went to the Grove of the Blind for the day's abiding.

Then a certain monk went to Ven. Sāriputta and, on arrival, said to him: "Friend Sāriputta, the monk named Puṇṇa Mantāṇiputta whom you have so often praised—instructed, urged, roused, & encouraged with the Blessed One's Dhamma talk; delighting & approving of the Blessed One's words—has gotten up from his seat, bowed down to the Blessed One, circumambulated him, and has gone to the Grove of the Blind for the day's abiding." So Ven. Sāriputta quickly picked up a sitting cloth and followed right behind Ven. Puṇṇa, keeping his head in sight. Ven. Puṇṇa plunged into the Grove of the Blind and sat down in the shade of a tree for the day's abiding. Ven. Sāriputta also plunged into the Grove of the Blind and sat down in the shade of a tree for the day's abiding.

Then Ven. Sāriputta emerged from his seclusion in the late afternoon and went to Ven. Puṇṇa. On arrival, he exchanged courteous greetings with him. After an exchange of friendly greetings & courtesies, he sat to one side. As he was sitting there, he said to Ven. Puṇṇa, "My friend, is the holy life lived under the Blessed One?"

"Yes, my friend."

"And is the holy life lived under the Blessed One for the sake of purity in terms of virtue?"[2]

"No, my friend."

"Then is the holy life lived under the Blessed One for the sake of purity in terms of mind [concentration]?"

"No, my friend."

"Then is the holy life lived under the Blessed One for the sake of purity in terms of view?"

"No, my friend."

"Then is the holy life lived under the Blessed One for the sake of purity in terms of the overcoming of perplexity?"

"No, my friend."

"Then is the holy life lived under the Blessed One for the sake of purity in terms of knowledge & vision of what is & is not the path?"

"No, my friend."

"Then is the holy life lived under the Blessed One for the sake of purity in terms of knowledge & vision of the way?"

"No, my friend."

"Then is the holy life lived under the Blessed One for the sake of purity in terms of knowledge & vision?"

"No, my friend."

"When asked if the holy life is lived under the Blessed One for the sake of purity in terms of virtue, you say, 'No, my friend.' When asked if the holy life is lived under the Blessed One for the sake of purity in terms of mind... view... the overcoming of perplexity... knowledge & vision of what is & is not the path... knowledge & vision of the way... knowledge & vision, you say, 'No, my friend.' For the sake of what, then, my friend, is the holy life lived under the Blessed One?"

"The holy life is lived under the Blessed One, my friend, for the sake of total unbinding through lack of clinging."[3]

"But is purity in terms of virtue total unbinding through lack of clinging?"

"No, my friend."

"Then is purity in terms of mind... view... the overcoming of perplexity... knowledge & vision of what is & is not the path...

knowledge & vision of the way... knowledge & vision total unbinding through lack of clinging?"

"No, my friend."

"Then is total unbinding through lack of clinging something apart from these qualities?"

"No, my friend."

"When asked if purity in terms of virtue... mind... view... the overcoming of perplexity... knowledge & vision of what is & is not the path... knowledge & vision of the way... knowledge & vision is total unbinding through lack of clinging, you say, 'No, my friend.' But when asked if total unbinding through lack of clinging is something apart from these qualities, you say, 'No, my friend.' Now how, my friend, is the meaning of these statements to be understood?"

"If the Blessed One had described purity in terms of virtue as total unbinding through lack of clinging, my friend, then he would have defined something still accompanied by clinging as total unbinding through lack of clinging. If he had described purity in terms of mind... view... the overcoming of perplexity... knowledge & vision of what is & is not the path... knowledge & vision of the way... knowledge & vision as total unbinding through lack of clinging, then he would have defined something still accompanied by clinging as total unbinding through lack of clinging. But if total unbinding through lack of clinging were apart from these qualities, then a run-of-the-mill person would be totally unbound, inasmuch as a run-of-the-mill person is apart from these qualities.

"So, my friend, I will give you an analogy, for there are cases where it's through analogies that observant people can understand the meaning of what is being said. Suppose that while King Pasenadi Kosala was staying at Sāvatthī, some urgent business were to arise at Sāketa; and that between Sāvatthī and Sāketa seven relay chariots were made ready for him. Coming out the door of the inner palace in Sāvatthī, he would get in the first relay chariot. By means of the first relay chariot he would reach the second relay chariot. Getting out of the first relay chariot he would get in the second relay chariot. By means of the second relay chariot he would reach the third... by means of the third he would reach the fourth... by means of the fourth, the fifth... by means of the fifth, the sixth... by means of the sixth he would reach the seventh relay chariot. Getting out of the sixth relay chariot he would get in the seventh relay chariot. By means of the seventh relay chariot he would finally arrive at the door of the inner palace at Sāketa. As he arrived there, his friends & companions, relatives & kin would ask him, 'Great king, did you come from Sāvatthī to the door of the inner palace in Sāketa by means of this chariot?' Answering in what way, my friend, would King Pasenadi Kosala answer them correctly?"

"Answering in this way, my friend, he would answer them correctly: 'Just now, as I was staying at Sāvatthī, some urgent business arose at Sāketa; and between Sāvatthī and Sāketa seven relay chariots were made ready for me. Coming out the door of the inner palace in Sāvatthī, I got in the first relay chariot. By means of the first relay chariot I reached the second relay chariot. Getting out of the first relay chariot I got in the second relay chariot. By means of the second relay chariot I reached the third... by means of the third I reached the fourth... by means of the fourth, the fifth... by means of the fifth, the sixth... by means of the sixth I reached the seventh relay chariot. Getting out of the sixth relay chariot I got in the seventh relay chariot. By means of the seventh relay chariot I finally arrived at the door of the inner palace at Sāketa.' Answering in this way, he would answer them correctly."

"In the same way, my friend, purity in terms of virtue is simply for the sake of purity in terms of mind. Purity in terms of mind is simply for the sake of purity in terms of view. Purity in terms of view is simply for the sake of purity in terms of the overcoming of perplexity. Purity in terms of the overcoming of perplexity is simply for the sake of purity in terms of knowledge & vision of what is & is not the path. Purity in terms of knowledge & vision of what is & is not the path is simply for the sake of purity in terms of knowledge & vision of the way. Purity in terms of knowledge & vision of the way is simply for the sake of purity in terms of knowledge & vision. Purity in terms of knowledge & vision is simply for the sake of total unbinding through lack of clinging. And it's for the sake of total unbinding through lack of clinging that the holy life is lived under the Blessed One."

When this was said, Ven. Sāriputta said to Ven. Puṇṇa Mantāṇiputta: "What is your name, friend, and how do your companions in the holy life know you?"

"My name is Puṇṇa, friend, and my companions in the holy life know me as Mantāṇiputta."

"How amazing, my friend, how astounding, that Ven. Puṇṇa Mantāṇiputta has answered point by point with profound, profound discernment in the manner of a learned disciple who has rightly understood the Teacher's message! It's a gain, a great gain, for any of his companions in the holy life who get to see him and visit with him. Even if they had to carry him around on a cushion placed on top of their heads in order to see him and visit with him, it would be a gain for them, a great gain. And the fact that I have gotten to see him and visit with him has been a gain, a great gain for me."

When this was said, Ven. Puṇṇa said to Ven. Sāriputta: "And what is your name, friend, and how do your companions in the holy life know you?"

"My name is Upatissa, friend, and my companions in the holy life know me as Sāriputta."

"What? I've been talking with the disciple who is like the Teacher himself without knowing that it is Ven. Sāriputta? Had I known it was Ven. Sāriputta, I wouldn't have answered at such length. How amazing, my friend, how astounding, that Ven. Sāriputta has questioned point by point with profound, profound discernment in the manner of a learned disciple who has rightly understood the Teacher's message! It's a gain, a great gain, for any of his companions in the holy life who get to see him and visit with him. Even if they had to carry him around on a cushion placed on top of their heads in order to see him and visit with him, it would be a gain for them, a great gain. And the fact that I have gotten to see him and visit with him has been a gain, a great gain for me."

In this way did both great beings rejoice in each other's good words.

NOTES

1. See AN 10:69

2. Ven. Sāriputta and Ven. Puṇṇa speak of this list of seven purities—purity in terms of virtue, mind, view, the overcoming of perplexity, knowledge & vision of what is & is not the path, knowledge & vision of the way, and knowledge & vision—as if it were a teaching familiar to both of them, and yet nowhere else is it mentioned as a Buddhist teaching in the discourses. The Aṭṭhaka Vagga (Sn 4), however, mentions various non-Buddhist sectarians who spoke of purity as the goal of their teaching and who variously defined that purity in terms of virtue, view, knowledge, & practice. Perhaps the seven types of purity listed in this discourse were originally non-Buddhist teachings that were adopted by the early Buddhist community and adapted to their own purpose for showing that these seven forms of purity functioned not as the goal of practice but as stages along the path to that goal. At any rate, this list of the seven purities formed the framework for Buddhaghosa's *Visuddhimagga (The Path of Purity)*, the cornerstone of his Pali commentaries, in which the seven purities cover all three parts of the threefold training in virtue, concentration, & discernment.

3. *Anupādā-parinibbāna.* The Commentary gives two interpretations of this term, both of them equating *anupādā* with *anupādāna* (without *upādāna*). The first, taking *upādāna* as *clinging,* is total unbinding through lack of clinging. This, it says, refers to the fact that total unbinding follows on the fruit of arahantship, which is devoid of clinging. The other meaning, taking *upādāna* as *sustenance,* is total unbinding with no sustenance. This, it says, refers to the fact that total unbinding is independent of any condition. For an explanation of these meanings of the word *upādāna*, see *The Mind Like Fire Unbound,* chapter 3.

See also: SN 51:15; AN 3:40; AN 4:159; AN 9:13; Sn 4:4; Sn 4:9

26 The Noble Search

Ariyapariyesana Sutta

INTRODUCTION

Some scholars have suggested that, of the many autobiographical accounts of the Buddha's awakening presented in the Pali Canon, this is the earliest. From that assumption, they have further suggested that because this account does not mention the four noble truths, either in connection with the awakening or with the Buddha's instructions to his first disciples, the four noble truths must have been a later doctrine.

There is little reason, however, to accept these suggestions. To begin with, the sutta does not recount the Buddha's period of austerities prior to his awakening, nor does it tell of how the group of five monks attended to him during that period and later left him when he abandoned his austerities, and yet toward the end of the sutta those two incidents are alluded to in a way that indicates that the Buddha assumes them to be familiar to his listeners. Thus, if anything, the accounts that do explicitly relate those events—such as the one in MN 36—would seem to be earlier.

Secondly, the lack of reference to the four noble truths does not indicate that they were not actually involved in the awakening or the first sermon. As is always the case in the Buddha's autobiographical accounts in the Canon, this account is designed to convey a lesson, and the lesson is clearly articulated toward the beginning of the sutta: the difference between noble search and ignoble search. The account then illustrates the Buddha's own noble search and his later teaching career in the terms introduced by the lesson: the search for the "unborn, aging-less, illness-less, deathless, sorrow-less, undefiled, unexcelled rest from the yoke: unbinding." In particular, all the events mentioned in the account revolve around the issue of the deathless: the discovery of the deathless, the teaching of the deathless, and the Buddha's success in helping others to attain the deathless. Had the lesson of the sutta concerned the four noble truths, they would probably have been mentioned in the account. Thus there seems little reason to regard this sutta as "proof" that the four noble truths were a later teaching.

Nevertheless, this sutta offers many excellent lessons in the Dhamma, in addition to mentioning a few incidents in the Buddha's life that are found nowhere else in the Sutta Piṭaka.

* * *

I have heard that on one occasion the Blessed One was staying at Sāvatthī in Jeta's Grove, Anāthapiṇḍika's monastery. Then early in the morning—having adjusted his under robe and carrying his bowl & outer robe—he went into Sāvatthī for alms. Then a large number of monks went to Ven. Ānanda and said, "It has been a long time, friend Ānanda, since we have heard a Dhamma talk in the Blessed One's presence. It would be good if we could get to hear a Dhamma talk in the Blessed One's presence."

"In that case, venerable ones, go to the hermitage of Rammaka the brahman. Perhaps you will get to hear a Dhamma talk in the Blessed One's presence."

"As you say, friend," the monks replied to Ven. Ānanda and left.

Then the Blessed One, having gone for alms, after his meal, on returning from his alms round, said to Ven. Ānanda, "Ānanda, let's go to the Eastern Park, the palace of Migāra's mother, for the day's abiding."

"As you say, lord," Ven. Ānanda replied to the Blessed One.

So the Blessed One, together with Ven. Ānanda, went to the Eastern Park, the palace of Migāra's mother, for the day's abiding. Then, emerging from his seclusion in the late afternoon, he said to Ven. Ānanda, "Ānanda, let's go to the Eastern Gatehouse to bathe our limbs."

"As you say, lord," Ven. Ānanda replied to the Blessed One.

So the Blessed One, together with Ven. Ānanda, went to the Eastern Gatehouse to bathe his limbs. Having bathed his limbs at the Eastern Gatehouse, coming out of the water, he stood in his lower robe, drying his limbs. Then Ven. Ānanda said to him, "Lord, the hermitage of Rammaka the brahman is not far away. Pleasing is the hermitage of Rammaka the brahman. Delightful is the hermitage of Rammaka the brahman. It would be good if the Blessed One went to the hermitage of Rammaka the brahman out of sympathy." The Blessed One acquiesced through silence.

So the Blessed One went to the hermitage of Rammaka the brahman. Now at that time a large number of monks had gathered in the hermitage of Rammaka the brahman for a Dhamma discussion. The Blessed One stood outside the door waiting for the discussion to end. On knowing that the discussion had ended, clearing his throat, he tapped at the door. The monks opened the door for him. Entering the hermitage of Rammaka the brahman, the Blessed One sat down on a seat made ready. As he was sitting there, he addressed the monks: "For what discussion are you gathered together here? In the midst of what discussion have you been interrupted?"

"Lord, our interrupted Dhamma discussion was about the Blessed One himself, and then the Blessed One arrived."

"Good, monks. It's fitting that you, as sons of good families who have gone forth out of faith from home to the homeless life, should gather for Dhamma discussion. When you have gathered you have two duties: either Dhamma discussion or noble silence.[1]

"Monks, there are these two searches: ignoble search & noble search. And which is the ignoble search? There is the case where a person, being subject himself to birth, seeks (happiness in) what is likewise subject to birth. Being subject himself to aging… illness… death…sorrow… defilement, he seeks (happiness in) what is likewise subject to aging… illness… death…sorrow… defilement.

"And what may be said to be subject to birth? Spouses & children are subject to birth. Men & women slaves… goats & sheep… fowl & pigs… elephants, cattle, horses, & mares… gold & silver are subject to birth. Subject to birth are these acquisitions, and one who is tied to them, infatuated with them, who has totally fallen for them, being subject to birth, seeks what is likewise subject to birth.

"And what may be said to be subject to aging… illness… death… sorrow… defilement? Spouses & children… men & women slaves… goats & sheep… fowl & pigs… elephants, cattle, horses, & mares… gold & silver[2] are subject to aging… illness… death… sorrow… defilement. Subject to aging… illness… death… sorrow… defilement are these acquisitions, and one who is tied to them, infatuated with them, who has totally fallen for them, being subject to birth, seeks what is likewise subject to aging… illness… death… sorrow… defilement. This is ignoble search.

"And which is the noble search? There is the case where a person, himself being subject to birth, seeing the drawbacks of birth, seeks the unborn, unexcelled rest from the yoke: unbinding. Himself being subject to aging… illness… death…sorrow… defilement, seeing the drawbacks of aging… illness… death… sorrow… defilement, seeks the aging-less, illness-less, deathless, sorrow-less, undefiled, unexcelled rest from the yoke: unbinding. This is the noble search.

"I, too, monks, before my self-awakening, when I was still just an unawakened Bodhisatta, being subject myself to birth, sought what was likewise subject to birth. Being subject myself to aging… illness… death… sorrow… defilement, sought (happiness in) what was likewise subject to aging… illness… death… sorrow…

defilement. The thought occurred to me, 'Why do I, being subject myself to birth, seek what is likewise subject to birth? Being subject myself to aging... illness... death... sorrow... defilement, why do I seek what is likewise subject to aging... illness... death... sorrow... defilement? What if I, being subject myself to birth, seeing the drawbacks of birth, were to seek the unborn, unexcelled rest from the yoke: unbinding? What if I, being subject myself to aging... illness... death... sorrow... defilement, seeing the drawbacks of aging... illness... death... sorrow... defilement, were to seek the aging-less, illness-less, deathless, sorrow-less, unexcelled rest from the yoke: unbinding?'

"So, at a later time, while still young, a black-haired young man endowed with the blessings of youth in the first stage of life—and while my parents, unwilling, were crying with tears streaming down their faces—I shaved off my hair & beard, put on the ochre robe, and went forth from the home life into homelessness.

"Having thus gone forth in search of what might be skillful, seeking the unexcelled state of sublime peace, I went to Āḷāra Kālāma and, on arrival, said to him: 'Friend Kālāma, I want to practice in this Dhamma & discipline.'

"When this was said, he replied to me, 'You may stay here, my friend. This Dhamma is such that an observant person can soon enter & dwell in his own teacher's knowledge, having realized it for himself through direct knowledge.'

"It was not long before I quickly learned that Dhamma. As far as mere lip-reciting & repetition, I could speak the words of knowledge, the words of the elders, and I could affirm that I knew & saw—I, along with others.

"I thought: 'It isn't through mere conviction alone that Āḷāra Kālāma declares, "I have entered & dwell in this Dhamma, having realized it for myself through direct knowledge." Certainly he dwells knowing & seeing this Dhamma.' So I went to him and said, 'To what extent do you declare that you have entered & dwell in this Dhamma?' When this was said, he declared the dimension of nothingness.

"I thought: 'Not only does Āḷāra Kālāma have conviction, persistence, mindfulness, concentration, & discernment. I, too, have conviction, persistence, mindfulness, concentration, & discernment. What if I were to endeavor to realize for myself the Dhamma that Āḷāra Kālāma declares he has entered & dwells in, having realized it for himself through direct knowledge.' So it was not long before I quickly entered & dwelled in that Dhamma, having realized it for myself through direct knowledge. I went to him and said,

'Friend Kālāma, is this the extent to which you have entered & dwell in this Dhamma, having realized it for yourself through direct knowledge?'

"'Yes, my friend....'

"'This, friend, is the extent to which I, too, have entered & dwell in this Dhamma, having realized it for myself through direct knowledge.'

"'It is a gain for us, my friend, a great gain for us, that we have such a companion in the holy life. So the Dhamma I declare I have entered & dwell in, having realized it for myself through direct knowledge, is the Dhamma you declare you have entered & dwell in, having realized it for yourself through direct knowledge. And the Dhamma you declare you have entered & dwell in, having realized it for yourself through direct knowledge, is the Dhamma I declare I have entered & dwell in, having realized it for myself through direct knowledge. The Dhamma I know is the Dhamma you know; the Dhamma you know is the Dhamma I know. As I am, so are you; as you are, so am I. Come friend, let us now lead this community together.'

"In this way did Āḷāra Kālāma, my teacher, place me, his pupil, on the same level with himself and pay me great honor. But the thought occurred to me, 'This Dhamma leads not to disenchantment, to dispassion, to cessation, to stilling, to direct knowledge, to self-awakening, nor to unbinding, but only to reappearance in the dimension of nothingness.' So, dissatisfied with that Dhamma, I left.

"In search of what might be skillful, seeking the unexcelled state of sublime peace, I went to Uddaka Rāmaputta and, on arrival, said to him: 'Friend Uddaka, I want to practice in this Dhamma & discipline.'

"When this was said, he replied to me, 'You may stay here, my friend. This Dhamma is such that an observant person can soon enter & dwell in his own teacher's knowledge, having realized it for himself through direct knowledge.'

"It was not long before I quickly learned that Dhamma. As far as mere lip-reciting & repetition, I could speak the words of knowledge, the words of the elders, and I could affirm that I knew & saw—I, along with others.

"I thought: 'It wasn't through mere conviction alone that Rāma declared, "I have entered & dwell in this Dhamma, having realized it for myself through direct knowledge." Certainly he dwelled knowing & seeing this Dhamma.' So I went to Uddaka and said, 'To what extent did Rāma declare that he had entered & dwelled in this Dhamma?' When this was said, Uddaka declared the dimension of neither perception nor non-perception.

"I thought: 'Not only did Rāma have conviction, persistence, mindfulness, concentration, & discernment. I, too, have conviction, persistence, mindfulness, concentration, & discernment. What if I were to endeavor to realize for myself the Dhamma that Rāma declared he entered & dwelled in, having realized it for himself through direct knowledge.' So it was not long before I quickly entered & dwelled in that Dhamma, having realized it for myself through direct knowledge. I went to Uddaka and said, 'Friend Uddaka, is this the extent to which Rāma entered & dwelled in this Dhamma, having realized it for himself through direct knowledge?'

"'Yes, my friend....'

"'This, friend, is the extent to which I, too, have entered & dwell in this Dhamma, having realized it for myself through direct knowledge.'

"'It is a gain for us, my friend, a great gain for us, that we have such a companion in the holy life. So the Dhamma Rāma declared he entered & dwelled in, having realized it for himself through direct knowledge, is the Dhamma you declare you have entered & dwell in, having realized it for yourself through direct knowledge. And the Dhamma you declare you have entered & dwell in, having realized it for yourself through direct knowledge, is the Dhamma Rāma declared he entered & dwelled in, having realized it for himself through direct knowledge. The Dhamma he knew is the Dhamma you know; the Dhamma you know is the Dhamma he knew. As he was, so are you; as you are, so was he. Come friend, lead this community.'

"In this way did Uddaka Rāmaputta, my companion in the holy life, place me in the position of teacher and pay me great honor. But the thought occurred to me, 'This Dhamma leads not to disenchantment, to dispassion, to cessation, to stilling, to direct knowledge, to self-awakening, nor to unbinding, but only to reappearance in the dimension of neither perception nor non-perception.' So, dissatisfied with that Dhamma, I left.

"In search of what might be skillful, seeking the unexcelled state of sublime peace, I wandered by stages in the Magadhan country and came to the military town of Uruvelā. There I saw some delightful countryside, with an inspiring forest grove, a clear-flowing river with fine, delightful banks, and villages for alms-going on all sides. The thought occurred to me: 'How delightful is this countryside, with its inspiring forest grove, clear-flowing river with fine, delightful banks, and villages for alms-going on all sides. This is just right for the exertion of a clansman intent on exertion.' So I sat down right there, thinking, 'This is just right for exertion.'

"Then, monks, being subject myself to birth, seeing the drawbacks of birth, seeking the unborn, unexcelled rest from the yoke, unbinding, I reached the unborn, unexcelled rest from the yoke: unbinding. Being subject myself to aging… illness… death… sorrow… defilement, seeing the drawbacks of aging… illness… death… sorrow… defilement, seeking the aging-less, illness-less, deathless, sorrow-less, unexcelled rest from the yoke, unbinding, I reached the aging-less, illness-less, deathless, sorrow-less, unexcelled rest from the yoke: unbinding. Knowledge & vision arose in me: 'Unprovoked is my release.[3] This is the last birth. There is now no further becoming.'

"The then thought occurred to me, 'This Dhamma that I have attained is deep, hard to see, hard to realize, peaceful, refined, beyond the scope of conjecture, subtle, to-be-experienced by the wise.[4] But this generation delights in attachment, is excited by attachment, enjoys attachment. For a generation delighting in attachment, excited by attachment, enjoying attachment, this/that conditionality & dependent co-arising are hard to see. This state, too, is hard to see: the pacification of all fabrications, the relinquishment of all acquisitions, the ending of craving; dispassion; cessation; unbinding. And if I were to teach the Dhamma and others would not understand me, that would be tiresome for me, troublesome for me.'

"Just then these verses, unspoken in the past, unheard before, occurred to me:

'Enough now with teaching
    what
    only with difficulty
    I reached.
This Dhamma is not easily realized
by those overcome
with aversion & passion.

What is abstruse, subtle,
    deep,
    hard to see,
going against the flow—
those delighting in passion,
cloaked in the mass of darkness,
    won't see.'

"As I reflected thus, my mind inclined to dwelling at ease, not to teaching the Dhamma.

"Then Brahmā Sahampati, having known with his own awareness the line of thinking in my awareness, thought: 'The world is lost! The world is destroyed! The mind of the Tathāgata, the Arahant, the Rightly Self-awakened One inclines to dwelling at ease, not to teaching the Dhamma!' Then, just as a strong man might extend his flexed arm or flex his extended arm, Brahmā Sahampati disappeared from the Brahmā world and reappeared in front me. Arranging his upper robe over one shoulder, he knelt down with his right knee on the ground, saluted me with his hands before his heart, and said to me: 'Lord, let the Blessed One teach the Dhamma! Let the One-Well-Gone teach the Dhamma! There are beings with little dust in their eyes who are falling away because they do not hear the Dhamma. There will be those who will understand the Dhamma.'

"That is what Brahmā Sahampati said. Having said that, he further said this:

'In the past
there appeared among the Magadhans
an impure Dhamma
devised by the stained.
Throw open the door to the deathless!
Let them hear the Dhamma
realized by the Stainless One!

Just as one standing on a rocky crag
might see people
all around below,
so, intelligent one, with all-around vision,
ascend the palace
fashioned of Dhamma.
Free from sorrow, behold the people
submerged in sorrow,
oppressed by birth & aging.

Rise up, hero, victor in battle!
O Teacher, wander without debt in the world.
Teach the Dhamma, O Blessed One:
There will be those who will understand.'

"Then, having understood Brahmā's invitation, out of compassion for beings, I surveyed the world with the eye of an Awakened

One. As I did so, I saw beings with little dust in their eyes and those with much, those with keen faculties and those with dull, those with good attributes and those with bad, those easy to teach and those hard, some of them seeing disgrace & danger in the other world. Just as in a pond of blue or red or white lotuses, some lotuses—born & growing in the water—might flourish while immersed in the water, without rising up from the water; some might stand at an even level with the water; while some might rise up from the water and stand without being smeared by the water—so too, surveying the world with the eye of an Awakened One, I saw beings with little dust in their eyes and those with much, those with keen faculties and those with dull, those with good attributes and those with bad, those easy to teach and those hard, some of them seeing disgrace & danger in the other world.

"Having seen this, I answered Brahmā Sahampati in verse:

'Open are the doors to the deathless.
Let those with ears show their conviction.
Perceiving trouble, O Brahmā,
I did not tell people
  the refined,
  sublime Dhamma.'

"Then Brahmā Sahampati, thinking, 'I'm the one who created the opportunity for the teaching of the Dhamma by the Blessed One!' bowed down to me and, circling me on the right, disappeared right there.

"Then the thought occurred to me, 'To whom should I teach the Dhamma first? Who will quickly understand this Dhamma?' Then the thought occurred to me, 'This Āḷāra Kālāma is wise, competent, intelligent. He has long had little dust in his eyes. What if I were to teach him the Dhamma first? He will quickly understand this Dhamma.' Then a devatā came to me and said, 'Lord, Āḷāra Kālāma died seven days ago.' And knowledge & vision arose within me: 'Āḷāra Kālāma died seven days ago.' The thought occurred to me, 'A great loss has Āḷāra Kālāma suffered. If he had heard this Dhamma, he would have quickly understood it.'

"Then the thought occurred to me, 'To whom should I teach the Dhamma first? Who will quickly understand this Dhamma?' Then the thought occurred to me, 'This Uddaka Rāmaputta is wise, competent, intelligent. He has long had little dust in his eyes. What if I were to teach him the Dhamma first? He will quickly understand this Dhamma.' Then a devatā came to me and said, 'Lord, Uddaka

Rāmaputta died last night.' And knowledge & vision arose within me: 'Uddaka Rāmaputta died last night.' The thought occurred to me, 'A great loss has Uddaka Rāmaputta suffered. If he had heard this Dhamma, he would have quickly understood it.'

"Then the thought occurred to me, 'To whom should I teach the Dhamma first? Who will quickly understand this Dhamma?' Then the thought occurred to me, 'They were very helpful to me, the group of five monks who attended to me when I was resolute in exertion. What if I were to teach them the Dhamma first?' Then the thought occurred to me, 'Where are the group of five monks staying now?' And with the divine eye, purified & surpassing the human, I saw that they were staying near Bārāṇasī in the Deer Park at Isipatana.

"Then, having stayed at Uruvelā as long as I liked, I set out to wander by stages to Bārāṇasī. Upaka the Ājīvaka saw me on the road between Gayā and the (place of) Awakening, and on seeing me said to me, 'Clear, my friend, are your faculties. Pure your complexion, and bright. On whose account have you gone forth? Who is your teacher? In whose Dhamma do you delight?'

"When this was said, I replied to Upaka the Ājīvaka in verses:

'All-vanquishing,
all-knowing am I,
with regard to all things,
unadhering.
All-abandoning,
released in the ending of craving:
having fully known on my own,
to whom should I point as my teacher?[5]

I have no teacher,
and one like me can't be found.
In the world with its devas,
I have no counterpart.

For I am an arahant in the world;
I, the unexcelled teacher.
I, alone, am rightly self-awakened.
Cooled am I, unbound.

To set rolling the wheel of Dhamma
I go to the city of Kāsi.
In a world become blind,
I beat the drum of the deathless.'

"'From your claims, my friend, you must be an infinite conqueror.'

"'Conquerors are those like me
who have reached effluents' end.
I've conquered evil qualities,
and so, Upaka, I'm a conqueror.'

"When this was said, Upaka said, 'May it be so, my friend,' and—shaking his head, taking a side-road—he left.

"Then, wandering by stages, I arrived at Bārāṇasī, at the Deer Park in Isipatana, to where the group of five monks were staying. From afar they saw me coming and, on seeing me, made a pact with one another, (saying,) 'Friends, here comes Gotama the contemplative: living luxuriously, straying from his exertion, backsliding into abundance. He doesn't deserve to be bowed down to, to be greeted by standing up, or to have his robe & bowl received. Still, a seat should be set out; if he wants to, he can sit down.' But as I approached, they were unable to keep to their pact. One, standing up to greet me, received my robe & bowl. Another spread out a seat. Another set out water for washing my feet. However, they addressed me by name and as 'friend.'

"So I said to them, 'Don't address the Tathāgata by name and as "friend." The Tathāgata, friends, is a worthy one, rightly self-awakened. Lend ear, friends: the deathless has been attained. I will instruct you. I will teach you the Dhamma. Practicing as instructed, you will in no long time reach & remain in the supreme goal of the holy life for which clansmen rightly go forth from home into homelessness, knowing & realizing it for yourselves in the here & now.'

"When this was said, the group of five monks replied to me, 'By that practice, that conduct, that performance of austerities you did not attain any superior human states, any distinction in knowledge & vision worthy of a noble one. So how can you now—living luxuriously, straying from your exertion, backsliding into abundance—have attained any superior human states, any distinction in knowledge & vision worthy of a noble one?'

"When this was said, I replied to them, 'The Tathāgata, monks, is not living luxuriously, has not strayed from his exertion, has not backslid into abundance. The Tathāgata, friends, is a worthy one, rightly self-awakened. Lend ear, friends: the deathless has been attained. I will instruct you. I will teach you the Dhamma. Practicing as instructed, you will in no long time reach & remain in the supreme goal of the holy life for which clansmen rightly go forth from home into homelessness, knowing & realizing it for yourselves in the here & now.'

A second time.... A third time, the group of five monks said to me, 'By that practice, that conduct, that performance of austerities you did not attain any superior human states, any distinction in knowledge & vision worthy of a noble one. So how can you now—living luxuriously, straying from your exertion, backsliding into abundance—have attained any superior human states, any distinction in knowledge & vision worthy of a noble one?'

"When this was said, I replied to the group of five monks, 'Do you recall my ever having spoken in this way before?'

"'No, lord.'

"'The Tathāgata, monks, is not living luxuriously, has not strayed from his exertion, has not backslid into abundance. The Tathāgata, friends, is a worthy one, rightly self-awakened. Lend ear, friends: the deathless has been attained. I will instruct you. I will teach you the Dhamma. Practicing as instructed, you will in no long time reach & remain in the supreme goal of the holy life for which clansmen rightly go forth from home into homelessness, knowing & realizing it for yourselves in the here & now.'

"And so I was able to convince them. I would teach two monks while three went for alms, and we six lived off what the three brought back from their alms round. Then I would teach three monks while two went for alms, and we six lived off what the two brought back from their alms round. Then the group of five monks—thus exhorted, thus instructed by me— being subject themselves to birth, seeing the drawbacks of birth, seeking the unborn, unexcelled rest from the yoke, unbinding, reached the unborn, unexcelled rest from the yoke: unbinding. Being subject themselves to aging... illness... death... sorrow... defilement, seeing the drawbacks of aging... illness... death... sorrow... defilement, seeking the aging-less, illness-less, deathless, sorrow-less, unexcelled rest from the yoke, unbinding, they reached the aging-less, illness-less, deathless, sorrow-less, unexcelled rest from the yoke: unbinding. Knowledge & vision arose in them: 'Unprovoked is our release. This is the last birth. There is now no further becoming.'

"Monks, there are these five strings of sensuality. Which five? Forms cognizable via the eye—agreeable, pleasing, charming, endearing, fostering desire, enticing. Sounds cognizable via the ear—agreeable, pleasing, charming, endearing, fostering desire, enticing. Aromas cognizable via the nose—agreeable, pleasing, charming, endearing, fostering desire, enticing. Tastes cognizable via the tongue—agreeable, pleasing, charming, endearing, fostering desire, enticing. Tactile sensations cognizable via the body—agreeable, pleasing, charming, endearing, fostering desire, enticing. These are the five strings of sensuality.

"And any contemplatives or brahmans tied to these five strings of sensuality—infatuated with them, have totally fallen for them, consuming them without seeing their drawbacks or discerning the escape from them—should be known as having met with misfortune, having met with ruin; Māra can do with them as he will. Just as if a wild deer were to lie bound on a heap of snares: it should be known as having met with misfortune, having met with ruin; the hunter can do with it as he will. When the hunter comes, it won't get away as it would like. In the same way, any contemplatives or brahmans tied to these five strings of sensuality—infatuated with them, have totally fallen for them, consuming them without seeing their drawbacks or discerning the escape from them—should be known as having met with misfortune, having met with ruin; Māra can do with them as he will.

"But any contemplatives or brahmans not tied to these five strings of sensuality—uninfatuated with them, having not totally fallen for them, consuming them seeing their drawbacks and discerning the escape from them—should be known as not having met with misfortune, not having met with ruin; Māra cannot do with them as he will. Just as if a wild deer were to lie unbound on a heap of snares: it should be known as not having met with misfortune, not having met with ruin; the hunter cannot do with it as he will. When the hunter comes, it will get away as it would like. In the same way, any contemplatives or brahmans not tied to these five strings of sensuality—uninfatuated with them, having not totally fallen for them, consuming them seeing their drawbacks and discerning the escape from them—should be known as not having met with misfortune, not having met with ruin; Māra cannot do with them as he will.

"Suppose that a wild deer is living in wilderness glen. Carefree it walks, carefree it stands, carefree it sits, carefree it lies down. Why is that? Because it has gone beyond the hunter's range.[6] In the same way, a monk—quite secluded from sensuality, secluded from unskillful qualities—enters & remains in the first jhāna: rapture & pleasure born of seclusion, accompanied by directed thought & evaluation. This monk is said to have put Māra in the dark. Having destroyed Māra's vision and leaving no trace, he has become invisible to the Evil One.[7]

"And further, the monk, with the stilling of directed thoughts & evaluations, enters & remains in the second jhāna: rapture & pleasure born of concentration, unification of awareness free from directed thought & evaluation—internal assurance. This monk is said to have put Māra in the dark. Having destroyed Māra's vision and leaving no trace, he has become invisible to the Evil One.

"And further, the monk, with the fading of rapture, remains equanimous, mindful, & alert, senses pleasure with the body, and enters & remains in the third jhāna, of which the noble ones declare, 'Equanimous & mindful, he has a pleasant abiding.' This monk is said to have put Māra in the dark. Having destroyed Māra's vision and leaving no trace, he has become invisible to the Evil One.

"And further, the monk, with the abandoning of pleasure & pain—as with the earlier disappearance of elation & distress—enters & remains in the fourth jhāna: purity of equanimity & mindfulness, neither pleasure nor pain. This monk is said to have put Māra in the dark. Having destroyed Māra's vision and leaving no trace, he has become invisible to the Evil One.

"And further, the monk, with the complete transcending of perceptions of (physical) form, with the disappearance of perceptions of resistance, and not attending to perceptions of multiplicity, (perceiving,) 'Infinite space,' enters & remains in the dimension of the infinitude of space. This monk is said to have put Māra in the dark. Having destroyed Māra's vision and leaving no trace, he has become invisible to the Evil One.

"And further, the monk, with the complete transcending of the dimension of the infinitude of space, (perceiving,) 'Infinite consciousness,' enters & remains in the dimension of the infinitude of consciousness. This monk is said to have put Māra in the dark. Having destroyed Māra's vision and leaving no trace, he has become invisible to the Evil One.

"And further, the monk, with the complete transcending of the dimension of the infinitude of consciousness, (perceiving,) 'There is nothing,' enters & remains in the dimension of nothingness. This monk is said to have put Māra in the dark. Having destroyed Māra's vision and leaving no trace, he has become invisible to the Evil One.

"And further, the monk, with the complete transcending of the dimension of nothingness, enters & remains in the dimension of neither perception nor non-perception. This monk is said to have put Māra in the dark. Having destroyed Māra's vision and leaving no trace, he has become invisible to the Evil One.

"And further, the monk, with the complete transcending of the dimension of neither perception nor non-perception, enters & remains in the cessation of perception & feeling. And, having seen (that) with discernment, his mental effluents are completely ended. This monk is said to have put Māra in the dark. Having destroyed Māra's vision and leaving no trace, he has become invisible to the Evil One, having crossed over attachment in the cosmos. Carefree he walks, carefree he stands, carefree he sits, carefree he lies down. Why is that? Because he has gone beyond the Evil One's range."

That is what the Blessed One said. Gratified, the monks delighted in the Blessed One's words.

NOTES

1. See Ud 2:2 and AN 10:69. Noble silence = the levels of jhāna beginning with the second.

2. The Burmese, Sri Lankan, and PTS editions of the Canon exclude gold and silver from the list of objects subject to illness, death, and sorrow, apparently on the grounds that they themselves do not grow ill, die, or feel sorrow. The Thai edition of the Canon includes gold and silver in the list of objects subject to illness, death, and sorrow in the sense that any happiness based on them is subject to change because of one's own illness, death, and sorrow.

3. See MN 29, note 3.

4. The section from here to Brahmā Sahampati's disappearance is recounted in the third person at SN 6:1.

5. This verse = Dhp 353.

6. For another use of the wild deer as a symbol for a free mind, see Ud 2:10.

7. As the Commentary points out, simply attaining the states of concentration from the first jhāna through the dimension of neither perception nor non-perception blinds Māra only temporarily. Only with the arising of discernment is Māra blinded for good. On Māra's blindness, see Sn 5:15, AN 9:39, and SN 22:87 (the last in *The Mind Like Fire Unbound*). For the meaning of "leaving no trace," see Dhp 92–93, 179–180.

See also: MN 4; MN 19; MN 36; AN 3:39; Iti 54–55; Sn 3:1; Sn 3:2

27 The Shorter Elephant Footprint Simile

Cūḷa Hatthipadopama Sutta

I have heard that on one occasion the Blessed One was staying near Sāvatthī in Jeta's Grove, Anāthapiṇḍika's monastery. Now at that time, Jāṇussoṇin the brahman was driving out of Sāvatthī in the middle of the day in a totally white roofed-chariot.[1] He saw Pilotika the wanderer coming from afar and, on seeing him, said to him, "Now where is Master Vacchāyana[2] coming from in the middle of the day?"

"Sir, I have come here from the presence of Gotama the contemplative."

"And what does a wise person think about Gotama the contemplative's acuity of discernment?"

"Sir, who am I to know Gotama the contemplative's acuity of discernment? Wouldn't one have to be his equal to know his acuity of discernment?"

"Master Vacchāyana praises Gotama the contemplative with lavish praise indeed!"

"Sir, who am I to praise Gotama the contemplative. He is praised by the praised as the best of beings, human & divine."

"Seeing what reasons does Master Vacchāyana have such high confidence in Gotama the contemplative?"

"Sir, suppose an elephant hunter were to enter an elephant forest and were to see there a large elephant footprint, long in extent and broad in width. He would come to the conclusion, 'What a big bull elephant!' In the same way, when I saw four footprints in Gotama the contemplative, I came to the conclusion, 'The Blessed One is rightly self-awakened, the Dhamma is well-taught by the Blessed One, the Saṅgha of the Blessed One's disciples has practiced rightly.' Which four?

"There is the case where I see certain noble warriors who are pundits, subtle, skilled in debate, like hair-splitting marksmen. They prowl about, as it were, shooting philosophical positions to pieces with their dialectic. They hear, 'Gotama the contemplative, they say, will visit that village or town.' They formulate a question thus: 'Having gone to Gotama the contemplative, we will ask him this question of ours. If, having been asked like this, he answers like this, we will refute his teaching like this. And, if having been asked like this, he answers like that, we will refute his teaching like that.'

"They hear, 'Gotama the contemplative is visiting that village or town.' They go to him, and he instructs, urges, rouses, & encourages them with a talk on Dhamma. Having been instructed, urged, roused, & encouraged by him with a talk on Dhamma, they don't even ask him their question, so since when could they refute him? As it turns out, they become his disciples. When I saw this first footprint in Gotama the contemplative, I came to the conclusion, 'The Blessed One is rightly self-awakened; the Dhamma is well-taught by the Blessed One; the Saṅgha of the Blessed One's disciples has practiced rightly.'

"Then there is the case where I see certain brahmans....

"Then there is the case where I see certain householders....

"Then there is the case where I see certain contemplatives who are pundits, subtle, skilled in debate, like hair-splitting marksmen. They prowl about, as it were, shooting philosophical positions to pieces with their dialectic. They hear, 'Gotama the contemplative, they say, will visit that village or town.' They formulate a question thus: 'Having gone to Gotama the contemplative, we will ask him this question of ours. If, having been asked like this, he answers like this, we will refute his teaching like this. And, if having been asked like this, he answers like that, we will refute his teaching like that.'

"They hear, 'Gotama the contemplative is visiting that village or town.' They go to him, and he instructs, urges, rouses, & encourages them with a talk on Dhamma. Having been instructed, urged, roused, & encouraged by him with a talk on Dhamma, they don't even ask him their question, so since when could they refute him? As it turns out, they ask him for the opportunity to go forth from the home life into homelessness. He gives them the Going-forth. Having gone forth there—dwelling alone, secluded, heedful, ardent, & resolute—they in no long time reach & remain in the supreme goal of the holy life, for which clansmen rightly go forth from home into homelessness, knowing & realizing it for themselves in the here & now. They say, 'How near we were to being lost! How near we were to being lost! Before, though we weren't contemplatives, we claimed to be contemplatives. Though we weren't brahmans, we claimed to be brahmans. Though we weren't arahants, we claimed to be arahants. But now we *are* contemplatives, now we *are* brahmans, now we *are* arahants.'

When I saw this fourth footprint in Gotama the contemplative, I came to the conclusion, 'The Blessed One is rightly self-awakened; the Dhamma is well-taught by the Blessed One; the Saṅgha of the Blessed One's disciples has practiced rightly.'

When this was said, Jāṇussoṇin the brahman got down from his totally white roofed-chariot and—arranging his upper robe over one shoulder and extending his hands in reverent salutation in the direction of the Blessed One—exclaimed this exclamation three times:

"Homage to the Blessed One, worthy & rightly self-awakened!
"Homage to the Blessed One, worthy & rightly self-awakened!
"Homage to the Blessed One, worthy & rightly self-awakened!

"May I, at some time or another, meet with Master Gotama! May there be some conversation!"

Then Jāṇussoṇin the brahman went to the Blessed One and, on arrival, exchanged courteous greetings with him. After an exchange of friendly greetings & courtesies, he sat to one side. As he was sitting there, he told the Blessed One the entirety of his conversation with Pilotika the wanderer. When he was finished, the Blessed One said to him, "It's not to that extent, brahman, that the elephant footprint simile is complete in its details. As to how it *is* complete in its details, listen & pay close attention. I will speak."

"As you say, sir," Jāṇussoṇin the brahman responded.

The Blessed One said: "Suppose an elephant hunter were to enter an elephant forest and were to see there a large elephant footprint, long in extent and broad in width. A skilled elephant hunter would not yet come to the conclusion, 'What a big bull elephant!' Why is that? Because in an elephant forest there are dwarf female elephants with big feet. The footprint might be one of theirs.

"So he follows along and sees in the elephant forest a large elephant footprint, long in extent and broad in width, and some scratch marks high up. A skilled elephant hunter would not yet come to the conclusion, 'What a big bull elephant!' Why is that? Because in an elephant forest there are tall female elephants with prominent teeth & big feet. The footprint might be one of theirs.

"So he follows along and sees in the elephant forest a large elephant footprint, long in extent and broad in width, with some scratch marks and tusk slashes high up. A skilled elephant hunter would not yet come to the conclusion, 'What a big bull elephant!' Why is that? Because in an elephant forest there are tall female elephants with tusks & big feet. The footprint might be one of theirs.

"So he follows along and sees in the elephant forest a large elephant footprint, long in extent and broad in width, with some scratch marks and tusk slashes high up and some broken-off branches. And he sees that bull elephant at the foot of the tree or in an open clearing, walking, standing, sitting, or lying down. He comes to the conclusion, 'That's the big bull elephant.'

"In the same way, brahman, there is the case where a Tathāgata appears in the world, worthy & rightly self-awakened. He teaches the Dhamma admirable in its beginning, admirable in its middle, admirable in its end. He proclaims the holy life both in its particulars and in its essence, entirely perfect, surpassingly pure.

"A householder or householder's son, hearing the Dhamma, gains conviction in the Tathāgata and reflects: 'Household life is confining, a dusty path. Life gone forth is the open air. It isn't easy, living at home, to practice the holy life totally perfect, totally pure, a polished shell. What if I, having shaved off my hair & beard and putting on the ochre robe, were to go forth from the household life into homelessness?'

"So after some time he abandons his mass of wealth, large or small; leaves his circle of relatives, large or small; shaves off his hair and beard, puts on the ochre robes, and goes forth from the household life into homelessness.

VIRTUE

"When he has thus gone forth, endowed with the monks' training & livelihood, then—abandoning the taking of life—he abstains from the taking of life. He dwells with his rod laid down, his knife laid down, scrupulous, merciful, compassionate for the welfare of all living beings.

"Abandoning the taking of what is not given, he abstains from taking what is not given. He takes only what is given, accepts only what is given, lives not by stealth but by means of a self that has become pure. This, too, is part of his virtue.

"Abandoning uncelibacy, he lives a celibate life, aloof, refraining from the sexual act that is the villager's way.

"Abandoning the telling of lies, he abstains from telling lies. He speaks the truth, holds to the truth, is firm, reliable, no deceiver of the world.

"Abandoning divisive speech, he abstains from divisive speech. What he has heard here he does not tell there to break those people apart from these people here. What he has heard there he does not tell here to break these people apart from those people there. Thus reconciling those who have broken apart or cementing those who are united, he loves concord, delights in concord, enjoys concord, speaks things that create concord.

"Abandoning abusive speech, he abstains from abusive speech. He speaks words that are soothing to the ear, that are affectionate, that go to the heart, that are polite, appealing and pleasing to people at large.

"Abandoning idle chatter, he abstains from idle chatter. He speaks in season, speaks what is factual, what is in accordance with the goal, the Dhamma, and the Vinaya. He speaks words worth treasuring, seasonable, reasonable, circumscribed, connected with the goal.

"He abstains from damaging seed & plant life.

"He eats only once a day, refraining from the evening meal and from food at the wrong time of day.

"He abstains from dancing, singing, instrumental music, and from watching shows.

"He abstains from wearing garlands and from beautifying himself with scents & cosmetics.

"He abstains from high and luxurious beds & seats.

"He abstains from accepting gold & money.

"He abstains from accepting uncooked grain… raw meat… women & girls… male & female slaves… goats & sheep… fowl & pigs… elephants, cattle, steeds, & mares… fields & property.

"He abstains from running messages… from buying & selling… from dealing with false scales, false metals, & false measures… from bribery, deception, & fraud.

"He abstains from mutilating, executing, imprisoning, highway robbery, plunder, and violence.

"He is content with a set of robes to provide for his body and alms food to provide for his hunger. Just as a bird, wherever it goes, flies with its wings as its only burden; so too is he content with a set of robes to provide for his body and alms food to provide for his hunger. Wherever he goes, he takes only his barest necessities along.

"Endowed with this noble aggregate of virtue, he is inwardly sensitive to the pleasure of being blameless.

SENSE RESTRAINT

"On seeing a form with the eye, he doesn't grasp at any theme or details by which—if he were to dwell without restraint over the faculty of the eye—evil, unskillful qualities such as greed or distress might assail him. On hearing a sound with the ear…. On smelling an aroma with the nose…. On tasting a flavor with the tongue…. On touching a tactile sensation with the body…. On cognizing an idea with the intellect, he doesn't grasp at any theme or details by which—if he were to dwell without restraint over the faculty of the intellect—evil, unskillful qualities such as greed or distress might assail him. Endowed with this noble restraint over the sense faculties, he is inwardly sensitive to the pleasure of being blameless.

MINDFULNESS & ALERTNESS

"When going forward and returning, he makes himself alert. When looking toward and looking away… when bending and extending his limbs… when carrying his outer cloak, his upper robe, and his bowl… when eating, drinking, chewing, and tasting… when urinating and defecating… when walking, standing, sitting, falling asleep, waking up, talking, and remaining silent, he makes himself alert.

ABANDONING THE HINDRANCES

"Endowed with this noble aggregate of virtue, this noble restraint over the sense faculties, this noble mindfulness & alertness, he seeks out a secluded dwelling: a wilderness, the shade of a tree, a mountain, a glen, a hillside cave, a charnel ground, a forest grove, the open air, a heap of straw. After his meal, returning from his alms round, he sits down, crosses his legs, holds his body erect, and brings mindfulness to the fore.

"Abandoning covetousness with regard to the world, he dwells with an awareness devoid of covetousness. He cleanses his mind of covetousness. Abandoning ill will & anger, he dwells with an awareness devoid of ill will, sympathetic with the welfare of all living beings. He cleanses his mind of ill will & anger. Abandoning sloth & drowsiness, he dwells with an awareness devoid of sloth & drowsiness, mindful, alert, percipient of light. He cleanses his mind of sloth & drowsiness. Abandoning restlessness & anxiety, he dwells undisturbed, his mind inwardly stilled. He cleanses his mind of restlessness & anxiety. Abandoning uncertainty, he dwells having crossed over uncertainty, with no perplexity with regard to skillful qualities. He cleanses his mind of uncertainty.

THE FOUR JHĀNAS

"Having abandoned these five hindrances—imperfections of awareness that weaken discernment—then, quite secluded from sensuality, secluded from unskillful qualities, he enters and remains in the first jhāna: rapture & pleasure born of seclusion, accompanied by directed thought & evaluation.

"This, brahman, is called a footprint of the Tathāgata, a scratch mark of the Tathāgata, a tusk slash of the Tathāgata, but a disciple of the noble ones would not yet come to the conclusion, 'The Blessed One is rightly self-awakened; the Dhamma is well-taught by the Blessed One; the Saṅgha of the Blessed One's disciples has practiced rightly.'

"Then, with the stilling of directed thoughts & evaluations, he enters and remains in the second jhāna: rapture & pleasure born of concentration, unification of awareness free from directed thought and evaluation—internal assurance.

"This, too, is called a footprint of the Tathāgata, a scratch mark of the Tathāgata, a tusk slash of the Tathāgata, but a disciple of the noble ones would not yet come to the conclusion, 'The Blessed One is rightly self-awakened; the Dhamma is well-taught by the Blessed One; the Saṅgha of the Blessed One's disciples has practiced rightly.'

"Then, with the fading of rapture, he remains equanimous, mindful, & alert, and senses pleasure with the body. He enters and remains in the third jhāna, of which the noble ones declare, 'Equanimous & mindful, he has a pleasant abiding.'

"This, too, is called a footprint of the Tathāgata, a scratch mark of the Tathāgata, a tusk slash of the Tathāgata, but a disciple of the noble ones would not yet come to the conclusion, 'The Blessed One is rightly self-awakened; the Dhamma is well-taught by the Blessed One; the Saṅgha of the Blessed One's disciples has practiced rightly.'

"Then, with the abandoning of pleasure & pain—as with the earlier disappearance of joy & distress—he enters and remains in the fourth jhāna: purity of equanimity & mindfulness, neither-pleasure-nor-pain.

"This, too, is called a footprint of the Tathāgata, a scratch mark of the Tathāgata, a tusk slash of the Tathāgata, but a disciple of the noble ones would not yet come to the conclusion, 'The Blessed One is rightly self-awakened; the Dhamma is well-taught by the Blessed One; the Saṅgha of the Blessed One's disciples has practiced rightly.'

THE THREE KNOWLEDGES

"With his mind thus concentrated, purified, and bright, unblemished, free from defects, pliant, malleable, steady, and attained to imperturbability, he directs and inclines it to knowledge of the recollection of past lives [lit: previous homes]. He recollects his manifold past lives, i.e., one birth, two births, three births, four, five, ten, twenty, thirty, forty, fifty, one hundred, one thousand, one hundred thousand, many eons of cosmic contraction, many eons of cosmic expansion, many eons of cosmic contraction and expansion, (recollecting,) 'There I had such a name, belonged to such a clan, had such an appearance. Such was my food, such my experience of pleasure and pain, such the end of my life. Passing away from that state, I re-arose there. There too I had such a name, belonged to such a clan, had such an appearance. Such was my food, such my experience of pleasure and pain, such the end of my life. Passing away from that state, I re-arose here.' Thus he recollects his manifold past lives in their modes and details.

"This, too, is called a footprint of the Tathāgata, a scratch mark of the Tathāgata, a tusk slash of the Tathāgata, but a disciple of the noble ones would not yet come to the conclusion, 'The Blessed One is rightly self-awakened; the Dhamma is well-taught by the Blessed One; the Saṅgha of the Blessed One's disciples has practiced rightly.'

"With his mind thus concentrated, purified, and bright, unblemished, free from defects, pliant, malleable, steady, and attained to imperturbability, he directs and inclines it to knowledge of the passing away and re-appearance of beings. He sees—by means of the divine eye, purified and surpassing the human—beings passing away and re-appearing, and he discerns how they are inferior and superior, beautiful and ugly, fortunate and unfortunate in accordance with their kamma: 'These beings—who were endowed with bad conduct of body, speech, and mind, who reviled the noble ones, held wrong views and undertook actions under the influence of wrong views—with the break-up of the body, after death, have re-appeared in a plane of deprivation, a bad destination, a lower realm, hell. But these beings—who were endowed with good conduct of body, speech, and mind, who did not revile the noble ones, who held right views and undertook actions under the influence of right views—with the break-up of the body, after death, have re-appeared in a good destination, a heavenly world.' Thus—by means of the divine eye, purified and surpassing the human—he sees beings passing away and re-appearing, and he discerns how they are inferior and superior, beautiful and ugly, fortunate and unfortunate in accordance with their kamma.

"This, too, is called a footprint of the Tathāgata, a scratch mark of the Tathāgata, a tusk slash of the Tathāgata, but a disciple of the noble ones would not yet come to the conclusion, 'The Blessed One is rightly self-awakened; the Dhamma is well-taught by the Blessed One; the Saṅgha of the Blessed One's disciples has practiced rightly.'

"With his mind thus concentrated, purified, and bright, unblemished, free from defects, pliant, malleable, steady, and attained to imperturbability, the monk directs and inclines it to the knowledge of the ending of the mental effluents. He discerns, as it has come to be, that 'This is stress… This is the origination of stress… This is the cessation of stress… This is the way leading to the cessation of stress… These are effluents… This is the origination of effluents... This is the cessation of effluents... This is the way leading to the cessation of effluents.'

"This, too, is called a footprint of the Tathāgata, a scratch mark of the Tathāgata, a tusk slash of the Tathāgata. A disciple of the noble ones has not yet come to conclusion, but he comes to the conclusion,[3] 'The Blessed One is rightly self-awakened; the Dhamma is well-taught by the Blessed One; the Saṅgha of the Blessed One's disciples has practiced rightly.'[4]

"His heart, thus knowing, thus seeing, is released from the effluent of sensuality, released from the effluent of becoming, released from the effluent of ignorance. With release, there is the knowledge, 'Released.' He discerns that 'Birth is ended, the holy life fulfilled, the task done. There is nothing further for this world.'

"This, too, is called a footprint of the Tathāgata, a scratch mark of the Tathāgata, a tusk slash of the Tathāgata, and it is here that a disciple of the noble ones has come to conclusion: 'The Blessed One is rightly self-awakened; the Dhamma is well-taught by the Blessed One; the Saṅgha of the Blessed One's disciples has practiced rightly.'"

When this was said, Jāṇussoṇin the brahman said to the Blessed One: "Magnificent, lord! Magnificent! Just as if he were to place upright what was overturned, to reveal what was hidden, to show the way to one who was lost, or to carry a lamp into the dark so that those with eyes could see forms, in the same way has the Blessed One—through many lines of reasoning—made the Dhamma clear. I go to the Blessed One for refuge, to the Dhamma, and to the Saṅgha of monks. May the Blessed One remember me as a lay follower who has gone to him for refuge, from this day forward, for life."

NOTES

1. The Thai version of the Canon here reads *vaḷavābhirathena,* which seems to be a mixture of two readings recognized in the PTS Dictionary: *vaḷabhi-rathena,* "in a roofed chariot"; and *vaḷavā-rathena,* "in a chariot drawn by mares."

2. Vacchāyana is Pilotika's clan name.

3. This is a pun. For an explanation, see the next note.

4. This stage in the practice would seem to correspond to reaching stream-entry, inasmuch as one of the standard definitions of stream-entry is direct vision of the four noble truths. It is also the stage at which one reaches verified conviction in the Buddha, Dhamma, and Saṅgha.

The sentence stating that the stream-enterer has come to a conclusion without coming to conclusion appears to be a pun. The idiomatic expression for coming to a conclusion—*niṭṭhaṁ gacchati*—can also mean coming to a finish, reaching completion, or coming to an end. To distinguish these two meanings, the text here uses the form *niṭṭhaṅgato* to mean having come to a finish, and *niṭṭhaṁ gacchati* to mean coming to a conclusion.

This particular way of distinguishing the meanings, however, is not adhered to consistently across the Canon. On the one hand, Dhp 351—like this sutta—uses the word *niṭṭhaṅgato* to describe an arahant. On the other, in a series of suttas beginning at AN 6:131 (AN 6:124 in the Thai numbering), some lay disciples are each described as *tathāgate niṭṭhaṅgato,* which could either mean that they have come to a definite conclusion about the Tathāgata or that they have concluded their training under the Tathāgata. Some of the disciples named in these suttas—such as Citta, Mahānāma, Ugga, Anāthapiṇḍika, and Jīvaka Komārabhacca—are, in other parts of the Canon, described as stream-winners or non-returners. However, the description of their attainment here contains a mixture of terms, some normally associated with stream-entry, some with arahantship. The pattern of the suttas is this: "Endowed with six qualities, Tapussa the householder has come to conclusion in the Tathāgata, seen the deathless, and goes about having realized the deathless. Which six? Verified confidence in the Buddha, verified confidence in the Dhamma, verified confidence in the Saṅgha, noble virtue, noble knowledge, noble release." Of these six qualities, the first four are normally associated with stream-entry, the last two with arahantship. It may be that the last two are meant here in a non-technical sense, which would mean that *niṭṭhaṅgato* here means simply coming to a definite conclusion about the Tathāgata.

AN 10:63 plays with the two meanings of *niṭṭha* in another way. The Buddha describes ten types of individuals, all of whom, he says, are "*niṭṭhaṅgatā* in me." In this case, *niṭṭhaṅgato* would simply mean having come to a definite conclusion. Of the ten types, he adds, the *niṭṭhā*—or conclusion of the training—of five occurs (or will occur) here in the human realm, the *niṭṭhā* of five occurs away from here. In the first five, he includes three types of stream-winners, once-returners (this item is omitted from the PTS translation), and those who attain arahantship in the present life. In the latter five, he includes five types of non-returners.

Thus, as with the suttas in AN 6, *niṭṭhaṅgato* here means simply coming to a definite conclusion about the Tathāgata. And the lack of consistency surrounding this term in the suttas suggests that it is not a technical term. This would confirm the impression the two meanings of *niṭṭha* are used more as an opportunity for word play, a game in which inconsistency is not a vice.

For more on word play in the Canon, see the introduction to Sn 4.

See also: DN 2; AN 3:65; MN 70; MN 95

28 The Great Elephant Footprint Simile

Mahā Hatthipadopama Sutta

I have heard that on one occasion the Blessed One was staying near Sāvatthī in Jeta's Grove, Anāthapiṇḍika's monastery. There Ven. Sāriputta addressed the monks, "Friend monks!"

"Yes, friend," the monks responded to him.

Ven. Sāriputta said, "Friends, just as the footprints of all legged animals are encompassed by the footprint of the elephant, and the elephant's footprint is reckoned the foremost among them in terms of size; in the same way, all skillful qualities are included in the four noble truths. In which four? In the noble truth of stress, in the noble truth of the origination of stress, in the noble truth of the cessation of stress, and in the noble truth of the path of practice leading to the cessation of stress.

"And what is the noble truth of stress? Birth is stressful, aging is stressful, death is stressful; sorrow, lamentation, pain, distress, & despair are stressful; not getting what is wanted is stressful. In short, the five clinging-aggregates are stressful. And which are the five clinging-aggregates? The form clinging-aggregate, the feeling clinging-aggregate, the perception clinging-aggregate, the fabrication clinging-aggregate, and the consciousness clinging-aggregate.

"And what is the form clinging-aggregate? The four great existents and the form derived from them. And what are the four great existents? The earth property, the liquid property, the fire property, & the wind property.

THE EARTH PROPERTY

"And what is the earth property? The earth property can be either internal or external. What is the internal earth property? Whatever internal, within oneself, is hard, solid, & sustained (by craving): head hairs, body hairs, nails, teeth, skin, flesh, tendons, bones, bone marrow, kidneys, heart, liver, pleura, spleen, lungs, large intestines, small intestines, contents of the stomach, feces, or whatever else internal, within oneself, is hard, solid, & sustained: This is called the internal earth property. Now both the internal earth property and the external earth property are simply earth property. And that should be seen as it has come to be with right discernment: 'This is not mine, this is not what I am, this is not my self.' When one sees it thus as it has come to be with right discernment, one becomes disenchanted with the earth property and makes the mind dispassionate toward the earth property.

"Now there comes a time, friends, when the external liquid property is provoked,[1] and at that time the external earth property vanishes. So when even in the external earth property—so vast—inconstancy will be discerned, destructibility will be discerned, a tendency to decay will be discerned, changeability will be discerned, then what of this short-lasting body, sustained by clinging, is 'I' or 'mine' or 'what I am'? It has here only a 'no.'

"Now if other people insult, malign, exasperate, & harass a monk (who has discerned this), he discerns that 'A painful feeling, born of ear-contact, has arisen within me. And that is dependent, not independent. Dependent on what? Dependent on contact.' And he sees that contact is inconstant, feeling is inconstant, perception is inconstant, consciousness is inconstant. His mind, with the (earth) property as its object/support, leaps up, grows confident, steadfast, & released.

"And if other people attack the monk in ways that are undesirable, displeasing, & disagreeable—through contact with fists, contact with stones, contact with sticks, or contact with knives—the monk discerns that 'This body is of such a nature that contacts with fists come, contacts with stones come, contacts with sticks come, & contacts with knives come. Now the Blessed One has said, in his exhortation of the simile of the saw [MN 21], "Monks, even if bandits were to carve you up savagely, limb by limb, with a two-handled saw, he among you who let his heart get angered even at that would not be doing my bidding." So my persistence will be aroused & untiring, my mindfulness established & unconfused, my body calm & unaroused, my mind centered & unified. And now let contact with fists come to this body, let contact with stones, with sticks, with knives come to this body, for this is how the Buddha's bidding is done.'

"And if, in the monk recollecting the Buddha, Dhamma, & Saṅgha in this way, equanimity based on what is skillful is not established, he feels apprehensive at that and gives rise to a sense of urgency: 'It is a loss for me, not a gain; ill-gotten for me, not well-gotten, that when I recollect the Buddha, Dhamma, & Saṅgha in this way, equanimity based on what is skillful is not established within me.' Just as when a daughter-in-law, on seeing her father-in-law, feels apprehensive and gives rise to a sense of urgency (to please him), in the same way, if, in the monk recollecting the Buddha, Dhamma, & Saṅgha in this way, equanimity based on what is skillful is not established, he feels apprehensive at that and gives rise to a sense of urgency: 'It is a loss for me, not a gain; ill-gotten for me, not well-gotten, that when I recollect the Buddha, Dhamma, & Saṅgha in this way, equanimity based on what is skillful is not established within me.'

"But if, in the monk recollecting the Buddha, Dhamma, & Saṅgha in this way, equanimity based on what is skillful is established, then he is gratified at that. And even to this extent, friends, the monk has accomplished a great deal.

THE LIQUID PROPERTY

"And what is the liquid property? The liquid property may be either internal or external. What is the internal liquid property? Whatever internal, belonging to oneself, is liquid, watery, & sustained: bile, phlegm, pus, blood, sweat, fat, tears, skin-oil, saliva, mucus, fluid in the joints, urine, or whatever else internal, within oneself, is liquid, watery, & sustained: This is called the internal liquid property. Now both the internal liquid property and the external liquid property are simply liquid property. And that should be seen as it has come to be with right discernment: 'This is not mine, this is not what I am, this is not my self.' When one sees it thus as it has come to be with right discernment, one becomes disenchanted with the liquid property and makes the mind dispassionate toward the liquid property.

"Now there comes a time, friends, when the external liquid property is provoked and washes away village, town, city, district, & country. There comes a time when the water in the great ocean drops down one hundred leagues, two hundred… three hundred… four hundred… five hundred… six hundred… seven hundred leagues. There comes a time when the water in the great ocean stands seven palm-trees deep, six… five… four… three… two palm-trees deep, one palm-tree deep. There comes a time when the water in the great ocean stands seven fathoms deep, six… five… four… three… two fathoms deep, one fathom deep. There comes a time when the water in the great ocean stands half a fathom deep, hip-deep, knee-deep, ankle deep. There comes a time when the water in the great ocean is not even the depth of the first joint of a finger.

"So when even in the external liquid property—so vast—inconstancy will be discerned, destructibility will be discerned, a tendency to decay will be discerned, changeability will be discerned, then what of this short-lasting body, sustained by clinging, is 'I' or 'mine' or 'what I am'? It has here only a 'no.'

"Now if other people insult, malign, exasperate, & harass a monk (who has discerned this), he discerns that 'A painful feeling, born of ear-contact, has arisen within me. And that is dependent, not independent. Dependent on what? Dependent on contact.' And he sees that contact is inconstant, feeling is inconstant, perception is inconstant, consciousness is inconstant. His mind, with the (liquid) property as its object/support, leaps up, grows confident, steadfast, & released.

"And if other people attack the monk in ways that are undesirable, displeasing, & disagreeable—through contact with fists, contact with stones, contact with sticks, or contact with knives—the monk discerns that 'This body is of such a nature that contacts with fists come, contacts with stones come, contacts with sticks come, & contacts with knives come. Now the Blessed One has said, in his exhortation of the simile of the saw, "Monks, even if bandits were to carve you up savagely, limb by limb, with a two-handled saw, he among you who let his heart get angered even at that would not be doing my bidding." So my persistence will be aroused & untiring, my mindfulness established & unconfused, my body calm & unaroused, my mind centered & unified. And now let contact with fists come to this body, let contact with stones, with sticks, with knives come to this body, for this is how the Buddha's bidding is done.'

"And if, in the monk recollecting the Buddha, Dhamma, & Saṅgha in this way, equanimity based on what is skillful is not established, he feels apprehensive at that and gives rise to a sense of urgency: 'It is a loss for me, not a gain; ill-gotten for me, not well-gotten, that when I recollect the Buddha, Dhamma, & Saṅgha in this way, equanimity based on what is skillful is not established within me.' Just as when a daughter-in-law, on seeing her father-in-law, feels apprehensive and gives rise to a sense of urgency (to please him), in the same way, if, in the monk recollecting the Buddha, Dhamma, & Saṅgha in this way, equanimity based on what is skillful is not established, he feels apprehensive at that and gives rise to a sense of urgency: 'It is a loss for me, not a gain; ill-gotten for me, not well-gotten, that when I recollect the Buddha, Dhamma, & Saṅgha in this way, equanimity based on what is skillful is not established within me.'

"But if, in the monk recollecting the Buddha, Dhamma, & Saṅgha in this way, equanimity based on what is skillful is established, then he is gratified at that. And even to this extent, friends, the monk has accomplished a great deal.

THE FIRE PROPERTY

"And what is the fire property? The fire property may be either internal or external. What is the internal fire property? Whatever internal, belonging to oneself, is fire, fiery, & sustained: that by which (the body) is warmed, aged, & consumed with fever; and that by which what is eaten, drunk, chewed, & savored gets properly digested, or whatever else internal, within oneself, is fire, fiery, & sustained: This is called the internal fire property. Now both the internal fire property and the external fire property are simply fire property. And that should be seen as it has come to be with right discernment: 'This is not mine, this is not what I am, this is not my self.' When one sees it thus as it has come to be with right discernment, one becomes disenchanted with the fire property and makes the mind dispassionate toward the fire property.

"Now there comes a time, friends, when the external fire property is provoked and consumes village, town, city, district, & country; and then, coming to the edge of a green district, the edge of a road, the edge of a rocky district, to the water's edge, or to a lush, well-watered area, goes out from lack of sustenance. There comes a time when people try to make fire using a wing-bone & tendon parings.[2]

"So when even in the external fire property—so vast—inconstancy will be discerned, destructibility will be discerned, a tendency to decay will be discerned, changeability will be discerned, then what of this short-lasting body, sustained by clinging, is 'I' or 'mine' or 'what I am'? It has here only a 'no.'

"Now if other people insult, malign, exasperate, & harass a monk (who has discerned this), he discerns that 'A painful feeling, born of ear-contact, has arisen within me. And that is dependent, not independent. Dependent on what? Dependent on contact.' And he sees that contact is inconstant, feeling is inconstant, perception is inconstant, consciousness is inconstant. His mind, with the (fire) property as its object/support, leaps up, grows confident, steadfast, & released.

"And if other people attack the monk in ways that are undesirable, displeasing, & disagreeable—through contact with fists, contact with stones, contact with sticks, or contact with knives—the monk discerns that 'This body is of such a nature that contacts with fists come, contacts with stones come, contacts with sticks come, & contacts with knives come. Now the Blessed One has said, in his exhortation of the simile of the saw, "Monks, even if bandits were to carve you up savagely, limb by limb, with a two-handled saw, he among you who let his heart get angered even at that would not be doing my bidding." So my persistence will be aroused & untiring, my mindfulness established & unconfused, my body calm & unaroused, my mind centered & unified. And now let contact with fists come to this body, let contact with stones, with sticks, with knives come to this body, for this is how the Buddha's bidding is done.'

"And if, in the monk recollecting the Buddha, Dhamma, & Saṅgha in this way, equanimity based on what is skillful is not established, he feels apprehensive at that and gives rise to a sense of urgency: 'It is a loss for me, not a gain; ill-gotten for me, not well-gotten, that when I recollect the Buddha, Dhamma, & Saṅgha in this way, equanimity based on what is skillful is not established within me.' Just as when a daughter-in-law, on seeing her father-in-law, feels apprehensive and gives rise to a sense of urgency (to please him), in the same way, if, in the monk recollecting the Buddha, Dhamma, & Saṅgha in this way, equanimity based on what is skillful is not established, he feels apprehensive at that and gives rise to a sense of urgency: 'It is a loss for me, not a gain; ill-gotten for me, not well-gotten, that when I recollect the Buddha, Dhamma, & Saṅgha in this way, equanimity based on what is skillful is not established within me.'

"But if, in the monk recollecting the Buddha, Dhamma, & Saṅgha in this way, equanimity based on what is skillful is established, then he is gratified at that. And even to this extent, friends, the monk has accomplished a great deal.

THE WIND PROPERTY

"And what is the wind property? The wind property may be either internal or external. What is the internal wind property? Whatever internal, belonging to oneself, is wind, windy, & sustained: up-going winds, down-going winds, winds in the stomach, winds in the intestines, winds that course through the body, in-&-out breathing, or whatever else internal, within oneself, is wind, windy, & sustained: This is called the internal wind property. Now both the internal wind property and the external wind property are simply wind property. And that should be seen as it has come to be with right discernment: 'This is not mine, this is not what I am, this is not my self.' When one sees it thus as it has come to be with right discernment, one becomes disenchanted with the wind property and makes the mind dispassionate toward the wind property.

"Now there comes a time, friends, when the external wind property is provoked and blows away village, town, city, district, & country. There comes a time when, in the last month of the hot season, people try to start a breeze with a fan or bellows, and even the grass at the fringe of a thatch roof doesn't stir.

"So when even in the external wind property—so vast—inconstancy will be discerned, destructibility will be discerned, a tendency to decay will be discerned, changeability will be discerned, then what of this short-lasting body, sustained by clinging, is 'I' or 'mine' or 'what I am'? It has here only a 'no.'

"Now if other people insult, malign, exasperate, & harass a monk (who has discerned this), he discerns that 'A painful feeling, born of ear-contact, has arisen within me. And that is dependent, not independent. Dependent on what? Dependent on contact.' And he sees that contact is inconstant, feeling is inconstant, perception is inconstant, consciousness is inconstant. His mind, with the (wind) property as its object/support, leaps up, grows confident, steadfast, & released.

"And if other people attack the monk in ways that are undesirable, displeasing, & disagreeable—through contact with fists, contact with stones, contact with sticks, or contact with knives—the monk discerns that 'This body is of such a nature that contacts with fists come, contacts with stones come, contacts with sticks come, & contacts with knives come. Now the Blessed One has said, in his exhortation of the simile of the saw, "Monks, even if bandits were to carve you up savagely, limb by limb, with a two-handled saw, he among you who let his heart get angered even at that would not be doing my bidding." So my persistence will be aroused & untiring, my mindfulness established & unconfused, my body calm & unaroused, my mind centered & unified. And now let contact with fists come to this body, let contact with stones, with sticks, with knives come to this body, for this is how the Buddha's bidding is done.'

"And if, in the monk recollecting the Buddha, Dhamma, & Saṅgha in this way, equanimity based on what is skillful is not established, he feels apprehensive at that and gives rise to a sense of urgency: 'It is a loss for me, not a gain; ill-gotten for me, not well-gotten, that when I recollect the Buddha, Dhamma, & Saṅgha in this way, equanimity based on what is skillful is not established within me.' Just as when a daughter-in-law, on seeing her father-in-law, feels apprehensive and gives rise to a sense of urgency (to please him), in the same way, if, in the monk recollecting the Buddha, Dhamma, & Saṅgha in this way, equanimity based on what is skillful is not established, he feels apprehensive at that and gives rise to a sense of urgency: 'It is a loss for me, not a gain; ill-gotten for me, not well-gotten, that when I recollect the Buddha, Dhamma, & Saṅgha in this way, equanimity based on what is skillful is not established within me.'

"But if, in the monk recollecting the Buddha, Dhamma, & Saṅgha in this way, equanimity based on what is skillful is established, then he is gratified at that. And even to this extent, friends, the monk has accomplished a great deal.

DEPENDENT CO-ARISING

"Friends, just as when—in dependence on timber, vines, grass, & clay—space is enclosed and is gathered under the term 'house,' in the same way, when space is enclosed in dependence on bones, tendons, muscle, & skin, it is gathered under the term, 'form.'

"Now if internally the eye is intact but externally forms do not come into range, nor is there a corresponding engagement, then there is no appearing of the corresponding type of consciousness. If internally the eye is intact and externally forms come into range, but there is no corresponding engagement, then there is no appearing of the corresponding type of consciousness. But when internally the eye is intact and externally forms come into range, and there is a corresponding engagement, then there is the appearing of the corresponding type of consciousness.

"The form of what has thus come into being is gathered under the form clinging-aggregate. The feeling of what has thus come into being is gathered under the feeling clinging-aggregate. The perception of what has thus come into being is gathered under the perception clinging-aggregate. The fabrications of what has thus come into being are gathered under the fabrication clinging-aggregate. The consciousness of what has thus come into being is gathered under the consciousness clinging-aggregate. One discerns, 'This, it seems, is how there is the gathering, meeting, & convergence of these five clinging-aggregates. Now, the Blessed One has said, "Whoever sees dependent co-arising sees the Dhamma; whoever sees the Dhamma sees dependent co-arising."[3] And these things—the five clinging-aggregates—are dependently co-arisen.[4] Any desire, embracing, grasping, & holding-on to these five clinging-aggregates is the origination of stress. Any subduing of desire & passion, any abandoning of desire & passion for these five clinging-aggregates is the cessation of stress.'[5] And even to this extent, friends, the monk has accomplished a great deal.

"Now if internally the ear is intact....

"Now if internally the nose... the tongue... the body is intact....

"Now if internally the intellect is intact but externally ideas do not come into range, nor is there a corresponding engagement, then there is no appearing of the corresponding type of consciousness. If internally the intellect is intact and externally ideas come into range, but there is no corresponding engagement, then there is no appearing of the corresponding type of consciousness. But when internally the intellect is intact and externally ideas come into range, and there is a corresponding engagement, then there is the appearing of the corresponding type of consciousness.

"The form of what has thus come into being is gathered under the form clinging-aggregate. The feeling of what has thus come into being is gathered under the feeling clinging-aggregate. The perception of what has thus come into being is gathered under the perception clinging-aggregate. The fabrications of what has thus come into being are gathered under the fabrication clinging-aggregate. The consciousness of what has thus come into being is gathered under the consciousness clinging-aggregate. One discerns, 'This, it seems, is how there is the gathering, meeting, & convergence of these five clinging-aggregates. Now, the Blessed One has said, "Whoever sees dependent co-arising sees the Dhamma; whoever sees the Dhamma sees dependent co-arising." And these things—the five clinging-aggregates—are dependently co-arisen. Any desire, embracing, grasping, & holding-on to these five clinging-aggregates is the origination of stress. Any subduing of desire & passion, any abandoning of desire & passion for these five clinging-aggregates is the cessation of stress.' And even to this extent, friends, the monk has accomplished a great deal."

That is what Ven. Sāriputta said. Gratified, the monks delighted in Ven. Sāriputta's words.

NOTES

1. The compilers of the Pali Canon used a common theory to explain the physics of heat & motion, meteorology, and the etiology of diseases. That theory centered on the concept of *dhātu:* property or potential. The physical properties presented in this theory were four: those of earth (solidity), liquid, fire, & wind (motion). Three of them—liquid, fire, & wind—were viewed as potentially active. When they were aggravated, agitated or provoked—the Pali term here, *'pakuppati'*, was used also on the psychological level, where it meant angered or upset—they acted as the underlying cause for activity in nature. For more on this topic, see *The Mind Like Fire Unbound,* Chapter 2.

2. AN 7:46 (quoted in *The Mind Like Fire Unbound)* cites a wing bone and tendon parings as examples of items that will not catch fire. Perhaps the passage was meant as a comical parody of someone who, having seen another person start fire with a fire stick, tried to imitate that person without understanding the basic principle involved. If you used a fire stick and wood shavings, you would get fire. If you used a

wing bone instead of a fire stick, and tendon parings instead of wood shavings, you wouldn't.

3. This statement has not been traced in any other part of the extant Pali Canon.

4. See SN 12:2.

5. Although the fourth noble truth—the path of practice leading to the cessation of stress—is not explicitly mentioned in this discussion, it is implicit as the path of practice leading to the subduing of desire & passion, the abandoning of desire & passion for the five clinging-aggregates.

See also: DN 22; MN 9; MN 43; MN 140; MN 147; SN 22:57

29 The Longer Heartwood Simile

Mahā Sāropama Sutta

I have heard that on one occasion the Blessed One was staying near Rājagaha on Vulture Peak mountain, not long after Devadatta had left. Referring to Devadatta, the Blessed One addressed the monks:

"Monks, there is the case where a certain son of good family, out of conviction, goes forth from the home life into homelessness, (thinking,) 'I am beset by birth, by aging-&-death, by sorrows, lamentations, pains, distresses, & despairs, beset by stress, overcome with stress. Perhaps the end of this entire mass of stress might be discerned!' Having thus gone forth, he encounters gain, offerings, & fame. He is gratified with that gain, offerings, & fame, his resolve fulfilled. Because of that gain, offerings, & fame he exalts himself and disparages others: 'I am a person with gain, offerings, & fame, but these other monks are unknown & of little influence.' He is intoxicated with that gain, offerings, & fame, heedless about it, and falls into heedlessness. Being heedless, he dwells in suffering & stress.

"Just as if a man in need of heartwood, seeking heartwood, wandering in search of heartwood—passing over the heartwood of a great standing tree possessed of heartwood, passing over the sapwood, passing over the inner bark, passing over the outer bark—cutting away the twigs & leaves, were to go off carrying them, thinking, 'heartwood.' A man with good eyesight, seeing him, would say, 'Ah, how this good man didn't know heartwood, didn't know sapwood, didn't know inner bark, didn't know outer bark, didn't know twigs & leaves! That's why he, in need of heartwood, seeking heartwood, wandering in search of heartwood—passing over the heartwood of a great standing tree possessed of heartwood, passing over the sapwood, passing over the inner bark, passing over the outer bark—cutting away the twigs & leaves, went off carrying them, thinking, "heartwood." Whatever heartwood-business he had with heartwood, his purpose won't be served.'

"In the same way, monks, there is the case where a certain son of good family, out of conviction, goes forth from the home life into homelessness, (thinking,) 'I am beset by birth, by aging-&-death,

by sorrows, lamentations, pains, distresses, & despairs, beset by stress, overcome with stress. Perhaps the end of this entire mass of stress might be discerned!' Having thus gone forth, he encounters gain, offerings, & fame. He is gratified with that gain, offerings, & fame, his resolve fulfilled. Because of that gain, offerings, & fame he exalts himself and disparages others: 'I am a person with gain, offerings, & fame, but these other monks are unknown & of little influence.' He is intoxicated with that gain, offerings, & fame, heedless about it, and falls into heedlessness. Being heedless, he dwells in suffering & stress. This, monks, is called a monk who grasps the twigs & leaves of the holy life, and with that he falls short.

"And further, there is the case where a certain son of good family, out of conviction, goes forth from the home life into homelessness, (thinking,) '… Perhaps the end of this entire mass of stress might be discerned!' Having thus gone forth, he encounters gain, offerings, & fame. He is not gratified with that gain, offerings, & fame, his resolve not fulfilled. He is not intoxicated with that gain, offerings, & fame, not heedless about it, and does not fall into heedlessness. Being heedful, he achieves consummation in virtue. He is gratified with that consummation in virtue, his resolve fulfilled. Because of that consummation in virtue he exalts himself and disparages others: 'I am a person of virtue, with fine qualities, but these other monks are unvirtuous, with evil qualities.' He is intoxicated with that consummation in virtue, heedless about it, and falls into heedlessness. Being heedless, he dwells in suffering & stress.

"Just as if a man in need of heartwood, seeking heartwood, wandering in search of heartwood—passing over the heartwood of a great standing tree possessed of heartwood, passing over the sapwood, passing over the inner bark—cutting away the outer bark, were to go off carrying it, thinking, 'heartwood.' A man with good eyesight, seeing him, would say, 'Ah, how this good man didn't know heartwood, didn't know sapwood, didn't know inner bark, didn't know outer bark, didn't know twigs & leaves! That's why he, in need of heartwood, seeking heartwood, wandering in search of heartwood—passing over the heartwood of a great standing tree possessed of heartwood, passing over the sapwood, passing over the inner bark—cutting away the outer bark, went off carrying it, thinking, "heartwood." Whatever heartwood-business he had with heartwood, his purpose won't be served.'

"In the same way, monks, there is the case where a certain son of good family, out of conviction, goes forth from the home life into homelessness, (thinking,) '… Perhaps the end of this entire mass of stress might be discerned!' Having thus gone forth, he encounters gain, offerings, & fame. He is not gratified with that gain, offerings, & fame, his resolve not fulfilled. He is not intoxicated with that gain, offerings, & fame, not heedless about it, and does not fall into heedlessness. Being heedful, he achieves consummation in virtue. He is gratified with that consummation in virtue, his resolve fulfilled. Because of that consummation in virtue he exalts himself and disparages others: 'I am a person of virtue, with fine qualities, but these other monks are unvirtuous, with evil qualities.' He is intoxicated with that consummation in virtue, heedless about it, and falls into heedlessness. Being heedless, he dwells in suffering & stress. This, monks, is called a monk who grasps the outer bark of the holy life, and with that he falls short.

"And further, there is the case where a certain son of good family, out of conviction, goes forth from the home life into homelessness, (thinking,) '... Perhaps the end of this entire mass of stress might be discerned!' Having thus gone forth, he encounters gain, offerings, & fame. He is not gratified with that gain, offerings, & fame, his resolve not fulfilled. He is not intoxicated with that gain, offerings, & fame, not heedless about it, and does not fall into heedlessness. Being heedful, he achieves consummation in virtue. He is gratified with that consummation in virtue, but his resolve is not fulfilled. Because of that consummation in virtue he does not exalt himself or disparage others. He is not intoxicated with that consummation in virtue, not heedless about it, and does not fall into heedlessness. Being heedful, he achieves consummation in concentration. He is gratified with that consummation in concentration, his resolve fulfilled. Because of that consummation in concentration he exalts himself and disparages others: 'I am concentrated, my mind at singleness, but these other monks are unconcentrated, their minds scattered.' He is intoxicated with that consummation in concentration, heedless about it, and falls into heedlessness. Being heedless, he dwells in suffering & stress.

"Just as if a man in need of heartwood, seeking heartwood, wandering in search of heartwood—passing over the heartwood of a great standing tree possessed of heartwood, passing over the sapwood—cutting away the inner bark, were to go off carrying it, thinking, 'heartwood.' A man with good eyesight, seeing him, would say, 'Ah, how this good man didn't know heartwood, didn't know sapwood, didn't know inner bark, didn't know outer bark, didn't know twigs & leaves! That's why he, in need of heartwood, seeking heartwood, wandering in search of heartwood—passing over the heartwood of a great standing tree possessed of heartwood, passing over the sapwood—cutting away the inner bark, went off carrying it, thinking, "heartwood." Whatever heartwood-business he had with heartwood, his purpose won't be served.'

"In the same way, monks, there is the case where a certain son of good family, out of conviction, goes forth from the home life into homelessness, (thinking,) '… Perhaps the end of this entire mass of stress might be discerned!' Having thus gone forth, he encounters gain, offerings, & fame. He is not gratified with that gain, offerings, & fame, his resolve not fulfilled. He is not intoxicated with that gain, offerings, & fame, not heedless about it, and does not fall into heedlessness. Being heedful, he achieves consummation in virtue. He is gratified with that consummation in virtue, but his resolve is not fulfilled. Because of that consummation in virtue he does not exalt himself or disparage others. He is not intoxicated with that consummation in virtue, not heedless about it, and does not fall into heedlessness. Being heedful, he achieves consummation in concentration. He is gratified with that consummation in concentration, his resolve fulfilled. Because of that consummation in concentration he exalts himself and disparages others: 'I am concentrated, my mind at singleness, but these other monks are unconcentrated, their minds scattered.' He is intoxicated with that consummation in concentration, heedless about it, and falls into heedlessness. Being heedless, he dwells in suffering & stress. This, monks, is called a monk who grasps the inner bark of the holy life, and with that he falls short.

"And further, there is the case where a certain son of good family, out of conviction, goes forth from the home life into homelessness, (thinking,) '… Perhaps the end of this entire mass of stress might be discerned!' Having thus gone forth, he encounters gain, offerings, & fame. He is not gratified with that gain, offerings, & fame, his resolve not fulfilled. He is not intoxicated with that gain, offerings, & fame, not heedless about it, and does not fall into heedlessness. Being heedful, he achieves consummation in virtue. He is gratified with that consummation in virtue, but his resolve is not fulfilled. Because of that consummation in virtue he does not exalt himself or disparage others. He is not intoxicated with that consummation in virtue, not heedless about it, and does not fall into heedlessness. Being heedful, he achieves consummation in concentration. He is gratified with that consummation in concentration, but his resolve is not fulfilled. He is not intoxicated with that consummation in concentration, not heedless about it, and does not fall into heedlessness. Being heedful, he achieves knowledge & vision.[1] He is gratified with that knowledge & vision, his resolve fulfilled. Because of that knowledge & vision he exalts himself and disparages others: 'I dwell knowing & seeing, but these other monks dwell not knowing & not seeing.' He is intoxicated with that knowledge & vision, heedless about it, and falls into heedlessness. Being heedless, he dwells in suffering & stress.

"Just as if a man in need of heartwood, seeking heartwood, wandering in search of heartwood—passing over the heartwood of a great standing tree possessed of heartwood—cutting away the sapwood, were to go off carrying it, thinking, 'heartwood.' A man with good eyesight, seeing him, would say, 'Ah, how this good man didn't know heartwood, didn't know sapwood, didn't know inner bark, didn't know outer bark, didn't know twigs & leaves! That's why he, in need of heartwood, seeking heartwood, wandering in search of heartwood—passing over the heartwood of a great standing tree possessed of heartwood—cutting away the sapwood, went off carrying it, thinking, "heartwood." Whatever heartwood-business he had with heartwood, his purpose won't be served.'

"In the same way, monks, there is the case where a certain son of good family, out of conviction, goes forth from the home life into homelessness, (thinking,) '… Perhaps the end of this entire mass of stress might be discerned!' Having thus gone forth, he encounters gain, offerings, & fame. He is not gratified with that gain, offerings, & fame, his resolve not fulfilled. He is not intoxicated with that gain, offerings, & fame, not heedless about it, and does not fall into heedlessness. Being heedful, he achieves consummation in virtue. He is gratified with that consummation in virtue, but his resolve is not fulfilled. Because of that consummation in virtue he does not exalt himself or disparage others. He is not intoxicated with that consummation in virtue, not heedless about it, and does not fall into heedlessness. Being heedful, he achieves consummation in concentration. He is gratified with that consummation in concentration, but his resolve is not fulfilled. He is not intoxicated with that consummation in concentration, not heedless about it, and does not fall into heedlessness. Being heedful, he achieves knowledge & vision. He is gratified with that knowledge & vision, his resolve fulfilled. Because of that knowledge & vision he exalts himself and disparages others: 'I dwell knowing & seeing, but these other monks dwell not knowing & not seeing.' He is intoxicated with that knowledge & vision, heedless about it, and falls into heedlessness. Being heedless, he dwells in suffering & stress. This, monks, is called a monk who grasps the sapwood of the holy life, and with that he falls short.

"And further, there is the case where a certain son of good family, out of conviction, goes forth from the home life into homelessness, (thinking,) 'I am beset by birth, by aging-&-death, by sorrows, lamentations, pains, distresses, & despairs, beset by stress, overcome with stress. Perhaps the end of this entire mass of stress might be discerned!' Having thus gone forth, he encounters gain, offerings, & fame. He is not gratified with that gain, offerings, & fame, his resolve not fulfilled. He is not intoxicated with that gain, offerings, & fame, not heedless about it, and does not fall into heedlessness. Being heedful, he achieves consummation in virtue. He is gratified with that consummation in virtue, but his resolve is not fulfilled. Because of that consummation in virtue he does not exalt himself or disparage others. He is not intoxicated with that consummation in virtue, not heedless about it, and does not fall into heedlessness. Being heedful, he achieves consummation in concentration. He is gratified with that consummation in concentration, but his resolve is not fulfilled. He is not intoxicated with that consummation in concentration, not heedless about it, and does not fall into heedlessness. Being heedful, he achieves knowledge & vision. He is gratified with that knowledge & vision, but his resolve is not fulfilled. Because of that knowledge & vision he does not exalt himself or disparage others. He is not intoxicated with that knowledge & vision, not heedless about it, and does not fall into heedlessness. Being heedful, he achieves a non-occasional liberation. And it is impossible, monks, there is no opportunity, for that monk to fall from that non-occasional release.[2]

"Just as if a man in need of heartwood, seeking heartwood, wandering in search of heartwood, cutting away just the heartwood of a great standing tree possessed of heartwood, were to go off carrying it, knowing, 'heartwood.' A man with good eyesight, seeing him, would say, 'Ah, how this good man *did* know heartwood, did know sapwood, did know inner bark, did know outer bark, did know twigs & leaves! That's why he, in need of heartwood, seeking heartwood, wandering in search of heartwood, cutting away just the heartwood of a great standing tree possessed of heartwood, were to go off carrying it, knowing, "heartwood." Whatever heartwood-business he had with heartwood, his purpose will be served.'

"In the same way, monks, there is the case where a certain son of good family, out of conviction, goes forth from the home life into homelessness, (thinking,) 'I am beset by birth, by aging-&-death, by sorrows, lamentations, pains, distresses, & despairs, beset by stress, overcome with stress. Perhaps the end of this entire mass of stress might be discerned!' Having thus gone forth, he encounters gain, offerings, & fame. He is not gratified with that gain, offerings, & fame, his resolve not fulfilled. He is not intoxicated with that gain, offerings, & fame, not heedless about it, and does not fall into heedlessness. Being heedful, he achieves consummation in virtue. He is gratified with that consummation in virtue, but his resolve is not fulfilled. Because of that consummation in virtue he does not exalt himself or disparage others. He is not intoxicated with that consummation in virtue, not heedless about it, and does not fall into heedlessness. Being heedful, he achieves consummation in concentration. He is gratified with that consummation in concentration, but his resolve is not fulfilled. Because of that consummation in concentration he does not exalt himself or disparage others. He is not intoxicated with that consummation in concentration, not heedless about it, and does not fall into heedlessness. Being heedful, he achieves knowledge & vision. He is gratified with that knowledge & vision, but his resolve is not fulfilled. Because of that knowledge & vision he does not exalt himself or disparage others. He is not intoxicated with that knowledge & vision, not heedless about it, and does not fall into heedlessness. Being heedful, he achieves a non-occasional liberation. And it is impossible, monks, there is no opportunity, for that monk to fall from that non-occasional release.

"Monks, this holy life doesn't have as its reward gain, offerings, & fame, doesn't have as its reward consummation of virtue, doesn't have as its reward consummation of concentration, doesn't have as its reward knowledge & vision, but the unprovoked[3] awareness-release: That is the purpose of this holy life, that is its heartwood, that its final end."

That is what the Blessed One said. Gratified, the monks delighted in the Blessed One's words.

NOTES

1. "Knowledge & vision" here apparently has the same meaning it does in AN 4:41—i.e., the various mundane psychic powers that can come from the development of concentration.

2.. This translation follows the Sri Lankan and Burmese editions of the Canon. The Thai and PTS editions at this point say, "Being heedful, he achieves an occasional liberation. And it is possible, monks, there is the opportunity, for that monk to fall from that occasional release." However, when the passage is repeated after the simile, these editions read, "Being heedful, he achieves a non-occasional liberation. And it is impossible, monks, there is no opportunity, for that monk to fall from that non-occasional release." Because this inconsistency is anomalous, the Sri Lankan/Burmese reading seems preferable.

Occasional liberation/release is the temporary release from such things as the hindrances, attained when entering right concentration, or the temporary release from some of the factors of lower states of jhāna, attained when entering higher states of jhāna. This release lasts only as long as the necessary causal factors are still in place. Non-occasional liberation/release, according to the Commentary, covers all of the transcendent attainments: the paths and fruitions of stream-entry, once-returning, non-returning, and arahantship, along with unbinding. Thus, if the Commentary is right here, non-occasional liberation/release has a broader meaning than the unprovoked release, mentioned below, as that covers only the fruition of arahantship and unbinding. Although the path factors are needed to reach these attainments, they do not cause them, just as a path to a mountain does not cause the mountain to be. This release is beyond time—and thus "non-occasional"—in that the falling away of the path factors would not end it.

3. *Akuppa.* This term is sometimes translated as "unshakable," but it literally means, "unprovoked." The reference is apparently to the theory of *dhātu,* or properties underlying physical or psychological events in nature. The physical properties according to this theory are four: earth (solidity), liquid, heat, and wind (motion). Three of them—liquid, heat, & wind—are potentially active. When they are aggravated, agitated, or provoked—the Pali term here, *pakuppati,* is used also on the psychological level, where it means angered or upset—they act as the underlying cause for natural activity. When the provocation ends, the corresponding activity subsides. (See the description of the properties in MN 28.)

A similar theory attributes the irruption of mental states to the provocation of the properties of sensuality, form, or formlessness.

> "In dependence on the property of sensuality there occurs the perception of sensuality. In dependence on the perception of sensuality there occurs the resolve for sensuality… the desire for sensuality… the fever for sensuality… the quest for sensuality. Searching for sensuality, monks, an uninstructed run-of-the-mill person conducts himself wrongly through three means: through body, through speech, & through mind."—*SN 14:12*

Even unbinding is described as a property (Iti 44). However, there is a crucial difference in how unbinding is attained, in that the unbinding property is not provoked. Any events that depend on the provocation of a property are inherently unstable and inconstant, subject to change when the provocation ends. But because true release is not caused by the provocation of anything, it is not subject to change.

See also: MN 43; SN 17:3; SN 17:5; SN 17:8; SN 22:88; AN 2:5; AN 6:60; AN 8:7–8; AN 10:58; Iti 35–36

30 *The Shorter Heartwood Simile*

Cūḷa Sāropama Sutta

I have heard that on one occasion the Blessed One was staying near Sāvatthī in Jeta's Grove, Anāthapiṇḍika's monastery. Then Piṅgalakoccha the brahman went to the Blessed One and, on arrival, having bowed down to him, sat to one side. As he was sitting there, he said to the Blessed One, "Master Gotama, these contemplatives & brahmans, each with his group, each with his community, each the teacher of his group, an honored leader, well-regarded by people at large—i.e., Pūraṇa Kassapa, Makkhali Gosāla, Ajita Kesakambalin, Pakudha Kaccāyana, Sañjaya Velaṭṭhaputta, & the Nigaṇṭha Nāṭaputta: Do they all have direct knowledge as they themselves claim, or do they all not have direct knowledge, or do some of them have direct knowledge and some of them not?"

"Enough, brahman. Put this question aside. I will teach you the Dhamma. Listen and pay close attention. I will speak."

"Yes, sir," Piṅgalakoccha the brahman responded to the Blessed One.

The Blessed One said, "Brahman, it's as if a man in need of heartwood, seeking heartwood, wandering in search of heartwood—passing over the heartwood of a great standing tree possessed of heartwood, passing over the sapwood, passing over the inner bark, passing over the outer bark—cutting away the twigs & leaves, were to go off carrying them, thinking, 'heartwood.' A man with good eyesight, seeing him, would say, 'Ah, how this good man didn't know heartwood, didn't know sapwood, didn't know inner bark, didn't know outer bark, didn't know twigs & leaves! That's why he, in need of heartwood, seeking heartwood, wandering in search of heartwood—passing over the heartwood of a great standing tree possessed of heartwood, passing over the sapwood, passing over the inner bark, passing over the outer bark—cutting away the twigs & leaves, went off carrying them, thinking, "heartwood." Whatever heartwood-business he had with heartwood, his purpose won't be served.'

"Or, brahman, it's as if a man in need of heartwood, seeking heartwood, wandering in search of heartwood—passing over the heartwood of a great standing tree possessed of heartwood, passing over the sapwood, passing over the inner bark—cutting away the outer bark, were to go off carrying it, thinking, 'heartwood.' A man with good eyesight, seeing him, would say, 'Ah, how this good man didn't know heartwood, didn't know sapwood, didn't know inner bark, didn't know outer bark, didn't know twigs & leaves! That's why he, in need of heartwood, seeking heartwood, wandering in search of heartwood—passing over the heartwood of a great standing tree possessed of heartwood, passing over the sapwood, passing over the inner bark—cutting away the outer bark, went off carrying it, thinking, "heartwood." Whatever heartwood-business he had with heartwood, his purpose won't be served.'

"Or, brahman, it's as if a man in need of heartwood, seeking heartwood, wandering in search of heartwood—passing over the heartwood of a great standing tree possessed of heartwood, passing over the sapwood—cutting away the inner bark, were to go off carrying it, thinking, 'heartwood.' A man with good eyesight, seeing him, would say, 'Ah, how this good man didn't know heartwood, didn't know sapwood, didn't know inner bark, didn't know outer bark, didn't know twigs & leaves! That's why he, in need of heartwood, seeking heartwood, wandering in search of heartwood—passing over the heartwood of a great standing tree possessed of heartwood, passing over the sapwood—cutting away the inner bark, went off carrying it, thinking, "heartwood." Whatever heartwood-business he had with heartwood, his purpose won't be served.'

"Or, brahman, it's as if a man in need of heartwood, seeking heartwood, wandering in search of heartwood—passing over the heartwood of a great standing tree possessed of heartwood—cutting away the sapwood, were to go off carrying it, thinking, 'heartwood.' A man with good eyesight, seeing him, would say, 'Ah, how this good man didn't know heartwood, didn't know sapwood, didn't know inner bark, didn't know outer bark, didn't know twigs & leaves! That's why he, in need of heartwood, seeking heartwood, wandering in search of heartwood—passing over the heartwood of a great standing tree possessed of heartwood—cutting away the sapwood, went off carrying it, thinking, "heartwood." Whatever heartwood-business he had with heartwood, his purpose won't be served.'

"Or, brahman, it's as if a man in need of heartwood, seeking heartwood, wandering in search of heartwood, cutting away just the heartwood of a great standing tree possessed of heartwood, were to go off carrying it, knowing, 'heartwood.' A man with good eyesight, seeing him, would say, 'Ah, how this good man *did* know heartwood, did know sapwood, did know inner bark, did know outer bark, did know twigs & leaves! That's why he, in need of heartwood, seeking heartwood, wandering in search of heartwood, cutting away just the heartwood of a great standing tree possessed of heartwood, went off carrying it, knowing, "heartwood." Whatever heartwood-business he had with heartwood, his purpose will be served.'

"In the same way, brahman, there is the case where a certain son of good family,[1] out of conviction, goes forth from the home life into homelessness, (thinking,) 'I am beset by birth, by aging-&-death, by sorrows, lamentations, pains, distresses, & despairs, beset by stress, overcome with stress. Perhaps the end of this entire mass of stress might be discerned!' Having thus gone forth, he encounters gain, offerings, & fame. He is gratified with that gain, offerings, & fame, his resolve fulfilled. Because of that gain, offerings, & fame he exalts himself and disparages others: 'I am a person with gain, offerings, & fame, but these other monks are unknown & of little influence.' He doesn't generate desire or exert himself for the realization of those qualities that are higher & more sublime than gain, offerings, & fame. He is drooping & lax.

"Just like the man who, in need of heartwood, seeking heartwood, wandering in search of heartwood—passing over the heartwood of a great standing tree possessed of heartwood, passing over the sapwood, passing over the inner bark, passing over the outer bark—cutting away the twigs & leaves, went off carrying them, thinking, 'heartwood': Whatever heartwood-business he had with heartwood, his purpose won't be served. This individual, I tell you, is similar to that.

"And further, there is the case where an individual, out of conviction, goes forth from the home life into homelessness, (thinking,) '...Perhaps the end of this entire mass of stress might be discerned!' Having thus gone forth, he encounters gain, offerings, & fame. He is not gratified with that gain, offerings, & fame, his resolve not fulfilled. He generates desire & exerts himself for the realization of those qualities that are higher & more sublime than gain, offerings, & fame. He is not drooping or lax. He achieves consummation in virtue. He is gratified with that consummation in virtue, his resolve fulfilled. Because of that consummation in virtue he exalts himself and disparages others: 'I am a person of virtue, with fine qualities, but these other monks are unvirtuous, with evil qualities.' He doesn't generate desire or exert himself for the realization of those qualities that are higher & more sublime than consummation in virtue. He is drooping & lax.

"Just like the man who, in need of heartwood, seeking heartwood, wandering in search of heartwood—passing over the heartwood of a great standing tree possessed of heartwood, passing over the sapwood, passing over the inner bark—cutting away the outer bark, went off carrying it, thinking, 'heartwood': Whatever heartwood-business he had with heartwood, his purpose won't be served. This individual, I tell you, is similar to that.

"And further, there is the case where an individual, out of conviction, goes forth from the home life into homelessness, (thinking,) '...Perhaps the end of this entire mass of stress might be discerned!' Having thus gone forth, he encounters gain, offerings, & fame. He is not gratified with that gain, offerings, & fame, his resolve not fulfilled. Because of that gain, offerings, & fame he does not exalt himself or disparage others. He generates desire & exerts himself for the realization of those qualities that are higher & more sublime than gain, offerings, & fame. He is not drooping or lax. He achieves consummation in virtue. He is gratified with that consummation in virtue, but his resolve is not fulfilled. Because of that consummation in virtue he does not exalt himself or disparage others. He generates desire & exerts himself for the realization of those qualities that are higher & more sublime than consummation in virtue. He is not drooping or lax. He achieves consummation in concentration. He is gratified with that consummation in concentration, his resolve fulfilled. Because of that consummation in concentration he exalts himself and disparages others: 'I am concentrated, my mind at singleness, but these other monks are unconcentrated, their minds scattered.' He doesn't generate desire or exert himself for the realization of those qualities that are higher & more sublime than consummation in concentration. He is drooping & lax.

"Just like the man who, in need of heartwood, seeking heartwood, wandering in search of heartwood—passing over the heartwood of a great standing tree possessed of heartwood, passing over the sapwood—cutting away the inner bark, went off carrying it, thinking, 'heartwood': Whatever heartwood-business he had with heartwood, his purpose won't be served. This individual, I tell you, is similar to that.

"And further, there is the case where an individual, out of conviction, goes forth from the home life into homelessness, (thinking,) 'I am beset by birth, by aging-&-death, by sorrows, lamentations, pains, distresses, & despairs, beset by stress, overcome with stress. Perhaps the end of this entire mass of stress might be discerned!' Having thus gone forth, he encounters gain, offerings, & fame. He is not gratified with that gain, offerings, & fame, his resolve not fulfilled. Because of that gain, offerings, & fame he does not exalt himself or disparage others. He generates desire & exerts himself for the realization of those qualities that are higher & more sublime than gain, offerings, & fame. He is not drooping or lax. He achieves consummation in virtue. He is gratified with that consummation in virtue, but his resolve is not fulfilled. Because of that consummation in virtue he does not exalt himself or disparage others. He generates desire & exerts himself for the realization of those qualities that are higher & more sublime than consummation in virtue. He is not drooping or lax. He achieves consummation in concentration. He is gratified with that consummation in concentration, but his resolve is not fulfilled. Because of that consummation in concentration he does not exalt himself or disparage others. He generates desire & exerts himself for the realization of those qualities that are higher & more sublime than consummation in concentration. He is not drooping or lax. He achieves knowledge & vision. He is gratified with that knowledge & vision, his resolve fulfilled. Because of that knowledge & vision he exalts himself and disparages others: 'I dwell knowing & seeing, but these other monks dwell not knowing & not seeing.' He doesn't generate desire or exert himself for the realization of those qualities that are higher & more sublime than knowledge & vision. He is drooping & lax.

"Just like the man who, in need of heartwood, seeking heartwood, wandering in search of heartwood—passing over the heartwood of a great standing tree possessed of heartwood—cutting away the sapwood, went off carrying it, thinking, 'heartwood': Whatever heartwood-business he had with heartwood, his purpose won't be served. This individual, I tell you, is similar to that.

"And further, there is the case where an individual, out of conviction, goes forth from the home life into homelessness, (thinking,) 'I am beset by birth, by aging-&-death, by sorrows, lamentations, pains, distresses, & despairs, beset by stress, overcome with stress. Perhaps the end of this entire mass of stress might be discerned!' Having thus gone forth, he encounters gain, offerings, & fame. He is not gratified with that gain, offerings, & fame, his resolve not fulfilled. Because of that gain, offerings, & fame he does not exalt himself or disparage others. He generates desire & exerts himself for the realization of those qualities that are higher & more sublime than gain, offerings, & fame. He is not drooping or lax. He achieves consummation in virtue. He is gratified with that consummation in virtue, but his resolve is not fulfilled. Because of that consummation in virtue does not exalt himself or disparage others. He generates desire & exerts himself for the realization of those qualities that are higher & more sublime than consummation in virtue. He is not drooping or lax. He achieves consummation in concentration. He is gratified with that consummation in concentration, but his resolve is not fulfilled. Because of that consummation in concentration he does not exalt himself or disparage others. He generates desire & exerts himself for the realization of those qualities that are higher & more sublime than consummation in concentration. He is not drooping or lax. He achieves knowledge & vision. He is gratified with that knowledge & vision, but his resolve is not fulfilled. Because of that knowledge & vision he does not exalt himself or disparage others. He generates desire & exerts himself for the realization of those qualities that are higher & more sublime than knowledge & vision. He is not drooping or lax.

"And which, brahman, are the qualities that are higher & more sublime than knowledge & vision?

"There is the case where a monk—quite secluded from sensuality, secluded from unskillful qualities—enters & remains in the first jhāna: rapture & pleasure born of seclusion, accompanied by directed thought & evaluation. This is a quality higher & more sublime than knowledge & vision.[2]

"And further, with the stilling of directed thoughts & evaluations, he enters & remains in the second jhāna: rapture & pleasure born of concentration, unification of awareness free from directed thought & evaluation—internal assurance. This too is a quality higher & more sublime than knowledge & vision.

"And further, with the fading of rapture, he remains equanimous, mindful, & alert, and senses pleasure with the body. He enters & remains in the third jhāna, of which the noble ones declare, 'Equanimous & mindful, he has a pleasant abiding.' This too is a quality higher & more sublime than knowledge & vision.

"And further, with the abandoning of pleasure & stress—as with the earlier disappearance of joys & distresses—he enters & remains in the fourth jhāna: purity of equanimity & mindfulness, neither-pleasure-nor-pain. This too is a quality higher & more sublime than knowledge & vision.

"And further, with the complete transcending of perceptions of (physical) form, with the disappearance of perceptions of resistance, and not attending to perceptions of multiplicity, (perceiving,) 'Infinite space,' he enters & remains in the dimension of the infinitude of space. This too is a quality higher & more sublime than knowledge & vision.

"And further, with the complete transcending of the dimension of the infinitude of space, (perceiving,) 'Infinite consciousness,' he enters & remains in the dimension of the infinitude of consciousness. This too is a quality higher & more sublime than knowledge & vision.

"And further, with the complete transcending of the dimension of the infinitude of consciousness, (perceiving,) 'There is nothing,' he enters & remains in the dimension of nothingness. This too is a quality higher & more sublime than knowledge & vision.

"And further, with the complete transcending of the dimension of nothingness, he enters & remains in the dimension of neither perception nor non-perception. This too is a quality higher & more sublime than knowledge & vision.

"And further, with the complete transcending of the dimension of neither perception nor non-perception, he enters & remains in the cessation of perception & feeling. And, having seen (that) with discernment, his effluents are completely ended. This too is a quality higher & more sublime than knowledge & vision.

"These are the qualities higher & more sublime than knowledge & vision.

"Just like the man who, in need of heartwood, seeking heartwood, wandering in search of heartwood, cutting away just the heartwood of a great standing tree possessed of heartwood, went off carrying it, knowing, 'heartwood': Whatever heartwood-business he had with heartwood, his purpose will be served. This individual, I tell you, is similar to that.

"Brahman, this holy life doesn't have as its reward gain, offerings, & fame, doesn't have as its reward consummation of virtue, doesn't have as its reward consummation of concentration, doesn't have as its reward knowledge & vision, but the unprovoked[3] awareness-release: That is the purpose of this holy life, that is its heartwood, that its final end."

When this was said, Piṅgalakoccha the brahman said to the Blessed One: "Magnificent, lord! Magnificent! Just as if he were to place upright what was overturned, to reveal what was hidden, to show the way to one who was lost, or to carry a lamp into the dark so that those with eyes could see forms, in the same way has the Blessed One—through many lines of reasoning—made the Dhamma clear. I go to the Blessed One for refuge, to the Dhamma, and to the Saṅgha of monks. May the Blessed One remember me as a lay follower who has gone to him for refuge, from this day forward, for life."

NOTES

1. Here I follow the Thai edition, which reads "son of good family" in this instance, and "individual" in all the remaining instances. Both the Sri Lankan and the Burmese editions read "individual" here and in all the remaining instances.

2. The Commentary explains that the first jhāna is listed as higher than knowledge & vision here because it is being presented in its role as a step toward cessation. The same principle holds for the other stages of concentration up through the dimension of neither perception nor non-perception.

3. *Akuppa.* See MN 29, note 3.

See also: MN 43; SN 17:3; SN 17:5; SN 17:8; AN 2:5; AN 6:60; AN 8:7–8; AN 10:58

33 *The Greater Cowherd Discourse*

Mahā Gopālaka Sutta

I have heard that on one occasion the Blessed One was staying near Sāvatthī in Jeta's Grove, Anāthapiṇḍika's monastery. There he addressed the monks: "Monks!"

"Yes, lord," the monks responded to him.

The Blessed One said, "Monks, a cowherd endowed with eleven factors is incapable of looking after a herd so that it prospers & grows. Which eleven? There is the case where a cowherd is not well-versed in forms [appearances], unskilled in characteristics,[1] doesn't pick out flies' eggs, doesn't dress wounds, doesn't fumigate (the cattle pen), doesn't know fords, doesn't know what it is (for the cattle) to have drunk, doesn't know the road, isn't skilled in pastures, milks dry, and shows no extra respect for the bulls who are fathers & leaders of the herd. A cowherd endowed with these eleven factors is incapable of looking after a herd so that it prospers & grows.

"A monk endowed with these eleven factors is incapable of attaining growth, increase, & abundance in this Dhamma-Vinaya. Which eleven? There is the case where a monk is not well-versed in forms, unskilled in characteristics, doesn't pick out flies' eggs, doesn't dress wounds, doesn't fumigate, doesn't know fords, doesn't know what it is to have drunk, doesn't know the road, is not skilled in pastures, milks dry, and shows no extra respect for the elder monks with seniority, who have been ordained long, who are fathers & leaders of the Saṅgha.

"And how is a monk not well-versed in forms? There is the case where a monk doesn't discern, as it has come to be, that every form whatsoever is composed of the four great existents [earth, water, fire, & wind] and the forms dependent on them. This is how a monk is not well-versed in forms.

"And how is a monk unskilled in characteristics? There is the case where a monk doesn't discern, as it has come to be, that a fool is characterized by his actions, a wise person is characterized by his actions.[2] This is how a monk is unskilled in characteristics.

"And how does a monk not pick out flies' eggs? There is the case where a monk acquiesces with an arisen thought of sensuality.

He doesn't abandon it, dispel it, demolish it, or wipe it out of existence. He acquiesces with an arisen thought of ill will… an arisen thought of harmfulness. He doesn't abandon it, dispel it, demolish it, or wipe it out of existence. He acquiesces with arisen evil, unskillful qualities. He doesn't abandon them, dispel them demolish them, or wipe the out of existence. This is how a monk doesn't pick out flies' eggs.

"And how does a monk not dress wounds? There is the case where a monk, on seeing a form with the eye, grasps at themes or details by which—as he dwells without restraint over the faculty of the eye—evil, unskillful qualities such as greed or distress might assail him. He doesn't practice for its restraint. He doesn't protect the faculty of the eye. On hearing a sound with the ear… On smelling an aroma with the nose… On tasting a flavor with the tongue… On touching a tactile sensation with the body… On cognizing an idea with the intellect, he grasps at themes or details by which—as he dwells without restraint over the faculty of the intellect—evil, unskillful qualities such as greed or distress might assail him. He doesn't practice for its restraint. He doesn't protect the faculty of the intellect. This is how a monk doesn't dress wounds.

"And how does a monk not fumigate? There is the case where a monk doesn't teach others in detail the Dhamma as he has heard and mastered it. This is how a monk doesn't fumigate.

"And how does a monk not know fords? There is the case where a monk goes time & again to the monks who are learned, well-versed in the tradition, who have memorized the Dhamma, the Vinaya, and the Mātikās,[3] but doesn't question them, doesn't present them with his problems: 'How is this, venerable sir? What is the meaning of this?' These venerable ones do not reveal what has not been revealed to him, do not make plain what has not been made plain to him, do not resolve his doubts about the many teachings that might give rise to doubt. This is how a monk doesn't know fords.

"And how does a monk not know what it is to have drunk? There is the case where a monk, when the Dhamma-Vinaya proclaimed by the Tathāgata is being taught, doesn't gain understanding of the meaning, doesn't gain understanding of the Dhamma, doesn't gain joy connected with the Dhamma. This is how a monk doesn't know what it is to have drunk.

"And how does a monk not know the road? There is the case where a monk doesn't discern, as it has come to be, the noble eightfold path. This is how a monk doesn't know the road.

"And how is a monk unskilled in pastures? There is the case where a monk doesn't discern, as they have come to be, the four establishings of mindfulness.[4] This is how a monk is unskilled in pastures.

"And how does a monk milk dry? There is the case where a monk—when faithful householders invite him to accept gifts of cloth, alms food, lodgings, and medicinal requisites for curing the sick—knows no moderation in taking. This is how a monk milks dry.

"And how does a monk show no extra respect for the elder monks with seniority, who have been ordained long, who are fathers & leaders of the Saṅgha? There is the case where a monk doesn't establish himself in bodily acts of goodwill, in public & in private, toward the elder monks with seniority, who have been ordained long, who are fathers & leaders of the Saṅgha. He doesn't establish himself in verbal acts of goodwill… in mental acts of goodwill, in public & in private, toward the elder monks with seniority, who have been ordained long, who are fathers & leaders of the Saṅgha.

"A monk endowed with these eleven factors is incapable of attaining growth, increase, & abundance in this Dhamma-Vinaya.

"Monks, a cowherd endowed with eleven factors is capable of looking after a herd so that it prospers & grows. Which eleven? There is the case where a cowherd is well-versed in forms (appearances), skilled in characteristics, picks out flies' eggs, dresses wounds, fumigates, knows fords, knows what it is to have drunk, knows the road, is skilled in pastures, doesn't milk dry, and shows extra respect for the bulls who are fathers & leaders of the herd. A cowherd endowed with these eleven factors is capable of looking after a herd so that it prospers & grows.

"A monk endowed with these eleven factors is capable of attaining growth, increase, & abundance in this Dhamma-Vinaya. Which eleven? There is the case where a monk is well-versed in forms, skilled in characteristics, picks out flies' eggs, dresses wounds, fumigates, knows fords, knows what it is to have drunk, knows the road, is skilled in pastures, doesn't milk dry, and shows extra respect for the elder monks with seniority, who have been ordained long, who are fathers & leaders of the Saṅgha.

"And how is a monk well-versed in forms? There is the case where a monk discerns, as it has come to be, that every form whatsoever is composed of the four great existents and the forms dependent on them. This is how a monk is well-versed in forms.

"And how is a monk skilled in characteristics? There is the case where a monk discerns, as it has come to be, that a fool is characterized by his actions, a wise person is characterized by his actions. This is how a monk is skilled in characteristics.

"And how does a monk pick out flies' eggs? There is the case where a monk doesn't acquiesce with an arisen thought of sensuality. He abandons it, dispels it, demolishes it, & wipes it out of existence. He doesn't acquiesce with an arisen thought of ill will… an arisen thought of harmfulness. He abandons it, dispels it, demolishes it, & wipes it out of existence. He doesn't acquiesce with arisen evil, unskillful qualities. He abandons them, dispels them, demolishes them, & wipes them out of existence. This is how a monk picks out flies' eggs.

"And how does a monk dress wounds? There is the case where a monk, on seeing a form with the eye, doesn't grasp at any theme or details by which—if he were to dwell without restraint over the faculty of the eye—evil, unskillful qualities such as greed or distress might assail him. He practices for its restraint. He protects the faculty of the eye. On hearing a sound with the ear… On smelling an aroma with the nose… On tasting a flavor with the tongue… On touching a tactile sensation with the body… On cognizing an idea with the intellect, he doesn't grasp at any theme or details by which—if he were to dwell without restraint over the faculty of the intellect—evil, unskillful qualities such as greed or distress might assail him. He practices for its restraint. He protects the faculty of the intellect. This is how a monk dresses wounds.

"And how does a monk fumigate? There is the case where a monk teaches others in detail the Dhamma as he has heard and mastered it. This is how a monk fumigates.

"And how does a monk know fords? There is the case where a monk goes time & again to the monks who are learned, well-versed in the tradition, who have memorized the Dhamma, the Vinaya, and the Mātikās. He questions them, presents them with his problems: 'How is this, venerable sir? What is the meaning of this?' These venerable ones reveal what has not been revealed to him, make plain what has not been made plain to him, resolve his doubts about the many teachings that might give rise to doubt. This is how a monk knows fords.

"And how does a monk know what it is to have drunk? There is the case where a monk, when the Dhamma-Vinaya proclaimed by the Tathāgata is being taught, gains understanding of the meaning, gains understanding of the Dhamma, gains joy connected with the Dhamma. This is how a monk knows what it is to have drunk.

"And how does a monk know the road? There is the case where a monk discerns, as it has come to be, the noble eightfold path. This is how a monk knows the roads.

"And how is a monk skilled in pastures? There is the case where a monk discerns, as they have come to be, the four establishings of mindfulness. This is how a monk is skilled in pastures.

"And how does a monk not milk dry? There is the case where a monk—when faithful householders invite him to accept gifts of cloth, alms food, lodgings, and medicinal requisites for curing the sick—knows moderation in taking. This is how a monk doesn't milk dry.

"And how does a monk show extra respect for the elder monks with seniority, who have been ordained long, who are fathers & leaders of the Saṅgha? There is the case where a monk establishes himself in bodily acts of goodwill, in public & in private, toward the elder monks with seniority, who have been ordained long, who are fathers & leaders of the Saṅgha. He establishes himself in verbal acts of goodwill... in mental acts of goodwill, in public & in private, toward the elder monks with seniority, who have been ordained long, who are fathers & leaders of the Saṅgha.

"A monk endowed with these eleven factors is capable of attaining growth, increase, & abundance in this Dhamma-Vinaya."

NOTES

1. According to the Commentary, a cowherd "unskilled in characteristics" is one who doesn't recognize the branding marks used on cattle.

2. See AN 3:2.

3. The Mātikā are lists of Dhamma topics that eventually were developed into the Abhidhamma.

4. See SN 47:6–7.

35 *The Shorter Discourse to Saccaka*

Cūḷa Saccaka Sutta

I have heard that on one occasion the Blessed One was staying near Vesālī at the Gabled Hall in the Great Forest. And on that occasion Saccaka the Nigaṇṭha-son was dwelling in Vesālī—a debater, a sophist,[1] well-regarded by people at large. He made this statement before the assembly in Vesālī: "I see no contemplative or brahman, the head of an order, the head of a group, or even one who claims to be an arahant, rightly self-awakened, who—engaged in debate with me—would not shiver, quiver, shake, & break out in sweat under the armpits. Even if I were to engage a senseless stump in debate, it—engaged with me in debate—would shiver, quiver, & shake, to say nothing of a human being."

Then early in the morning Ven. Assaji[2] adjusted his under robe and—carrying his bowl & outer robe—went into Vesālī for alms. Saccaka the Nigaṇṭha-son, walking & wandering around Vesālī to exercise his legs, saw Ven. Assaji coming from afar. On seeing him, he went up to him and exchanged courteous greetings with him. After an exchange of friendly greetings & courtesies, he stood to one side. As he was standing there, he said to him, "Master Assaji, how does Gotama the contemplative discipline his disciples? Or what part of his instruction is generally presented to his disciples?"

"Aggivessana,[3] the Blessed One disciplines his disciples in this way; this part of the Blessed One's instruction is generally presented to his disciples: 'Form is inconstant. Feeling is inconstant. Perception is inconstant. Fabrications are inconstant. Consciousness is inconstant. Form is not-self. Feeling is not-self. Perception is not-self. Fabrications are not-self. Consciousness is not-self. All fabrications are inconstant. All phenomena are not-self.' This, Aggivessana, is the way in which the Blessed One disciplines his disciples; this part of the Blessed One's instruction is generally presented to his disciples."

"What a bad thing to hear we have heard, Master Assaji, when we have heard that Gotama the contemplative teaches this sort of thing. Perhaps sooner or later we might go to meet with Gotama the contemplative. Perhaps there might be some discussion. Perhaps we might pry him away from that evil viewpoint."

Now on that occasion, five hundred Licchavis had gathered at a meeting hall on some business or other. So Saccaka the Nigaṇṭha-son went to those Licchavis and, on arrival, said to them, "Come out, good Licchavis! Come out, good Licchavis! Today will be my discussion with Gotama the contemplative! If he takes the position with me that was taken with me by his famous disciple, the monk named Assaji, then just as a strong man, seizing a long-haired ram by the hair, would drag him to and drag him fro and drag him all around, in the same way I, statement by statement, will drag Gotama the contemplative to and drag him fro and drag him all around. Just as a strong distillery worker, throwing a large distiller's strainer into a deep water tank and grabbing it by the corners, would drag it to and drag it fro and drag it all around, in the same way I, statement by statement, will drag Gotama the contemplative to and drag him fro and drag him all around. Just as a strong distillery ruffian, grabbing a horse-hair strainer by the corners, would shake it down and shake it out and thump it, in the same way I, statement by statement, will shake Gotama the contemplative down and shake him out and thump him. Just as a sixty-year old elephant, plunging into a deep pond, would amuse itself playing the game of hemp-washing, in the same way I will amuse myself playing the game of hemp-washing Gotama the contemplative, as it were. Come on out, good Licchavis! Come on out, good Licchavis! Today will be my discussion with Gotama the contemplative!"

Then some of the Licchavis said, "Who is Gotama the contemplative that he will refute the statement of Saccaka the Nigaṇṭha-son? It's Saccaka the Nigaṇṭha-son who will refute the statement of Gotama the contemplative." Some of the Licchavis said, "Who is Saccaka the Nigaṇṭha-son that he will refute the statement of Gotama the contemplative? It's Gotama the contemplative who will refute the statement of Saccaka the Nigaṇṭha-son."

So Saccaka the Nigaṇṭha-son, surrounded by five hundred Licchavis, went to the Gabled Hall in the Great Forest.

Now on that occasion a large number of monks were doing walking meditation in the open air. So Saccaka the Nigaṇṭha-son went up to the monks and said, "Where, masters, is Master Gotama now? We want to see Master Gotama."

"The Blessed One, Aggivessana, having plunged into the Great Forest, is sitting under a certain tree for the day's abiding."

Then Saccaka the Nigaṇṭha-son together with a large group of Licchavis plunged into the Great Forest and went to the Blessed One. On arrival, he exchanged courteous greetings with the Blessed One. After an exchange of friendly greetings & courtesies, he sat to one side. Some of the Licchavis, having bowed down to the Blessed One, sat to one side. Some of the Licchavis exchanged courteous greetings with the Blessed One and, after an exchange of friendly greetings & courtesies, sat to one side. Some of the Licchavis, having raised their hands palm-to-palm in front of the chest, sat to one side. Some of the Licchavis, after announcing their name and clan, sat to one side. Some of the Licchavis, staying silent, sat to one side.

As he was sitting there, he said to the Blessed One, "I would like to question Master Gotama on a certain point, if Master Gotama would grant me the favor of an answer to the question."

"Ask, Aggivessana, as you see fit."

"How does Master Gotama discipline his disciples? Or what part of his instruction is generally presented to his disciples?"

"Aggivessana, I discipline my disciples in this way; this part of my instruction is generally presented to my disciples: 'Form is inconstant. Feeling is inconstant. Perception is inconstant. Fabrications are inconstant. Consciousness is inconstant. Form is not-self. Feeling is not-self. Perception is not-self. Fabrications are not-self. Consciousness is not-self. All fabrications are inconstant. All phenomena are not-self.' This, Aggivessana, is the way in which I discipline my disciples; this part of my instruction is generally presented to my disciples."

"A simile occurs to me, Master Gotama."

"Let it occur to you, Aggivessana."

"Just as any seeds that exhibit growth, increase, & proliferation, all do so in dependence on the earth; or just as any activities requiring strength that are done, all are done in dependence on the earth; in the same way, Master Gotama, an individual with form as self, taking a stance on form, produces merit or demerit. An individual with feeling as self… with perception as self… with fabrications as self… with consciousness as self, taking a stance on consciousness, produces merit or demerit."

"Then, Aggivessana, are you saying, 'Form is my self, feeling is my self, perception is my self, fabrications are my self, consciousness is my self'?"

"Yes, Master Gotama, I'm saying that 'Form is my self, feeling is my self, perception is my self, fabrications are my self, consciousness is my self.' As does this great multitude."[4]

"What does this great multitude have to do with you? Please focus just on your own assertion."

"Yes, Master Gotama, I'm saying that 'Form is my self, feeling is my self, perception is my self, fabrications are my self, consciousness is my self.'"

"Very well then, Aggivessana, I will cross-question you on this matter. Answer as you see fit. What do you think? Would a consecrated, noble-warrior king—such as King Pasenadi of Kosala or King Ajātasattu Vedehiputta of Magadha—wield the power in his own domain to execute those (he has) sentenced to be executed, to fine those (he has) sentenced to be fined, or to banish those (he has) sentenced to be banished?"

"Yes, Master Gotama, he would wield the power in his own domain to execute those (he has) sentenced to be executed, to fine those (he has) sentenced to be fined, or to banish those (he has) sentenced to be banished. Even these oligarchic groups, such as the Vajjians & Mallans, wield the power in their own domains to execute to execute those (they've) sentenced to be executed, to fine those (they've) sentenced to be fined, or to banish those (they've) sentenced to be banished,[5] to say nothing of a consecrated, noble-warrior king such as King Pasenadi of Kosala, or King Ajātasattu Vedehiputta of Magadha. He would wield it, and he would deserve to wield it."

"What do you think, Aggivessana? When you say, 'Form is my self,' do you wield power over that form: 'May my form be thus, may my form not be thus'?"

When this was said, Saccaka the Nigaṇṭha-son was silent.

A second time, the Blessed One said to Saccaka the Nigaṇṭha-son: "What do you think, Aggivessana? When you say, 'Form is my self,' do you wield power over that form: 'May my form be thus, may my form not be thus'?"

When this was said, Saccaka the Nigaṇṭha-son was silent a second time.

Then the Blessed One said to him, "Answer now, Aggivessana. This is not the time to be silent. When anyone doesn't answer when asked a legitimate question by the Tathāgata up to three times, his head splits into seven pieces right here."

Now on that occasion the spirit *[yakkha]* Vajirapāṇin [Thunderbolt-in-Hand], carrying an iron thunderbolt, was poised in the air above Saccaka the Nigaṇṭha-son, (thinking,) "If Saccaka the Nigaṇṭha-son doesn't answer when asked a legitimate question by the Blessed One up to three times, I will split his head into seven pieces right here."

The Blessed One saw the spirit Vajirapāṇin, as did Saccaka the Nigaṇṭha-son. So Saccaka—afraid, terrified, his hair standing on end—seeking shelter in the Blessed One, seeking a cave/asylum in the Blessed One, seeking refuge in the Blessed One—said to the Blessed One, "Let Master Gotama ask me. I will answer."

"What do you think, Aggivessana? When you say, 'Form is my self,' do you wield power over that form: 'May my form be thus, may my form not be thus'?"

"No, Master Gotama."

"Pay attention, Aggivessana, and answer (only) after having paid attention! What you said after isn't consistent with what you said before, nor is what you said before consistent with what you said after.

"What do you think, Aggivessana? When you say, 'Feeling is my self… Perception is my self… Fabrications are my self… Consciousness is my self,' do you wield power over that consciousness: 'May my consciousness be thus, may my consciousness not be thus'?"

"No, Master Gotama."

"Pay attention, Aggivessana, and answer (only) after having paid attention! What you said after isn't consistent with what you said before, nor is what you said before consistent with what you said after.

"What do you think, Aggivessana? Is form constant or inconstant?"

"Inconstant, Master Gotama."

"And is that which is inconstant easeful or stressful?"

"Stressful, Master Gotama."

"And is it fitting to regard what is inconstant, stressful, subject to change as: 'This is mine. This is my self. This is what I am'?"

"No, Master Gotama."

"…Is feeling constant or inconstant?"

"Inconstant, Master Gotama."…

"…Is perception constant or inconstant?"

"Inconstant, Master Gotama."…

"…Are fabrications constant or inconstant?"

"Inconstant, Master Gotama."…

"What do you think, Aggivessana? Is consciousness constant or inconstant?"

"Inconstant, Master Gotama."

"And is that which is inconstant easeful or stressful?"

"Stressful, Master Gotama."

"And is it fitting to regard what is inconstant, stressful, subject to change as: 'This is mine. This is my self. This is what I am'?"

"No, Master Gotama."

"What do you think, Aggivessana? When one adheres to stress, holds to stress, is attached to stress, and envisions of stress that 'This is mine; this is my self; this is what I am,' would he comprehend stress or dwell having totally destroyed stress?"

"How could that be, Master Gotama? No, Master Gotama."

"That being the case, Aggivessana, don't you adhere to stress, hold to stress, aren't you attached to stress, and don't you envision of stress that 'This is mine. This is my self. This is what I am'?"

"How could that not be the case, Master Gotama? Yes, Master Gotama."

"Suppose a man—in need of heartwood, seeking heartwood, wandering in search of heartwood—were to enter a forest taking a sharp ax. There he would see a large plantain trunk: straight, young, immature. He would cut it at the root and, having cut it at the root, cut off the crown. Having cut off the crown, he would unfurl the leaf sheaths. Unfurling the leaf sheaths, he wouldn't even find sapwood there, to say nothing of heartwood. In the same way, Aggivessana, when you are interrogated, rebuked, & pressed by me with regard to your own statement, you are empty, void, mistaken. But it was you who made this statement before the assembly in Vesālī: 'I see no contemplative or brahman, the head of an order, the head of a group, or even one who claims to be an arahant, rightly self-awakened, who—engaged in debate with me—would not shiver, quiver, shake, & break out in sweat under the armpits. Even if I were to engage a senseless stump in debate, it—engaged with me in debate—would shiver, quiver, & shake, to say nothing of a human being.' But now some drops of sweat coming out of your forehead, drenching your upper robe, are landing on the ground, whereas now I have no sweat on my body." And the Blessed One uncovered his golden-colored body to the assembly.

When this was said, Saccaka the Nigaṇṭha-son fell silent, abashed, sitting with his shoulders drooping, his head down, brooding, at a loss for words.

Then Dummukha [BadMouth] the Licchavi-son—sensing that Saccaka the Nigaṇṭha-son was silent, abashed, sitting with his shoulders drooping, his head down, brooding, at a loss for words—said to the Blessed One, "Lord, a simile has come to me."

"Let it come to you, Dummukha," the Blessed One said.

"Suppose, lord, that not far from a village or town was a pond. There in it was a crab. Then a number of boys & girls, leaving the village or town, would go to the pond and, on arrival, would go down to bathe in it. Taking the crab out of the water, they would place it on the ground. And whenever the crab extended a leg, the boys or girls would cut it off, break it, and smash it with sticks or stones right there, so that the crab—with all its legs cut off, broken, & smashed—would be unable to get back in the water as before. In the same way, whatever Saccaka the Nigaṇṭha-son's writhings, capers, & contortions, the Blessed One has cut them off, broken them, and smashed them all, so that Saccaka the Nigaṇṭha-son is now unable to approach the Blessed One again for the purpose of debate."

When this was said, Saccaka the Nigaṇṭha-son said to Dummukha the Licchavi-son, "Just you wait, Dummukha. Just you wait, Dummukha. You're a big-mouth, Dummukha.[6] We're not taking counsel with you. We're here taking counsel with Master Gotama." [Then, turning to the Buddha,] "Let that be, Master Gotama, our words & those of other ordinary contemplatives & brahmans—prattled prattling, as it were.

"Now, Master Gotama, to what extent is a disciple of Master Gotama one who carries out his message, carries out his instruction, one who has crossed over & beyond doubt, one with no more questioning, one who has gained fearlessness and dwells independent of others with regard to the Teacher's message?"

"There is the case, Aggivessana, where a disciple of mine sees with right discernment any form whatsoever—past, future, or present; internal or external; blatant or subtle; common or sublime; far or near: every form as it has come to be—as 'This is not mine. This is not my self. This is not what I am.'

"He sees with right discernment any feeling… any perception… any fabrications… any consciousness whatsoever—past, future, or present; internal or external; blatant or subtle; common or sublime; far or near: every consciousness as it has come to be—as 'This is not mine. This is not my self. This is not what I am.'

"It's to this extent, Aggivessana, that a disciple of mine is one who carries out my message, carries out my instruction, one who has crossed over & beyond doubt, one with no more questioning, one who has gained fearlessness and dwells independent of others with regard to the Teacher's message."

"And to what extent, Master Gotama, is a monk an arahant, one whose mental effluents are ended, who has reached fulfillment, done the task, laid down the burden, attained the true goal, laid to waste the fetter of becoming, and is released through right gnosis?"

"There is the case, Aggivessana, where a monk—having seen with right discernment any form whatsoever—past, future, or present; internal or external; blatant or subtle; common or sublime; far or near: every form as it has come to be—as 'This is not mine. This is not my self. This is not what I am' is, through lack of clinging/sustenance, released.

"Having seen with right discernment any feeling… any perception… any fabrications… any consciousness whatsoever—past, future, or present; internal or external; blatant or subtle; common or sublime; far or near: every consciousness as it has come to be—as 'This is not mine. This is not my self. This is not what I am,' he is, through lack of clinging/sustenance, released.

"It's to this extent, Aggivessana, that a monk is an arahant, one whose mental effluents are ended, who has reached fulfillment, done the task, laid down the burden, attained the true goal, laid to waste the fetter of becoming, and is released through right gnosis.

"One thus released is endowed with three unsurpassables: unsurpassable vision, unsurpassable practice, unsurpassable release. And a monk whose mind is thus released still honors, respects, reveres, & worships the Tathāgata (in this way): "Awakened, the Blessed One teaches the Dhamma for awakening. Tamed, the Blessed One teaches the Dhamma for taming. Tranquil, the Blessed One teaches the Dhamma for tranquility. Having crossed over, the Blessed One teaches the Dhamma for crossing over. Totally unbound, the Blessed One teaches the Dhamma for total unbinding."

When this was said, Saccaka the Nigaṇṭha-son said to the Blessed One, "It is we, Master Gotama, who were insolent, we who were reckless, in that we supposed that Master Gotama could be attacked statement by statement. For there might be safety for a person who has attacked a rutting elephant, but there is no safety for a person who has attacked Master Gotama. There might be safety for a person who has attacked a mass of fire, but there is no safety for a person who has attacked Master Gotama. There might be safety for a person who has attacked a fanged snake, a poisonous snake, but there is no safety for a person who has attacked Master Gotama. It is we, Master Gotama, who were insolent, we who were reckless, in that we supposed that Master Gotama could be attacked statement by statement.

"May Master Gotama, together with the Saṅgha of monks, acquiesce to my offer of tomorrow's meal."

The Blessed One acquiesced with silence.

Then Saccaka the Nigaṇṭha-son, sensing the Blessed One's acquiescence, addressed the Licchavis, "Listen, Master Licchavis. Gotama the contemplative is invited for tomorrow together with the Saṅgha of monks. Offer to me what you think would be proper for him."

Then, after the night had passed, the Licchavis offered to Saccaka the Nigaṇṭha-son a food offering of approximately five hundred oblation-dishes. Saccaka the Nigaṇṭha-son, after having exquisite staple & non-staple food prepared in his own monastery, announced the time to the Blessed One: "It's time, Master Gotama. The meal is ready."

So the Blessed One early in the morning adjusted his under robe and—carrying his bowl & outer robe—went together with the Saṅgha of monks to Saccaka the Nigaṇṭha-son's monastery. On arrival, he sat down on a seat laid out. Saccaka the Nigaṇṭha-son, with his own hand, served & satisfied the Saṅgha of monks headed by the Blessed One with exquisite staple & non-staple food. Then, when the Blessed One had eaten and had rinsed his bowl & hands, Saccaka the Nigaṇṭha-son, taking a lower seat, sat down to one side. As he was sitting there, he said to the Blessed One, "Master Gotama, may the merit and accoutrements of the merit of this gift be exclusively for the happiness of the donors."

"Aggivessana, whatever has come from (giving to) a recipient such as you—not without passion, not without aversion, not without delusion—that will be for the donors. Whatever has come from (giving to) a recipient such as me—without passion, without aversion, without delusion—that will be for you."

NOTES

1. In Pali, *paṇḍita-vādo,* "one who teaches the teaching of the wise." Like the sophists ("wisdom-ists") of Greece who were near contemporaries of the Buddha, Saccaka claimed to be wise, but his wisdom was largely a matter of debater's tricks. Thus it seems appropriate to adopt the Greek label for him.

2. One of the five brethren to whom the Buddha delivered his first sermon (SN 56:11). Ven. Assaji was also the person who taught Sāriputta the wanderer the brief gist of the Buddha's teaching that immediately inspired Sāriputta to attain the Dhamma eye. See Mv 1.23.1–10.

3. Aggivessana is Saccaka's clan name.

4. Saccaka is here attempting to appeal to the prejudices of his audience, a cheap debater's trick.

5. Again, Saccaka is trying to appeal to the vanity of his audience. He doesn't realize, however, that he is setting himself up for a trap. By tying his audience's vanity to the Buddha's analogy, he cannot later deny that the analogy is valid.

6. Following the Thai edition here, which reads, *"Āgamehi tvaṁ Dummukha. Āgamehi tvaṁ Dummukha. Mukharo'si tvaṁ Dummukha."* The Burmese edition here reads, "Just you wait, Dummukha. Just you wait, Dummukha." The Sri Lankan edition reads, "Just you wait, Dummukha. You're a big-mouth, Dummukha."

For more on the Buddha's approach to argument and debate, see *Skill in Questions,* chapters one and five.

36 The Longer Discourse to Saccaka

Mahā Saccaka Sutta

I have heard that on one occasion the Blessed One was staying near Vesālī at the Gabled Hall in the Great Forest. And on that occasion, early in the morning, he had adjusted his under robe and was carrying his bowl & outer robe, planning to enter Vesālī for alms.

Then Saccaka, a Nigaṇṭha [Jain], while walking and wandering around to exercise his legs, went to the Gabled Hall in the Great Forest. Ven. Ānanda saw him coming from afar and, on seeing him, said to the Blessed One, "Venerable sir, here comes Saccaka the Nigaṇṭha: a debater, a sophist, well-regarded by people at large. He is intent on the disparagement of the Buddha, the disparagement of the Dhamma, the disparagement of the Saṅgha. It would be good if the Blessed One would sit down for a moment, out of sympathy (for him)." So the Blessed One sat down on a prepared seat. Then Saccaka the Nigaṇṭha went to the Blessed One and, on arrival, exchanged courteous greetings with him. After an exchange of friendly greetings & courtesies, he sat to one side.

As he was sitting there he said to the Blessed One, "There are, Master Gotama, some contemplatives & brahmans who live committed to the development of the body but not to the development of the mind. They are touched by bodily painful feeling. It has happened in the past that when one (of them) was touched by bodily painful feeling, his thighs would grow rigid, his heart would burst, hot blood would gush from his mouth, he would go mad, out of his mind. His mind was thus subservient to his body and fell under the power of the body. Why was that? A lack of development of the mind.

"Then there are some contemplatives & brahmans who live committed to the development of the mind but not to the development of the body. They are touched by mental painful feeling. It has happened in the past that when one (of them) was touched by mental painful feeling, his thighs would grow rigid, his heart would burst, hot blood would gush from his mouth, he would go mad, out of his mind. His body was thus subservient to his mind and fell under the power of the mind. Why was that? A lack of development of the body. The thought has occurred to me that the disciples of

Gotama the contemplative live committed to the development of the mind but not to the development of the body."

"But what have you learned, Aggivessana, about the development of the body?"

"There are, for example, Nanda Vaccha, Kisa Saṅkicca, and Makkhali Gosāla. They are cloth-less[1] ascetics, rejecting conventions, licking their hands, not coming when called, not staying when asked. They don't consent to food brought to them or food dedicated to them or to an invitation to a meal. They accept nothing from the mouth of a pot or from the mouth of a bowl. They accept nothing from across a threshold, across a stick, across a pestle, from two eating together, from a pregnant woman, from a nursing woman, from a woman living with a man, from where it is announced that food is to be distributed, from where a dog is waiting or flies are buzzing. They take no fish or meat. They drink no liquor, wine, or fermented drink. They limit themselves to one house & one morsel a day, or two houses & two morsels... seven houses & seven morsels. They live on one saucerful a day, two... seven saucerfuls a day. They take food once a day, once every two days... once every seven days, and so on up to a fortnight, devoted to regulating their intake of food."

"But, Aggivessana, do they survive just on that?"

"No, Master Gotama. Sometimes they eat outstanding staple foods, chew on outstanding non-staple foods, taste outstanding delicacies, and drink outstanding drinks. They rescue the body & its strength, fortify it, and fatten it."

"What they earlier abandoned, Aggivessana, they later gather up. This is how there is decrease & increase of the body. But what have you learned, Aggivessana, about the development of the mind?"

Yet Saccaka the Nigaṇṭha, when asked by the Blessed One about the development of the mind, was unable to respond.

Then the Blessed One said to Saccaka, "The ones you described just now as developed in the development of the body: That is not legitimate development of the body in the discipline of the noble ones. As you don't understand the development of the body, from where would you understand the development of the mind? Nevertheless, as to how one is undeveloped in body and undeveloped in mind, and developed in body and developed in mind, listen and pay close attention. I will speak."

"As you say, Master Gotama," Saccaka responded.

The Blessed One said, "And how is one undeveloped in body and undeveloped in mind? There is the case where a pleasant feeling arises in an uneducated run-of-the-mill person. On being touched by the pleasant feeling, he becomes impassioned with pleasure, and is reduced to being impassioned with pleasure. His pleasant feeling ceases. With the cessation of the pleasant feeling there arises a painful feeling. On being touched with the painful feeling, he sorrows, grieves, & laments, beats his breast, becomes distraught. When that pleasant feeling had arisen in him, it invaded his mind and remained because of his lack of development of the body. When that painful feeling had arisen in him, it invaded his mind and remained because of his lack of development of the mind. This is how one is undeveloped in body and undeveloped in mind.

"And how is one developed in body and developed in mind? There is the case where a pleasant feeling arises in a well-educated disciple of the noble ones. On being touched by the pleasant feeling, he doesn't become impassioned with pleasure, and is not reduced to being impassioned with pleasure. His pleasant feeling ceases. With the cessation of the pleasant feeling there arises a painful feeling. On being touched with the painful feeling, he doesn't sorrow, grieve, or lament, beat his breast or become distraught. When that pleasant feeling had arisen in him, it didn't invade his mind and remain because of his development of the body. When that painful feeling had arisen in him, it didn't invade his mind and remain because of his development of the mind. This is how one is developed in body and developed in mind."

"I have confidence in Master Gotama that Master Gotama is developed in body and developed in mind."

"Well, Aggivessana, you are certainly being rude and presumptuously speaking your words, but nevertheless I will respond to you.[2] Ever since I shaved my hair & beard, put on the ochre robe, and went forth from the home life into homelessness, it has not been possible for a pleasant feeling that has arisen to invade my mind and remain, or for a painful feeling that has arisen to invade my mind and remain."

"But perhaps there has never arisen in Master Gotama the sort of pleasant feeling that, having arisen, would invade the mind and remain. Perhaps there has never arisen in Master Gotama the sort of painful feeling that, having arisen, would invade the mind and remain."[3]

"Why wouldn't it have, Aggivessana? Before my self-awakening, when I was still just an unawakened Bodhisatta, the thought occurred to me: 'Household life is confining, a dusty path. Life gone forth is the open air. It isn't easy, living in a home, to practice the holy life totally perfect, totally pure, a polished shell. What if I, having shaved off my hair & beard and putting on the ochre robe, were to go forth from the household life into homelessness?'

"So at a later time, when I was still young, black-haired, endowed with the blessings of youth in the first stage of life, having shaved off my hair & beard—though my parents wished otherwise and were grieving with tears on their faces—I put on the ochre robe and went forth from the home life into homelessness.

"Having gone forth in search of what might be skillful, seeking the unexcelled state of sublime peace, I went to Āḷāra Kālāma and, on arrival, said to him: 'Friend Kālāma, I want to practice in this Dhamma & discipline.'

"When this was said, he replied to me, 'You may stay here, my friend. This Dhamma is such that an observant person can soon enter & dwell in his own teacher's knowledge, having realized it for himself through direct knowledge.'

"It wasn't long before I quickly learned that Dhamma. As far as mere lip-reciting & repetition, I could speak the words of knowledge, the words of the elders, and I could affirm that I knew & saw—I, along with others.

"I thought: 'It isn't through mere conviction alone that Āḷāra Kālāma declares, "I have entered & dwell in this Dhamma, having realized it for myself through direct knowledge." Certainly he dwells knowing & seeing this Dhamma.' So I went to him and said, 'To what extent do you declare that you have entered & dwell in this Dhamma?' When this was said, he declared the dimension of nothingness.

"I thought: 'Not only does Āḷāra Kālāma have conviction, persistence, mindfulness, concentration, & discernment. I, too, have conviction, persistence, mindfulness, concentration, & discernment. What if I were to endeavor to realize for myself the Dhamma that Āḷāra Kālāma declares he has entered & dwells in, having realized it for himself through direct knowledge.' So it was not long before I quickly entered & dwelled in that Dhamma, having realized it for myself through direct knowledge. I went to him and said, 'Friend Kālāma, is this the extent to which you have entered & dwell in this Dhamma, having realized it for yourself through direct knowledge?'

"'Yes, my friend....'

"'This, friend, is the extent to which I, too, have entered & dwell in this Dhamma, having realized it for myself through direct knowledge.'

"'It is a gain for us, my friend, a great gain for us, that we have such a companion in the holy life. So the Dhamma I declare I have entered & dwell in, having realized it for myself through direct knowledge, is the Dhamma you declare you have entered & dwell in, having realized it for yourself through direct knowledge. And the Dhamma you declare you have entered & dwell in, having realized it for yourself through direct knowledge, is the Dhamma I declare I have entered & dwell in, having realized it for myself through direct knowledge. The Dhamma I know is the Dhamma you know; the Dhamma you know is the Dhamma I know. As I am, so are you; as you are, so am I. Come friend, let us now lead this community together.'

"In this way did Āḷāra Kālāma, my teacher, place me, his pupil, on the same level with himself and pay me great honor. But the thought occurred to me, 'This Dhamma leads not to disenchantment, to dispassion, to cessation, to stilling, to direct knowledge, to self-awakening, nor to unbinding, but only to reappearance in the dimension of nothingness.' So, dissatisfied with that Dhamma, I left.

"In search of what might be skillful, seeking the unexcelled state of sublime peace, I went to Uddaka Rāmaputta and, on arrival, said to him: 'Friend Uddaka, I want to practice in this Dhamma & discipline.'

"When this was said, he replied to me, 'You may stay here, my friend. This doctrine is such that an observant person can soon enter & dwell in his own teacher's knowledge, having realized it for himself through direct knowledge.'

"It wasn't long before I quickly learned that Dhamma. As far as mere lip-reciting & repetition, I could speak the words of knowledge, the words of the elders, and I could affirm that I knew & saw—I, along with others.

"I thought: 'It wasn't through mere conviction alone that Rāma declared, "I have entered & dwell in this Dhamma, having realized it for myself through direct knowledge." Certainly he dwelled knowing & seeing this Dhamma.' So I went to Uddaka and said, 'To what extent did Rāma declare that he had entered & dwelled in this Dhamma?' When this was said, Uddaka declared the dimension of neither perception nor non-perception.

"I thought: 'Not only did Rāma have conviction, persistence, mindfulness, concentration, & discernment. I, too, have conviction, persistence, mindfulness, concentration, & discernment. What if I were to endeavor to realize for myself the Dhamma that Rāma declared he entered & dwelled in, having realized it for himself through direct knowledge.' So it was not long before I quickly entered & dwelled in that Dhamma, having realized it for myself through direct knowledge. I went to Uddaka and said, 'Friend

Uddaka, is this the extent to which Rāma entered & dwelled in this Dhamma, having realized it for himself through direct knowledge?'

"'Yes, my friend....'

"'This, friend, is the extent to which I, too, have entered & dwell in this Dhamma, having realized it for myself through direct knowledge.'

"'It is a gain for us, my friend, a great gain for us, that we have such a companion in the holy life. So the Dhamma Rāma declared he entered & dwelled in, having realized it for himself through direct knowledge, is the Dhamma you declare you have entered & dwell in, having realized it for yourself through direct knowledge. And the Dhamma you declare you have entered & dwell in, having realized it for yourself through direct knowledge, is the Dhamma Rāma declared he entered & dwelled in, having realized it for himself through direct knowledge. The Dhamma he knew is the Dhamma you know; the Dhamma you know is the Dhamma he knew. As he was, so are you; as you are, so was he. Come friend, lead this community.'

"In this way did Uddaka Rāmaputta, my companion in the holy life, place me in the position of teacher and pay me great honor. But the thought occurred to me, 'This Dhamma leads not to disenchantment, to dispassion, to cessation, to stilling, to direct knowledge, to self-awakening, nor to unbinding, but only to reappearance in the dimension of neither perception nor non-perception.' So, dissatisfied with that Dhamma, I left.

"In search of what might be skillful, seeking the unexcelled state of sublime peace, I wandered by stages in the Magadhan country and came to the military town of Uruvelā. There I saw some delightful countryside, with an inspiring forest grove, a clear-flowing river with fine, delightful banks, and villages for alms-going on all sides. The thought occurred to me: 'How delightful is this countryside, with its inspiring forest grove, clear-flowing river with fine, delightful banks, and villages for alms-going on all sides. This is just right for the striving of a clansman intent on striving.' So I sat down right there, thinking, 'This is just right for striving.'

"Then these three similes—spontaneous, never before heard—appeared to me. Suppose there were a wet, sappy piece of timber lying in the water, and a man were to come along with an upper fire-stick, thinking, 'I'll produce fire. I'll make heat appear.' Now what do you think? Would he be able to produce fire and make heat appear by rubbing the upper fire-stick in the wet, sappy timber lying in the water?"

"No, Master Gotama. Why is that? Because the timber is wet & sappy, and besides it is lying in the water. Eventually the man would reap only his share of weariness & disappointment."

"So it is with any contemplative or brahman who does not live withdrawn from sensuality in body & mind, and whose desire, infatuation, urge, thirst, & fever for sensuality is not relinquished & stilled within him: Whether or not he feels painful, racking, piercing feelings due to his striving (for awakening), he is incapable of knowledge, vision, & unexcelled self-awakening. This was the first simile—spontaneous, never before heard—that appeared to me.

"Then a second simile—spontaneous, never before heard—appeared to me. Suppose there were a wet, sappy piece of timber lying on land far from water, and a man were to come along with an upper fire-stick, thinking, 'I'll produce fire. I'll make heat appear.' Now what do you think? Would he be able to produce fire and make heat appear by rubbing the upper fire-stick in the wet, sappy timber lying on land far from water?"

"No, Master Gotama. Why is that? Because the timber is wet & sappy, even though it is lying on land far from water. Eventually the man would reap only his share of weariness & disappointment."

"So it is with any contemplative or brahman who lives withdrawn from sensuality in body only, but whose desire, infatuation, urge, thirst, & fever for sensuality is not relinquished & stilled within him: Whether or not he feels painful, racking, piercing feelings due to his striving, he is incapable of knowledge, vision, & unexcelled self-awakening. This was the second simile—spontaneous, never before heard—that appeared to me.

"Then a third simile—spontaneous, never before heard—appeared to me. Suppose there were a dry, sapless piece of timber lying on land far from water, and a man were to come along with an upper fire-stick, thinking, 'I'll produce fire. I'll make heat appear.' Now what do you think? Would he be able to produce fire and make heat appear by rubbing the upper fire-stick in the dry, sapless timber lying on land?"

"Yes, Master Gotama. Why is that? Because the timber is dry & sapless, and besides it is lying on land far from water."

"So it is with any contemplative or brahman who lives withdrawn from sensuality in body & mind, and whose desire, infatuation, urge, thirst, & fever for sensuality is relinquished & stilled within him: Whether or not he feels painful, racking, piercing feelings due to his striving, he is capable of knowledge, vision, & unexcelled self-awakening. This was the third simile—spontaneous, never before heard—that appeared to me.

"I thought: 'What if I, clenching my teeth and pressing my tongue against the roof of my mouth, were to beat down, constrain, & crush my mind with my awareness?' So, clenching my teeth and pressing my tongue against the roof of my mouth, I beat down, constrained, & crushed my mind with my awareness. Just as a strong man, seizing a weaker man by the head or the throat or the shoulders, would beat him down, constrain, & crush him, in the same way I beat down, constrained, & crushed my mind with my awareness. As I did so, sweat poured from my armpits. And although tireless persistence was aroused in me, and unmuddled mindfulness established, my body was aroused & uncalm because of the painful exertion. But the painful feeling that arose in this way did not invade my mind or remain.

"I thought: 'What if I were to become absorbed in the trance of non-breathing?' So I stopped the in-breaths & out-breaths in my nose & mouth. As I did so, there was a loud roaring of winds coming out my earholes, just like the loud roar of winds coming out of a smith's bellows.... So I stopped the in-breaths & out-breaths in my nose & mouth & ears. As I did so, extreme forces sliced through my head, just as if a strong man were slicing my head open with a sharp sword.... Extreme pains arose in my head, just as if a strong man were tightening a turban made of tough leather straps around my head.... Extreme forces carved up my stomach cavity, just as if a butcher or his apprentice were to carve up the stomach cavity of an ox.... There was an extreme burning in my body, just as if two strong men, grabbing a weaker man by the arms, were to roast & broil him over a pit of hot embers. And although tireless persistence was aroused in me, and unmuddled mindfulness established, my body was aroused & uncalm because of the painful exertion. But the painful feeling that arose in this way did not invade my mind or remain.

"Devas, on seeing me, said, 'Gotama the contemplative is dead.' Other devas said, 'He isn't dead, he's dying.' Others said, 'He's neither dead nor dying, he's an arahant, for this is the way arahants live.'

"I thought: 'What if I were to practice going altogether without food?' Then devas came to me and said, 'Dear sir, please don't practice going altogether without food. If you go altogether without food, we'll infuse divine nourishment in through your pores, and you will survive on that.' I thought, 'If I were to claim to be completely fasting while these devas are infusing divine nourishment in through my pores, I would be lying.' So I dismissed them, saying, 'Enough.'

"I thought: 'What if I were to take only a little food at a time, only a handful at a time of bean soup, lentil soup, vetch soup, or pea soup?' So I took only a little food at a time, only a handful at a time of bean soup, lentil soup, vetch soup, or pea soup. My body became extremely emaciated. Simply from my eating so little, my limbs became like the jointed segments of vine stems or bamboo stems.... My backside became like a camel's hoof.... My spine stood out like a string of beads.... My ribs jutted out like the jutting rafters of an old, run-down barn.... The gleam of my eyes appeared to be sunk deep in my eye sockets like the gleam of water deep in a well.... My scalp shriveled & withered like a green bitter gourd, shriveled & withered in the heat & the wind.... The skin of my belly became so stuck to my spine that when I thought of touching my belly, I grabbed hold of my spine as well; and when I thought of touching my spine, I grabbed hold of the skin of my belly as well.... If I urinated or defecated, I fell over on my face right there.... Simply from my eating so little, if I tried to ease my body by rubbing my limbs with my hands, the hair—rotted at its roots—fell from my body as I rubbed, simply from eating so little.

"People on seeing me would say, 'Gotama the contemplative is black. Other people would say, 'Gotama the contemplative isn't black, he's brown.' Others would say, 'Gotama the contemplative is neither black nor brown, he's golden-skinned.' So much had the clear, bright color of my skin deteriorated, simply from eating so little.

"I thought: 'Whatever contemplatives or brahmans in the past have felt painful, racking, piercing feelings due to their striving, this is the utmost. None have been greater than this. Whatever contemplatives or brahmans in the future will feel painful, racking, piercing feelings due to their striving, this is the utmost. None will be greater than this. Whatever contemplatives or brahmans in the present are feeling painful, racking, piercing feelings due to their striving, this is the utmost. None is greater than this. But with this racking practice of austerities I haven't attained any superior human state, any distinction in knowledge or vision worthy of the noble ones. Could there be another path to awakening?'

"I thought: 'I recall once, when my father the Sakyan was working, and I was sitting in the cool shade of a rose-apple tree, then—quite secluded from sensuality, secluded from unskillful qualities—I entered & remained in the first jhāna: rapture & pleasure born of seclusion, accompanied by directed thought & evaluation. Could that be the path to awakening?' Then there was the consciousness following on that memory: 'That is the path to awakening.' I thought: 'So why am I afraid of that pleasure that has nothing to do with sensuality, nothing to do with unskillful qualities?' I thought: 'I am no longer afraid of that pleasure that has nothing to do with sensuality, nothing to do with unskillful qualities, but that pleasure is not easy to achieve with a body so extremely emaciated. What if I were to take some solid food: some rice & porridge?' So I took some solid food: some rice & porridge. Now five monks had been attending on me, thinking, 'If Gotama, our contemplative, achieves some higher state, he will tell us.' But when they saw me taking some solid food—some rice & porridge—they were disgusted and left me, thinking, 'Gotama the contemplative is living luxuriously. He has abandoned his exertion and is backsliding into abundance.'

"So when I had taken solid food and regained strength, then—quite secluded from sensuality, secluded from unskillful qualities, I entered & remained in the first jhāna: rapture & pleasure born of seclusion, accompanied by directed thought & evaluation. But the pleasant feeling that arose in this way did not invade my mind or remain. With the stilling of directed thoughts & evaluations, I entered & remained in the second jhāna: rapture & pleasure born of concentration, unification of awareness free from directed thought & evaluation—internal assurance. But the pleasant feeling that arose in this way did not invade my mind or remain. With the fading of rapture I remained equanimous, mindful, & alert, and sensed pleasure with the body. I entered & remained in the third jhāna, of which the noble ones declare, 'Equanimous & mindful, he has a pleasant abiding.' But the pleasant feeling that arose in this way did not invade my mind or remain. With the abandoning of pleasure & pain—as with the earlier disappearance of elation & distress—I entered & remained in the fourth jhāna: purity of equanimity & mindfulness, neither pleasure nor pain. But the pleasant feeling that arose in this way did not invade my mind or remain.

"When the mind was thus concentrated, purified, bright, unblemished, rid of defilement, pliant, malleable, steady, & attained to imperturbability, I directed it to the knowledge of recollecting my past lives. I recollected my manifold past lives, i.e., one birth, two… five, ten… fifty, a hundred, a thousand, a hundred thousand, many eons of cosmic contraction, many eons of cosmic expansion, many eons of cosmic contraction & expansion: 'There I had such a name, belonged to such a clan, had such an appearance. Such was my food, such my experience of pleasure & pain, such the end of my life. Passing away from that state, I re-arose there. There too I had such a name, belonged to such a clan, had such an appearance.

Such was my food, such my experience of pleasure & pain, such the end of my life. Passing away from that state, I re-arose here.' Thus I recollected my manifold past lives in their modes & details.

"This was the first knowledge I attained in the first watch of the night. Ignorance was destroyed; knowledge arose; darkness was destroyed; light arose—as happens in one who is heedful, ardent, & resolute. But the pleasant feeling that arose in this way did not invade my mind or remain.

"When the mind was thus concentrated, purified, bright, unblemished, rid of defilement, pliant, malleable, steady, & attained to imperturbability, I directed it to the knowledge of the passing away & reappearance of beings. I saw—by means of the divine eye, purified & surpassing the human—beings passing away & re-appearing, and I discerned how they are inferior & superior, beautiful & ugly, fortunate & unfortunate in accordance with their kamma: 'These beings—who were endowed with bad conduct of body, speech, & mind, who reviled the noble ones, held wrong views and undertook actions under the influence of wrong views—with the break-up of the body, after death, have re-appeared in a plane of deprivation, a bad destination, a lower realm, hell. But these beings—who were endowed with good conduct of body, speech & mind, who did not revile the noble ones, who held right views and undertook actions under the influence of right views—with the break-up of the body, after death, have re-appeared in a good destinations, a heavenly world.' Thus—by means of the divine eye, purified & surpassing the human—I saw beings passing away & re-appearing, and I discerned how they are inferior & superior, beautiful & ugly, fortunate & unfortunate in accordance with their kamma.

"This was the second knowledge I attained in the second watch of the night. Ignorance was destroyed; knowledge arose; darkness was destroyed; light arose—as happens in one who is heedful, ardent, & resolute. But the pleasant feeling that arose in this way did not invade my mind or remain.

"When the mind was thus concentrated, purified, bright, unblemished, rid of defilement, pliant, malleable, steady, & attained to imperturbability, I directed it to the knowledge of the ending of the mental effluents. I discerned, as it had come to be, that 'This is stress... This is the origination of stress... This is the cessation of stress... This is the way leading to the cessation of stress... These are effluents... This is the origination of effluents... This is the cessation of effluents... This is the way leading to the cessation of effluents.' My heart, thus knowing, thus seeing, was released from the effluent of sensuality, released from the effluent of becoming, released from the effluent of ignorance. With release, there was the knowledge, 'Released.' I discerned that 'Birth is ended, the holy life fulfilled, the task done. There is nothing further for this world.'

"This was the third knowledge I attained in the third watch of the night. Ignorance was destroyed; knowledge arose; darkness was destroyed; light arose—as happens in one who is heedful, ardent, & resolute. But the pleasant feeling that arose in this way did not invade my mind or remain.

"I recall having taught the Dhamma to an assembly of many hundreds, and yet each one of them assumes of me, 'Gotama the contemplative is teaching the Dhamma attacking just me,' but it shouldn't be seen in that way. The Tathāgata rightly teaches them the Dhamma simply for the purpose of giving knowledge. At the end of that very talk I steady the mind inwardly, settle it, concentrate it, and unify it in the same theme of concentration as before, in which I almost constantly dwell."

"That is credible for the Master Gotama, as would be the case for one who is worthy & rightly self-awakened. But does the Master Gotama recall sleeping during the day?"

"I recall, Aggivessana, in the last month of the hot season, after the meal, returning from my almsround, setting out my outer robe folded in four, lying down on my right side, and falling asleep while mindful & alert."

"There are some contemplatives & brahmans, Master Gotama, who would call that dwelling in delusion."

"It's not to that extent that one is deluded or undeluded, Aggivessana. As to how one is deluded or undeluded, listen and pay close attention. I will speak."

"As you say, Master Gotama," Saccaka responded.

The Blessed One said: "In whomever the effluents that defile, that lead to renewed becoming, that give trouble, that ripen in stress, and lead to future birth, aging, & death are not abandoned: Him I call deluded. For it is from not abandoning the effluents that one is deluded. In whomever the effluents that defile, that lead to renewed becoming, that give trouble, that ripen in stress, and lead to future birth, aging, & death *are* abandoned: Him I call undeluded. For it is from abandoning the effluents that one is undeluded. In the Tathāgata, Aggivessana, the effluents that defile, that lead to renewed becoming, that give trouble, that ripen in stress, and lead to future birth, aging, & death have been abandoned, their root destroyed, made like a palmyra stump, deprived of the conditions of development, not destined for future arising.

Just as a palmyra cut off at the crown is incapable of further growth, in the same way in the Tathāgata the effluents that defile, that lead to renewed becoming, that give trouble, that ripen in stress, and lead to future birth, aging, & death have been abandoned, their root destroyed, made like a palmyra stump, deprived of the conditions of development, not destined for future arising."

When this was said, Saccaka the Nigaṇṭha said to the Blessed One: "It's amazing, Master Gotama. It's astounding—that when Master Gotama is addressed rudely again & again, is assailed by presumptuous courses of speech, the color of his skin brightens, the color of his face clears, as would be the case with one who is worthy & rightly self-awakened. I recall engaging Pūraṇa Kassapa in debate. He, when engaged in debate by me, spoke evasively and led the discussion astray, displayed irritation, aversion, & peevishness. But when Master Gotama is addressed rudely again & again, is assailed by presumptuous courses of speech, the color of his skin brightens, the color of his face clears, as would be the case with one who is worthy & rightly self-awakened. I recall engaging Makkhali Gosāla... Ajita Kesakambalin... Pakudha Kaccāyana... Sañjaya Velaṭṭhaputta... Nigaṇṭha Nāṭaputta in debate. He, when engaged in debate by me, spoke evasively and led the discussion astray, displayed irritation, aversion, & peevishness. But when Master Gotama is addressed rudely again & again, is assailed by presumptuous courses of speech, the color of his skin brightens, the color of his face clears, as would be the case with one who is worthy & rightly self-awakened.

"And now, Master Gotama, I am going. Many are my duties, many my responsibilities."

"Then do, Aggivessana, what you think it is now time to do."

So Saccaka the Nigaṇṭha, delighting in & approving of the Blessed One's words, got up from his seat and left.[4]

NOTES

1. *Acelaka,* sometimes translated as "naked." However, the description of *acelaka* ascetics in MN 45 shows that they might wear garments made out of items other than cloth, such as tree bark, antelope hide, strips of antelope hide, kusa-grass garments, bark garments, wood-shaving garments, head-hair garments, animal wool, or owl's wings.

2. In other words, Saccaka has been impolite not only in asking challenging personal questions about the Buddha, but also excessively familiar in claiming to know about the Buddha's personal attainments, even though his claim sounds like praise. For other cases in which what

sounds like praise is criticized for being presumptuous, see MN 127, AN 3:61 (AN 3:60 in the PTS numbering), and AN 4:35.

3. Saccaka is here implying that the reason the Buddha's mind has not been invaded by pleasant or painful feelings has nothing to do with any special quality of the Buddha's mind. Instead, it's because potentially invasive feelings simply have never arisen in him. This paragraph is mistranslated in both MLS and MLDB.

4. The suttas do not record what happened to Saccaka after this conversation. The Commentary claims that he was reborn many years later in Sri Lanka, where he became an arahant.

See also: MN 4; MN 19; MN 26; SN 36:7; SN 42:7; SN 52:10; AN 3:39; AN 4:252; AN 5:79

38 The Greater Craving-Destruction Discourse

Mahā Taṇhāsaṅkhaya Sutta

INTRODUCTION

This sutta teaches how to understand the relationship of consciousness to rebirth in a way that helps put an end to rebirth.

Although the Buddha never used any word corresponding to "rebirth" in his teachings, he did describe birth as a process following on death again and again as long as the appropriate conditions are present. In other words, even though he didn't use the word "rebirth," his teachings on birth are teachings on repeated birth: how it happens, how it inherently involves suffering and stress, and how it can be brought to an end.

The idea that death can be followed by birth was not universally accepted in India in the Buddha's time. As DN 1, DN 2, and MN 102 show, some prominent contemplative schools actively rejected the idea of rebirth while others affirmed it. So when the Buddha taught rebirth, he wasn't simply following an unexamined cultural assumption. He was consciously taking a stand on one of the controversial issues of his time. However, his explanation of rebirth differed from other schools on both sides of the issue in that he avoided the question of whether or not there's a "what" that gets reborn, or if there is a "what," what it is (SN 12:12; SN 12:35). He also discouraged such speculations as, "If I take rebirth, what was I in the past, and what will I be in the future?" (MN 2)

He put all these questions aside because they interfered with the path of practice leading to the end of suffering. Instead, he focused on the process of how birth happens, because the process involves factors that are immediately apparent to one's awareness throughout life and lie enough under one's control to turn them toward the ending of birth. An understanding of the process as process—and in particular, as an example of the process of dependent co-arising—can actually contribute to the end to suffering, because it gives guidance in how to apply the tasks appropriate for the four noble truths to all the factors in the process leading up to birth.

One of the salient features of dependent co-arising is its lack of outside context. In other words, it avoids any reference to the presence or absence of a self around or a world behind the processes it describes. This allows one to focus directly on the factors of the process as factors, parts of a causal chain. And this, in turn, makes it easier to notice which factors—such as ignorance—cause suffering and should thus be abandoned; which ones—such as attention and intention—can be converted to the path to the end of suffering, and so should be developed before they, too, are abandoned; and which ones—such as clinging and becoming—constitute suffering, and so should be comprehended to the point of disenchantment and dispassion, leading to release.

This sutta concerns a monk—Sāti, the Fisherman's Son—who refuses to heed the Buddha's care in treating all the elements of the process of wandering on from birth to birth as processes. Sāti states that, in his understanding of the Buddha's teachings, consciousness is the "what" that does the wandering on. His fellow monks and then the Buddha treat him and his erroneous view in a way that parallels the way they treat Ariṭṭha Formerly-of-the-Vulture-Killers in MN 22. First the narrator notes that the view is not merely wrong, but actually evil and pernicious: To adopt it would be to place an obstacle in one's path. The monks try, unsuccessfully, to dissuade Sāti from his view, after which they report the case to the Buddha. The Buddha calls Sāti into his presence, and after ascertaining that Sāti will not abandon his view even when reprimanded by the Buddha himself, he abandons Sāti as too recalcitrant to teach, and turns to cross-question the monks as to the relevant right view of how consciousness functions in the process leading to repeated birth.

The Buddha's treatment of Sāti might seem harsh, but he is actually acting out of compassion for the monks in the assembly, in case any of them might be swayed by Sāti's position. Seeing Sāti as a lost cause, the Buddha doesn't want this lost cause to cause further losses among the other monks. We have to remember that during the Buddha's lifetime there were no written accounts of his teachings; the monks and nuns all had to rely on their memory of what they had heard directly from him or through word-of-mouth from fellow members of the Saṅgha. Thus the Buddha saw the need to establish orthodoxy whenever a member of the Saṅgha was espousing false interpretations of his teaching.

Because Sāti's evil view deals with issues that are much more complex than those touched on in Ariṭṭha's, the Buddha's cross-questioning of the monks here is correspondingly longer and more complex than in MN 22. However, the complexity can be comprehended by keeping in mind that, essentially, the cross-questioning aims at accomplishing two things at once: In providing a correct understanding of consciousness as a conditioned phenomenon, it also shows why the sort of question Sāti was trying to answer is ill-conceived.

The first part of the cross-questioning treats the conditioned nature of consciousness as a process in the context of two frameworks: (1) the standard description of the factors of dependent co-arising, and (2) the four nutriments of consciousness.

Following the pattern of dependent co-arising, the Buddha first classifies consciousness in terms of the way it arises in dependence on the six sense-media. This analysis points to the way consciousness functions as a sub-factor under the factor of contact in dependent co-arising.

> *"It's in dependence on a pair that consciousness comes into play. And how does consciousness come into play in dependence on a pair? In dependence on the eye & forms there arises eye-consciousness. The eye is inconstant, changeable, of a nature to become otherwise. Forms are inconstant, changeable, of a nature to become otherwise. Thus this pair is both wavering & fluctuating—inconstant, changeable, of a nature to become otherwise.*
>
> *"Eye-consciousness is inconstant, changeable, of a nature to become otherwise. Whatever is the cause, the requisite condition, for the arising of eye-consciousness, that is inconstant, changeable, of a nature to become otherwise. Having arisen in dependence on an inconstant factor, how could eye-consciousness be constant?*
>
> *"The coming together, the meeting, the convergence of these three phenomena is eye-contact. [Similarly with ear-, nose-, tongue-, body-, and intellect-consciousness.]" — SN 35:93*

The discussion then switches to consciousness as dependent on four types of nutriment: physical food, contact, intellectual intention, and consciousness itself. Here the sutta focuses on the need—in practice—to see this dependence as it actually occurs, and on the need to use this view for the proper purpose. As other passages in the Canon point out, the purpose of all Dhamma teachings is to induce the disenchantment/distaste for the nutriment that will allow for release.

> *"For a monk practicing the Dhamma in accordance with the Dhamma, this is what accords with the Dhamma: that he keep cultivating disenchantment/distaste with regard to form… feeling… perception… fabrications… consciousness. As he keeps cultivating disenchantment/distaste with regard to form… feeling… perception… fabrications… consciousness, he comprehends form… feeling… perception… fabrications… consciousness. As he comprehends form… feeling… perception… fabrications… consciousness, he is totally released from form… feeling… perception… fabrications… consciousness. He is totally released from sorrows, lamentations, pains, distresses, &*

despairs. He is totally released, I tell you, from suffering & stress." — *SN 22:39*

"Just as the ocean has a single taste—that of salt—in the same way, this Dhamma-Vinaya has a single taste: that of release." — *Ud 5:5*

In other words, the ability of the monks to give, in unison, the right answers to the Buddha's questions does not fulfill the teaching's purpose. The right answers are meant to be used as tools to induce a sense of disenchantment/distaste for continued feeding on the processes leading to suffering. This sense of disenchantment/distaste is what leads to release.

The reference to the raft analogy here is another point on which this sutta parallels MN 22, in which the monks also give correct answers in unison to the Buddha's questions. Perhaps the reason for why the raft analogy is cited in both suttas is that it was seen as a corrective for the sort of complacency that can come when one can recite with others an orthodox view.

At any rate, the discussion of consciousness in the framework of nutriment is then tied into the discussion of dependent co-arising through the fact that nutriment is dependent on craving. This places nutriment in the position of clinging/sustenance in dependent co-arising—as dependent on craving, and acting as a condition for becoming. This placement is affirmed by passages elsewhere in the Canon that speak of consciousness plus its nutriment as among the sub-factors providing the conditions for further becoming:

"Kamma is the field, consciousness the seed, and craving the moisture. The consciousness of living beings hindered by ignorance & fettered by craving is established in/tuned to a lower property… a middling property… a refined property. Thus there is the production of renewed becoming in the future. This is how there is becoming." — *AN 3:76*

"Like the earth property, monks, is how the four standing-spots for consciousness [the properties of form, feeling, perception, and fabrications] should be seen. Like the liquid property is how delight & passion should be seen. Like the five types of propagation [through roots, stems, joints, cuttings, & seeds] is how consciousness together with its nutriment should be seen." — *SN 22:54*

Given that consciousness also functions at a point in dependent co-arising prior to sensory contact—as following on fabrication and preceding name-and-form—it thus plays a role at three stages in the process: as a factor following on fabrication, as a sub-factor of contact, and as a sub-factor of clinging.

The remainder of the Buddha's cross-questioning of the monks further explores the framework of dependent co-arising, arriving at the conclusion that a person thus trained in understanding dependent co-arising would no longer be interested in pursuing questions of identity and existence—such as, "Am I?" "Am I not?" "What am I?" "What was I?" "What will I be?" This is because, as MN 2 points out, such questions are instances of inappropriate attention; and as SN 12:2 points out, the framework of dependent co-arising classes inappropriate attention under the factor of "name" as a cause of suffering. Thus the discussion arrives at the reasons why the Buddha was so careful to put the sort of question asked and answered by Sāti aside.

The sutta then turns to the path of practice by which an understanding of dependent co-arising can gain the power and focus needed to put an end to suffering. It begins with an account of birth, noting that the birth of a human being requires not only that the parents have intercourse when the mother is in her season, but also that a "gandhabba" is present. Usually in the Canon, the term gandhabba means a being on the lowest level of the celestial devas—devas who are often represented as obsessed with lust. However, the Commentary notes that gandhabba in this context means a being whose kamma enables it to take birth on that occasion, an interpretation supported by a discussion in MN 93.

By introducing a being into the discussion, the Buddha might be suspected of introducing a "what" into his discussion of birth. However, on the level of dependent co-arising, the Buddha did not treat the concept of a being as a "what." His definition of a "being" shows that he recommended that it, too, be regarded as a process:

> *As he was sitting there, Ven. Rādha said to the Blessed One: "'A being,' lord. 'A being,' it's said. To what extent is one said to be 'a being'?"*
>
> *"Any desire, passion, delight, or craving for form, Rādha: When one is caught up [satta] there, tied up [visatta] there, one is said to be 'a being [satta].'*
>
> *"Any desire, passion, delight, or craving for feeling… perception… fabrications…*
>
> *"Any desire, passion, delight, or craving for consciousness, Rādha: When one is caught up there, tied up there, one is said to be 'a being.'" — SN 23:2*

Thus the Buddha advocated viewing a "being" simply as a process of attachment to desire, passion, delight, and craving. And it is precisely this attachment to craving that allows for rebirth after death:

> *[The Buddha:] "Just as a fire burns with sustenance and not without sustenance, even so I designate the rebirth of one who has sustenance and not of one without sustenance."*
>
> *[Vacchagotta:] "But, Master Gotama, at the moment a flame is being swept on by the wind and goes a far distance, what do you designate as its sustenance then?"*
>
> *"Vaccha, when a flame is being swept on by the wind and goes a far distance, I designate it as wind-sustained, for the wind is its sustenance at that time."*
>
> *"And at the moment when a being sets this body aside and is not yet reborn in another body, what do you designate as its sustenance then?"*
>
> *"Vaccha, when a being sets this body aside and is not yet reborn in another body, I designate it as craving-sustained, for craving is its sustenance at that time." — SN 44:9*

However, a being—in the Buddha's sense of the term—not only takes birth after the death of the body, it can also take birth, die, and be reborn many times in the course of a day—as attachment develops for one desire, ends, and then develops for another desire. This is why the processes leading to rebirth after death can be observed and redirected in the present moment during life. This is why the ability to understand and observe the processes of dependent co-arising is so important in putting an end to rebirth on all its many levels.

To emphasize the desirability of putting an end to rebirth, the sutta moves from the topic of conception to note the pains and anxieties suffered by the mother in carrying the fetus and giving birth. But then what does her child do? He spends his time in trivial pursuits, childish games, and then, as he grows older, the quest for sensual pleasures. If the child—now an adult—realizes the limited nature of such an existence, he gains conviction in the need to practice the Dhamma. He becomes a monk, develops virtue and concentration, and then on the basis of his attainment in concentration he approaches the senses in a way that overcomes the limitations experienced by one who approaches them simply for the pursuit of sensual pleasure. This, the Buddha says, is a short description of the destruction of craving—and, by implication, of the ending of the consciousness and the birth that depend on craving as a condition.

One of the ironies in the organization of the sutta is that, after a long detailed discussion of discernment, virtue, and concentration, the description of how these factors actually are brought together to arrive at the end of craving and birth leaves out many important details. For instance, there is no discussion of how, once the monk has attained concentration, he uses it wisely in such a way that actually puts an end to craving. As the Buddha states in other suttas—such as MN 29, MN 113, and AN 4:178—it is possible to attain strong states of concentration and use them, not as a basis of release, but as a basis for increased defilement and attachment.

This means that the Buddha is not being coy when he states at the end of this long sutta that his discussion of the destruction of craving is brief. It's up to the reader to put the elements of triple training together in practice to see how they lead from a limited awareness through a limitless awareness to total release.

* * *

I have heard that on one occasion the Blessed One was staying near Sāvatthī in Jeta's Grove, Anāthapiṇḍika's monastery. Now on that occasion this evil viewpoint *[diṭṭhigata]* had arisen in the monk Sāti the Fisherman's Son: "As I understand the Dhamma taught by the Blessed One, it is just this consciousness that runs and wanders on (from birth to birth), not another." A large number of monks heard, "They say that this evil viewpoint has arisen in the monk Sāti the Fisherman's Son: 'As I understand the Dhamma taught by the Blessed One, it is just this consciousness that runs and wanders on (from birth to birth), not another.'" So they went to the monk Sāti the Fisherman's Son and on arrival said to him, "Is it true, friend Sāti, that this evil viewpoint has arisen in you—'As I understand the Dhamma taught by the Blessed One, it is just this consciousness that runs and wanders on, not another'?"

"Exactly so, friends. I understand the Dhamma taught by the Blessed One such that it is just this consciousness that runs and wanders on, not another."

Then those monks, desiring to pry the monk Sāti the Fisherman's Son away from that evil viewpoint, quizzed him back & forth and rebuked him, saying, "Don't say that, friend Sāti. Don't slander the Blessed One, for it is not good to slander the Blessed One. The Blessed One would not say anything like that. In many ways, friend, the Blessed One has said of dependently co-arisen consciousness, 'Apart from a requisite condition, there is no coming-into-play of consciousness.'" And yet even though he was quizzed back & forth and rebuked by those monks, the monk Sāti the Fisherman's Son, through stubbornness and attachment to that very same evil viewpoint, continued to insist, "Exactly so, friends. I understand the Dhamma taught by the Blessed One such that it is just this consciousness that runs and wanders on, not another."

So when the monks were unable to pry the monk Sāti the Fisherman's Son away from that evil viewpoint, they went to the Blessed One and on arrival, having bowed down to him, sat to one side. As they were sitting there, they [told him what had happened].

So the Blessed One told a certain monk, "Come, monk. In my name, call the monk Sāti the Fisherman's Son, saying, 'The Teacher calls you, friend Sāti.'"

"As you say, lord," the monk answered and, having gone to the monk Sāti the Fisherman's Son, on arrival he said, "The Teacher calls you, friend Sāti."

"As you say, friend," the monk Sāti the Fisherman's Son replied. Then he went to the Blessed One and, on arrival, having bowed down to him, sat to one side. As he was sitting there, the Blessed One said to him, "Is it true, Sāti, that this evil viewpoint has arisen in you—'As I understand the Dhamma taught by the Blessed One, it is just this consciousness that runs and wanders on, not another'?"

"Exactly so, lord. As I understand the Dhamma taught by the Blessed One, it is just this consciousness that runs and wanders on, not another."

"Which consciousness, Sāti, is that?"[1]

"This speaker, this knower, lord, that is sensitive here & there to the ripening of good & evil actions."

"And to whom, worthless man, do you understand me to have taught the Dhamma like that? Haven't I, in many ways, said of dependently co-arisen consciousness, 'Apart from a requisite condition, there is no coming-into-play of consciousness'?[2] But you, through your own poor grasp, not only slander us but also dig yourself up (by the root) and produce much demerit for yourself. That will lead to your long-term harm & suffering."

Then the Blessed One said to the monks, "What do you think, monks? Is this monk Sāti, the Fisherman's Son, even warm in this Dhamma & Vinaya?"

"How could he be, lord? No, lord."

When this was said, the monk Sāti, the Fisherman's Son, sat silent, abashed, his shoulders drooping, his head down, brooding, at a loss for words.

Then the Blessed One, seeing that the monk Sāti, the Fisherman's Son, was sitting silent, abashed, his shoulders drooping, his head down, brooding, at a loss for words, said to him, "Worthless man, you will be recognized for your own evil viewpoint. I will cross-question the monks on this matter."

Then the Blessed One addressed the monks, "Monks, do you too understand the Dhamma as taught by me in the same way that the monk Sāti, the Fisherman's Son, does when, through his own poor grasp (of the Dhamma), he not only slanders us but also digs himself up (by the root) and produces much demerit for himself?"

"No, lord, for in many ways the Blessed One has said of dependently co-arisen consciousness, 'Apart from a requisite condition, there is no coming-into-play of consciousness.'"

"It's good, monks, that you understand the Dhamma taught by me in this way, for in many ways I have said of dependently co-arisen consciousness, 'Apart from a requisite condition, there is no coming-into-play of consciousness.' But this monk Sāti, the Fisherman's Son, through his own poor grasp (of the Dhamma), has not only slandered us but has also dug himself up (by the root), producing much demerit for himself. That will lead to this worthless man's long-term harm & suffering.

CONSCIOUSNESS CLASSIFIED BY REQUISITE CONDITION

"Consciousness, monks, is classified simply by the requisite condition in dependence on which it arises. Consciousness that arises in dependence on the eye & forms is classified simply as eye-consciousness. Consciousness that arises in dependence on the ear & sounds is classified simply as ear-consciousness. Consciousness that arises in dependence on the nose & aromas is classified simply as nose-consciousness. Consciousness that arises in dependence on the tongue & flavors is classified simply as tongue-consciousness. Consciousness that arises in dependence on the body & tactile sensations is classified simply as body-consciousness. Consciousness that arises in dependence on the intellect & ideas is classified simply as intellect-consciousness.

"Just as fire is classified simply by whatever requisite condition in dependence on which it burns—a fire that burns in dependence on wood is classified simply as a wood-fire, a fire that burns in dependence on wood-chips is classified simply as a wood-chip-fire; a fire that burns in dependence on grass is classified simply as a grass-fire; a fire that burns in dependence on cow-dung is classified simply as a cow-dung-fire; a fire that burns in dependence on chaff is classified simply as a chaff-fire; a fire that burns in dependence on rubbish is classified simply as a rubbish-fire—in the same way, consciousness is classified simply by the requisite condition in dependence on which it arises. Consciousness that arises in dependence on the eye & forms is classified simply as eye-consciousness. Consciousness that arises in dependence on the ear & sounds is classified simply as ear-consciousness. Consciousness that arises in dependence on the nose & aromas is classified simply as nose-consciousness. Consciousness that arises in dependence on the tongue & flavors is classified simply as tongue-consciousness. Consciousness that arises in dependence on the body & tactile sensations is classified simply as body-consciousness. Consciousness that arises in dependence on the intellect & ideas is classified simply as intellect-consciousness.

ON BECOMING

"Monks, do you see, 'This has come to be'?"[3]

"Yes, lord."

"Monks, do you see, 'It comes into play from that nutriment'?"

"Yes, lord."

"Monks, do you see, 'From the cessation of that nutriment, what has come to be is subject to cessation'?"

"Yes, lord."

"From the doubt—'Has this come to be?'—does uncertainty arise?"

"Yes, lord."

"From the doubt—'Does it come into play from that nutriment?'—does uncertainty arise?"

"Yes, lord."

"From the doubt—'From the cessation of that nutriment, is what has come to be subject to cessation?'—does uncertainty arise?"

"Yes, lord."

"Monks, for one who sees with right discernment, as it has come to be, that 'This has come to be,' is that uncertainty abandoned?"

"Yes, lord."

"For one who sees with right discernment, as it has come to be, that 'It comes into play from that nutriment,' is that uncertainty abandoned?"

"Yes, lord."

"For one who sees with right discernment, as it has come to be, that 'From the cessation of that nutriment, what has come to be is subject to cessation,' is that uncertainty abandoned?"

"Yes, lord."

"Monks, are you thus free from uncertainty here that 'This has come to be'?"

"Yes, lord."

"Are you thus free from uncertainty here that 'It comes into play from that nutriment'?"

"Yes, lord."

"Are you thus free from uncertainty here that 'From the cessation of that nutriment, what has come to be is subject to cessation'?"

"Yes, lord."

"Monks, is it well seen (by you) that 'This has come to be'?"

"Yes, lord."

"Is it well seen (by you) that 'It comes into play from that nutriment'?"

"Yes, lord."

"Is it well seen (by you) that 'From the cessation of that nutriment, what has come to be is subject to cessation'?"

"Yes, lord."

"Monks, if you were to adhere to this view—so pure, so bright—if you were to cherish it, treasure it, regard it as 'mine,' would you understand the Dhamma taught as analogous to a raft,[4] for crossing over, not for holding on to?"

"No, lord."

"If you were not to adhere to this view—so pure, so bright—if you were to not to cherish it, not to treasure it, not to regard it as 'mine,' would you understand the Dhamma taught as analogous to a raft, for crossing over, not for holding on to?"

"Yes, lord."

NUTRIMENT & DEPENDENT CO-ARISING

"Monks, there are these four nutriments for the maintenance of beings who have come into being or for the support of those in search of a place to be born. Which four? Physical food, gross or refined; contact as the second, intellectual intention the third, and consciousness the fourth.

"Now, these four nutriments have what as their cause, what as their origination, through what are they born, through what are they brought into being? These four nutriments have craving as their cause, craving as their origination, are born from craving, are brought into being from craving.

"And this craving has what as its cause, what as its origination, through what is it born, through what is it brought into being?

"Craving has feeling as its cause... is brought into being through feeling.

"And this feeling has what as its cause... through what is it brought into being?

"Feeling has contact as its cause....

"And this contact has what as its cause... through what is it brought into being?

"Contact has the six sense-media as its cause....

"And these six sense-media have what as their cause... through what are they brought into being?

"The six sense-media have name-&-form as their cause....

"And this name-&-form has what as its cause... through what is it brought into being?

"Name-&-form has consciousness as its cause....

"And this consciousness has what as its cause... through what is it brought into being?

"Consciousness has fabrications as its cause....

"And these fabrications have what as their cause... through what are they brought into being?

"Fabrications have ignorance as their cause, ignorance as their origination, are born from ignorance, are brought into being from ignorance.

THE ARISING OF STRESS & SUFFERING

"Thus:

From ignorance as a requisite condition come fabrications.

From fabrications as a requisite condition comes consciousness.

From consciousness as a requisite condition comes name-&-form.

From name-&-form as a requisite condition come the six sense media.

From the six sense media as a requisite condition comes contact.

From contact as a requisite condition comes feeling.

From feeling as a requisite condition comes craving.

From craving as a requisite condition comes clinging/sustenance.

From clinging/sustenance as a requisite condition comes becoming.

From becoming as a requisite condition comes birth.

From birth as a requisite condition, then aging-&-death, sorrow, lamentation, pain, distress, & despair come into play. Such is the origination of this entire mass of stress & suffering.

"'From birth as a requisite condition comes aging-&-death': Thus was it said. Now, monks, is it the case that from birth as a requisite condition comes aging-&-death, or not, or how is it here?"

"Lord, from birth as a requisite condition comes aging-&-death. That's how it is for us here: From birth as a requisite condition comes aging-&-death."

[Similarly with the remaining requisite conditions down to:]

"'From ignorance as a requisite condition come fabrications': Thus was it said. Now, monks, is it the case that from ignorance as a requisite condition come fabrications, or not, or how is it here?"

"Lord, from ignorance as a requisite condition come fabrications. That's how it is for us here: From ignorance as a requisite condition come fabrications."

"It's good, monks, that you say that, and I say that,[5] too.

When this is, that is.

From the arising of this comes the arising of that.

In other words:

From ignorance as a requisite condition come fabrications.

From fabrications as a requisite condition comes consciousness.

From consciousness as a requisite condition comes name-&-form.

From name-and-form as a requisite condition come the six sense media.

From the six sense media as a requisite condition comes contact.

From contact as a requisite condition comes feeling.

From feeling as a requisite condition comes craving.

From craving as a requisite condition comes clinging/sustenance.

From clinging/sustenance as a requisite condition comes becoming.

From becoming as a requisite condition comes birth.

From birth as a requisite condition, then aging-&-death, sorrow, lamentation, pain, distress, and despair come into play. Such is the origination of this entire mass of stress & suffering.

THE CESSATION OF STRESS & SUFFERING

"Now from the remainderless fading and cessation of that very ignorance comes the cessation of fabrications.

From the cessation of fabrications comes the cessation of consciousness.

From the cessation of consciousness comes the cessation of name-&-form.

From the cessation of name-&-form comes the cessation of the six sense media.

From the cessation of the six sense media comes the cessation of contact.

From the cessation of contact comes the cessation of feeling.

From the cessation of feeling comes the cessation of craving.

From the cessation of craving comes the cessation of clinging/sustenance.

From the cessation of clinging/sustenance comes the cessation of becoming.

From the cessation of becoming comes the cessation of birth.

From the cessation of birth, then aging-&-death, sorrow, lamentation, pain, distress, and despair all cease. Such is the cessation of this entire mass of stress & suffering.

"'From the cessation of birth comes the cessation of aging-&-death': Thus was it said. Now, monks, is it the case that from the cessation of birth comes the cessation of aging-&-death, or not, or how is it here?"

"Lord, from the cessation of birth comes the cessation of aging-&-death. That's how it is for us here: From the cessation of birth comes the cessation of aging-&-death."

[Similarly with the remaining requisite conditions down to:]

"'From the cessation of ignorance comes the cessation of fabrications': Thus was it said. Now, monks, is it the case that from cessation of ignorance comes the cessation of fabrications, or not, or how is it here?"

"Lord, from the cessation of ignorance comes the cessation of fabrications. That's how it is for us here: From the cessation of ignorance comes the cessation of fabrications."

"It's good, monks, that you say that, and I say that,[5] too.

When this isn't, that isn't.

From the cessation of this comes the cessation of that.

In other words:

"From the cessation of ignorance comes the cessation of fabrications.

From the cessation of fabrications comes the cessation of consciousness.

From the cessation of consciousness comes the cessation of name-&-form.

From the cessation of name-&-form comes the cessation of the six sense media.

From the cessation of the six sense media comes the cessation of contact.

From the cessation of contact comes the cessation of feeling.

From the cessation of feeling comes the cessation of craving.

From the cessation of craving comes the cessation of clinging/sustenance.

From the cessation of clinging/sustenance comes the cessation of becoming.

From the cessation of becoming comes the cessation of birth.

From the cessation of birth, then aging-&-death, sorrow, lamentation, pain, distress, & despair all cease. Such is the cessation of this entire mass of stress & suffering.

INAPPROPRIATE QUESTIONS AVOIDED

"Now, monks, knowing thus and seeing thus, would you run after the past, thinking, *'Were we in the past? Were we not in the past? What were we in the past? How were we in the past? Having been what, what were we in the past'?"*

"No, lord."

"Knowing thus and seeing thus, would you run after the future, thinking, *'Shall we be in the future? Shall we not be in the future? What shall we be in the future? How shall we be in the future? Having been what, what shall we be in the future'?"*

"No, lord."

"Knowing thus and seeing thus, would you be inwardly perplexed about the immediate present, thinking, *'Am I? Am I not? What am I? How am I? Where has this being come from? Where is it bound'?"*[6]

"No, lord."

"Knowing thus and seeing thus, would you say, 'The Teacher is our respected mentor. We speak thus out of respect for the Teacher'?"

"No, lord."

"Knowing thus and seeing thus, would you say, 'The Contemplative says this. We speak thus in line with the Contemplative's words'?"

"No, lord."

"Knowing thus and seeing thus, would you dedicate yourselves to another teacher?"

"No, lord."

"Knowing thus and seeing thus, would you return to the observances, grand ceremonies, & auspicious rites of common contemplatives & brahmans as having any essence?"

"No, lord."

"Is it the case that you speak simply in line with what you have known, seen, & understood for yourselves?"

"Yes, lord."

"Good, monks. You have been guided by me in this Dhamma which is to be seen here & now, timeless, inviting verification, pertinent, to be realized by the observant for themselves. For it has been said, 'This Dhamma is to be seen here & now, timeless, inviting verification, pertinent, to be by the observant for themselves,' and it was in reference to this that it was said.

THE BIRTH & GROWTH OF A BEING

"Monks, the descent of the embryo occurs with the union of three things. There is the case where there is no union of the mother & father, the mother is not in her season, and a gandhabba[7] is not present, nor is there a descent of an embryo. There is the case where there is a union of the mother & father, and the mother is in her season, but a gandhabba is not present, nor is there a descent of an embryo. But when there is a union of the mother & father, the mother is in her season, and a gandhabba is present, then with this union of three things the descent of the embryo occurs.

"Then for nine or ten months the mother shelters the embryo in her womb with great anxiety, as a heavy burden. Then, at the end of nine or ten months, she gives birth with great anxiety, as a heavy burden. Then, when the child is born, she feeds it with her own blood—for mother's milk is called blood in the discipline of the noble ones.

"Then, as the child grows and his faculties mature, he plays at children's[8] games: toy plows, stick games, somersaults, toy windmills, toy measures, toy carts, and a toy bow & arrow.

"As he grows and his faculties mature (still further), he enjoys himself provided & endowed with the five strings of sensuality: forms cognizable via the eye—agreeable, pleasing, charming, endearing, enticing, accompanied with sensual desire; sounds cognizable via the ear... aromas cognizable via the nose... flavors cognizable via the tongue... tactile sensations cognizable via the body— agreeable, pleasing, charming, endearing, enticing, accompanied with sensual desire.

LIMITED AWARENESS

"On seeing a form with the eye, he is infatuated with pleasing forms, and gets upset over unpleasing forms. He dwells with body-mindfulness unestablished,[9] with limited awareness. He doesn't discern, as it has come to be, the awareness-release & discernment-release where those evil, unskillful qualities cease without remainder. Engaged thus in predilection & opposition, he relishes any feeling he feels—pleasure, pain, neither-pleasure-nor-pain—welcomes it, & remains fastened to it. As he relishes that feeling, welcomes it, & remains fastened to it, delight arises. Now, any delight in feeling is clinging/sustenance. From his clinging/sustenance as a requisite condition comes becoming. From becoming as a requisite condition comes birth. From birth as a requisite condition, then aging-&-death, sorrow, lamentation, pain, distress, and despair come into play. Such is the origination of this entire mass of stress & suffering.

"On hearing a sound with the ear....

"On smelling an aroma with the nose....

"On tasting a flavor with the tongue....

"On sensing a tactile sensation with the body....

"On cognizing an idea with the intellect, he is infatuated with pleasing ideas, and gets upset over unpleasing ideas. He dwells with body-mindfulness unestablished, with limited awareness. He doesn't discern, as it has come to be, the awareness-release & discernment-release where those evil, unskillful qualities cease without remainder. Engaged thus in compliance & opposition, he relishes any feeling he feels—pleasure, pain, neither-pleasure-nor-pain—welcomes it, & remains fastened to it. As he relishes that feeling, welcomes it, & remains fastened to it, delight arises. Now, any delight in feeling is clinging/sustenance. From his clinging/sustenance as a requisite condition comes becoming. From becoming as a requisite condition comes birth. From birth as a requisite condition, then aging-&-death, sorrow, lamentation, pain, distress, & despair come into play. Such is the origination of this entire mass of stress & suffering.

THE PATH TO UNLIMITED AWARENESS

"Now, there is the case where a Tathāgata appears in the world, worthy & rightly self-awakened. He teaches the Dhamma admirable in its beginning, admirable in its middle, admirable in its end. He proclaims the holy life both in its particulars and in its essence, entirely perfect, surpassingly pure.

"He [the person discussed above], hearing the Dhamma, gains conviction in the Tathāgata and reflects: 'Household life is confining, a dusty path. Life gone forth is the open air. It isn't easy, living at home, to practice the holy life totally perfect, totally pure, a polished shell. What if I, having shaved off my hair & beard and putting on the ochre robe, were to go forth from the household life into homelessness?'

"So after some time he abandons his mass of wealth, large or small; leaves his circle of relatives, large or small; shaves off his hair and beard, puts on the ochre robes, and goes forth from the household life into homelessness.

VIRTUE

"When he has thus gone forth, endowed with the monks' training & livelihood, then—abandoning the taking of life—he abstains from the taking of life. He dwells with his rod laid down, his knife laid down, scrupulous, merciful, compassionate for the welfare of all living beings.

"Abandoning the taking of what is not given, he abstains from taking what is not given. He takes only what is given, accepts only what is given, lives not by stealth but by means of a self that has become pure. This, too, is part of his virtue.

"Abandoning uncelibacy, he lives a celibate life, aloof, refraining from the sexual act that is the villager's way.

"Abandoning the telling of lies, he abstains from telling lies. He speaks the truth, holds to the truth, is firm, reliable, no deceiver of the world.

"Abandoning divisive speech, he abstains from divisive speech. What he has heard here he does not tell there to break those people apart from these people here. What he has heard there he does not tell here to break these people apart from those people there. Thus reconciling those who have broken apart or cementing those who are united, he loves concord, delights in concord, enjoys concord, speaks things that create concord.

"Abandoning abusive speech, he abstains from abusive speech. He speaks words that are soothing to the ear, that are affectionate, that go to the heart, that are polite, appealing and pleasing to people at large.

"Abandoning idle chatter, he abstains from idle chatter. He speaks in season, speaks what is factual, what is in accordance with the goal, the Dhamma, and the Vinaya. He speaks words worth treasuring, seasonable, reasonable, circumscribed, connected with the goal.

"He abstains from damaging seed & plant life.

"He eats only once a day, refraining from the evening meal and from food at the wrong time of day.

"He abstains from dancing, singing, instrumental music, and from watching shows.

"He abstains from wearing garlands and from beautifying himself with scents & cosmetics.

"He abstains from high and luxurious beds & seats.

"He abstains from accepting gold & money.

"He abstains from accepting uncooked grain… raw meat… women & girls… male & female slaves… goats & sheep… fowl & pigs… elephants, cattle, steeds, & mares… fields & property.

"He abstains from running messages… from buying & selling… from dealing with false scales, false metals, & false measures… from bribery, deception, & fraud.

"He abstains from mutilating, executing, imprisoning, highway robbery, plunder, and violence.

"He is content with a set of robes to provide for his body and alms food to provide for his hunger. Just as a bird, wherever it goes, flies with its wings as its only burden; so too is he content with a set of robes to provide for his body and alms food to provide for his hunger. Wherever he goes, he takes only his barest necessities along.

"Endowed with this noble aggregate of virtue, he is inwardly sensitive to the pleasure of being blameless.

SENSE RESTRAINT

"On seeing a form with the eye, he doesn't grasp at any theme or details by which—if he were to dwell without restraint over the faculty of the eye—evil, unskillful qualities such as greed or distress might assail him. On hearing a sound with the ear.... On smelling an aroma with the nose.... On tasting a flavor with the tongue.... On touching a tactile sensation with the body.... On cognizing an idea with the intellect, he doesn't grasp at any theme or details by which—if he were to dwell without restraint over the faculty of the intellect—evil, unskillful qualities such as greed or distress might assail him. Endowed with this noble restraint over the sense faculties, he is inwardly sensitive to the pleasure of being blameless.

MINDFULNESS & ALERTNESS

"When going forward and returning, he makes himself alert. When looking toward and looking away... when bending and extending his limbs... when carrying his outer cloak, his upper robe, and his bowl... when eating, drinking, chewing, and tasting... when urinating and defecating... when walking, standing, sitting, falling asleep, waking up, talking, and remaining silent, he makes himself alert.

ABANDONING THE HINDRANCES

"Endowed with this noble aggregate of virtue, this noble restraint over the sense faculties, this noble mindfulness & alertness, he seeks out a secluded dwelling: a wilderness, the shade of a tree, a mountain, a glen, a hillside cave, a charnel ground, a forest grove, the open air, a heap of straw. After his meal, returning from his alms round, he sits down, crosses his legs, holds his body erect, and brings mindfulness to the fore.

"Abandoning covetousness with regard to the world, he dwells with an awareness devoid of covetousness. He cleanses his mind of covetousness. Abandoning ill will & anger, he dwells with an awareness devoid of ill will, sympathetic with the welfare of all living beings. He cleanses his mind of ill will & anger. Abandoning sloth & drowsiness, he dwells with an awareness devoid of sloth & drowsiness, mindful, alert, percipient of light. He cleanses his mind of sloth & drowsiness. Abandoning restlessness & anxiety, he dwells undisturbed, his mind inwardly stilled. He cleanses his mind of restlessness & anxiety. Abandoning uncertainty, he dwells having crossed over uncertainty, with no perplexity with regard to skillful qualities. He cleanses his mind of uncertainty.

THE FOUR JHĀNAS

"Having abandoned these five hindrances—imperfections of awareness that weaken discernment—then, quite secluded from sensuality, secluded from unskillful qualities, he enters and remains in the first jhāna: rapture & pleasure born of seclusion, accompanied by directed thought & evaluation.

"With the stilling of directed thoughts & evaluations, he enters and remains in the second jhāna: rapture & pleasure born of concentration, unification of awareness free from directed thought & evaluation—internal assurance.

"With the fading of rapture, he remains equanimous, mindful, & alert, and senses pleasure with the body. He enters and remains in the third jhāna, of which the noble ones declare, 'Equanimous & mindful, he has a pleasant abiding.'

"With the abandoning of pleasure & pain—as with the earlier disappearance of joy & distress—he enters and remains in the fourth jhāna: purity of equanimity & mindfulness, neither pleasure nor pain.

UNLIMITED AWARENESS

"On seeing a form with the eye, he isn't infatuated with pleasing forms, and doesn't get upset over unpleasing forms. He dwells with body-mindfulness established,[9] with unlimited awareness. He discerns, as it has come to be, the awareness-release & discernment-release where those evil, unskillful qualities cease without remainder. Having thus abandoned compliance & opposition, he doesn't relish any feeling he feels—pleasure, pain, neither pleasure nor pain—doesn't welcome it, doesn't remain fastened to it. As he doesn't relish that feeling, doesn't welcome it, & doesn't remain fastened to it, delight doesn't arise. From the cessation of his delight comes the cessation of clinging/sustenance. From the cessation of clinging/sustenance comes the cessation of becoming. From the cessation of becoming comes the cessation of birth. From the cessation of birth, then aging-&-death, sorrow, lamentation, pain, distress, & despair all cease. Such is the cessation of this entire mass of stress & suffering.

"On hearing a sound with the ear....

"On smelling an aroma with the nose....

"On tasting a flavor with the tongue....

"On sensing a tactile sensation with the body....

"On cognizing an idea with the intellect, he isn't infatuated with pleasing ideas, and doesn't get upset over unpleasing ideas. He dwells with body-mindfulness established, with unlimited awareness. He discerns, as it has come to be, the awareness-release & discernment-release where those evil, unskillful qualities cease without remainder. Having thus abandoned compliance & opposition, he doesn't relish any feeling he feels—pleasure, pain, neither pleasure nor pain—doesn't welcome it, doesn't remain fastened to it. As he doesn't relish that feeling, doesn't welcome it, & doesn't remain fastened to it, delight doesn't arise. From the cessation of his delight comes the cessation of clinging/sustenance. From the cessation of clinging/sustenance comes the cessation of becoming.

From the cessation of becoming comes the cessation of birth. From the cessation of birth, then aging-&-death, sorrow, lamentation, pain, distress, & despair all cease. Such is the cessation of this entire mass of stress & suffering.

"Monks, remember this, my brief (account of) release through the destruction of craving; and Sāti, the Fisherman's Son, as tied up in the great net of craving, the great tangle of craving."

That is what the Blessed One said. Gratified, the monks delighted in the Blessed One's words.

NOTES

1. The Buddha, knowing that there are two types of consciousness—the consciousness aggregate *(viññāṇakkhandha),* which is experienced in conjunction with the six sense media, and consciousness without surface *(viññāṇaṁ anidassanaṁ),* which is experienced independently of the six sense media (MN 49)—is here giving Sāti the chance to identify which of the two types he has interpreted as running and wandering on. Sāti's answer shows that he is talking about the first type. The remaining discussion of consciousness throughout this sutta is thus directed at this first type. It would have been interesting to see how the Buddha would have attacked Sāti's misunderstanding had Sāti stated that he was talking about the second.

On the topic of consciousness without surface, see DN 11, note 2, and MN 49, note 9.

2. The Pali here is, *Nanu mayā moghapurisa anekapariyāyena paṭiccasamuppannaṁ viññāṇaṁ vuttaṁ, 'Aññatra paccayā n'atthi viññāṇassa sambhavoti'?*

If the first part of this sentence were a complete sentence, its syntax—putting the topic of what is described in the nominative (*paṭiccasamuppannaṁ viññāṇaṁ*), followed by the word *vuttaṁ* ("described") plus the speaker in the instrumental *(mayā)*—could be translated in line with either of two patterns.

An example of the first pattern is in SN 12:24: *Paṭiccasamuppannaṁ kho ānanda dukkhaṁ vuttaṁ mayā*—"Ānanda, stress has been described by me as dependently co-arisen." In other words, the pattern is: "X has been described as Y by the speaker."

An example of the second pattern is in AN 3:74: *Sekhampi kho mahānāma sīlaṁ vuttaṁ bhagavatā, asekhampi sīlaṁ vuttaṁ bhagavatā*—"Mahānāma, the virtue of one in training has been described by the Blessed One, and the virtue of one beyond training has been described by the Blessed One." This pattern is: "X has been described by the speaker." Another example of this pattern is in SN 41:2: *Idaṁ kho gahapati dhātu-nānattaṁ vuttaṁ bhagavatā: cakkhu-dhātu, rūpa-dhātu, cakkhu-viññāṇa-dhātu... mano-dhātu, dhamma-dhātu, mano-viññāṇa-dhātu*—"Householder, this diversity of properties has been described by the Blessed One: eye-property, form property, eye-consciousness property... intellect-property, idea property, intellect-consciousness property." Again: "X has been described by the speaker."

To make a literal translation of the passage here in line with the first pattern would yield: "Worthless man, hasn't consciousness been described as dependently co-arisen by me in many ways (that), 'Apart from a requisite condition, there is no coming-into-play of consciousness'?"

To make a literal translation in line with the second pattern would yield: "Worthless man, hasn't dependently co-arisen consciousness been described by me in many ways (that), 'Apart from a requisite condition, there is no coming-into-play of consciousness'?"

The translator of MLS renders the sentence both ways. When it earlier appears in the mouths of the monks reprimanding Sāti, she renders it in line with the first pattern: "For, reverend Sāti, in many a figure is conditioned genesis spoken of in connection with consciousness by the Lord, saying: 'Apart from condition there is no origination of consciousness.'" When the sentence appears in the Buddha's mouth, she renders it in line with the second pattern: "Foolish man, has not consciousness generated by conditions been spoken of in many a figure by me, saying: Apart from condition there is no origination of consciousness?"

The translators of MLDB consistently follow the first pattern in rendering this sentence: "Misguided man, have I not stated in many ways consciousness to be dependently arisen since without a condition there is no origination of consciousness?" (It might be noted that this rendering inserts a "since" where there is none in the Pali, and ignores the quotation marks *(ti)* around the sentence beginning, "Apart from" or "without." More on this below.)

At any rate, the substantive difference in these two patterns is that the first could be taken as implying that all consciousness is dependently co-arisen, whereas the second states explicitly that the Buddha's words, "Apart from condition there is no origination of consciousness," apply specifically to one type of consciousness—consciousness arising in dependence on the co-arising of conditions—leaving open the possibility that there is another type of consciousness to which these words do not apply.

Arguing from translations rendered in line with the first pattern, people have asserted that the two passages in the Canon (in DN 11 and

MN 49) referring to consciousness without surface are not in keeping with the principle, expressed here, that all consciousness is dependently co-arisen. Thus, the argument continues, those two passages cannot be accepted as coming genuinely from the Buddha, whereas this passage in MN 38 definitely can.

There are three main problems with this argument. The first is that, throughout the suttas, when consciousness as an active agent is discussed without modifiers, it is always with reference to the consciousness aggregate, as that is the sort of consciousness occurring within the territory delimited by the way the Buddha explicitly defines the term, "all" (see SN 35:23). That is clearly the topic of discussion here. Consciousness without surface (see note 1) is discussed explicitly only in passages where the Buddha is citing the superiority of his attainment over that of Brahmās: In knowing this sort of consciousness, which performs no active role and lies outside of the term "all" (MN 49), he knows something that Brahmās do not. Because the consciousness discussed in this sutta is an active agent and definitely lies within the term "all," all references can be understood to apply solely to the consciousness aggregate. What this means is that even if we follow the first pattern in translating this sentence, it would not require that we adopt the argument drawn from it; the people advancing this argument force the passage to say more than it actually says when taken in the context of the suttas as a whole.

Second, it is a poor interpretative strategy to give unnecessary privilege to one passage of the Canon at the expense of two others when we have no way of proving which passages in the suttas are most authentic. This is especially true in light of the fact that the passage here—if we took it as a complete sentence—would not demand a single, unequivocal interpretation. To force such an interpretation on it, knowing that that would discredit other passages as inauthentic, is unfair to the texts.

The third problem with the argument for using this passage to reject DN 11 and MN 49, however, is the most telling: The first part of the above sentence is not a complete sentence. It is followed by a passage in quotation marks: *'Aññatra paccayā n'atthi viññāṇassa sambhavoti'?* The only way to make sense of this punctuation is to take this passage in quotation marks as constituting what is said *(vuttaṁ)* about X as named in the first part of the sentence. In other words, this constitutes the description that the Buddha has made about dependently-coarisen consciousness. The second pattern is the only one that make sense in this context: "Worthless man, hasn't dependently co-arisen consciousness been described by me in many ways (that), 'Apart from a requisite condition, there is no coming-into-play of consciousness'?"

Thus it is clear that the Buddha here is discussing dependently co-arisen consciousness in a way that does not preclude the possibility that there is also a consciousness that lies beyond the six sense-media, is not dependently co-arisen, and is neither momentary nor eternal, as it stands outside the dimension of time.

3. See SN 12:31.

4. See MN 22.

5. Both MLS and MLDB treat the "that" here as referring to what follows—MLDB puts what follows into single quotation marks to underline this interpretation—but there are no quotation-marks-within-quotation-marks around what follows, and it would appear that the "that" here refers to the statements made above.

6. MN 2 identifies these questions as topics of inappropriate attention. For a discussion of these questions, and the way in which an understanding of dependent co-arising leaves the mind disinterested in them, see *Skill in Questions,* Chapter 8.

7. "Gandhabba" usually means a low level of celestial deva. Devas on this level are frequently represented in the Canon as obsessed with sexual desire. However, the Commentary here notes that "gandhabba" here does not mean a being standing near, watching the couple have sexual intercourse. Rather, it means the being, driven by kamma, who will take birth on that occasion. This interpretation is seconded by a passage in MN 93, which builds on the brahman assumption that a person maintains the same caste from one life to the next:

> "[Devala the Dark (an ancient brahman seer):] 'Do you know how there is the descent of an embryo?'
>
> "[Seven brahman seers:] 'Yes, master, we know how there is the descent of an embryo. There is the case where the mother & father have come together, the mother is fertile, and a *gandhabba* is standing present. The coming together of these three is the descent of the embryo.'
>
> "'But do you know for sure whether the *gandhabba* is a noble warrior, a brahman, a merchant, or a worker?'
>
> "'No, master.'
>
> "'That being the case, do you know who you are?'
>
> "'That being the case, master, we don't know who we are.'"

8. This word, present in all editions of the Canon and in MLS, is missing in MLDB.

9. See SN 35:206.

See also: DN 2; MN 2; MN 43; SN 12:20; AN 10:81

39 *The Greater Discourse at Assapura*

Mahā Assapura Sutta

I have heard that on one occasion the Blessed One was staying among the Aṅgas. Now, the Aṅgas have a town named Assapura. There the Blessed One addressed the monks, "Monks!"

"Yes, lord," the monks responded to him.

The Blessed One said, "'Contemplatives, contemplatives': That is how people perceive you. And when asked, 'What are you?' you claim that 'We are contemplatives.' So, with this being your designation and this your claim, this is how you should train yourselves: 'We will undertake & practice those qualities that make one a contemplative, that make one a brahman, so that our designation will be true and our claim accurate; so that the services of those whose robes, alms-food, lodging, and medicinal requisites we use will bring them great fruit & great reward; and so that our going forth will not be barren, but fruitful & fertile.'[1]

SHAME & COMPUNCTION

"And what, monks, are the qualities that make one a contemplative, that make one a brahman? 'We will be endowed with shame (at the idea of wrong-doing) & compunction (for the consequences of wrong-doing)': That's how you should train yourselves. Now the thought may occur to you, 'We are endowed with shame & compunction. That much is enough, that much means we're done, so that the goal of our contemplative state has been reached. There's nothing further to be done,' and you may rest content with just that. So I tell you, monks. I exhort you, monks. Don't let those of you who seek the contemplative state fall away from the goal of the contemplative state when there is more to be done.

PURITY OF CONDUCT

"And what more is to be done? 'Our bodily conduct will be pure, clear & open, unbroken & restrained. We will not exalt ourselves nor disparage others on account of that pure bodily conduct': That's how you should train yourselves. Now the thought may occur to you, 'We are endowed with shame & compunction. Our bodily conduct is pure. That much is enough, that much means we're done, so that the goal of our contemplative state has been reached. There's nothing further to be done,' and you may rest content with just that. So I tell you, monks. I exhort you, monks. Don't let those of you who seek the contemplative state fall away from the goal of the contemplative state when there is more to be done.

"And what more is to be done? 'Our verbal conduct… our mental conduct will be pure, clear & open, unbroken & restrained. We will not exalt ourselves nor disparage others on account of that pure verbal… mental conduct': That's how you should train yourselves. Now the thought may occur to you, 'We are endowed with shame & compunction. Our bodily conduct is pure. Our verbal conduct… our mental conduct is pure. That much is enough, that much means we're done, so that the goal of our contemplative state has been reached. There's nothing further to be done,' and you may rest content with just that. So I tell you, monks. I exhort you, monks. Don't let those of you who seek the contemplative state fall away from the goal of the contemplative state when there is more to be done.

"And what more is to be done? 'Our livelihood will be pure, clear & open, unbroken & restrained. We will not exalt ourselves nor disparage others on account of that pure livelihood': That's how you should train yourselves. Now the thought may occur to you, 'We are endowed with shame & compunction. Our bodily conduct is pure. Our verbal conduct… our mental conduct is pure. Our livelihood is pure. That much is enough, that much means we're done, so that the goal of our contemplative state has been reached. There's nothing further to be done,' and you may rest content with just that. So I tell you, monks. I exhort you, monks. Don't let those of you who seek the contemplative state fall away from the goal of the contemplative state when there is more to be done.

RESTRAINT OF THE SENSES

"And what more is to be done? 'We will guard the doors to our sense faculties. On seeing a form with the eye, we will not grasp at any theme or variations by which—if we were to dwell without restraint over the faculty of the eye—evil, unskillful qualities such as greed or distress might assail us. We will practice for its restraint. We will protect the faculty of the eye. We will achieve restraint with regard to the faculty of the eye. On hearing a sound with the ear… On smelling an aroma with the nose… On tasting a flavor with the tongue… On feeling a tactile sensation with the body... On cognizing an idea with the intellect, we will not grasp at any theme or variations by which—if we were to dwell without restraint over the faculty of the intellect—evil, unskillful qualities such as greed or distress might assail us. We will practice for its restraint. We will protect the faculty of the intellect. We will achieve restraint with regard to the faculty of the intellect': That's how you should train yourselves. Now the thought may occur to you, 'We are endowed with shame & compunction. Our bodily conduct is pure. Our verbal conduct... our mental conduct is pure. Our livelihood is pure. We guard the doors to our sense faculties. That much is enough, that much means we're done, so that the goal of our contemplative state has been reached. There's nothing further to be done,' and you may rest content with just that. So I tell you, monks. I exhort you, monks. Don't let those of you who seek the contemplative state fall away from the goal of the contemplative state when there is more to be done.

MODERATION IN EATING

"And what more is to be done? 'We will have a sense of moderation in eating. Considering it appropriately, we will take food not playfully, nor for intoxication, nor for putting on bulk, nor for beautification, but simply for the survival & continuance of this body, for ending its afflictions, for the support of the holy life, thinking, "I will destroy old feelings (of hunger) & not create new feelings (from overeating). Thus I will maintain myself, be blameless, & live in comfort"': That's how you should train yourselves. Now the thought may occur to you, 'We are endowed with shame & compunction. Our bodily conduct is pure. Our verbal conduct... our mental conduct is pure. Our livelihood is pure. We guard the doors to our sense faculties. We have a sense of moderation in eating. That much is enough, that much means we're done, so that the goal of our contemplative state has been reached. There's nothing further to be done,' and you may rest content with just that. So I tell you, monks. I exhort you, monks. Don't let those of you who seek the contemplative state fall away from the goal of the contemplative state when there is more to be done.

WAKEFULNESS

"And what more is to be done? 'We will be devoted to wakefulness. During the day, sitting & pacing back & forth, we will cleanse the mind of any qualities that would hold it in check.

During the first watch of the night [dusk to 10 p.m.], sitting & pacing back & forth, we will cleanse the mind of any qualities that would hold it in check. During the second watch of the night [10 p.m. to 2 a.m.], reclining on our right side, we will take up the lion's posture, one foot placed on top of the other, mindful, alert, with the mind set on getting up [either as soon as we awaken or at a particular time]. During the last watch of the night [2 a.m. to dawn], sitting & pacing back & forth, we will cleanse the mind of any qualities that would hold it in check': That's how you should train yourselves. Now the thought may occur to you, 'We are endowed with shame & compunction. Our bodily conduct is pure. Our verbal conduct… our mental conduct is pure. Our livelihood is pure. We guard the doors to our sense faculties. We have a sense of moderation in eating. We are devoted to wakefulness. That much is enough, that much means we're done, so that the goal of our contemplative state has been reached. There's nothing further to be done,' and you may rest content with just that. So I tell you, monks. I exhort you, monks. Don't let those of you who seek the contemplative state fall away from the goal of the contemplative state when there is more to be done.

MINDFULNESS & ALERTNESS

"And what more is to be done? We will be possessed of mindfulness & alertness. When going forward and returning, we will act with alertness. When looking toward and looking away… when bending and extending our limbs… when carrying our outer cloak, upper robe, & bowl… when eating, drinking, chewing, & tasting… when urinating & defecating… when walking, standing, sitting, falling asleep, waking up, talking, & remaining silent, we will act with alertness': That's how you should train yourselves. Now the thought may occur to you, 'We are endowed with shame & compunction. Our bodily conduct is pure. Our verbal conduct… our mental conduct is pure. Our livelihood is pure. We guard the doors to our sense faculties. We have a sense of moderation in eating. We are devoted to wakefulness. We are possessed of mindfulness & alertness. That much is enough, that much means we're done, so that the goal of our contemplative state has been reached. There's nothing further to be done,' and you may rest content with just that. So I tell you, monks. I exhort you, monks. Don't let those of you who seek the contemplative state fall away from the goal of the contemplative state when there is more to be done.

ABANDONING THE HINDRANCES

"And what more is to be done? There is the case where a monk seeks out a secluded dwelling: a forest, the shade of a tree, a mountain, a glen, a hillside cave, a charnel ground, a forest grove, the open air, a heap of straw. After his meal, returning from his alms round, he sits down, crosses his legs, holds his body erect, and brings mindfulness to the fore.

"Abandoning covetousness with regard to the world, he dwells with an awareness devoid of covetousness. He cleanses his mind of covetousness. Abandoning ill will and anger, he dwells with an awareness devoid of ill will, sympathetic with the welfare of all living beings. He cleanses his mind of ill will and anger. Abandoning sloth and drowsiness, he dwells with an awareness devoid of sloth and drowsiness, mindful, alert, percipient of light. He cleanses his mind of sloth and drowsiness. Abandoning restlessness and anxiety, he dwells undisturbed, his mind inwardly stilled. He cleanses his mind of restlessness and anxiety. Abandoning uncertainty, he dwells having crossed over uncertainty, with no perplexity with regard to skillful qualities. He cleanses his mind of uncertainty.

"Suppose that a man, taking a loan, invests it in his business affairs. His business affairs succeed. He repays his old debts and there is extra left over for maintaining his wife. The thought would occur to him, 'Before, taking a loan, I invested it in my business affairs. Now my business affairs have succeeded. I have repaid my old debts and there is extra left over for maintaining my wife.' Because of that he would experience joy and happiness.

"Now suppose that a man falls sick—in pain and seriously ill. He does not enjoy his meals, and there is no strength in his body. As time passes, he eventually recovers from that sickness. He enjoys his meals and there is strength in his body. The thought would occur to him, 'Before, I was sick... Now I am recovered from that sickness. I enjoy my meals and there is strength in my body.' Because of that he would experience joy and happiness.

"Now suppose that a man is bound in prison. As time passes, he eventually is released from that bondage, safe and sound, with no loss of property. The thought would occur to him, 'Before, I was bound in prison. Now I am released from that bondage, safe and sound, with no loss of my property.' Because of that he would experience joy and happiness.

"Now suppose that a man is a slave, subject to others, not subject to himself, unable to go where he likes. As time passes, he eventually is released from that slavery, subject to himself, not subject to others, freed, able to go where he likes. The thought would occur to him, 'Before, I was a slave… Now I am released from that slavery, subject to myself, not subject to others, freed, able to go where I like.' Because of that he would experience joy and happiness.

"Now suppose that a man, carrying money and goods, is traveling by a road through desolate country. As time passes, he eventually emerges from that desolate country, safe and sound, with no loss of property. The thought would occur to him, 'Before, carrying money and goods, I was traveling by a road through desolate country. Now I have emerged from that desolate country, safe and sound, with no loss of my property.' Because of that he would experience joy and happiness.

"In the same way, when these five hindrances are not abandoned in himself, the monk regards it as a debt, a sickness, a prison, slavery, a road through desolate country. But when these five hindrances are abandoned in himself, he regards it as unindebtedness, good health, release from prison, freedom, a place of security. When he sees that they have been abandoned within him, gladness is born. In one who is gladdened, rapture is born. Enraptured at heart, his body grows calm. His body calm, he is sensitive to pleasure. Feeling pleasure, his mind becomes concentrated.

THE FOUR JHĀNAS

"Quite secluded from sensuality, secluded from unskillful qualities, he enters and remains in the first jhāna: rapture & pleasure born of seclusion, accompanied by directed thought and evaluation. He permeates and pervades, suffuses and fills this very body with the rapture and pleasure born of seclusion. Just as if a dexterous bathman or bathman's apprentice would pour bath powder into a brass basin and knead it together, sprinkling it again and again with water, so that his ball of bath powder—saturated, moisture-laden, permeated within and without—would nevertheless not drip; even so, the monk permeates… this very body with the rapture & pleasure born of seclusion. There's nothing of his entire body unpervaded by rapture & pleasure born of seclusion.

"Furthermore, with the stilling of directed thoughts & evaluations, he enters and remains in the second jhāna: rapture & pleasure born of concentration, unification of awareness free from directed thought and evaluation—internal assurance. He permeates and pervades, suffuses and fills this very body with the rapture & pleasure born of concentration. Just like a lake with spring-water welling up from within, having no inflow from the east, west, north, or south, and with the skies supplying abundant showers time and again,[2] so that the cool fount of water welling up from within the lake would permeate and pervade, suffuse and fill it with cool waters, there being no part of the lake unpervaded by the cool waters; even so, the monk permeates… this very body with the rapture & pleasure born of concentration. There's nothing of his entire body unpervaded by rapture & pleasure born of concentration.

"And furthermore, with the fading of rapture, he remains equanimous, mindful, & alert, and senses pleasure with the body. He enters and remains in the third jhāna, of which the noble ones declare, 'Equanimous & mindful, he has a pleasant abiding.' He permeates and pervades, suffuses and fills this very body with the pleasure divested of rapture. Just as in a lotus pond, some of the lotuses, born and growing in the water, stay immersed in the water and flourish without standing up out of the water, so that they are permeated and pervaded, suffused and filled with cool water from their roots to their tips, and nothing of those lotuses would be unpervaded with cool water; even so, the monk permeates… this very body with the pleasure divested of rapture. There's nothing of his entire body unpervaded with pleasure divested of rapture.

"And furthermore, with the abandoning of pleasure & pain—as with the earlier disappearance of joy & distress—he enters and remains in the fourth jhāna: purity of equanimity & mindfulness, neither-pleasure nor stress. He sits, permeating the body with a pure, bright awareness. Just as if a man were sitting covered from head to foot with a white cloth so that there would be no part of his body to which the white cloth did not extend; even so, the monk sits, permeating the body with a pure, bright awareness. There's nothing of his entire body unpervaded by pure, bright awareness.

THE THREE KNOWLEDGES

"With his mind thus concentrated, purified, and bright, unblemished, free from defects, pliant, malleable, steady, and attained to imperturbability, he directs and inclines it to knowledge of the recollection of past lives [lit: previous homes]. He recollects his manifold past lives, i.e., one birth, two births, three births, four, five, ten, twenty, thirty, forty, fifty, one hundred, one thousand, one hundred thousand, many eons of cosmic contraction, many eons of cosmic expansion, many eons of cosmic contraction and expansion, (recollecting,) 'There I had such a name, belonged to such a clan, had such an appearance. Such was my food, such my experience of pleasure and pain, such the end of my life. Passing away from that state, I re-arose there. There too I had such a name, belonged to such a clan, had such an appearance. Such was my food, such my experience of pleasure and pain, such the end of my life. Passing away from that state, I re-arose here.' Thus he recollects his manifold past lives in their modes and details.

"Just as if a man were to go from his home village to another village, and then from that village to yet another village, and then from that village back to his home village. The thought would occur to him, 'I went from my home village to that village over there. There I stood in such a way, sat in such a way, talked in such a way, and remained silent in such a way. From that village I went to that village over there, and there I stood in such a way, sat in such a way, talked in such a way, and remained silent in such a way. From that village I came back home.' In the same way—with his mind thus concentrated, purified, and bright, unblemished, free from defects, pliant, malleable, steady, and attained to imperturbability—the monk directs and inclines it to knowledge of the recollection of past lives. He recollects his manifold past lives… in their modes and details.

"With his mind thus concentrated, purified, and bright, unblemished, free from defects, pliant, malleable, steady, and attained to imperturbability, he directs and inclines it to knowledge of the passing away and re-appearance of beings. He sees—by means of the divine eye, purified and surpassing the human—beings passing away and re-appearing, and he discerns how they are inferior and superior, beautiful and ugly, fortunate and unfortunate in accordance with their kamma: 'These beings—who were endowed with bad conduct of body, speech, and mind, who reviled the noble ones, held wrong views and undertook actions under the influence of wrong views—with the break-up of the body, after death, have re-appeared in a plane of deprivation, a bad destination, a lower realm, hell. But these beings—who were endowed with good conduct of body, speech, and mind, who did not revile the noble ones, who held right views and undertook actions under the influence of right views—with the break-up of the body, after death, have re-appeared in a good destination, a heavenly world.' Thus—by means of the divine eye, purified and surpassing the human—he sees beings passing away and re-appearing, and he discerns how they are inferior and superior, beautiful and ugly, fortunate and unfortunate in accordance with their kamma.

"Just as if there were a tall building in the central square (of a town), and a man with good eyesight standing on top of it were to see people entering a house, leaving it, walking along the street, and sitting in the central square. The thought would occur to him, 'These people are entering a house, leaving it, walking along the streets, and sitting in the central square.' In the same way—with his mind thus concentrated, purified, and bright, unblemished, free from defects, pliant, malleable, steady, and attained to imperturbability—the monk directs and inclines it to knowledge of the passing away and re-appearance of beings. He sees—by means of the divine eye, purified and surpassing the human—beings passing away and re-appearing, and he discerns how they are inferior and superior, beautiful and ugly, fortunate and unfortunate in accordance with their kamma....

"With his mind thus concentrated, purified, and bright, unblemished, free from defects, pliant, malleable, steady, and attained to imperturbability, the monk directs and inclines it to the knowledge of the ending of the effluents. He discerns, as it is has come to be, that 'This is stress... This is the origination of stress... This is the cessation of stress... This is the way leading to the cessation of stress... These are effluents... This is the origination of effluents... This is the cessation of effluents... This is the way leading to the cessation of effluents.' His heart, thus knowing, thus seeing, is released from the effluent of sensuality, released from the effluent of becoming, released from the effluent of ignorance. With release, there is the knowledge, 'Released.' He discerns that 'Birth is ended, the holy life fulfilled, the task done. There is nothing further for this world.'

"Just as if there were a pool of water in a mountain glen—clear, limpid, and unsullied—where a man with good eyesight standing on the bank could see shells, gravel, and pebbles, and also shoals of fish swimming about and resting, and it would occur to him, 'This pool of water is clear, limpid, and unsullied. Here are these shells, gravel, and pebbles, and also these shoals of fish swimming about and resting.' In the same way—with his mind thus concentrated, purified, and bright, unblemished, free from defects, pliant, malleable, steady, and attained to imperturbability—the monk directs and inclines it to the knowledge of the ending of the effluents. He discerns, as it has come to be, that 'This is stress... This is the origination of stress... This is the cessation of stress... This is the way leading to the cessation of stress... These are effluents... This is the origination of effluents... This is the cessation of effluents... This is the way leading to the cessation of effluents.' His heart, thus knowing, thus seeing, is released from the effluent of sensuality, released from the effluent of becoming, released from the effluent of ignorance. With release, there is the knowledge, 'Released.' He discerns that 'Birth is ended, the holy life fulfilled, the task done. There is nothing further for this world.'

"This, monks, is called a monk who is a contemplative, a brahman, washed, a master, learned, noble, an arahant.[3]

"And how is a monk a contemplative *[samaṇa]?* His evil, unskillful qualities that are defiled, that lead to further becoming, create trouble, ripen in stress, and lead to future birth, aging, & death have been calmed *[samita].* This is how a monk is a contemplative.

"And how is a monk a brahman? His evil, unskillful qualities that are defiled, that lead to further becoming, create trouble, ripen in stress, and lead to future birth, aging, & death have been expelled *[bahita].* This is how a monk is a brahman.

"And how is a monk washed? His evil, unskillful qualities that are defiled, that lead to further becoming, create trouble, ripen in stress, and lead to future birth, aging, & death have been washed away. This is how a monk is washed.

"And how is a monk a master? His evil, unskillful qualities that are defiled, that lead to further becoming, create trouble, ripen in stress, and lead to future birth, aging, & death have been mastered. This is how a monk is a master.

"And how is a monk learned *[sottiya]?* His evil, unskillful qualities that are defiled, that lead to further becoming, create trouble, ripen in stress, and lead to future birth, aging, & death have streamed away *[nissuta].* This is how a monk is learned.

"And how is a monk noble *[ariya]?* His evil, unskillful qualities that are defiled, that lead to further becoming, create trouble, ripen in stress, and lead to future birth, aging, & death have gone far away *[ārakā].* This is how a monk is noble.

"And how is a monk an arahant? His evil, unskillful qualities that are defiled, that lead to further becoming, create trouble, ripen in stress, and lead to future birth, aging, & death have gone far away *[ārakā].* This is how a monk is an arahant."

That is what the Blessed One said. Gratified, the monks delighted in the Blessed One's words.

NOTES

1. Given the widespread misperception that arahantship is a selfish goal, it's important to take note of this statement—that part of the motivation to become an arahant is how it will benefit other people.

2. Reading, *Devo ca kālena kālaṁ sammādhāraṁ anuppaveccheyya,* with the Thai edition.

3. The following passages are all based on word play in the Pali.

See also: DN 2; MN 29–30

41 (Brahmans) of Sāla

Sāleyyaka Sutta

I have heard that on one occasion, while the Blessed One was on a wandering tour among the Kosalans with a large Saṅgha of monks, he arrived at a brahman village of the Kosalans called Sāla.

The brahman householders of Sāla heard it said: "Gotama the contemplative—the son of the Sakyans, having gone forth from the Sakyan clan—on a wandering tour among the Kosalans with a large Saṅgha of monks—has arrived at Sāla. And of that Master Gotama this fine reputation has spread: 'He is indeed a Blessed One, worthy & rightly self-awakened, consummate in clear-knowing & conduct, well-gone, an expert with regard to the cosmos, unexcelled trainer of people fit to be tamed, teacher of devas & human beings, awakened, blessed. He makes known—having realized it through direct knowledge—this world with its devas, Māras, & Brahmās, this generation with its contemplatives & brahmans, its rulers & commonfolk; he explains the Dhamma admirable in the beginning, admirable in the middle, admirable in the end; he expounds the holy life both in its particulars & in its essence, entirely perfect, surpassingly pure. It is good to see such a worthy one.'"

So the brahman householders of Sāla went to the Blessed One. On arrival, some of them, bowing down to him, sat to one side. Some of them exchanged courteous greetings with him and, after an exchange of friendly greetings & courtesies, sat to one side. Some of them, placing their hands palm-to-palm over the heart in his direction, sat to one side. Some of them, announcing their name and clan in his presence, sat to one side. Some of them, remaining silent, sat to one side.

As they were sitting there, the brahman householders of Sāla said to the Blessed One, "What is the reason, Master Gotama, what is the condition, whereby some beings here, with the break-up of the body, after death, reappear in a plane of deprivation, a bad destination, a lower realm, hell? And what is the reason, what is the condition, whereby some beings here, with the break-up of the body, after death, reappear in a good destination, a heavenly world?"

"Householders, it's by reason of un-Dhamma conduct, dissonant[1] conduct that some beings here, with the break-up of the body, after death, reappear in a plane of deprivation, a bad destination, a lower realm, hell. It's by reason of Dhamma conduct, harmonious[1] conduct that some beings here, with the break-up of the body, after death, reappear in a good destination, a heavenly world."

"We don't understand the detailed meaning of Master Gotama's brief statement, the detailed meaning of what he hasn't analyzed. It would be good if Master Gotama would teach the Dhamma so that we would understand the detailed meaning of Master Gotama's brief statement, the detailed meaning of what he hasn't analyzed."

"Very well, in that case, householders, listen & pay careful attention. I will speak."

"As you say, master," the brahman householders of Sāla responded to the Blessed One.

The Blessed One said: "Householders, there are three sorts of un-Dhamma conduct, dissonant conduct with the body; four sorts of un-Dhamma conduct, dissonant conduct with speech; and three sorts of un-Dhamma conduct, dissonant conduct with the mind.

UNSKILLFUL BODILY ACTION

"And how are there three sorts of un-Dhamma conduct, dissonant conduct with the body?

"There is the case where a certain person takes life, is brutal, bloody-handed, devoted to killing & slaying, showing no mercy to living beings.

"He takes what is not given. He takes, in the manner of a thief, things in a village or a wilderness that belong to others and have not been given by them.

"He engages in sexual misconduct. He gets sexually involved with those who are protected by their mothers, their fathers, their brothers, their sisters, their relatives, or their Dhamma; those with husbands, those who entail punishments, or even those crowned with flowers by another man.

"This is how there are three sorts of un-Dhamma conduct, dissonant conduct with the body.

UNSKILLFUL VERBAL ACTION

"And how are there four sorts of un-Dhamma conduct, dissonant conduct with speech?

"There is the case where a certain person tells lies. When he has been called to a town meeting, a group meeting, a gathering of his relatives, his guild, or of the royalty [i.e., a royal court proceeding], if he is asked as a witness, 'Come & tell, good man, what you know': If he doesn't know, he says, 'I know.' If he does know, he says, 'I don't know.' If he hasn't seen, he says, 'I have seen.' If he has seen, he says, 'I haven't seen.' Thus he consciously tells lies for his own sake, for the sake of another, or for the sake of a certain reward.

"He engages in divisive speech.[2] What he has heard here he tells there to break those people apart from these people here. What he has heard there he tells here to break these people apart from those people there. Thus breaking apart those who are united and stirring up strife between those who have broken apart, he loves factionalism, delights in factionalism, enjoys factionalism, speaks things that create factionalism.

"He engages in abusive speech. He speaks words that are harsh, cutting, bitter to others, abusive of others, provoking anger and destroying concentration.

"He engages in idle chatter. He speaks out of season, speaks what isn't factual, what isn't in accordance with the goal, the Dhamma, & the Vinaya, words that are not worth treasuring.

"This is how there are four sorts of un-Dhamma conduct, dissonant conduct with speech.

UNSKILLFUL MENTAL ACTION

"And how are there three sorts of un-Dhamma conduct, dissonant conduct with the mind?

"There is the case where a certain person is covetous. He covets the belongings of others, thinking, 'O, that what belongs to others would be mine!'

"He bears ill will, corrupt in the resolves of his heart: 'May these beings be killed or cut apart or crushed or destroyed, or may they not exist at all!'

"He has wrong view, is warped in the way he sees things: 'There is nothing given, nothing offered, nothing sacrificed. There is no fruit or result of good or bad actions. There is no this world, no next world, no mother, no father, no spontaneously reborn beings; no contemplatives or brahmans who, faring rightly & practicing rightly, proclaim this world & the next after having directly known & realized it for themselves.'[3]

"This is how there are three sorts of un-Dhamma conduct, dissonant conduct with the mind.

"It's by reason of this un-Dhamma conduct & dissonant conduct that some beings here, with the break-up of the body, after death, re-appear in a plane of deprivation, a bad destination, a lower realm, hell.

"Householders, there are three sorts of Dhamma conduct, harmonious conduct with the body; four sorts of Dhamma conduct, harmonious conduct with speech; and three sorts of Dhamma conduct, harmonious conduct with the mind.

SKILLFUL BODILY ACTION

"And how are there three sorts of Dhamma conduct, harmonious conduct with the body?

"There is the case where a certain person, abandoning the taking of life, abstains from the taking of life. He dwells with his rod laid down, his knife laid down, scrupulous, merciful, compassionate for the welfare of all living beings.

"Abandoning the taking of what is not given, he abstains from taking what is not given. He doesn't take, in the manner of a thief, things in a village or a wilderness that belong to others and have not been given by them.

"Abandoning sexual misconduct, he abstains from sexual misconduct. He doesn't get sexually involved with those who are protected by their mothers, their fathers, their brothers, their sisters, their relatives, or their Dhamma; those with husbands, those who entail punishments, or even those crowned with flowers by another man.

"This is how there are three sorts of Dhamma conduct, harmonious conduct with the body.

SKILLFUL VERBAL ACTION

"And how are there three sorts of Dhamma conduct, harmonious conduct with speech?

"There is the case where a certain person, abandoning the telling of lies, abstains from telling lies. When he has been called to a town meeting, a group meeting, a gathering of his relatives, his guild, or of the royalty, if he is asked as a witness, 'Come & tell, good man, what you know': If he doesn't know, he says, 'I don't know.' If he does know, he says, 'I know.' If he hasn't seen, he says, 'I haven't seen.' If he has seen, he says, 'I have seen.' Thus he doesn't consciously tell a lie for his own sake, for the sake of another, or for the sake of any reward.

"Abandoning divisive speech, he abstains from divisive speech. What he has heard here he doesn't tell there to break those people apart from these people here. What he has heard there he doesn't tell here to break these people apart from those people there. Thus reconciling those who have broken apart or cementing those who are united, he loves concord, delights in concord, enjoys concord, speaks things that create concord.

"Abandoning abusive speech, he abstains from abusive speech. He speaks words that are soothing to the ear, that are affectionate, that go to the heart, that are polite, appealing & pleasing to people at large.

"Abandoning idle chatter, he abstains from idle chatter. He speaks in season, speaks what is factual, what is in accordance with the goal, the Dhamma, & the Vinaya. He speaks words worth treasuring, seasonable, reasonable, circumscribed, connected with the goal.

"This is how there are four sorts of Dhamma conduct, harmonious conduct with speech.

SKILLFUL MENTAL ACTION

"And how are there three sorts of Dhamma conduct, harmonious conduct with the mind?

"There is the case where a certain person is not covetous. He doesn't covet the belongings of others, thinking, 'O, that what belongs to others would be mine!'

"He bears no ill will and is not corrupt in the resolves of his heart. (He thinks,) 'May these beings be free from animosity, free from oppression, free from trouble, and may they look after themselves with ease!'[4]

"He has right view and is not warped in the way he sees things: 'There is what is given, what is offered, what is sacrificed. There are fruits & results of good & bad actions. There is this world & the next world. There is mother & father. There are spontaneously reborn beings; there are contemplatives & brahmans who, faring rightly & practicing rightly, proclaim this world & the next after having directly known & realized it for themselves.'[5]

"This is how there are three sorts of Dhamma conduct, harmonious conduct with the mind.

"It's by reason of this Dhamma conduct & harmonious conduct that some beings here, with the break-up of the body, after death, reappear in a good destination, a heavenly world.

"Householders, if one—a person of Dhamma conduct, harmonious conduct—should wish: 'O if I, with the break-up of the body, after death, were to reappear among well-to-do noble warriors,' it is possible that one—with the break-up of the body, after death—would appear among well-to-do noble warriors. Why is that? Because one is a person of Dhamma conduct, harmonious conduct.[6]

"If one—a person of Dhamma conduct, harmonious conduct—should wish: 'O if I, with the break-up of the body, after death, were to reappear among well-to-do brahmans,' it is possible that one—with the break-up of the body, after death—would appear among well-to-do brahmans. Why is that? Because one is a person of Dhamma conduct, harmonious conduct.

"If one—a person of Dhamma conduct, harmonious conduct—should wish: 'O if I, with the break-up of the body, after death, were to reappear among well-to-do householders,' it is possible that one—with the break-up of the body, after death—would appear among well-to-do householders. Why is that? Because one is a person of Dhamma conduct, harmonious conduct.

"If one—a person of Dhamma conduct, harmonious conduct—should wish: 'O if I, with the break-up of the body, after death, were to reappear among the devas of the Four Great Kings,' it is possible that one—with the break-up of the body, after death—would appear among the devas of the Four Great Kings. Why is that? Because one is a person of Dhamma conduct, harmonious conduct.

"If one—a person of Dhamma conduct, harmonious conduct—should wish: 'O if I, with the break-up of the body, after death, were to reappear among the devas of the Thirty-three... the devas of the Hours... the Contented devas... the devas Delighting in Creation... the devas Wielding Power over the Creations of Others,' it is possible that one—with the break-up of the body, after death—would appear among the devas Wielding Power over the Creations of Others. Why is that? Because one is a person of Dhamma conduct, harmonious conduct.[7]

"If one—a person of Dhamma conduct, harmonious conduct—should wish: 'O if I, with the break-up of the body, after death, were to reappear among the devas in Brahmā's retinue... the Radiant devas... the devas of Limited Radiance... the devas of Immeasurable Radiance... the devas of Streaming Radiance... the Beautiful devas ... the devas of Limited Beauty... the devas of Immeasurable Beauty... the Beautiful Black devas... the Sky-fruit devas,' it is possible that one—with the break-up of the body, after death—would appear among the Sky-fruit devas. Why is that? Because one is a person of Dhamma conduct, harmonious conduct.[8]

"If one—a person of Dhamma conduct, harmonious conduct—should wish: 'O if I, with the break-up of the body, after death, were to reappear among the Not Falling Away devas... the Untroubled devas... the Good-looking devas... the Clear-seeing devas... the Peerless devas,' it is possible that one—with the break-up of the body, after death—would appear among the Peerless devas.

Why is that? Because one is a person of Dhamma conduct, harmonious conduct.[9]

"If one—a person of Dhamma conduct, harmonious conduct—should wish: 'O if I, with the break-up of the body, after death, were to reappear among the devas who have reached the dimension of the infinitude of space... the devas who have reached the dimension of the infinitude of consciousness... the devas who have reached the dimension of nothingness... the devas who have reached the dimension of neither perception nor non-perception,' it is possible that one—with the break-up of the body, after death—would appear among the devas who have reached the dimension of neither perception nor non-perception. Why is that? Because one is a person of Dhamma conduct, harmonious conduct.[10]

"If one—a person of Dhamma conduct, harmonious conduct—should wish: 'O if I—with the ending of the effluents—were to enter & remain in the effluent-free awareness-release & discernment-release, having directly known and realized them for myself right in the here & now,' it is possible that one—with the ending of the effluents—would enter & remain in the effluent-free awareness-release & discernment-release, having directly known and realized them for oneself right in the here & now.[11] Why is that? Because one is a person of Dhamma conduct, harmonious conduct."

When this was said, the brahman householders of Sāla said to the Blessed One: "Magnificent, Master Gotama! Magnificent! Just as if he were to place upright what was overturned, to reveal what was hidden, to show the way to one who was lost, or to carry a lamp into the dark so that those with eyes could see forms, in the same way has Master Gotama—through many lines of reasoning—made the Dhamma clear. We go to Master Gotama for refuge, to the Dhamma, & to the Saṅgha of monks. May Master Gotama remember us as lay followers who have gone for refuge from this day forward, for life."

NOTES

1. Dissonant and harmonious *(visama* and *sama):* Throughout ancient cultures, the terminology of music was used to describe the moral quality of people and acts. Dissonant intervals or poorly-tuned musical instruments were metaphors for evil; harmonious intervals and well-tuned instruments were metaphors for good. In Pali, the term *sama*—"even"—describes an instrument tuned on-pitch. AN 6:55 contains a famous passage where the Buddha reminds Soṇa Koḷivisa—

who had been over-exerting himself in the practice—that a lute sounds appealing only if the strings are neither too taut nor too lax, but "evenly" tuned.

2. *Pisuṇā vācā:* Some translators mistakenly render this term as "slander," which is actually a form of false speech. *Pisuṇā vācā* deals with true matters but is intended to break friendships or to prevent them from happening.

3. This is the materialist view espoused by Ajita Kesakambalin (DN 2), who maintained that there was no birth after death and that actions bore no results. "Nothing given" means that the act of generosity bears no karmic fruit. "No this world, no next world" means that there is no life after death. "No spontaneously reborn beings" means that there are no inhabitants of heaven or hell.

4. This passage is the basis for the expressions of goodwill that are often chanted in Theravada countries.

5. This definition of right view—called "mundane" right view in MN 117—is a level of right view that is a preliminary to transcendent right view, i.e., right view in terms of the four noble truths. Mundane right view establishes two principles—that actions bear fruit and that death is normally followed by rebirth—as basic working hypotheses for the practice. MN 60 notes that if a person who does not accept these principles, "it can be expected that, shunning these three skillful activities—good bodily conduct, good verbal conduct, good mental conduct—they will adopt & practice these three unskillful activities: bad bodily conduct, bad verbal conduct, bad mental conduct. Why is that? Because (they) do not see, in unskillful activities, the drawbacks, the degradation, and the defilement; nor in skillful activities the rewards of renunciation, resembling cleansing."

6. This and the following passages on the power of a wish made by a virtuous person are apparently related to a principle—expressed in SN 41:10—that a wish made by a virtuous person can succeed through the purity of his/her virtue. However, other passages in the Canon suggest that virtue on its own—even when combined with the levels of conviction and discernment embodied in the three types of skillful mental action—may not be enough for any of the attainments listed here. In other words, the ten types of skillful action may be necessary causes for these attainments, but they may not be sufficient causes.

For example, MN 135 states that one must be generous in order to be born into a wealthy family. AN 3:71 states that the rebirth into the six deva realms beginning with the devas of the Four Great Kings is based on five qualities: conviction, virtue, learning, generosity, and discernment. AN 7:49 correlates different motivations for giving with the attainment of different levels of rebirth among these realms after death. AN 4:123 and 125 state that rebirth in Brahmā's retinue can follow on the attainment of the first jhāna or the meditative development of immeasurable goodwill.

It should also be noted, in line with MN 136, that skillful conduct in this lifetime is not always rewarded in the immediate next birth, either because of previous bad actions or because of bad actions adopted toward the end of one's life. In such a case, the desired destination will be delayed to a later lifetime. This may be why the Buddha states that "it is possible" that a person of Dhamma conduct will attain his/her desired destination in the next life. Only with the attainment of stream-entry is one guaranteed not to fall into the lower realms.

Conversely, it is not always the case that a person who engages in unskillful conduct in this lifetime will go to a lower destination in the next. There is always the possibility that such a person may have good kamma from the past, or may change his/her ways later in this lifetime. In SN 42:8 the Buddha criticizes those who teach that misdeeds inevitably lead to a bad destination in the next lifetime, saying that anyone who believed such a teaching and knew that he/she had already committed misdeeds would feel that he/she had already been consigned to hell. A more skillful way to regard past misdeeds would be to recognize that they were wrong, to resolve not to repeat them, and to develop attitudes of immeasurable goodwill, compassion, empathetic joy, and equanimity to reinforce one's resolve not to treat anyone in an unskillful way.

AN 3:101 adds that the results of past misdeeds can be mitigated both through the practice of the four immeasurables and through training the mind so that it is not overcome by feelings of pleasure or pain.

7. The six deva realms listed here, beginning with the Four Great Kings, are the realms of the sensual heavens.

8. These are the devas (also called Brahmās) on the level of form. The commentary notes that the term "Radiant devas" is actually a class name encompassing the following three levels: the devas of Limited Radiance, the devas of Immeasurable Radiance, and the devas of Streaming Radiance. Similarly, the "Beautiful devas" encompass the devas of Limited Beauty, the devas of Immeasurable Beauty, and the Beautiful Black devas. According to AN 4:123 and 125, rebirth among the devas of Streaming Radiance can follow on the attainment of the second jhāna or the meditative development of immeasurable compassion; rebirth among the Beautiful Black devas can follow on the attainment of the third jhāna or the meditative development of immeasurable empathetic joy; rebirth among the Sky-fruit devas can follow on the attainment of the fourth jhāna or the meditative development of immeasurable equanimity.

An Abhidhamma text, the Vibhaṅga—drawing on a passage in DN 1—mentions another level of devas of form not listed here: the Non-percipient beings, a level in which there is no perception at all. The commentary explains that they are not listed here because this attainment is open to hermits and seers outside the Buddha's teaching, and does not require virtue. This, however, ignores the fact that the four jhānas and four formless states are also open to people outside the Buddha's teaching; and although virtue helps with the attainment of jhāna, it is nowhere stated in the Canon that the jhānas cannot be attained by a person whose virtue is not pure. A more likely reason for omitting the Non-percipient beings here is that this state, unlike the jhānas and four formless states, is not conducive to the arising of insight, and so would not be considered a desirable goal.

9. These are the Pure Abodes: the Brahmā heavens into which non-returners are reborn and where they attain total unbinding. AN 4:124 and 126 state that, to attain these realms, one masters any of the four jhānas or four immeasurable abidings (based on goodwill, etc.), and then contemplates the resulting mental state in this way: "One regards whatever phenomena there that are connected with form, feeling, perception, fabrications, & consciousness, as inconstant, stressful, a disease, a cancer, an arrow, painful, an affliction, alien, a disintegration, an emptiness, not-self. At the break-up of the body, after death, he reappears among the devas of the Pure Abodes. This rebirth is not in common with run-of-the-mill people."

10. These are the devas (also called Brahmās) of the formless levels, corresponding to the four formless attainments.

11. This is the standard description of arahantship, which requires not only heightened virtue, but also heightened mastery of concentration and heightened discernment (see AN 3:88).

See also: MN 9; MN 60; MN 135; AN 3:71; AN 4:123–126; AN 7:49; AN 8:54; AN 10:165

43 *The Greater Set of Questions & Answers*

Mahā Vedalla Sutta

I have heard that on one occasion the Blessed One was staying near Sāvatthī in Jeta's Grove, Anāthapiṇḍika's monastery. Then Ven. Mahā Koṭṭhita, emerging from his seclusion in the late afternoon, went to Ven. Sāriputta and, on arrival, exchanged courteous greetings with him. After an exchange of friendly greetings & courtesies, he sat to one side.

DISCERNMENT

As he was sitting there, he said to Ven. Sāriputta, "Friend, 'One of poor discernment, one of poor discernment': Thus is it said. To what extent is one said to be 'one of poor discernment'?"

"'One doesn't discern, one doesn't discern': Thus, friend, one is said to be 'one of poor discernment.' And what doesn't one discern? One doesn't discern, 'This is stress.' One doesn't discern, 'This is the origination of stress.' One doesn't discern, 'This is the cessation of stress.' One doesn't discern, 'This is the practice leading to the cessation of stress.' 'One doesn't discern, one doesn't discern': Thus one is said to be 'one of poor discernment.'"

Saying, "Very good, friend," Ven. Mahā Koṭṭhita—delighting in & approving of Ven. Sāriputta's statement—asked him a further question: "Discerning, discerning': Thus is it said. To what extent, friend, is one said to be 'discerning'?"

"'One discerns, one discerns': Thus, friend, one is said to be 'discerning.' And what does one discern? One discerns, 'This is stress.' One discerns, 'This is the origination of stress.' One discerns, 'This is the cessation of stress.' One discerns, 'This is the practice leading to the cessation of stress.' 'One discerns, one discerns': Thus one is said to be 'discerning.'"

CONSCIOUSNESS

"'Consciousness, consciousness': Thus is it said. To what extent, friend, is it said to be 'consciousness'?"

"'It cognizes, it cognizes': Thus, friend, it is said to be 'consciousness.' And what does it cognize? It cognizes 'pleasant.' It cognizes 'painful.' It cognizes 'neither painful nor pleasant.' 'It cognizes, it cognizes': Thus it is said to be 'consciousness.'"

"Discernment & consciousness, friend: Are these qualities conjoined or disjoined? Is it possible, having separated them one from the other, to delineate the difference between them?"

"Discernment & consciousness are conjoined, friend, not disjoined. It's not possible, having separated them one from the other, to delineate the difference between them. For what one discerns, that one cognizes. What one cognizes, that one discerns. Therefore these qualities are conjoined, not disjoined, and it is not possible, having separated them one from another, to delineate the difference between them."

"Discernment & consciousness, friend: What is the difference between these qualities that are conjoined, not disjoined?"

"Discernment & consciousness, friend: Of these qualities that are conjoined, not disjoined, discernment is to be developed, consciousness is to be fully comprehended."[1]

FEELING

"'Feeling, feeling': Thus is it said. To what extent, friend, is it said to be 'feeling'?"

"'It feels, it feels': Thus, friend, it is said to be 'feeling.' And what does it feel? It feels pleasure. It feels pain. It feels neither pleasure nor pain. 'It feels, it feels': Thus it is said to be 'feeling.'"

PERCEPTION

"'Perception, perception': Thus is it said. To what extent, friend, is it said to be 'perception'?"

"'It perceives, it perceives': Thus, friend, it is said to be 'perception.' And what does it perceive? It perceives blue. It perceives yellow. It perceives red. It perceives white. 'It perceives, it perceives': Thus it is said to be 'perception.'"

"Feeling, perception, & consciousness, friend: Are these qualities conjoined or disjoined? Is it possible, having separated them one from another, to delineate the difference among them?"

"Feeling, perception, & consciousness are conjoined, friend, not disjoined. It is not possible, having separated them one from another, to delineate the difference among them. For what one feels, that one perceives. What one perceives, that one cognizes. Therefore these qualities are conjoined, not disjoined, and it is not possible, having separated them one from another, to delineate the difference among them."

THE EYE OF DISCERNMENT

"Friend, what can be known with the purified intellect-consciousness divorced from the five (sense) faculties?"

"Friend, with the purified intellect-consciousness divorced from the five faculties, the dimension of the infinitude of space can be known (as) 'infinite space,' the dimension of the infinitude of consciousness can be known (as) 'infinite consciousness,' the dimension of nothingness can be known (as) 'There is nothing.'[2]

"With what does one know a quality that can be known?"

"One knows a quality that can be known with the eye of discernment."

"And what is the purpose of discernment?"

"The purpose of discernment is direct knowledge, its purpose is full comprehension, its purpose is abandoning."

RIGHT VIEW

"Friend, how many conditions are there for the arising of right view?"

"Friend, there are two conditions for the arising of right view: the voice of another and appropriate attention. These are the two conditions for the arising of right view."

"And assisted by how many factors does right view have awareness-release as its fruit & reward, and discernment-release as its fruit & reward?"

"Assisted by five factors, right view has awareness-release as its fruit & reward, and discernment-release as its fruit & reward. There is the case where right view is assisted by virtue, assisted by learning, assisted by discussion, assisted by tranquility, assisted by insight. Assisted by these five factors, right view has awareness-release as its fruit & reward, and discernment-release as its fruit & reward."

BECOMING

"Friend, how many kinds of becoming are there?"

"Friend, there are these three kinds of becoming: sensual becoming, form becoming, formless becoming."

"And how is further becoming in the future brought about?"

"The delight, now here, now there, of beings hindered by ignorance & fettered by craving: That's how further becoming in the future is brought about."

"And how is further becoming in the future not brought about?"

"Through the fading of ignorance, the arising of clear knowing, & the cessation of craving: That's how further becoming in the future is not brought about."

THE FIRST JHĀNA

"What, friend, is the first jhāna?"

"There is the case, friend, where a monk—quite secluded from sensuality, secluded from unskillful qualities—enters & remains in the first jhāna: rapture & pleasure born of seclusion, accompanied by directed thought & evaluation. This is called the first jhāna."

"And how many factors does the first jhāna have?"

"The first jhāna has five factors. There is the case where, in a monk who has attained the five-factored first jhāna, there occurs directed thought, evaluation, rapture, pleasure, & singleness of mind. It's in this way that the first jhāna has five factors."

"And how many factors are abandoned in the first jhāna, and with how many is it endowed?"

"Five factors are abandoned in the first jhāna, and with five is it endowed. There is the case where, in a monk who has attained the first jhāna, sensual desire is abandoned, ill will is abandoned, sloth & torpor is abandoned, restlessness & anxiety is abandoned, uncertainty is abandoned. And there occur directed thought, evaluation, rapture, pleasure, & singleness of mind. It's in this way that five factors are abandoned in the first jhāna, and with five it is endowed."

THE FIVE FACULTIES

"Friend, there are these five faculties each with a separate range, a separate domain, and they do not experience one another's range & domain: the eye-faculty, the ear-faculty, the nose-faculty, the tongue-faculty, & the body-faculty. Now what do these five faculties—each with a separate range, a separate domain, not experiencing one another's range & domain: the eye-faculty, the ear-faculty, the nose-faculty, the tongue-faculty, & the body-faculty—have as their (common) arbitrator? What experiences (all) their ranges & domains?"

"Friend, these five faculties—each with a separate range, a separate domain, not experiencing one another's range & domain: the eye-faculty, the ear-faculty, the nose-faculty, the tongue-faculty, & the body-faculty—have the intellect as their (common) arbitrator. The intellect is what experiences (all) their ranges & domains."

"Now, these five faculties—the eye-faculty, the ear-faculty, the nose-faculty, the tongue-faculty, & the body-faculty: In dependence on what do they remain standing?"

"These five faculties—the eye-faculty, the ear-faculty, the nose-faculty, the tongue-faculty, & the body-faculty—remain standing in dependence on vitality."[3]

"And vitality remains standing in dependence on what?"

"Vitality remains standing in dependence on heat."

"And heat remains standing in dependence on what?"

"Heat remains standing in dependence on vitality."

"Just now, friend Sāriputta, we understood you to say, 'Vitality remains standing in dependence on heat.' And just now we understood you to say, 'Heat remains standing in dependence on vitality.' Now how is the meaning of these statements to be seen?"

"In that case, friend, I will give you analogy, for there are cases where it is through an analogy that an intelligent person understands the meaning of a statement. Suppose an oil lamp is burning. Its radiance is discerned in dependence on its flame, and its flame is discerned in dependence on its radiance. In the same way, vitality remains standing in dependence on heat, and heat remains standing in dependence on vitality.

VITALITY-FABRICATIONS

"Friend, are vitality-fabrications[4] the same thing as feeling-states? Or are vitality-fabrications one thing, and feeling-states another?"

"Vitality-fabrications are not the same thing as feeling-states, friend. If vitality-fabrications were the same thing as feeling-states, the emergence of a monk from the attainment of the cessation of feeling & perception would not be discerned. It's because vitality-fabrications are one thing and feeling-states another that the emergence of a monk from the attainment of the cessation of perception & feeling is discerned."

"When this body lacks how many qualities does it lie discarded & forsaken, like a senseless log?"

"When this body lacks these three qualities—vitality, heat, & consciousness—it lies discarded & forsaken like a senseless log."

"What is the difference between one who is dead, who has completed his time, and a monk who has attained the cessation of perception & feeling?"

"In the case of the one who is dead, who has completed his time, his bodily fabrications have ceased & subsided, his verbal fabrications… his mental fabrications have ceased & subsided, his vitality is exhausted, his heat subsided, & his faculties are scattered. But in the case of a monk who has attained the cessation of perception & feeling, his bodily fabrications have ceased & subsided, his verbal fabrications… his mental fabrications have ceased

& subsided, his vitality is not exhausted, his heat has not subsided, & his faculties are exceptionally clear. This is the difference between one who is dead, who has completed his time, and a monk who has attained the cessation of perception & feeling."

AWARENESS-RELEASE

"Friend, how many conditions are there for the attainment of the neither-pleasant-nor-painful awareness-release?"

"Friend, there are four conditions for the attainment of the neither-pleasant-nor-painful awareness-release. There is the case where a monk, with the abandoning of pleasure & pain—as with the earlier disappearance of elation & distress—enters & remains in the fourth jhāna: purity of equanimity & mindfulness, neither pleasure nor pain. These are the four conditions for the attainment of the neither-pleasant-nor-painful awareness-release.

"How many conditions are there for the attainment of the theme-less awareness-release?"[5]

"There are two conditions for the attainment of the theme-less awareness-release: lack of attention to all themes and attention to the theme-less property. These are the two conditions for the attainment of the theme-less awareness-release."

"And how many conditions are there for the persistence of the theme-less awareness-release?"

"There are three conditions for the persistence of the theme-less awareness-release: lack of attention to all themes, attention to the theme-less property, and a prior act of will. These are the three conditions for the persistence of the theme-less awareness-release."

"And how many conditions are there for the emergence from the theme-less awareness-release?"

"There are two conditions for the emergence from the theme-less awareness-release: attention to all themes and lack of attention to the theme-less property. These are the two conditions for the emergence from the theme-less awareness-release."

"The immeasurable awareness-release, the nothingness awareness-release, the emptiness awareness-release, the theme-less awareness-release: Are these qualities different in meaning & different in name, or are they one in meaning and different only in name?"

"The immeasurable awareness-release, the nothingness awareness-release, the emptiness awareness-release, the theme-less awareness-release: There is a way of explanation by which these qualities are different in meaning & different in name, and there is a way of explanation by which these qualities are one in meaning and different only in name.

"And what is the way of explanation by which these qualities are different in meaning & different in name? There is the case where a monk keeps pervading the first direction [the east]—as well as the second direction, the third, & the fourth—with an awareness imbued with goodwill. Thus he keeps pervading above, below, & all around, everywhere & in every respect the all-encompassing world with an awareness imbued with goodwill: abundant, enlarged, immeasurable, free from hostility, free from ill will.

"He keeps pervading the first direction—as well as the second direction, the third, & the fourth—with an awareness imbued with compassion... an awareness imbued with empathetic joy....

"He keeps pervading the first direction—as well as the second direction, the third, & the fourth—with an awareness imbued with equanimity. Thus he keeps pervading above, below, & all around, everywhere & in every respect the all-encompassing world with an awareness imbued with equanimity: abundant, enlarged, immeasurable, free from hostility, free from ill will.

"This is called the immeasurable awareness-release.

"And what is the nothingness awareness-release? There is the case where a monk, with the complete transcending of the dimension of the infinitude of consciousness, thinking, 'There is nothing,' enters & remains in the dimension of nothingness. This is called the nothingness awareness-release.

"And what is the emptiness awareness-release? There is the case where a monk, having gone into the wilderness, to the root of a tree, or into an empty dwelling, considers this: 'This is empty of self or of anything pertaining to self.'[6] This is called the emptiness awareness-release.

"And what is the theme-less awareness-release? There is the case where a monk, through not attending to all themes, enters & remains in the theme-less concentration of awareness.[5] This is called the theme-less awareness-release.

"This is the way of explaining by which these qualities are different in meaning & different in name.

"And what is the way of explaining whereby these qualities are one in meaning and different only in name?

"Passion, friend, is a making of measurement. Aversion is a making of measurement. Delusion is a making of measurement. In a monk whose effluents are ended, these have been abandoned, their root destroyed, made like a palmyra stump, deprived of the conditions of development, not destined for future arising. Now, to the extent that there is immeasurable awareness-release, the unprovoked awareness-release is declared the foremost. And this unprovoked awareness-release is empty of passion, empty of aversion, empty of delusion.

"Passion is a something. Aversion is a something. Delusion is a something. In a monk whose effluents are ended, these have been abandoned, their root destroyed, made like a palmyra stump, deprived of the conditions of development, not destined for future arising. Now, to the extent that there is nothingness awareness-release, the unprovoked awareness-release is declared the foremost. And this unprovoked awareness-release is empty of passion, empty of aversion, empty of delusion.

"Passion is a making of themes. Aversion is a making of themes. Delusion is a making of themes. In a monk whose effluents are ended, these have been abandoned, their root destroyed, made like a palmyra stump, deprived of the conditions of development, not destined for future arising. Now, to the extent that there is theme-less awareness-release, the unprovoked awareness-release is declared the foremost. And this unprovoked awareness-release is empty of passion, empty of aversion, empty of delusion.

"This, friend, is the way of explaining whereby these qualities are one in meaning and different only in name."

That is what Ven. Sāriputta said. Gratified, Ven. Mahā Koṭṭhita delighted in Ven. Sāriputta's words.

NOTES

1. Discernment is to be developed because it is part of the fourth noble truth, the path of practice leading to the end of suffering. Consciousness is to be fully comprehended because, as an object of clinging, it is part of the first noble truth, the truth of suffering & stress. See SN 56:11.

2. The import of this passage is that while one is in any of these three formless states, one can analyze them with discernment in a way that can lead to release. On the fact that this cannot be done with regard to the fourth formless state, see MN 111. On the fact that the external senses can fall silent while one is in these states, see AN 9:37.

3. Vitality *(āyu)* is the force that determines the length of one's life.

4. Vitality-fabrications are the intentions to continue living. The Buddha entered total nibbāna three months after abandoning his vitality-fabrications. See DN 16.

5. See MN 121.

6. See MN 106.

See also: MN 44; MN 122; SN 22:23; SN 22:79; AN 9:37

44 *The Shorter Set of Questions & Answers*

Cūḷa Vedalla Sutta

The Buddha praised Dhammadinnā the nun as the foremost Dhamma teacher among his nun disciples. In this discourse she answers questions put to her by a layman—Visākha—who, according to the commentary, was her former husband, a merchant of Rājagaha, and a non-returner.

I have heard that on one occasion the Blessed One was staying near Rājagaha in the Bamboo Grove, the Squirrels' Sanctuary. Then Visākha the lay follower went to Dhammadinnā the nun and, on arrival, having bowed down to her, sat to one side.

SELF-IDENTIFICATION

As he was sitting there he said to her, "'Self-identification, self-identification,' it is said, lady. Which self-identification is described by the Blessed One?"

"There are these five clinging-aggregates, friend Visākha: the form clinging-aggregate, the feeling clinging-aggregate, the perception clinging-aggregate, the fabrications clinging-aggregate, the consciousness clinging-aggregate. These five clinging-aggregates are the self-identification described by the Blessed One."

Saying, "Yes, lady," Visākha the lay follower delighted & rejoiced in what Dhammadinnā the nun had said. Then he asked her a further question: "'The origination of self-identification, the origination of self-identification,' it is said, lady. Which origination of self-identification is described by the Blessed One?"

"The craving that makes for further becoming—accompanied by passion & delight, relishing now here & now there—i.e., craving for sensual pleasure, craving for becoming, craving for non-becoming: This, friend Visākha, is the origination of self-identification described by the Blessed One."

"'The cessation of self-identification, the cessation of self-identification,' it is said, lady. Which cessation of self-identification is described by the Blessed One?"

"The remainderless fading & cessation, renunciation, relinquishment, release, & letting go of that very craving: This, friend Visākha, is the cessation of self-identification described by the Blessed One."

"'The way of practice leading to the cessation of self-identification, the way of practice leading to the cessation of self-identification,' it is said, lady. Which way of practice leading to the cessation of self-identification is described by the Blessed One?"

"Precisely this noble eightfold path—right view, right resolve, right speech, right action, right livelihood, right effort, right mindfulness, right concentration: This, friend Visākha, is the way of practice leading to the cessation of self-identification described by the Blessed One."

"Is it the case, lady, that clinging is the same thing as the five clinging-aggregates or is it something separate?"

"Friend Visākha, neither is clinging the same thing as the five clinging-aggregates, nor is it something separate. Whatever desire & passion there is with regard to the five clinging-aggregates, that is the clinging there."

"But, lady, how does self-identification view come about?"

"There is the case, friend Visākha, where an uninstructed run-of-the-mill person—who has no regard for noble ones, is not well-versed or disciplined in their Dhamma; who has no regard for people of integrity, is not well-versed or disciplined in their Dhamma—assumes form [e.g., the body] to be the self, or the self as possessing form, or form as in the self, or the self as in form.

"He assumes feeling to be the self....

"He assumes perception to be the self....

"He assumes fabrications to be the self....

"He assumes consciousness to be the self, or the self as possessing consciousness, or consciousness as in the self, or the self as in consciousness. This is how self-identification view comes about."

"But, lady, how does self-identification view not come about?"

"There is the case where a well-instructed disciple of the noble ones—who has regard for noble ones, is well-versed & disciplined in their Dhamma; who has regard for people of integrity, is well-versed & disciplined in their Dhamma—doesn't assume form to be the self, or the self as possessing form, or form as in the self, or the self as in form.

"He doesn't assume feeling to be the self....

"He doesn't assume perception to be the self....

"He doesn't assume fabrications to be the self...."

"He doesn't assume consciousness to be the self, or the self as possessing consciousness, or consciousness as in the self, or the self as in consciousness. This is how self-identification view does not come about."

THE NOBLE EIGHTFOLD PATH

"Now, again, lady, what is the noble eightfold path?"

"This is the noble eightfold path, friend Visākha: right view, right resolve, right speech, right action, right livelihood, right effort, right mindfulness, right concentration."

"Is the noble eightfold path fabricated or unfabricated?"

"The noble eightfold path is fabricated."

"And are the three aggregates [of virtue, concentration, & discernment] included under the noble eightfold path, lady, or is the noble eightfold path included under the three aggregates?"

"The three aggregates are not included under the noble eightfold path, friend Visākha, but the noble eightfold path is included under the three aggregates. Right speech, right action, & right livelihood come under the aggregate of virtue. Right effort, right mindfulness, & right concentration come under the aggregate of concentration. Right view & right resolve come under the aggregate of discernment."

"Now what is concentration, lady, what qualities are its themes, what qualities are its requisites, and what is its development?"

"Singleness of mind is concentration, friend Visākha; the four establishings of mindfulness are its themes; the four right exertions are its requisites; and any cultivation, development, & pursuit of these qualities is its development."

FABRICATIONS

"Now, lady, what are fabrications?"

"These three fabrications, friend Visākha: bodily fabrications, verbal fabrications, & mental fabrications."

"But what are bodily fabrications? What are verbal fabrications? What are mental fabrications?"

"In-&-out breaths are bodily fabrications. Directed thought & evaluation are verbal fabrications. Perceptions & feelings are mental fabrications."

"But why are in-&-out breaths bodily fabrications? Why are directed thought & evaluation verbal fabrications? Why are perceptions & feelings mental fabrications?"

"In-&-out breaths are bodily; these are things tied up with the body. That's why in-&-out breaths are bodily fabrications. Having first directed one's thoughts and made an evaluation, one then breaks out into speech. That's why directed thought & evaluation are verbal fabrications. Perceptions & feelings are mental; these are things tied up with the mind. That's why perceptions & feelings are mental fabrications."

"Now, lady, how does the attainment of the cessation of perception & feeling come about?"

"The thought does not occur to a monk as he is attaining the cessation of perception & feeling that 'I am about to attain the cessation of perception & feeling' or that 'I am attaining the cessation of perception & feeling' or that 'I have attained the cessation of perception & feeling.' Instead, the way his mind has previously been developed leads him to that state."

"But when a monk is attaining the cessation of perception & feeling, which things cease first: bodily fabrications, verbal fabrications, or mental fabrications?"

"When a monk is attaining the cessation of perception & feeling, friend Visākha, verbal fabrications cease first, then bodily fabrications, then mental fabrications."[1]

"Now, lady, how does emergence from the cessation of perception & feeling come about?"

"The thought does not occur to a monk as he is emerging from the cessation of perception & feeling that 'I am about to emerge from the cessation of perception & feeling' or that 'I am emerging from the cessation of perception & feeling' or that 'I have emerged from the cessation of perception & feeling.' Instead, the way his mind has previously been developed leads him to that state."

"But when a monk is emerging from the cessation of perception & feeling, which things arise first: bodily fabrications, verbal fabrications, or mental fabrications?"

"When a monk is emerging from the cessation of perception & feeling, friend Visākha, mental fabrications arise first, then bodily fabrications, then verbal fabrications."

"When a monk has emerged from the cessation of perception & feeling, lady, how many contacts make contact?"

"When a monk has emerged from the cessation of perception & feeling, friend Visākha, three contacts make contact: contact with emptiness, contact with the signless, & contact with the undirected."[2]

"When a monk has emerged from the cessation of perception & feeling, lady, to what does his mind lean, to what does it tend, to what does it incline?"

"When a monk has emerged from the cessation of perception & feeling, friend Visākha, his mind leans to seclusion, tends to seclusion, inclines to seclusion."[3]

FEELING

"Now, lady, how many kinds of feeling are there?"

"These three kinds of feeling: pleasant feeling, painful feeling, & neither-pleasant-nor-painful feeling."

"What is pleasant feeling? What is painful feeling? What is neither-pleasant-nor-painful feeling?"

"Whatever is experienced physically or mentally as pleasant & gratifying is pleasant feeling. Whatever is experienced physically or mentally as painful & hurting is painful feeling. Whatever is experienced physically or mentally as neither gratifying nor hurting is neither-pleasant-nor-painful feeling."

"In what way is pleasant feeling pleasant, lady, and in what way painful?"

"Pleasant feeling is pleasant in remaining, & painful in changing, friend Visākha. Painful feeling is painful in remaining & pleasant in changing. Neither-pleasant-nor-painful feeling is pleasant in occurring together with knowledge, and painful in occurring without knowledge."

"What obsession gets obsessed with pleasant feeling? What obsession gets obsessed painful feeling? What obsession gets obsessed with neither-pleasant-nor-painful feeling?"

"Passion-obsession gets obsessed with pleasant feeling. Resistance-obsession gets obsessed with painful feeling. Ignorance-obsession gets obsessed with neither-pleasant-nor-painful feeling."

"Does passion-obsession get obsessed with all pleasant feeling? Does resistance-obsession get obsessed with all painful feeling? Does ignorance-obsession get obsessed with all neither-pleasant-nor-painful feeling?"

"No…."

"But what is to be abandoned with regard to pleasant feeling? What is to be abandoned with regard to painful feeling? What is to be abandoned with regard to neither-pleasant-nor-painful feeling?"

"Passion-obsession is to be abandoned with regard to pleasant feeling. Resistance-obsession is to be abandoned with regard to painful feeling. Ignorance-obsession is to be abandoned with regard to neither-pleasant-nor-painful feeling."

"Is passion-obsession to be abandoned with regard to all pleasant feeling? Is resistance-obsession to be abandoned with regard to all painful feeling? Is ignorance-obsession to be abandoned with regard to all neither-pleasant-nor-painful feeling?"

"No .... There is the case where a monk—quite secluded from sensuality, secluded from unskillful qualities—enters & remains in the first jhāna: rapture & pleasure born of seclusion, accompanied by directed thought & evaluation. With that he abandons passion. No passion-obsession gets obsessed there.[4] There is the case where a monk considers, 'O when will I enter & remain in the dimension that those who are noble now enter & remain in?' And as he thus nurses this yearning for the unexcelled liberations, there arises within him sorrow based on that yearning. With that he abandons resistance. No resistance-obsession gets obsessed there.[5] There is the case where a monk, with the abandoning of pleasure & pain—as with the earlier disappearance of elation & distress—enters & remains in the fourth jhāna: purity of equanimity & mindfulness, neither pleasure nor pain. With that he abandons ignorance. No ignorance-obsession gets obsessed there."[6]

"Now what, lady, lies on the other side of pleasant feeling?"

"Passion lies on the other side of pleasant feeling."

"And what lies on the other side of painful feeling?"

"Resistance lies on the other side of painful feeling."[7]

"What lies on the other side of neither-pleasant-nor-painful feeling?"

"Ignorance lies on the other side of neither-pleasant-nor-painful feeling."

"What lies on the other side of ignorance?"

"Clear knowing lies on the other side of ignorance."

"What lies on the other side of clear knowing?"

"Release lies on the other side of clear knowing."

"What lies on the other side of release?"

"Unbinding lies on the other side of release."

"What lies on the other side of unbinding?"

"You've gone too far, friend Visākha. You can't keep holding on up to the limit of questions. For the holy life gains a footing in unbinding, culminates in unbinding, has unbinding as its final end. If you wish, go to the Blessed One and ask him the meaning of these things. Whatever he says, that's how you should remember it."

Then Visākha the lay follower, delighting & rejoicing in what Dhammadinnā the nun had said, bowed down to her and, keeping her to his right, went to the Blessed One. On arrival, having bowed down to the Blessed One, he sat to one side. As he was sitting there he told the Blessed One the full extent of the conversation he had had with Dhammadinnā the nun. When this was said, the Blessed One said to him, "Dhammadinnā the nun is wise, Visākha, a woman of great discernment. If you had asked me those things, I would have answered you in the same way she did. That is the meaning of those things. That is how you should remember it."

That is what the Blessed One said. Gratified, Visākha the lay follower delighted in the Blessed One's words.

NOTES

1. Verbal fabrication grows still on attaining the second jhāna; bodily fabrication grows still on attaining the fourth jhāna; mental fabrication grows still on attaining the cessation of perception & feeling.

2. Emptiness, the signless, & the undirected are names for a state of concentration that lies on the threshold of unbinding. They differ only in how they are approached. According to the commentary, they color one's first apprehension of unbinding: a meditator who has been focusing on the theme of inconstancy will first apprehend unbinding as signless; one who has been focusing on the theme of stress will first apprehend it as undirected; one who has been focusing on the theme of not-self will first apprehend it as emptiness.

3. According to the commentary, "seclusion" here stands for unbinding. On emerging from the cessation of perception & feeling, and having had contact with emptiness/the signless/the undirected, the mind inclines naturally to a direct experience of unbinding.

4. In other words, once the pleasure of the first jhāna has been used as a basis for giving rise to the discernment that leads to arahantship, the mind has no further passion-obsession with pleasant feeling. (The commentary says that this is true at the attainment of non-returning, but this must be a mistake, as non-returners are still subject to passion for form and formless phenomena.)

5. Once this sorrow has been used as a basis for giving rise to the discernment that leads to non-returning, the mind has no further resistance-obsession with painful feeling.

6. Once this feeling of neither pleasure nor pain has been used as a basis for giving rise to the discernment that leads to arahantship, the mind has no further ignorance-obsession with feelings of neither pleasure nor pain.

7. This reading follows the Thai edition of the Pali Canon. The PTS edition gives the first two questions and answers of this exchange as follows:

"Now what, lady, lies on the other side of pleasant feeling?"
"Painful feeling lies on the other side of pleasant feeling."
"And what lies on the other side of painful feeling?"
"Pleasant feeling lies on the other side of painful feeling."

For some reason, the editors of neither edition seen to have been aware of the reading in the other edition.

See also: MN 109; MN 111; MN 148; SN 22:121; SN 36:6; SN 36:11; AN 5:200; AN 7:11–12; AN 8:70; AN 10:20

45 *The Shorter Discourse on Taking on Practices*

Cūḷa Dhammasamādāna Sutta

I have heard that on one occasion the Blessed One was staying near Sāvatthī in Jeta's Grove, Anāthapiṇḍika's monastery. There he addressed the monks: "Monks!"

"Yes, lord," the monks responded to him.

"Monks, there are these four ways of taking on practices. Which four? There is the taking on of a practice that is pleasant in the present but yields pain in the future. There is the taking on of a practice that is painful in the present and yields pain in the future. There is the taking on of a practice that is painful in the present but yields pleasure in the future. There is the taking on of a practice that is pleasant in the present and yields pleasure in the future.

"Now, what is the taking on of a practice that is pleasant in the present but yields pain in the future? There are some contemplatives & brahmans who hold to a doctrine, a view like this: 'There is no harm in sensual pleasures.' Thus they meet with their downfall through sensual pleasures. They consort with women wanderers who wear their hair coiled in a topknot.

"The thought occurs to them: 'Now what future danger concerning sensual pleasures do those (other) contemplatives & brahmans foresee that they have spoken of the relinquishment of sensual pleasures and describe the full comprehension of sensual pleasures? It's pleasant, the touch of this woman wanderer's soft, tender, downy arm.'

"Thus they meet with their downfall through sensual pleasures. Then, having met with their downfall through sensual pleasures, with the break-up of the body, after death, they go to a plane of deprivation, a bad destination, a lower realm, hell. There they experience sharp, burning pains. They say: '*This* was the future danger concerning sensual pleasures those contemplatives & brahmans foresaw that they spoke of the relinquishment of sensual pleasures and described the full comprehension of sensual pleasures. It's because of sensual pleasures, as a result of sensual pleasures, that we're now experiencing these sharp, burning pains.'

"Just as if a māluvā creeper pod were to burst open in the last month of the hot season, and a māluvā creeper seed were to fall at the foot of a Sal tree. The deva living in the tree would become frightened, apprehensive, & anxious. Her friends & companions, relatives & kin—garden devas, forest devas, tree devas, devas living in herbs, grass, & forest monarchs—would gather together to console her: 'Have no fear, have no fear. In all likelihood a peacock is sure to swallow this māluvā creeper seed, or a deer will eat it, or a brush fire will burn it up, or woodsmen will pick it up, or termites will carry it off, and anyway it probably isn't really a seed.'

"And then no peacock swallowed it, no deer ate it, no brush fire burned it up, no woodsmen picked it up, no termites carried it off, and it really *was* a seed. Watered by a rain-laden cloud, it sprouted in due course and curled its soft, tender, downy tendril around the Sal tree.

"The thought occurred to the deva living in the Sal tree: 'Now what future danger did my friends & companions, relatives & kin—garden devas, forest devas, tree devas, devas living in herbs, grass, & forest monarchs—foresee in that māluvā creeper seed that they gathered together to console me: "Have no fear, have no fear. In all likelihood a peacock is sure to swallow this māluvā creeper seed, or a deer will eat it, or a brush fire will burn it up, or woodsmen will pick it up, or termites will carry it off, and anyway it probably isn't really a seed." It's pleasant, the touch of this māluvā creeper's soft, tender, downy tendril.'

"Then the creeper, having enwrapped the Sal tree, having made a canopy over it, & cascading down around it, caused the massive limbs of the Sal tree to come crashing down. The thought occurred to the deva living in the tree: '*This* was the future danger my friends… foresaw in that māluvā creeper seed, that they gathered together to console me.… It's because of that māluvā creeper seed that I'm now experiencing sharp, burning pains.'

"In the same way, monks, there are some contemplatives & brahmans who hold to a doctrine, a view like this: 'There is no harm in sensual pleasures.' Thus they meet with their downfall through sensual pleasures. They consort with women wanderers who wear their hair coiled in a topknot.

"The thought occurs to them: 'Now, what future danger do those (other) contemplatives & brahmans foresee that they teach the relinquishment & analysis of sensual pleasures? It's pleasant, the touch of this woman wanderer's soft, tender, downy arm.'

Thus they meet with their downfall through sensual pleasures. Then, having met with their downfall through sensual pleasures, with the break-up of the body, after death, they reappear in a plane of deprivation, a bad destination, a lower realm, hell. There they experience sharp, burning pains. They say: '*This* was the future danger concerning sensual pleasures those contemplatives & brahmans foresaw that they spoke of the relinquishment of sensual pleasures and described the full comprehension of sensual pleasures. It's because of sensual pleasures, as a result of sensual pleasures, that we're now experiencing these sharp, burning pains.'

"This is called the taking on of a practice that is pleasant in the present but yields pain in the future.

"And what is the taking on of a practice that is painful in the present and yields pain in the future?

"There is the case where someone is a cloth-less[1] ascetic, rejecting conventions, licking his hands, not coming when called, not staying when asked. He doesn't consent to food brought to him or food dedicated to him or to an invitation to a meal. He accepts nothing from the mouth of a pot or from the mouth of a bowl. He accepts nothing from across a threshold, across a stick, across a pestle, from two eating together, from a pregnant woman, from a nursing woman, from a woman living with a man, from where it is announced that food is to be distributed, from where a dog is waiting or flies are buzzing. He takes no fish or meat. He drinks no liquor, wine, or fermented drink. He limits himself to one house & one morsel a day, or two houses & two morsels… seven houses & seven morsels. He lives on one saucerful a day, two… seven saucerfuls a day. He takes food once a day, once every two days… once every seven days, and so on up to a fortnight, devoted to regulating his intake of food. He is an eater of greens, millet, wild rice, hide-parings, moss, rice bran, rice-scum, sesame flour, grass, or cow dung. He lives on forest roots & berries. He feeds on fallen fruits. He wears hemp, canvas, shrouds, refuse rags, tree bark, antelope hide, strips of antelope hide, kusa-grass garments, bark garments, wood-shaving garments, head-hair garments, animal wool, owl's wings. He is a hair-&-beard puller, one devoted to the practice of pulling out his hair & beard. He is a stander, one who rejects seats. He is a hands-around-the-knees sitter, one devoted to the exertion of sitting with his hands around his knees. He is a spike-mattresser, one who makes his bed on a bed of spikes. He is a third-time-in-the-evening bather, one who stays devoted to the practice of bathing in water. Thus in a variety of ways he stays devoted to the practice of tormenting & afflicting the body. With the break-up of the body, after death, he reappears in a plane of deprivation, a bad destination, a lower realm, hell.

"This is called the taking on of a practice that is painful in the present and yields pain in the future.

"And what is the taking on of a practice that is painful in the present but yields pleasure in the future? There is the case of a person who is normally strongly passionate by nature and frequently experiences pain & grief born of passion; a person who is normally strongly aversive by nature and frequently experiences pain & grief born of aversion; a person who is normally strongly deluded by nature and frequently experiences pain & grief born of delusion. Even though touched with pain & grief, crying with a tearful face, he lives the holy life that is utterly perfect, surpassingly pure. With the break-up of the body, after death, he reappears in a good destination, a heavenly world. This is called the taking on of a practice that is painful in the present but yields pleasure in the future.

"And what is the taking on of a practice that is pleasant in the present and yields pleasure in the future? There is the case of a person who is not normally strongly passionate by nature and doesn't frequently experience pain & grief born of passion; who is not normally strongly aversive by nature and doesn't frequently experience pain & grief born of aversion; who is not normally strongly deluded by nature and doesn't frequently experience pain & grief born of delusion. Quite secluded from sensuality, secluded from unskillful qualities, he enters & remains in the first jhāna: rapture & pleasure born of seclusion, accompanied by directed thought & evaluation. With the stilling of directed thoughts & evaluations, he enters & remains in the second jhāna: rapture & pleasure born of concentration, unification of awareness free from directed thought & evaluation—internal assurance. With the fading of rapture, he remains equanimous, mindful, & alert, and senses pleasure with the body. He enters & remains in the third jhāna, of which the noble ones declare, 'Equanimous & mindful, he has a pleasant abiding.' With the abandoning of pleasure & pain—as with the earlier disappearance of elation & distress—he enters & remains in the fourth jhāna: purity of equanimity & mindfulness, neither pleasure nor pain. With the break-up of the body, after death, he reappears in a good destination, a heavenly world. This is called the taking on of a practice that is pleasant in the present and yields pleasure in the future.

"And these are the four ways of taking on practices."

That is what the Blessed One said. Gratified, the monks delighted in the Blessed One's words.

NOTE: 1. *Acelaka:* "One without cloth." Often translated as "naked," but as the description shows, such a person might wear garments made of something other than cloth.

See also: MN 13; MN 14; AN 4:115; AN 4:192; AN 6:63

48 Kosambiyā Sutta

In Kosambī

I have heard that on one occasion the Blessed One was staying near Kosambī at Ghosita's monastery. And on that occasion the monks in Kosambī were given to arguing and quarreling and disputing, stabbing one another with weapons of the mouth. They did not persuade one another, and did not agree to be persuaded by one another. They did not convince one another, and did not agree to be convinced by one another.[1]

Then a certain monk went to the Blessed One and, on arrival, having bowed down to him, sat to one side. As he was sitting there, he said to the Blessed One: "Lord, the monks in Kosambī are now given to arguing and quarreling and disputing, stabbing one another with weapons of the mouth. They don't persuade one another, and don't agree to be persuaded by one another. They don't convince one another, and don't agree to be convinced by one another.

Then the Blessed One told a certain monk, "Come, monk. In my name, call those monks, saying, 'The Teacher calls you, venerable ones.'"

Responding, "As you say, lord," to the Blessed One, the monk went to those monks, and on arrival he said to them, "The Teacher calls you, venerable ones."

Responding, "As you say, my friend," to the monk, those monks went to the Blessed One and, on arrival, having bowed down to him, sat to one side.

As they were sitting there, the Blessed One said to them, "Is it true, monks, that you are given to arguing and quarreling and disputing, stabbing one another with weapons of the mouth? That you don't persuade one another, and don't agree to be persuaded by one another? That you don't convince one another, and don't agree to be convinced by one another?"

"Yes, lord."

"And while you are given to arguing and quarreling and disputing, stabbing one another with weapons of the mouth, are you set on bodily acts of good will with regard to your companions in the holy life, to their faces & behind their backs? Are you set on verbal acts of good will with regard to your companions in the holy life, to their faces & behind their backs? Are you set on mental acts of good will with regard to your companions in the holy life, to their faces & behind their backs?"

"No, lord."

"So then, while you are given to arguing and quarreling and disputing, stabbing one another with weapons of the mouth, you are not set on bodily acts of good will with regard to your companions in the holy life, to their faces & behind their backs; you are not set on verbal acts of good will with regard to your companions in the holy life, to their faces & behind their backs; you are not set on mental acts of good will with regard to your companions in the holy life, to their faces & behind their backs. Then what could you worthless men possibly know or see that you are given to arguing and quarreling and disputing, stabbing one another with weapons of the mouth? That will be to your long-term harm and suffering."

Then the Blessed One addressed the monks: "Monks, these six are conditions that are conducive to amiability, that engender feelings of endearment, engender feelings of respect, leading to a sense of fellowship, a lack of disputes, harmony, & a state of unity. Which six?

"There is the case where a monk is set on bodily acts of good will with regard to his companions in the holy life, to their faces & behind their backs. This is a condition that is conducive to amiability, that engenders feelings of endearment, engenders feelings of respect, leading to a sense of fellowship, a lack of disputes, harmony, & a state of unity.

"And further, the monk is set on verbal acts of good will with regard to his companions in the holy life, to their faces & behind their backs. This, too, is a condition that is conducive to amiability, that engenders feelings of endearment, engenders feelings of respect, leading to a sense of fellowship, a lack of disputes, harmony, & a state of unity.

"And further, the monk is set on mental acts of good will with regard to his companions in the holy life, to their faces & behind their backs. This, too, is a condition that is conducive to amiability, that engenders feelings of endearment, engenders feelings of respect, leading to a sense of fellowship, a lack of disputes, harmony, & a state of unity.

"And further, whatever righteous gains the monk may obtain in a righteous way—even if only the alms in his bowl—he does not consume them alone. He consumes them after sharing them in common with his virtuous companions in the holy life. This, too, is a condition that is conducive to amiability, that engenders feelings of endearment, engenders feelings of respect, leading to a sense of fellowship, a lack of disputes, harmony, & a state of unity.

"And further—with reference to the virtues that are untorn, unbroken, unspotted, unsplattered, liberating, praised by the observant, ungrasped at, leading to concentration—the monk dwells with his virtue in tune with that of his companions in the holy life, to their faces & behind their backs. This, too, is a condition that is conducive to amiability, that engenders feelings of endearment, engenders feelings of respect, leading to a sense of fellowship, a lack of disputes, harmony, & a state of unity.

"And further—with reference to the view that is noble, leading outward, that leads those who act in accordance with it to the right ending of suffering & stress—the monk dwells with a view in tune with those of his companions in the holy life, to their faces & behind their backs. This, too, is a condition that is conducive to amiability, that engenders feelings of endearment, engenders feelings of respect, leading to a sense of fellowship, a lack of disputes, harmony, & a state of unity.

"These are the six conditions that are conducive to amiability, that engender feelings of endearment, engender feelings of respect, leading to a sense of fellowship, a lack of disputes, harmony, & a state of unity.

"Of these six conditions conducive to amiability, this is the summit, this the girding, this the kingpin: the view that is noble, leading outward, that leads those who act in accordance with it to the right ending of suffering & stress. Just as in a building with a ridged roof, this is the summit, this the girding, this the kingpin: the ridge beam; in the same way, of these six conditions conducive to amiability, this is the summit, this the girding, this the kingpin: the view that is noble, leading outward, that leads those who act in accordance with it to the right ending of suffering & stress.[2]

"And how is there the view that is noble, leading outward, that leads those who act in accordance with it to the right ending of suffering & stress?

"There is the case where a monk, having gone to the wilderness, to the root of a tree, or to an empty dwelling, considers thus: 'Is there any internal subjugation unabandoned in me that, subjugated by which, my subjugated mind would not know or see things as they have come to be?' If a monk is subjugated by sensual passion, monks, then his mind is subjugated. If he is subjugated by ill will, then his mind is subjugated. If he is subjugated by sloth & torpor, then his mind is subjugated. If he is subjugated by restlessness & anxiety, then his mind is subjugated. If he is subjugated by uncertainty, then his mind is subjugated. If a monk is absorbed in speculation about this world, then his mind is enthralled. If a monk is absorbed in speculation about the other world, then his mind is subjugated. If a monk is given to arguing and quarreling and disputing, stabbing others with weapons of the mouth, then his mind is subjugated.

"He discerns that, 'There is no subjugation unabandoned in me that, subjugated by which, my subjugated mind would not know and see things as they have come to be. My mind is well directed for awakening to the truths.' This is the first knowledge attained by him that is noble, transcendent, not held in common with run-of-the-mill people.

"And further, the disciple of the noble ones considers thus: 'When I cultivate, develop, and pursue this view, do I personally obtain tranquility, do I personally obtain unbinding?'

"He discerns that, 'When I cultivate, develop, and pursue this view, I personally obtain tranquility, I personally obtain unbinding.' This is the second knowledge attained by him that is noble, transcendent, not held in common with run-of-the-mill people.

"And further, the disciple of the noble ones considers thus: 'Is there, outside of this (Dhamma & Vinaya), any other contemplative or brahman endowed with the sort of view with which I am endowed?'

"He discerns that, 'There is no other contemplative or brahman outside (the Dhamma & Vinaya) endowed with the sort of view with which I am endowed.' This is the third knowledge attained by him that is noble, transcendent, not held in common with run-of-the-mill people.

"And further, the disciple of the noble ones considers thus: 'I am endowed with the character of a person consummate in view?'[3] And what, monks, is the character of a person consummate in view? This is the character of a person consummate in view: Although he may commit some kind of offence for which a means of rehabilitation has been laid down, still he immediately confesses, reveals, and discloses it to the Teacher or to observant companions in the holy life; having done that, he undertakes restraint for the future. Just as a young, tender infant lying on his back, when he has hit a live ember with his hand or his foot, immediately draws back; in the same way, this is the character of a person consummate in view: Although he may commit some kind of offence for which a means of rehabilitation has been laid down, still he immediately confesses, reveals, and discloses it to the Teacher or to observant companions in the holy life; having done that, he undertakes restraint for the future.

"He discerns that, 'I am endowed with the character of a person consummate in view.' This is the fourth knowledge attained by him that is noble, transcendent, not held in common with run-of-the-mill people.

"And further, the disciple of the noble ones considers thus: 'I am endowed with the character of a person consummate in view?' And what, monks, is the character of a person consummate in view? This is the character of a person consummate in view: Although he may be active in the various affairs of his companions in the holy life, he still has a keen regard for training in heightened virtue, training in heightened mind, & training in heightened discernment. Just as a cow with a new calf watches after her calf all the while she is grazing on grass, in the same way, this is the character of a person consummate in view: Although he may be active in the various affairs of his companions in the holy life, he still has a keen regard for training in heightened virtue, training in heightened mind, & training in heightened discernment.

"He discerns that, 'I am endowed with the character of a person consummate in view.' This is the fifth knowledge attained by him that is noble, transcendent, not held in common with run-of-the-mill people.

"And further, the disciple of the noble ones considers thus: 'I am endowed with the strength of a person consummate in view?' And what, monks, is the strength of a person consummate in view? This is the strength of a person consummate in view: When the Dhamma & Vinaya proclaimed by the Tathāgata is being taught, he heeds it, gives it attention, engages it with all his mind, hears the Dhamma with eager ears.

"He discerns that, 'I am endowed with the strength of a person consummate in view.' This is the sixth knowledge attained by him that is noble, transcendent, not held in common with run-of-the-mill people.

"And further, the disciple of the noble ones considers thus: 'I am endowed with the strength of a person consummate in view?' And what, monks, is the strength of a person consummate in view? This is the strength of a person consummate in view: When the Dhamma & Vinaya proclaimed by the Tathāgata is being taught, he gains understanding of the meaning, gains understanding of the Dhamma, gains joy connected with the Dhamma.

"He discerns that, 'I am endowed with the strength of a person consummate in view.' This is the seventh knowledge attained by him that is noble, transcendent, not held in common with run-of-the-mill people.

"A disciple of the noble ones thus endowed with seven factors has well examined the character for the realization of the fruit of stream entry. A disciple of the noble ones thus endowed with seven factors is endowed with the fruit of stream entry."

That is what the Blessed One said. Gratified, the monks delighted in the Blessed One's words.

NOTES

1. This is apparently not the same Kosambī quarrel as that described in Mv X. This quarrel seems to have been settled in Kosambī with the discourse the Buddha gives here. That quarrel was much harder to settle. The Buddha had to leave Kosambī and take up residence in Sāvatthī before the monks in Kosambī came to their senses, followed him to Sāvatthī, and settled their differences there.

2. SN 48:52 contains a similar image, applied to the five faculties, to make the point that the lower, supporting faculties are not solid until the highest faculty—discernment—is in place, just as the rafters in the roof of a ridge-roofed building are not stable or firm until the ridge-beam is in place.

3. In this and the remaining three considerations, the words of the consideration follow the syntax of a declarative sentence, but the context seems to require a question. There are other instances in the Canon where this happens, suggesting that—as in, say, English or French—a native speaker of Pali could phrase a question in the declarative, indicating the question by the tone of voice.

See also: DN 16; SN 48:53; AN 3:74; AN 5:179; AN 6:12; AN 10:92

49 *The Brahmā Invitation*

Brahma-nimantanika Sutta

INTRODUCTION

In this sutta, the Buddha faces two antagonists: Baka, a Brahmā who believes that his Brahmā-attainment is the highest attainment there is; and Māra, who wants (1) to keep Baka under his power by allowing Baka to maintain his deluded opinion, and (2) to prevent the Buddha from sharing his awakened knowledge with others. Of the two, Māra is the more insidious, a point illustrated by the fact that Māra always speaks through someone else and never directly shows his face. (Another interesting point is illustrated by the fact that Māra is the source of the demand that one obey a creator god.)

In overcoming his antagonists, the Buddha asserts the superiority of his knowledge in two major fashions: through a description of his awakened knowledge and through a display of psychic powers.

The Buddha describes his awakened knowledge in a variety of ways:

—by identifying Māra whenever he possesses an attendant of Baka's assembly,

—by describing the full extent of Baka's power,

—by identifying levels of being that Baka does not know,

—by describing an awakened consciousness that is not known by means of any of the six senses at all,

—by asserting an awareness that avoids delight in both becoming and the quest for non-becoming, and

—by asserting that he has abandoned all possible conditions that would lead to further rebirth.

Some of these assertions—in particular, the assertion of a consciousness not mediated by any of the six senses—are extremely important Dhamma lessons, which are further explained in the notes. But as the sutta shows, even the Buddha's description of these teachings was not enough to win over Baka or the members of his following. They were convinced only when the Buddha then performed a feat of psychic power that (1) even Baka could not fathom and (2) illustrated the Buddha's major point. Up to then, in identifying Māra and the range of Baka's power, the Buddha was in effect saying, "I see you, but you don't see me." With his display of psychic power, in which Brahmā and his following could not see him but could hear his voice, he demonstrated his point in such graphic terms that Baka and his following were immediately won over.

In this way, the protagonists of this sutta react in a way very different from that of a typical modern reader. We at present, when reading this sutta, may be more impressed with the Buddha's explanation of his awakened knowledge than we are with the account of his display of psychic power, for after all, both aspects of the sutta—the description of the Buddha's knowledge and the description of his psychic power—are, for us, just that: descriptions. But, for those who witnessed it, his display of power was an undeniable fact that went beyond words. They saw him go beyond their range. Prior to that display, they regarded his claims of knowledge simply as that: mere claims. When he showed, however, that he could perform a miracle that even Baka could not perform, they were forced to concede his superiority. Thus this sutta imparts a lesson often forgotten at present, that the Buddha taught not only by word but also by example, and that some of his examples required a dimension of power that even the gods could not match.

Strictly speaking, of course, the Buddha's display of power did not prove that he had gone beyond becoming. After all, in becoming invisible to Baka, he may simply have gone to another level of becoming of which Baka was unaware. However, the Buddha correctly surmised that a display of power would subdue the pride of his listeners, awaken a sense of conviction in his attainment, and thus enable them to enter the path of practice. As he states in MN 27, only when one sees the four noble truths—usually a synonym for stream-entry—is one's conviction in the Buddha's awakening confirmed. Only when one puts an end to one's mental effluents does one have firm proof of the Buddha's awakening. The Buddha notes in DN 11 that a display of psychic powers can sometimes backfire, in that one's audience might assume that one is engaging in cheap magic tricks. Thus, instead of inspiring conviction, the display simply increases doubt. Nevertheless, there are other instances in the Canon—most notably in the story of the Kassapa brothers (Mv.I.15-22) and that of Aṅgulimāla (MN 86)—where the Buddha was able to display his powers to good effect. But because he could not trust even his arahant disciples to possess his same sense of when such powers would work and when they would backfire, he forbade his disciples from displaying psychic powers to lay people. (See Cv.V.8; Buddhist Monastic Code, vol. 2, chapter 10.)

The conclusion of the sutta states that the sutta's name comes from two facets of the story: the fact that it contains an invitation from a Brahmā—when Baka welcomes the Buddha to his realm—and from the silencing of Māra. The first point is clear enough, but the second requires explanation. It is a play on the word Brahmā, *which is not only a noun denoting the highest levels of devas, but also an adjective meaning "of great or high power." The Buddha's last statement, in which he declares his freedom from rebirth, is something of an invitation to Māra: Māra is welcome to refute it if he can. Up to that point, Māra has phrased his threats to the Buddha in terms of the fortunate rebirths the Buddha will experience if he obeys Māra's advice, and the unfortunate ones he will experience if he doesn't. Now that the Buddha declares, in a way that Māra cannot refute, that he has abandoned all possible conditions for rebirth, Māra has nothing more on which to base his threats. Thus he is left speechless. In this way, the Buddha's last statement is a brahma-invitation: a statement that anyone is welcome to refute, but of such great power that no one can refute it at all.*

* * *

I have heard that on one occasion the Blessed One was staying near Sāvatthī in Jeta's Grove, Anāthapiṇḍika's monastery. There he addressed the monks, "Monks!"

"Yes, lord," the monks responded to him.

The Blessed One said: "On one occasion recently I was staying in Ukkaṭṭha in the Subhaga forest at the root of a royal Sal tree. Now on that occasion an evil viewpoint had arisen to Baka Brahmā: 'This is constant. This is permanent. This is eternal. This is total. This is not subject to falling away—for this does not take birth, does not age, does not die, does not fall away, does not reappear.[1] And there is no other, higher escape.'

"So I—having known with my awareness the line of thinking in Baka Brahmā's awareness—as a strong man would extend his flexed arm or flex his extended arm, vanished into the root of the royal Sal tree in the Subhaga forest in Ukkaṭṭha and appeared in that Brahmā world. Baka Brahmā saw me coming in the distance and, on seeing me, said, 'Come, good sir. You are well-come, good sir. It has been long, good sir, since you arranged to come here—for this, good sir, is constant. This is permanent. This is eternal. This is total. This is not subject to falling away—for here one does not take birth, does not age, does not die, does not fall away, does not reappear. And there is no other, higher escape.'

"When this was said, I told Baka Brahmā, 'How immersed in ignorance is Baka Brahmā! How immersed in ignorance is Baka Brahmā! — in that what is actually inconstant he calls "constant." What is actually impermanent he calls "permanent." What is actually non-eternal he calls "eternal." What is actually partial he calls "total." What is actually subject to falling away he calls "not subject to falling away." Where one takes birth, ages, dies, falls away, and reappears, he says, "For here one does not take birth, does not age, does not die, does not fall away, does not reappear." And there being another, higher escape, he says, "There is no other, higher escape."'

"Then Māra, the Evil One, taking possession of an attendant of the Brahmā assembly, said to me, 'Monk! Monk! Don't attack him! Don't attack him! For this Brahmā, monk, is the Great Brahmā, the Conqueror, the Unconquered, the All-Seeing, All-Powerful, the Sovereign Lord, the Maker, Creator, Chief, Appointer and Ruler, Father of All That Have Been and Shall Be. There were, monk, before your time, contemplatives & brahmans in the world

who found fault with earth and were disgusted with earth,
who found fault with liquid and were disgusted with liquid,
who found fault with fire and were disgusted with fire,
who found fault with wind and were disgusted with wind,
who found fault with beings and were disgusted with beings,
who found fault with devas and were disgusted with devas,
who found fault with Pajāpati and were disgusted with Pajāpati,[2]
who found fault with Brahmā and were disgusted with Brahmā.

"'They, with the break-up of the body, with the cutting off of life, were established in a coarse body.[3] There were, monk, before your time, contemplatives & brahmans in the world

who praised earth and were delighted with earth,
who praised liquid and were delighted with liquid,
who praised fire and were delighted with fire,
who praised wind and were delighted with wind,
who praised beings and were delighted with beings,
who praised devas and were delighted with devas,
who praised Pajāpati and were delighted with Pajāpati,
who praised Brahmā and were delighted with Brahmā.

"'They, with the break-up of the body, with the cutting off of life, were established in a refined body. So I tell you, monk, "Please, good sir, do only as Brahmā says. Don't defy the word of Brahmā. If you defy the word of Brahmā, then—as a man, when the goddess of fortune approaches, chases her away with a stick, or as a man, falling into hell, loses hold of the earth with his hands and feet—that will be what you have accomplished. Please, good sir, do only as Brahmā says. Don't defy the word of Brahmā. Don't you see that Brahmā's assembly has gathered?"' And so Māra the Evil One directed my attention to Brahmā's assembly.

"When this was said, I told Māra the Evil One, 'I know you, Evil One. Don't assume, "He doesn't know me." You are Māra, Evil One. And Brahmā, and Brahmā's assembly, and the attendants of Brahmā's assembly have all fallen into your hands. They have all fallen under your sway. And you think, "This one, too, has come into my hands, has come under my sway." But, Evil One, I have neither come into your hands nor have I come under your sway.'

"When this was said, Baka Brahmā told me, 'But, good sir, what is actually constant I call "constant." What is actually permanent I call "permanent." What is actually eternal I call "eternal." What is actually total I call "total." What is actually not subject to falling away I call "not subject to falling away." Where one does not take birth, age, die, fall away, or reappear, I say, "For this does not take birth, does not age, does not die, does not fall away, does not reappear." And there being no other, higher escape, I say, "There is no other, higher escape."

"'There were, monk, before your time, contemplatives & brahmans in the world whose ascetic practice lasted as long as your entire life span. They knew, when there was another, higher escape, that there was another, higher escape; or, when there was no other, higher escape, that there was no other, higher escape. So I tell you, monk, both that you will not find another, higher escape, and that, to that extent, you will reap your share of trouble & weariness. Monk, if you relish earth, you will lie close to me, lie within my domain, for me to banish and to do with as I like. If you relish liquid… fire… wind… beings… devas… Pajāpati… Brahmā, you will lie close to me, lie within my domain, for me to banish and to do with as I like.'

"'I, too, know that, Brahmā. If I relish earth, I will lie close to you, lie within your domain, for you to banish and to do with as you like. If I relish liquid… fire… wind… beings… devas… Pajāpati… Brahmā, I will lie close to you, lie within your domain, for you to banish and to do with as you like. Moreover, I discern your sphere, I discern your splendor: "Baka Brahmā has this much great power. Baka Brahmā has this much great might. Baka Brahmā has this much great influence."'

"'Well, monk, how do you discern my sphere, how do you discern my splendor: "Baka Brahmā has this much great power. Baka Brahmā has this much great might. Baka Brahmā has this much great influence"?'

"'As far as suns & moons revolve,
shining, illuminating the directions,
over a thousand-fold world
    your control holds sway.
There you know those above & below,
those with lust & those without,

the state of what is as it is,
the state of what becomes otherwise,
the coming & going of beings.

"'That, Brahmā, is how I discern your sphere, that is how I discern your splendor: "Baka Brahmā has this much great power. Baka Brahmā has this much great might. Baka Brahmā has this much great influence." There are, Brahmā, bodies other than yours that you don't know, don't see, but that I know, I see. There is, Brahmā, the body named Ābhassarā [Radiant] from which you fell away & reappeared here.[4] From your having lived here so long, your memory of that has become muddled. That is why you don't know it, don't see it, but I know it, I see it. Thus I am not your mere equal in terms of direct knowing, so how could I be inferior? I am actually superior to you.

"'There is, Brahmā, the body named Subhakiṇhā [Beautiful Black]… the body named Vehapphalā [Sky-fruit], {the body named Abhibhū [Conqueror]}[5] which you don't know, don't see, but that I know, I see. Thus I am not your mere equal in terms of direct knowing, so how could I be your inferior? I am actually superior to you.

"'Having directly known earth as earth, and having directly known the extent of what has not been experienced through the earthness of earth,[6] I wasn't earth, I wasn't in earth, I wasn't coming from earth, I wasn't "Earth is mine." I didn't affirm earth.[7] Thus I am not your mere equal in terms of direct knowing, so how could I be inferior? I am actually superior to you.

"'Having directly known liquid as liquid… fire as fire… wind as wind… beings as beings… devas as devas… Pajāpati as Pajāpati… Brahmā as Brahmā… the radiant as radiant… the beautiful black as the beautiful black… the sky-fruit as the sky-fruit… the conqueror as the conqueror…

"'Having directly known the all as the all,[8] and having directly known the extent of what has not been experienced through the allness of the all, I wasn't the all, I wasn't in the all, I wasn't coming forth from the all, I wasn't "The all is mine." I didn't affirm the all. Thus I am not your mere equal in terms of direct knowing, so how could I be inferior? I am actually superior to you.'

"'If, good sir, you have directly known the extent of what has not been experienced through the allness of the all, may it not turn out to be actually vain and void for you.'

"'Consciousness without surface,
endless, radiant all around,

has not been experienced through the earthness of earth… the liquidity of liquid… the fieriness of fire… the windiness of wind… the allness of the all.'[9]

"'Well then, good sir, I will disappear from you.'

"'Well then, Brahmā, disappear from me if you can.'

"Then Baka Brahmā, (thinking,) 'I will disappear from Gotama the contemplative. I will disappear from Gotama the contemplative,' was not able to disappear from me. When this was said, I said to Baka Brahmā, 'Well then, Brahmā, I will disappear from you.'

"'Well then, good sir, disappear from me if you can.'

"So then, monks, I fabricated a fabrication of psychic power to the extent that Brahmā, the Brahmā assembly, and the attendants of the Brahmā assembly heard my voice but did not see me. Having disappeared, I recited this verse:

'Having seen
danger
right in becoming,
and becoming
in searching for non-becoming,[10]
I didn't affirm
any kind of becoming,
or cling to any delight.'

"Then in Brahmā, the Brahmā assembly, and the attendants of the Brahmā assembly there arose a sense of amazement & astonishment: 'How amazing! How astounding! — The great power, the great might of Gotama the contemplative! Never before have we seen or heard of any other contemplative or brahman of such great power, such great might as that of this Gotama the contemplative, who went forth from a Sakyan clan! Living in a generation that so delights in becoming, so rejoices in becoming, is so fond of becoming, he has pulled out becoming by the root!'

"Then Māra, the Evil One, taking possession of an attendant of the Brahmā assembly, said to me, 'If, good sir, this is what you discern, if this is what you have awakened to, do not lead (lay) disciples or those gone forth. Do not teach the Dhamma to (lay) disciples or those gone forth. Do not yearn for (lay) disciples or those gone forth. There were, good sir, before your time, contemplatives & brahmans in the world who claimed to be worthy & rightly self-awakened. They led (lay) disciples & those gone forth. They taught the Dhamma to (lay) disciples & those gone forth. They yearned for (lay) disciples & those gone forth. Having led (lay) disciples & those gone forth, having taught the Dhamma to (lay) disciples & those gone forth, having yearned for (lay) disciples & those gone forth, they—on the break-up of the body, with the cutting off of life—were established in a coarse body.

"'There were, good sir, before your time, contemplatives & brahmans in the world who claimed to be worthy & rightly self-awakened. They did not lead (lay) disciples or those gone forth. They did not teach the Dhamma to (lay) disciples or those gone forth. They did not yearn for (lay) disciples or those gone forth. Having not led (lay) disciples or those gone forth, having not taught the Dhamma to (lay) disciples or those gone forth, having not yearned for (lay) disciples or those gone forth, they—on the break-up of the body, with the cutting off of life—were established in a refined body.

"'So, monk, I tell you this: Please, good sir, be effortless. Abide committed to a pleasant abiding in the here-&-now—for it's skillful, good sir, that this not be taught. Don't instruct others.'

"When this was said, I told Māra the Evil One, 'I know you, Evil One. Don't assume, "He doesn't know me." You are Māra, Evil One. And it's not sympathetic to welfare that you speak thus to me. It's sympathetic to what is not welfare that you speak thus to me. You think this, Evil One: "Those to whom Gotama the contemplative will teach the Dhamma will defy my sovereignty. Without being rightly self-awakened, Evil One, your contemplatives & brahmans claimed to be rightly self-awakened. I, however, being rightly self-awakened claim to be rightly self-awakened. For when the Tathāgata is teaching the Dhamma to his disciples, he is Such. When he is not teaching the Dhamma to his disciples, he is Such. When leading his disciples he is Such. When not leading his disciples he is Such. Why is that? The effluents that defile, that lead to further becoming, that disturb, that ripen in stress, that tend to future birth, aging, & death: Those the Tathāgata has abandoned, their root destroyed, made like a palmyra stump, deprived of the conditions of development, not destined for future arising. Just as a palmyra tree with its crown cut off is incapable of growing again; so, too, the effluents that defile, that lead to further becoming, that disturb, that ripen in stress, that tend to future birth, aging, & death: Those the Tathāgata has abandoned, their root destroyed, made like a palmyra stump, deprived of the conditions of development, not destined for future arising.'"

Thus, because of the silencing of Māra, and because of the Brahmā's invitation, this discourse is entitled, "The Brahmā Invitation."

NOTES

1. Baka Brahmā here appears to be referring both to his Brahmā world and to the state of mind that enables one to inhabit his Brahmā world.

2. *Pajāpati* has different meanings in different contexts. In some contexts, it refers to a creator deva dwelling in a Brahmā world of form. In other contexts, it refers to the chief wife of a major deva.

3. The word *body* in this discourse refers to three things: an individual body, a group of beings on a particular level of being, and the level of being as a whole. The Commentary says that *coarse body* here refers to the four levels of deprivation, and *refined body,* further on, to the Brahmā worlds.

4. The Ābhassarā Brahmā-body is attained through mastering and relishing the second jhāna. The next two Brahmā-bodies are attained through mastering and relishing the third and fourth. See AN 4:123 & 125, and in particular note 2 under the latter sutta.

5. The phrase in braces is from the Burmese edition of the Canon.

6. What is not experienced through the earthness of earth (and so on through the list of categories up through the allness of the all) is nibbāna, or unbinding. It is described in these terms because it is directly known, without intermediary of any sort.

7. These statements can be read in two ways. The first way is to regard them in light of the standard definition of self-identification view (see, for instance, MN 44, MN 109, and SN 22.1) in which one defines self either as identical with an aggregate, as possessing an aggregate, as being contained in an aggregate, or as containing an aggregate within it. The second way is to regard the statements in light of the parallel passage from MN 1, in which one engages in metaphysical speculation as to whether one's being is identical with something, lies within something, or comes from something. For more on this topic, see the introduction to MN 1.

8. "What is the All? Simply the eye & forms, ear & sounds, nose & aromas, tongue & flavors, body & tactile sensations, intellect & ideas. This is termed the All. Anyone who would say, 'Repudiating this All, I will describe another,' if questioned on what exactly might be the grounds for his assertion, would be unable to explain, and furthermore, would be put to grief. Why is that? Because it lies beyond range." — *SN 35:23*

For more on this topic, see *The Mind Like Fire Unbound,* Chapter 1.

9. Consciousness without surface *(viññāṇaṁ anidassanaṁ):* This term appears to be related to the following image from SN 12:64:

"Just as if there were a roofed house or a roofed hall having windows on the north, the south, or the east. When the sun rises, and a ray has entered by way of the window, where does it land?"

"On the western wall, lord."

"And if there is no western wall, where does it land?"

"On the ground, lord."

"And if there is no ground, where does it land?"

"On the water, lord."

"And if there is no water, where does it land?"

"It doesn't land, lord."

"In the same way, where there is no passion for the nutriment of physical food... contact... intellectual intention... consciousness, where there is no delight, no craving, then consciousness does not land there or grow. Where consciousness does not land or grow, name-&-form does not alight. Where name-&-form does not alight, there is no growth of fabrications. Where there is no growth of fabrications, there is no production of renewed becoming in the future. Where there is no production of renewed becoming in the future, there is no future birth, aging, & death. That, I tell you, has no sorrow, affliction, or despair."

In other words, normal sensory consciousness is experienced because it has a "surface" against which it lands: the sense organs and their objects, which constitute the "all." For instance, we experience visual consciousness because of the eye and forms of which we are conscious. Consciousness without surface, however, is directly known, without intermediary, free from any dependence on conditions at all.

This consciousness thus differs from the consciousness factor in dependent co-arising, which is defined in terms of the six sense media. Lying outside of time and space, it would also not come under the consciousness-aggregate, which covers all consciousness near and far; past, present, and future. And, as SN 35:23 notes, the word "all" in the Buddha's teaching covers only the six sense media, which is another reason for not including this consciousness under the aggregates. However, the fact that it is outside of time and space—in a dimension where there is no here, there, or in between (Ud 1:10), no coming, no going, or staying (Ud 8:1)—means that it cannot be described as permanent or omnipresent, terms that have meaning only within space and time.

Some have objected to the equation of this consciousness with nibbāna, on the grounds that nibbāna is nowhere else in the Canon described as a form of consciousness. Thus they have proposed that consciousness without surface be regarded as an arahant's consciousness of nibbāna in meditative experience, and not nibbāna itself. This argument, however, contains a flaw: If nibbāna is an object of mental consciousness (as a dhamma), it would come under the all, as an object of the intellect. There are passages in the Canon (such as AN 9:36) that describe meditators experiencing nibbāna as a dhamma, but these passages seem to indicate that this description applies up through the level of non-returning. Other passages, however, describe nibbāna as the ending of all dhammas. For instance, Sn 5:6 quotes the Buddha as calling the attainment of the goal the transcending of all dhammas. Sn 4:6 and Sn 4:10 state that the arahant has transcended dispassion, said to be the highest dhamma. Thus, for the arahant, nibbāna is not an object of consciousness. Instead it is directly known without mediation. Because consciousness without feature is directly known without mediation, there seems good reason to equate the two.

Also, given that this consciousness is independent of the six senses, and that at the death of the arahant the six senses simply grow cold (Iti 44), then such an event should have no effect on it.

10. In other words, the act of searching for non-becoming—or annihilation—is also a type of becoming. Although the Buddhist path aims at the cessation of becoming *(bhava)*, it does not attempt this cessation by trying to annihilate the process of becoming. Instead, it does so by focusing on what has already come to be *(bhūta)*, developing dispassion for what has come to be and for the nutriment—the causes—of what has come to be. With no more passion, there is no clinging to or taking sustenance from the causes of what has come to be. And through this lack of clinging or sustenance comes release. On this point see SN 12:31 and Iti 49.

See also: DN 11; MN 1; MN 72; MN 86; SN 4:19; SN 35:117; AN 4:173

52 *To the Man from Aṭṭhakanagara*

Aṭṭhakanāgara Sutta

I have heard that on one occasion Ven. Ānanda was staying near Vesālī at Veḷuvagāmaka. Now on that occasion Dasama the householder from Aṭṭhakanagara[1] had arrived at Pāṭaliputta on some business. Then he went to a certain monk at Kukkaṭa Monastery and on arrival, having bowed down to him, sat to one side. As he was sitting there he said to the monk, "Where is Ven. Ānanda staying now? I'd like to see him."

"Householder, the Ven. Ānanda is staying near Vesālī at Veḷuvagāmaka."

Then Dasama the householder from Aṭṭhakanagara, on completing his business at Pāṭaliputta, went to Ven. Ānanda at Veḷuvagāmaka near Vesālī. On arrival, having bowed down to him, he sat to one side. As he was sitting there, he said to Ven. Ānanda: "Venerable sir, is there a single quality declared by the Blessed One—the one who knows, the one who sees, worthy & rightly self-awakened—where the unreleased mind of a monk who dwells there heedful, ardent, & resolute becomes released, or his unended effluents go to their total ending, or he attains the unexcelled security from the yoke that he had not attained before?"

"Yes, householder, there is...."

"And what is that one quality, venerable sir...?"

"There is the case, householder, where a monk, quite secluded from sensuality, secluded from unskillful qualities, enters & remains in the first jhāna: rapture & pleasure born from seclusion, accompanied by directed thought & evaluation. He reflects on this and discerns, 'This first jhāna is fabricated & intended. Now whatever is fabricated & intended is inconstant & subject to cessation.' Staying right there, he reaches the ending of the effluents. Or, if not, then—through this very Dhamma-passion, this Dhamma-delight, and from the total wasting away of the five lower fetters [self-identification views, grasping at habits & practices, uncertainty, sensual passion, and irritation]—he is due to arise spontaneously (in the Pure Abodes), there to be totally unbound, never again to return from that world.

"This, householder, is a single quality declared by the Blessed One—the one who knows, the one who sees, worthy & rightly self-awakened—where the unreleased mind of a monk who dwells there heedful, ardent, & resolute becomes released, or his unended effluents go to their total ending, or he attains the unexcelled security from the yoke that he had not attained before.

[Similarly with the second, third, and fourth jhānas.]

"Then again, a monk keeps pervading the first direction [the east] with an awareness imbued with goodwill, likewise the second, likewise the third, likewise the fourth. Thus above, below, & all around, everywhere, in its entirety, he keeps pervading the all-encompassing cosmos with an awareness imbued with goodwill—abundant, enlarged, unlimited, without hostility, without ill will. He reflects on this and discerns, 'This awareness-release through goodwill is fabricated & intended. Now whatever is fabricated & intended is inconstant & subject to cessation.' Staying right there, he reaches the ending of the effluents. Or, if not, then—through this very Dhamma-passion, this Dhamma-delight, and from the total wasting away of the five lower fetters—he is due to arise spontaneously (in the Pure Abodes), there to be totally unbound, never again to return from that world.

"This too, householder, is a single quality declared by the Blessed One—the one who knows, the one who sees, worthy & rightly self-awakened—where the unreleased mind of a monk who dwells there heedful, ardent, & resolute becomes released, or his unended effluents go to their total ending, or he attains the unexcelled security from the yoke that he had not attained before.

[Similarly with awareness-release through compassion, through empathetic joy, & through equanimity.]

"Then again, a monk—with the complete transcending of perceptions of (physical) form, with the disappearance of perceptions of resistance, and not attending to perceptions of multiplicity, (perceiving,) 'Infinite space'—enters & remains in the dimension of the infinitude of space. He reflects on this and discerns, 'This attainment of the infinitude of space is fabricated & intended. Now whatever is fabricated & intended is inconstant & subject to cessation.' Staying right there, he reaches the ending of the effluents. Or, if not, then—through this very Dhamma-passion, this Dhamma-delight, and from the total wasting away of the five lower fetters—he is due to arise spontaneously (in the Pure Abodes), there to be totally unbound, never again to return from that world.

"This too, householder, is a single quality declared by the Blessed One—the one who knows, the one who sees, worthy &

rightly self-awakened—where the unreleased mind of a monk who dwells there heedful, ardent, & resolute becomes released, or his unended effluents go to their total ending, or he attains the unexcelled security from the yoke that he had not attained before.

[Similarly with the dimension of the infinitude of consciousness and the dimension of nothingness.]

When this was said, Dasama the householder from Aṭṭhakanagara said to Ven. Ānanda, "Venerable Ānanda, just as if a man seeking a single opening onto treasure were all at once to come upon eleven openings onto treasure, in the same way I—seeking a single doorway to the deathless—have all at once come to hear of eleven doorways to the deathless. And just as if a man whose house had eleven doors could take himself to safety by means of any one of those doors, in the same way I can take myself to safety by means of any one of these eleven doors to the deathless. Venerable sir, when sectarians search for a teacher's fee for their teachers, why shouldn't I pay homage to Ven. Ānanda?"

So Dasama the householder from Aṭṭhakanagara, having assembled the Saṅgha of monks from Vesāli and Pāṭaliputta, with his own hands served & satisfied them with refined staple & non-staple foods. He presented a pair of cloths to each monk, and a triple robe to Ven. Ānanda. And for Ven. Ānanda he had a dwelling built worth five hundred (kahāpanas).

NOTE

1. The term *aṭṭhakanāgara* in the title of this sutta—with the fourth "a" marked with a macron—means, "a person from Aṭṭhakanagara."

See also: MN 140; AN 9:36

53 The Practice for One in Training

Sekha-paṭipadā Sutta

I have heard that on one occasion the Blessed One was staying among the Sakyans at Kapilavatthu in the Banyan Park. Now at that time a new reception hall[1] had just been built by the Kapilavatthu Sakyans, and it had not yet been dwelled in by any contemplative, brahman, or anyone at all in human form. So the Kapilavatthu Sakyans went to the Blessed One and, on arrival, having bowed down to him, sat to one side. As they were sitting there they said to him, "Lord, a new reception hall has just been built by the Kapilavatthu Sakyans, and it has not yet been dwelled in by any contemplative, brahman, or anyone at all in human form. May the Blessed One be the first to use it. When the Blessed One has used it first, the Kapilavatthu Sakyans will use it afterwards. That will be for their long-term welfare & happiness."

The Blessed One acquiesced with silence. Sensing his acquiescence, the Kapilavatthu Sakyans got up from their seats, bowed down to him, circumambulated him, and then went to the new reception hall. On arrival, they spread it all over with felt rugs, arranged seats, set out a water vessel, and raised an oil lamp. Then they went to the Blessed One and, on arrival, having bowed down to him, stood to one side. As they were standing there they said to him, "Lord, the reception hall has been covered all over with felt rugs, seats have been arranged, a water vessel has been set out, and an oil lamp raised. It is now time for the Blessed One to do as he sees fit."

So the Blessed One—after adjusting his under robe and carrying his bowl & outer robe—went together with a Saṅgha of monks to the reception hall. On arrival he washed his feet, entered the hall, and sat with his back to the central post, facing east. The Saṅgha of monks washed their feet, entered the hall, and sat with their backs to the western wall, facing east, ranged around the Blessed One. The Kapilavatthu Sakyans washed their feet, entered the hall, and sat with their backs to the eastern wall, facing west, ranged around the Blessed One. Then the Blessed One—having spent most of the night instructing, urging, rousing, & encouraging the Kapilavatthu

Sakyans with a Dhamma talk—said to Ven. Ānanda, "Ānanda, speak to the Kapilavatthu Sakyans about the person who follows the practice for one in training.[2] My back aches. I will rest it."

"As you say, lord," Ven. Ānanda responded to him.

Then the Blessed One, having arranged his outer robe folded in four, lay down on his right side in the lion's sleeping posture, with one foot on top of the other, mindful & alert, having made a mental note to get up.

Then Ven. Ānanda addressed Mahānāma the Sakyan[3]: "There is the case, Mahānāma, where a disciple of the noble ones is consummate in virtue, guards the doors to his sense faculties, knows moderation in eating, is devoted to wakefulness, is endowed with seven qualities, and obtains at will—without trouble or difficulty—the four jhānas that constitute heightened awareness and a pleasant abiding in the here-&-now.

"And how is the disciple of the noble ones consummate in virtue? There is the case where the disciple of the noble ones is virtuous. He dwells restrained in accordance with the Pāṭimokkha, consummate in his behavior & sphere of activity. He trains himself, having undertaken the training rules, seeing danger in the slightest faults. This is how the disciple of the noble ones is consummate in virtue.

"And how does the disciple of the noble ones guard the doors to his sense faculties? There is the case where the disciple of the noble ones, on seeing a form with the eye, doesn't grasp at any theme or variations by which—if he were to dwell without restraint over the faculty of the eye—evil, unskillful qualities such as greed or distress might assail him. He practices with restraint. He guards the faculty of the eye. He achieves restraint with regard to the faculty of the eye.

"On hearing a sound with the ear....

"On smelling an aroma with the nose....

"On tasting a flavor with the tongue....

"On feeling a tactile sensation with the body....

"On cognizing an idea with the intellect, he doesn't grasp at any theme or variations by which—if he were to dwell without restraint over the faculty of the intellect—evil, unskillful qualities such as greed or distress might assail him. He practices with restraint. He guards the faculty of the intellect. He achieves restraint with regard to the faculty of the intellect. This is how the disciple of the noble ones guards the doors to his sense faculties.

"And how does the disciple of the noble ones know moderation in eating? There is the case where the disciple of the noble ones, considering it appropriately, takes his food not playfully, nor for intoxication, nor for putting on bulk, nor for beautification, but simply for the survival & continuance of this body, for ending its afflictions, for the support of the holy life, thinking, 'I will destroy old feelings (of hunger) & not create new feelings (from overeating). Thus I will maintain myself, be blameless, & live in comfort.' This is how the disciple of the noble ones knows moderation in eating.

"And how is the disciple of the noble ones devoted to wakefulness? There is the case where a monk during the day, sitting & pacing back & forth, cleanses his mind of any qualities that would hold the mind in check. During the first watch of the night [dusk to 10 p.m.], sitting & pacing back & forth, he cleanses his mind of any qualities that would hold the mind in check. During the second watch of the night [10 p.m. to 2 a.m.], reclining on his right side, he takes up the lion's posture, one foot placed on top of the other, mindful, alert, with his mind set on getting up [either as soon as he awakens or at a particular time]. During the last watch of the night [2 a.m. to dawn], sitting & pacing back & forth, he cleanses his mind of any qualities that would hold the mind in check. This is how the monk is devoted to wakefulness.

"And how is the disciple of the noble ones endowed with seven qualities?

"[1] There is the case where the disciple of the noble ones has conviction, is convinced of the Tathāgata's awakening: 'Indeed, the Blessed One is worthy & rightly self-awakened, consummate in clear-knowing & conduct, well-gone, an expert with regard to the cosmos, unexcelled trainer of people fit to be tamed, teacher of devas & human beings, awakened, blessed.'

"[2] He feels shame at (the thought of engaging in) bodily misconduct, verbal misconduct, mental misconduct.

"[3] He feels compunction over (the suffering that would result from) bodily misconduct, verbal misconduct, mental misconduct.

"[4] He has heard much, has retained what he has heard, has stored what he has heard. Whatever teachings are admirable in the beginning, admirable in the middle, admirable in the end, that—in their meaning & expression—proclaim the holy life that is entirely complete & pure: those he has listened to often, retained, discussed, accumulated, examined with his mind, and well-penetrated in terms of his views.

"[5] He keeps his persistence aroused for abandoning unskillful qualities and taking on skillful qualities. He is steadfast, solid in his effort, not shirking his duties with regard to skillful qualities.

"[6] He is mindful, highly meticulous, remembering & able to call to mind even things that were done & said long ago.

"[7] He is discerning, endowed with discernment of arising & passing away—noble, penetrating, leading to the right ending of stress.

"This is how the disciple of the noble ones is endowed with seven qualities.

"And how does the disciple of the noble ones obtain at will—without trouble or difficulty—the four jhānas that constitute heightened awareness and a pleasant abiding in the here-&-now? There is the case where, quite secluded from sensuality, secluded from unskillful qualities, the disciple of the noble ones enters & remains in the first jhāna: rapture & pleasure born of seclusion, accompanied by directed thought & evaluation. With the stilling of directed thoughts & evaluations, he enters & remains in the second jhāna: rapture & pleasure born of concentration, unification of awareness free from directed thought & evaluation—internal assurance. With the fading of rapture he remains equanimous, mindful, & alert, and senses pleasure with the body. He enters & remains in the third jhāna, of which the noble ones declare, 'Equanimous & mindful, he has a pleasant abiding.' With the abandoning of pleasure & pain—as with the earlier disappearance of elation & distress—he enters & remains in the fourth jhāna: purity of equanimity & mindfulness, neither pleasure nor pain. This is how the disciple of the noble ones obtains at will—without trouble or difficulty—the four jhānas that constitute heightened awareness and a pleasant abiding in the here-&-now.

"Now, when a disciple of the noble ones is consummate in virtue in this way, guards the doors to his sense faculties in this way, knows moderation in eating in this way, is devoted to wakefulness in this way, is endowed with seven qualities in this way, and obtains at will—without trouble or difficulty—the four jhānas that constitute heightened awareness and a pleasant abiding in the here-&-now in this way, then he is called a disciple of the noble ones who follows the practice for one in training, whose eggs are unspoiled, who is capable of breaking out, capable of awakening, capable of attaining the supreme rest from the yoke.[4]

"Just as if a hen had eight, ten, or twelve eggs that she covered rightly, warmed rightly, & incubated rightly: Even though this wish did not occur to her—'O that my chicks might break through the egg shells with their spiked claws or beaks and hatch out safely!'—still it is possible that the chicks would break through the shells with their spiked claws or beaks and hatch out safely. In the same way, when a disciple of the noble ones is consummate in virtue in this way, guards the doors to his sense faculties in this way, knows moderation in eating in this way, is devoted to wakefulness in this way, is endowed with seven qualities in this way, and obtains at will—without trouble or difficulty—the four jhānas that constitute heightened awareness and a pleasant abiding in the here-&-now in this way, then he is called a disciple of the noble ones who follows the practice for one in training, whose eggs are unspoiled, who is capable of breaking out, capable of awakening, capable of attaining the supreme rest from the yoke.

"Now when the disciple of the noble ones has arrived at this purity of equanimity & mindfulness, he recollects his manifold past lives, i.e., one birth, two… five, ten… fifty, a hundred, a thousand, a hundred thousand, many eons of cosmic contraction, many eons of cosmic expansion, many eons of cosmic contraction & expansion: 'There I had such a name, belonged to such a clan, had such an appearance. Such was my food, such my experience of pleasure & pain, such the end of my life. Passing away from that state, I re-arose there. There too I had such a name, belonged to such a clan, had such an appearance. Such was my food, such my experience of pleasure & pain, such the end of my life. Passing away from that state, I re-arose here.' Thus he recollects his manifold past lives in their modes & details. This is his first breaking out, like that of the hen's chicks from their shells.

"When the disciple of the noble ones has arrived at this purity of equanimity & mindfulness, he sees—by means of the divine eye, purified & surpassing the human—beings passing away & re-appearing, and he discerns how they are inferior & superior, beautiful & ugly, fortunate & unfortunate in accordance with their kamma: 'These beings—who were endowed with bad conduct of body, speech & mind, who reviled noble ones, held wrong views and undertook actions under the influence of wrong views—with the break-up of the body, after death, have re-appeared in a plane of deprivation, a bad destination, a lower realm, hell. But these beings—who were endowed with good conduct of body, speech, & mind, who did not revile noble ones, who held right views and undertook actions under the influence of right views—with the break-up of the body, after death, have re-appeared in a good destination, a heavenly world.' Thus—by means of the divine eye, purified & surpassing the human—he sees beings passing away & re-appearing, and he discerns how they are inferior & superior, beautiful & ugly, fortunate & unfortunate in accordance with their kamma. This is his second breaking out, like that of the hen's chicks from their shells.

"When the disciple of the noble ones has arrived at this purity of equanimity & mindfulness, he enters & remains in the effluent-free awareness-release & discernment-release, having directly known & realized them for himself right in the here & now.[5] This is his third breaking out, like that of the hen's chicks from their shells.

"Now, when the disciple of the noble ones is consummate in virtue, that is a matter of his conduct. When he guards the doors to his sense faculties... knows moderation in eating... is devoted to wakefulness... is endowed with seven qualities, that is a matter of his conduct. When he obtains at will—without trouble or difficulty—the four jhānas that constitute heightened awareness and a pleasant abiding in the here-&-now, that is a matter of his conduct.

"When he recollects his manifold past lives... in their modes & details, that is a matter of his clear-knowing. When he sees—by means of the divine eye, purified & surpassing the human—beings passing away & re-appearing.... When he enters & remains in the effluent-free awareness-release & discernment-release, having directly known & realized them for himself right in the here & now, that is a matter of his clear knowing.

"This, Mahānāma, is called a disciple of the noble ones who is consummate in clear-knowing, consummate in conduct, consummate in clear-knowing & conduct. And by the Brahmā Sanaṅkumāra this verse was said:

> 'The noble warrior is the best among people
> when judging by clan.
> But a person consummate
> in clear-knowing & conduct,
> is the best of beings
> human & divine.'

"This verse was well-sung by the Brahmā Sanaṅkumāra, not ill-sung; well-said, not ill-said; connected with the goal, not unconnected with the goal. It was endorsed by the Blessed One."

Then the Blessed One got up and said to Ven. Ānanda, "Good, good, Ānanda. What you have said to the Kapilavatthu Sakyans about the person who follows the practice for one in training is good."

That is what Ven. Ānanda said, and the Teacher approved. Gratified, the Kapilavatthu Sakyans delighted in Ven. Ānanda's words.

NOTES

1. According to the Commentary, this was a hall built to receive royal guests, together with their entourages. See SN 35:202.

2. This phrase—"the person who follows the practice for one in higher training"—translates the Pali phrase, *sekho pāṭipado.* Although this phrase may be taken as two separate words, the Commentary treats it as a compound and translates it as "one who follows the *sekha-paṭipadā.*" Grammatically, as a compound, the form is strange, with the first member maintaining its case ending, instead of being reduced to a stem form connected with the following member of the compound, as in a normal compound. However, this form has been found in other parts of the Canon as well, and modern grammarians have coined a term to describe it: a syntactical compound. I have thus followed the Commentary in my translation.

"One in training" is a person who has attained at least stream entry, but not yet arahantship.

3. The chief of the Kapilavatthu Sakyans. See AN 3:73; AN 11:12; and AN 11:13.

4. The yoke is fourfold: the yoke of sensuality, the yoke of becoming, the yoke of views, & the yoke of ignorance. See AN 4:10.

5. At this point, one becomes an *asekha,* one no longer in training because one's training is complete. In other words, one is an arahant.

See also: SN 22:101; SN 48:53; SN 55:1; AN 4:37; AN 7:6

54 To Potaliya (Excerpt)

Potaliya Sutta

In this passage, the Buddha teaches Potaliya the householder what it means, in the discipline of a noble one, to have entirely cut off one's worldly affairs.

...."Suppose a dog, overcome with weakness & hunger, were to come across a slaughterhouse, and there a dexterous butcher or butcher's apprentice were to fling him a chain of bones—thoroughly scraped, without any flesh, smeared with blood. What do you think? Would the dog, gnawing on that chain of bones—thoroughly scraped, without any flesh, smeared with blood—appease its weakness & hunger?"

"No, lord. And why is that? Because the chain of bones is thoroughly scraped, without any flesh, & smeared with blood. The dog would get nothing but its share of weariness & vexation."

"In the same way, householder, a disciple of the noble ones considers this point: 'The Blessed One has compared sensuality to a chain of bones, of much stress, much despair, & greater drawbacks.' Seeing this with right discernment, as it has come to be, then avoiding the equanimity coming from multiplicity, dependent on multiplicity, he develops the equanimity coming from singleness, dependent on singleness,[1] where sustenance/clinging for the baits of the world ceases without trace.

"Now suppose a vulture, a kite, or a hawk, seizing a lump of flesh, were to take off, and other vultures, kites, or hawks—following right after it—were to tear at it with their beaks & pull at it with their claws. What do you think? If that vulture, kite, or hawk were not quickly to drop that lump of flesh, would it meet with death from that cause, or with death-like pain?"

"Yes, lord."

"In the same way, householder, a disciple of the noble ones considers this point: 'The Blessed One has compared sensuality to a lump of flesh, of much stress, much despair, & greater drawbacks.' Seeing this with right discernment, as it has come to be, then avoiding the equanimity coming from multiplicity, dependent on multiplicity, he develops the equanimity coming from singleness, dependent on singleness, where sustenance/clinging for the baits of the world ceases without trace.

"Now suppose a man were to come against the wind, carrying a burning grass torch. What do you think? If he were not quickly to drop that grass torch, would he burn his hand or his arm or some other part of his body, so that he would meet with death from that cause, or with death-like pain?"

"Yes, lord."

"In the same way, householder, a disciple of the noble ones considers this point: 'The Blessed One has compared sensuality to a grass torch, of much stress, much despair, & greater drawbacks.' Seeing this with right discernment, as it has come to be, then avoiding the equanimity coming from multiplicity, dependent on multiplicity, he develops the equanimity coming from singleness, dependent on singleness, where sustenance/clinging for the baits of the world ceases without trace.

"Now suppose there were a pit of glowing embers, deeper than a man's height, full of embers that were neither flaming nor smoking, and a man were to come along—loving life, hating death, loving pleasure, abhorring pain—and two strong men, grabbing him with their arms, were to drag him to the pit of embers. What do you think? Wouldn't the man twist his body this way & that?"

"Yes, lord. And why is that? Because he would realize, 'If I fall into this pit of glowing embers, I will meet with death from that cause, or with death-like pain.'"

"In the same way, householder, a disciple of the noble ones considers this point: 'The Blessed One has compared sensuality to a pit of glowing embers, of much stress, much despair, & greater drawbacks.' Seeing this with right discernment, as it has come to be, then avoiding the equanimity coming from multiplicity, dependent on multiplicity, he develops the equanimity coming from singleness, dependent on singleness, where sustenance/clinging for the baits of the world ceases without trace.

"Now suppose a man, when dreaming, were to see delightful parks, delightful forests, delightful stretches of land, & delightful lakes, and on awakening were to see nothing. In the same way, householder, a disciple of the noble ones considers this point: 'The Blessed One has compared sensuality to a dream, of much stress, much despair, & greater drawbacks.' Seeing this with right discernment, as it has come to be, then avoiding the equanimity coming from multiplicity, dependent on multiplicity, he develops the equanimity coming from singleness, dependent on singleness, where sustenance/clinging for the baits of the world ceases without trace.

"Now suppose a man having borrowed some goods—a manly carriage, fine jewels, & ear ornaments—were to go into the market preceded & surrounded by his borrowed goods, and people seeing him would say, 'How wealthy this man is, for this is how the wealthy enjoy their possessions,' but the actual owners, wherever they might see him, would strip him then & there of what is theirs. What do you think? Should the man rightly be upset?"

"No, lord.[2] And why is that? The owners are stripping him of what is theirs."

"In the same way, householder, a disciple of the noble ones considers this point: 'The Blessed One has compared sensuality to borrowed goods, of much stress, much despair, & greater drawbacks.' Seeing this with right discernment, as it has come to be, then avoiding the equanimity coming from multiplicity, dependent on multiplicity, he develops the equanimity coming from singleness, dependent on singleness, where sustenance/clinging for the baits of the world ceases without trace.

"Now suppose that, not far from a village or town, there were a dense forest grove, and there in the grove was a tree with delicious fruit, abundant fruit, but with no fruit fallen to the ground. A man would come along, desiring fruit, looking for fruit, searching for fruit. Plunging into the forest grove, he would see the tree... and the thought would occur to him, 'This is a tree with delicious fruit, abundant fruit, and there is no fruit fallen to the ground, but I know how to climb a tree. Why don't I climb the tree, eat what I like, and fill my clothes with the fruit?' So, having climbed the tree, he would eat what he liked and fill his clothes with the fruit. Then a second man would come along, desiring fruit, looking for fruit, searching for fruit and carrying a sharp ax. Plunging into the forest grove, he would see the tree... and the thought would occur to him, 'This is a tree with delicious fruit, abundant fruit, and there is no fruit fallen to the ground, and I don't know how to climb a tree. Why don't I chop down this tree at the root, eat what I like, and fill my clothes with the fruit?' So he would chop the tree at the root. What do you think? If the first man who climbed the tree didn't quickly come down, wouldn't the falling tree crush his hand or foot or some other part of his body, so that he would meet with death from that cause, or with death-like pain?"

"Yes, lord."

"In the same way, householder, a disciple of the noble ones considers this point: 'The Blessed One has compared sensuality to the fruits of a tree, of much stress, much despair, & greater drawbacks.' Seeing this with right discernment, as it has come to be, then avoiding the equanimity coming from multiplicity, dependent on multiplicity, he develops the equanimity coming from singleness, dependent on singleness, where sustenance/clinging for the baits of the world ceases without trace.

"Now when the disciple of the noble ones has arrived at this purity of equanimity & mindfulness, he recollects his manifold past lives, i.e., one birth, two… five, ten… fifty, a hundred, a thousand, a hundred thousand, many eons of cosmic contraction, many eons of cosmic expansion, many eons of cosmic contraction & expansion: 'There I had such a name, belonged to such a clan, had such an appearance. Such was my food, such my experience of pleasure & pain, such the end of my life. Passing away from that state, I re-arose there. There too I had such a name, belonged to such a clan, had such an appearance. Such was my food, such my experience of pleasure & pain, such the end of my life. Passing away from that state, I re-arose here.' Thus he recollects his manifold past lives in their modes & details.

"When the disciple of the noble ones has arrived at this purity of equanimity & mindfulness, he sees—by means of the divine eye, purified & surpassing the human—beings passing away & re-appearing, and he discerns how they are inferior & superior, beautiful & ugly, fortunate & unfortunate in accordance with their kamma: 'These beings—who were endowed with bad conduct of body, speech & mind, who reviled noble ones, held wrong views and undertook actions under the influence of wrong views—with the break-up of the body, after death, have re-appeared in a plane of deprivation, a bad destination, a lower realm, hell. But these beings—who were endowed with good conduct of body, speech, & mind, who did not revile noble ones, who held right views and undertook actions under the influence of right views—with the break-up of the body, after death, have re-appeared in a good destination, a heavenly world.' Thus—by means of the divine eye, purified & surpassing the human—he sees beings passing away & re-appearing, and he discerns how they are inferior & superior, beautiful & ugly, fortunate & unfortunate in accordance with their kamma.

"When the disciple of the noble ones has arrived at this purity of equanimity & mindfulness, he enters & remains in the effluent-free awareness-release & discernment-release, having directly known & realized them for himself right in the here & now.

"It's to this extent, householder, that there is the all-around in-every-way cutting off of one's affairs in the discipline of a noble one"….

NOTES

1. MN 137 (passage 179 in *The Wings to Awakening)* identifies "equanimity based on multiplicity" as equanimity with regard to forms, sounds, smells, tastes, and tactile sensations. It identifies "equanimity based on singleness" as the four formless attainments. In the context of this sutta, however, the Commentary defines equanimity based on singleness as the fourth jhāna, and this interpretation seems correct. Toward the end of this passage, the equanimity based on singleness functions as the basis for the three knowledges, a function normally filled by the fourth jhāna.

2. Following the Thai edition. The Burmese and PTS editions say, "Yes, lord," apparently reading the Buddha's question as meaning, "Would that be enough for the man to be upset?" This, however, ignores the monks' reason for their answer. The fact that the owners are taking what is theirs does not relate to the question of whether the man would be upset, but it does relate to the question of whether he would *rightly* be upset.

See also: MN 13; MN 14; MN 22; MN 82; AN 5:76; AN 7:70; Dhp 146–156; Sn 4:1; Thig 13:1; Thig 13:5; Thig 14

58 To Prince Abhaya

Abhaya Rāja-kumāra Sutta

INTRODUCTION

In this discourse, the Buddha shows the factors that go into deciding what is and is not worth saying. The main factors are three: whether or not a statement is true, whether or not it is beneficial, and whether or not it is pleasing to others. The Buddha himself would state only those things that are true and beneficial, and would have a sense of time for when pleasing and unpleasing things should be said. Notice that the possibility that a statement might be untrue yet beneficial is not even entertained.

This discourse also shows, in action, the Buddha's teaching on the four categories of questions and how they should be answered (see AN 4:42). The prince asks him two questions, and in both cases he responds first with a counter-question, before going on to give an analytical answer to the first question and a categorical answer to the second. Each counter-question serves a double function: to give the prince a familiar reference point for understanding the answer about to come, and also to give him a chance to speak of his own intelligence and good motives. This provides him with the opportunity to save face after being stymied in his desire to best the Buddha in argument. The Commentary notes that the prince had placed his infant son on his lap as a cheap debater's trick: If the Buddha had put him in an uncomfortable spot in the debate, the prince would have pinched his son, causing him to cry and thus effectively bringing the debate to a halt. The Buddha, however, uses the infant's presence to remove any sense of a debate and also to make an effective point. Taking Nigaṇṭha Nāṭaputta's image of a dangerous object stuck in the throat, he applies it to the infant, and then goes on to make the point that, unlike the Nigaṇṭhas—who were content to leave someone with a potentially lethal object in the throat—the Buddha's desire is to remove such objects, out of sympathy and compassion. In this way, he brings the prince over to his side, converting a potential opponent into a disciple.

Thus this discourse is not only about *right speech, but also shows right speech in action.*

* * *

I have heard that on one occasion the Blessed One was staying near Rājagaha in the Bamboo Grove, the Squirrels' Sanctuary.

Then Prince Abhaya went to Nigaṇṭha Nāṭaputta and on arrival, having bowed down to him, sat to one side. As he was sitting there, Nigaṇṭha Nāṭaputta said to him, "Come, now, prince. Refute the words of Gotama the contemplative, and this admirable report about you will spread afar: 'The words of Gotama the contemplative—so mighty, so powerful—were refuted by Prince Abhaya!'"

"But how, lord, will I refute the words of Gotama the contemplative—so mighty, so powerful?"

"Come now, prince. Go to Gotama the contemplative and on arrival say this: 'Lord, would the Tathāgata say words that are unendearing & disagreeable to others?' If Gotama the contemplative, thus asked, answers, 'The Tathāgata would say words that are unendearing & disagreeable to others,' then you should say, 'Then how is there any difference between you, lord, and run-of-the-mill people? For even run-of-the-mill people say words that are unendearing & disagreeable to others.' But if Gotama the contemplative, thus asked, answers, 'The Tathāgata would not say words that are unendearing & disagreeable to others,' then you should say, 'Then how, lord, did you say of Devadatta that "Devadatta is doomed to deprivation, Devadatta is doomed to hell, Devadatta will stay for an eon, Devadatta is incurable"? For Devadatta was upset & disgruntled at those words of yours.' When Gotama the contemplative is asked this two-pronged question by you, he won't be able to swallow it down or spit it up. Just as if a two-horned chestnut[1] were stuck in a man's throat: He would not be able to swallow it down or spit it up. In the same way, when Gotama the contemplative is asked this two-pronged question by you, he won't be able to swallow it down or spit it up."

Responding, "As you say, lord," to Nigaṇṭha Nāṭaputta, Prince Abhaya got up from his seat, bowed down to Nigaṇṭha Nāṭaputta, circumambulated him, and then went to the Blessed One. On arrival, having bowed down to the Blessed One, he sat to one side. As he was sitting there, he glanced up at the sun and thought, "Today is not the time to refute the Blessed One's words. Tomorrow in my own home I will refute the Blessed One's words." So he said to the Blessed One, "Lord, may the Blessed One, together with three others, acquiesce to my offer of tomorrow's meal."

The Blessed One acquiesced with silence.

Then Prince Abhaya, understanding the Blessed One's acquiescence, got up from his seat, bowed down to the Blessed One, circumambulated him, and left.

Then, after the night had passed, the Blessed One early in the morning adjusted his under robe and, carrying his bowl & outer robe, went to Prince Abhaya's home. On arrival, he sat down on a seat made ready. Prince Abhaya, with his own hand, served & satisfied the Blessed One with fine staple & non-staple foods. Then, when the Blessed One had eaten and had rinsed his bowl & hands, Prince Abhaya took a lower seat and sat to one side. As he was sitting there he said to the Blessed One, "Lord, would the Tathāgata say words that are unendearing & disagreeable to others?"

"Prince, there is no categorical yes-or-no answer to that."

"Then right here, lord, the Nigaṇṭhas are destroyed."

"But prince, why do you say, 'Then right here, lord, the Nigaṇṭhas are destroyed'?"

"Just yesterday, lord, I went to Nigaṇṭha Nāṭaputta and… he said to me… 'Come now, prince. Go to Gotama the contemplative and on arrival say this: "Lord, would the Tathāgata say words that are unendearing & disagreeable to others?" … Just as if a two-horned chestnut were stuck in a man's throat: He would not be able to swallow it down or spit it up. In the same way, when Gotama the contemplative is asked this two-pronged question by you, he won't be able to swallow it down or spit it up.'"

Now at that time a baby boy was lying face-up on the prince's lap. So the Blessed One said to the prince, "What do you think, prince? If this young boy, through your own negligence or that of the nurse, were to take a stick or a piece of gravel into its mouth, what would you do?"

"I would take it out, lord. If I couldn't get it out right away, then holding its head in my left hand and crooking a finger of my right, I would take it out, even if it meant drawing blood. Why is that? Because I have sympathy for the young boy."

"In the same way, prince:

[1] In the case of words that the Tathāgata knows to be unfactual, untrue, unbeneficial [or: not connected with the goal], unendearing & disagreeable to others, he does not say them.

[2] In the case of words that the Tathāgata knows to be factual, true, unbeneficial, unendearing & disagreeable to others, he does not say them.

[3] In the case of words that the Tathāgata knows to be factual, true, beneficial, but unendearing & disagreeable to others, he has a sense of the proper time for saying them.

[4] In the case of words that the Tathāgata knows to be unfactual, untrue, unbeneficial, but endearing & agreeable to others, he does not say them.

[5] In the case of words that the Tathāgata knows to be factual, true, unbeneficial, but endearing & agreeable to others, he does not say them.

[6] In the case of words that the Tathāgata knows to be factual, true, beneficial, and endearing & agreeable to others, he has a sense of the proper time for saying them. Why is that? Because the Tathāgata has sympathy for living beings."

"Lord, when wise nobles or brahmans, householders or contemplatives, having formulated questions, come to the Tathāgata and ask him, does this line of reasoning appear to his awareness beforehand—'If those who approach me ask this, I—thus asked—will answer in this way'—or does the Tathāgata come up with the answer on the spot?"

"In that case, prince, I will ask you a counter-question. Answer as you see fit. What do you think? Are you skilled in the parts of a chariot?"

"Yes, lord. I am skilled in the parts of a chariot."

"And what do you think? When people come & ask you, 'What is the name of this part of the chariot?' does this line of reasoning appear to your awareness beforehand—'If those who approach me ask this, I—thus asked—will answer in this way'—or do you come up with the answer on the spot?"

"Lord, I am renowned for being skilled in the parts of a chariot. All the parts of a chariot are well-known to me. I come up with the answer on the spot."

"In the same way, prince, when wise nobles or brahmans, householders or contemplatives, having formulated questions, come to the Tathāgata and ask him, he comes up with the answer on the spot. Why is that? Because the property of the Dhamma is thoroughly penetrated by the Tathāgata. From his thorough penetration of the property of the Dhamma, he comes up with the answer on the spot."[2]

When this was said, Prince Abhaya said to the Blessed One: "Magnificent, lord! Magnificent! Just as if he were to place upright what was overturned, to reveal what was hidden, to show the way to one who was lost, or to carry a lamp into the dark so that those with eyes could see forms, in the same way has the Blessed One—

through many lines of reasoning—made the Dhamma clear. I go to the Blessed One for refuge, to the Dhamma, and to the Saṅgha of monks. May the Blessed One remember me as a lay follower who has gone to him for refuge, from this day forward, for life."

NOTES

1. A two-horned chestnut is the nut of a tree *(Trapa bicornis)* growing in south and southeast Asia. Its shell looks like the head of a water buffalo, with two nasty, curved "horns" sticking out of either side.

2. This statement is apparently related to the more abstract statement in AN 4:24, that what the Tathāgata knows is not "established" in him. In other words, he does not define himself or the awakened mind in terms of knowledge or views, even concerning the Dhamma, although the knowledge that led to his awakening is fully available for him to draw on at any time.

See also: SN 11:5; AN 4:42; AN 4:183; AN 5:198; AN 8:7–8; AN 10:165; Sn 3:3

59 Many Things To Be Felt

Bahuvedanīya Sutta

I have heard that on one occasion the Blessed One was staying near Sāvatthī in Jeta's Grove, Anāthapiṇḍika's monastery.

Then Pañcakaṅga the carpenter[1] went to Ven. Udāyin and, on arrival, having bowed down to him, sat to one side. As he was sitting there, he said to Ven. Udāyin, "Venerable Udāyin, how many feelings have been described by the Blessed One?"

"The Blessed One has described three feelings, householder: a feeling of pleasure, a feeling of pain, a feeling of neither pleasure nor pain. These are the three feelings described by the Blessed One."

When this was said, Pañcakaṅga the carpenter said to Ven. Udāyin, "No, Venerable Udāyin, the Blessed One hasn't described three feelings, he's described two feelings: a feeling of pleasure & a feeling of pain. As for the feeling of neither pleasure nor pain, that has been described by the Blessed One as a peaceful, sublime pleasure."

A second time... A third time, Ven. Udāyin said to Pañcakaṅga the carpenter, "No, householder, the Blessed One hasn't described two feelings, he's described three feelings: a feeling of pleasure, a feeling of pain, a feeling of neither pleasure nor pain. These are the three feelings described by the Blessed One."

A second time... A third time, Pañcakaṅga the carpenter said to Ven. Udāyin, "No, Venerable Udāyin, the Blessed One hasn't described three feelings, he's described two feelings: a feeling of pleasure & a feeling of pain. As for the feeling of neither pleasure nor pain, that has been described by the Blessed One as a peaceful, sublime pleasure."

But neither was Ven. Udāyin able to convince Pañcakaṅga the carpenter, nor was Pañcakaṅga the carpenter able to convince Ven. Udāyin.

Ven. Ānanda heard of Ven. Udāyin's conversation with Pañcakaṅga the carpenter. So he went to the Blessed One and, on arrival, having bowed down to him, sat to one side. As he was sitting there, he told the Blessed One the entire extent of Ven. Udāyin's conversation with Pañcakaṅga the carpenter.

(The Blessed One said,) "Ānanda, it was a genuine exposition that Pañcakaṅga the carpenter didn't accept from Udāyin the monk, and it was a genuine exposition that Udāyin the monk didn't accept from Pañcakaṅga the carpenter. There is the exposition whereby I have spoken of two feelings, the exposition whereby I have spoken of three feelings… five… six… eighteen… thirty-six… one hundred and eight feelings.[2]

"Thus I have taught the Dhamma by means of exposition. When I have taught the Dhamma by means of exposition, if there are those who do not concede, allow, or approve of what has been well-spoken & well-stated by one another, it can be expected that they will dwell arguing, quarreling, & disputing, stabbing one another with weapons of the mouth.

Thus I have taught the Dhamma by means of exposition. When I have taught the Dhamma by means of exposition, if there are those who concede, allow, & approve of what has been well-spoken & well-stated by one another, it can be expected that they will dwell harmoniously, cordially, without dispute, becoming like milk mixed with water, regarding one another with affectionate eyes.

"Ānanda, there are these five strings of sensuality. Which five? Forms cognizable via the eye—agreeable, pleasing, charming, endearing, enticing, linked with sensual desire. Sounds cognizable via the ear… Aromas cognizable via the nose… Flavors cognizable via the tongue… Tactile sensations cognizable via the body—agreeable, pleasing, charming, endearing, enticing, linked with sensual desire. Now, whatever pleasure & joy arises in dependence on these five strings of sensuality, that is called sensual pleasure.

"Though there are those who say, 'They [i.e., beings] experience this as the highest existing pleasure & joy,'[3] I do not grant them that. Why is that? Because there is another pleasure more excellent than that pleasure and more sublime.

"And which, Ānanda, is the other pleasure more excellent than that pleasure and more sublime? There is the case where a monk—quite secluded from sensuality, secluded from unskillful qualities—enters & remains in the first jhāna: rapture & pleasure born of seclusion, accompanied by directed thought & evaluation. This is the other pleasure more excellent than that pleasure and more sublime.

"Though there are those who say, 'They experience this as the highest existing pleasure & joy,' I do not grant them that. Why is that? Because there is another pleasure more excellent than that pleasure and more sublime.

"And which, Ānanda, is the other pleasure more excellent than that pleasure and more sublime? There is the case where, with the stilling of directed thoughts & evaluations, a monk enters & remains in the second jhāna: rapture & pleasure born of concentration, unification of awareness free from directed thought & evaluation—internal assurance. This is the other pleasure more excellent than that pleasure and more sublime.

"Though there are those who say, 'They experience this as the highest existing pleasure & joy,' I do not grant them that. Why is that? Because there is another pleasure more excellent than that pleasure and more sublime.

"And which, Ānanda, is the other pleasure more excellent than that pleasure and more sublime? There is the case where a monk, with the fading of rapture, remains equanimous, mindful, & alert, and senses pleasure with the body. He enters & remains in the third jhāna, of which the noble ones declare, 'Equanimous & mindful, he has a pleasant abiding.' This is the other pleasure more excellent than that pleasure and more sublime.

"Though there are those who say, 'They experience this as the highest existing pleasure & joy,' I do not grant them that. Why is that? Because there is another pleasure more excellent than that pleasure and more sublime.

"And which, Ānanda, is the other pleasure more excellent than that pleasure and more sublime? There is the case where a monk, with the abandoning of pleasure & pain—as with the earlier disappearance of elation & distress—enters & remains in the fourth jhāna: purity of equanimity & mindfulness, neither pleasure nor pain. This is the other pleasure more excellent than that pleasure and more sublime.[4]

"Though there are those who say, 'They experience this as the highest existing pleasure & joy,' I do not grant them that. Why is that? Because there is another pleasure more excellent than that pleasure and more sublime.

"And which, Ānanda, is the other pleasure more excellent than that pleasure and more sublime? There is the case where a monk, with the complete transcending of perceptions of form, with the disappearance of perceptions of resistance,[5] and not attending to perceptions of multiplicity,[6] (perceiving,) 'Infinite space,' enters & remains in the dimension of the infinitude of space. This is the other pleasure more excellent than that pleasure and more sublime.

"Though there are those who say, 'They experience this as the highest existing pleasure & joy,' I do not grant them that. Why is that? Because there is another pleasure more excellent than that pleasure and more sublime.

"And which, Ānanda, is the other pleasure more excellent than that pleasure and more sublime? There is the case where a monk, with the complete transcending of the dimension of the infinitude of space, (perceiving,) 'Infinite consciousness,' enters & remains in the dimension of the infinitude of consciousness. This is the other pleasure more excellent than that pleasure and more sublime.

"Though there are those who say, 'They experience this as the highest existing pleasure & joy,' I do not grant them that. Why is that? Because there is another pleasure more excellent than that pleasure and more sublime.

"And which, Ānanda, is the other pleasure more excellent than that pleasure and more sublime? There is the case where a monk, with the complete transcending of the dimension of the infinitude of consciousness, (perceiving,) 'There is nothing,' enters & remains in the dimension of nothingness. This is the other pleasure more excellent than that pleasure and more sublime.

"Though there are those who say, 'They experience this as the highest existing pleasure & joy,' I do not grant them that. Why is that? Because there is another pleasure more excellent than that pleasure and more sublime.

"And which, Ānanda, is the other pleasure more excellent than that pleasure and more sublime? There is the case where a monk, with the complete transcending of the dimension of nothingness, enters & remains in the dimension of neither perception nor non-perception. This is the other pleasure more excellent than that pleasure and more sublime.

"Though there are those who say, 'They experience this as the highest existing pleasure & joy,' I do not grant them that. Why is that? Because there is another pleasure more excellent than that pleasure and more sublime.

"And which, Ānanda, is the other pleasure more excellent than that pleasure and more sublime? There is the case where a monk, with the complete transcending of the dimension of neither perception nor non-perception, enters & remains in the cessation of perception & feeling.[7] This is the other pleasure more excellent than that pleasure and more sublime.

"Now, it's possible, Ānanda, that some wanderers of other persuasions might say, 'Gotama the contemplative speaks of the cessation of perception & feeling and yet describes it as pleasure. What is this? How is this?' When they say that, they are to be told, 'It's not the case, friends, that the Blessed One describes only pleasant feeling as included under pleasure. Wherever pleasure is found, in whatever terms, the Blessed One describes it as pleasure.'"

That is what the Blessed One said. Gratified, Ven. Ānanda delighted in the Blessed One's words.

NOTES

1. See MN 78.

2. See SN 36:22. SN 48:38–9 provide further explanations of the five feelings. MN 137 provides a further explanation of the eighteen and thirty-six feelings.

The two types of feelings described in SN 36:22 do not correspond to the two types cited here by Pañcakaṅga, but see note 4, below. As for the three types described in SN 36:22, they do correspond to the three types cited here by Ven. Udayin. It may be that, in this sutta, Ven. Udāyin is still smarting from the rebuke he received from the Buddha in MN 136 for trying to apply the teaching that all feelings are stressful—essentially, an assertion that there is only one type of feeling—to a question about the results of kamma: a question that, the Buddha said, should have been answered with an explanation of the three types of feeling, corresponding to the three types of action.

3. Reading, *'etaṁ paramaṃ santaṁ sukhaṁ somanassaṁ paṭisaṃvedentīti,'* with the Thai edition.

4. By identifying the neither-pleasure nor pain of the fourth jhāna as a kind of pleasure, the Buddha shows that Pañcakaṅga was, at least partially, right.

5. "Resistance" is a translation of the Pali term, *paṭigha.* According to DN 15, resistance-contact results from the characteristics of physical form and allows mental activity to know the presence of form. In other words, if form did not put up resistance to something else taking its place, one would not know that form is present. Thus the disappearance of perceptions of resistance aids in the mind's ability to transcend perceptions of form and to sense, in its place, infinite space.

6. "Multiplicity" is a translation of the Pali term, *nānattā*. MN 137 identifies multiplicity as the input of the five physical senses. See the essay, "Silence Isn't Mandatory."

7. Notice that this description of the cessation of perception & feeling lacks the statement often added in some passages where this attainment is described (as in MN 26 and AN 9:38): "and, as he sees (that) with discernment, his effluents are completely ended." This suggests that the arising of discernment may not be an automatic feature of this attainment.

See also: DN 2; DN 9; MN 14; MN 140; AN 9:33; AN 9:34; Dhp 202–204; Thag 9

60 *A Safe Bet*

Apaṇṇaka Sutta

INTRODUCTION

The Buddha often likened himself to a doctor, offering a treatment for the sufferings of the heart. Unlike ordinary doctors, however, he could not show newcomers the state of health—nibbāna—that his teaching was supposed to produce. If they followed his teaching, they would see it for themselves. But until they followed his teaching, he could offer them no empirical proof that nibbāna was a genuine possibility. As he stated in MN 27, the proof that he was awakened—and that awakening was a good thing—came with one's first taste of the deathless, at the first level of awakening, called stream-entry. However, stream-entry could be attained only through a serious commitment to the practice. Thus he had to provide other, non-empirical, means of persuasion to induce his listeners to give his teachings a serious try.

One of these means was the pragmatic argument, which differs from empirical arguments as follows. An empirical argument presents facts that logically imply that A must be true or false. A pragmatic argument focuses not on the facts related to A, but on the behavior that can be expected from a person who believes or rejects A. The Buddha's main pragmatic argument is that if one accepted his teachings, one would be likely to pay careful attention to one's actions, so as to do no harm. This in and of itself is a worthy activity regardless of whether the rest of the path was true. When applying this argument to the issue of rebirth and karmic results, the Buddha sometimes coupled it with a second pragmatic argument that resembles Pascal's wager: If one practices the Dhamma, one leads a blameless life in the here-and-now. Even if the afterlife and karmic results do not exist, one has not lost the wager, for the blamelessness of one's life is a reward in and of itself. If there is an afterlife with karmic results, then one has won a double reward: the blamelessness of one's life here and now, and the good rewards of one's actions in the afterlife. These two pragmatic arguments form the central message of this sutta.

The Pali title of this sutta is an adjective that has no exact equivalent in English. It is used in two different contexts. In the context of gambling, it describes a die that has not been loaded to favor one side or the other. In the context of an argument, it describes a position that is true regardless of which side of the argument is right. In other words, if there is an argument as to whether A or not-A is true, if C is true regardless of whether A is true or not, C is an apaṇṇaka position.

Although this sutta is primarily concerned with the second context, the Buddha implicitly makes the connection between this context and the first in stating that a person who rightly grasps the apaṇṇaka position has made a lucky throw, whereas a person who has wrongly grasped it has made an unlucky throw. Thus, to preserve this double context, I have translated apaṇṇaka as "safe-bet." "Cover-your-bets" might have been a more accurate translation, but it would have been unwieldy.

The sutta falls into two parts, the first part covering his "safe-bet" arguments, and the second part extolling the person who practices the Dhamma for tormenting neither himself nor others. The two parts are connected in that they both present pragmatic arguments for accepting the Buddha's teaching.

The safe-bet arguments in the first part of the sutta follow two patterns. The first pattern covers controversies over whether there is a life after death, whether actions bear results, and whether there is a causal connection between one's actions and one's experience of pleasure and pain. The pattern here is as follows:

(A) a statement of the anti-Dhamma position;

(B) a rejection of the anti-Dhamma position;

(A1) a pragmatic argument against holding to A—a person who does so is likely to act, speak, and think in unskillful ways;

(A2) further unfortunate consequences that follow from holding to A, given that A is wrong;

(A3) further unfortunate consequences that come from holding to A whether or not it is right;

(B1) a pragmatic argument for holding to B—a person who does so is likely to act, speak, and think in skillful ways;

(B2) further fortunate consequences that follow from holding to B, given that B is right;

(B3) further fortunate consequences that come from holding to B whether or not it is right.

It's noteworthy that the arguments in A2 and B2 are not safe-bet arguments, for they assume that A is wrong and B is right. Whether these arguments date from the Buddha or were added at a later date, no one knows.

The second pattern in the first part covers two controversies: whether or not a person can attain a total state of formlessness, and whether or not a person can attain total cessation of becoming. In the context of the first controversy, the safe-bet position is that even if there is no total attainment of formlessness, that still opens the possibility that one could become a deva on the level of form. In the context of the second, the safe-bet position is that even if there is no total cessation of becoming, that still leaves open the possibility that one could become a deva on the formless level. One further reflects that total formlessness would open the way to greater peace than the level of form; and that the cessation of becoming would open the way to greater freedom than formlessness. These last observations in no way prove that there is total formlessness or total cessation of becoming, but they do incline the mind to view those possibilities favorably.

The second part of the sutta divides people into four sorts: (1) those who torment themselves, (2) those who torment others, (3) those who torment themselves and others, and (4) those who torment neither themselves nor others. The first and third alternatives describe styles of religious practice that were common in the Buddha's time: practices of self-torture and self-affliction, and the offering of sacrifices. The second alternative covers any and all bloody occupations. In opposition to these alternatives, the Buddha presents the fourth alternative as ideal: the practice of his teachings all the way to full liberation.

For other pragmatic arguments for accepting and practicing the Dhamma, see AN 3:61, AN 3:66, and SN 42:8. AN 3:66 also contains a variant on the wager argument given in this sutta.

* * *

I have heard that on one occasion, when the Blessed One was on a wandering tour among the Kosalans with a large Saṅgha of monks, he arrived at the brahman village of the Kosalans called Sāla.

The brahman householders heard, "Master Gotama the contemplative—the son of the Sakyans, having gone forth from the Sakyan clan—on a wandering tour among the Kosalans with a large Saṅgha of monks—has arrived at Sāla. And of that master Gotama this fine reputation has spread: 'He is indeed a Blessed One, worthy & rightly self-awakened, consummate in clear-knowing & conduct, well-gone, an expert with regard to the cosmos, unexcelled trainer of people fit to be tamed, teacher of devas & human beings, awakened, blessed. He makes known—having realized it through direct knowledge—this world with its devas, Māras, & Brahmās, this generation with its contemplatives & brahmans, its rulers & commonfolk; he explains the Dhamma admirable in the beginning, admirable in the middle, admirable in the end; he expounds the holy life both in its particulars & in its essence, entirely perfect, surpassingly pure. It is good to see such a worthy one.'"

So the brahman householders of Sāla went to the Blessed One. On arrival, some of them bowed down to the Blessed One and sat to one side. Some of them exchanged courteous greetings with him and, after an exchange of friendly greetings & courtesies, sat to one side. Some of them sat to one side having saluted him with their hands palm-to-palm over their hearts. Some of them sat to one side having announced their name & clan. Some of them sat to one side in silence.

As they were sitting there, the Blessed One asked them, "Householders, is there any teacher agreeable to you, in whom you have found grounded conviction?"

"No, lord, there is no teacher agreeable to us, in whom we have found grounded conviction."

"As you have not found an agreeable teacher, you should adopt and practice this safe-bet teaching, for this safe-bet teaching—when accepted and adopted—will be to your long-term welfare & happiness.

"And what is the safe-bet teaching?

EXISTENCE & NON-EXISTENCE

A. "There are some contemplatives & brahmans who hold this doctrine, hold this view: 'There is nothing given, nothing offered, nothing sacrificed. There is no fruit or result of good or bad actions. There is no this world, no next world, no mother, no father, no spontaneously reborn beings; no contemplatives or brahmans who, faring rightly and practicing rightly, proclaim this world and the next after having directly known and realized it for themselves.'[1]

B. "Some contemplatives & brahmans, speaking in direct opposition to those contemplatives & brahmans, say this: 'There is what is given, what is offered, what is sacrificed. There are fruits & results of good & bad actions. There is this world & the next world. There is mother & father. There are spontaneously reborn beings; there are contemplatives & brahmans who, faring rightly & practicing rightly, proclaim this world & the next after having directly known & realized it for themselves.'

"What do you think, householders? Don't these contemplatives & brahmans speak in direct opposition to each other?"

"Yes, lord."

A1. "Now, householders, of those contemplatives & brahmans who hold this doctrine, hold this view—'There is nothing given, nothing offered, nothing sacrificed. There is no fruit or result of good or bad actions. There is no this world, no next world, no mother, no father, no spontaneously reborn beings; no contemplatives or brahmans who, faring rightly and practicing rightly, proclaim this world and the next after having directly known and realized it for themselves'—it can be expected that, shunning these three skillful activities—good bodily conduct, good verbal conduct, good mental conduct—they will adopt & practice these three unskillful activities: bad bodily conduct, bad verbal conduct, bad mental conduct. Why is that? Because those venerable contemplatives & brahmans do not see, in unskillful activities, the drawbacks, the degradation, and the defilement; nor in skillful activities the rewards of renunciation, resembling cleansing.

A2. "Because there actually is the next world, the view of one who thinks, 'There is no next world' is his wrong view. Because there actually is the next world, when he is resolved that 'There is no next world,' that is his wrong resolve. Because there actually is the next world, when he speaks the statement, 'There is no next world,' that is his wrong speech. Because there actually is the next world, when he says that 'There is no next world,' he makes himself an opponent to those arahants who know the next world. Because there actually is the next world, when he persuades another that 'There is no next world,' that is persuasion in what is not true Dhamma. And in that persuasion in what is not true Dhamma, he exalts himself and disparages others. Whatever good habituation he previously had is abandoned, while bad habituation is manifested. And this wrong view, wrong resolve, wrong speech, opposition to the arahants, persuasion in what is not true Dhamma, exaltation of self, & disparagement of others: These many evil, unskillful activities come into play, in dependence on wrong view.

A3. "With regard to this, an observant person considers thus: 'If there is no next world, then—with the breakup of the body, after death—this venerable person has made himself safe. But if there is the next world, then this venerable person—on the breakup of the body, after death—will reappear in a plane of deprivation, a bad destination, a lower realm, hell. Even if we didn't speak of the next world, and there weren't the true statement of those venerable contemplatives & brahmans, this venerable person is still criticized in the here-&-now by the observant as a person of bad habits & wrong view[2]: one who holds to a doctrine of non-existence.' If there really is a next world, then this venerable person has made a bad throw twice: in that he is criticized by the observant here-&-now, and in that—with the breakup of the body, after death—he will reappear in a plane of deprivation, a bad destination, a lower realm, hell. Thus this safe-bet teaching, when poorly grasped &

poorly adopted by him, covers (only) one side, and leaves behind the possibility of the skillful.

B1. "Now, householders, of those contemplatives & brahmans who hold this doctrine, hold this view—'There is what is given, what is offered, what is sacrificed. There are fruits & results of good & bad actions. There is this world & the next world. There is mother & father. There are spontaneously reborn beings; there are contemplatives & brahmans who, faring rightly & practicing rightly, proclaim this world & the next after having directly known & realized it for themselves'—it can be expected that, shunning these three unskillful activities—bad bodily conduct, bad verbal conduct, bad mental conduct—they will adopt & practice these three skillful activities: good bodily conduct, good verbal conduct, good mental conduct. Why is that? Because those venerable contemplatives & brahmans see in unskillful activities the drawbacks, the degradation, and the defilement; and in skillful activities the rewards of renunciation, resembling cleansing.

B2. "Because there actually is the next world, the view of one who thinks, 'There is a next world' is his right view. Because there actually is the next world, when he is resolved that 'There is a next world,' that is his right resolve. Because there actually is the next world, when he speaks the statement, 'There is a next world,' that is his right speech. Because there actually is the next world, when he says that 'There is a next world,' he doesn't make himself an opponent to those arahants who know the next world. Because there actually is the next world, when he persuades another that 'There is a next world,' that is persuasion in what is true Dhamma. And in that persuasion in what is true Dhamma, he doesn't exalt himself or disparage others. Whatever bad habituation he previously had is abandoned, while good habituation is manifested. And this right view, right resolve, right speech, non-opposition to the arahants, persuasion in what is true Dhamma, non-exaltation of self, & non-disparagement of others: These many skillful activities come into play, in dependence on right view.

B3. "With regard to this, an observant person considers thus: 'If there is the next world, then this venerable person—on the breakup of the body, after death—will reappear in a good destination, a heavenly world. Even if we didn't speak of the next world, and there weren't the true statement of those venerable contemplatives & brahmans, this venerable person is still praised in the here-&-now by the observant as a person of good habits & right view: one who holds to a doctrine of existence.' If there really is a next world, then this venerable person has made a good throw twice, in that he is praised by the observant here-&-now; and in that—with the breakup of the body, after death—he will reappear in a good destination, a heavenly world. Thus this safe-bet teaching, when well grasped & adopted by him, covers both sides, and leaves behind the possibility of the unskillful.

ACTION & NON-ACTION

A. "There are some contemplatives & brahmans who hold this doctrine, hold this view: 'In acting or getting others to act, in mutilating or getting others to mutilate, in torturing or getting others to torture, in inflicting sorrow or in getting others to inflict sorrow, in tormenting or getting others to torment, in intimidating or getting others to intimidate, in taking life, taking what is not given, breaking into houses, plundering wealth, committing burglary, ambushing highways, committing adultery, telling lies—one does no evil. If with a razor-edged disk one were to turn all the living beings on this earth to a single heap of flesh, a single pile of flesh, there would be no evil from that cause, no coming of evil. Even if one were to go along the right bank of the Ganges, killing and getting others to kill, mutilating and getting others to mutilate, torturing and getting others to torture, there would be no evil from that cause, no coming of evil. Even if one were to go along the left bank of the Ganges, giving and getting others to give, making sacrifices and getting others to make sacrifices, there would be no merit from that cause, no coming of merit. Through generosity, self-control, restraint, and truthful speech there is no merit from that cause, no coming of merit.'[3]

B. "Some contemplatives & brahmans, speaking in direct opposition to those contemplatives & brahmans, say this: 'In acting or getting others to act, in mutilating or getting others to mutilate, in torturing or getting others to torture, in inflicting sorrow or in getting others to inflict sorrow, in tormenting or getting others to torment, in intimidating or getting others to intimidate, in taking life, taking what is not given, breaking into houses, plundering wealth, committing burglary, ambushing highways, committing adultery, telling lies—one does evil. If with a razor-edged disk one were to turn all the living beings on this earth to a single heap of flesh, a single pile of flesh, there would be evil from that cause, there would be a coming of evil. If one were to go along the right bank of the Ganges, killing and getting others to kill, mutilating and getting others to mutilate, torturing and getting others to torture, there would be evil from that cause, there would be a coming of evil. If one were to go along the left bank of the Ganges, giving and getting others to give, making sacrifices and getting others to make sacrifices, there would be merit from that cause, there would be a coming of merit. Through generosity, self-control, restraint, and truthful speech there is merit from that cause, there is a coming of merit.'

"What do you think, householders? Don't these contemplatives & brahmans speak in direct opposition to each other?"

"Yes, lord."

A1. "Now, householders, of those contemplatives & brahmans who hold this doctrine, hold this view—'In acting or getting others to act, in mutilating or getting others to mutilate, in torturing or getting others to torture... one does no evil ... Through generosity, self-control, restraint, and truthful speech there is no merit from that cause, no coming of merit'—it can be expected that, shunning these three skillful activities—good bodily conduct, good verbal conduct, good mental conduct—they will adopt & practice these three unskillful activities: bad bodily conduct, bad verbal conduct, bad mental conduct. Why is that? Because those venerable contemplatives & brahmans do not see, in unskillful activities, the drawbacks, the degradation, and the defilement; nor in skillful activities the rewards of renunciation, resembling cleansing.

A2. "Because there actually is action, the view of one who thinks, 'There is no action' is his wrong view. Because there actually is action, when he is resolved that 'There is no action,' that is his wrong resolve. Because there actually is action, when he speaks the statement, 'There is no action,' that is his wrong speech. Because there actually is action, when he says that 'There is no action,' he makes himself an opponent to those arahants who teach action. Because there actually is action, when he persuades another that 'There is no action,' that is persuasion in what is not true Dhamma. And in that persuasion in what is not true Dhamma, he exalts himself and disparages others. Whatever good habituation he previously had is abandoned, while bad habituation is manifested. And this wrong view, wrong resolve, wrong speech, opposition to the arahants, persuasion in what is not true Dhamma, exaltation of self, & disparagement of others: These many evil, unskillful activities come into play, in dependence on wrong view.

A3. "With regard to this, an observant person considers thus: 'If there is no action, then—with the breakup of the body, after death—this venerable person has made himself safe. But if there is action, then this venerable person—on the breakup of the body, after death—will reappear in a plane of deprivation, a bad destination, a lower realm, hell. Even if we didn't speak of action, and there weren't the true statement of those venerable contemplatives & brahmans, this venerable person is still criticized in the here-&-now by the observant as a person of bad habits & wrong view: one who holds to a doctrine of non-action.' If there really is action, then this venerable person has made a bad throw twice: in that he is criticized by the observant here-&-now; and in that—with the breakup of the body, after death—he will reappear in a plane of deprivation, a bad destination, a lower realm, hell. Thus this safe-bet teaching, when poorly grasped & poorly adopted by him, covers (only) one side, and leaves behind the possibility of the skillful.

B1. "Now, householders, of those contemplatives & brahmans who hold this doctrine, hold this view—'In acting or getting others to act, in mutilating or getting others to mutilate, in torturing or getting others to torture... one does evil.... Through generosity, self-control, restraint, and truthful speech there is merit from that cause, there is a coming of merit'—it can be expected that, shunning these three unskillful activities—bad bodily conduct, bad verbal conduct, bad mental conduct—they will adopt & practice these three skillful activities: good bodily conduct, good verbal conduct, good mental conduct. Why is that? Because those venerable contemplatives & brahmans see in unskillful activities the drawbacks, the degradation, and the defilement; and in skillful activities the rewards of renunciation, resembling cleansing.

B2. "Because there actually is action, the view of one who thinks, 'There is action' is his right view. Because there actually is action, when he is resolved that 'There is action,' that is his right resolve. Because there actually is action, when he speaks the statement, 'There is action,' that is his right speech. Because there actually is action, when he says that 'There is action,' he doesn't make himself an opponent to those arahants who teach action. Because there actually is action, when he persuades another that 'There is action,' that is persuasion in what is true Dhamma. And in that persuasion in what is true Dhamma, he doesn't exalt himself or disparage others. Whatever bad habituation he previously had is abandoned, while good habituation is manifested. And this right view, right resolve, right speech, non-opposition to the arahants, persuasion in what is true Dhamma, non-exaltation of self, & non-disparagement of others: These many skillful activities come into play, in dependence on right view.

B3. "With regard to this, an observant person considers thus: 'If there is action, then this venerable person—on the breakup of the body, after death—will reappear in a good destination, a heavenly world. Even if we didn't speak of action, and there weren't the true statement of those venerable contemplatives & brahmans, this venerable person is still praised in the here-&-now by the observant as a person of good habits & right view: one who holds to a doctrine of action.' If there really is a next world, then this venerable person has made a good throw twice, in that he is praised by the observant here-&-now; and in that—with the breakup of the body, after death—he will reappear in a good destination, a heavenly world. Thus this safe-bet teaching, when well grasped & adopted by him, covers both sides, and leaves behind the possibility of the unskillful.

CAUSALITY & NON-CAUSALITY

A. "There are some contemplatives & brahmans who hold this doctrine, hold this view: 'There is no causality, no requisite condition, for the defilement of beings. Beings are defiled without causality, without requisite condition. There is no causality, no requisite condition, for the purification of beings. Beings are purified without causality, without requisite condition. There is no strength, no effort, no human energy, no human endeavor. All living beings, all life, all beings, all souls are powerless, devoid of strength, devoid of effort. Subject to the changes of fate, serendipity, and nature, they experience pleasure and pain in the six great classes of birth.'[4]

B. "Some contemplatives & brahmans, speaking in direct opposition to those contemplatives & brahmans, say this: 'There is causality, there is requisite condition, for the defilement of beings. Beings are defiled with causality, with requisite condition. There is causality, there is requisite condition, for the purification of beings. Beings are purified with causality, with requisite condition. There is strength, there is effort, there is human energy, there is human endeavor. It's not the case that all living beings, all life, all beings, all souls are powerless, devoid of strength, devoid of effort; or that subject to the changes of fate, serendipity, and nature, they experience pleasure and pain in the six great classes of birth.'

"What do you think, householders? Don't these contemplatives & brahmans speak in direct opposition to each other?"

"Yes, lord."

A1. "Now, householders, of those contemplatives & brahmans who hold this doctrine, hold this view—'There is no cause, no requisite condition, for the defilement of beings.... Subject to the changes of fate, serendipity, and nature, they experience pleasure and pain in the six great classes of birth'—it can be expected that, shunning these three skillful activities—good bodily conduct, good verbal conduct, good mental conduct—they will adopt & practice these three unskillful activities: bad bodily conduct, bad verbal conduct, bad mental conduct. Why is that? Because those venerable contemplatives & brahmans do not see, in unskillful activities, the drawbacks, the degradation, and the defilement; nor in skillful activities the rewards of renunciation, resembling cleansing.

A2. "Because there actually is causality, the view of one who thinks, 'There is no causality' is his wrong view. Because there actually is causality, when he is resolved that 'There is no causality,' that is his wrong resolve. Because there actually is causality, when he speaks the statement, 'There is no causality,' that is his wrong speech. Because there actually is causality, when he says that 'There is no causality,' he makes himself an opponent to those arahants who teach causality. Because there actually is causality, when he persuades another that 'There is no causality,' that is persuasion in what is not true Dhamma. And in that persuasion in what is not true Dhamma, he exalts himself and disparages others. Whatever good habituation he previously had is abandoned, while bad habituation is manifested. And this wrong view, wrong resolve, wrong speech, opposition to the arahants, persuasion in what is not true Dhamma, exaltation of self, & disparagement of others: These many evil, unskillful activities come into play, in dependence on wrong view.

A3. "With regard to this, an observant person considers thus: 'If there is no causality, then—with the breakup of the body, after death—this venerable person has made himself safe. But if there is causality, then this venerable person—on the breakup of the body, after death—will reappear in a plane of deprivation, a bad destination, a lower realm, hell. Even if we didn't speak of causality, and there weren't the true statement of those venerable contemplatives & brahmans, this venerable person is still criticized in the here-&-now by the observant as a person of bad habits & wrong view: one who holds to a doctrine of non-causality.' If there really is a next world, then this venerable person has made a bad throw twice: in that he is criticized by the observant here-&-now, and in that—with the breakup of the body, after death—he will reappear in a plane of deprivation, a bad destination, a lower realm, hell. Thus this safe-bet teaching, when poorly grasped & poorly adopted by him, covers (only) one side, and leaves behind the possibility of the skillful.

B1. "Now, householders, of those contemplatives & brahmans who hold this doctrine, hold this view—'There is causality, there is requisite condition, for the defilement of beings.... It's not the case that all living beings, all life, all beings, all souls are powerless, devoid of strength, devoid of effort; or that subject to the changes of fate, serendipity, and nature, they experience pleasure and pain in the six great classes of birth'—it can be expected that, shunning these three unskillful activities—bad bodily conduct, bad verbal conduct, bad mental conduct—they will adopt & practice these three skillful activities: good bodily conduct, good verbal conduct, good mental conduct. Why is that? Because those venerable contemplatives & brahmans see in unskillful activities the drawbacks, the degradation, and the defilement; and in skillful activities the rewards of renunciation, resembling cleansing.

B2. "Because there actually is causality, the view of one who thinks, 'There is causality' is his right view. Because there actually is causality, when he is resolved that 'There is causality,' that is his right resolve. Because there actually causality, when he speaks the statement, 'There is causality,' that is his right speech. Because there actually is causality, when he says that 'There is causality,' he doesn't make himself an opponent to those arahants who teach causality. Because there actually is causality, when he persuades another that 'There is causality,' that is persuasion in what is true Dhamma. And in that persuasion in what is true Dhamma, he doesn't exalt himself or disparage others. Whatever bad habituation he previously had is abandoned, while good habituation is manifested. And this right view, right resolve, right speech, non-opposition to the arahants, persuasion in what is true Dhamma, non-exaltation of self, & non-disparagement of others: These many skillful activities come into play, in dependence on right view.

B3. "With regard to this, an observant person considers thus: 'If there is causality, then this venerable person—on the breakup of the body, after death—will reappear in a good destination, a heavenly world. Even if we didn't speak of causality, and there weren't the true statement of those venerable contemplatives & brahmans, this venerable person is still praised in the here-&-now by the observant as a person of good habits & right view: one who holds to a doctrine of causality.' If there really is causality, then this venerable person has made a good throw twice, in that he is praised by the observant here-&-now; and in that—with the breakup of the body, after death—he will reappear in a good destination, a heavenly world. Thus this safe-bet teaching, when well grasped & adopted by him, covers both sides, and leaves behind the possibility of the unskillful.

FORMLESSNESS

"There are some contemplatives & brahmans who hold this doctrine, hold this view: 'There is no total formlessness.' Some contemplatives & brahmans, speaking in direct opposition to those contemplatives & brahmans, say this: 'There is total formlessness.' What do you think, householders? Don't these contemplatives & brahmans speak in direct opposition to each other?"

"Yes, lord."

"With regard to this, an observant person considers thus: 'As for those venerable contemplatives & brahmans who hold this doctrine, hold this view—"There is no total formlessness"—I haven't seen that. As for those venerable contemplatives & brahmans who hold this doctrine, hold this view—"There is total formlessness"—I haven't known that. If I, not knowing, not seeing, were to take one side and declare, "Only this is true, anything otherwise is worthless," that would not be fitting for me. As for those venerable contemplatives & brahmans who hold this doctrine, hold this view—"There is no total formlessness": If their statement is true, there's the safe-bet possibility that I might reappear among the mind-made devas of form. As for those venerable contemplatives & brahmans who hold this doctrine, hold this view—"There is total formlessness": If their statement is true, there's the safe-bet possibility that I might reappear among the perception-made devas of no form. The taking up of rods & weapons, quarrels, contention, disputes, recrimination, divisiveness, & the telling of lies are seen to arise from form, but not from total formlessness.' Reflecting thus, he practices for disenchantment toward forms, for dispassion toward forms, and for the cessation of forms.

CESSATION OF BECOMING

"There are some contemplatives & brahmans who hold this doctrine, hold this view: 'There is no total cessation of becoming.' Some contemplatives & brahmans, speaking in direct opposition to those contemplatives & brahmans, say this: 'There is total cessation of becoming.' What do you think, householders? Don't these contemplatives & brahmans speak in direct opposition to each other?"

"Yes, lord."

"With regard to this, an observant person considers thus: 'As for those venerable contemplatives & brahmans who hold this doctrine, hold this view—"There is no total cessation of becoming"—I haven't seen that. As for those venerable contemplatives & brahmans who hold this doctrine, hold this view—"There is total cessation of becoming"—I haven't known that. If I, not knowing, not seeing, were to take one side and declare, "Only this is true, anything otherwise is worthless," that would not be fitting for me. As for those venerable contemplatives & brahmans who hold this doctrine, hold this view—"There is no total cessation of becoming": If their statement is true, there's the safe-bet possibility that I might reappear among the perception-made devas of no form. As for those venerable contemplatives & brahmans who hold this doctrine, hold this view—"There is total cessation of becoming": If their statement is true, it is possible that I will be totally unbound in the here-&-now. As for those venerable contemplatives & brahmans who hold this doctrine, hold this view—"There is no total cessation of becoming": This view of theirs borders on passion, borders on fettering, borders on relishing, borders on grasping, borders on clinging. As for those venerable contemplatives & brahmans who hold this doctrine, hold this view—"There is total cessation of becoming": This view of theirs borders on non-passion, borders on non-fettering, borders on non-relishing, borders on non-grasping, borders on non-clinging.' Reflecting thus, he practices for disenchantment toward becomings, for dispassion toward becomings, and for the cessation of becomings.

FOUR INDIVIDUALS

"Householders, there are these four types of individuals to be found existing in the world. Which four? There is the case where a certain individual torments himself and is devoted to the practice of torturing himself. There is the case where a certain individual torments others and is devoted to the practice of torturing others. There is the case where a certain individual torments himself and is devoted to the practice of torturing himself, and also torments others and is devoted to the practice of torturing others. There is the case where a certain individual neither torments himself nor is he devoted to the practice of torturing himself, neither torments others nor is he devoted to the practice of torturing others. Neither tormenting himself nor tormenting others, he dwells in the here-&-now free of hunger, unbound, cooled, sensitive to happiness, with a Brahmā-like mind.

"And which is the individual who torments himself and is devoted to the practice of torturing himself? There is the case where a certain individual goes without cloth, rejecting conventions, licking his hands, not coming when called, not staying when asked. He does not accept food brought or specially made. He does not consent to an invitation (to a meal). He doesn't receive anything from the mouth of a pot, from the mouth of a container, across a threshold, across a stick, across a pestle, from two eating together, from a pregnant woman, from a woman nursing a child, from a woman living with a man, from where it is announced that food is to be distributed, from where a dog is waiting, from where flies are buzzing. He accepts no meat, no distilled liquor, no wine, no fermented liquor. He limits himself to one house for one morsel, to two houses for two morsels... to seven houses for seven morsels. He lives on one saucerful a day, two saucerfuls a day... seven saucerfuls a day. He takes food once a day, once every two days... once every seven days, and so on up to once every half-month. He remains devoted to the practice of taking food at stated intervals. He eats a diet of green vegetables or millet or wild rice or hide-parings or moss or rice bran or rice-water or sesame flour or grass or cow dung. He lives off forest roots & fruits. He eats fallen fruits. He clothes himself in hemp, in canvas, in shrouds, in thrown-away rags, in tree bark, in antelope hide, in wood-shavings fabric, in head-hair wool, in wild-animal wool, in owls' wings. He is a hair-&-beard puller, one devoted to the practice of pulling out his hair & beard. He is a stander, one who rejects seats. He is a hands-around-the-knees sitter, one devoted to the exertion of sitting with his hands around his knees. He is a spike-mattresser, one who makes his bed on a bed of spikes. He is a third-time-in-the-evening bather, one who stays devoted to the practice of bathing in water. Thus, in these many ways, he is devoted to the practice of tormenting & persecuting the body. This is called an individual who torments himself and is devoted to the practice of torturing himself.

"And which is the individual who torments others and is devoted to the practice of torturing others? There is the case where a certain individual is a butcher of sheep, a butcher of pigs, a butcher of fowl, a trapper, a hunter, a fisherman, a thief, an executioner,[5] a prison warden, or anyone who follows any other bloody occupation. This is called an individual who torments others and is devoted to the practice of torturing others.

"And which is the individual who torments himself and is devoted to the practice of torturing himself, and also torments others and is devoted to the practice of torturing others? There is the case where an individual is a head-anointed noble warrior king, or a brahman of great wealth. Having had a new temple built to the east of the city, having shaved off his hair & beard, having dressed himself in a rough hide, having smeared his body with ghee & oil, and scratching his back with a deer horn, he enters the new temple along with his chief queen & brahman high priest. There he makes his bed on the bare ground strewn with grass. The king lives off the milk from the first teat of a cow with an identical calf; the queen lives off the milk from the second teat; the brahman high priest, off the milk from the third teat. The milk from the fourth teat they pour[6] into the fire. The calf lives on what is left.

"He says, 'Let so many bulls be slaughtered for the sacrifice. Let so many bullocks… so many heifers… so many goats… so many sheep…. Let so many horses be slaughtered for the sacrifice.[7] Let so many trees be cut down for the sacrificial posts; let so many plants be mowed down for the sacrificial grass.' And his slaves, servants, & workers make preparations, weeping with tearful faces, spurred on by punishment, spurred on by fear. This is called an individual who torments himself and is devoted to the practice of torturing himself, and also torments others and is devoted to the practice of torturing others.

"And which is the individual who neither torments himself nor is devoted to the practice of torturing himself, neither torments others nor is devoted to the practice of torturing others; who—neither tormenting himself nor tormenting others—dwells in the here-&-now free of hunger, unbound, cooled, sensitive to happiness with a Brahmā-like mind?

"There is the case where a Tathāgata appears in the world, worthy & rightly self-awakened. He teaches the Dhamma admirable in its beginning, admirable in its middle, admirable in its end. He proclaims the holy life both in its particulars and in its essence, entirely perfect, surpassingly pure.

"A householder or householder's son, hearing the Dhamma, gains conviction in the Tathāgata and reflects: 'Household life is confining, a dusty path. Life gone forth is the open air. It isn't easy, living at home, to practice the holy life totally perfect, totally pure, a polished shell. What if I, having shaved off my hair & beard and putting on the ochre robe, were to go forth from the household life into homelessness?'

"So after some time he abandons his mass of wealth, large or small; leaves his circle of relatives, large or small; shaves off his hair and beard, puts on the ochre robes, and goes forth from the household life into homelessness.

VIRTUE

"When he has thus gone forth, endowed with the monks' training & livelihood, then—abandoning the taking of life—he abstains from the taking of life. He dwells with his rod laid down, his knife laid down, scrupulous, merciful, compassionate for the welfare of all living beings.

"Abandoning the taking of what is not given, he abstains from taking what is not given. He takes only what is given, accepts only what is given, lives not by stealth but by means of a self that has become pure.

"Abandoning uncelibacy, he lives a celibate life, aloof, refraining from the sexual act that is the villager's way.

"Abandoning the telling of lies, he abstains from telling lies. He speaks the truth, holds to the truth, is firm, reliable, no deceiver of the world.

"Abandoning divisive speech, he abstains from divisive speech. What he has heard here he does not tell there to break those people apart from these people here. What he has heard there he does not tell here to break these people apart from those people there. Thus reconciling those who have broken apart or cementing those who are united, he loves concord, delights in concord, enjoys concord, speaks things that create concord.

"Abandoning abusive speech, he abstains from abusive speech. He speaks words that are soothing to the ear, that are affectionate, that go to the heart, that are polite, appealing and pleasing to people at large.

"Abandoning idle chatter, he abstains from idle chatter. He speaks in season, speaks what is factual, what is in accordance with the goal, the Dhamma, and the Vinaya. He speaks words worth treasuring, seasonable, reasonable, circumscribed, connected with the goal.

"He abstains from damaging seed and plant life.

"He eats only once a day, refraining from the evening meal and from food at the wrong time of day.

"He abstains from dancing, singing, instrumental music, and from watching shows.

"He abstains from wearing garlands and from beautifying himself with scents and cosmetics.

"He abstains from high and luxurious beds and seats.

"He abstains from accepting gold and money.

"He abstains from accepting uncooked grain... raw meat... women and girls... male and female slaves... goats and sheep... fowl and pigs... elephants, cattle, steeds, and mares... fields and property.

"He abstains from running messages... from buying and selling... from dealing with false scales, false metals, and false measures... from bribery, deception, and fraud.

"He abstains from mutilating, executing, imprisoning, highway robbery, plunder, and violence.

"He is content with a set of robes to provide for his body and alms food to provide for his hunger. Just as a bird, wherever it goes, flies with its wings as its only burden; so too is he content with a set of robes to provide for his body and alms food to provide for his hunger. Wherever he goes, he takes only his barest necessities along.

"Endowed with this noble aggregate of virtue, he is inwardly sensitive to the pleasure of being blameless.

SENSE RESTRAINT

"On seeing a form with the eye, he does not grasp at any theme or details by which—if he were to dwell without restraint over the faculty of the eye—evil, unskillful qualities such as greed or distress might assail him. On hearing a sound with the ear.... On smelling an aroma with the nose.... On tasting a flavor with the tongue.... On touching a tactile sensation with the body.... On cognizing an idea with the intellect, he does not grasp at any theme or details by which—if he were to dwell without restraint over the faculty of the intellect—evil, unskillful qualities such as greed or distress might assail him. Endowed with this noble restraint over the sense faculties, he is inwardly sensitive to the pleasure of being blameless.

MINDFULNESS & ALERTNESS

"When going forward and returning, he makes himself alert. When looking toward and looking away... when bending and extending his limbs... when carrying his outer cloak, his upper robe, and his bowl... when eating, drinking, chewing, and tasting... when urinating and defecating... when walking, standing, sitting, falling asleep, waking up, talking, and remaining silent, he makes himself alert.

ABANDONING THE HINDRANCES

"Endowed with this noble aggregate of virtue, this noble restraint over the sense faculties, this noble mindfulness & alertness, he seeks out a secluded dwelling: a wilderness, the shade of a tree, a mountain, a glen, a hillside cave, a charnel ground, a forest grove, the open air, a heap of straw. After his meal, returning from his alms round, he sits down, crosses his legs, holds his body erect, and brings mindfulness to the fore.

"Abandoning covetousness with regard to the world, he dwells with an awareness devoid of covetousness. He cleanses his mind of covetousness. Abandoning ill will and anger, he dwells with an awareness devoid of ill will, sympathetic with the welfare of all living beings. He cleanses his mind of ill will and anger. Abandoning sloth and drowsiness, he dwells with an awareness devoid of sloth and drowsiness, mindful, alert, percipient of light. He cleanses his mind of sloth and drowsiness. Abandoning restlessness and anxiety, he dwells undisturbed, his mind inwardly stilled. He cleanses his mind of restlessness and anxiety. Abandoning uncertainty, he dwells having crossed over uncertainty, with no perplexity with regard to skillful qualities. He cleanses his mind of uncertainty.

THE FOUR JHĀNAS

"Having abandoned these five hindrances—imperfections of awareness that weaken discernment—then, quite secluded from sensuality, secluded from unskillful qualities, he enters and remains in the first jhāna: rapture & pleasure born of seclusion, accompanied by directed thought & evaluation.

"Then, with the stilling of directed thoughts & evaluations, he enters and remains in the second jhāna: rapture & pleasure born of concentration, unification of awareness free from directed thought & evaluation—internal assurance.

"Then, with the fading of rapture, he remains equanimous, mindful, & alert, and senses pleasure with the body. He enters and remains in the third jhāna, of which the noble ones declare, 'Equanimous & mindful, he has a pleasant abiding.'

"Then, with the abandoning of pleasure & pain—as with the earlier disappearance of elation & distress—he enters and remains in the fourth jhāna: purity of equanimity & mindfulness, neither pleasure nor pain.

THE THREE KNOWLEDGES

"With his mind thus concentrated, purified, and bright, unblemished, free from defects, pliant, malleable, steady, and attained to imperturbability, he directs and inclines it to knowledge of the recollection of past lives (lit: previous homes). He recollects his manifold past lives, i.e., one birth, two births, three births, four, five, ten, twenty, thirty, forty, fifty, one hundred, one thousand, one hundred thousand, many eons of cosmic contraction, many eons of cosmic expansion, many eons of cosmic contraction and expansion, (recollecting,) 'There I had such a name, belonged to such a clan, had such an appearance. Such was my food, such my experience of pleasure and pain, such the end of my life. Passing away from that state, I re-arose there. There too I had such a name, belonged to such a clan, had such an appearance. Such was my food, such my experience of pleasure and pain, such the end of my life. Passing away from that state, I re-arose here.' Thus he recollects his manifold past lives in their modes and details. This, too, is how striving is fruitful, how exertion is fruitful.

"With his mind thus concentrated, purified, and bright, unblemished, free from defects, pliant, malleable, steady, and attained to imperturbability, he directs and inclines it to knowledge of the passing away and re-appearance of beings. He sees—by means of the divine eye, purified and surpassing the human—beings passing away and re-appearing, and he discerns how they are inferior and superior, beautiful and ugly, fortunate and unfortunate in accordance with their kamma: 'These beings—who were endowed with bad conduct of body, speech, and mind, who reviled the noble ones, held wrong views and undertook actions under the influence of wrong views—with the breakup of the body, after death, have re-appeared in a plane of deprivation, a bad destination, a lower realm, hell. But these beings—who were endowed with good conduct of body, speech, and mind, who did not revile the noble ones, who held right views and undertook actions under the influence of right views—with the breakup of the body, after death, have re-appeared in a good destination, a heavenly world.' Thus—by means of the divine eye, purified and surpassing the human—he sees beings passing away and re-appearing, and he discerns how they are inferior and superior, beautiful and ugly, fortunate and unfortunate in accordance with their kamma.

"With his mind thus concentrated, purified, and bright, unblemished, free from defects, pliant, malleable, steady, and attained to imperturbability, the monk directs and inclines it to the knowledge of the ending of the effluents. He discerns, as it has come to be, that 'This is stress... This is the origination of stress... This is the cessation of stress... This is the way leading to the cessation of stress... These are effluents... This is the origination of effluents... This is the cessation of effluents... This is the way leading to the cessation of effluents.' His heart, thus knowing, thus seeing, is released from the effluent of sensuality, released from the effluent of becoming, released from the effluent of ignorance. With release, there is the knowledge, 'Released.' He discerns that 'Birth is ended, the holy life fulfilled, the task done. There is nothing further for this world.'

"This is called an individual who neither torments himself nor is devoted to the practice of torturing himself, who neither torments others nor is devoted to the practice of torturing others. Neither tormenting himself nor tormenting others, he dwells in the here-&-now free of hunger, unbound, cooled, sensitive to happiness, with a Brahmā-like mind."

When this was said, the brahman householders of Sāla said, "Magnificent, master Gotama! Magnificent! Just as if he were to place upright what was overturned, to reveal what was hidden, to show the way to one who was lost, or to carry a lamp into the dark so that those with eyes could see forms, in the same way has master Gotama—through many lines of reasoning—made the Dhamma clear. We go to master Gotama for refuge, to the Dhamma, and to the Saṅgha of monks. May master Gotama remember us as lay followers who have gone to him for refuge, from this day forward, for life."

NOTES

1. This was the view of Ajita Kesakambalin. See DN 2.

2. In this context—where that actual truth or falseness of the doctrine is not being addressed—"wrong view" would have to mean a view that leads a person to engage in bad conduct in body, speech, or mind.

3. This was the view of Pūraṇa Kassapa. See DN 2.

4. This was the view of Makkhali Gosāla. See DN 2.

5. The Burmese edition of the Canon here adds, "a slaughterer of cows."

6. This follows the Sinhalese, Burmese, and PTS editions of the Canon. The Thai edition reads, "he pours."

7. The PTS and Sinhalese editions omit the sentence, "Let so many horses be slaughtered for the sacrifice."

See also: MN 41; MN 95; AN 3:62; AN 3:66

61 *The Exhortation to Rāhula at Mango Stone*

Ambalaṭṭhikā Rāhulovāda Sutta

I have heard that on one occasion the Blessed One was staying near Rājagaha in the Bamboo Grove, the Squirrels' Sanctuary.

At that time Ven. Rāhula[1] was staying at the Mango Stone. Then the Blessed One, emerging from his seclusion in the late afternoon, went to where Ven. Rāhula was staying at the Mango Stone. Ven. Rāhula saw him coming from afar and, on seeing him, set out a seat & water for washing the feet. The Blessed One sat down on the seat set out and, having sat down, washed his feet. Ven. Rāhula, bowing down to the Blessed One, sat to one side.

Then the Blessed One, having left a little bit of the remaining water in the water dipper, said to Ven. Rāhula, "Rāhula, do you see this little bit of remaining water left in the water dipper?"

"Yes sir."

"That's how little of a contemplative[2] there is in anyone who feels no shame at telling a deliberate lie."

Having tossed away the little bit of remaining water, the Blessed One said to Ven. Rāhula, "Rāhula, do you see how this little bit of remaining water is tossed away?"

"Yes, sir."

"Rāhula, whatever there is of a contemplative in anyone who feels no shame at telling a deliberate lie is tossed away just like that."

Having turned the water dipper upside down, the Blessed One said to Ven. Rāhula, "Rāhula, do you see how this water dipper is turned upside down?"

"Yes, sir."

"Rāhula, whatever there is of a contemplative in anyone who feels no shame at telling a deliberate lie is turned upside down just like that."

Having turned the water dipper right-side up, the Blessed One said to Ven. Rāhula, "Rāhula, do you see how empty & hollow this water dipper is?"

"Yes, sir."

"Rāhula, whatever there is of a contemplative in anyone who feels no shame at telling a deliberate lie is empty & hollow just like that.

"Rāhula, it's like a royal elephant: immense, pedigreed, accustomed to battles, its tusks like chariot poles. Having gone into battle, it uses its forefeet & hindfeet, its forequarters & hindquarters, its head & ears & tusks & tail, but will simply hold back its trunk. The elephant trainer notices that and thinks, 'This royal elephant has not given up its life to the king.' But when the royal elephant... having gone into battle, uses its forefeet & hindfeet, its forequarters & hindquarters, its head & ears & tusks & tail & his trunk, the trainer notices that and thinks, 'This royal elephant has given up its life to the king. There is nothing it will not do.'

"In the same way, Rāhula, when anyone feels no shame in telling a deliberate lie, there is no evil, I tell you, he will not do. Thus, Rāhula, you should train yourself, 'I will not tell a deliberate lie even in jest.'

"What do you think, Rāhula? What is a mirror for?"

"For reflection, sir."

"In the same way, Rāhula, bodily actions, verbal actions, & mental actions are to be done with repeated reflection.

"Whenever you want to do a bodily action, you should reflect on it: 'This bodily action I want to do—would it lead to self-affliction, to the affliction of others, or to both? Would it be an unskillful bodily action, with painful consequences, painful results?' If, on reflection, you know that it would lead to self-affliction, to the affliction of others, or to both; it would be an unskillful bodily action with painful consequences, painful results, then any bodily action of that sort is absolutely unfit for you to do. But if on reflection you know that it would not cause affliction... it would be a skillful bodily action with pleasant consequences, pleasant results, then any bodily action of that sort is fit for you to do.

"While you are doing a bodily action, you should reflect on it: 'This bodily action I am doing—is it leading to self-affliction, to the affliction of others, or to both? Is it an unskillful bodily action, with painful consequences, painful results?' If, on reflection, you know that it is leading to self-affliction, to affliction of others, or both... you should give it up. But if on reflection you know that it is not... you may continue with it.

"Having done a bodily action, you should reflect on it: 'This bodily action I have done—did it lead to self-affliction, to the affliction of others, or to both? Was it an unskillful bodily action, with painful consequences, painful results?' If, on reflection, you know that it led to self-affliction, to the affliction of others, or to both; it was an unskillful bodily action with painful consequences, painful results, then you should confess it, reveal it, lay it open to the Teacher or to an observant companion in the holy life. Having confessed it… you should exercise restraint in the future. But if on reflection you know that it did not lead to affliction… it was a skillful bodily action with pleasant consequences, pleasant results, then you should stay mentally refreshed & joyful, training day & night in skillful qualities.

"Whenever you want to do a verbal action, you should reflect on it: 'This verbal action I want to do—would it lead to self-affliction, to the affliction of others, or to both? Would it be an unskillful verbal action, with painful consequences, painful results?' If, on reflection, you know that it would lead to self-affliction, to the affliction of others, or to both; it would be an unskillful verbal action with painful consequences, painful results, then any verbal action of that sort is absolutely unfit for you to do. But if on reflection you know that it would not cause affliction… it would be a skillful verbal action with pleasant consequences, pleasant results, then any verbal action of that sort is fit for you to do.

"While you are doing a verbal action, you should reflect on it: 'This verbal action I am doing—is it leading to self-affliction, to the affliction of others, or to both? Is it an unskillful verbal action, with painful consequences, painful results?' If, on reflection, you know that it is leading to self-affliction, to affliction of others, or both… you should give it up. But if on reflection you know that it is not… you may continue with it.

"Having done a verbal action, you should reflect on it: 'This verbal action I have done—did it lead to self-affliction, to the affliction of others, or to both? Was it an unskillful verbal action, with painful consequences, painful results?' If, on reflection, you know that it led to self-affliction, to the affliction of others, or to both; it was an unskillful verbal action with painful consequences, painful results, then you should confess it, reveal it, lay it open to the Teacher or to an observant companion in the holy life. Having confessed it… you should exercise restraint in the future. But if on reflection you know that it did not lead to affliction… it was a skillful verbal action with pleasant consequences, pleasant results, then you should stay mentally refreshed & joyful, training day & night in skillful qualities.

"Whenever you want to do a mental action, you should reflect on it: 'This mental action I want to do—would it lead to self-affliction, to the affliction of others, or to both? Would it be an unskillful mental action, with painful consequences, painful results?' If, on reflection, you know that it would lead to self-affliction, to the affliction of others, or to both; it would be an unskillful mental action with painful consequences, painful results, then any mental action of that sort is absolutely unfit for you to do. But if on reflection you know that it would not cause affliction... it would be a skillful mental action with pleasant consequences, pleasant results, then any mental action of that sort is fit for you to do.

"While you are doing a mental action, you should reflect on it: 'This mental action I am doing—is it leading to self-affliction, to the affliction of others, or to both? Is it an unskillful mental action, with painful consequences, painful results?' If, on reflection, you know that it is leading to self-affliction, to affliction of others, or both... you should give it up. But if on reflection you know that it is not... you may continue with it.

"Having done a mental action, you should reflect on it: 'This mental action I have done—did it lead to self-affliction, to the affliction of others, or to both? Was it an unskillful mental action, with painful consequences, painful results?' If, on reflection, you know that it led to self-affliction, to the affliction of others, or to both; it was an unskillful mental action with painful consequences, painful results, then you should feel distressed, ashamed, & disgusted with it. Feeling distressed... you should exercise restraint in the future. But if on reflection you know that it did not lead to affliction... it was a skillful mental action with pleasant consequences, pleasant results, then you should stay mentally refreshed & joyful, training day & night in skillful qualities.

"Rāhula, all those contemplatives & brahmans in the course of the past who purified their bodily actions, verbal actions, & mental actions, did it through repeated reflection on their bodily actions, verbal actions, & mental actions in just this way.

"All those contemplatives & brahmans in the course of the future who will purify their bodily actions, verbal actions, & mental actions, will do it through repeated reflection on their bodily actions, verbal actions, & mental actions in just this way.

"All those contemplatives & brahmans at present who purify their bodily actions, verbal actions, & mental actions, do it through repeated reflection on their bodily actions, verbal actions, & mental actions in just this way.

"Thus, Rāhula, you should train yourself: 'I will purify my bodily actions through repeated reflection. I will purify my verbal actions through repeated reflection. I will purify my mental actions through repeated reflection.' That's how you should train yourself."

That is what the Blessed One said. Gratified, Ven. Rāhula delighted in the Blessed One's words.

NOTES

1. Rāhula: the Buddha's son, who according to the Commentary was seven years old when this discourse was delivered to him.

2. *Sāmañña.* Throughout ancient cultures, the terminology of music was used to describe the moral quality of people and actions. Discordant intervals or poorly-tuned musical instruments were metaphors for evil; harmonious intervals and well-tuned instruments, metaphors for good. In Pali, the term *sama*—"even"—described an instrument tuned on-pitch. There is a famous passage (AN 6:55) where the Buddha reminds Soṇa Koḷivisa—who had been over-exerting himself in the practice—that a lute sounds appealing only if the strings are neither too taut nor too lax, but "evenly" tuned. This image would have special resonances with the Buddha's teaching on the middle way. It also adds meaning to the term *samaṇa*—monk or contemplative—which the texts frequently mention as being derived from *sama.* The word *sāmañña*—"evenness," the quality of being in tune—also means the quality of being a contemplative: The true contemplative is always in tune with what is proper and good.

See also: MN 19; MN 24; MN 95; MN 121; AN 3:66; AN 4:115; AN 4:183; AN 5:140; AN 7:80; AN 8:53; Iti 25

62 *The Greater Exhortation to Rāhula*

Mahā Rāhulovāda Sutta

I have heard that on one occasion the Blessed One was staying near Sāvatthī in Jeta's Grove, Anāthapiṇḍika's Monastery. Then the Blessed One, early in the morning, adjusted his under robe and, carrying his bowl & outer robe, went into Sāvatthī for alms. And Ven. Rāhula, early in the morning, adjusted his under robe and, carrying his bowl & outer robe, went into Sāvatthī for alms following right behind the Blessed One.[1] Then the Blessed One, looking back at Rāhula, addressed him: "Rāhula, any form whatsoever that is past, future, or present; internal or external; blatant or subtle; common or sublime; far or near: Every form is to be seen as it has come to be with right discernment as: 'This is not mine. This is not my self. This is not what I am.'"

"Just form, O Blessed One? Just form, O One Well-Gone?"

"Form, Rāhula, & feeling & perception & fabrications & consciousness."

Then the thought occurred to Ven. Rāhula, "Who, having been exhorted face-to-face by the Blessed One, would go into the town for alms today?" So he turned back and sat down at the foot of a tree, folding his legs crosswise, holding his body erect, & setting mindfulness to the fore.

Ven. Sāriputta saw Ven. Rāhula sitting at the foot of a tree, his legs folded crosswise, his body held erect, & with mindfulness set to the fore. On seeing him, he said to him, "Rāhula, develop the meditation *[bhāvanā]* of mindfulness of in-&-out breathing. The meditation of mindfulness of in-&-out breathing, when developed & pursued, is of great fruit, of great benefit."

Then Ven. Rāhula, emerging from his seclusion in the late afternoon, went to the Blessed One and, having bowed down to him, sat to one side. As he was sitting there he said to him, "How, lord, is mindfulness of in-&-out breathing to be developed & pursued so as to be of great fruit, or great benefit?"

{"Rāhula, any form whatsoever that is past, future, or present; internal or external; blatant or subtle; common or sublime; far or near: Every form is to be seen as it has come to be with right discernment as: 'This is not mine. This is not my self. This is not what

I am.' There are these five properties, Rāhula. Which five? The earth property, the water property, the fire property, the wind property, & the space property.

"And what is the earth property? The earth property may be either internal or external. What is the internal earth property?}[2] Anything internal, within oneself, that's hard, solid, & sustained (by craving): head hairs, body hairs, nails, teeth, skin, flesh, tendons, bones, bone marrow, kidneys, heart, liver, membranes, spleen, lungs, large intestines, small intestines, contents of the stomach, feces, or anything else internal, within oneself, that's hard, solid, and sustained: This is called the internal earth property. Now both the internal earth property & the external earth property are simply earth property. And that should be seen as it has come to be with right discernment: 'This is not mine, this is not me, this is not my self.' When one sees it thus as it has come to be with right discernment, one becomes disenchanted with the earth property and makes the earth property fade from the mind.

"And what is the water property? The water property may be either internal or external. What is the internal water property? Anything internal, belonging to oneself, that's water, watery, & sustained: bile, phlegm, pus, blood, sweat, fat, tears, oil, saliva, mucus, oil-of-the-joints, urine, or anything else internal, within oneself, that's water, watery, & sustained: This is called the internal water property. Now both the internal water property & the external water property are simply water property. And that should be seen as it has come to be with right discernment: 'This is not mine, this is not me, this is not my self.' When one sees it thus as it has come to be with right discernment, one becomes disenchanted with the water property and makes the water property fade from the mind.

"And what is the fire property? The fire property may be either internal or external. What is the internal fire property? Anything internal, belonging to oneself, that's fire, fiery, & sustained: that by which (the body) is warmed, aged, & consumed with fever; and that by which what is eaten, drunk, chewed, & savored gets properly digested; or anything else internal, within oneself, that's fire, fiery, & sustained: This is called the internal fire property. Now both the internal fire property & the external fire property are simply fire property. And that should be seen as it has come to be with right discernment: 'This is not mine, this is not me, this is not my self.' When one sees it thus as it has come to be with right discernment, one becomes disenchanted with the fire property and makes the fire property fade from the mind.

"And what is the wind property? The wind property may be either internal or external. What is the internal wind property? Anything internal, belonging to oneself, that's wind, windy, & sustained: up-going winds, down-going winds, winds in the stomach, winds in the intestines, winds that course through the body, in-and-out breathing, or anything else internal, within oneself, that's wind, windy, & sustained: This is called the internal wind property. Now both the internal wind property & the external wind property are simply wind property. And that should be seen as it has come to be with right discernment: 'This is not mine, this is not me, this is not my self.' When one sees it thus as it has come to be with right discernment, one becomes disenchanted with the wind property and makes the wind property fade from the mind.

"And what is the space property? The space property may be either internal or external. What is the internal space property? Anything internal, belonging to oneself, that's space, spatial, & sustained: the holes of the ears, the nostrils, the mouth, the (passage) whereby what is eaten, drunk, consumed, & tasted gets swallowed, and where it collects, and whereby it is excreted from below, or anything else internal, within oneself, that's space, spatial, & sustained: This is called the internal space property. Now both the internal space property & the external space property are simply space property. And that should be seen as it has come to be with right discernment: 'This is not mine, this is not me, this is not my self.' When one sees it thus as it has come to be with right discernment, one becomes disenchanted with the space property and makes the space property fade from the mind.

"Rāhula, develop the meditation in tune with earth. For when you are developing the meditation in tune with earth, agreeable & disagreeable sensory impressions that have arisen will not stay in charge of your mind. Just as when people throw what is clean or unclean on the earth—feces, urine, saliva, pus, or blood—the earth is not horrified, humiliated, or disgusted by it; in the same way, when you are developing the meditation in tune with earth, agreeable & disagreeable sensory impressions that have arisen will not stay in charge of your mind.

"Develop the meditation in tune with water. For when you are developing the meditation in tune with water, agreeable & disagreeable sensory impressions that have arisen will not stay in charge of your mind. Just as when people wash what is clean or unclean in water—feces, urine, saliva, pus, or blood—the water is not horrified, humiliated, or disgusted by it; in the same way, when you are developing the meditation in tune with water, agreeable &

disagreeable sensory impressions that have arisen will not stay in charge of your mind.

"Develop the meditation in tune with fire. For when you are developing the meditation in tune with fire, agreeable & disagreeable sensory impressions that have arisen will not stay in charge of your mind. Just as when fire burns what is clean or unclean—feces, urine, saliva, pus, or blood—it is not horrified, humiliated, or disgusted by it; in the same way, when you are developing the meditation in tune with fire, agreeable & disagreeable sensory impressions that have arisen will not stay in charge of your mind.

"Develop the meditation in tune with wind. For when you are developing the meditation in tune with wind, agreeable & disagreeable sensory impressions that have arisen will not stay in charge of your mind. Just as when wind blows what is clean or unclean—feces, urine, saliva, pus, or blood—it is not horrified, humiliated, or disgusted by it; in the same way, when you are developing the meditation in tune with wind, agreeable & disagreeable sensory impressions that have arisen will not stay in charge of your mind.

"Develop the meditation in tune with space. For when you are developing the meditation in tune with space, agreeable & disagreeable sensory impressions that have arisen will not stay in charge of your mind. Just as space is not established anywhere, in the same way, when you are developing the meditation in tune with space, agreeable & disagreeable sensory impressions that have arisen will not stay in charge of your mind.

"Develop the meditation of goodwill. For when you are developing the meditation of goodwill, ill-will will be abandoned.

"Develop the meditation of compassion. For when you are developing the meditation of compassion, cruelty will be abandoned.

"Develop the meditation of empathetic joy. For when you are developing the meditation of empathetic joy, resentment will be abandoned.

"Develop the meditation of equanimity. For when you are developing the meditation of equanimity, irritation will be abandoned.

"Develop the meditation of the unattractive. For when you are developing the meditation of the unattractive, passion will be abandoned.

"Develop the meditation of the perception of inconstancy. For when you are developing the meditation of the perception of inconstancy, the conceit 'I am' will be abandoned.

"Develop the meditation of mindfulness of in-&-out breathing. Mindfulness of in-&-out breathing, when developed & pursued, is of great fruit, of great benefit.

"And how, Rāhula, is mindfulness of in-&-out breathing developed & pursued so as to be of great fruit, of great benefit?

"There is the case where a monk, having gone to the wilderness, to the shade of a tree, or to an empty building, sits down folding his legs crosswise, holding his body erect, and setting mindfulness to the fore.[3] Always mindful, he breathes in; mindful he breathes out.

"[1] Breathing in long, he discerns, 'I am breathing in long'; or breathing out long, he discerns, 'I am breathing out long.' [2] Or breathing in short, he discerns, 'I am breathing in short'; or breathing out short, he discerns, 'I am breathing out short.' [3] He trains himself, 'I will breathe in sensitive to the entire body.' He trains himself, 'I will breathe out sensitive to the entire body.' [4] He trains himself, 'I will breathe in calming bodily fabrication.' He trains himself, 'I will breathe out calming the bodily fabrication.'

"[5] He trains himself, 'I will breathe in sensitive to rapture.' He trains himself, 'I will breathe out sensitive to rapture.' [6] He trains himself, 'I will breathe in sensitive to pleasure.' He trains himself, 'I will breathe out sensitive to pleasure.' [7] He trains himself, 'I will breathe in sensitive to mental fabrication.' He trains himself, 'I will breathe out sensitive to mental fabrication.' [8] He trains himself, 'I will breathe in calming mental fabrication.' He trains himself, 'I will breathe out calming mental fabrication.'

"[9] He trains himself, 'I will breathe in sensitive to the mind.' He trains himself, 'I will breathe out sensitive to the mind.' [10] He trains himself, 'I will breathe in satisfying the mind.' He trains himself, 'I will breathe out satisfying the mind.' [11] He trains himself, 'I will breathe in steadying the mind.' He trains himself, 'I will breathe out steadying the mind. [12] He trains himself, 'I will breathe in releasing the mind.' He trains himself, 'I will breathe out releasing the mind.'

"[13] He trains himself, 'I will breathe in focusing on inconstancy.' He trains himself, 'I will breathe out focusing on inconstancy.' [14] He trains himself, 'I will breathe in focusing on dispassion [lit: fading].' He trains himself, 'I will breathe out focusing on dispassion.' [15] He trains himself, 'I will breathe in focusing on cessation.' He trains himself, 'I will breathe out focusing on cessation.' [16] He trains himself, 'I will breathe in focusing on relinquishment.' He trains himself, 'I will breathe out focusing on relinquishment.'

"This, Rāhula, is how mindfulness of in-&-out breathing is developed & pursued so as to be of great fruit, of great benefit.

"When mindfulness of in-&-out breathing is developed & pursued in this way, even one's final in-breaths & out-breaths are known as they cease, not unknown."[4]

That is what the Blessed One said. Gratified, Ven. Rāhula delighted in the Blessed One's words.

NOTES

1. According to the Commentary, Ven. Rāhula was 18 years old when this discourse took place.

2. The preceding passage in braces is missing from the editions on which both *MLS* and *MLDB* are based.

3. For notes on these sixteen steps, see MN 118.

4. In other words, one dies fully alert.

See also: MN 28; MN 61; MN 118; MN 140; MN 147; AN 9:1

63 *The Shorter Exhortation to Māluṅkya*

Cūḷa Māluṅkyovāda Sutta

I have heard that on one occasion the Blessed One was staying near Sāvatthī in Jeta's Grove, Anāthapiṇḍika's monastery. Then, as Ven. Māluṅkyaputta was alone in seclusion, this line of thinking arose in his awareness: "These positions that are undisclosed, set aside, discarded by the Blessed One—'The cosmos is eternal,' 'The cosmos is not eternal,' 'The cosmos is finite,' 'The cosmos is infinite,' 'The soul & the body are the same,' 'The soul is one thing and the body another,' 'After death a Tathāgata exists,' 'After death a Tathāgata does not exist,' 'After death a Tathāgata both exists & does not exist,' 'After death a Tathāgata neither exists nor does not exist'—I don't approve, I don't accept that the Blessed One has not disclosed them to me. I'll go ask the Blessed One about this matter. If he discloses to me that 'The cosmos is eternal,' that 'The cosmos is not eternal,' that 'The cosmos is finite,' that 'The cosmos is infinite,' that 'The soul & the body are the same,' that 'The soul is one thing and the body another,' that 'After death a Tathāgata exists,' that 'After death a Tathāgata does not exist,' that 'After death a Tathāgata both exists & does not exist,' or that 'After death a Tathāgata neither exists nor does not exist,' then I will live the holy life under him. If he does not disclose to me that 'The cosmos is eternal,' ... or that 'After death a Tathāgata neither exists nor does not exist,' then I will renounce the training and return to the lower life."

Then, emerging from his seclusion in the late afternoon, Ven. Māluṅkyaputta went to the Blessed One and, on arrival, having bowed down to him, sat to one side. As he was sitting there he said to the Blessed One, "Lord, just now, as I was alone in seclusion, this line of thinking arose in my awareness: 'These positions that are undisclosed, set aside, discarded by the Blessed One... I don't approve, I don't accept that the Blessed One has not disclosed them to me. I'll go ask the Blessed One about this matter. If he discloses to me that "The cosmos is eternal," ... or that "After death a Tathāgata neither exists nor does not exist," then I will live the holy life under him. If he does not disclose to me that "The cosmos is eternal," ... or that "After death a Tathāgata neither exists nor does not exist," then I will renounce the training and return to the lower life.'

"Lord, if the Blessed One knows that 'The cosmos is eternal,' then may he disclose to me that 'The cosmos is eternal.' If he knows that 'The cosmos is not eternal,' then may he disclose to me that 'The cosmos is not eternal.' But if he doesn't know or see whether the cosmos is eternal or not eternal, then, in one who is unknowing & unseeing, the straightforward thing is to admit, 'I don't know. I don't see.' ... If he doesn't know or see whether after death a Tathāgata exists... does not exist... both exists & does not exist... neither exists nor does not exist,' then, in one who is unknowing & unseeing, the straightforward thing is to admit, 'I don't know. I don't see.'"

"Māluṅkyaputta, did I ever say to you, 'Come, Māluṅkyaputta, live the holy life under me, and I will disclose to you that 'The cosmos is eternal,' or 'The cosmos is not eternal,' or 'The cosmos is finite,' or 'The cosmos is infinite,' or 'The soul & the body are the same,' or 'The soul is one thing and the body another,' or 'After death a Tathāgata exists,' or 'After death a Tathāgata does not exist,' or 'After death a Tathāgata both exists & does not exist,' or 'After death a Tathāgata neither exists nor does not exist'?"

"No, lord."

"And did you ever say to me, 'Lord, I will live the holy life under the Blessed One and (in return) he will disclose to me that 'The cosmos is eternal,' or 'The cosmos is not eternal,' or 'The cosmos is finite,' or 'The cosmos is infinite,' or 'The soul & the body are the same,' or 'The soul is one thing and the body another,' or 'After death a Tathāgata exists,' or 'After death a Tathāgata does not exist,' or 'After death a Tathāgata both exists & does not exist,' or 'After death a Tathāgata neither exists nor does not exist'?"

"No, lord."

"Then that being the case, foolish man, who are you to be claiming grievances/making demands of anyone?

"Māluṅkyaputta, if anyone were to say, 'I won't live the holy life under the Blessed One as long as he does not disclose to me that "The cosmos is eternal," ... or that "After death a Tathāgata neither exists nor does not exist,"' the man would die and those things would still remain undisclosed by the Tathāgata.

"It's just as if a man were wounded with an arrow thickly smeared with poison. His friends & companions, kinsmen & relatives would provide him with a surgeon, and the man would say, 'I won't have this arrow removed until I know whether the man who wounded me was a noble warrior, a brahman, a merchant, or a worker.' He would say, 'I won't have this arrow removed until I know the given name & clan name of the man who wounded me... until I know whether he was tall, medium, or short... until I know whether he was dark, ruddy-brown, or golden-colored... until I know his home village, town, or city… until I know whether the bow with which I was wounded was a long bow or a crossbow… until I know whether the bowstring with which I was wounded was fiber, bamboo threads, sinew, hemp, or bark… until I know whether the shaft with which I was wounded was wild or cultivated… until I know whether the feathers of the shaft with which I was wounded were those of a vulture, a stork, a hawk, a peacock, or another bird… until I know whether the shaft with which I was wounded was bound with the sinew of an ox, a water buffalo, a langur, or a monkey.' He would say, 'I won't have this arrow removed until I know whether the shaft with which I was wounded was that of a common arrow, a curved arrow, a barbed, a calf-toothed, or an oleander arrow.' The man would die and those things would still remain unknown to him.

"In the same way, if anyone were to say, 'I won't live the holy life under the Blessed One as long as he does not disclose to me that "The cosmos is eternal," … or that "After death a Tathāgata neither exists nor does not exist,"' the man would die and those things would still remain undisclosed by the Tathāgata.

"Māluṅkyaputta, it's not the case that when there is the view, 'The cosmos is eternal,' there is the living of the holy life. And it's not the case that when there is the view, 'The cosmos is not eternal,' there is the living of the holy life. When there is the view, 'The cosmos is eternal,' and when there is the view, 'The cosmos is not eternal,' there is still the birth, there is the aging, there is the death, there is the sorrow, lamentation, pain, despair, & distress whose destruction I make known right in the here & now.

"It's not the case that when there is the view, 'The cosmos is finite,' there is the living of the holy life. And it's not the case that when there is the view, 'The cosmos is infinite,' there is the living of the holy life. When there is the view, 'The cosmos is finite,' and when there is the view, 'The cosmos is infinite,' there is still the birth, there is the aging, there is the death, there is the sorrow, lamentation, pain, despair, & distress whose destruction I make known right in the here & now.

"It's not the case that when there is the view, 'The soul & the body are the same,' there is the living of the holy life. And it's not the case that when there is the view, 'The soul is one thing and the body another,' there is the living of the holy life. When there is the view, 'The soul & the body are the same,' and when there is the view, 'The soul is one thing and the body another,' there is still the birth, there is the aging, there is the death, there is the sorrow, lamentation, pain, despair, & distress whose destruction I make known right in the here & now.

"It's not the case that when there is the view, 'After death a Tathāgata exists,' there is the living of the holy life. And it's not the case that when there is the view, 'After death a Tathāgata does not exist,' there is the living of the holy life. And it's not the case that when there is the view, 'After death a Tathāgata both exists & does not exist,' there is the living of the holy life. And it's not the case that when there is the view, 'After death a Tathāgata neither exists nor does not exist' there is the living of the holy life. When there is the view, 'After death a Tathāgata exists' ... 'After death a Tathāgata does not exist' ... 'After death a Tathāgata both exists & does not exist' ... 'After death a Tathāgata neither exists nor does not exist,' there is still the birth, there is the aging, there is the death, there is the sorrow, lamentation, pain, despair, & distress whose destruction I make known right in the here & now.

"So, Māluṅkyaputta, remember what is undisclosed by me as undisclosed, and what is disclosed by me as disclosed. And what is undisclosed by me? 'The cosmos is eternal,' is undisclosed by me. 'The cosmos is not eternal,' is undisclosed by me. 'The cosmos is finite' ... 'The cosmos is infinite' ... 'The soul & the body are the same' ... 'The soul is one thing and the body another' ... 'After death a Tathāgata exists' ... 'After death a Tathāgata does not exist' ... 'After death a Tathāgata both exists & does not exist' ... 'After death a Tathāgata neither exists nor does not exist,' is undisclosed by me.

"And why are they undisclosed by me? Because they are not connected with the goal, are not fundamental to the holy life. They do not lead to disenchantment, dispassion, cessation, calming, direct knowledge, self-awakening, unbinding. That's why they are undisclosed by me.

"And what is disclosed by me? 'This is stress,' is disclosed by me. 'This is the origination of stress,' is disclosed by me. 'This is the cessation of stress,' is disclosed by me. 'This is the path of practice leading to the cessation of stress,' is disclosed by me. And why are they disclosed by me? Because they are connected with the goal, are fundamental to the holy life. They lead to disenchantment, dispassion, cessation, calming, direct knowledge, self-awakening, unbinding. That's why they are disclosed by me.

"So, Māluṅkyaputta, remember what is undisclosed by me as undisclosed, and what is disclosed by me as disclosed."

That is what the Blessed One said. Gratified, Ven. Māluṅkyaputta delighted in the Blessed One's words.

See also: DN 9; MN 72; SN 12:35; SN 22:85-86; SN 44; SN 56:31; AN 4:42; AN 7:51; AN 10:93; AN 10:96, Sn 4:9

66 The Quail Simile

Laḍukikopama Sutta

I have heard that on one occasion the Blessed One was staying among the Aṅguttarāpans at an Aṅguttarāpan town named Āpaṇa. Then, early in the morning—adjusting his under robe and carrying his outer robe & bowl—he went into Āpaṇa for alms. Having gone for alms in Āpaṇa and returning from his alms round after his meal, he went to a certain forest grove for the day's abiding. Plunging into the grove, he sat down for his day's abiding at the root of a certain tree.

Ven. Udāyin, too, early in the morning—adjusting his under robe and carrying his outer robe & bowl—went into Āpaṇa for alms. Having gone for alms in Āpaṇa and returning from his alms round after his meal, he went to that forest grove for the day's abiding. Plunging into the grove, he sat down for his day's abiding at the root of a certain tree. Then, as he was alone in seclusion, this line of thinking arose in his awareness: "So many painful things has the Blessed One taken away from us! So many pleasant things has he brought us! So many unskillful qualities has the Blessed One taken away from us! So many skillful qualities has he brought us!"

Then, Ven. Udāyin, emerging from his seclusion in the late afternoon, went to the Blessed One and, on arrival, having bowed down to him, sat to one side. As he was sitting there he said to the Blessed One: "Just now, lord, as I was alone in seclusion, this line of thinking arose in my awareness: 'So many painful things has the Blessed One taken away from us! So many pleasant things has he brought us! So many unskillful qualities has the Blessed One taken away from us! So many skillful qualities has he brought us!' For in the past, lord, we used to eat in the morning, in the evening, and in the day at the wrong time (the afternoon). Then there was the time when the Blessed One addressed the monks, saying, 'Monks, please discontinue that daytime meal at the wrong time.' At the time I was upset, at the time I was sad, (thinking,) 'The exquisite staple & non-staple foods that faithful householders give us during the day at the wrong time: even that the Blessed One has us abandon; even that the One Well-Gone has us relinquish!' But, out of consideration for our love & respect for the Blessed One, out of consideration for shame & fear of wrong-doing, we abandoned that daytime meal at the wrong time.

"So we ate both in the evening & in the morning. Then there was the time when the Blessed One addressed the monks, saying, 'Monks, please discontinue that evening meal at the wrong time.' At the time I was upset, at the time I was sad, (thinking,) 'The more exquisitely prepared of our two meals: even that the Blessed One has us abandon; even that the One Well-Gone has us relinquish!' In the past, lord, a man—obtaining some soup during the day—would say to his wife, 'Put this aside and we will all eat it together in the evening.' (Almost) all food preparation is done in the evening, and almost none during the day. But, out of consideration for our love & respect for the Blessed One, out of consideration for shame & fear of wrong-doing, we abandoned that evening meal at the wrong time.

"In the past, lord, monks going for alms in the pitch black of the night have walked into a waste-water pool, fallen into a cesspit, stumbled over a thorn patch, or stumbled over a sleeping cow. They have encountered young hooligans on the way to or from a crime. They have been propositioned by women. Once I went for alms in the pitch black of night. A woman washing a pot saw me by a lightning flash and, on seeing me, screamed out: 'I'm done for! A demon is after me!' When this was said, I said to her, 'I'm no demon, sister. I'm a monk waiting for alms.' 'Then you're a monk whose daddy's dead and whose mommy's dead. Better for you, monk, that your belly were slit open with a sharp butcher's knife than this prowling for alms for your belly's sake in the pitch black of the night!" On recollecting that, lord, the thought occurred to me: 'So many painful things has the Blessed One taken away from us! So many pleasant things has he brought us! So many unskillful qualities has the Blessed One taken away from us! So many skillful qualities has he brought us!'"

"In the same way, Udāyin, there are some worthless men who, when I tell them, 'Abandon this,' say: 'What? Over this little, trifling thing? He's too much of a stickler, this contemplative.' They don't abandon it. They're rude to me and to the monks keen on training. For them that's a strong snare, a thick snare, a heavy snare, an unrotting snare, and a thick yoke.

"Suppose a quail were snared by a rotting creeper, by which it could expect injury, captivity, or death, and someone were to say, 'This rotting creeper by which this quail is snared, and by which she could expect injury, captivity, or death, is for her a weak snare, a feeble snare, a rotting snare, an insubstantial snare.' Would the person speaking that way be speaking rightly?"

"No, lord. That rotting creeper… is for her a strong snare, a thick snare, a heavy snare, an unrotting snare, and a thick yoke.

"In the same way, Udāyin, there are some worthless men who, when I tell them, 'Abandon this,' say: 'What? This little, trifling thing? He's too much of a stickler, this contemplative.' They don't abandon it. They're rude to me and to the monks keen on training. For them that's a strong snare, a thick snare, a heavy snare, an unrotting snare, and a thick yoke.

"Now there are some clansmen who, when I tell them, 'Abandon this,' say: 'What? The Blessed One has us abandon, the One Well-Gone has us relinquish this little, trifling thing?' But they abandon it and are not rude to me or to the monks keen on training. Having abandoned it, they live unconcerned, unruffled, their wants satisfied, with their mind like a wild deer. For them that's a weak snare, a feeble snare, a rotting snare, an insubstantial snare.

"Suppose a royal elephant—immense, pedigreed, accustomed to battles, its tusks like chariot poles—were snared with thick leather snares, but by twisting its body a bit it could break & burst those snares and go off wherever it liked. And suppose someone were to say, 'Those thick leather snares by which the royal elephant… was snared, but which—by twisting its body a bit— it could break & burst and go off wherever it liked: for him they were a strong snare, a thick snare, a heavy snare, an unrotting snare, and a thick yoke.' Would the person speaking that way be speaking rightly?'

"No, lord. Those thick leather snares… were for him a weak snare, a feeble snare, a rotting snare, an insubstantial snare."

"In the same way, Udāyin, there are some clansmen who, when I tell them, 'Abandon this,' say: 'What? The Blessed One has us abandon, the One Well-Gone has us relinquish this little, trifling thing?' But they abandon it and are not rude to me or to the monks keen on training. Having abandoned it, they live unconcerned, unruffled, their wants satisfied, with their mind like a wild deer. For them that's a weak snare, a feeble snare, a rotting snare, an insubstantial snare.

"Suppose there were a poor person, penniless & indigent, with a single little shack—dilapidated, open to the crows, not the best sort; and a single bed—dilapidated, not the best sort; and a single pot of rice & gourd seeds—not the best sort; and a single wife, not the best sort. He would go to a park and see a monk—his hands & feet washed, after a delightful meal, sitting in the cool shade, committed to the heightened mind. The thought would occur to him: How happy the contemplative state! How free of disease the contemplative state! O that I—shaving off my hair & beard and donning the ochre robe—might go forth from the household life into homelessness!' But being unable to abandon his single little shack—dilapidated, open to the crows, not the best sort; to abandon his single bed—dilapidated, not the best sort; to abandon his single pot of rice & gourd seeds—not the best sort; and to abandon his single wife, not the best sort, he wouldn't be able to shave off his hair & beard, to don the ochre robe, or to go forth from the household life into homelessness. And suppose someone were to say, 'That single little shack—dilapidated, open to the crows, not the best sort; that single bed—dilapidated, not the best sort; that single pot of rice & gourd seeds—not the best sort; and that single wife, not the best sort by which that man was snared, which he was unable to abandon, and because of which he couldn't shave off his hair & beard, don the ochre robe, and go forth from the household life into homelessness: for him they were a weak snare, a feeble snare, a rotting snare, an insubstantial snare.' Would the person speaking that way be speaking rightly?"

"No, lord. That single hut… that single bed… that single pot… that single wife… were for that man a strong snare, a thick snare, a heavy snare, an unrotting snare, and a thick yoke."

"In the same way, Udāyin, there are some worthless men who, when I tell them, 'Abandon this,' say: 'What? This little, trifling thing? He's too much of a stickler, this contemplative.' They don't abandon it. They're rude to me and to the monks keen on training. For them that's a strong snare, a thick snare, a heavy snare, an unrotting snare, and a thick yoke.

"Now suppose, Udāyin, that there were a householder or householder's son—rich, prosperous, & wealthy—with vast amounts of gold ingots, vast amounts of grain, a vast number of fields, a vast amount of land, a vast number of wives, and a vast number of male & female slaves. He would go to a park and see a monk—his hands & feet washed, after a delightful meal, sitting in the cool shade, committed to the heightened mind. The thought would occur to him: How happy the contemplative state! How free of disease the contemplative state! O that I—shaving off my hair & beard and donning the ochre robe—might go forth from the household life into homelessness!' And being able to abandon his vast amounts of gold ingots, his vast amounts of grain, his vast number of fields, his vast amount of land, his vast number of wives, and his vast number of male & female slaves, he would be able to shave off his hair & beard, to don the ochre robe, and to go forth from the household life into homelessness. Now suppose someone were to say, 'Those vast amounts of gold ingots… and a vast number of male & female slaves by which that householder or householder's son was snared but which he was able to abandon so that he could shave off his hair & beard, don the ochre robe, and go forth from the household life into homelessness: for him they were a strong snare, a thick snare, a heavy snare, an unrotting snare, and a thick yoke.' Would the person speaking that way be speaking rightly?"

"No, lord. Those vast amounts of gold ingots… were for him a weak snare, a feeble snare, a rotting snare, an insubstantial snare.'

"In the same way, Udāyin, there are some clansmen who, when I tell them, 'Abandon this,' say: 'What? The Blessed One has us abandon, the One Well-Gone has us relinquish this little, trifling thing?' But they abandon it and are not rude to me or to the monks keen on training. Having abandoned it, they live unconcerned, unruffled, their wants satisfied, with their mind like a wild deer. For them that's a weak snare, a feeble snare, a rotting snare, an insubstantial snare.

"Udāyin, there are these four types of people to be found existing in the world. Which four? There is the case where a certain person is practicing for the abandoning & relinquishing of acquisitions. As he is practicing for the abandoning & relinquishing of acquisitions, memories & resolves associated with acquisitions assail him. He acquiesces to them. He does not abandon them, destroy them, dispel them, or wipe them out of existence. I tell you, Udāyin, that this sort of person is fettered, not unfettered. Why is that? Because I have known the diversity of faculties with regard to this type of person.

"Then there is the case where a certain person practicing for the abandoning & relinquishing of acquisitions. As he is practicing for the abandoning & relinquishing of acquisitions, memories & resolves associated with acquisitions assail him. He does not acquiesce to them. He abandons them, destroys them, dispels them, & wipes them out of existence. I tell you, Udāyin, that this sort of person is fettered, not unfettered. Why is that? Because I have known the diversity of faculties with regard to this type of person.

"Then there is the case where a certain person is practicing for the abandoning & relinquishing of acquisitions. As he is practicing for the abandoning & relinquishing of acquisitions, then—from time to time, owing to lapses in mindfulness—he is assailed by memories & resolves associated with acquisitions. Slow is the arising of his mindfulness, but then he quickly abandons (those memories & resolves), destroys them, dispels them, & wipes them out of existence. Just as when two or three drops of water fall onto an iron pan heated all day: Slow is the falling of the drops of water, but they quickly vanish & disappear. In the same way, there is the case where a certain person is practicing for the abandoning & relinquishing of acquisitions. As he is practicing for the abandoning &

relinquishing of acquisitions, then—from time to time, owing to lapses in mindfulness—he is assailed by memories & resolves associated with acquisitions. Slow is the arising of his mindfulness, but then he quickly abandons (those memories & resolves), destroys them, dispels them, & wipes them out of existence. I tell you, Udāyin, that this sort of person is fettered, not unfettered. Why is that? Because I have known the diversity of faculties with regard to this type of person.

"Then there is the case where a certain person, realizing that acquisitions are the root of suffering & stress, is without acquisitions, released in the ending of acquisitions. I tell you, Udāyin, that this sort of person is unfettered, not fettered. Why is that? Because I have known the diversity of faculties with regard to this type of person.

"There are these four types of people to be found existing in the world.

"And, Udāyin, there are these five strings of sensuality. Which five? Forms cognizable via the eye—agreeable, pleasing, charming, endearing, enticing, linked with sensual desire. Sounds cognizable via the ear.... Aromas cognizable via the nose.... Flavors cognizable via the tongue.... Tactile sensations cognizable via the body—agreeable, pleasing, charming, endearing, enticing, linked with sensual desire. These are the five strings of sensuality. Now, any pleasure & happiness that arises dependent on these five strings of sensuality is called sensual pleasure, a filthy pleasure, a run-of-the-mill pleasure, an ignoble pleasure. And of this pleasure I say that it is not to be associated with, not to be developed, not to be pursued, that it is to be feared.

"Now, there is the case where a monk—quite secluded from sensuality, secluded from unskillful qualities—enters & remains in the first jhāna: rapture & pleasure born of seclusion, accompanied by directed thought & evaluation. With the stilling of directed thoughts & evaluations, he enters & remains in the second jhāna: rapture & pleasure born of concentration, unification of awareness free from directed thought & evaluation—internal assurance. With the fading of rapture, he remains equanimous, mindful, & alert, and senses pleasure with the body. He enters & remains in the third jhāna, of which the noble ones declare, 'Equanimous & mindful, he has a pleasant abiding.' With the abandoning of pleasure & pain—as with the earlier disappearance of elation & distress—he enters & remains in the fourth jhāna: purity of equanimity & mindfulness, neither pleasure nor pain. This is called renunciation-pleasure, seclusion-pleasure, calm-pleasure, self-awakening-pleasure. And of this pleasure I say that it is to be associated with, to be developed, to be pursued, that it is not to be feared.

"Now, there is the case where a monk—quite secluded from sensuality, secluded from unskillful qualities—enters & remains in the first jhāna: rapture & pleasure born of seclusion, accompanied by directed thought & evaluation. That, I tell you, comes under the perturbable. And what comes under the perturbable there? The directed thoughts & evaluations that have not ceased there: That's what comes under the perturbable there.

"There is the case where a monk, with the stilling of directed thoughts & evaluations, enters & remains in the second jhāna: rapture & pleasure born of concentration, unification of awareness free from directed thought & evaluation—internal assurance. That, I tell you, comes under the perturbable. And what comes under the perturbable there? The rapture-pleasure that has not ceased there: That's what comes under the perturbable there.

"There is the case where a monk, with the fading of rapture, remains equanimous, mindful, & alert, and senses pleasure with the body. He enters & remains in the third jhāna, of which the noble ones declare, 'Equanimous & mindful, he has a pleasant abiding.' That, I tell you, comes under the perturbable. And what comes under the perturbable there? The equanimity-pleasure that has not ceased there: That's what comes under the perturbable there.

"There is the case where a monk, with the abandoning of pleasure & pain—as with the earlier disappearance of elation & distress—enters & remains in the fourth jhāna: purity of equanimity & mindfulness, neither pleasure nor pain. Now that, I tell you, comes under the imperturbable.[1]

"Now there is the case where a monk… enters & remains in the first jhāna: rapture & pleasure born of seclusion, accompanied by directed thought & evaluation. That, I tell you, isn't enough. Abandon it, I tell you. Transcend it, I tell you. And what is its transcending?

"There is the case where a monk… enters & remains in the second jhāna…. That is its transcending. But that, too, I tell you, isn't enough. Abandon it, I tell you. Transcend it, I tell you. And what is its transcending?

"There is the case where a monk… enters & remains in the third jhāna …. That is its transcending. But that, too, I tell you, isn't enough. Abandon it, I tell you. Transcend it, I tell you. And what is its transcending?

"There is the case where a monk… enters & remains in the fourth jhāna…. That is its transcending. But that, too, I tell you, isn't enough. Abandon it, I tell you. Transcend it, I tell you. And what is its transcending?

"Then there is the case where a monk, with the complete transcending of perceptions of (physical) form, with the disappearance of perceptions of resistance, and not attending to perceptions of multiplicity, (perceiving,) 'Infinite space,' enters & remains in the dimension of the infinitude of space. That is its transcending. But that, too, I tell you, isn't enough. Abandon it, I tell you. Transcend it, I tell you. And what is its transcending?

"Then there is the case where a monk, with the complete transcending of the dimension of the infinitude of space, (perceiving,) 'Infinite consciousness,' enters & remains in the dimension of the infinitude of consciousness. That is its transcending. But that, too, I tell you, isn't enough. Abandon it, I tell you. Transcend it, I tell you. And what is its transcending?

"Then there is the case where a monk, with the complete transcending of the dimension of the infinitude of consciousness, (perceiving,) 'There is nothing,' enters & remains in the dimension of nothingness. That is its transcending. But that, too, I tell you, isn't enough. Abandon it, I tell you. Transcend it, I tell you. And what is its transcending?

"Then there is the case where a monk, with the complete transcending of the dimension of nothingness, enters & remains in the dimension of neither perception nor non-perception. That is its transcending. But that, too, I tell you, isn't enough. Abandon it, I tell you. Transcend it, I tell you. And what is its transcending?

"There is the case where a monk, with the complete transcending of the dimension of neither perception nor non-perception, enters & remains in the cessation of perception & feeling. That is its transcending.

"Thus, Udāyin, I speak even of the abandoning of the dimension of neither perception nor non-perception. Do you see any fetter, large or small, of whose abandoning I don't speak?"

"No, lord."

That is what the Blessed One said. Gratified, Ven. Udāyin delighted in the Blessed One's words.

NOTE: 1. According to the commentaries, "imperturbable" denotes not only the fourth jhāna but also the four formless attainments. MN 106, however, explicitly does *not* include the dimension of nothingness under the term—and the same, apparently, holds for any of the formless attainments higher than that.

See also: MN 106; MN 137; MN 152; AN 5:30; AN 9:34; Ud 3:3

70 At Kīṭāgiri

Kīṭāgiri Sutta

I have heard that on one occasion the Blessed One was wandering on a tour of Kāsi with a large Saṅgha of monks. There he addressed the monks: "I abstain from the nighttime meal.[1] As I am abstaining from the nighttime meal, I sense next-to-no illness, next-to-no affliction, lightness, strength, & and comfortable abiding. Come, now. You, too, abstain from the nighttime meal. As you are abstaining from the nighttime meal, you, too, will sense next-to-no illness, next-to-no affliction, lightness, strength, & and comfortable abiding."

"As you say, lord," the monks responded to him.

Then, as he was wandering by stages in Kāsi, the Blessed One eventually arrived at a Kāsi town called Kīṭāgiri. And there he stayed in the Kāsi town, Kīṭāgiri.

Now at that time the monks led by Assaji & Punabbasu[2] were residing in Kīṭāgiri. Then a large number of monks went to them and, on arrival, said to them, "The Blessed One and the Saṅgha of monks abstain from the nighttime meal. As they are abstaining from the nighttime meal, they sense next-to-no illness, next-to-no affliction, lightness, strength, & and comfortable abiding. Come now, friends. You, too, abstain from the nighttime meal. As you are abstaining from the nighttime meal, you, too, will sense next-to-no illness, next-to-no affliction, lightness, strength, & and comfortable abiding."

When this was said, the monks led by Assaji & Punabbasu said to those monks, "Friends, we eat in the evening, in the morning, & in the wrong-time during the day. As we are eating in the evening, and in the morning, & in the wrong-time during the day, we sense next-to-no illness, next-to-no affliction, lightness, strength, & and comfortable abiding. Why should we, abandoning what is immediately visible, chase after something subject to time? We will eat in the evening, in the morning, & in the wrong-time during the day."

When they were unable to convince the monks led by Assaji & Punabbasu, those monks went to the Blessed One [and told him what had happened].

Then the Blessed One told a certain monk, "Come, monk. In my name, call the monks led by Assaji & Punabbasu, saying, 'The Teacher calls you, friends.'"

"As you say, lord," the monk answered and, having gone to the monks led by Assaji & Punabbasu, on arrival he said, "The Teacher calls you, friends."

"As you say, friend," the monks led by Assaji & Punabbasu replied. Then they went to the Blessed One and, on arrival, having bowed down to him, sat to one side. As they were sitting there, the Blessed One said to him, "Is it true, monks, that a large number of monks went to you… and you said, '…Why should we, abandoning what is immediately visible, chase after something subject to time? We will eat in the evening, in the morning, & in the wrong-time during the day.'"

"Yes, lord."

"Monks, have you ever understood me to teach the Dhamma in this way: 'Whatever a person experiences—pleasant, painful, or neither-pleasant-nor-painful—his unskillful qualities decrease and his skillful qualities grow'?"

"No, lord."

"And haven't you understood me to teach the Dhamma in this way: 'For someone feeling a pleasant feeling of this sort, unskillful qualities grow and skillful qualities decrease. But there is the case where, for someone feeling a pleasant feeling of that sort, unskillful qualities decrease and skillful qualities grow. For someone feeling a painful feeling of this sort, unskillful qualities grow and skillful qualities decrease. But there is the case where, for someone feeling a painful feeling of that sort, unskillful qualities decrease and skillful qualities grow. For someone feeling a neither-pleasant-nor-painful feeling of this sort, unskillful qualities grow and skillful qualities decrease. But there is the case where, for someone feeling a neither-pleasant-nor-painful feeling of that sort, unskillful qualities decrease and skillful qualities grow.'"

"Yes, lord."

"Good, monks. And if it were not known by me—not seen, not observed, not realized, not touched through discernment—that 'For someone feeling a pleasant feeling of this sort, unskillful qualities grow and skillful qualities decrease,' then would it be fitting for me, not knowing that, to say, 'Abandon that sort of pleasant feeling'?"

"No, lord."

"But because it is known by me—seen, observed, realized, touched through discernment—that 'For someone feeling a pleasant feeling of this sort, unskillful qualities grow and skillful qualities decrease,' I therefore say, 'Abandon that sort of pleasant feeling.'

"If it were not known by me—not seen, not observed, not realized, not touched through discernment—that 'For someone feeling a pleasant feeling of this sort, unskillful qualities decrease and skillful qualities grow,' then would it be fitting for me, not knowing that, to say, 'Enter & remain in that sort of pleasant feeling'?"

"No, lord."

"But because it is known by me—seen, observed, realized, touched through discernment—that 'For someone feeling a pleasant feeling of this sort, unskillful qualities decrease and skillful qualities grow,' I therefore say, 'Enter & remain in that sort of pleasant feeling.'

[Similarly for painful feelings and neither-pleasant-nor-painful feelings.]

"Monks, I don't say of all monks that they have a task to do with heedfulness; nor do I say of all monks that they have no task to do with heedfulness.

"Monks who are arahants, whose mental effluents are ended, who have reached fulfillment, done the task, laid down the burden, attained the true goal, totally destroyed the fetter of becoming, and who are released through right gnosis: I don't say of them that they have a task to do with heedfulness. Why is that? They have done their task with heedfulness. They are incapable of being heedless. But as for monks in higher training, who have not yet reached their hearts' goal, who still aspire for the unexcelled freedom from bondage: I say of them that they have a task to do with heedfulness. Why is that? (I think:) 'Perhaps these venerable ones, when making use of suitable resting places, associating with admirable friends, balancing their (mental) faculties,[3] will reach & remain in the supreme goal of the holy life for which clansmen rightly go forth from home into homelessness, knowing & realizing it for themselves in the here & now.' Envisioning this fruit of heedfulness for these monks, I say that they have a task to do with heedfulness.

"Monks, there are these seven individuals to be found in the world. Which seven? One (released) both ways, one released through discernment, a bodily witness, one attained to view, one released through conviction, a Dhamma-follower, and a conviction-follower.

"And what is the individual (released) both ways? There is the case where a certain individual remains touching with his body those peaceful liberations that transcend form, that are formless, and—having seen with discernment—his effluents are ended. This is called an individual (released) both ways.[4] Regarding this monk, I do not say that he has a task to do with heedfulness. Why is that? He has done his task with heedfulness. He is incapable of being heedless.

"And what is the individual released through discernment? There is the case where a certain individual does not remain touching with his body those peaceful liberations that transcend form, that are formless, but—having seen with discernment—his effluents are ended. This is called an individual who is released through discernment.[5] Regarding this monk, I do not say that he has a task to do with heedfulness. Why is that? He has done his task with heedfulness. He is incapable of being heedless.

"And what is the individual who is a bodily witness? There is the case where a certain individual remains touching with his body those peaceful liberations that transcend form, that are formless, and—having seen with discernment—some of his effluents are ended. This is called an individual who is a bodily witness.[6] Regarding this monk, I say that he has a task to do with heedfulness. Why is that? (I think:) 'Perhaps this venerable one, when making use of suitable resting places, associating with admirable friends, balancing his (mental) faculties, will reach & remain in the supreme goal of the holy life for which clansmen rightly go forth from home into homelessness, knowing & realizing it for himself in the here & now.' Envisioning this fruit of heedfulness for this monk, I say that he has a task to do with heedfulness.

"And what is the individual attained to view? There is the case where a certain individual does not remain touching with his body those peaceful liberations that transcend form, that are formless, but—having seen with discernment—some of his effluents are ended, and he has reviewed & examined with discernment the qualities (or: teachings) proclaimed by the Tathāgata. This is called an individual who is attained to view.[7] Regarding this monk, I say that he has a task to do with heedfulness. Why is that? (I think:) 'Perhaps this venerable one, when making use of suitable resting places, associating with admirable friends, balancing his (mental) faculties, will reach & remain in the supreme goal of the holy life for which clansmen rightly go forth from home into homelessness, knowing & realizing it for himself in the here & now.' Envisioning this fruit of heedfulness for this monk, I say that he has a task to do with heedfulness.

"And what is the individual released through conviction? There is the case where a certain individual does not remain touching with his body those peaceful liberations that transcend form, that are formless, but—having seen with discernment—some of his effluents are ended, and his conviction in the Tathāgata is settled, rooted, and established. This is called an individual who is released through conviction. Regarding this monk, I say that he has a task to do with heedfulness. Why is that? (I think:) 'Perhaps this venerable one, when making use of suitable resting places, associating with admirable friends, balancing his (mental) faculties, will reach & remain in the supreme goal of the holy life for which clansmen rightly go forth from home into homelessness, knowing & realizing it for himself in the here & now.' Envisioning this fruit of heedfulness for this monk, I say that he has a task to do with heedfulness.

"And what is the individual who is a Dhamma-follower? There is the case where a certain individual does not remain touching with his body those peaceful liberations that transcend form, that are formless, nor—having seen with discernment—are his effluents ended. But with a (sufficient) measure of reflection through discernment he has come to an agreement with the teachings proclaimed by the Tathāgata. And he has these qualities: the faculty of conviction, the faculty of persistence, the faculty of mindfulness, the faculty of concentration, & the faculty of discernment. This is called an individual who is a Dhamma-follower.[8] Regarding this monk, I say that he has a task to do with heedfulness. Why is that? (I think:) 'Perhaps this venerable one, when making use of suitable resting places, associating with admirable friends, balancing his (mental) faculties, will reach & remain in the supreme goal of the holy life for which clansmen rightly go forth from home into homelessness, knowing & realizing it for himself in the here & now.' Envisioning this fruit of heedfulness for this monk, I say that he has a task to do with heedfulness.

"And what is the individual who is a conviction-follower? There is the case where a certain individual does not remain touching with his body those peaceful liberations that transcend form, that are formless, nor—having seen with discernment—are his effluents ended. But he has a (sufficient) measure of conviction in & love for the Tathāgata. And he has these qualities: the faculty of conviction, the faculty of persistence, the faculty of mindfulness, the faculty of concentration, & the faculty of discernment. This is called an individual who is a conviction-follower. Regarding this monk, I say that he has a task to do with heedfulness. Why is that? (I think:) 'Perhaps this venerable one, when making use of suitable resting places, associating with admirable friends, balancing his (mental) faculties, will reach & remain in the supreme goal of the holy life for which clansmen rightly go forth from home into homelessness, knowing & realizing it for himself in the here & now.' Envisioning this fruit of heedfulness for this monk, I say that he has a task to do with heedfulness.

"Monks, I do not say that the attainment of gnosis is all at once. Rather, the attainment of gnosis is after gradual training, gradual action, gradual practice. And how is there the attainment of gnosis after gradual training, gradual action, gradual practice? There is the case where, when conviction has arisen, one visits (a teacher). Having visited, one grows close. Having grown close, one lends ear. Having lent ear, one hears the Dhamma. Having heard the Dhamma, one remembers it. Remembering, one penetrates the meaning of the teachings. Penetrating the meaning, one comes to an agreement through pondering the teachings. There being an agreement through pondering the teachings, desire arises. When desire has arisen, one is willing. When one is willing, one contemplates. Having contemplated, one makes an exertion. Having made an exertion, one realizes with the body the ultimate truth and, having penetrated it with discernment, sees it.[9]

"Now, monks, there hasn't been that conviction, there hasn't been that visiting, there hasn't been that growing close… that lending ear… that hearing of the Dhamma… that remembering… that penetration of the meaning of the teachings… that agreement through pondering the teachings… that desire… that willingness… that contemplation… that exertion. You have lost the way, monks. You have gone the wrong way, monks. How far have you strayed, foolish men, from this Dhamma & Discipline!

"Monks, there is a four-phrased statement that, when it is recited, an observant man will in no long time learn the meaning through discernment. I will recite it, and you learn it from me."

"But, lord, who are we to be learners of the Dhamma?"

"Monks, even with a teacher devoted to material things, an heir of material things, who lives attached to material things, this sort of haggling (by his students) wouldn't be proper: 'If we get this, we'll do it; if we don't, we won't.' So how could it be with regard to the Tathāgata, who dwells entirely detached from material things?

"For a disciple who has conviction in the Teacher's message & lives to penetrate it, what accords with the Dhamma is this: 'The Blessed One is the Teacher, I am a disciple. He is the one who knows, not I.' For a disciple who has conviction in the Teacher's message & lives to penetrate it, the Teacher's message is healing & nourishing. For a disciple who has conviction in the Teacher's message & lives to penetrate it, what accords with the Dhamma is this: 'Gladly would I let the flesh & blood in my body dry up, leaving just the skin, tendons, & bones, but if I have not attained what can be reached through manly firmness, manly persistence, manly striving, there will be no relaxing my persistence.' For a disciple who has conviction in the Teacher's message & lives to penetrate it, one of two fruits can be expected: either gnosis here & now, or—if there be any remnant of clinging-sustenance—non-return."

That is what the Blessed One said. Gratified, the monks delighted in the Blessed One's words.

NOTES

1. Pācittiya 37 forbids monks from eating during the period from noon until the following dawn. According to MN 66, the Buddha introduced this restriction in stages, first forbidding the afternoon meal, and then the nighttime meal.

2. Assaji and Punabbasu were two of the six ringleaders of the notorious "group-of-six" monks, whose misbehavior led to the formulation of many rules in the Vinaya. (The group is named after the number of ringleaders, not the number of members, which—according to the Commentary—reached more than one thousand.) In the origin story to Saṅghādisesa 13, the monks led by Assaji and Punabbasu behaved in many inappropriate ways to please the lay families of Kīṭāgiri, to the point where the Kīṭāgiri laypeople ridiculed well-behaved monks and refused to give them alms.

The Pali phrase for "monks led by Assaji and Punabbasu" is *assaji-punabbusakā bhikkhū*. Both *MLS* and *MLDB* mistakenly treat this phrase as the names of two monks, Assaji and Punabbasuka. Actually, the *-kā* at the end of the compound name is a suffix that converts it into an adjective, describing a group following Assaji and Punabbasu.

3. On the mental faculties, see SN 48:10. On heedfulness, see SN 48:56 and SN 55:40.

4. See DN 15 and AN 9:45.

5. See AN 9:44.

6. See AN 9:43. According to the Commentary, this category includes all noble ones (except for those who have reached the fruit of arahantship) who have also attained any of the formless dimensions.

7. According to the Commentary, this category and the following one include all noble ones (except for those who have reached the fruit of arahantship) who have not attained any of the formless dimensions.

8. According to the Commentary, this category and the following one include those who have reached the path to stream-entry, but not yet the fruit of stream-entry.

9. The steps of the practice, as presented here, follow the same sequence as that discussed in MN 95. However, in that sutta, the sequence is prefaced by instructions on how to determine whether a teacher is worthy of conviction.

See also: MN 22; MN 27; MN 95; SN 25:1–10; SN 48:44; AN 3:66; AN 3:87–88; AN 4:131

72 To Vacchagotta on Fire

Aggi-vacchagotta Sutta

I have heard that on one occasion the Blessed One was staying near Sāvatthī in Jeta's Grove, Anāthapiṇḍika's monastery. Then Vacchagotta the wanderer went to the Blessed One and, on arrival, exchanged courteous greetings with him. After an exchange of friendly greetings & courtesies, he sat to one side. As he was sitting there, he asked the Blessed One: "How is it, Master Gotama—does Master Gotama hold the view: 'The cosmos is eternal: only this is true, anything otherwise is worthless'?"

"... no..."

"Then does Master Gotama hold the view: 'The cosmos is not eternal: only this is true, anything otherwise is worthless'?"

"... no..."

"Then does Master Gotama hold the view: 'The cosmos is finite: only this is true, anything otherwise is worthless'?"

"... no..."

"Then does Master Gotama hold the view: 'The cosmos is infinite: only this is true, anything otherwise is worthless'?"

"... no..."

"Then does Master Gotama hold the view: 'The soul & the body are the same: only this is true, anything otherwise is worthless'?"

"... no..."

"Then does Master Gotama hold the view: 'The soul is one thing and the body another: only this is true, anything otherwise is worthless'?"

"... no..."

"Then does Master Gotama hold the view: 'After death a Tathāgata exists: only this is true, anything otherwise is worthless'?"

"... no..."

"Then does Master Gotama hold the view: 'After death a Tathāgata does not exist: only this is true, anything otherwise is worthless'?"

"... no ..."

"Then does Master Gotama hold the view: 'After death a Tathāgata both exists & does not exist: only this is true, anything otherwise is worthless'?"

" … no… "

"Then does Master Gotama hold the view: 'After death a Tathāgata neither exists nor does not exist: only this is true, anything otherwise is worthless'?"

" … no… "

"How is it, Master Gotama, when Master Gotama is asked if he holds the view 'the cosmos is eternal…' … 'after death a Tathāgata neither exists nor does not exist: only this is true, anything otherwise is worthless,' he says ' … no…' in each case. Seeing what drawback, then, is Master Gotama thus entirely dissociated from each of these ten positions?"

"Vaccha, the position that 'the cosmos is eternal' is a thicket of views, a wilderness of views, a contortion of views, a writhing of views, a fetter of views. It is accompanied by suffering, distress, despair, & fever, and it does not lead to disenchantment, dispassion, cessation; to calm, direct knowledge, self-awakening, unbinding.

"The position that 'the cosmos is not eternal'…

"…'the cosmos is finite'…

"…'the cosmos is infinite'…

"…'the soul & the body are the same'…

"…'the soul is one thing and the body another'…

"…'after death a Tathāgata exists'…

"…'after death a Tathāgata does not exist'…

"…'after death a Tathāgata both exists & does not exist'…

"…'after death a Tathāgata neither exists nor does not exist'… does not lead to disenchantment, dispassion, cessation; to calm, direct knowledge, self-awakening, unbinding."

"Does Master Gotama have any position at all?"

"A 'position,' Vaccha, is something that a Tathāgata has done away with. What a Tathāgata sees is this: 'Such is form, such its origination, such its disappearance; such is feeling, such its origination, such its disappearance; such is perception… such are fabrications… such is consciousness, such its origination, such its disappearance.' Because of this, I say, a Tathāgata—with the ending, fading away, cessation, renunciation, & relinquishment of all suppositions, all excogitations, all I-making & mine-making & obsessions with conceit—is, through lack of clinging/sustenance, released."

"But, Master Gotama, the monk whose mind is thus released: Where does he reappear?"

"'Reappear,' Vaccha, doesn't apply."

"In that case, Master Gotama, he does not reappear."

"'Does not reappear,' Vaccha, doesn't apply."

"…both does & does not reappear."

"...doesn't apply."

"...neither does nor does not reappear."

"...doesn't apply."

"How is it, Master Gotama, when Master Gotama is asked if the monk reappears... does not reappear... both does & does not reappear... neither does nor does not reappear, he says, '... doesn't apply' in each case. At this point, Master Gotama, I am befuddled; at this point, confused. The modicum of clarity coming to me from your earlier conversation is now obscured."

"Of course you're befuddled, Vaccha. Of course you're confused. Deep, Vaccha, is this phenomenon, hard to see, hard to realize, tranquil, refined, beyond the scope of conjecture, subtle, to-be-experienced by the wise. For those with other views, other practices, other satisfactions, other aims, other teachers, it is difficult to know. That being the case, I will counter-question you on this matter. Answer as you see fit. What do you think, Vaccha? If a fire were burning in front of you, would you know that 'This fire is burning in front of me'?"

"...yes..."

"And if someone were to ask you, Vaccha, 'This fire burning in front of you, dependent on what is it burning?': Thus asked, how would you reply?"

"...I would reply, 'This fire burning in front of me is burning dependent on grass & timber as its sustenance.'"

"If the fire burning in front of you were to go out, would you know that, 'This fire burning in front of me has gone out'?"

"...yes..."

"And if someone were to ask you, 'This fire that has gone out in front of you, in which direction from here has it gone? East? West? North? Or south?': Thus asked, how would you reply?"

"That doesn't apply, Master Gotama. Any fire burning dependent on a sustenance of grass & timber, being unnourished—from having consumed that sustenance and not being offered any other—is classified simply as 'out' [unbound]."

"In the same way, Vaccha, any form by which one describing the Tathāgata would describe him: That the Tathāgata has abandoned, its root destroyed, made like a palmyra stump, deprived of the conditions of development, not destined for future arising. Freed from the classification of form, Vaccha, the Tathāgata is deep, boundless, hard to fathom, like the sea. 'Reappears' doesn't apply. 'Does not reappear' doesn't apply. 'Both does & does not reappear' doesn't apply. 'Neither reappears nor does not reappear' doesn't apply.

"Any feeling.... Any perception.... Any fabrication....

"Any consciousness by which one describing the Tathāgata would describe him: That the Tathāgata has abandoned, its root destroyed, made like a palmyra stump, deprived of the conditions of development, not destined for future arising. Freed from the classification of consciousness, Vaccha, the Tathāgata is deep, boundless, hard to fathom, like the sea. 'Reappears' doesn't apply. 'Does not reappear' doesn't apply. 'Both does & does not reappear' doesn't apply. 'Neither reappears nor does not reappear' doesn't apply."

When this was said, Vacchagotta the wanderer said to the Blessed One: "Master Gotama, it's as if there were a great Sal tree not far from a village or town: From inconstancy, its branches and leaves would wear away, its bark would wear away, its sapwood would wear away, so that on a later occasion—divested of branches, leaves, bark, & sapwood—it would stand as pure heartwood. In the same way, Master Gotama's words are divested of branches, leaves, bark, & sapwood and stand as pure heartwood.

"Magnificent, Master Gotama! Magnificent! Just as if he were to place upright what was overturned, to reveal what was hidden, to show the way to one who was lost, or to carry a lamp into the dark so that those with eyes could see forms, in the same way has Master Gotama—through many lines of reasoning—made the Dhamma clear. I go to Master Gotama for refuge, to the Dhamma, and to the Saṅgha of monks. May Master Gotama remember me as a lay follower who has gone to him for refuge, from this day forward, for life."

See also: DN 15; MN 29–30; SN 6:15; SN 22:36; SN 22:85–86; SN 23:2; SN 35:117; SN 44:1; SN 44:9; AN 4:24; AN 4:173; AN 10:81; AN 10:93; Ud 8:9–10; Iti 63; Iti 112; Sn 5:6; Thig 5:10

74 *To LongNails*

Dīghanakha Sutta

I have heard that on one occasion the Blessed One was staying near Rājagaha on Vulture's Peak Mountain, in the Boar's Cave. Then LongNails the wanderer[1] went to the Blessed One and, on arrival, exchanged courteous greetings with him. After an exchange of friendly greetings & courtesies, he stood to one side. As he was standing there, he said to the Blessed One, "Master Gotama, I am of the view, of the opinion, that 'All is not pleasing to me.'"

"But even this view of yours, Aggivessana—'All is not pleasing to me'—is even that not pleasing to you?'"

"Even if this view of mine were pleasing to me, Master Gotama, it would still be the same, it would still be the same."

"Well, Aggivessana, there are more than many in the world who say, 'It would still be the same, it would still be the same,' yet they both do not abandon that view and they cling to another view. There are fewer than few in the world who say, 'It would still be the same, it would still be the same,' and they both abandon that view and do not cling to another view.

"There are some contemplatives & brahmans who are of the view, of the opinion, that 'All is pleasing to me.' There are some contemplatives & brahmans who are of the view, of the opinion, that 'All is not pleasing to me.' There are some contemplatives & brahmans who are of the view, of the opinion, that 'A part is pleasing to me; a part is not pleasing to me.'

"With regard to those contemplatives & brahmans who are of the view, of the opinion, that 'All is pleasing to me': That view of theirs is close to being impassioned, close to bondage, close to delighting, close to holding, close to clinging. With regard to those contemplatives & brahmans who are of the view, of the opinion, that 'All is not pleasing to me': That view of theirs is close to not being impassioned, close to non-bondage, close to not-delighting, close to not-holding, close to not-clinging."

When this was said, LongNails the wanderer said to the Blessed One, "Master Gotama commends my viewpoint. Master Gotama recommends my viewpoint."

"With regard to those contemplatives & brahmans who are of the view, of the opinion that 'A part is pleasing to me; a part is not pleasing to me': Whatever is pleasing to them, their view is close to being impassioned, close to bondage, close to delighting, close to holding, close to clinging. Whatever is not pleasing to them, their view is close to not being impassioned, close to non-bondage, close to not-delighting, close to not-holding, close to not-clinging.

"With regard to those contemplatives & brahmans who are of the view, of the opinion, 'All is pleasing to me': An observant person among them considers that 'If I were to grasp and insist firmly on this view of mine that "All is pleasing to me," and to state that "Only this is true, all else is worthless," I would clash with two—the contemplative or brahman who is of the view, of the opinion that "All is not pleasing to me" and the contemplative or brahman who is of the view, of the opinion that "A part is pleasing to me; a part is not pleasing to me." I would clash with these two. Where there is a clash, there is dispute. Where there is a dispute, quarreling. Where there is quarreling, annoyance. Where there is annoyance, frustration.' Envisioning for himself clash, dispute, quarreling, annoyance, frustration, he both abandons that view and does not cling to another view. Thus there is the abandoning of these views; thus there is the relinquishing of these views.

"With regard to those contemplatives & brahmans who are of the view, of the opinion that 'All is not pleasing to me': An observant person among them considers that 'If I were to grasp and insist firmly on this view of mine that "All is not pleasing to me," and to state that "Only this is true, all else is worthless," I would clash with two—the contemplative or brahman who is of the view, of the opinion that "All is pleasing to me" and the contemplative or brahman who is of the view, of the opinion that "A part is pleasing to me; a part is not pleasing to me." I would clash with these two. Where there is a clash, there is dispute. Where there is a dispute, quarreling. Where there is quarreling, annoyance. Where there is annoyance, frustration.' Envisioning for himself clash, dispute, quarreling, annoyance, frustration, he both abandons that view and does not cling to another view. Thus there is the abandoning of these views; thus there is the relinquishing of these views.

"With regard to those contemplatives & brahmans who are of the view, of the opinion that 'A part is pleasing to me; a part is not pleasing to me': An observant person among them considers that 'If I were to grasp and insist firmly on this view of mine that "A part is pleasing to me; a part is not pleasing to me," and to state that "Only this is true, all else is worthless," I would clash with two—the contemplative or brahman who is of the view, of the opinion that "All is pleasing to me" and the contemplative or brahman who is of the view, of the opinion that "All is not pleasing to me." I would clash with these two. Where there is a clash, there is dispute. Where there is a dispute, quarreling. Where there is quarreling, annoyance. Where there is annoyance, frustration.' Envisioning for himself clash, dispute, quarreling, annoyance, frustration, he both abandons that view and does not cling to another view. Thus there is the abandoning of these views; thus there is the relinquishing of these views.

"Now, Aggivessana, this body—endowed with form, composed of the four primary elements, born from mother & father, nourished with rice & porridge, subject to inconstancy, rubbing, pressing, dissolution, and dispersion—should be envisioned as inconstant, stressful, a disease, a cancer, an arrow, painful, an affliction, alien, a disintegration, an emptiness, not-self. In one who envisions the body as inconstant, stressful, a disease, a cancer, an arrow, painful, an affliction, alien, a disintegration, an emptiness, not-self, any desire for the body, attraction to the body, following after the body is abandoned.

"There are these three kinds of feeling: a pleasant feeling, a painful feeling, and neither-pleasant-nor-painful feeling. On the occasion when one feels a pleasant feeling, one does not feel either a painful feeling or a neither-pleasant-nor-painful feeling. One feels only a pleasant feeling on that occasion. On the occasion when one feels a painful feeling, one does not feel either a pleasant feeling or a neither-pleasant-nor-painful feeling. One feels only a painful feeling on that occasion. On the occasion when one feels a neither-pleasant-nor-painful feeling, one does not feel either a pleasant feeling or a painful feeling. One feels only a neither-pleasant-nor-painful feeling on that occasion.

"A pleasant feeling is inconstant, fabricated, dependently co-arisen, subject to ending, subject to vanishing, fading, ceasing. A painful feeling is also inconstant, fabricated, dependently co-arisen, subject to ending, subject to vanishing, fading, ceasing. A neither-pleasant-nor-painful feeling is also inconstant, fabricated, dependently co-arisen, subject to ending, subject to vanishing, fading, ceasing.

"Seeing this, an instructed disciple of the noble ones grows disenchanted with pleasant feeling, disenchanted with painful feeling, disenchanted with neither-pleasant-nor-painful feeling. Disenchanted, he grows dispassionate. From dispassion, he is released. With release, there is the knowledge, 'Released.' He discerns, 'Birth is ended, the holy life fulfilled, the task done. There is nothing further for this world.' A monk whose mind is thus released does not take sides with anyone, does not dispute with anyone. He words things by means of what is said in the world but without grasping at it."

Now at that time Ven. Sāriputta was sitting[2] behind the Blessed One, fanning him. The thought occurred to him, "Indeed, it seems that the Blessed One speaks to us of the abandoning of each of these qualities through direct knowledge.[3] Indeed, it seems that the One Well-Gone speaks to us of the relinquishing of each of these qualities through direct knowledge."[4] As Ven. Sāriputta was reflecting thus, his mind was released from effluents through not-clinging. While in LongNails the wanderer there arose the dustless, stainless Dhamma eye: "Whatever is subject to origination is all subject to cessation."

Then LongNails the wanderer—having seen the Dhamma, having attained the Dhamma, having known the Dhamma, having fathomed the Dhamma, having crossed over and beyond uncertainty, having no more perplexity, having gained fearlessness, having becoming independent of others with regard to the Teacher's message—said to the Blessed One: "Magnificent, Master Gotama! Magnificent! Just as if he were to place upright what was overturned, to reveal what was hidden, to show the way to one who was lost, or to carry a lamp into the dark so that those with eyes could see forms, in the same way has Master Gotama—through many lines of reasoning—made the Dhamma clear. I go to Master Gotama for refuge, to the Dhamma, and to the Saṅgha of monks. May Master Gotama remember me as a lay follower who has gone to him for refuge, from this day forward, for life."[5]

NOTES

1. The Commentary states that LongNails (Dīghanakha) was a nephew of Ven. Sāriputta.

2. Following the Thai edition of the Canon. The Burmese and PTS editions say that Ven. Sāriputta was standing.

3. The Pali word *no* in this sentence can mean either "indeed" or "to us."

4. Compare this account of Ven. Sāriputta's awakening with the account given in MN 111.

5. The Commentary states that after delivering this discourse the Buddha returned to the Bamboo Grove outside of Rājagaha and met with 1,250 arahant disciples to deliver the Ovāda Pāṭimokkha—the event commemorated every year on Māgha Pūjā.

See also: MN 18; AN 3:68; Sn 4:3; Sn 4:8; Sn 4:12–13

75 To Māgaṇḍiya (Excerpt)

Māgaṇḍiya Sutta

In this passage, the Buddha discusses the nature of true pleasure and true health with a wanderer belonging to a hedonist sect.

… "Māgaṇḍiya, suppose that there was a leper covered with sores and infections, devoured by worms, picking the scabs off the openings of his wounds with his nails, cauterizing his body over a pit of glowing embers. His friends, companions, & relatives would take him to a doctor. The doctor would concoct medicine for him, and thanks to the medicine he would be cured of his leprosy: well & happy, free, master of himself, going wherever he liked. Then suppose two strong men, having seized hold of him by both arms, were to drag him to a pit of glowing embers. What do you think? Wouldn't he twist his body this way & that?"

"Yes, Master Gotama. Why is that? The fire is painful to the touch, very hot & scorching."

"Now what do you think, Māgaṇḍiya? Is the fire painful to the touch, very hot & scorching, only now, or was it also that way before?"

"Both now & before is it painful to the touch, very hot & scorching, Master Gotama. It's just that when the man was a leper covered with sores and infections, devoured by worms, picking the scabs off the openings of his wounds with his nails, his faculties were impaired, which was why, even though the fire was actually painful to the touch, he had the skewed perception of 'pleasant.'"

"In the same way, Māgaṇḍiya, sensual pleasures in the past were painful to the touch, very hot & scorching; sensual pleasures in the future will be painful to the touch, very hot & scorching; sensual pleasures at present are painful to the touch, very hot & scorching; but when beings are not free from passion for sensual pleasures—devoured by sensual craving, burning with sensual fever—their faculties are impaired, which is why, even though sensual pleasures are actually painful to the touch, they have the skewed perception of 'pleasant.'

"Now suppose that there was a leper covered with sores & infections, devoured by worms, picking the scabs off the openings of his wounds with his nails, cauterizing his body over a pit of glowing embers. The more he cauterized his body over the pit of glowing embers, the more disgusting, foul-smelling, & putrid the openings of his wounds would become, and yet he would feel a modicum of enjoyment & satisfaction because of the itchiness of his wounds. In the same way, beings not free from passion for sensual pleasures—devoured by sensual craving, burning with sensual fever—indulge in sensual pleasures. The more they indulge in sensual pleasures, the more their sensual craving increases and the more they burn with sensual fever, and yet they feel a modicum of enjoyment & satisfaction dependent on the five strands of sensuality.

"Now what do you think, Māgaṇḍiya? Have you ever seen or heard of a king or king's minister—enjoying himself, provided & endowed with the five strands of sensual pleasure, without abandoning sensual craving, without removing sensual fever—who has dwelt or will dwell or is dwelling free from thirst, his mind inwardly at peace?"

"No, Master Gotama."

"Very good, Māgaṇḍiya. Neither have I ever seen or heard of a king or king's minister—enjoying himself, provided & endowed with the five strands of sensual pleasure, without abandoning sensual craving, without removing sensual fever—who has dwelt or will dwell or is dwelling free from thirst, his mind inwardly at peace. But whatever contemplatives or brahmans who have dwelt or will dwell or are dwelling free from thirst, their minds inwardly at peace, all have done so having realized—as it has come to be—the origination & disappearance, the allure, the danger, & the escape from sensual pleasures, having abandoned sensual craving and removed sensual fever."

Then at that moment the Blessed One exclaimed,

"Freedom from disease: the foremost good fortune.
Unbinding: the foremost ease.
The eightfold: the foremost of paths
going to the
Deathless,
Secure.'

When this was said, Māgaṇḍiya the wanderer said to the Blessed One, "It's amazing, Master Gotama. It's astounding, how this, too, is well-stated by Master Gotama: 'Freedom from disease: the foremost good fortune. Unbinding: the foremost ease.' We have also heard this said by earlier wanderers in the lineage of our teachers: 'Freedom from disease: the foremost good fortune. Unbinding: the foremost ease.' This agrees with that."

"But as for what you have heard said by earlier wanderers in the lineage of your teachers, Māgaṇḍiya—'Freedom from disease: the foremost good fortune. Unbinding: the foremost ease'—which freedom from disease is that, which unbinding?"

When this was said, Māgaṇḍiya the wanderer rubbed his own limbs with his hand. "This is that freedom from disease, Master Gotama," he said. "This is that unbinding. For I am now free from disease, happy, and nothing afflicts me."

"Māgaṇḍiya, it's just as if there were a man blind from birth who couldn't see black objects... white... blue... yellow... red... or pink objects; who couldn't see even or uneven places, the stars, the sun, or the moon. He would hear a man with good eyesight saying, 'How wonderful, good sirs, is a white cloth—beautiful, spotless, & clean.' He would go in search of something white. Then another man would fool him with a grimy, oil-stained rag: 'Here, my good man, is a white cloth—beautiful, spotless, & clean.' The blind man would take it and put it on. Having put it on, gratified, he would exclaim words of gratification, 'How wonderful, good sirs, is a white cloth—beautiful, spotless, & clean.' Now what do you think, Māgaṇḍiya? When that man blind from birth took the grimy, oil-stained rag and put it on; and, having put it on, gratified, exclaimed words of gratification, 'How wonderful, good sirs, is a white cloth—beautiful, spotless, & clean': Did he do so knowing & seeing, or out of faith in the man with good eyesight?"

"Of course he did it not knowing & not seeing, Master Gotama, but out of faith in the man with good eyesight."

"In the same way, Māgaṇḍiya, the wanderers of other sects are blind & eyeless. Without knowing freedom from disease, without seeing unbinding, they still speak this verse:

'Freedom from disease: the foremost good fortune.
Unbinding: the foremost ease.'

This verse was stated by earlier worthy ones, fully self-awakened:

'Freedom from disease: the foremost good fortune.
Unbinding: the foremost ease.
The eightfold: the foremost of paths
going to the
Deathless,
Secure.'

"But now it has gradually become a verse of run-of-the-mill people.

"This body, Māgaṇḍiya, is a disease, a cancer, an arrow, painful, an affliction. And yet you say, with reference to this body, which is a disease, a cancer, an arrow, painful, an affliction: 'This is that freedom from disease, Master Gotama. This is that unbinding,' for you don't have the noble vision with which you would know freedom from disease and see unbinding."

"I'm convinced, Master Gotama, that you can teach me the Dhamma in such a way that I would know freedom from disease, that I would see unbinding."

"Māgaṇḍiya, it's just as if there were a man blind from birth who couldn't see black objects... white... blue... yellow... red... the sun or the moon. His friends, companions, & relatives would take him to a doctor. The doctor would concoct medicine for him, but in spite of the medicine his eyesight would not appear or grow clear. What do you think, Māgaṇḍiya? Would that doctor have nothing but his share of weariness & disappointment?"

"Yes, Master Gotama."

"In the same way, Māgaṇḍiya, if I were to teach you the Dhamma—'This is that freedom from disease; this is that unbinding'—and you on your part did not know freedom from disease or see unbinding, that would be wearisome for me; that would be troublesome for me."

"I'm convinced, Master Gotama, that you can teach me the Dhamma in such a way that I would know freedom from disease, that I would see unbinding."

"Māgaṇḍiya, it's just as if there were a man blind from birth who couldn't see black objects... white... blue... yellow... red... the sun or the moon. Now suppose that a certain man were to take a grimy, oil-stained rag and fool him, saying, 'Here, my good man, is a white cloth—beautiful, spotless, & clean.' The blind man would take it and put it on.

"Then his friends, companions, & relatives would take him to a doctor. The doctor would concoct medicine for him: purges from above & purges from below, ointments & counter-ointments and treatments through the nose. And thanks to the medicine his eyesight would appear & grow clear. Then together with the arising of his eyesight, he would abandon whatever passion & delight he felt for that grimy, oil-stained rag. And he would regard that man as an enemy & no friend at all, and think that he deserved to be killed. 'My gosh, how long have I been fooled, cheated, & deceived by that man & his grimy, oil-stained rag!—"Here, my good man, is a white cloth—beautiful, spotless, & clean."'

"In the same way, Māgaṇḍiya, if I were to teach you the Dhamma—'This is that freedom from Disease; this is that unbinding'—and you on your part were to know that freedom from Disease and see that unbinding, then together with the arising of your eyesight you would abandon whatever passion & delight you felt with regard for the five clinging-aggregates. And it would occur to you, 'My gosh, how long have I been fooled, cheated, & deceived by this mind! For in clinging, it was just form that I was clinging to… it was just feeling… just perception… just fabrications… just consciousness that I was clinging to. With my clinging as a requisite condition, there arises becoming… birth… aging & death… sorrow, lamentation, pains, distresses, & despairs. And thus is the origin of this entire mass of stress.'"

"I'm convinced, Master Gotama, that you can teach me the Dhamma in such a way that I might rise up from this seat cured of my blindness."

"In that case, Māgaṇḍiya, associate with people of integrity. When you associate with people of integrity, you will hear the true Dhamma. When you hear the true Dhamma, you will practice the Dhamma in accordance with the Dhamma. When you practice the Dhamma in accordance with the Dhamma, you will know & see for yourself: 'These things are diseases, cancers, arrows. And here is where diseases, cancers, & arrows cease without trace. With the cessation of my clinging comes the cessation of becoming. With the cessation of becoming comes the cessation of birth. With the cessation of birth then aging & death, sorrow, lamentation, pain, distress, & despair all cease. Such is the cessation of this entire mass of suffering & stress."

When this was said, Māgaṇḍiya the wanderer said, "Magnificent, Master Gotama! Magnificent! Just as if he were to place upright what was overturned, to reveal what was hidden, to show the way to one who was lost, or to carry a lamp into the dark so that those with eyes could see forms, in the same way has Master Gotama—through many lines of reasoning—made the Dhamma clear. I go to Master Gotama for refuge, to the Dhamma, and to the Saṅgha of monks. Let me obtain the going forth in Master Gotama's presence; let me obtain the acceptance."

"Anyone, Māgaṇḍiya, who has previously belonged to another sect and who desires the going forth & acceptance in this doctrine & discipline, must first undergo probation for four months. If, at the end of four months, the monks feel so moved, they give him the going forth & accept him into the monk's state. But I know distinctions among individuals in this matter."

"Master Gotama, if anyone who has previously belonged to another sect and desires the going forth & acceptance in this doctrine & discipline must first undergo probation for four months; and if, at the end of four months, the monks feel so moved, they give him the going forth & accept him into the monk's state; then I am willing to undergo probation for four years. If, at the end of four years, the monks feel so moved, let them give me the going forth & accept me into the monk's state."

Then Māgaṇḍiya the wanderer received the going forth & the acceptance in the Blessed One's presence. And not long after his acceptance—dwelling alone, secluded, heedful, ardent, & resolute—he in no long time reached & remained in the supreme goal of the holy life, for which clansmen rightly go forth from home into homelessness, knowing & realizing it for himself in the here & now. He knew: "Birth is ended, the holy life fulfilled, the task done. There is nothing further for the sake of this world." And thus Ven. Māgaṇḍiya became another one of the arahants.

See also: MN 13; MN 14; MN 105; SN 22:1; Sn 4:1; Dhp 203–204; Thig 13:5

78 *Muṇḍika the Contemplative*

Samaṇa-Muṇḍika Sutta

I have heard that on one occasion the Blessed One was staying near Sāvatthī in Jeta's Grove, Anāthapiṇḍika's monastery. Now on that occasion Uggāhamāna, a follower of Muṇḍika the contemplative,[1] together with a large following of about 500 wanderers, had taken up residence in the debating hall near the Tiṇḍuka tree in the single-pavilion park of Queen Mallikā. Then Pañcakaṅga the carpenter left Sāvatthī in the middle of the day to see the Blessed One, but the thought occurred to him, "Now is not the right time to see the Blessed One, for he is in seclusion. And it's not the right time to see the mind-developing monks, for they too are in seclusion. Why don't I go to the debating hall near the Tiṇḍuka tree in the single-pavilion park of Queen Mallikā to see Uggāhamāna, a follower of Muṇḍika the contemplative?" So he headed to the debating hall near the Tiṇḍuka tree in the single-pavilion park of Queen Mallikā.

Now on that occasion Uggāhamāna was sitting with his large following of wanderers, all making a great noise & racket, discussing many kinds of bestial topics of conversation: conversation about kings, robbers, & ministers of state; armies, alarms, & battles; food & drink; clothing, furniture, garlands, & scents; relatives; vehicles; villages, towns, cities, the countryside; women & heroes; the gossip of the street & the well; tales of the dead; tales of diversity, the creation of the world & of the sea; talk of whether things exist or not. Then Uggāhamāna saw Pañcakaṅga the carpenter coming from afar, and on seeing him, hushed his following: "Be quiet, good sirs. Don't make any noise. Here comes Pañcakaṅga the carpenter, a disciple of Gotama the contemplative. He is one of those disciples of Gotama the contemplative, clad in white, who lives in Sāvatthī. These people are fond of quietude, trained in quietude, and speak in praise of quietude. Maybe, if he perceives our group as quiet, he will consider it worth his while to come our way." So the wanderers fell silent.

Then Pañcakaṅga went to Uggāhamāna and, on arrival, greeted him courteously. After an exchange of friendly greetings & courtesies, he sat down to one side. As he was sitting there, Uggāhamāna said to him, "I describe an individual endowed with four qualities as being consummate in what is skillful, foremost in what is skillful, an invincible contemplative attained to the highest attainments. Which four? There is the case where he does no evil action with his body, speaks no evil speech, resolves on no evil resolve, and maintains himself with no evil means of livelihood. An individual endowed with these four qualities I describe as being consummate in what is skillful, foremost in what is skillful, an invincible contemplative attained to the highest attainments."

Then Pañcakaṅga neither delighted in Uggāhamāna's words nor did he scorn them. Expressing neither delight nor scorn, he got up from his seat & left, thinking, "I will learn the meaning of this statement in the Blessed One's presence."

Then he went to the Blessed One and, on arrival, after bowing down to him, sat to one side. As he was sitting there, he told the Blessed One the entire conversation he had had with Uggāhamāna.

When this was said, the Blessed One said to Pañcakaṅga: "In that case, carpenter, then according to Uggāhamāna's words a stupid baby boy, lying on its back, is consummate in what is skillful, foremost in what is skillful, an invincible contemplative attained to the highest attainments. For even the thought 'body' doesn't occur to a stupid baby boy lying on its back, so from where would it do any evil action with its body, aside from a little kicking? Even the thought 'speech' doesn't occur to it, so from where would it speak any evil speech, aside from a little crying? Even the thought 'resolve' doesn't occur to it, so from where would it resolve on any evil resolve, aside from a little bad temper? Even the thought 'livelihood' doesn't occur to it, so from where would it maintain itself with any evil means of livelihood, aside from its mother's milk? So, according to Uggāhamāna's words, a stupid baby boy, lying on its back is consummate in what is skillful, foremost in what is skillful, an invincible contemplative attained to the highest attainments.

"If an individual is endowed with these four qualities, I do not describe him as consummate in what is skillful, foremost in what is skillful, an invincible contemplative attained to the highest attainments. Rather, he stands on the same level as a stupid baby boy lying on its back. Which four? There is the case where he does no evil action with his body, speaks no evil speech, resolves on no evil resolve, and maintains himself with no evil means of livelihood. If an individual is endowed with these four qualities, I do not describe him as consummate in what is skillful, foremost in what is skillful, an invincible contemplative attained to the highest attainments. Rather, he stands on the same level as a stupid baby boy lying on its back.

"An individual endowed with *ten* qualities is one whom I describe as being consummate in what is skillful, foremost in what is skillful, an invincible contemplative attained to the highest attainments. With regard to that point, one should know that 'These are unskillful habits,' I say. With regard to that point, one should know that 'That is the cause of unskillful habits' ... 'Here unskillful habits cease without trace' ... 'This sort of practice is the practice leading to the cessation of unskillful habits,' I say.

"With regard to that point, one should know that 'These are skillful habits' ... 'That is the cause of skillful habits' ... 'Here skillful habits cease without trace' ... 'This sort of practice is the practice leading to the cessation of skillful habits,' I say.

"With regard to that point, one should know that 'These are unskillful resolves' ... 'That is the cause of unskillful resolves' ... 'Here unskillful resolves cease without trace' ... 'This sort of practice is the practice leading to the cessation of unskillful resolves' I say.

"With regard to that point, one should know that 'These are skillful resolves' ... 'That is the cause of skillful resolves' ... 'Here skillful resolves cease without trace' ... 'This sort of practice is the practice leading to the cessation of skillful resolves,' I say.

"Now what are unskillful habits? Unskillful bodily actions, unskillful verbal actions, evil means of livelihood. These are called unskillful habits. What is the cause of unskillful habits? Their cause is stated, and they are said to be mind-caused. Which mind?—for the mind has many modes & permutations. Any mind with passion, aversion or delusion: That is the cause of unskillful habits. Now where do unskillful habits cease without trace? Their cessation has been stated: There is the case where a monk abandons wrong bodily conduct & develops right bodily conduct, abandons wrong verbal conduct & develops right verbal conduct, abandons wrong livelihood & maintains his life with right livelihood. This is where unskillful habits cease without trace. And what sort of practice is the practice leading to the cessation of unskillful habits? There is the case where a monk generates desire, endeavors, arouses persistence, upholds & exerts his intent for the sake of the non-arising of evil, unskillful qualities that have not yet arisen... for the sake of the abandoning of evil, unskillful qualities that have arisen... for the sake of the arising of skillful qualities that have not yet arisen... (and) for the maintenance, non-confusion, increase, plenitude, development & culmination of skillful qualities that have arisen. This sort of practice is the practice leading to the cessation of unskillful habits.

"And what are skillful habits? Skillful bodily actions, skillful verbal actions, purity of livelihood. These are called skillful habits. What is the cause of skillful habits? Their cause, too, has been stated, and they are said to be mind-caused. Which mind?—for the mind has many modes & permutations. Any mind without passion, without aversion, without delusion: That is the cause of skillful habits. Now where do skillful habits cease without trace? Their cessation, too, has been stated: There is the case where a monk is virtuous, but not fashioned of virtue.[2] He discerns, as it has come to be, the awareness-release & discernment-release where his skillful habits cease without trace. And what sort of practice is the practice leading to the cessation of skillful habits? There is the case where a monk generates desire… for the sake of the non-arising of evil, unskillful qualities that have not yet arisen… for the sake of the abandoning of evil, unskillful qualities that have arisen… for the sake of the arising of skillful qualities that have not yet arisen… (and) for the… development & culmination of skillful qualities that have arisen. This sort of practice is the practice leading to the cessation of skillful habits.

"And what are unskillful resolves? Being resolved on sensuality, on ill will, on harmfulness. These are called unskillful resolves. What is the cause of unskillful resolves? Their cause, too, has been stated, and they are said to be perception-caused. Which perception?—for perception has many modes & permutations. Any sensuality-perception, ill will-perception or harmfulness-perception: That is the cause of unskillful resolves. Now where do unskillful resolves cease without trace? Their cessation, too, has been stated: There is the case where a monk, quite secluded from sensuality, secluded from unskillful qualities, enters & remains in the first jhāna: rapture & pleasure born of seclusion, accompanied by directed thought & evaluation. This is where unskillful resolves cease without trace. And what sort of practice is the practice leading to the cessation of unskillful resolves? There is the case where a monk generates desire… for the sake of the non-arising of evil, unskillful qualities that have not yet arisen… for the sake of the abandoning of evil, unskillful qualities that have arisen… for the sake of the arising of skillful qualities that have not yet arisen… (and) for the… development & culmination of skillful qualities that have arisen. This sort of practice is the practice leading to the cessation of unskillful resolves.

"And what are skillful resolves? Being resolved on renunciation [freedom from sensuality], on non-ill will, on harmlessness. These are called skillful resolves. What is the cause of skillful resolves?

Their cause, too, has been stated, and they are said to be perception-caused. Which perception?—for perception has many modes & permutations. Any renunciation-perception, non-ill will-perception or harmlessness-perception: That is the cause of skillful resolves. Now where do skillful resolves cease without trace? Their cessation, too, has been stated: There is the case where a monk, with the stilling of directed thoughts & evaluations, enters & remains in the second jhāna: rapture & pleasure born of concentration, unification of awareness free from directed thought & evaluation—internal assurance. This is where skillful resolves cease without trace. And what sort of practice is the practice leading to the cessation of skillful resolves? There is the case where a monk generates desire...for the sake of the non-arising of evil, unskillful qualities that have not yet arisen...for the sake of the abandoning of evil, unskillful qualities that have arisen... for the sake of the arising of skillful qualities that have not yet arisen... (and) for the... development & culmination of skillful qualities that have arisen. This sort of practice is the practice leading to the cessation of skillful resolves.

"Now, an individual endowed with which ten qualities is one whom I describe as being consummate in what is skillful, foremost in what is skillful, an invincible contemplative attained to the highest attainments? One endowed with the right view of one beyond training, the right resolve of one beyond training, the right speech... the right action... the right livelihood... the right effort... the right mindfulness... the right concentration... the right knowledge... the right release of one beyond training. An individual endowed with these ten qualities is one whom I describe as being consummate in what is skillful, foremost in what is skillful, an invincible contemplative attained to the highest attainments."

That is what the Blessed One said. Gratified, Pañcakaṅga the carpenter delighted in the Blessed One's words.

NOTES

1. This can also mean "the shaven-headed contemplative," in which case Uggāhamāna might have belonged to one of the Jain sects.

2. The Pali here is: *no ca sīla-mayo.* According to the Commentary, this means that he does not regard virtue as the consummation of the path. It may also mean that he does not define himself by his virtue. This term is apparently related to the state called *atammayatā,* or non-fashioning. On this topic, see *The Wings to Awakening,* especially the introduction to section II/B and passage §179.

See also: MN 101; MN 113; MN 117; MN 152

82 About Raṭṭhapāla

Raṭṭhapāla Sutta

I have heard that on one occasion the Blessed One, on a wandering tour among the Kurus with a large Saṅgha of monks, arrived at Thullakoṭṭhita, a town of the Kurus. The brahmans & householders of Thullakoṭṭhita heard it said, "Gotama the contemplative— the son of the Sakyans, having gone forth from the Sakyan clan—has arrived at Kesaputta. And of that Master Gotama this fine reputation has spread: 'He is indeed a Blessed One, worthy & rightly self-awakened, consummate in clear-knowing & conduct, well-gone, an expert with regard to the cosmos, unexcelled trainer of people fit to be tamed, teacher of devas & human beings, awakened, blessed. He makes known—having realized it through direct knowledge—this world with its devas, Māras, & Brahmās, this generation with its contemplatives & brahmans, its rulers & commonfolk; he explains the Dhamma admirable in the beginning, admirable in the middle, admirable in the end; he expounds the holy life both in its particulars & in its essence, entirely perfect, surpassingly pure. It's good to see such a worthy one.'"

So the brahmans & householders of Thullakoṭṭhita went to the Blessed One. On arrival, some of them bowed down to the Blessed One and sat to one side. Some of them exchanged courteous greetings with him and, after an exchange of friendly greetings & courtesies, sat to one side. Some of them sat to one side having saluted him with their hands palm-to-palm over their hearts. Some of them sat to one side having announced their name & clan. Some of them sat to one side in silence. As they were sitting there, the Blessed One instructed, urged, roused, and encouraged them with a talk on Dhamma.

Now at that time a clansman named Raṭṭhapāla, the son of the leading clan in that same Thullakoṭṭhita, was sitting in that assembly. The thought occurred to him, "As I understand the Dhamma taught by the Blessed One, it's not easy, living at home, to practice the holy life totally perfect, totally pure, a polished shell. What if I, having shaved off my hair & beard and putting on the ochre robe, were to go forth from the household life into homelessness?"

Then the brahmans & householders of Thullakoṭṭhita, having been instructed, urged, roused, & encouraged by the Blessed One's talk on Dhamma, delighted & rejoiced in his words. Rising from their seats, bowing down to him, they left, keeping him on their right.

Then Raṭṭhapāla, not long after the brahmans & householders of Thullakoṭṭhita had left, approached the Blessed One and, on arrival, said to him, "As I understand the Dhamma taught by the Blessed One, it's not easy, living at home, to practice the holy life totally perfect, totally pure, a polished shell. Lord, I want—having shaved off my hair & beard and putting on the ochre robe—to go forth from the household life into homelessness. May I receive the going-forth in the Blessed One's presence? May I receive acceptance?"

"Do you have your parents' permission, Raṭṭhapāla, to go forth from the household life into homelessness?"

"No, lord, I haven't."

"Raṭṭhapāla, Tathāgatas do not give the going-forth to anyone who doesn't have his parents' permission."

"Lord, I will do what needs to be done so that my parents will give their permission for me to go forth from the household life into homelessness."

Then Raṭṭhapāla, rising from his seat, bowing down to the Blessed One and keeping him on his right, went to his parents and said, "Mom, Dad, as I understand the Dhamma taught by the Blessed One, it's not easy, living at home, to practice the holy life totally perfect, totally pure, a polished shell. I want—having shaved off my hair & beard and putting on the ochre robe—to go forth from the household life into homelessness. Please give me your permission to go forth from the household life into homelessness."

When this was said, Raṭṭhapāla's parents said to him, "Raṭṭhapāla, dear, you are our only son, dear & beloved, raised in comfort, brought up in comfort. You know nothing of suffering. Eat, drink, & enjoy yourself. While eating, drinking, & looking after yourself, you may enjoy yourself by indulging in sensual pleasures & making merit. We don't give our permission for you to go forth from the household life into homelessness.[1] Even with your death we would not want to be separated from you, so how could we—while you're alive—give our permission for you to go forth from the household life into homelessness?"

A second time… A third time, Raṭṭhapāla said to his parents, "Mom, Dad, as I understand the Dhamma taught by the Blessed One, it's not easy, living at home, to practice the holy life totally perfect, totally pure, a polished shell. I want—having shaved off my hair & beard and putting on the ochre robe—to go forth from the household life into homelessness. Please give me your permission to go forth from the household life into homelessness."

A third time, Raṭṭhapāla's parents said to him, "Raṭṭhapāla, dear, you are our only son, dear & beloved, raised in comfort, brought up in comfort. You know nothing of suffering. Eat, drink, & enjoy yourself. While eating, drinking, & looking after yourself, you may enjoy yourself by indulging in sensual pleasures & making merit. We don't give our permission for you to go forth from the household life into homelessness.[1] Even with your death we would not want to be separated from you, so how could we—while you're alive—give our permission for you to go forth from the household life into homelessness?"

Then Raṭṭhapāla, not getting his parents' permission to go forth from the household life into homelessness, lay down right there on the bare floor, (saying,) "Here will be my death or my going-forth." And he went without food for one day… two days… three days, four… five… six days. He went without food for seven days.[2]

His parents said to him, "Raṭṭhapāla, dear, you are our only son, dear & beloved, raised in comfort, brought up in comfort. You know nothing of suffering. Get up, dear. Eat, drink, & enjoy yourself. While eating, drinking, & looking after yourself, you may enjoy yourself by indulging in sensual pleasures & making merit. We don't give our permission for you to go forth from the household life into homelessness. Even with your death we would not want to be separated from you, so how could we—while you're alive—give our permission for you to go forth from the household life into homelessness?"

When this was said, Raṭṭhapāla remained silent.

A second time… A third time, Raṭṭhapāla's parents said to him, "Raṭṭhapāla, dear, you are our only son, dear & beloved, raised in comfort, brought up in comfort. You know nothing of suffering. Get up, dear. Eat, drink, & enjoy yourself. While eating, drinking, & looking after yourself, you may enjoy yourself by indulging in sensual pleasures & making merit. We don't give our permission for you to go forth from the household life into homelessness. Even with your death we would not want to be separated from you, so how could we—while you're alive—give our permission for you to go forth from the household life into homelessness?"

A third time, Raṭṭhapāla remained silent.

Then Raṭṭhapāla's parents went to his friends and said to them, "My dears, Raṭṭhapāla has lain down on the bare floor, (saying,) 'Here will be my death or my going-forth.' Please, dears, go to Raṭṭhapāla and say to him, 'Friend Raṭṭhapāla, you are your parents' only son... Get up, friend Raṭṭhapāla. Eat, drink, & enjoy yourself... How could your parents—while you're alive—give their permission for you to go forth from the household life into homelessness?'"[3]

So Raṭṭhapāla's friends went to Raṭṭhapāla and, on arrival, said to him, "Friend Raṭṭhapāla, you are your parents' only son... Get up, friend Raṭṭhapāla. Eat, drink, & enjoy yourself... How could your parents—while you're alive—give their permission for you to go forth from the household life into homelessness?"

When this was said, Raṭṭhapāla remained silent.

A second time... A third time, his friends said to him, "Friend Raṭṭhapāla, you are your parents' only son... Get up, friend Raṭṭhapāla. Eat, drink, & enjoy yourself... How could your parents—while you're alive—give their permission for you to go forth from the household life into homelessness?"

A third time, Raṭṭhapāla remained silent.

So Raṭṭhapāla's friends went to his parents and, on arrival, said to them, "Mom, Dad, Raṭṭhapāla is lying there on the bare floor, (having said,) 'Here will be my death or my going-forth.' If you don't give him your permission to go forth from the household life into homelessness, right there will be his death. But if you do give him your permission... then even when he has gone forth, you will see him. And if he does not enjoy going forth from the household life into homelessness, where else will he go? He'll return right here. So please give him permission to go forth from the household life into homelessness."

"Then, dears, we give our permission for Raṭṭhapāla to go forth from the household life into homelessness. But when he has gone forth, he should visit his parents."

Then Raṭṭhapāla's friends went to him and said, "Get up, Raṭṭhapāla.[4] Your parents give their permission for you to go forth from the household life into homelessness. But when you have gone forth, you should visit your parents."

Then Raṭṭhapāla got up and, on regaining strength, went to the Blessed One. On arrival, having bowed down to him, he sat to one side. As he was sitting there, he said to the Blessed One, "I have received my parents' permission, lord, to go forth from the household life into homelessness. May the Blessed One give me the going-forth!"

Then Raṭṭhapāla the clansman obtained the going-forth in the Blessed One's presence, he obtained the acceptance. And not long after his acceptance, one half month after his acceptance, the Blessed One–having stayed at Thullakoṭṭhita as long as he liked—set out wandering to Sāvatthī. Wandering by stages, he eventually arrived at Sāvatthī. There he lived near Sāvatthī in Jeta's Grove, Anāthapiṇḍika's monastery.

As for Ven. Raṭṭhapāla—dwelling alone, secluded, heedful, ardent, & resolute—he in no long time reached & remained in the supreme goal of the holy life, for which clansmen rightly go forth from home into homelessness, knowing & realizing it for himself in the here & now. He knew: "Birth is ended, the holy life fulfilled, the task done. There is nothing further for the sake of this world." And thus Ven. Raṭṭhapāla became another one of the arahants.

Then Ven. Raṭṭhapāla went to the Blessed One and, on arrival, having bowed down to him, sat to one side. As he was sitting there he said to the Blessed One, "Lord, I want to visit my parents, if you give me permission." Then the Blessed One, encompassing Ven. Raṭṭhapāla's awareness with his awareness, considered & understood, "Ven. Raṭṭhapāla is incapable of leaving the training and reverting to the lower life." So he said to him, "Now is the time, Raṭṭhapāla, for you to do as you see fit."

Then Ven. Raṭṭhapāla, rising from his seat, bowing down to the Blessed One and keeping him on his right, (left). Putting his lodgings in order and, carrying his bowl & robes, set out wandering toward Thullakoṭṭhita. Wandering by stages, he eventually arrived at Thullakoṭṭhita. There he stayed in Thullakoṭṭhita in King Koravya's Migācīra (garden). Then, early in the morning—having adjusted his under robe and carrying his bowl & outer robe—he went into Thullakoṭṭhita for alms. As he went for alms from house to house in Thullakoṭṭhita, he came to his own father's house.

Now at that time Ven. Raṭṭhapāla's father was in the middle door-porch having his hair combed. He saw Ven. Raṭṭhapāla coming from afar and, on seeing him, said, "It was by these shaven-headed contemplatives that our only son, dear & beloved, was made to go forth!" So Ven. Raṭṭhapāla—instead of receiving a gift or a polite refusal at his own father's house—got nothing but abuse.

Just then a slavewoman belonging to one of his relatives was about to throw away some day-old porridge. So Ven. Raṭṭhapāla said to her, "Sister, if that is to be thrown away, pour it here into my bowl." While she was pouring the day-old porridge into this bowl, she recognized his hands, feet, & voice. So she went to his mother and said, "May it please you to know, my lady, that master-son Raṭṭhapāla has arrived."

"Hey, if what you say is true, I give you your freedom!"

Then Ven. Raṭṭhapāla's mother went to his father and said, "May it please you to know, householder, that they say the clansman Raṭṭhapāla has arrived."

Now at that time Ven. Raṭṭhapāla was sitting by a wall, eating the day-old porridge. His father went to him and said, "Raṭṭhapāla, my dear, isn't there... What? You're eating day-old porridge? Don't you have your own home to go to?"

"How could we have a home, householder? We have gone forth from the household life into homelessness. We are homeless, householder. We went to your house, but—instead of receiving a gift or a polite refusal—we got nothing but abuse."

"Come, dear Raṭṭhapāla. Let's go home."

"Enough, householder. My meal for today is finished."

"In that case, dear Raṭṭhapāla, acquiesce to the meal for tomorrow."

So Ven. Raṭṭhapāla acquiesced in silence.

Understanding Ven. Raṭṭhapāla's acquiescence, his father went to his house and, having the floor smeared with fresh cow dung, had a great heap of gold & silver made, two great heaps made—one of gold, one of silver—so large that a man standing on the near side could not see a man standing on the far side, just as a man standing on the far side could not see a man standing on the near. Hiding them behind screens, he set out a seat between them, surrounded by a curtain.[5] Addressing Ven. Raṭṭhapāla's former wives, he said to them, "Come, daughters-in-law. Adorn yourself in the ornaments that our son, Raṭṭhapāla, used to find dear & loveable."

Then, as the night was ending, Ven. Raṭṭhapāla's father had exquisite staple & non-staple foods prepared in his own house and had the time announced to Ven. Raṭṭhapāla: "It's time, dear Raṭṭhapāla. The meal is ready."

Then, early in the morning—having adjusted his under robe and carrying his bowl & outer robe—Ven. Raṭṭhapāla went to his father's house and, on arrival, sat down on the seat made ready. Then his father revealed the heap of gold & silver, said to him, "This, my dear Raṭṭhapāla, is your mother's inheritance. The other is your fathers; the other, your grandfather's—(enough that) you can enjoy wealth and make merit. Come, my dear Raṭṭhapāla. Leave the training and revert to the lower life. Enjoy wealth and make merit!"

"Householder, if you'd do as I say, you would have this heap of gold & silver loaded on carts and hauled away to be dumped midstream in the river Ganges. Why is that? This (wealth) will be the cause of your sorrow, lamentation, pain, distress, & despair."

Then, clasping each of his feet, Ven. Raṭṭhapāla's former wives said to him, "What are they like, dear master-son: those nymphs for whose sake you lead the holy life?"

"Sisters, we don't lead the holy life for the sake of nymphs."

"'Sisters' he calls us!" And they fell down right there in a faint.

Then Ven. Raṭṭhapāla said to his father, "Householder, if there's food to be given, then give it. Don't harass us."

"Eat, then, my dear Raṭṭhapāla. The meal is ready."

So, with his own hands, Ven. Raṭṭhapāla's father served and satisfied him with exquisite staple and non-staple foods. When he had finished his meal and rinsed his bowl & hands, Ven. Raṭṭhapāla stood up and recited these verses:

> Look at the image beautified,
> a heap of festering wounds, shored up:
> ill, but the object
>   of many resolves,
> where there is nothing
>   lasting or sure.[6]
>
> Look at the form beautified
> with earrings & gems:
>   a skeleton wrapped in skin,
>   made attractive with clothes.
>
> Feet reddened with henna,
> a face smeared with powder:
>   enough to deceive a fool,
>   but not a seeker for the further shore.
>
> Hair plaited in eight pleats,
> eyes smeared with unguent:
>   enough to deceive a fool,
>   but not a seeker for the further shore.
>
> Like a newly painted unguent pot—
> a putrid body adorned:
>   enough to deceive a fool,
>   but not a seeker for the further shore.
>
> The hunter set out the snares
> but the deer didn't go near the trap.
> Having eaten the bait,
>   I go,
>   leaving the hunters
>   to weep.

After reciting these verses while standing, Ven. Raṭṭhapāla went to King Koravya's Migācīra. On arrival, he sat down in the shade of a tree for the day's abiding.

Then King Koravya said to his gamekeeper: "Clean up the Migācīra pleasure garden. I am going there to see the beautiful grounds."

"As you say, your majesty," the gamekeeper responded to the king. As he was cleaning up Migācīra he saw Ven. Raṭṭhapāla sitting in the shade of a tree for the day's abiding. On seeing him, he went to the king and said, "Migācīra has been cleaned up for you, your majesty. And the clansman Raṭṭhapāla—the son of the leading clan in this Thullakoṭṭhita, of whom you have often spoken highly—is there, sitting in the shade of a tree for the day's abiding."

"In that case, my dear gamekeeper, never mind about the pleasure garden for today. I am now going to pay my respects to that Master Raṭṭhapāla."

Then, saying, "Give away all the staple and non-staple foods that have been prepared," King Koravya had auspicious vehicles harnessed. Mounting an auspicious vehicle he set out from Thullakoṭṭhita accompanied by other auspicious vehicles in full royal pomp to see Ven. Raṭṭhapāla. Going as far by vehicle as the ground would permit, he dismounted and went to Ven. Raṭṭhapāla, accompanied by many eminent members of his court. On arrival, he exchanged courteous greetings with Ven. Raṭṭhapāla. After an exchange of friendly greetings & courtesies, he stood to one side. As he was standing there, he said to Ven. Raṭṭhapāla, "May Master Raṭṭhapāla sit here on the elephant rug."

"Never mind, great king. You sit there. I am sitting on my own seat."

So King Koravya sat down on the seat prepared. As he was sitting there, he said to Ven. Raṭṭhapāla, "There are cases where, having suffered these four kinds of loss, men shave off their hair & beard, put on the ochre robe, and go forth from the home life into homelessness. Which four? Loss through aging, loss through illness, loss of wealth, & loss of relatives.... But Master Raṭṭhapāla has suffered none of these. What did he know or see or hear that Master Raṭṭhapāla went forth from the home life into homelessness?"

"Great king, there are four Dhamma summaries stated by the Blessed One who knows & sees, worthy & rightly self-awakened. Having known & seen & heard them, I went forth from the home life into homelessness. Which four?

"'The world[7] is swept away. It does not endure': This is the first Dhamma summary stated by the Blessed One who knows & sees, worthy & rightly self-awakened. Having known & seen & heard it, I went forth from the home life into homelessness.

"'The world is without shelter, without protector': This is the second Dhamma summary....

"'The world is without ownership. One has to pass on, leaving everything behind': This is the third Dhamma summary....

"'The world is insufficient, insatiable, a slave to craving': This is the fourth Dhamma summary....

"These, great king, are the four Dhamma summaries stated by the Blessed One who knows & sees, worthy & rightly self-awakened. Having known & seen & heard them, I went forth from the home life into homelessness."

"Master Raṭṭhapāla, you say, 'The world is swept away. It does not endure.' Now how is the meaning of this statement to be understood?"

"What do you think, great king? When you were twenty or twenty-five years old—an expert elephant rider, an expert horseman, an expert charioteer, an expert archer, an expert swordsman—were you strong in arm & strong in thigh, fit, & seasoned in warfare?"

"Yes, Master Raṭṭhapāla, when I was twenty or twenty-five years old... I was strong in arm & strong in thigh, fit, & seasoned in warfare. It was as if I had supernormal power. I do not see anyone who was my equal in strength."

"And what do you think, great king? Are you even now as strong in arm & strong in thigh, as fit, & as seasoned in warfare?"

"Not at all, Master Raṭṭhapāla. I'm now aged, old, elderly, advanced in years, having come to the last stage of life, 80 years old. Sometimes, thinking, 'I will place my foot here,' I place it somewhere else."

"It was in reference to this, great king, that the Blessed One who knows & sees, worthy & rightly self-awakened, said: 'The world is swept away. It does not endure.' Having known & seen & heard this, I went forth from the home life into homelessness."

"It's amazing, Master Raṭṭhapāla. It's astounding, how well that has been said by the Blessed One who knows & sees, worthy & rightly self-awakened: 'The world is swept away. It does not endure.' For the world really is swept away, Master Raṭṭhapāla. It does not endure.

"Now, in this royal court there are elephant troops & cavalry & chariot troops & infantry that will serve to defend us from dangers. And yet you say, 'The world is without shelter, without protector.' How is the meaning of this statement to be understood?"

"What do you think, great king? Do you have any recurring illness?"

"Yes, Master Raṭṭhapāla, I have a recurring wind-illness.[8] Sometimes my friends & advisors, relatives & blood-kinsmen, stand around me saying, 'This time King Koravya will die. This time King Koravya will die.'"

"And what do you think, great king? Can you say to your friends & advisors, relatives & blood-kinsmen, 'My friends & advisors, relatives & blood-kinsmen are commanded: all of you who are present, share out this pain so that I may feel less pain'? Or do you have to feel that pain all alone?"

"Oh, no, Master Raṭṭhapāla, I can't say to my friends & advisors, relatives & blood-kinsmen, 'All of you who are present, share out this pain so that I may feel less pain.' I have to feel that pain all alone."

"It was in reference to this, great king, that the Blessed One who knows & sees, worthy & rightly self-awakened, said: 'The world is without shelter, without protector.' Having known & seen & heard this, I went forth from the home life into homelessness."

"It's amazing, Master Raṭṭhapāla. It's astounding, how well that has been said by the Blessed One who knows & sees, worthy & rightly self-awakened: 'The world is without shelter, without protector.' For the world really is without shelter, Master Raṭṭhapāla. It is without protector.

"Now, in this royal court there is a great deal of gold & silver stashed away underground & in attic vaults. And yet you say, 'The world is without ownership. One has to pass on, leaving everything behind.' How is the meaning of this statement to be understood?"

"What do you think, great king? As you now enjoy yourself endowed & replete with the pleasures of the five senses, can you say, 'Even in the afterlife I will enjoy myself in the same way, endowed & replete with the very same pleasures of the five senses'? Or will this wealth fall to others, while you pass on in accordance with your kamma?"

"Oh, no, Master Raṭṭhapāla, I can't say, 'Even in the afterlife I will enjoy myself in the same way, endowed & replete with the very same pleasures of the five senses.' This wealth will fall to others, while I pass on in accordance with my kamma."

"It was in reference to this, great king, that the Blessed One who knows & sees, worthy & rightly self-awakened, said: 'The world is without ownership. One has to pass on, leaving everything behind.' Having known & seen & heard this, I went forth from the home life into homelessness."

"It's amazing, Master Raṭṭhapāla. It's astounding, how well that has been said by the Blessed One who knows & sees, worthy & rightly self-awakened: 'The world is without ownership. One has to pass on, leaving everything behind.' For the world really is without ownership, Master Raṭṭhapāla. One has to pass on, leaving everything behind.

"Now, Master Raṭṭhapāla, you say, 'The world is insufficient, insatiable, a slave to craving.' How is the meaning of this statement to be understood?"

"What do you think, great king? Do you now rule over the prosperous country of Kuru?"

"That is so, Master Raṭṭhapāla. I rule over the prosperous country of Kuru."

"What do you think, great king? Suppose a trustworthy, reliable man of yours were to come to you from the east. On arrival he would say to you, 'May it please your majesty to know, I have come from the east. There I saw a great country, powerful & prosperous, populous & crowded with people. Plenty are the elephant troops there, plenty the cavalry troops, chariot troops, & infantry troops. Plenty is the ivory-work there, plenty the gold & silver, both worked & unworked. Plenty are the women for the taking. It is possible, with the forces you now have, to conquer it. Conquer it, great king!' What would you do?"

"Having conquered it, Master Raṭṭhapāla, I would rule over it."

"Now what do you think, great king? Suppose a trustworthy, reliable man of yours were to come to you from the west... the north... the south... the other side of the ocean. On arrival he would say to you, 'May it please your majesty to know, I have come from the other side of the ocean. There I saw a great country, powerful & prosperous, populous & crowded with people. Plenty are the elephant troops there, plenty the cavalry troops, chariot troops, & infantry troops. Plenty is the ivory-work there, plenty the gold & silver, both worked & unworked. Plenty are the women for the taking. It is possible, with the forces you now have, to conquer it. Conquer it, great king!' What would you do?"

"Having conquered it, Master Raṭṭhapāla, I would rule over it, too."

"It was in reference to this, great king, that the Blessed One who knows & sees, worthy & rightly self-awakened, said: 'The world is insufficient, insatiable, a slave to craving.' Having known & seen & heard this, I went forth from the home life into homelessness."

"It's amazing, Master Raṭṭhapāla. It's astounding, how well that has been said by the Blessed One who knows & sees, worthy &

rightly self-awakened: 'The world is insufficient, insatiable, a slave to craving.' For the world really is insufficient, Master Raṭṭhapāla. It's insatiable, a slave to craving."

That is what Ven. Raṭṭhapāla said. Having said that, he further said this:

I see in the world
    people with wealth
who, from delusion,
    don't make a gift
    of the treasure they've gained.
Greedy, they stash it away,
hoping for even more
sensual pleasures.

A king who, by force,
has conquered the world
and rules over the Earth
to the edge of the sea,
dissatisfied with the ocean's near shore,
    longs for the ocean's
    far shore as well.

Kings & others
    —plenty of people—
go to death with craving
    unabated. Unsated,
they leave the body behind,
having not had enough
of the world's sensual pleasures.

One's relatives weep
& pull out their hair.
'Oh woe, our loved one is dead,' they cry.
Carrying him off,
wrapped in a piece of cloth,
they place him
    on a pyre,
    then set him on fire.

So he burns, poked with sticks,
in just one piece of cloth,
leaving all his possessions behind.
They are not shelters for one who has died—
    not relatives,

friends,
or companions.

His heirs take over his wealth,
while the being goes on,
in line with his kamma.
No wealth at all
follows the dead one—
not children, wives,
dominion, or riches.

Long life
can't be gotten with wealth,
nor aging
warded off with treasure.
The wise say this life
is next to nothing—
impermanent,
subject to change.

The rich & the poor
touch the touch of Death.
The foolish & wise
are touched by it, too.
But while fools lie as if slain by their folly,
the wise don't tremble
when touched by the touch.

Thus the discernment by which
one attains to mastery,
is better than wealth—
for those who haven't reached mastery
go from becomings to becomings,
out of delusion,
doing bad deeds.

One goes to a womb
& to the next world,
falling into the wandering on
—one thing
after another—
while those of weak discernment,
trusting in one,
also go to a womb
& to the next world.

Just as an evil thief
caught at the break-in
    is destroyed
    by his own act,
so evil people
—after dying, in the next world—
    are destroyed
    by their own acts.

Sensual pleasures—
    variegated,
    enticing,
    sweet—
in various ways disturb the mind.
Seeing the drawbacks in sensual objects:
that's why, O king, I went forth.

Just like fruits, people fall
    —young & old—
at the break-up of the body.
Knowing this, O king,
    I went forth.
The contemplative life is better
        for sure.

NOTES

1. The preceding three sentences appear in this location only in the Thai edition of the Canon, although they appear below in all editions of the Canon.

2. This reference to the number of days Raṭṭhapāla went without food appears only in the Thai edition of the Canon.

3. This paragraph is not in the Thai edition of the Canon.

4. This first sentence in quotation marks is not in the Thai edition of the Canon.

5. This passage in the Thai edition of the Canon is much more elaborate than the corresponding passage in other editions of the Canon. The other editions mention simply that the father went home and had a heap of gold & silver made and concealed with a screen. The detail of the height of the heaps seems to have been adopted from the Commentary, for the commentators—in discussing this passage—feel called upon to explain how tall the piles were. If that detail had been in the original Pali, they wouldn't have had to supply it. As for the two heaps,

that detail seems required by the later passage where Ven. Raṭṭhapāla's father points out three separate inheritances, although that passage—as indicated in the translation—mentions "heap" in the singular.

Apparently there were some discrepancies in the original discourse that subsequent editors tried to correct, but it's hard to reach a definitive conclusion as to which version is closer to the original. On the one hand, it might be that the two extra heaps were mentioned in the original, but later deleted in some editions to bring the description in line with the fact that the later passage mentions "heap" in the singular; on the other hand, it might be that the original described the father making one heap, and the editors later amended the passage to account for his later reference to three inheritances.

6. This verse is identical with Dhp 147.

7. For the meaning of the word "world" in this discourse, see SN 35:82.

8. In ancient Indian medicine, a variety of illnesses—such as indigestion, sharp pains running through the body, etc.—were said to be caused by an imbalance of the wind-property *(vāyo-dhātu)* in the body.

See also: MN 13; MN 14; MN 54; SN 3:25; SN 4:20; SN 12:65; AN 3:39; Ud 2:10; Sn 3:8; Sn 4:6; Sn 4:7; Thag 6:13

86 *About Aṅgulimāla*

Aṅgulimāla Sutta

I have heard that on one occasion the Blessed One was staying near Sāvatthī in Jeta's Grove, Anāthapiṇḍika's monastery. And at that time in King Pasenadi's realm there was a bandit named Aṅgulimāla: brutal, bloody-handed, devoted to killing & slaying, showing no mercy to living beings. He turned villages into non-villages, towns into non-towns, settled countryside into unsettled countryside. Having repeatedly killed human beings, he wore a garland *[māla]* made of fingers *[aṅguli].*

Then the Blessed One, early in the morning, having adjusted his under robe and carrying his bowl & outer robe, went into Sāvatthī for alms. Having gone for alms in Sāvatthī and returning from his alms round after his meal, he set his lodging in order. Carrying his bowl & robe, he went along the road to where Aṅgulimāla was staying. Cowherds, shepherds, & farmers saw him going along the road to where Aṅgulimāla was staying, and on seeing him said to him, "Don't go along that road, contemplative, for on that road is Aṅgulimāla: brutal, bloody-handed, devoted to killing & slaying, showing no mercy to living beings. He has turned villages into non-villages, towns into non-towns, settled countryside into unsettled countryside. Having repeatedly killed human beings, he wears a garland made of fingers. Groups of ten, twenty, thirty, & forty men have gone along that road, and even they have fallen into Aṅgulimāla's hands." When this was said, the Blessed One kept going in silence.

A second time.... A third time, cowherds, shepherds, & farmers said to the Blessed One, "Don't go along that road, contemplative.... Groups of ten, twenty, thirty, & forty men have gone along that road, and even they have fallen into Aṅgulimāla's hands." When this was said, the Blessed One kept going in silence.

Then Aṅgulimāla saw the Blessed One coming from afar and on seeing him, this thought occurred to him: "Isn't it amazing! Isn't it astounding! Groups of ten, twenty, thirty, & forty men have gone along this road, and even they have fallen into my hands, and yet now this contemplative comes attacking, as it were, alone and without a companion. Why don't I kill him?" So Aṅgulimāla, taking up his sword & shield, buckling on his bow & quiver, followed right behind the Blessed One.

Then the Blessed One willed a feat of psychic power such that Aṅgulimāla, though running with all his might, could not catch up with the Blessed One walking at normal pace. Then the thought occurred to Aṅgulimāla: "Isn't it amazing! Isn't it astounding! In the past I've chased & seized even a swift-running elephant, a swift-running horse, a swift-running chariot, a swift-running deer. But now, even though I'm running with all my might, I can't catch up with this contemplative walking at normal pace." So he stopped and called out to the Blessed One, "Stop, contemplative! Stop!"

"I *have* stopped, Aṅgulimāla. *You* stop."

Then the thought occurred to Aṅgulimāla, "These Sakyan contemplatives are speakers of the truth, asserters of the truths, and yet this contemplative, even while walking, says, 'I have stopped, Aṅgulimāla. *You* stop.' Why don't I question him?"

So Aṅgulimāla the bandit addressed this verse to the Blessed One:

"While walking, contemplative,
you say, 'I have stopped.'
But when *I* have stopped
you say I haven't.
I ask you the meaning of this:
How have you stopped?
How haven't I?"

The Buddha:

"I have stopped, Aṅgulimāla,
once & for all,
having cast off violence
toward all living beings.
You, though,
are unrestrained toward beings.
That's how I've stopped
and you haven't."

Aṅgulimāla:

"At long last a greatly revered great seer
for my sake
has come to the great forest.
Having heard your verse
in line with the Dhamma,

I will go about
having abandoned evil."

So saying, the bandit
hurled his sword & weapons
over a cliff
into a chasm,
a pit.
Then the bandit paid homage
to the feet of the One Well-Gone,
and right there requested the Going-forth.

The Awakened One,
the compassionate great seer,
the teacher of the world, along with its devas,
said to him then:
"Come, bhikkhu."
That in itself
was bhikkhuhood for him.

Then the Blessed One set out wandering toward Sāvatthī with Ven. Aṅgulimāla as his attendant monk. After wandering by stages he reached Sāvatthī, and there he lived near Sāvatthī in Jeta's Grove, Anāthapiṇḍika's monastery.

Now at that time a large crowd of people, loud & noisy, had gathered at the gates to King Pasenadi Kosala's inner palace, (calling out,) "There is a bandit in your realm, sire, named Aṅgulimāla: brutal, bloody-handed, devoted to killing & slaying, showing no mercy to living beings. He has turned villages into non-villages, towns into non-towns, settled countryside into unsettled countryside. Having repeatedly killed human beings, he wears a garland made of fingers. The king must stamp him out!"

Then King Pasenadi Kosala, with a cavalry of roughly 500 horsemen, drove out of Sāvatthī in the middle of the dayand entered the monastery. Driving as far as the ground was passable for chariots, he got down from his chariot and proceeded on foot to the Blessed One. On arrival, having bowed down to the Blessed One, he sat to one side. As he was sitting there, the Blessed One said to him, "What is it, great king? Has King Seniya Bimbisāra of Magadha provoked you, or have the Licchavis of Vesālī or some other hostile king?"

"No, lord. King Seniya Bimbisāra of Magadha hasn't provoked me, nor have the Licchavis of Vesālī, nor has some other hostile king. There is a bandit in my realm, lord, named Aṅgulimāla: brutal, bloody-handed, devoted to killing & slaying, showing no mercy to living beings. He has turned villages into non-villages, towns into non-towns, settled countryside into unsettled countryside. Having repeatedly killed human beings, he wears a garland made of fingers. I am going to stamp him out."[1]

"Great king, suppose you were to see Aṅgulimāla with his hair & beard shaved off, wearing the ochre robe, having gone forth from the home life into homelessness, refraining from killing living beings, refraining from taking what is not given, refraining from telling lies, living the holy life on one meal a day, virtuous & of fine character: what would you do to him?"

"We would bow down to him, lord, or rise up to greet him, or offer him a seat, or offer him robes, almsfood, lodgings, or medicinal requisites for curing illness; or we would arrange a lawful guard, protection, & defense. But how could there be such virtue & restraint in an unvirtuous, evil character?"

Now at that time Ven. Aṅgulimāla was sitting not far from the Blessed One. So the Blessed One, pointing with his right arm, said to King Pasenadi Kosala, "That, great king, is Aṅgulimāla." Then King Pasenadi Kosala was frightened, terrified, his hair standing on end. So the Blessed One, sensing the king's fear & hair-raising awe, said to him, "Don't be afraid, great king. Don't be afraid. He poses no danger to you.

Then the king's fear, his terror, his hair-standing-on-end subsided. He went over to Ven. Aṅgulimāla and said, "Are you really Aṅgulimāla, lord?"

"Yes, great king."

"What is your father's clan? What is your mother's clan?"

"My father is a Gagga, great king, and my mother a Mantāṇi."

"Then may Master Gagga Mantāṇiputta delight (in staying here). I will be responsible for your robes, almsfood, lodgings, & medicinal requisites for curing illness."

Now it so happened that at that time Ven. Aṅgulimāla was a wilderness-dweller, an alms-goer, wearing one set of the triple robe made of cast-off cloth. So he said to King Pasenadi Kosala, "Enough, great king. My triple robe is complete."

So King Pasenadi Kosala went to the Blessed One and on arrival, having bowed down to him, sat to one side. As he was sitting there he said to the Blessed One, "It's amazing, lord. It's astounding, how the Blessed One has tamed the untamed, pacified the unpeaceful, and brought to unbinding those who were not unbound. For what we could not tame even with blunt or bladed weapons, the Blessed One has tamed without blunt or bladed weapons. Now, lord, we must go. Many are our duties, many our responsibilities."

"Then do, great king, what you think it is now time to do."

Then King Pasenadi Kosala got up from his seat, bowed down to the Blessed One and—keeping him to his right—departed.

Then Ven. Aṅgulimāla, early in the morning, having adjusted his under robe and carrying his bowl & outer robe, went into Sāvatthī for alms. As he was going from house to house for alms, he saw a woman suffering a breech birth. On seeing her, the thought occurred to him: "How tormented are living beings! How tormented are living beings!" Then, having gone for alms in Sāvatthī and returning from his alms round after his meal, he went to the Blessed One. On arrival, having bowed down to him, he sat to one side. As he was sitting there he said to the Blessed One, "Just now, lord, early in the morning, having adjusted my under robe and carrying my bowl & outer robe, I went into Sāvatthī for alms. As I was going from house to house for alms, I saw a woman suffering a breech birth. On seeing her, the thought occurred to me: 'How tormented are living beings! How tormented are living beings!'"

"In that case, Aṅgulimāla, go to that woman and on arrival say to her, 'Sister, since I was born I do not recall intentionally killing a living being. Through this truth may there be wellbeing for you, wellbeing for your fetus.'"

"But, lord, wouldn't that be a lie for me? For I have intentionally killed many living beings."

"Then in that case, Aṅgulimāla, go to that woman and on arrival say to her, 'Sister, since I was born in the noble birth, I do not recall intentionally killing a living being. Through this truth may there be wellbeing for you, wellbeing for your fetus.'"[2]

Responding, "As you say, lord," to the Blessed One, Aṅgulimāla went to that woman and on arrival said to her, "Sister, since I was born in the noble birth, I do not recall intentionally killing a living being. Through this may there be wellbeing for you, wellbeing for your fetus." And there was wellbeing for the woman, wellbeing for her fetus.

Then Ven. Aṅgulimāla, dwelling alone, secluded, heedful, ardent, & resolute, in no long time reached & remained in the supreme goal of the holy life for which clansmen rightly go forth from home into homelessness, knowing & realizing it for himself in the here & now. He knew: "Birth is ended, the holy life fulfilled, the task done. There is nothing further for the sake of this world." And thus Ven. Aṅgulimāla became another one of the arahants.

Then Ven. Aṅgulimāla, early in the morning, having adjusted his under robe and carrying his bowl & outer robe, went into Sāvatthī for alms. Now at that time a clod thrown by one person hit

Ven. Aṅgulimāla on the body, a stone thrown by another person hit him on the body, and a potsherd thrown by still another person hit him on the body. So Ven. Aṅgulimāla—his head broken open and dripping with blood, his bowl broken, and his outer robe ripped to shreds—went to the Blessed One. The Blessed One saw him coming from afar and on seeing him said to him: "Bear with it, brahman! Bear with it! The fruit of the kamma that would have burned you in hell for many years, many hundreds of years, many thousands of years, you are now experiencing in the here-&-now!"[3]

Then Ven. Aṅgulimāla, having gone alone into seclusion, experienced the bliss of release. At that time he exclaimed:

Who once was heedless,
but later is not,
    brightens the world
    like the moon set free from a cloud.[4]

His evil-done deed
is replaced with skillfulness:
    he brightens the world
    like the moon set free from a cloud.[5]

Whatever young monk
devotes himself
to the Buddha's bidding:
    he brightens the world
    like the moon set free from a cloud.

May even my enemies
hear talk of the Dhamma.
May even my enemies
devote themselves
to the Buddha's bidding.
May even my enemies
associate with those people
who—peaceful, good—
get others to accept the Dhamma.
May even my enemies
hear the Dhamma time & again
from those who advise   endurance,
                                    forbearance,
who praise non-opposition,
    and may they follow it.

For surely he wouldn't harm me,
or anyone else;
he would attain the foremost peace,
would protect the feeble & firm.

Irrigators guide the water.
Fletchers shape the arrow shaft.
Carpenters shape the wood.
The wise control
themselves.[6]

Some tame with a blunt stick,
with hooks, & with whips
But without blunt or bladed weapons
I was tamed by the one who is Such.

"Doer of No Harm" is my name,
but I used to be a doer of harm.
Today I am true to my name,
for I harm no one at all.

A bandit
I used to be,
renowned as Aṅgulimāla.
Swept along by a great flood,
I went to the Buddha as refuge.

Bloody-handed
I used to be,
renowned as Aṅgulimāla.
See my going for refuge!
Uprooted is [craving],
the guide to becoming.

Having done the type of kamma
that would lead to many
bad destinations,
touched by the fruit of (that) kamma,
unindebted, I eat my food.[7]
They're addicted to heedlessness
—dullards, fools—
while one who is wise
cherishes heedfulness
as his highest wealth.[8]
Don't give way to heedlessness
or to intimacy
with sensual delight—

for a heedful person,
absorbed in jhāna,
attains an abundant bliss.[9]

This[10] has come well & not gone away,
it was not badly thought through for me.
From among well-analyzed qualities,
I have obtained
the best.

This has come well & not gone away,
it was not badly thought through for me.
The three knowledges
have been attained;
the Buddha's bidding,
done.

NOTES

1. The PTS reading here, followed in *MLS* and *MLDB*—"I will not stamp him out"—is surely a mistake. I follow the Thai reading of this passage, even though it is somewhat ungrammatical. There are passages in MN 90 where King Pasenadi's sentences don't quite parse, and perhaps this is another example of his brusque language.

2. This blessing is often chanted at house blessings in Theravada countries.

3. This incident illustrates the kammic principle stated in AN 3:101.

4. This verse = Dhp 172.

5. This verse = Dhp 173.

6. This verse = Dhp 80.

7. This verse is another illustration of the principle stated in AN 3:101.

8. This verse = Dhp 26.

9. This verse = Dhp 27.

10. "This" apparently refers to the abundant bliss mentioned in the previous verse.

See also: DN 11; SN 41:4

87 From One Who Is Dear

Piyajātika Sutta

Many discourses depict King Pasenadi Kosala as a Buddhist. This discourse relates how—through the astuteness of Queen Mallikā—he first became favorably disposed toward the Buddha.

I have heard that on one occasion the Blessed One was staying near Sāvatthī in Jeta's Grove, Anāthapiṇḍika's monastery. Now at that time a certain householder's dear & beloved little son, his only child, had died. Because of his death, the father had no desire to work or to eat. He kept going to the cemetery and crying out, "Where have you gone, my only little child? Where have you gone, my only little child?"

Then he went to the Blessed One and, on arrival, having bowed down to him, sat to one side. As he was sitting there the Blessed One said to him, "Householder, your faculties are not those of one who is steady in his own mind. There is an aberration in your faculties."

"Lord, how could there not be an aberration in my faculties? My dear & beloved little son, my only child, has died. Because of his death, I have no desire to work or to eat. I keep going to the cemetery and crying out, 'Where have you gone, my only little child? Where have you gone, my only little child?'"

"That's the way it is, householder. That's the way it is—for sorrow, lamentation, pain, distress, & despair are born from one who is dear, come springing from one who is dear."

"But lord, who would ever think that sorrow, lamentation, pain, distress, & despair are born from one who is dear, come springing from one who is dear? Happiness & joy are born from one who is dear, come springing from one who is dear." So the householder, not delighting in the Blessed One's words, rejecting the Blessed One's words, got up from his seat and left.

Now at that time a large number of gamblers were playing dice not far from the Blessed One. So the householder went to them and, on arrival, said to them, "Just now, venerable sirs, I went to Gotama the contemplative and, on arrival, having bowed down to him, sat to one side. As I was sitting there, Gotama the contemplative said to me, 'Householder, your faculties are not those of one who is steady in his own mind. There is an aberration in your faculties.'

"When this was said, I said to him, 'Lord, how could there not be an aberration in my faculties? My dear & beloved little son, my only child, has died. Because of his death, I have no desire to work or to eat. I keep going to the cemetery and crying out, "Where have you gone, my only little child? Where have you gone, my only little child?"'

"'That's the way it is, householder. That's the way it is—for sorrow, lamentation, pain, distress, & despair are born from one who is dear, come springing from one who is dear.'

"'But, lord, who would ever think that sorrow, lamentation, pain, distress, & despair are born from one who is dear, come springing from one who is dear? Happiness & joy are born from one who is dear, come springing from one who is dear.' So, not delighting in the words of Gotama the contemplative, rejecting them, I got up from my seat and left."

"That's the way it is, householder (said the gamblers). That's the way it is. Happiness & joy are born from one who is dear, come springing from one who is dear."

So the householder left, thinking, "I agree with the gamblers."

Eventually, word of this conversation made its way into the king's inner chambers. Then King Pasenadi Kosala addressed Queen Mallikā, "Mallikā, your contemplative, Gotama, has said this: 'Sorrow, lamentation, pain, distress, & despair are born from one who is dear, come springing from one who is dear.'"

"If that was said by the Blessed One, great king, then that's the way it is."

"No matter what Gotama the contemplative says, Mallikā endorses it: 'If that was said by the Blessed One, great king, then that's the way it is.' Just as, no matter what his teacher says, a pupil endorses it: 'That's the way it is, teacher. That's the way is.' In the same way, no matter what Gotama the contemplative says, Mallikā endorses it: 'If that was said by the Blessed One, great king, then that's the way it is.' Go away, Mallikā! Out of my sight!"

Then Queen Mallikā called for the brahman Nāḷijaṅgha: "Come, brahman. Go to the Blessed One and, on arrival, showing reverence with your head to his feet in my name, ask whether he is free from illness & affliction, is carefree, strong, & living in comfort, saying: 'Queen Mallikā, lord, shows reverence with her head to your feet and asks whether you are free from illness & affliction, are carefree, strong, & living in comfort.' And then say: 'Lord, did the Blessed One say that sorrow, lamentation, pain, distress, &

despair are born from one who is dear, come springing from one who is dear?' Whatever the Blessed One says, remember it well and tell it to me—for Tathāgatas do not speak untruthfully."

"Yes, madam," the brahman Nāḷijaṅgha responded to Queen Mallikā. Going to the Blessed One, on arrival he exchanged courteous greetings with the Blessed One. After an exchange of friendly greetings & courtesies, he sat to one side. As he was sitting there he said to the Blessed One: "Master Gotama, Queen Mallikā shows reverence with her head to your feet and asks whether you are free from illness & affliction, are carefree, strong, & living in comfort. And she says further: 'Lord, did the Blessed One say that sorrow, lamentation, pain, distress, & despair are born from one who is dear, come springing from one who is dear?'"

"That's the way it is, brahman. That's the way it is. Sorrow, lamentation, pain, distress, & despair are born from one who is dear, come springing from one who is dear. And it's through this line of reasoning that it may be understood how sorrow, lamentation, pain, distress, & despair are born from one who is dear, come springing from one who is dear.

"Once in this same Sāvatthī there was a woman whose mother died. Owing to her mother's death she went mad, out of her mind, and wandering from street to street, crossroads to crossroads, would say, 'Have you seen my mother? Have you seen my mother?' It's through this line of reasoning that it may be understood how sorrow, lamentation, pain, distress, & despair are born from one who is dear, come springing from one who is dear.

"Once in this same Sāvatthī there was a woman whose father died... whose brother died... whose sister died... whose son died... whose daughter died... whose husband died. Owing to his death she went mad, out of her mind, and wandering from street to street, crossroads to crossroads, would say, 'Have you seen my husband? Have you seen my husband?' It's through this line of reasoning that it may be understood how sorrow, lamentation, pain, distress, & despair are born from one who is dear, come springing from one who is dear.

"Once in this same Sāvatthī there was a man whose mother died. Owing to her death he went mad, out of his mind, and wandering from street to street, crossroads to crossroads, would say, 'Have you seen my mother? Have you seen my mother?' It's through this line of reasoning that it may be understood how sorrow, lamentation, pain, distress, & despair are born from one who is dear, come springing from one who is dear.

"Once in this same Sāvatthī there was a man whose father died... whose brother died... whose sister died... whose son died... whose daughter died... whose wife died. Owing to her death he went mad, out of his mind, and wandering from street to street, crossroads to crossroads, would say, 'Have you seen my wife? Have you seen my wife?' It's through this line of reasoning that it may be understood how sorrow, lamentation, pain, distress, & despair are born from one who is dear, come springing from one who is dear.

"Once in this same Sāvatthī there was a wife who went to her relatives' home. Her relatives, having separated her from her husband, wanted to give her to another against her will. So she said to her husband, 'These relatives of mine, having separated us, want to give me to another against my will,' whereupon he cut her in two and slashed himself open, thinking, 'Dead we will be together.' It's through this line of reasoning that it may be understood how sorrow, lamentation, pain, distress, & despair are born from one who is dear, come springing from one who is dear."

Then the brahman Nāḷijaṅgha, delighting in & approving of the Blessed One's words, got up from his seat and went to Queen Mallikā. On arrival, he told her all that had been said in his conversation with the Blessed One.

Then Queen Mallikā went to King Pasenadi Kosala and on arrival said to him, "What do you think, great king? Is Princess Vajirī dear to you?"

"Yes, Mallikā, Princess Vajirī is dear to me."

"And what do you think? Would sorrow, lamentation, pain, distress, & despair arise in you from any change & aberration in Princess Vajirī?"

"Mallikā, any change & aberration in Princess Vajirī would mean an aberration of my very life. How could sorrow, lamentation, pain, distress, & despair not arise in me?"

"Great king, it was in connection with this that the Blessed One—the One who knows, the One who sees, worthy & rightly self-awakened—said, 'Sorrow, lamentation, pain, distress, & despair are born from one who is dear, come springing from one who is dear.'

"Now what do you think, great king? Is the noble Queen Vāsabhā dear to you? .... Is [your son] General Viḍūḍabha dear to you? .... Am I dear to you?"

"Yes, Mallikā, you are dear to me."

"And what do you think? Would sorrow, lamentation, pain, distress, & despair arise in you from any change & aberration in me?"

"Mallikā, any change & aberration in you would mean an aberration of my very life. How could sorrow, lamentation, pain, distress, & despair not arise in me?"

"Great king, it was in connection with this that the Blessed One—the One who knows, the One who sees, worthy & rightly self-awakened—said, 'Sorrow, lamentation, pain, distress, & despair are born from one who is dear, come springing from one who is dear.'

"Now what do you think, great king? Are [your subjects] the Kāsis & Kosalans dear to you?"

"Yes, Mallikā, the Kāsis & Kosalans are dear to me. It's through the might of the Kāsis & Kosalans that we use Kāsi sandalwood and wear garlands, scents, & ointments."

"And what do you think? Would sorrow, lamentation, pain, distress, & despair arise in you from any change & aberration in the Kāsis & Kosalans?"

"Mallikā, any change & aberration in the Kāsis & Kosalans would mean an aberration of my very life. How could sorrow, lamentation, pain, distress, & despair not arise in me?"

"Great king, it was in connection with this that the Blessed One—the One who knows, the One who sees, worthy & rightly self-awakened—said, 'Sorrow, lamentation, pain, distress, & despair are born from one who is dear, come springing from one who is dear.'"

"It's amazing, Mallikā. It's astounding: how deeply the Blessed One sees, having pierced through, as it were, with discernment. Come Mallikā: Give me the ablution water." Then King Pasenadi Kosala, rising from his seat and arranging his upper robe over one shoulder, paid homage in the direction of the Blessed One with his hands palm-to-palm in front of his heart, and exclaimed three times:

"Homage to the Blessed One, worthy & rightly self-awakened!
Homage to the Blessed One, worthy & rightly self-awakened!
Homage to the Blessed One, worthy & rightly self-awakened!"

See also: DN 21; SN 3; SN 4:8; SN 42:11; AN 3:63; AN 4:200; AN 5:49; Ud 2:7; Ud 5:1; Ud 8:8; Sn 1:3; Sn 4:11; Thig 3:5; Thig 6:1

90 At Kaṇṇakatthala

Kaṇṇakatthala Sutta

INTRODUCTION

The frame story of this sutta presents a gentle satire of royal life. Despite his position, King Pasenadi Kosala must still act the role of messenger for his wives. Because of his position, he finds himself surrounded by people he cannot trust—he never gets to the bottom of the question of who brought misinformation into the palace—and whose minds fasten on issues of overthrowing and banishing, possibly him. He is so preoccupied with his responsibilities that he doesn't pick up on the Buddha's gentle joke about his servitude to the sisters Somā and Sakulā, can't stick with an issue for any length of time, sometimes can't even phrase his questions properly, and can arrive at no greater certainty about the Buddha's teachings than that they seem reasonable. At the end of the sutta he has to leave, not because he has exhausted the issues he would like to discuss, but because one of his courtiers tells him it is time to go. All in all, not an enviable position.

The substance of the discussion, however, does touch on some serious issues. The topic treated in greatest detail concerns the differences among the castes of the Buddha's time, and the Buddha's remarks can profitably be applied to issues of racism in ours.

The discussion and the frame story, of course, play off one another. Because of his social position, King Pasenadi is unable to pursue the path to release that is open to all regardless of race or caste. His social advantages are a spiritual liability. Like many people in the modern world, he has plenty of things but no time.

* * *

I have heard that on one occasion the Blessed One was staying among the Udaññans, in the Deer Park at Kaṇṇakatthala. And at that time King Pasenadi Kosala had arrived at Udañña on some business or other. So King Pasenadi Kosala said to one of his men, "Come, my good man. Go to the Blessed One and, on arrival, showing reverence with your head to his feet in my name, ask whether he is free from illness & affliction, is carefree, strong, & living in comfort, saying: 'King Pasenadi Kosala, lord, shows reverence with his head to your feet and asks whether you are free from illness & affliction, are carefree, strong, & living in comfort.' And then say: 'Lord, today King Pasenadi Kosala will come to see the Blessed One after his morning meal.'"

Having responded, "As you say, sire," the man went to the Blessed One and, on arrival, having bowed down to him, sat to one side. As he was sitting there, he said to him, "King Pasenadi Kosala, lord, shows reverence with his head to your feet and asks whether you are free from illness & affliction, are carefree, strong, & living in comfort." And then he said, "Lord, today King Pasenadi Kosala will come to see the Blessed One after his morning meal."

Now, the sisters Somā and Sakulā[1] heard, "Today, they say, King Pasenadi Kosala will go to see the Blessed One after his morning meal." So they approached King Pasenadi while his meal was being served and on arrival said to him, "Well in that case, great king, show reverence with your head to his feet in our name, too, and ask whether he is free from illness & affliction, is carefree, strong, & living in comfort, saying: 'The sisters Somā and Sakulā, lord, show reverence with their heads to your feet and asks whether you are free from illness & affliction, are carefree, strong, & living in comfort.'"

Then, after his morning meal, King Pasenadi Kosala went to the Blessed One and, on arrival, having bowed down to him, sat to one side. As he was sitting there, he said to the Blessed One, "The sisters Somā and Sakulā, lord, show reverence with their heads to your feet and asks whether you are free from illness & affliction, are carefree, strong, & living in comfort."

"But, great king, couldn't the sisters Somā and Sakulā get another messenger?"

"Lord, the sisters Somā and Sakulā heard, 'Today, they say, King Pasenadi Kosala will go to see the Blessed One after his morning meal.' So they approached me while my meal was being served and on arrival said to me, 'In that case, great king, show reverence with your head to his feet in our name, too, and ask whether he is free from illness & affliction, is carefree, strong, & living in comfort, saying: "The sisters Somā and Sakulā, lord, show reverence with their heads to your feet and asks whether you are free from illness & affliction, are carefree, strong, & living in comfort."' Lord, the sisters Somā and Sakulā show reverence with their heads to your feet and asks whether you are free from illness & affliction, are carefree, strong, & living in comfort."

"May the sisters Somā and Sakulā be happy, great king."

Then King Pasenadi Kosala said to the Blessed One, "Lord, I have heard that 'Gotama the contemplative says this: "It is not possible that a contemplative or brahman would claim a knowledge and vision that is all-knowing and all-seeing without exception."' Those who say this: are they speaking in line with what the Blessed One has said? Are they not misrepresenting the Blessed One with what is unfactual? Are they answering in line with the Dhamma, so that no one whose thinking is in line with the Dhamma would have grounds for criticizing them?"

"Great king, those who say that are not speaking in line with what I have said, and are misrepresenting me with what is untrue and unfactual."

Then King Pasenadi Kosala turned to General Viḍūḍabha: "General, who brought this topic into the palace?"

"Sañjaya, the brahman of the Ākāsa clan, great king."

So King Pasenadi turned to one of his men, "Come, my good man. Summon Sañjaya the brahman of the Ākāsa clan, saying, 'King Pasenadi Kosala summons you.'"

Responding, "As you say, sire," the man went to Sañjaya the brahman of the Ākāsa clan and on arrival said to him, "King Pasenadi Kosala summons you."

Then King Pasenadi Kosala said to the Blessed One, "Could it be that something was said by the Blessed One in reference to something else, which a person could have misunderstood? In what way does the Blessed One recall having said (such) a statement?"

"Great king, I recall having said, 'It is not possible that a contemplative or brahman could know everything and see everything all at once.'"

"What the Blessed One says, lord, seems reasonable. What the Blessed One says seems logical: 'It is not possible that a contemplative or brahman could know everything and see everything all at once.'

"Lord, there are these four castes: noble warriors, brahmans, merchants, & workers. Is there any distinction or difference among them?"

"Great king, of these four castes, two—noble warriors & brahmans—are held to be foremost in terms of receiving homage, hospitality, salutation, & polite services."

"I'm not asking about the present life, lord. I'm asking about the future life. Is there any distinction or difference among these four castes?"

"Great king, there are these five factors for exertion. Which five?

"There is the case where a monk has conviction, is convinced of the Tathāgata's Awakening: 'Indeed, the Blessed One is worthy & rightly self-awakened, consummate in clear-knowing & conduct, well-gone, an expert with regard to the cosmos, unexcelled trainer of people fit to be tamed, teacher of devas & human beings, awakened, blessed.'

"He is free from illness & discomfort, endowed with good digestion—not too cold, not too hot, of moderate strength—fit for exertion.

"He is neither fraudulent nor deceitful. He declares himself to the Teacher or to his observant companions in the holy life in line with what he actually is.

"He keeps his persistence aroused for abandoning unskillful qualities and taking on skillful qualities. He is steadfast, solid in his effort, not shirking his duties with regard to skillful qualities.

"He is discerning, endowed with discernment leading to the arising of the goal—noble, penetrating, leading to the right ending of stress.

"These are the five factors for exertion.

"As for the four castes, great king: If they were endowed with these five factors for exertion, that would be for their long-term welfare & happiness."

"Lord, if these four castes were endowed with these five factors for exertion, would there be any distinction or difference among them in that respect?"

"I tell you, great king: The difference among them would lie in the diversity of their exertion. Suppose that there were two tamable elephants, tamable horses, or tamable oxen that were well-tamed & well-trained; and two tamable elephants, tamable horses, or tamable oxen that were untamed & untrained. What do you think? Would the two tamable elephants, tamable horses, or tamable oxen that were well-tamed & well-trained acquire the habits of the tamed and reach the status of the tamed?"

"Yes, lord."

"And would the two tamable elephants, tamable horses, or tamable oxen that were untamed & untrained acquire the habits of the tamed and reach the status of the tamed?"

"No, lord."

"In the same way, great king, it is impossible that what could be attained by one who has confidence, who is free from illness, who is neither fraudulent nor deceitful, whose persistence is aroused, and who is discerning could also be attained by one who is without conviction, who is sickly, fraudulent & deceitful, lazy, and dull."

"What the Blessed One says, lord, seems reasonable. What the Blessed One says seems logical. But with regard to these four castes: if they were endowed with these five factors for exertion, and they had right exertion, would there be any distinction or difference among them in that respect?"

"I tell you, great king, that there would be no difference among them with regard to the release of one and the release of another. Suppose that a man, taking dry Sal wood, were to generate a fire and make heat appear. And suppose that another man, taking dry saka [teak?] wood, were to generate a fire and make heat appear. And suppose that another man, taking dry mango wood, were to generate a fire and make heat appear. And suppose that another man, taking dry fig wood, were to generate a fire and make heat appear. Now what do you think, great king? Among those fires generated from different kinds of wood, would there be any difference between the glow of one and the glow of another, the color of one and the color of another, the radiance of one and the radiance of another?"

"No, lord."

"In the same way, great king, in the power that is kindled by persistence and generated by exertion, I say that there is no difference with regard to the release of one and the release of another."

"What the Blessed One says, lord, seems reasonable. What the Blessed One says seems logical. But, lord, are there devas?"

"But why do you ask, 'But, lord, are there devas?'?"

"Whether the devas come back to this life, lord, or whether they don't."

"Those devas who are afflicted[2] come back to this life, whereas those devas who are unafflicted don't come back to this life."

When this was said, General Viḍūḍabha said to the Blessed One, "Lord, can the afflicted devas oust or expel the unafflicted devas from that place?"

Then the thought occurred to Ven. Ānanda, "This General Viḍūḍabha is the son of King Pasenadi Kosala, and I am the son of the Blessed One. Now is the time for the son to counsel the son." So Ven. Ānanda turned to General Viḍūḍabha and said, "In that case, general, I will ask you a counter question. Answer as you see fit. Through the extent of land conquered by King Pasenadi Kosala—where he exercises sovereign & independent kingship—is he able to oust or expel a contemplative or brahman from that place, regardless of whether that person has merit or not, or follows the holy life or not?"

"Sir, through the extent of land conquered by King Pasenadi Kosala—where he exercises sovereign & independent kingship—he *is* able to oust or expel a contemplative or brahman from that place, regardless of whether that person has merit or not, or follows the holy life or not."

"And what do you think, general? Through the extent of land *not* conquered by King Pasenadi Kosala—where he does not exercise sovereign & independent kingship—is he able to oust or expel a contemplative or brahman from that place, regardless of whether that person has merit or not, or follows the holy life or not?"

"Sir, through the extent of land not conquered by King Pasenadi Kosala—where he does not exercise sovereign & independent kingship—he is *not* able to oust or expel a contemplative or brahman from that place, regardless of whether that person has merit or not, or follows the holy life or not."

"And what do you think, general? Have you heard of the Devas of the Thirty-three?"

"Yes, sir, I have heard of the Devas of the Thirty-three, as has King Pasenadi Kosala."

"And what do you think, general? Could King Pasenadi Kosala oust or expel the Devas of the Thirty-three from that place?"

"Sir, King Pasenadi Kosala can't even see the Devas of the Thirty-three. How could he oust or expel them from that place?"

"In the same way, general, afflicted devas, who will come back to this life, can't even see the unafflicted devas who don't come back to this life. How could they oust or expel them from that place?"

Then King Pasenadi Kosala said to the Blessed One, "Lord, what is the name of this monk?"

"His name is Ānanda [Joy], great king."

"What a joy he is! What a true joy! But, lord, are there Brahmās?"

"But why do you ask, 'But, lord, are there Brahmās?'?"

"Whether the Brahmās come back to this life, lord, or whether they don't."

"Those Brahmās who are afflicted come back to this life, whereas those Brahmās who are unafflicted don't come back to this life."

Then a man said to King Pasenadi Kosala, "Great king, Sañjaya the brahman of the Ākāsa clan has come."

Then King Pasenadi Kosala said to Sañjaya the brahman of the Ākāsa clan, "Who brought that topic into the royal palace?"

"General Viḍūḍabha, great king."

General Viḍūḍabha said, "Sañjaya the brahman of the Ākāsa clan, great king."

Then a man said to King Pasenadi Kosala, "Time to go, great king."

So King Pasenadi Kosala said to the Blessed One, "Lord, we have asked the Blessed One about omniscience, the Blessed One has answered about omniscience, and that is pleasing & agreeable to us, and we are gratified because of it. We have asked the Blessed One about the purity of the four castes, the Blessed One has answered about the purity of the four castes, and that is pleasing & agreeable to us, and we are gratified because of it. We have asked the Blessed One about the higher devas, the Blessed One has answered about the higher devas, and that is pleasing & agreeable to us, and we are gratified because of it. We have asked the Blessed One about the higher Brahmās, the Blessed One has answered about the higher Brahmās, and that is pleasing & agreeable to us, and we are gratified because of it. Whatever we have asked the Blessed One about, that he has answered, and that is pleasing & agreeable to us, and we are gratified because of it. Now, lord, we must go. Many are our duties, many our responsibilities."

"Then do, great king, what you think it is now time to do."

Then King Pasenadi Kosala, delighting in and approving of the Blessed One's words, got up from his seat, bowed down to the Blessed One and—keeping him to his right—departed.

NOTES

1. According to the Commentary, Somā and Sakulā were two wives of the king. The Commentary's treatment of this incident as a whole, however, seems aimed at taking the teeth out of the satire, perhaps to appease the royal patrons of the monks who compiled the Commentary. It insists that the two sisters did not barge in on the king as his meal was being served, but were actually taking part in the meal-serving ceremony. However, the sisters' tone of voice in delivering their request to the king is anything but servile. So perhaps the Commentary is mistaken about their identity as well.

2. According to the Commentary, "afflicted" here means still subject to suffering; "unafflicted" means free from the roots of suffering.

See also: SN 3:7; SN 3:14–15; SN 3:24; AN 3:58

93 With Assalāyana

Assalāyana Sutta

I have heard that on one occasion the Blessed One was staying near Sāvatthī in Jeta's Grove, Anāthapiṇḍika's monastery. And on that occasion 500 brahmans from various provinces were staying at Sāvatthī on some business or other. The thought occurred to them, "This Gotama the contemplative prescribes purity for the four castes. Now who is capable of disputing with him on this statement. And on that occasion the brahman student Assalāyana was staying at Sāvatthī. Young, shaven-headed, sixteen years old, he was a master of the Three Vedas with their vocabularies, liturgy, phonology, etymology, & histories as a fifth; skilled in philology & grammar, he was fully versed in cosmology and in the marks of a Great Man. The thought occurred to the brahmans, "This brahman student Assalāyana is staying in Sāvatthī... He is capable of disputing with Gotama the contemplative on this statement."

So the brahmans went to the brahman student Assalāyana and said to him, "Master Assalāyana, this Gotama the contemplative prescribes purity for the four castes. Come and dispute with him on this statement."

When this was said, the brahman student Assalāyana said to the brahmans, "Sirs, Gotama the contemplative is one who speaks Dhamma. And those who speak Dhamma are hard to dispute with. I can't dispute with him on this statement."

A second time.... A third time, the brahmans said to the brahman student Assalāyana, "Master Assalāyana, this Gotama the contemplative prescribes purity for the four castes. Come and dispute with him on this statement, for you have lived the life of a wanderer. Don't be defeated without being defeated in battle."

When this was said, the brahman student Assalāyana said to the brahmans, "Apparently, sirs, I don't get leave from you (to avoid the matter by saying), 'Gotama the contemplative is one who speaks Dhamma. And those who speak Dhamma are hard to dispute with. I can't dispute with him on this statement.' But at your bidding I will go."

Then the brahman student Assalāyana went with a large group of brahmans to the Blessed One and, on arrival, exchanged courteous greetings with him. After an exchange of friendly greetings & courtesies, he sat to one side. As he was sitting there he said to the Blessed One: "Master Gotama, the brahmans say, 'Brahmans are the superior caste; any other caste is inferior. Only brahmans are the fair caste; any other caste is dark. Only brahmans are pure, not non-brahmans. Only brahmans are the sons & offspring of Brahmā: born of his mouth, born of Brahmā, created by Brahmā, heirs of Brahmā.' What does Master Gotama have to say with regard to that?"

"But, Assalāyana, the brahmans' brahman-women are plainly seen having their periods, becoming pregnant, giving birth, and nursing (their children). And yet the brahmans, being born through the birth canal, say, 'Brahmans are the superior caste; any other caste is inferior. Only brahmans are the fair caste; any other caste is dark. Only brahmans are pure, not non-brahmans. Only brahmans are the sons & offspring of Brahmā: born of his mouth, born of Brahmā, created by Brahmā, heirs of Brahmā.'"

"Even though Master Gotama says that, still the brahmans think, 'Brahmans are the superior caste… the sons & offspring of Brahmā: born of his mouth, born of Brahmā, created by Brahmā, heirs of Brahmā.'"

"What do you think, Assalāyana? Have you heard that in Yona & Kamboja and other outlying countries there are only two castes—masters & slaves—and that having been a master one (can) become a slave, and that having been a slave one (can) become a master?"

"Yes, Master Gotama…."

"So what strength is there, Assalāyana, what assurance, when the brahmans say, 'Brahmans are the superior caste… the sons & offspring of Brahmā: born of his mouth, born of Brahmā, created by Brahmā, heirs of Brahmā'?"

"Even though Master Gotama says that, still the brahmans think, 'Brahmans are the superior caste… the sons & offspring of Brahmā: born of his mouth, born of Brahmā, created by Brahmā, heirs of Brahmā.'"

"What do you think, Assalāyana? Is it only a noble warrior who—taking life, stealing, engaging in sexual misconduct, telling lies, speaking divisively, speaking harshly, engaging in idle chatter, greedy, bearing thoughts of ill will, and holding wrong views—on the break-up of the body, after death, reappears in a plane of deprivation, a bad destination, a lower realm, hell, and not a brahman? Is it only a merchant…? Is it only a worker who—taking life, stealing, engaging in sexual misconduct, telling lies, speaking divisively, speaking harshly, engaging in idle chatter, greedy, bearing thoughts of ill will, and holding wrong views—on the break-up of the body, after death, reappears in a plane of deprivation, a bad destination, a lower realm, hell, and not a brahman?"

"No, Master Gotama. Even a noble warrior.... Even a brahman.... Even a merchant.... Even a worker.... (Members of) all four castes—if they take life, steal, engage in sexual misconduct, tell lies, speak divisively, speak harshly, engage in idle chatter, are greedy, bear thoughts of ill will, & hold wrong views—on the break-up of the body, after death, reappear in a plane of deprivation, a bad destination, a lower realm, hell."

"So what strength is there, Assalāyana, what assurance, when the brahmans say, 'Brahmans are the superior caste... the sons & offspring of Brahmā: born of his mouth, born of Brahmā, created by Brahmā, heirs of Brahmā'?"

"Even though Master Gotama says that, still the brahmans think, 'Brahmans are the superior caste... the sons & offspring of Brahmā: born of his mouth, born of Brahmā, created by Brahmā, heirs of Brahmā.'"

"What do you think, Assalāyana? Is it only a brahman who—refraining from taking life, from stealing, from sexual misconduct, from telling lies, from speaking divisive speech, from harsh speech, & from idle chatter, not greedy, bearing no thoughts of ill-will, & holding to right view—on the break-up of the body, after death, reappears in a good destination, a heavenly world, and not a noble warrior, not a merchant, not a worker?"

"No, Master Gotama. Even a noble warrior.... Even a brahman.... Even a merchant.... Even a worker.... (Members of) all four castes—if they refrain from taking life, from stealing, from sexual misconduct, from telling lies, from speaking divisive speech, from harsh speech, & from idle chatter, are not greedy, bear no thoughts of ill-will, & hold to right view—on the break-up of the body, after death, reappear in a good destination, a heavenly world."

"So what strength is there, Assalāyana, what assurance, when the brahmans say, 'Brahmans are the superior caste... the sons & offspring of Brahmā: born of his mouth, born of Brahmā, created by Brahmā, heirs of Brahmā'?"

"Even though Master Gotama says that, still the brahmans think, 'Brahmans are the superior caste... the sons & offspring of Brahmā: born of his mouth, born of Brahmā, created by Brahmā, heirs of Brahmā.'"

"What do you think, Assalāyana? Is it only a brahman who is capable of developing in any direction a heart of good will—free from animosity, free from ill will—and not a noble warrior, not a merchant, not a worker?"

"No, Master Gotama. Even a noble warrior.... Even a brahman.... Even a merchant.... Even a worker.... (Members of) all four castes are capable of developing in any direction a heart of good will—free from animosity, free from ill will."

"So what strength is there, Assalāyana, what assurance, when the brahmans say, 'Brahmans are the superior caste... the sons & offspring of Brahmā: born of his mouth, born of Brahmā, created by Brahmā, heirs of Brahmā'?"

"Even though Master Gotama says that, still the brahmans think, 'Brahmans are the superior caste... the sons & offspring of Brahmā: born of his mouth, born of Brahmā, created by Brahmā, heirs of Brahmā.'"

"What do you think, Assalāyana? Is it only a brahman who is capable of taking a loofah & bath powder, going to a river, and scrubbing off dust & dirt, and not a noble warrior, not a merchant, not a worker?"

"No, Master Gotama. Even a noble warrior.... Even a brahman.... Even a merchant.... Even a worker.... (Members of) all four castes are capable of taking a loofah & bath powder, going to a river, and scrubbing off dust & dirt."

"So what strength is there, Assalāyana, what assurance, when the brahmans say, 'Brahmans are the superior caste... Only brahmans are pure, not non-brahmans. Only brahmans are the sons & offspring of Brahmā: born of his mouth, born of Brahmā, created by Brahmā, heirs of Brahmā'?"

"Even though Master Gotama says that, still the brahmans think, 'Brahmans are the superior caste... Only brahmans are pure, not non-brahmans. Only brahmans are the sons & offspring of Brahmā: born of his mouth, born of Brahmā, created by Brahmā, heirs of Brahmā.'"

"What do you think, Assalāyana? There is the case where a consecrated noble warrior king might call together 100 men of different births (and say to them), 'Come, masters. Those of you there born from a noble warrior clan, from a brahman clan, or from a royal clan: taking an upper fire-stick of Sal wood, salaḷa wood, sandalwood, or padumaka wood, produce fire & make heat appear. And come, masters. Those of you there born from an outcast clan, a trapper clan, a wicker workers' clan, a cartwrights' clan, or a scavengers' clan: taking an upper fire-stick from a dog's drinking trough, from a pig's trough, from a dustbin, or of castor-oil wood, produce fire & make heat appear.' What do you think, Assalāyana? Would the fire made by those born from a noble warrior clan, a brahman clan, or a royal clan—who had produced fire & made heat appear by taking an upper fire-stick of Sal wood, salaḷa wood, sandalwood, or padumaka wood—be the only one with flame, color, & radiance, able to do whatever a fire might be needed to do? And would the fire made by those born those born from an outcast clan, a trapper clan, a wicker workers' clan, a cartwrights' clan, or a scavengers' clan—who had produced fire & made heat appear by taking an upper fire-stick from a dog's drinking trough, from a pig's trough, from a dustbin, or of castor-oil wood—be without flame, color, & radiance, unable to do what a fire might be needed to do?"

"No, Master Gotama. The fire made by those born from a noble warrior clan, a brahman clan, or a royal clan… would have flame, color, & radiance, able to do whatever a fire might be needed to do. And the fire made by those born from an outcast clan, a trapper clan, a wicker workers' clan, a cartwrights' clan, or a scavengers' clan… would have flame, color, & radiance, able to do whatever a fire might be needed to do. For all fire has flame, color, & radiance, and is able to do whatever a fire might be needed to do."

"So what strength is there, Assalāyana, what assurance, when the brahmans say, 'Brahmans are the superior caste… Only brahmans are pure, not non-brahmans. Only brahmans are the sons & offspring of Brahmā: born of his mouth, born of Brahmā, created by Brahmā, heirs of Brahmā'?"

"Even though Master Gotama says that, still the brahmans think, 'Brahmans are the superior caste… Only brahmans are pure, not non-brahmans. Only brahmans are the sons & offspring of Brahmā: born of his mouth, born of Brahmā, created by Brahmā, heirs of Brahmā.'"

"What do you think, Assalāyana? There is the case where a noble warrior youth might cohabit with a brahman maiden, and from their cohabitation a son would be born. Would the son born from the noble warrior youth and brahman maiden be like the father and like the mother? Should it be called a noble warrior & a brahman?"

"Yes, Master Gotama…."

"What do you think, Assalāyana? There is the case where a brahman youth might cohabit with a noble warrior maiden, and from their cohabitation a son would be born. Would the son born from the brahman youth and noble warrior maiden be like the father and like the mother? Should it be called a noble warrior & a brahman?"

"Yes, Master Gotama…."

"What do you think, Assalāyana? There is the case where a mare might mate with a donkey, and from their mating a foal would be born. Would the foal born from the mare & the donkey be like the father and like the mother? Should it be called a horse & a donkey?"

"Master Gotama, from the mixed breeding it would be a mule. Here I see that it [the mixed breeding] makes a difference, but there [in the other two cases] I don't see that it makes a difference."

"What do you think, Assalāyana? There is the case where there might be two brahman-student brothers, born of the same mother: one learned & initiated, the other not learned & uninitiated. Which of the two would the brahmans serve first at a funeral feast, a milk-rice offering, a sacrifice, or a feast for guests?"

"The brahman student who was learned & initiated, Master Gotama.... For what great fruit would there be for what is given to one who is not learned & uninitiated?"

"What do you think, Assalāyana? There is the case where there might be two brahman-student brothers, born of the same mother: one learned & initiated (but) unvirtuous & of evil character, the other not learned & uninitiated, (but) virtuous & of fine character. Which of the two would the brahmans serve first at a funeral feast, a milk-rice offering, a sacrifice, or a feast for guests?"

"The brahman student who was not learned & uninitiated, (but) virtuous & of fine character, Master Gotama.... For what great fruit would there be for what is given to one who is unvirtuous & of evil character?"

"First, Assalāyana, you went by birth. Then, having gone by birth, you went by mantras. Then, having gone by mantras, putting them both aside, you have come around to the purity of the four castes that I prescribe."

When this was said, the brahman student Assalāyana sat silent, abashed, his shoulders drooping, his head down, brooding, at a loss for words.

Then the Blessed One—seeing that the brahman student Assalāyana was sitting silent, abashed, his shoulders drooping, his head down, brooding, at a loss for words—said to him, "Once, Assalāyana, this evil viewpoint arose in the seven brahman seers as they were consulting together in leaf huts in the wilderness: 'Brahmans are the superior caste; any other caste is inferior. Only brahmans are the fair caste; any other caste is dark. Only brahmans are pure, not non-brahmans. Only brahmans are the sons & offspring of Brahmā: born of his mouth, born of Brahmā, created by Brahmā, heirs of Brahmā.' Then the seer Devala the Dark heard, 'This evil viewpoint has arisen in the seven brahman seers as they are consulting together in leaf huts in the wilderness: "Brahmans are the superior caste; any other caste is inferior.... Only brahmans are the sons & offspring of Brahmā: born of his mouth, born of Brahmā, created by Brahmā, heirs of Brahmā." So, arranging his hair & beard, putting on crimson garments, wearing multi-layered sandals, and carrying a staff made of gold, he appeared in the courtyard of the seven brahman seers. Then he walked back & forth in the courtyard of the seven brahman seers saying, 'Well, now, where have these masters, the brahman seers, gone? Well, now, where have these masters, the brahman seers, gone?'

"Then the seven brahman seers said to the seer Devala the Dark, 'Now who is this, walking back & forth in the courtyard of the seven brahman seers like a village lout, saying, "Well, now, where have these masters, the brahman seers, gone? Well, now, where have these masters, the brahman seers, gone?" Let's curse him!' So the seven brahman seers cursed the seer Devala the Dark: 'Be ashes, dribble-spit![1] Be ashes, dribble-spit! Be ashes, dribble-spit!' But the more they cursed him, the more beautiful, good-looking, & inspiring he became. Then the thought occurred to the seven brahman seers, 'Our asceticism is in vain! Our holy-life is fruitless! For before, whenever we cursed anyone, "Be ashes, dribble-spit!" he would always become ashes. But the more we curse this one, the more beautiful, good-looking, & inspiring he becomes!'

"'Masters, your asceticism is not in vain, and your holy-life not fruitless. Please, masters, abandon your hatred toward me.'

"'We abandon our hatred toward you, master. Who are you?'

"'Have you heard of the seer Devala the Dark?'

"'Yes, master.'

"'I am he.'

"Then the seven brahman seers approached him to bow down to him, and he said to them, 'I have heard that this evil viewpoint has arisen in the seven brahman seers as they are consulting together in leaf huts in the wilderness: "Brahmans are the superior caste; any other caste is inferior.... Only brahmans are the sons & offspring of Brahmā: born of his mouth, born of Brahmā, created by Brahmā, heirs of Brahmā."'

"That is so, master.'

"'But do you know, masters, if the mother who bore you went only with a brahman, and not with a non-brahman?'

"'No, master.'

"'And do you know if the mothers of the mother who bore you—back seven generations of mothers—went only with brahmans, and not with non-brahmans?'

"'No, master.'

"'And do you know if the father who sired you went only with a brahman woman, and not with a non-brahman woman?'

"'No, master.'

"'And do you know if the fathers of the father who bore you—back seven generations of fathers—went only with brahman women, and not with non-brahman women?'

"'No, master.'

"'Do you know how there is the descent of an embryo?'

"'Yes, master, we know how there is the descent of an embryo. There is the case where the mother & father have come together, the mother is fertile, and a *gandhabba* [the being about to be reborn] is standing present. The coming together of these three is the descent of the embryo.'[2]

"'But do you know for sure whether the gandhabba is a noble warrior, a brahman, a merchant, or a worker?'

"'No, master.'

"'That being the case, do you know who you are?'

"'That being the case, master, we don't know who we are.'

"Now, Assalāyana, when those seven brahman seers couldn't defend their own birth-statement when interrogated, pressed, & rebuked by the seer Devala the Dark, how can you now defend your own birth-statement when interrogated, pressed, & rebuked by me—you, their lineage holder, but not (the equal of) Puṇṇa, their ladle holder?"

When this was said, the brahman student Assalāyana said to the Blessed One: "Magnificent, Master Gotama! Magnificent! Just as if he were to place upright what was overturned, to reveal what was hidden, to show the way to one who was lost, or to carry a lamp into the dark so that those with eyes could see forms, in the same way has Master Gotama—through many lines of reasoning—made the Dhamma clear. I go to Master Gotama for refuge, to the Dhamma, and to the Saṅgha of monks. May Master Gotama remember me as a lay follower who has gone to him for refuge, from this day forward, for life."

NOTES

1. Reading *capalī* with the Thai edition of the Canon. The PTS edition has *vasalī* ("one having a vile person (as a mother?)"); the Sri Lankan edition, *vasala,* "vile person."

2. This description of the conditions for birth is identical with one the Buddha himself gives in MN 38. Apparently in the Buddha's time it was a common feature among those who taught rebirth.

See also: SN 3:24; AN 5:191; Sn 1:11

95 *With Caṅkī (Excerpt)*

Caṅkī Sutta

... Now at that time the Blessed One was sitting & exchanging courtesies & conversation with some very senior brahmans. It so happened that a brahman student named Kāpadika[1] was seated in the assembly: young, shaven-headed, sixteen years old, a master of the Three Vedas with their vocabularies, liturgy, phonology, & etymologies, and the histories as a fifth; skilled in philology & grammar, well-versed in cosmology & the marks of a great man. While the very senior brahmans were conversing with the Blessed One, he kept breaking in & interrupting their talk. So the Blessed One scolded him, "Venerable Bhāradvāja, don't break in & interrupt while the very senior brahmans are conversing. Wait until they are finished talking."

When this was said, the brahman Caṅkī said to the Blessed One, "Master Gotama, don't scold the brahman student Kāpadika. He is a clansman, learned, wise, with good delivery. He is capable of taking part in this discussion with Master Gotama."

Then the thought occurred to the Blessed One, "Yes, this brahman student Kāpadika must be accomplished in the texts of the Three Vedas, inasmuch as the brahmans honor him so."

Then the thought occurred to Kāpadika, "When Gotama the contemplative meets my gaze with his, I will ask him a question."

And so the Blessed One, encompassing Kāpadika's awareness with his awareness, met his gaze. Kāpadika thought, "Gotama the contemplative has turned to me. Suppose I ask him a question." So he said to the Blessed One, "Master Gotama, with regard to the ancient hymns of the brahmans—passed down through oral transmission & included in their canon—the brahmans have come to the definite conclusion that "Only this is true; anything else is worthless." What does Master Gotama have to say to this?"

"Tell me, Bhāradvāja, is there among the brahmans even one brahman who says, 'This I know; this I see; only this is true; anything else is worthless?'"

"No, Master Gotama."

"And has there been among the brahmans even one teacher or teacher's teacher back through seven generations who said, 'This I know; this I see; only this is true; anything else is worthless?'"

"No, Master Gotama."

"And among the brahman seers of the past, the creators of the hymns, the composers of the hymns—those ancient hymns, sung, repeated, & collected, which brahmans at present still sing, still chant, repeating what was said, repeating what was spoken—i.e., Aṭṭhaka, Vāmaka, Vāmadeva, Vessāmitta, Yamataggi, Aṅgīrasa, Bhāradvāja, Vāseṭṭha, Kassapa & Bhagu: was there even one of these who said, 'This we know; this we see; only this is true; anything else is worthless?'"

"No, Master Gotama."

"So then, Bhāradvāja, it seems that there isn't among the brahmans even one brahman who says, 'This I know; this I see; only this is true; anything else is worthless.' And there hasn't been among the brahmans even one teacher or teacher's teacher back through seven generations who said, 'This I know; this I see; only this is true; anything else is worthless.' And there hasn't been among the brahman seers of the past, the creators of the hymns, the composers of the hymns... even one who said, 'This we know; this we see; only this is true; anything else is worthless.' Suppose there were a row of blind men, each holding on to the one in front of him: the first one doesn't see, the middle one doesn't see, the last one doesn't see. In the same way, the statement of the brahmans turns out to be a row of blind men, as it were: the first one doesn't see, the middle one doesn't see, the last one doesn't see. So what do you think, Bhāradvāja? This being the case, doesn't the conviction of the brahmans turn out to be groundless?"

"It's not only out of conviction, Master Gotama, that the brahmans honor this. They also honor it as unbroken tradition."

"Bhāradvāja, first you went by conviction. Now you speak of unbroken tradition. There are five things that can turn out in two ways in the here-&-now. Which five? Conviction, liking, unbroken tradition, reasoning by analogy, & an agreement through pondering views. These are the five things that can turn out in two ways in the here-&-now. Now some things are firmly held in conviction and yet vain, empty, & false. Some things are not firmly held in conviction, and yet they are genuine, factual, & unmistaken. Some things are well-liked... truly an unbroken tradition... well-reasoned... Some things are well-pondered and yet vain, empty, & false. Some things are not well-pondered, and yet they are genuine, factual, & unmistaken. In these cases it isn't proper for a observant person who safeguards the truth to come to a definite conclusion, 'Only this is true; anything else is worthless."

"But to what extent, Master Gotama, is there the safeguarding of the truth? To what extent does one safeguard the truth? We ask Master Gotama about the safeguarding of the truth."

"If a person has conviction, his statement, 'This is my conviction,' safeguards the truth. But he doesn't yet come to the definite conclusion that 'Only this is true; anything else is worthless.' To this extent, Bhāradvāja, there is the safeguarding of the truth. To this extent one safeguards the truth. I describe this as the safeguarding of the truth. But it is not yet an awakening to the truth.

"If a person likes something... holds an unbroken tradition... has something reasoned through analogy... has something he agrees to, having pondered views, his statement, 'This is what I agree to, having pondered views,' safeguards the truth. But he doesn't yet come to the definite conclusion that 'Only this is true; anything else is worthless.' To this extent, Bhāradvāja, there is the safeguarding of the truth. To this extent one safeguards the truth. I describe this as the safeguarding of the truth. But it is not yet an awakening to the truth."

"Yes, Master Gotama, to this extent there is the safeguarding of the truth. To this extent one safeguards the truth. We regard this as the safeguarding of the truth. But to what extent is there an awakening to the truth? To what extent does one awaken to the truth? We ask Master Gotama about awakening to the truth."

"There is the case, Bhāradvāja, where a monk lives in dependence on a certain village or town. Then a householder or householder's son goes to him and observes him with regard to three qualities—qualities based on greed, qualities based on aversion, qualities based on delusion: 'Are there in this venerable one any such qualities based on greed that, with his mind overcome by these qualities, he might say, "I know," while not knowing, or say, "I see," while not seeing; or that he might urge another to act in a way that was for his/her long-term harm & pain?' As he observes him, he comes to know, 'There are in this venerable one no such qualities based on greed.... His bodily behavior & verbal behavior are those of one not greedy. And the Dhamma he teaches is deep, hard to see, hard to realize, tranquil, refined, beyond the scope of conjecture, subtle, to-be-experienced by the wise. This Dhamma can't easily be taught by a person who's greedy.

"When, on observing that the monk is purified with regard to qualities based on greed, he next observes him with regard to qualities based on aversion: 'Are there in this venerable one any such qualities based on aversion that, with his mind overcome by these qualities, he might say, "I know," while not knowing, or say, "I see," while not seeing; or that he might urge another to act in a way that was for his/her long-term harm & pain?' As he observes him, he comes to know, 'There are in this venerable one no such qualities based on aversion.... His bodily behavior & verbal behavior are those of one not aversive. And the Dhamma he teaches is deep, hard to see, hard to realize, tranquil, refined, beyond the scope of conjecture, subtle, to-be-experienced by the wise. This Dhamma can't easily be taught by a person who's aversive.

"When, on observing that the monk is purified with regard to qualities based on aversion, he next observes him with regard to qualities based on delusion: 'Are there in this venerable one any such qualities based on delusion that, with his mind overcome by these qualities, he might say, "I know," while not knowing, or say, "I see," while not seeing; or that he might urge another to act in a way that was for his/her long-term harm & pain?' As he observes him, he comes to know, 'There are in this venerable one no such qualities based on delusion.... His bodily behavior & verbal behavior are those of one not deluded. And the Dhamma he teaches is deep, hard to see, hard to realize, tranquil, refined, beyond the scope of conjecture, subtle, to-be-experienced by the wise. This Dhamma can't easily be taught by a person who's deluded.

"When, on observing that the monk is purified with regard to qualities based on delusion, he places conviction in him. With the arising of conviction, he visits him & grows close to him. Growing close to him, he lends ear. Lending ear, he hears the Dhamma. Hearing the Dhamma, he remembers it. Remembering it, he penetrates the meaning of those dhammas. Penetrating the meaning, he comes to an agreement through pondering those dhammas. There being an agreement through pondering those dhammas, desire arises. With the arising of desire, he becomes willing. Willing, he contemplates [lit: weighs, compares]. Contemplating, he makes an exertion. Exerting himself, he both realizes the ultimate meaning of the truth with his body and sees by penetrating it with discernment.

"To this extent, Bhāradvāja, there is an awakening to the truth. To this extent one awakens to the truth. I describe this as an awakening to the truth. But it is not yet the final attainment of the truth."

"Yes, Master Gotama, to this extent there is an awakening to the truth. To this extent one awakens to the truth. We regard this as an awakening to the truth. But to what extent is there the final attainment of the truth? To what extent does one finally attain the truth? We ask Master Gotama about the final attainment of the truth."

"The cultivation, development, & pursuit of those very same qualities: to this extent, Bhāradvāja, there is the final attainment of the truth. To this extent one finally attains the truth. I describe this as the final attainment of the truth."

"Yes, Master Gotama, to this extent there is the final attainment of the truth. To this extent one finally attains the truth. We regard this as the final attainment of the truth. But what quality is most helpful for the final attainment of the truth? We ask Master Gotama about the quality most helpful for the final attainment of the truth."

"Exertion is most helpful for the final attainment of the truth, Bhāradvāja. If one didn't make an exertion, one wouldn't finally attain the truth. Because one makes an exertion, one finally attains the truth. Therefore, exertion is most helpful for the final attainment of the truth."

"But what quality is most helpful for exertion? We ask Master Gotama about the quality most helpful for exertion."

"Contemplating is most helpful for exertion, Bhāradvāja. If one didn't contemplate, one wouldn't make an exertion. Because one contemplates, one makes an exertion. Therefore, contemplating is most helpful for exertion."

"But what quality is most helpful for contemplating? ..."

"Being willing.... If one weren't willing, one wouldn't contemplate...."

"But what quality is most helpful for being willing? ..."

"Desire.... If desire didn't arise, one wouldn't be willing...."

"But what quality is most helpful for desire? ..."

"Coming to an agreement through pondering dhammas.... If one didn't come to an agreement through pondering dhammas, desire wouldn't arise...."

"But what quality is most helpful for coming to an agreement through pondering dhammas? ..."

"Penetrating the meaning.... If one didn't penetrate the meaning, one wouldn't come to an agreement through pondering dhammas...."

"But what quality is most helpful for penetrating the meaning?...."

"Remembering the Dhamma.... If one didn't remember the Dhamma, one wouldn't penetrate the meaning...."

"But what quality is most helpful for remembering the Dhamma?... "

"Hearing the Dhamma.... If one didn't hear the Dhamma, one wouldn't remember the Dhamma...."

"But what quality is most helpful for hearing the Dhamma? ..."

"Lending ear.... If one didn't lend ear, one wouldn't hear the Dhamma...."

"But what quality is most helpful for lending ear? ... "

"Growing close.... If one didn't grow close, one wouldn't lend ear...."

"But what quality is most helpful for growing close? ... "

"Visiting.... If one didn't visit, one wouldn't grow close...."

"But what quality is most helpful for visiting? We ask Master Gotama about the quality most helpful for visiting."

"Conviction is most helpful for visiting, Bhāradvāja. If conviction (in a person) didn't arise, one wouldn't visit (that person).

Because conviction arises, one visits. Therefore, conviction is most helpful for visiting."

"We have asked Master Gotama about safeguarding the truth, and Master Gotama has answered about safeguarding the truth. We like that & agree with that,[2] and so we are gratified. We have asked Master Gotama about awakening to the truth, and Master Gotama has answered about awakening to the truth. We like that & agree with that, and so we are gratified. We have asked Master Gotama about finally attaining the truth, and Master Gotama has answered about finally attaining the truth. We like that & agree with that, and so we are gratified. We have asked Master Gotama about the quality most helpful for finally attaining the truth, and Master Gotama has answered about the quality most helpful for finally attaining the truth. We like that & agree with that, and so we are gratified. Whatever we have asked Master Gotama, Master Gotama has answered it. We like that & agree with that, and so we are gratified.

"We used to think, 'Who are these bald-headed 'contemplatives,' these menial, dark offspring of the Kinsman's [Brahmā's] feet[3]? Who are they to know the Dhamma?' But now Master Gotama has inspired within us a contemplative-love for contemplatives, a contemplative-confidence in contemplatives, a contemplative-respect for contemplatives. Magnificent, Master Gotama! Magnificent! Just as if he were to place upright what was overturned, to reveal what was hidden, to show the way to one who was lost, or to carry a lamp into the dark so that those with eyes could see forms, in the same way has Master Gotama—through many lines of reasoning—made the Dhamma clear. I go to Master Gotama for refuge, to the Dhamma, & to the Saṅgha of monks. May Master Gotama remember me as a lay follower who has gone for refuge from this day forward, for life."

NOTES

1. Alternative readings: Kāpaṭhika, Kāpaṭhaka.

2. Notice that Kāpadika is careful to safeguard the truth in the way he expresses his approval for the Buddha's teachings.

3. The brahmans regarded Brahmā as their original ancestor, and so called him their "Kinsman." The commentary notes that they regarded themselves as born from his mouth, while other castes were born from lower parts of his body, down to contemplatives *(samaṇa)*, who they said were born from his feet.

See also: AN 3:66; AN 9:1

97 To Dhanañjānin

Dhanañjānin Sutta

I have heard that on one occasion the Blessed One was staying near Rājagaha in the Bamboo Grove, the Squirrels' Sanctuary. Now, on that occasion Ven. Sāriputta was wandering in the Southern Mountains with a large Saṅgha of monks. Then a certain monk who had spent the Rains in Rājagaha went to the Southern Mountains, to Ven. Sāriputta. On arrival, he exchanged courteous greetings with Ven. Sāriputta and—after an exchange of friendly greetings & courtesies—sat to one side. As he was sitting there, Ven. Sāriputta said to him, "I trust, friend, that the Blessed One is strong & free from illness?"

"The Blessed One, friend, is strong & free from illness."

"I trust that the Saṅgha of monks is strong & free from illness?"

"The Saṅgha of monks is also strong & free from illness."

"At the Taṇḍulapāla Gate is a brahman named Dhanañjānin.[1] I trust that he is strong & free from illness?"

"Dhanañjānin the brahman is also strong & free from illness."

"And I trust that Dhanañjānin the brahman is heedful?"

"From where would our Dhanañjānin the brahman get any heedfulness, friend? Relying on the king, he plunders brahmans & householders. Relying on the brahmans & householders, he plunders the king. His wife—a woman of faith, fetched from a family with faith—has died. He has fetched another wife—a woman of no faith—from a family with no faith."

"What a bad thing to hear, my friend—when we hear that Dhanañjānin the brahman is heedless. Perhaps sooner or later we might meet with Dhanañjānin the brahman. Perhaps there might be some conversation."

Then Ven. Sāriputta, having stayed in the Southern Mountains as long as he liked, wandered in the direction of Rājagaha. After wandering by stages, he arrived at Rājagaha. There he stayed near Rājagaha in the Squirrels' Sanctuary.

Then early in the morning, Ven. Sāriputta, having adjusted his under robe and carrying his bowl & outer robe, went into Rājagaha for alms. And on that occasion Dhanañjānin the brahman was milking cows in a cow pen outside the city. Then Ven. Sāriputta, having gone for alms in Rājagaha, after his meal, on his way back from his almsround, went to Dhanañjānin the brahman. Dhanañjānin the brahman saw Ven. Sāriputta coming from afar. On seeing him, he went to him and said, "Drink some of this fresh milk, master Sāriputta. It must be time for your meal."

"That's all right, brahman. I have finished my meal for today. My day's abiding will be under that tree over there. You may come there."

"As you say, master," Dhanañjānin responded to Ven. Sāriputta. Then after he had finished his morning meal, he went to Ven. Sāriputta. On arrival, he exchanged courteous greetings with Ven. Sāriputta and—after an exchange of friendly greetings & courtesies—sat to one side. As he was sitting there, Ven. Sāriputta said to him, "I trust, Dhanañjānin, that you are heedful?"

"From where would we get any heedfulness, master?—when parents are to be supported, wife & children are to be supported, slaves & workers are to be supported, friend-&-companion duties are to be done for friends & companions, kinsmen-&-relative duties for kinsmen & relatives, guest duties for guests, departed-ancestor duties for departed ancestors, devatā duties for devatās, king duties for the king, and this body also has to be refreshed & nourished."

"What do you think, Dhanañjānin? There is the case where a certain person, for the sake of his mother & father, does what is unrighteous, does what is dissonant. Then, because of his unrighteous, dissonant conduct, hell-wardens drag him off to hell. Would he gain anything by saying, 'I did what is unrighteous, what is dissonant, for the sake of my mother & father. Don't (throw) me into hell, hell-wardens!' Or would his mother & father gain anything for him by saying, 'He did what is unrighteous, what is dissonant, for our sake. Don't (throw) him into hell, hell-wardens!'?"

"No, master Sāriputta. Even right while he was wailing, they'd cast him into hell."

"What do you think, Dhanañjānin? There is the case where a certain person, for the sake of his wife & children... his slaves & workers... his friends & companions... his kinsmen & relatives... his guests... his departed ancestors... the devatās... the king, does what is unrighteous, does what is dissonant. Then, because of his unrighteous, dissonant conduct, hell-wardens drag him off to hell. Would he gain anything by saying, 'I did what is unrighteous, what is dissonant, for the sake of the king. Don't (throw) me into hell, hell-wardens!' Or would the king gain anything for him by saying, 'He did what is unrighteous, what is dissonant, for our sake. Don't (throw) him into hell, hell-wardens!'?"

"No, master Sāriputta. Even right while he was wailing, they'd cast him into hell."

"What do you think, Dhanañjānin? There is the case where a certain person, for the sake of refreshing & nourishing his body, does what is unrighteous, does what is dissonant. Then, because of his unrighteous, dissonant conduct, hell-wardens drag him off to hell. Would he gain anything by saying, 'I did what is unrighteous, what is dissonant, for the sake of refreshing & nourishing my body. Don't (throw) me into hell, hell-wardens!' Or would others gain anything for him by saying, 'He did what is unrighteous, what is dissonant, for the sake of refreshing & nourishing his body. Don't (throw) him into hell, hell-wardens!'?"

"No, master Sāriputta. Even right while he was wailing, they'd cast him into hell."

"Now, what do you think, Dhanañjānin? Which is the better: one who, for the sake of his mother & father, would do what is unrighteous, what is dissonant; or one who, for the sake of his mother & father, would do what is righteous, what is harmonious?

"Master Sāriputta, the one who, for the sake of his mother & father, would do what is unrighteous, what is dissonant, is not the better one. The one who, for the sake of his mother & father, would do what is righteous, what is harmonious would be the better one there. Righteous conduct, harmonious conduct, is better than unrighteous conduct, dissonant conduct.[2]

"Dhanañjānin, there are other activities—reasonable, righteous—by which one can support one's mother & father, and at the same time both not do evil and practice the practice of merit.

"What do you think, Dhanañjānin? Which is the better: one who, for the sake of his wife & children... his slaves & workers... his friends & companions... his kinsmen & relatives... his guests... his departed ancestors... the devatās... the king... refreshing & nourishing his body, would do what is unrighteous, what is dissonant; or one who, for the sake of refreshing & nourishing his body, would do what is righteous, what is harmonious?

"Master Sāriputta, the one who, for the sake of refreshing & nourishing his body, would do what is unrighteous, what is dissonant, is not the better one. The one who, for the sake of refreshing & nourishing his body, would do what is righteous, what is harmonious would be the better one there. Righteous conduct, harmonious conduct, is better than unrighteous conduct, dissonant conduct.

"Dhanañjānin, there are other activities—reasonable, righteous—by which one can refresh & nourish one's body, and at the same time both not do evil and practice the practice of merit."

Then Dhanañjānin the brahman, delighting & rejoicing in Ven. Sāriputta's words, got up from his seat and left.

Then on a later occasion, Dhanañjānin the brahman became diseased, in pain, severely ill. So he said to one of his men, "Come, my good man. Go to the Blessed One and, on arrival, pay homage to his feet with your head in my name and say 'Lord, Dhanañjānin the brahman is diseased, in pain, severely ill. He pays homage with his head to the Blessed One's feet.' Then go to Ven. Sāriputta and, on arrival, pay homage to his feet with your head in my name and say 'Venerable sir, Dhanañjānin the brahman is diseased, in pain, severely ill. He pays homage with his head to Ven. Sāriputta's feet.' Then say, 'It would be good if Ven. Sāriputta would visit Dhanañjānin's home, out of sympathy for him.'"

Responding, "As you say, lord," to Dhanañjānin the brahman, the man went to the Blessed One and, on arrival, bowed down to him and sat to one side. As he was sitting there he said, "Lord, Dhanañjānin the brahman is diseased, in pain, severely ill. He pays homage with his head to the Blessed One's feet." Then he went to Ven. Sāriputta and, on arrival, bowed down to him and sat to one side. As he was sitting there he said, 'Venerable sir, Dhanañjānin the brahman is diseased, in pain, severely ill. He pays homage with his head to Ven. Sāriputta's feet." Then he said, "It would be good if Ven. Sāriputta would visit Dhanañjānin's home, out of sympathy for him." Ven. Sāriputta acquiesced through silence.

Then Ven. Sāriputta, having adjusted his under robe and carrying his bowl & outer robe, went to Dhanañjānin's home. On arrival, he sat down on a prepared seat and said to him, "I trust you are getting better, Dhanañjānin? I trust you are comfortable? I trust that your pains are lessening and not increasing? I trust that there are signs of their lessening, and not of their increasing?"

"I am not getting better, Master Sāriputta. I am not comfortable. My severe pains are increasing, not lessening. There are signs of their increasing, and not of their lessening. Extreme forces slice through my head, just as if a strong man were slicing my head open with a sharp sword.... Extreme pains have arisen in my head, just as if a strong man were tightening a turban on my head with a tough leather strap.... Extreme forces carve up my stomach cavity, just as if an expert butcher or his apprentice were to carve up the stomach cavity of an ox with a sharp butcher's knife.... There is an extreme burning in my body, just as if two strong men, seizing a weaker man with their arms, were to roast and broil him over a pit of hot embers. I am not getting better, venerable sir. I am not comfortable. My severe pains are increasing, not lessening. There are signs of their increasing, and not of their lessening."

"What do you think, Dhanañjānin? Which is better: hell or the animal womb?"

"The animal womb is better than hell, Master Sāriputta."

"... Which is better: the animal womb or the realm of the hungry ghosts?"

"... the realm of the hungry ghosts...."

"... the realm of the hungry ghosts or human beings?"

"... human beings...."

"... human beings or the Devas of the Four Great Kings?"

"... the Devas of the Four Great Kings...."

"... the Devas of the Four Great Kings or the Devas of the Thirty-three?"

"... the Devas of the Thirty-three...."

"... the Devas of the Thirty-three or the Devas of the Hours?"

"... the Devas of the Hours...."

"... the Devas of the Hours or the Contented Devas?"

"... the Contented Devas...."

"... the Contented Devas or the Devas Delighting in Creation?"

"... the Devas Delighting in Creation...."

"... the Devas Delighting in Creation or the Devas Wielding Power over the Creations of Others?"

"... the Devas Wielding Power over the Creations of Others...."

"... the Devas Wielding Power over the Creations of Others or the Brahmā world?"

"Did Master Sāriputta say, 'Brahmā world'? Did Master Sāriputta say, 'Brahmā world'?"

Then the thought occurred to Ven. Sāriputta, "These brahmans are set on the Brahmā world. What if I were to teach Dhanañjānin the brahman the path to union with the Brahmās?" (So he said:) "Dhanañjānin, I will teach you the path to union with the Brahmās. Listen and pay careful attention to that. I will speak."

"As you say, master," Dhanañjānin the brahman responded to Ven. Sāriputta.

Ven. Sāriputta said: "And what is the path to union with the Brahmās? There is the case where a monk keeps pervading the first direction [the east] with an awareness imbued with good will, likewise the second, likewise the third, likewise the fourth. Thus above, below, & all around, everywhere, in its entirety, he keeps pervading the all-encompassing cosmos with an awareness imbued with good will—abundant, enlarged, immeasurable, without hostility, without ill will. He keeps pervading the first direction with an awareness imbued with compassion... empathetic joy... equanimity, likewise the second, likewise the third, likewise the fourth. Thus above, below, & all around, everywhere, in its entirety, he keeps pervading the all-encompassing cosmos with an awareness imbued with equanimity—abundant, enlarged, immeasurable, without hostility, without ill will. This, Dhanañjānin, is the path to union with the Brahmās."

"In that case, Master Sāriputta, pay homage to the Blessed One's feet with your head in my name and say 'Lord, Dhanañjānin the brahman is diseased, in pain, severely ill. He pays homage with his head to the Blessed One's feet.'"

So Ven. Sāriputta—when there was still more to be done, having established Dhanañjānin the brahman in the inferior[3] Brahmā world—got up from his seat and left. Then, not long after Ven. Sāriputta's departure, Dhanañjānin the brahman died and reappeared in the Brahmā world.

And the Blessed One said to the monks, "Monks, Sāriputta—when there was still more to be done, having established Dhanañjānin the brahman in the inferior Brahmā world—has gotten up from his seat and left."

Then Ven. Sāriputta went to the Blessed One and, on arrival, having bowed down to him, sat to one side. As he was sitting there he said to the Blessed One, "Lord, Dhanañjānin the brahman is diseased, in pain, severely ill. He pays homage with his head to the Blessed One's feet."

"But why, Sāriputta—when there was still more to be done, having established Dhanañjānin the brahman in the inferior Brahmā world—did you get up from your seat and leave?"

"The thought occurred to me, lord, 'These brahmans are set on the Brahmā worlds. What if I were to teach Dhanañjānin the brahman the path to union with the Brahmās?'"

"Sāriputta, Dhanañjānin the brahman has died and reappeared in the Brahmā world."

NOTES

1. The PTS edition of the canon gives this name as Dhānañjānin, whereas the Thai and Sri Lankan editions give it as Dhanañjānin. This discourse is unusual in that Ven. Sāriputta addresses Dhanañjānin not as "householder," but by his personal name. This would seem to indicate that the two of them were on especially familiar terms.

2. This sentence appears in the Thai and Sri Lankan editions of the canon, and in MLS, but not in MLDB.

3. I.e., inferior to any of the noble attainments. The Brahmā world can be attained simply through the power of concentration applied to unlimited goodwill, etc., or to any of the jhānas. Only if discernment is developed to overcome passion and delight for these mundane attainments can the noble attainments be realized. For discussions of this issue see MN 106, AN 4:123–126, and AN 4:178.

See also: MN 130; MN 143; SN 3:17; SN 41:7; SN 41:10; SN 55:54; AN 4:178; AN 5:130; AN 10:15

101 *At Devadaha*

Devadaha Sutta

INTRODUCTION

In this sutta, the Buddha refutes the theories of the Jains—here called the Nigaṇṭhas—an order of contemplatives flourishing in India during his time. Although on the surface this sutta may seem to be of strictly historical interest, it makes two important points that are very relevant to some common misunderstandings about Buddhism alive today.

The first point concerns the Buddhist teaching on action, or kamma (karma). The general understanding of this teaching is that actions from the past determine present pleasure and pain, while present actions determine future pleasure and pain. Or, to quote a recent book devoted to the topic, "Karma is the moral principle that governs human conduct. It declares that our present experience is conditioned by our past conduct and that our present conduct will condition our future experience." This, however, does not accurately describe the Buddha's teaching on karma, and is instead a fairly accurate account of the Nigaṇṭha teaching, which the Buddha explicitly refutes here. As he interrogates the Nigaṇṭhas, he makes the point that if all pleasure and pain experienced in the present were determined by past action, why is it that they now feel the pain of harsh treatment when they practice asceticism, and no pain of harsh treatment when they don't? If past action were the sole determining factor, then present action should have no effect on their present experience of pleasure or pain.

In this way, the Buddha points to one of the most distinctive features of his own teaching on kamma: that the present experience of pleasure and pain is a combined result of both past and present actions. This seemingly small addition to the notion of kamma plays an enormous role in allowing for the exercise of free will and the possibility of putting an end to suffering before the effects of all past actions have ripened. In other words, this addition is what makes Buddhist practice possible, and makes it possible for a person who has completed the practice to survive and teach it with full authority to others. For more on these points, see the articles, "Karma," "A Refuge in Skillful Action," and "Five Piles of Bricks"; see also the Introduction to The Wings to Awakening, along with the introductions to the sections on Skillfulness and Kamma & the End of Kamma in that book.

The second important point touched on in this sutta—how to put an end to pain and suffering—relates to the first. If the cause of present suffering were located exclusively in the past, no one could do anything in the present moment to stop that suffering; the most that could be done would be to endure the suffering while not creating any new kamma leading to future suffering. Although this was the Jain approach to practice, many people at present believe that it is the Buddhist approach as well. Meditation, according to this understanding, is the process of purifying the mind of old kamma by training it to look on with non-reactive equanimity as pain arises. The pain is the result of old kamma, the equanimity adds no new kamma, and thus over time all old kamma can be burned away.

In this sutta, however, the Buddha heaps ridicule on this idea. First he notes that none of the Nigaṇṭhas have ever come to the end of pain by trying to burn it away in this way; then he notes that they have based their belief in this practice entirely on their faith in their teacher and their approval of his ideas, but neither faith nor approval can act as guarantees of the truth. As he illustrates with his simile of the man shot with an arrow, only a person who has succeeded in going beyond pain would be in a position to speak with authority of the method that actually puts an end to pain. (What is not mentioned in this sutta is the Nigaṇṭha idea that the practice of austerities, to succeed completely in burning away old kamma, must culminate in a suicide by starvation. Thus there could be no living person who would be able to vouch for the efficacy of their method.)

The Buddha then provides his own account of how meditation actually works in putting an end to pain and suffering. His discussion shows that the problem underlying pain is not past action, but passion—in the present—for the causes of pain. In other words, pain is not inevitable. Present suffering can be prevented by changing one's understanding of, and attitude toward, the cause of suffering in the present. The Buddha illustrates this principle with the simile of a man in love with a woman: As long as he feels passion for her, he will suffer when he sees her enjoying the company of another man; when, seeing the connection between his suffering and his passion, he abandons that passion, he will no longer suffer from that cause.

Thus the practice must focus on ways to understand and bring about dispassion for the causes of stress and pain here and now. As the Buddha points out in MN 106, equanimity plays an important role in this practice, but it can also become an object for passion and delight, which would then stand in the way of true release. Thus he notes here that, in some cases, dispassion can arise simply from on-looking equanimity directed at the causes of stress. In other cases, it can come only through exertion: the mental effort—through the fabrications of directed thought, evaluation, and perception—to develop the discernment needed to see through and abandon any and all passion.

The remainder of the sutta is devoted to a standard map of how the practice develops over time, showing how the proper mixture of on-looking equanimity combined with fabrication and exertion can lead to dispassion, and through dispassion to release from all stress and suffering.

* * *

I have heard that on one occasion the Blessed One was staying among the Sakyans. Now the Sakyans have a city named Devadaha, and there the Blessed One addressed the monks: "Monks!"

"Yes, lord," the monks responded to him.

The Blessed One said, "Monks, there are some contemplatives & brahmans who teach in this way, who have this view: 'Whatever a person experiences—pleasure, pain, or neither pleasure nor pain—all is caused by what was done in the past. Thus, with the destruction of old actions through asceticism, and with the non-doing of new actions, there will be no flow into the future. With no flow into the future, there is the ending of action. With the ending of action, the ending of stress. With the ending of stress, the ending of feeling. With the ending of feeling, all suffering & stress will be exhausted.' Such is the teaching of the Nigaṇṭhas.

"Going to Nigaṇṭhas who teach in this way, I have asked them, 'Is it true, friend Nigaṇṭhas, that you teach in this way, that you have this view: "Whatever a person experiences—pleasure, pain, or neither pleasure nor pain—all is caused by what was done in the past. Thus, with the destruction of old actions through asceticism, and with the non-doing of new actions, there will be no flow into the future. With no flow into the future, there is the ending of action. With the ending of action, the ending of stress. With the ending of stress, the ending of feeling. With the ending of feeling, all suffering & stress will be exhausted"?'

"Having been asked this by me, the Nigaṇṭhas admitted it, 'Yes.'

"So I said to them, 'But friends, do you know that you existed in the past, and that you did not not exist?'

"'No, friend.'

"'And do you know that you did evil actions in the past, and that you did not not do them?'

"'No, friend.'

"'And do you know that you did such-and-such evil actions in the past?'

"'No, friend.'

"'And do you know that so-and-so much stress has been exhausted, or that so-and-so much stress remains to be exhausted, or that with the exhaustion of so-and-so much stress all stress will be exhausted?'

"'No, friend.'

"'But do you know what is the abandoning of unskillful qualities and the attainment of skillful qualities in the here-&-now?'

"'No, friend.'

"'So, friends, it seems that you don't know that you existed in the past, and that you did not not exist... you don't know what is the abandoning of unskillful qualities and the attainment of skillful qualities in the here-&-now. That being the case, it is not proper for you to assert that, "Whatever a person experiences—pleasure, pain, or neither pleasure nor pain—all is caused by what was done in the past. Thus, with the destruction of old actions through asceticism, and with the non-doing of new actions, there will be no flow into the future. With no flow into the future, there is the ending of action. With the ending of action, the ending of stress. With the ending of stress, the ending of feeling. With the ending of feeling, all suffering & stress will be exhausted."

"'If, however, you knew that you existed in the past, and that you did not not exist; if you knew that you did evil actions in the past, and that you did not not do them; if you knew that you did such-and-such evil actions in the past; if you knew that so-and-so much stress has been exhausted, or that so-and-so much stress remains to be exhausted, or that with the exhaustion of so-and-so much stress all stress will be exhausted; if you knew what is the abandoning of unskillful qualities and the attainment of skillful qualities in the here-&-now, then—that being the case—it would be proper for you to assert that, "Whatever a person experiences—pleasure, pain, or neither pleasure nor pain—all is caused by what was done in the past. Thus, with the destruction of old actions through asceticism, and with the non-doing of new actions, there will be no flow into the future. With no flow into the future, there is the ending of action. With the ending of action, the ending of stress. With the ending of stress, the ending of feeling. With the ending of feeling, all suffering & stress will be exhausted."

"'Friend Nigaṇṭhas, it's as if a man were shot with an arrow thickly smeared with poison. As a result of being shot with the arrow, he would feel fierce, sharp, racking pains. His friends & companions, kinsmen & relatives would provide him with a surgeon. The surgeon would cut around the opening of the wound with a knife. As a result of the surgeon's cutting around the opening of the wound with a knife, the man would feel fierce, sharp, racking pains. The surgeon would probe for the arrow with a probe. As a result of the surgeon's probing for the arrow with a probe, the man would feel fierce, sharp, racking pains. The surgeon would then pull out the arrow. As a result of the surgeon's pulling out the arrow, the man would feel fierce, sharp, racking pains. The surgeon would then apply a burning medicine to the mouth of the wound. As a result of the surgeon's applying a burning medicine to the mouth of the wound, the man would feel fierce, sharp, racking pains. But then at a later time, when the wound had healed and was covered with skin, he would be well & happy, free, master of himself, able to go wherever he liked. The thought would occur to him, "Before, I was shot with an arrow thickly smeared with poison. As a result of being shot with the arrow, I felt fierce, sharp, racking pains. My friends & companions, kinsmen & relatives provided me with a surgeon… The surgeon cut around the opening of the wound with a knife… probed for the arrow with a probe… pulled out the arrow… applied a burning medicine to the mouth of the wound. As a result of his applying a burning medicine to the mouth of the wound, I felt fierce, sharp, racking pains. But now that the wound is healed and covered with skin, I am well & happy, free, master of myself, able to go wherever I like."

"'In the same way, friend Nigaṇṭhas, if you knew that you existed in the past, and that you did not not exist… if you knew what is the abandoning of unskillful qualities and the attainment of skillful qualities in the here-&-now, then—that being the case—it would be proper for you to assert that, "Whatever a person experiences—pleasure, pain, or neither pleasure nor pain—all is caused by what was done in the past. Thus, with the destruction of old actions through asceticism, and with the non-doing of new actions, there will be no flow into the future. With no flow into the future, there is the ending of action. With the ending of action, the ending of stress. With the ending of stress, the ending of feeling. With the ending of feeling, all suffering & stress will be exhausted." But because you do not know that you existed in the past… you do not know what is the abandoning of unskillful qualities and the attainment of skillful qualities in the here-&-now, then—that being the case—it is not proper for you to assert that, "Whatever a person experiences—pleasure, pain, or neither pleasure nor pain—all is caused by what was done in the past. Thus, with the destruction of old actions through asceticism, and with the non-doing of new actions, there will be no flow into the future. With no flow into the future, there is the ending of action. With the ending of action, the ending of stress. With the ending of stress, the ending of feeling. With the ending of feeling, all suffering & stress will be exhausted."

"When this was said, the Nigaṇṭhas said to me, 'Friend, the Nigaṇṭha Nāṭaputta [the leader of the Nigaṇṭhas] is all-knowing, all-seeing, and claims total knowledge & vision thus: "Whether I am walking or standing, sleeping or awake, knowledge & vision are continuously & continually established in me." He has told us, "Nigaṇṭhas, there are evil actions that you have done in the past. Exhaust them with these painful austerities. When in the present you are restrained in body, restrained in speech, and restrained in mind, that is the non-doing of evil action for the future. Thus, with the destruction of old actions through asceticism, and with the non-doing of new actions, there will be no flow into the future. With no flow into the future, there is the ending of action. With the ending of action, the ending of stress. With the ending of stress, the ending of feeling. With the ending of feeling, all suffering & stress will be exhausted." We approve of that (teaching), prefer it, and are gratified by it.'

"When this was said, I said to the Nigaṇṭhas, 'Friend Nigaṇṭhas, there are five things that can turn out in two ways in the here-&-now. Which five? Conviction, liking, unbroken tradition, reasoning by analogy, & an agreement through pondering views. These are the five things that can turn out in two ways in the here-&-now. That being the case, what kind of conviction do you have for your teacher with regard to the past? What kind of liking? What kind of unbroken tradition? What kind of reasoning by analogy? What kind of agreement through pondering views?' But when I said this, I did not see that the Nigaṇṭhas had any legitimate defense of their teaching.

"So I asked them further, 'Friend Nigaṇṭhas, what do you think? When there is fierce striving, fierce exertion, do you feel fierce, sharp, racking pains from harsh treatment? And when there is no fierce striving, no fierce exertion, do you feel no fierce, sharp, racking pains from harsh treatment?'

"'Yes, friend…'

"'… Then it's not proper for you to assert that, "Whatever a person experiences—pleasure, pain, or neither pleasure nor pain—all is caused by what was done in the past. Thus, with the destruction of old actions through asceticism, and with the non-doing of new actions, there will be no flow into the future. With no flow into the future, there is the ending of action. With the ending of action, the ending of stress. With the ending of stress, the ending of feeling. With the ending of feeling, all suffering & stress will be exhausted."

"'If it were the case that when there was fierce striving, fierce exertion, you felt fierce, sharp, racking pains from harsh treatment; and when there was no fierce striving, no fierce exertion, you still felt fierce, sharp, racking pains from harsh treatment, then—that being the case—it would be proper for you to assert that, "Whatever a person experiences—pleasure, pain, or neither pleasure nor pain—all is caused by what was done in the past. Thus, with the destruction of old actions through asceticism, and with the non-doing of new actions, there will be no flow into the future. With no flow into the future, there is the ending of action. With the ending of action, the ending of stress. With the ending of stress, the ending of feeling. With the ending of feeling, all suffering & stress will be exhausted." But because when there is fierce striving, fierce exertion, you feel fierce, sharp, racking pains from harsh treatment; and when there was no fierce striving, no fierce exertion, you feel no fierce, sharp, racking pains from harsh treatment, then—that being the case—it is not proper for you to assert that, "Whatever a person experiences—pleasure, pain, or neither pleasure nor pain—all is caused by what was done in the past. Thus, with the destruction of old actions through asceticism, and with the non-doing of new actions, there will be no flow into the future. With no flow into the future, there is the ending of action. With the ending of action, the ending of stress. With the ending of stress, the ending of feeling. With the ending of feeling, all suffering & stress will be exhausted."' But when I said this, I did not see that the Niganṭhas had any legitimate defense of their teaching.

"So I asked them further, 'Friend Niganṭhas, what do you think? Can an action to be experienced in the here-&-now be turned, through striving & exertion, into an action to be experienced in the future life?'

"'No, friend.'

"'Can an action to be experienced in the future life be turned, through striving & exertion, into an action to be experienced in the here-&-now?'

"'No, friend.'

"What do you think? Can an action to be experienced as pleasure be turned, through striving & exertion, into an action to be experienced as pain?'

"'No, friend.'

"'Can an action to be experienced as pain be turned, through striving & exertion, into an action to be experienced as pleasure?'

"'No, friend.'

"What do you think? Can an action ripe to be experienced be turned, through striving & exertion, into an action not ripe to be experienced?'

"'No, friend.'

"'Can an action not ripe to be experienced be turned, through striving & exertion, into an action ripe to be experienced?'

"'No, friend.'

"What do you think? Can an action greatly to be experienced be turned, through striving & exertion, into an action barely to be experienced?'

"'No, friend.'

"'Can an action barely to be experienced be turned, through striving & exertion, into an action greatly to be experienced?'

"'No, friend.'

"What do you think? Can an action to be experienced be turned, through striving & exertion, into an action not to be experienced?'

"'No, friend.'

"'Can an action not to be experienced be turned, through striving & exertion, into an action to be experienced?'

"'No, friend.'

"'So, friends, it seems that an action to be experienced in the here-&-now cannot be turned, through striving & exertion, into an action to be experienced in the future life. An action to be experienced in the future life cannot be turned, through striving & exertion, into an action to be experienced in the here-&-now.... An action to be experienced cannot be turned, through striving & exertion, into an action not to be experienced. An action not to be experienced cannot be turned, through striving & exertion, into an action to be experienced. That being the case, the striving of the Nigaṇṭhas is fruitless, their exertion is fruitless.'

"Such is the teaching of the Nigaṇṭhas. And, such being the teaching of the Nigaṇṭhas, ten legitimate deductions can be drawn that give grounds for censuring them.

"[1] If beings experience pleasure & pain based on what was done in the past, then obviously the Nigaṇṭhas have done bad things in the past, which is why they now feel such fierce, sharp, racking pains.

"[2] If beings experience pleasure & pain based on the creative act of a supreme god, then obviously the Nigaṇṭhas have been created by an evil supreme god, which is why they now feel such fierce, sharp, racking pains.

"[3] If beings experience pleasure & pain based on sheer luck, then obviously the Nigaṇṭhas have evil luck, which is why they now feel such fierce, sharp, racking pains.

"[4] If beings experience pleasure & pain based on birth, then obviously the Nigaṇṭhas have had an evil birth, which is why they now feel such fierce, sharp, racking pains.

"[5] If beings experience pleasure & pain based on efforts in the here-&-now, then obviously the Nigaṇṭhas have evil efforts in the here-&-now, which is why they now feel such fierce, sharp, racking pains.

"[6] If beings experience pleasure & pain based on what was done in the past, the Nigaṇṭhas deserve censure. Even if not, they still deserve censure.

"[7] If beings experience pleasure & pain based on the creative act of a supreme god, the Nigaṇṭhas deserve censure. Even if not, they still deserve censure.

"[8] If beings experience pleasure & pain based on sheer luck, the Nigaṇṭhas deserve censure. Even if not, they still deserve censure.

"[9] If beings experience pleasure & pain based on birth, the Nigaṇṭhas deserve censure. Even if not, they still deserve censure.

"[10] If beings experience pleasure & pain based on efforts in the here-&-now, the Nigaṇṭhas deserve censure. Even if not, they still deserve censure.

"Such is the teaching of the Nigaṇṭhas, monks. And, such being the teaching of the Nigaṇṭhas, these ten legitimate deductions can be drawn that give grounds for censuring them. This is how striving is fruitless, how exertion is fruitless.

"And how is striving fruitful, how is exertion fruitful? There is the case where a monk, when not loaded down, does not load himself down with pain, nor does he reject pleasure that accords with the Dhamma, although he is not infatuated with that pleasure. He discerns that 'When I exert a [physical, verbal, or mental] fabrication against this cause of stress, then from the fabrication of exertion there is dispassion. When I look on with equanimity at that cause of stress, then from the development of equanimity there is dispassion.' So he exerts a fabrication against the cause of stress for which dispassion comes from the fabrication of exertion, and develops equanimity with regard to the cause of stress for which dispassion comes from the development of equanimity. Thus the stress coming from the cause of stress where there is dispassion from the fabrication of exertion is exhausted, and the stress coming from the cause of stress where there is dispassion from the development of equanimity is exhausted.

"Suppose that a man is in love with a woman, his mind ensnared with fierce desire, fierce passion. He sees her standing with another man, chatting, joking, & laughing. What do you think, monks? As he sees her standing with another man, chatting, joking, & laughing, would sorrow, lamentation, pain, distress, & despair arise in him?"

"Yes, lord. Why is that? Because he is in love with her, his mind ensnared with fierce desire, fierce passion...."

"Now suppose the thought were to occur to him, 'I am in love with this woman, my mind ensnared with fierce desire, fierce passion. When I see her standing with another man, chatting, joking, & laughing, then sorrow, lamentation, pain, distress, & despair arise within me. Why don't I abandon my desire & passion for that woman?' So he abandons his desire & passion for that woman, and afterwards sees her standing with another man, chatting, joking, & laughing. What do you think, monks? As he sees her standing with another man, chatting, joking, & laughing, would sorrow, lamentation, pain, distress, & despair arise in him?"

"No, lord. Why is that? He is dispassionate toward that woman...."

"In the same way, the monk, when not loaded down, does not load himself down with pain, nor does he reject pleasure that accords with the Dhamma, although he is not infatuated with that pleasure. He discerns that 'When I exert a [physical, verbal, or mental] fabrication against this cause of stress, then from the fabrication of exertion there is dispassion. When I look on with equanimity at that cause of stress, then from the development of equanimity there is dispassion.' So he exerts a fabrication against the cause of stress for which dispassion comes from the fabrication of exertion, and develops equanimity with regard to the cause of stress for which dispassion comes from the development of equanimity. Thus the stress coming from the cause of stress where there is dispassion from the fabrication of exertion is exhausted, and the stress coming from the cause of stress where there is dispassion from the development of equanimity is exhausted.

"And further, the monk notices this: 'When I live according to my pleasure, unskillful qualities increase in me & skillful qualities decline. When I exert myself with stress & pain, though, unskillful qualities decline in me & skillful qualities increase. Why don't I exert myself with stress & pain?' So he exerts himself with stress & pain, and while he is exerting himself with stress & pain, unskillful qualities decline in him, & skillful qualities increase. Then at a later time he would no longer exert himself with stress & pain. Why is that? Because he has attained the goal for which he was exerting himself with stress & pain. That is why, at a later time, he would no longer exert himself with stress & pain.

"Suppose a fletcher were to heat & warm an arrow shaft between two flames, making it straight & pliable. Then at a later time he would no longer heat & warm the shaft between two flames, making it straight & pliable. Why is that? Because he has attained the goal for which he was heating & warming the shaft. That is why at a later time he would no longer heat & warm the shaft between two flames, making it straight & pliable.

"In the same way, the monk notices this: 'When I live according to my pleasure, unskillful qualities increase in me & skillful qualities decline. When I exert myself with stress & pain, though, unskillful qualities decline in me & skillful qualities increase. Why don't I exert myself with stress & pain?' So he exerts himself with stress & pain, and while he is exerting himself with stress & pain, unskillful qualities decline in him, & skillful qualities increase. Then at a later time he would no longer exert himself with stress & pain. Why is that? Because he has attained the goal for which he was exerting himself with stress & pain. That is why, at a later time, he would no longer exert himself with stress & pain.

"This is how striving is fruitful, how exertion is fruitful.

"And further, there is the case where a Tathāgata appears in the world, worthy & rightly self-awakened. He teaches the Dhamma admirable in its beginning, admirable in its middle, admirable in its end. He proclaims the holy life both in its particulars and in its essence, entirely perfect, surpassingly pure.

"A householder or householder's son, hearing the Dhamma, gains conviction in the Tathāgata and reflects: 'Household life is confining, a dusty path. Life gone forth is the open air. It isn't easy, living at home, to practice the holy life totally perfect, totally pure, a polished shell. What if I, having shaved off my hair & beard and putting on the ochre robe, were to go forth from the household life into homelessness?'

"So after some time he abandons his mass of wealth, large or small; leaves his circle of relatives, large or small; shaves off his hair and beard, puts on the ochre robes, and goes forth from the household life into homelessness.

VIRTUE

"When he has thus gone forth, endowed with the monks' training & livelihood, then—abandoning the taking of life—he abstains from the taking of life. He dwells with his rod laid down, his knife laid down, scrupulous, merciful, compassionate for the welfare of all living beings.

"Abandoning the taking of what is not given, he abstains from taking what is not given. He takes only what is given, accepts only what is given, lives not by stealth but by means of a self that has become pure. This, too, is part of his virtue.

"Abandoning uncelibacy, he lives a celibate life, aloof, refraining from the sexual act that is the villager's way.

"Abandoning the telling of lies, he abstains from telling lies. He speaks the truth, holds to the truth, is firm, reliable, no deceiver of the world.

"Abandoning divisive speech, he abstains from divisive speech. What he has heard here he does not tell there to break those people apart from these people here. What he has heard there he does not tell here to break these people apart from those people there. Thus reconciling those who have broken apart or cementing those who are united, he loves concord, delights in concord, enjoys concord, speaks things that create concord.

"Abandoning abusive speech, he abstains from abusive speech. He speaks words that are soothing to the ear, that are affectionate, that go to the heart, that are polite, appealing and pleasing to people at large.

"Abandoning idle chatter, he abstains from idle chatter. He speaks in season, speaks what is factual, what is in accordance with the goal, the Dhamma, and the Vinaya. He speaks words worth treasuring, seasonable, reasonable, circumscribed, connected with the goal.

"He abstains from damaging seed and plant life.

"He eats only once a day, refraining from the evening meal and from food at the wrong time of day.

"He abstains from dancing, singing, instrumental music, and from watching shows.

"He abstains from wearing garlands and from beautifying himself with scents and cosmetics.

"He abstains from high & luxurious beds and seats.

"He abstains from accepting gold & money.

"He abstains from accepting uncooked grain… raw meat… women & girls… male & female slaves… goats & sheep… fowl & pigs… elephants, cattle, steeds, & mares… fields & property.

"He abstains from running messages… from buying & selling… from dealing with false scales, false metals, & false measures… from bribery, deception, & fraud.

"He abstains from mutilating, executing, imprisoning, highway robbery, plunder, & violence.

"He is content with a set of robes to provide for his body and alms food to provide for his hunger. Just as a bird, wherever it goes, flies with its wings as its only burden; so too is he content with a set of robes to provide for his body and alms food to provide for his hunger. Wherever he goes, he takes only his barest necessities along.

"Endowed with this noble aggregate of virtue, he is inwardly sensitive to the pleasure of being blameless.

SENSE RESTRAINT

"On seeing a form with the eye, he does not grasp at any theme or details by which—if he were to dwell without restraint over the faculty of the eye—evil, unskillful qualities such as greed or distress might assail him. On hearing a sound with the ear.... On smelling an aroma with the nose.... On tasting a flavor with the tongue.... On touching a tactile sensation with the body.... On cognizing an idea with the intellect, he does not grasp at any theme or details by which—if he were to dwell without restraint over the faculty of the intellect—evil, unskillful qualities such as greed or distress might assail him. Endowed with this noble restraint over the sense faculties, he is inwardly sensitive to the pleasure of being blameless.

MINDFULNESS & ALERTNESS

"When going forward & returning, he acts with alertness. When looking toward & looking away... when bending & extending his limbs... when carrying his outer cloak, upper robe, & bowl... when eating, drinking, chewing, & tasting... when urinating & defecating... when walking, standing, sitting, falling asleep, waking up, talking, & remaining silent, he acts with alertness.

ABANDONING THE HINDRANCES

"Endowed with this noble aggregate of virtue, this noble restraint over the sense faculties, this noble mindfulness & alertness, he seeks out a secluded dwelling: a wilderness, the shade of a tree, a mountain, a glen, a hillside cave, a charnel ground, a forest grove, the open air, a heap of straw. After his meal, returning from his alms round, he sits down, crosses his legs, holds his body erect, and brings mindfulness to the fore.

"Abandoning covetousness with regard to the world, he dwells with an awareness devoid of covetousness. He cleanses his mind of covetousness. Abandoning ill will and anger, he dwells with an awareness devoid of ill will, sympathetic with the welfare of all living beings. He cleanses his mind of ill will and anger. Abandoning sloth & drowsiness, he dwells with an awareness devoid of sloth and drowsiness, mindful, alert, percipient of light. He cleanses his mind of sloth and drowsiness. Abandoning restlessness & anxiety, he dwells undisturbed, his mind inwardly stilled. He cleanses his mind of restlessness and anxiety. Abandoning uncertainty, he dwells having crossed over uncertainty, with no perplexity with regard to skillful qualities. He cleanses his mind of uncertainty.

THE FOUR JHĀNAS

"Having abandoned these five hindrances—imperfections of awareness that weaken discernment—then, quite secluded from sensuality, secluded from unskillful qualities, he enters and remains in the first jhāna: rapture & pleasure born of seclusion, accompanied by directed thought & evaluation. This, too, is how striving is fruitful, how exertion is fruitful.

"Then, with the stilling of directed thoughts & evaluations, he enters and remains in the second jhāna: rapture & pleasure born of concentration, unification of awareness free from directed thought & evaluation—internal assurance. This, too, is how striving is fruitful, how exertion is fruitful.

"Then, with the fading of rapture, he remains equanimous, mindful, & alert, and senses pleasure with the body. He enters and remains in the third jhāna, of which the noble ones declare, 'Equanimous & mindful, he has a pleasant abiding.' This, too, is how striving is fruitful, how exertion is fruitful.

"Then, with the abandoning of pleasure & pain—as with the earlier disappearance of elation & distress—he enters and remains in the fourth jhāna: purity of equanimity & mindfulness, neither pleasure nor pain. This, too, is how striving is fruitful, how exertion is fruitful.

THE THREE KNOWLEDGES

"With his mind thus concentrated, purified, and bright, unblemished, free from defects, pliant, malleable, steady, and attained to imperturbability, he directs and inclines it to knowledge of the recollection of past lives [lit: previous homes]. He recollects his manifold past lives, i.e., one birth, two births, three births, four, five, ten, twenty, thirty, forty, fifty, one hundred, one thousand, one hundred thousand, many eons of cosmic contraction, many eons of cosmic expansion, many eons of cosmic contraction and expansion, (recollecting,) 'There I had such a name, belonged to such a clan, had such an appearance. Such was my food, such my experience of pleasure and pain, such the end of my life. Passing away from that state, I re-arose there. There too I had such a name, belonged to such a clan, had such an appearance. Such was my food, such my experience of pleasure and pain, such the end of my life. Passing away from that state, I re-arose here.' Thus he recollects his manifold past lives in their modes and details. This, too, is how striving is fruitful, how exertion is fruitful.

"With his mind thus concentrated, purified, and bright, unblemished, free from defects, pliant, malleable, steady, and attained to imperturbability, he directs and inclines it to knowledge of the passing away and re-appearance of beings. He sees—by means of the divine eye, purified and surpassing the human—beings passing away & reappearing, and he discerns how they are inferior & superior, beautiful & ugly, fortunate & unfortunate in accordance with their kamma: 'These beings—who were endowed with bad conduct of body, speech, & mind, who reviled the noble ones, held wrong views and undertook actions under the influence of wrong views—with the break-up of the body, after death, have re-appeared in a plane of deprivation, a bad destination, a lower realm, hell. But these beings—who were endowed with good conduct of body, speech, & mind, who did not revile the noble ones, who held right views and undertook actions under the influence of right views—with the break-up of the body, after death, have re-appeared in a good destination, a heavenly world.' Thus—by means of the divine eye, purified and surpassing the human—he sees beings passing away & reappearing, and he discerns how they are inferior & superior, beautiful & ugly, fortunate & unfortunate in accordance with their kamma. This, too, is how striving is fruitful, how exertion is fruitful.

"With his mind thus concentrated, purified, and bright, unblemished, free from defects, pliant, malleable, steady, & attained to imperturbability, the monk directs and inclines it to the knowledge of the ending of effluents. He discerns, as it is has come to be, that 'This is stress… This is the origination of stress… This is the cessation of stress… This is the way leading to the cessation of stress… These are effluents… This is the origination of effluents… This is the cessation of effluents… This is the way leading to the cessation of effluents.' His heart, thus knowing, thus seeing, is released from the effluent of sensuality, the effluent of becoming, the effluent of ignorance. With release, there is the knowledge, 'Released.' He discerns that 'Birth is ended, the holy life fulfilled, the task done. There is nothing further for this world.' This, too, is how striving is fruitful, how exertion is fruitful.

"Such is the teaching of the Tathāgata. And, such being the teaching of the Tathāgata, ten legitimate deductions can be drawn that give grounds for praising him.

"[1] If beings experience pleasure & pain based on what was done in the past, then obviously the Tathāgata has done good things in the past, which is why he now feels such pleasure free from effluents.

"[2] If beings experience pleasure & pain based on the creative act of a supreme god, then obviously the Tathāgata has been created by an excellent supreme god, which is why he now feels such pleasure free from effluents.

"[3] If beings experience pleasure & pain based on sheer luck, then obviously the Tathāgata has admirable luck, which is why he now feels such pleasure free from effluents.

"[4] If beings experience pleasure & pain based on birth, then obviously the Tathāgata has had an admirable birth, which is why he now feels such pleasure free from effluents.

"[5] If beings experience pleasure & pain based on efforts in the here-&-now, then obviously the Tathāgata has admirable efforts in the here-&-now, which is why he now feels such pleasure free from effluents.

"[6] If beings experience pleasure & pain based on what was done in the past, the Tathāgata deserves praise. Even if not, he still deserves praise.

"[7] If beings experience pleasure & pain based on the creative act of a supreme god Tathāgata deserves praise. Even if not, he still deserves praise.

"[8] If beings experience pleasure & pain based on sheer luck, the Tathāgata deserves praise. Even if not, he still deserves praise.

"[9] If beings experience pleasure & pain based on birth, Tathāgata deserves praise. Even if not, he still deserves praise.

"[10] If beings experience pleasure & pain based on efforts in the here-&-now, the Tathāgata deserves praise. Even if not, he still deserves praise.

"Such is the teaching of the Tathāgata. And, such being the teaching of the Tathāgata, these ten legitimate deductions can be drawn that give grounds for praising him."

That is what the Blessed One said. Gratified, the monks delighted in the Blessed One's words.

See also: MN 14; MN 26; MN 78; SN 35:145; SN 36:21; SN 42:8; SN 42:11; AN 3:62; AN 3:99; AN 9:13; AN 10:54

102 *Five & Three*

Pañcattaya Sutta (Excerpt)

INTRODUCTION

This discourse has two striking features. The first is that it seems to contain an interpolation. The introduction summarizes the topic of the discourse: five alternative ways in which a person might theorize or speculate about the future state of a person after death. What seems to be the interpolation begins after the first four ways have been discussed, and there are two reasons for regarding it as a later addition. (1) It announces that all five alternatives mentioned in the summary have been discussed, whereas only four have. (2) It then treats a topic not mentioned in the summary at all: alternatives ways in which a person might speculate about the past. Only when this section is finished does the discourse pick up the fifth alternative mentioned in the introductory summary.

Because this apparent interpolation interrupts the flow of the discourse, I have here translated just the remaining parts, to give some sense of how they fit together without the interruption.

The second striking feature of the discourse is its resemblance to DN 1 in covering two of the three main topics covered by that discourse: speculations about the future and false views of unbinding here-and-now. This resemblance, in fact, may have been what inspired the apparent interpolation, for the third topic covered by DN 1—speculations about the past—is precisely the topic covered in that passage. Perhaps the monks who collected, organized, and memorized the Majjhima Nikāya wanted their own discourse treating the same range of topics covered in DN 1, and so inserted the section on speculations about the past here. (This, by the way, is not to say that this section is less authentic than the rest of the discourse; just that its insertion is awkward. The redactors may have simply borrowed an authentic teaching from another Dhamma talk.)

At any rate, a comparison of the remaining sections with their parallels in DN 1 shows that the Buddha's approach here differs in 3 ways from the approach taken there.

1) To begin with, DN 1 focuses primary attention on the source of the various speculative views about the future, based on ways in which the self is defined in the present. The Buddha then rejects these views, both on the basis of their sources and on the basis of the future destinations that such views, as actions, lead to after death. Here, however, the Buddha focuses on (a) the ways in which people who hold these views refute one another's views; (b) the Buddha's own refutation of these views, showing either why they make no sense or why they do not lead to freedom from clinging.

2) In DN 1, speculations about the future and false views of unbinding here-and-now are treated as two separate categories. Here, false views of unbinding here-and-now are treated as a type of speculation about the future. The reason for this may be that the claim of having attained unbinding carries an implicit claim about the future: There is no further birth for that person (see DN 29, quoted in Skill in Questions*).*

3) The most interesting difference between the two discourses, however, centers on the final claim to unbinding given here. All the views listed in DN 1, and all the preceding theories given in this discourse, are attributed to contemplatives who are not followers of the Buddha's teachings. In contrast, this final view could easily be one of a person who has followed the Buddha's instructions but has simply misread his/her ability to complete those instructions, mistaking a state that still harbors some clinging for one that is totally free of it.

It's easy to imagine that the monks listening to this discourse might have been brought up short by this last example. After hearing of the failings of contemplatives outside the Buddha's teachings, they are presented with a failing to which they themselves could easily fall prey.

This discourse thus contains a useful warning for Buddhist meditators today.

* * *

I have heard that on one occasion the Blessed One was staying near Sāvatthī in Jeta's Grove, Anāthapiṇḍika's monastery. There he addressed the monks, "Monks!"

"Yes, lord," the monks responded to him.

The Blessed One said: "Monks, there are some contemplatives & brahmans who theorize about the future state, who speculate about the future state. They assert many various beliefs concerning the future state. Some assert that 'The self is percipient & free from disease after death.' Some assert that 'The self is non-percipient & free from disease after death.' Some assert that 'The self is neither percipient nor non-percipient & free from disease after death.' Or they describe the destruction, annihilation, & non-becoming of the existing being after death. Or some assert unbinding in the here-&-now.

"Thus, being five, these become three. Being three, they become five. This is the summary of the five-&-three.

"Now, monks, as for those contemplatives & brahmans who describe the self as percipient & free from disease after death, they describe the self that is percipient & free from disease after death as possessed of form... as formless... as both possessed of form & formless... as neither possessed of form nor formless... as percipient of singleness... as percipient of multiplicity[1]... as percipient of what is limited... or as percipient of what is immeasurable. Or some, among the few who go beyond this, assert the consciousness-totality: immeasurable & imperturbable.[2]

"With regard to this, the Tathāgata discerns[3] that 'Those venerable contemplative & brahmans who describe the self as percipient & free from disease after death, describe the self that is percipient & free from disease after death as possessed of form... as formless... as both possessed of form & formless... as neither possessed of form nor formless... as percipient of singleness... as percipient of multiplicity... as percipient of what is limited... or as percipient of what is immeasurable. Or some assert the dimension of nothingness, "There is nothing"—which is declared the purest, foremost, highest, most unexcelled of (all) perceptions, whether perceptions of form, perceptions of formlessness, perceptions of singleness, or perceptions of multiplicity—as immeasurable & imperturbable.[4] With regard to that—fabricated, gross—there is still the cessation of fabrications: There *is* this.' Knowing that, seeing the escape from it, the Tathāgata has gone beyond it.

"Now, as for those contemplatives & brahmans who describe the self as non-percipient & free from disease after death, they describe the self that is non-percipient & free from disease after death as possessed of form... as formless... as both possessed of form & formless... as neither possessed of form nor formless. They criticize those contemplatives & brahmans who describe the self as percipient & free from disease after death. For what reason? (They say,) 'Perception is a disease, perception is a tumor, perception is an arrow. This is peaceful, this is exquisite: non-perception.'

"With regard to this, the Tathāgata discerns that 'Those venerable contemplative & brahmans who describe the self as non-percipient & free from disease after death, describe the self that is non-percipient & free from disease after death as possessed of form... as formless... as both possessed of form & formless... as neither possessed of form nor formless. But if any contemplative or brahman were to say, "I will describe a coming, a going, a passing away, an arising, a growth, an increase, or a proliferation of consciousness apart from form, apart from feeling, apart from perception, apart from fabrications," that would be impossible.[5] With regard to that—fabricated, gross—there is still the cessation of fabrications: There *is* this.' Knowing that, seeing the escape from it, the Tathāgata has gone beyond it.

"Now, as for those contemplatives & brahmans who describe the self as neither percipient nor non-percipient & free from disease after death, they describe the self that is neither percipient nor non-percipient & free from disease after death as possessed of form… as formless… as both possessed of form & formless… as neither possessed of form nor formless. They criticize those contemplatives & brahmans who describe the self as percipient & free from disease after death and they criticize those contemplatives & brahmans who describe the self as non-percipient & free from disease after death. For what reason? (They say,) 'Perception is a disease, perception is a tumor, perception is an arrow. Non-perception is dullness. This is peaceful, this is exquisite: neither perception nor non-perception.'

"With regard to this, the Tathāgata discerns that 'Those venerable contemplative & brahmans who describe the self as neither percipient nor non-percipient & free from disease after death, describe the self that is neither percipient nor non-percipient & free from disease after death as possessed of form… as formless… as both possessed of form & formless… as neither possessed of form nor formless. But if any contemplative or brahman were to describe the entry into that dimension as based on a modicum of fabrication with regard to what is seen, heard, sensed, or cognized, that, monks, is declared to be a disaster for the entry into that dimension. For that dimension is said not to be attained as a fabrication-attainment. It is to be attained as a remnant-of-fabrication-attainment. With regard to that—fabricated, gross—there is still the cessation of fabrications: There *is* this.' Knowing that, seeing the escape from it, the Tathāgata has gone beyond it.

"Now, as for those contemplatives & brahmans who describe the destruction, annihilation, & non-becoming of the existing being after death, they criticize the contemplatives & brahmans who describe the self as percipient & free from disease after death and they criticize the contemplatives & brahmans who describe the self as non-percipient & free from disease after death and they criticize the contemplatives & brahmans who describe the self as neither percipient nor non-percipient & free from disease after death. For what reason? (They say,) 'These venerable contemplatives & brahmans, rushing ahead, assert nothing but their attachment: "I will be this after death. I will be this after death." Just as when a merchant going to market thinks, "From this, that will be mine. By means of this I will get that"; in the same way, these venerable contemplatives & brahmans act like merchants, as it were: "I will be this after death. I will be this after death."'

"With regard to this, the Tathāgata discerns that 'Those venerable contemplative & brahmans who describe the destruction, annihilation, & non-becoming of the existing being after death, they—through fear of self-identity, through disgust for self-identity—(nevertheless) keep running & circling around self-identity.[6] Just as a dog, tied by a leash to a post or stake, keeps running around and circling around that very post or stake; in the same way, these venerable contemplative & brahmans—through fear of self-identity, through disgust for self-identity—(nevertheless) keep running & circling around self-identity. With regard to that—fabricated, gross—there is still the cessation of fabrications: There *is* this.' Knowing that, seeing the escape from it, the Tathāgata has gone beyond it. ...

"There is the case, monks, where a certain contemplative or brahman, with the relinquishing of speculations about the past and the relinquishing of speculations about the future, from being totally not determined on the fetters of sensuality, enters & remains in the rapture of seclusion [the first jhāna]. (He thinks,) 'This is peaceful, this is exquisite, that I enter & remain in the rapture of seclusion.' His rapture of seclusion ceases. With the cessation of the rapture of seclusion, sadness arises; with the cessation of sadness, the rapture of seclusion arises. Just as what the shade leaves the sunlight pervades, and what the sunlight leaves the shade pervades; in the same way, with the cessation of the rapture of seclusion, sadness arises; with the cessation of sadness, the rapture of seclusion arises.

"With regard to this, the Tathāgata discerns that 'This venerable contemplative or brahman, with the relinquishing of speculations about the past and the relinquishing of speculations about the future, from being totally not determined on the fetters of sensuality, enters & remains in the rapture of seclusion. (He thinks,) "This is peaceful, this is exquisite, that I enter & remain in the rapture of seclusion." His rapture of seclusion ceases. With the cessation of the rapture of seclusion, sadness arises; with the cessation of sadness, the rapture of seclusion arises. With regard to that—fabricated, gross—there is still the cessation of fabrications: There *is* this.' Knowing that, seeing the escape from it, the Tathāgata has gone beyond it.

"There is the case, monks, where a certain contemplative or brahman, with the relinquishing of speculations about the past and the relinquishing of speculations about the future, from being totally not determined on the fetters of sensuality, and surmounting the rapture of seclusion, enters & remains in pleasure not-of-the-flesh [the third jhāna]. (He thinks,) 'This is peaceful, this is exquisite, that I enter & remain in pleasure not-of-the-flesh.' His pleasure not-of-the-flesh ceases. With the cessation of pleasure not-of-the-flesh, the rapture of seclusion arises; with the cessation of the rapture of seclusion, pleasure not-of-the-flesh arises. Just as what the shade leaves the sunlight pervades, and what the sunlight leaves the shade pervades; in the same way, with the cessation of pleasure not-of-the-flesh, the rapture of seclusion arises; with the cessation of the rapture of seclusion, pleasure not-of-the-flesh arises.

"With regard to this, the Tathāgata discerns that 'This venerable contemplative or brahman, with the relinquishing of speculations about the past and the relinquishing of speculations about the future, from being totally not determined on the fetters of sensuality, and surmounting the rapture of seclusion, enters & remains in pleasure not-of-the-flesh. (He thinks,) "This is peaceful, this is exquisite, that I enter & remain in pleasure not-of-the-flesh." His pleasure not-of-the-flesh ceases. With the cessation of pleasure not-of-the-flesh, the rapture of seclusion arises; with the cessation of the rapture of seclusion, pleasure not-of-the-flesh arises. With regard to that—fabricated, gross—there is still the cessation of fabrications: There *is* this.' Knowing that, seeing the escape from it, the Tathāgata has gone beyond it.

"There is the case, monks, where a certain contemplative or brahman, with the relinquishing of speculations about the past and the relinquishing of speculations about the future, from being totally not determined on the fetters of sensuality, surmounting the rapture of seclusion, surmounting pleasure not-of-the flesh, enters & remains in a feeling of neither pleasure nor pain [the fourth jhāna]. (He thinks,) 'This is peaceful, this is exquisite, that I enter & remain in a feeling of neither pleasure nor pain.' His feeling of neither pleasure nor pain ceases. With the cessation of the feeling of neither pleasure nor pain, the pleasure not-of-the flesh arises; with the cessation of pleasure not-of-the flesh, the feeling of neither pleasure nor pain arises. Just as what the shade leaves the sunlight pervades, and what the sunlight leaves the shade pervades; in the same way, with the cessation of the feeling of neither pleasure nor pain, the pleasure not-of-the flesh arises; with the cessation of pleasure not-of-the flesh, the feeling of neither pleasure nor pain arises.

"With regard to this, the Tathāgata discerns that 'This venerable contemplative or brahman, with the relinquishing of speculations about the past and the relinquishing of speculations about the future, from being totally not determined on the fetters of sensuality, surmounting the rapture of seclusion, surmounting pleasure not-of-the flesh, enters & remains in a feeling of neither pleasure nor pain. (He thinks,) "This is peaceful, this is exquisite, that I enter & remain in a feeling of neither pleasure nor pain." His feeling of neither pleasure nor pain ceases. With the cessation of the feeling of neither pleasure nor pain, the pleasure not-of-the flesh arises; with the cessation of pleasure not-of-the flesh, the feeling of neither pleasure nor pain arises. With regard to that—fabricated, gross—there is still the cessation of fabrications: There *is* this.' Knowing that, seeing the escape from it, the Tathāgata has gone beyond it.

"There is the case, monks, where a certain contemplative or brahman, with the relinquishing of speculations about the past and the relinquishing of speculations about the future, from being totally not determined on the fetters of sensuality, surmounting the rapture of seclusion, surmounting pleasure not-of-the-flesh, and surmounting the feeling of neither pleasure nor pain, envisions that 'I am at peace, I am unbound, I am without clinging/sustenance!'

"With regard to this, the Tathāgata discerns that 'This venerable contemplative or brahman, with the relinquishing of speculations about the past and the relinquishing of speculations about the future, from being totally not determined on the fetters of sensuality, surmounting the rapture of seclusion, surmounting pleasure not-of-the-flesh, and surmounting the feeling of neither pleasure nor pain, envisions that "I am at peace, I am unbound, I am without clinging/sustenance!" Yes, he affirms a practice conducive to unbinding. But still he clings, clinging to a speculation about the past; or he clings, clinging to a speculation about the future; or he clings, clinging to a fetter of sensuality; or he clings, clinging to the rapture of seclusion; or he clings, clinging to pleasure not-of-the-flesh; or he clings, clinging to a feeling of neither pleasure nor pain. And the fact that he envisions that "I am at peace, I am unbound, I am without clinging/sustenance!"—that in itself points to his clinging.[7] With regard to that—fabricated, gross—there is still the cessation of fabrications: There *is* this.' Knowing that, seeing the escape from it, the Tathāgata has gone beyond it.

"Thus, monks, the Tathāgata has awakened to the unexcelled state of foremost peace: liberation through lack of clinging/sustenance, having known, as they have come to be, the origination, passing away, allure, drawbacks of—and escape from—the six media of contact."[8]

That is what the Blessed One said. Gratified, the monks delighted in the Blessed One's words.

NOTES

1. MN 137 indicates that perceptions of multiplicity deal with the six senses, whereas perceptions of singleness form the basis of the four formless attainments.

2. This is apparently equivalent to the formless attainment of the dimension of the infinitude of consciousness, which MN 106 classes as imperturbable. AN 10:29 has this to say about the consciousness-totality:

> "There are these ten totality-dimensions. Which ten? One perceives the earth-totality above, below, all-around: non-dual *[advayaṁ],* immeasurable. One perceives the water-totality… the fire-totality… the wind-totality… the blue-totality… the yellow-totality… the red-totality… the white-totality… the space-totality… the consciousness-totality above, below, all-around: non-dual, immeasurable. These are the ten totality-dimensions. Now, of these ten totality-dimensions, this is supreme: when one perceives the consciousness-totality above, below, all-around: non-dual, immeasurable. And there are beings who are percipient in this way. Yet even in the beings who are percipient in this way there is still aberration, there is change. Seeing this, the instructed disciple of the noble ones grows disenchanted with that. Being disenchanted with that, he becomes dispassionate toward what is supreme, and even more so toward what is inferior."

3. Reading *pajānāti* with the Thai edition. The Burmese edition here, and in all the following passages describing what the Buddha knows about the various contemplatives and brahmans, has *abhijānāti:* "directly knows."

4. Both MLS and MLDB mistakenly insert a quotation mark after this statement, here and in all the parallel passages in this discourse. This changes the meaning of the last sentence in each of these passages with regard to what is meant by "that" in the phrase, "Knowing that."

Unlike the contemplatives and brahmans quoted in this passage, the Buddha—in MN 106—does not apply the adjective "imperturbable" to the dimension of nothingness. See note 1 to that sutta.

5. See SN 22:54.

6. Craving for non-becoming *(vibhava-taṇhā)* is one of the three types of craving that lead to becoming. On this point, see, *The Paradox of Becoming.*

7. The "I am," here, is what points to the clinging. It shows that conceit, one of the ten fetters, has not been cut—"conceit," here, not meaning pride, but simply a sense of what one's identity consists of. As MN 52 and AN 9:36 point out, it is possible, even when experiencing the deathless, to develop a sense of passion and delight for it, thus giving rise to a subtle sense of "I am" that prevents full awakening. The passage here gives useful directions as to where to look for the lurking clinging that may contribute to that sense of "I am."

Actual, spontaneous expressions of full awakening are phrased in impersonal terms. See, for instance, MN 4, SN 56:11, AN 6:49, and AN 6:55.

8. Compare this passage with the refrain in DN 1:

> "This, monks, the Tathāgata discerns. And he discerns that these standpoints, thus seized, thus grasped at, lead to such & such a destination, to such & such a state in the world beyond. And he discerns what is higher than this. And yet discerning that, he does not grasp at that act of discerning. And as he is not grasping at it, unbinding *[nibbuti]* is experienced right within. Knowing, as they have come to be, the origin, ending, allure, & drawbacks of feelings, along with the escape from feelings, the Tathāgata, monks—through lack of clinging/ sustenance—is released."

See also: MN 2; MN 106; SN 36:31

105 To Sunakkhatta

Sunakkhatta Sutta

This discourse gives guidance on how to judge whether another person's claim to enlightenment might be true or false. It ends with a warning: Anyone who claims enlightenment as license for unrestrained behavior is like someone who (1) has undergone surgery but does not follow doctor's orders for healing the wound; (2) knowingly drinks a cup of poison; (3) extends his hand or finger to a deadly poisonous snake.

I have heard that on one occasion the Blessed One was staying near Vesālī at the Gabled Hall in the Great Forest. Now at that time a large number of monks had declared final gnosis in the Blessed One's presence: "We discern that 'Birth is ended, the holy life fulfilled, the task done. There is nothing further for the sake of this world.'"

Sunakkhatta the Licchavi heard that "A large number of monks, it seems, have declared final gnosis in the Blessed One's presence: 'We discern that "Birth is ended, the holy life fulfilled, the task done. There is nothing further for the sake of this world."'" Then Sunakkhatta the Licchavi went to the Blessed One and, on arrival, having bowed down to him, sat to one side. As he was sitting there he said to the Blessed One: "I have heard, lord, that a large number of monks have declared final gnosis in the Blessed One's presence: 'We discern that "Birth is ended, the holy life fulfilled, the task done. There is nothing further for the sake of this world."' Now, have they rightly declared final gnosis, or is it the case that some of them have declared final gnosis out of over-estimation?"

"Sunakkhatta, of the monks who have declared final gnosis in my presence… it is the case that some have rightly declared final gnosis, whereas others have declared final gnosis out of over-estimation. As for those who have rightly declared final gnosis, that is their truth. As for those who have declared final gnosis out of over-estimation, the thought occurs to the Tathāgata, 'I will teach them the Dhamma.' But there are cases when the thought has occurred to the Tathāgata, 'I will teach them the Dhamma,' but there are worthless men who come to him having formulated question after question, so that his thought, 'I will teach them the Dhamma,' changes into something else."

"Now is the time, O Blessed One. Now is the time, O One Well-Gone, for the Blessed One to teach the Dhamma. Having heard the Blessed One, the monks will remember it."

"Then in that case, Sunakkhatta, listen & pay close attention. I will speak."

"As you say, lord," Sunakkhatta the Licchavi responded to the Blessed One.

The Blessed One said: "Sunakkhatta, there are these five strands of sensuality. Which five? Forms cognizable via the eye—agreeable, pleasing, charming, endearing, enticing, linked with sensual desire. Sounds cognizable via the ear... Aromas cognizable via the nose... Flavors cognizable via the tongue... Tactile sensations cognizable via the body—agreeable, pleasing, charming, endearing, enticing, linked with sensual desire. These are the five strands of sensuality.

"Now there's the possible case where a certain person is intent on the baits of the world. When a person is intent on the baits of the world, that sort of talk interests him, his thinking & evaluating follow along those lines, he feels at home with that sort of person, and his mind gets along with that sort of person. But when talk concerning the imperturbable [the fourth jhāna and the dimensions of the infinitude of space & the infinitude of consciousness] is going on, he does not listen, does not lend ear, and does not exert his mind to know. He does not get along with that sort of person; his mind does not feel at home with him.

"Suppose that there were a man who had left his home village or town a long time ago. And he were to meet with a man who had left the village or town only a short time ago. He would ask if the people in the village or town were secure, well-fed, & free of disease, and the second man would tell him if they were secure, well-fed, & free of disease. Now, what do you think, Sunakkhatta? Would the first man listen to the second man, lend ear, and exert his mind to know? Would he get along with the second man; would his mind feel at home with him?"

"Yes, lord."

"In the same way, it is possible that there is the case where a certain person is intent on the baits of the world. When a person is intent on the baits of the world, that sort of talk interests him, his thinking & evaluating follow along those lines, he feels at home with that sort of person, and his mind gets along with that sort of person. But when talk concerning the imperturbable [the fourth jhāna and the dimensions of the infinitude of space and the infinitude of consciousness] is going on, he does not listen, does not lend ear, and does not exert his mind to know. He does not get along with that sort of person; his mind does not feel at home with him. This is how it can be known that 'This person is intent on the baits of the world.'

"Now, there's the possible case where a certain person is intent on the imperturbable. When a person is intent on the imperturbable, that sort of talk interests him, his thinking & evaluating follow along those lines, he feels at home with that sort of person, and his mind gets along with that sort of person. But when talk concerning the baits of the world is going on, he does not listen, does not lend ear, and does not exert his mind to know. He does not get along with that sort of person; his mind does not feel at home with him.

"Just as a yellow leaf released from its stem is incapable of ever again becoming green, in the same way, when a person is intent on the imperturbable, he is released from the fetter of the baits of the world. This is how it can be known that 'This person, disjoined from the fetter of the baits of the world, is intent on the imperturbable.'

"Now, there's the possible case where a certain person is intent on the dimension of nothingness. When a person is intent on the dimension of nothingness, that sort of talk interests him, his thinking & evaluating follow along those lines, he feels at home with that sort of person, and his mind gets along with that sort of person. But when talk concerning the imperturbable is going on, he does not listen, does not lend ear, and does not exert his mind to know. He does not get along with that sort of person; his mind does not feel at home with him.

"Just as a thick rock broken in two cannot be put back together again, in the same way, when a person is intent on the dimension of nothingness, he has broken the fetter of the imperturbable. This is how it can be known that 'This person, disjoined from the fetter of the imperturbable, is intent on the dimension of nothingness.'

"Now, there's the possible case where a certain person is intent on the dimension of neither perception nor non-perception. When a person is intent on the dimension of neither perception nor non-perception, that sort of talk interests him, his thinking & evaluating follow along those lines, he feels at home with that sort of person, and his mind gets along with that sort of person. But when talk concerning the dimension of nothingness is going on, he does not listen, does not lend ear, and does not exert his mind to know. He does not get along with that sort of person; his mind does not feel at home with him.

"Sunakkhatta, suppose that a person, having eaten some delicious food, were to vomit it up. What do you think? Would he have any desire for that food?"

"No, lord. Why is that? Because he would consider that food to be disgusting."

"In the same way, when a person is intent on the dimension of neither perception nor non-perception, he has vomited up the fetter of the dimension of nothingness. This is how it can be known that 'This person, disjoined from the fetter of the dimension of nothingness, is intent on the dimension of neither perception nor non-perception.'

"Now, there's the possible case where a certain person is rightly intent on unbinding. When a person is rightly intent on unbinding, that sort of talk interests him, his thinking & evaluating follow along those lines, he feels at home with that sort of person, and his mind gets along with that sort of person. But when talk concerning the dimension of neither perception nor non-perception is going on, he does not listen, does not lend ear, and does not exert his mind to know. He does not get along with that sort of person; his mind does not feel at home with him.

"Just as a palmyra tree with its top cut off is incapable of further growth, in the same way, when a person is rightly intent on unbinding, he has destroyed the fetter of the dimension of neither perception nor non-perception, has destroyed it by the root, made it like a palmyra stump, deprived of the conditions of development, not destined for future arising. This is how it can be known that 'This person, disjoined from the fetter of the dimension of neither perception nor non-perception, is intent on unbinding.'

"Now, there's the possible case where a certain monk thinks, 'Craving is said by the Contemplative [the Buddha] to be an arrow. The poison of ignorance spreads its toxin through desire, passion, & ill will. I have abandoned the arrow. I have expelled the poison of ignorance. I am rightly intent on unbinding.' Because this is not true of him, he might pursue those things that are unsuitable for a person rightly intent on unbinding. He might pursue unsuitable forms & sights with the eye. He might pursue unsuitable sounds with the ear... unsuitable aromas with the nose... unsuitable flavors with the tongue... unsuitable tactile sensations with the body. He might pursue unsuitable ideas with the intellect. When he pursues unsuitable forms & sights with the eye... pursues unsuitable ideas with the intellect, lust invades the mind. With his mind invaded by lust, he incurs death or death-like suffering.

"Suppose that a man were wounded with an arrow thickly smeared with poison. His friends & companions, kinsmen & relatives would provide him with a surgeon. The surgeon would cut around the opening of the wound with a knife and then would probe for the arrow with a probe. He then would pull out the arrow and extract the poison, leaving a residue behind. Knowing that a residue was left behind, he would say, 'My good man, your arrow has been pulled out. The poison has been extracted, with a residue left behind, but it is not enough to do you harm. Eat suitable food. Don't eat unsuitable food, or else the wound will fester. Wash the wound frequently, smear it with an ointment frequently, so that blood & pus don't fill the opening of the wound. Don't walk around in the wind & sun, or else dust & dirt may contaminate the opening of the wound. Keep looking after the wound, my good man, and work for its healing.'

"The thought would occur to the man: 'My arrow has been pulled out. The poison has been extracted, with a residue left behind, but it is not enough to do me harm.' He would eat unsuitable food, so the wound would fester. He wouldn't wash the wound or smear it with an ointment frequently, so blood & pus would fill the opening of the wound. He would walk around in the wind & sun, so dust & dirt would contaminate the opening of the wound. He wouldn't keep looking after the wound or work for its healing. Now, both because of these unsuitable actions of his and because of the residue of the dirty poison left behind, the wound would swell. With the swelling of the wound he would incur death or death-like suffering.

"In the same way, there's the possible case where a certain monk thinks, 'Craving is said by the Contemplative to be an arrow. The poison of ignorance spreads its toxin through desire, passion, & ill will. I have abandoned the arrow. I have expelled the poison of ignorance. I am rightly intent on unbinding.' Because this is not true of him, he might pursue those things that are unsuitable for a person rightly intent on unbinding. He might pursue unsuitable forms & sights with the eye. He might pursue unsuitable sounds with the ear… unsuitable aromas with the nose… unsuitable flavors with the tongue… unsuitable tactile sensations with the body. He might pursue unsuitable ideas with the intellect. When he pursues unsuitable forms & sights with the eye… pursues unsuitable ideas with the intellect, lust invades the mind. With his mind invaded by lust, he incurs death or death-like suffering. For this is death in the discipline of the noble ones: when one renounces the training and returns to the lower life. And this is death-like suffering: when one commits a defiled offense.

"Now, there's the possible case where a certain monk thinks, 'Craving is said by the Contemplative to be an arrow. The poison of ignorance spreads its toxin through desire, passion, & ill will. I have abandoned the arrow. I have expelled the poison of ignorance. I am rightly intent on unbinding.' Because he is rightly intent on unbinding, he wouldn't pursue those things that are unsuitable for a person rightly intent on unbinding. He wouldn't pursue unsuitable forms & sights with the eye. He wouldn't pursue unsuitable sounds with the ear... unsuitable aromas with the nose... unsuitable flavors with the tongue... unsuitable tactile sensations with the body. He wouldn't pursue unsuitable ideas with the intellect. When he doesn't pursue unsuitable forms & sights with the eye... doesn't pursue unsuitable ideas with the intellect, lust doesn't invade the mind. With his mind not invaded by lust, he doesn't incur death or death-like suffering.

"Suppose that a man were wounded with an arrow thickly smeared with poison. His friends & companions, kinsmen & relatives would provide him with a surgeon. The surgeon would cut around the opening of the wound with a knife and then would probe for the arrow with a probe. He then would pull out the arrow and extract the poison, leaving no residue behind. Knowing that no residue was left behind, he would say, 'My good man, your arrow has been pulled out. The poison has been extracted, with no residue left behind, so it is not enough to do you harm. Eat suitable food. Don't eat unsuitable food, or else the wound will fester. Wash the wound frequently, smear it with an ointment frequently, so that blood & pus don't fill the opening of the wound. Don't walk around in the wind & sun, or else dust & dirt may contaminate the opening of the wound. Keep looking after the wound, my good man, and work for its healing.'

"The thought would occur to the man: 'My arrow has been pulled out. The poison has been extracted with no residue left behind, so it is not enough to do me harm.' He would eat suitable food, so the wound wouldn't fester. He would wash the wound and smear it with an ointment frequently, so blood & pus wouldn't fill the opening of the wound. He would not walk around in the wind & sun, so dust & dirt wouldn't contaminate the opening of the wound. He would keep looking after the wound and would work for its healing. Now, both because of these suitable actions of his and because of there being no residue of the poison left behind, the wound would heal. With the healing of the wound and its being covered with skin, he wouldn't incur death or death-like suffering.

"In the same way, there's the possible case where a certain monk thinks, 'Craving is said by the Contemplative to be an arrow. The poison of ignorance spreads its toxin through desire, passion, & ill will. I have abandoned the arrow. I have expelled the poison of ignorance. I am rightly intent on unbinding.' Because he is rightly intent on unbinding, he wouldn't pursue those things that are unsuitable for a person rightly intent on unbinding. He wouldn't pursue unsuitable forms & sights with the eye. He wouldn't pursue unsuitable sounds with the ear... unsuitable aromas with the nose... unsuitable flavors with the tongue... unsuitable tactile sensations with the body. He wouldn't pursue unsuitable ideas with the intellect. When he doesn't pursue unsuitable forms & sights with the eye... doesn't pursue unsuitable ideas with the intellect, lust doesn't invade the mind. With his mind not invaded by lust, he doesn't incur death or death-like suffering.

"I have given this simile to convey a meaning. The meaning is this: the wound stands for the six internal sense media; the poison, for ignorance; the arrow, for craving; the probe, for mindfulness; the knife, for noble discernment; the surgeon, for the Tathāgata, worthy & rightly self-awakened.

"Now, when a monk—maintaining restraint over the six spheres of contact, knowing that 'Acquisition is the root of stress'—is free from acquisition, released in the total ending of acquisition, it's not possible that, with regard to acquisition, he would stir his body or arouse his mind.

"Suppose there were a beverage in a bronze cup—consummate in its color, smell, & flavor—but mixed with poison. And suppose a man were to come along, wanting to live, not wanting to die, desiring pleasure, & abhorring pain. What do you think, Sunakkhatta? Would he drink the beverage in the bronze cup knowing that 'Having drunk this, I will incur death or death-like suffering'?"

"No, lord."

"In the same way, when a monk—maintaining restraint over the six spheres of contact, knowing that 'Acquisition is the root of stress'—is free from acquisition, released in the total ending of acquisition, it's not possible that, with regard to acquisition, he would stir his body or arouse his mind.

"Suppose there were a deadly poisonous viper, and a man were to come along, wanting to live, not wanting to die, desiring pleasure, & abhorring pain. What do you think, Sunakkhatta? Would he give his hand or finger to the snake knowing that 'Having been bitten by this, I will incur death or death-like suffering'?"

"No, lord."

"In the same way, when a monk—maintaining restraint over the six spheres of contact, knowing that 'Acquisition is the root of stress'—is free from acquisition, released in the total ending of acquisition, it's not possible that, with regard to acquisition, he would stir his body or arouse his mind."

That is what the Blessed One said. Gratified, Sunakkhatta the Licchavi delighted in the Blessed One's words.

See also: MN 75; AN 6:49; AN 6:55; AN 9:7; AN 10:24

106 *Conducive to the Imperturbable*

Āneñja-sappāya Sutta

I have heard that on one occasion the Blessed One was staying in the Kuru country. Now there is a town of the Kurus called Kammāsadhamma. There the Blessed One addressed the monks, "Monks!"

"Yes, lord," the monks responded to him.

The Blessed One said: "Monks, sensuality is inconstant, hollow, vain, deceptive. It is illusory, the babble of fools. Sensuality here & now; sensuality in lives to come; sensual perceptions here & now; sensual perceptions in lives to come: both are Māra's realm, Māra's domain, Māra's bait, Māra's range. They lead to these evil, unskillful mental states: greed, ill will, & contentiousness. They arise for the obstruction of a disciple of the noble ones here in training.

"In that case, the disciple of the noble ones considers this: 'Sensuality here & now; sensuality in lives to come; sensual perceptions here & now; sensual perceptions in lives to come: Both are Māra's realm, Māra's domain, Māra's bait, Māra's range. They lead to these evil, unskillful mental states: greed, ill will, & contentiousness. They arise for the obstruction of a disciple of the noble ones here in training. What if I—overpowering the world [of the five senses] and having determined my mind—were to dwell with an awareness that was abundant & enlarged? Having done so, these evil, unskillful mental states—greed, ill will, & contentiousness—would not come into being. With their abandoning, my mind would become unlimited, immeasurable, & well developed.' Practicing & frequently abiding in this way, his mind acquires confidence in that dimension. There being full confidence, he either attains the imperturbable[1] now or else is committed to discernment. With the breakup of the body, after death, it's possible that this leading-on consciousness of his will go to the imperturbable. This is declared to be the first practice conducive to the imperturbable.

"Then again, the disciple of the noble ones considers this: 'Sensuality here & now; sensuality in lives to come; sensual perceptions here & now; sensual perceptions in lives to come: Whatever is form, every form, is the four great elements or a form derived from the four great elements.' Practicing & frequently abiding in this way, his mind acquires confidence in that dimension. There being full confidence, he either attains the imperturbable now or else is committed to discernment. With the break-up of the body, after death, it's possible that this leading-on consciousness of his will go to the imperturbable. This is declared to be the second practice conducive to the imperturbable.

"Then again, the disciple of the noble ones considers this: 'Sensuality here & now; sensuality in lives to come; sensual perceptions here & now; sensual perceptions in lives to come; forms here & now; forms in lives to come; form-perceptions here & now; form-perceptions in lives to come: Both are inconstant. Whatever is inconstant is not worth relishing, is not worth welcoming, is not worth remaining fastened to." Practicing & frequently abiding in this way, his mind acquires confidence in that dimension. There being full confidence, he either attains the imperturbable now or else is committed to discernment. With the break-up of the body, after death, it's possible that this leading-on consciousness of his will go to the imperturbable. This is declared to be the third practice conducive to the imperturbable.

"Then again, the disciple of the noble ones considers this: 'Sensuality here & now; sensuality in lives to come; sensual perceptions here & now; sensual perceptions in lives to come; forms here & now; forms in lives to come; form-perceptions here & now; form-perceptions in lives to come; perceptions of the imperturbable: All are perceptions. Where they cease without remainder: that is peaceful, that is exquisite, i.e., the dimension of nothingness.' Practicing & frequently abiding in this way, his mind acquires confidence in that dimension. There being full confidence, he either attains the dimension of nothingness now or else is committed to discernment. With the break-up of the body, after death, it's possible that this leading-on consciousness of his will go to the dimension of nothingness. This is declared to be the first practice conducive to the dimension of nothingness.

"Then again, the disciple of the noble ones, having gone into the wilderness, to the root of a tree, or into an empty dwelling, considers this: 'This is empty of self or of anything pertaining to self.' Practicing & frequently abiding in this way, his mind acquires confidence in that dimension. There being full confidence, he either attains the dimension of nothingness now or else is committed to discernment. With the break-up of the body, after death, it's possible that this leading-on consciousness of his will go to the dimension of nothingness. This is declared to be the second practice conducive to the dimension of nothingness.

"Then again, the disciple of the noble ones considers this: 'I am not anyone's anything anywhere; nor is anything of mine in anyone anywhere.' Practicing & frequently abiding in this way, his mind acquires confidence in that dimension. There being full confidence, he either attains the dimension of nothingness now or else is committed to discernment. With the break-up of the body, after death, it's possible that this leading-on consciousness of his will go to the dimension of nothingness. This is declared to be the third practice conducive to the dimension of nothingness.

"Then again, the disciple of the noble ones considers this: 'Sensuality here & now; sensuality in lives to come; sensual perceptions here & now; sensual perceptions in lives to come; forms here & now; forms in lives to come; form-perceptions here & now; form-perceptions in lives to come; perceptions of the imperturbable; perceptions of the dimension of nothingness: All are perceptions. Where they cease without remainder: That is peaceful, that is exquisite, i.e., the dimension of neither perception nor non-perception.' Practicing & frequently abiding in this way, his mind acquires confidence in that dimension. There being full confidence, he either attains the dimension of neither perception nor non-perception now or else is committed to discernment. With the break-up of the body, after death, it's possible that this leading-on consciousness of his will go to the dimension of neither perception nor non-perception. This is declared to be the practice conducive to the dimension of neither perception nor non-perception.

When this was said, Ven. Ānanda said to the Blessed One: "There is the case, lord, where a monk, having practiced in this way—'It should not be, it should not occur to me; it will not be, it will not occur to me. What is, what has come to be, that I abandon'—obtains equanimity. Now, would this monk be totally unbound, or not?"

"A certain such monk might, Ānanda, and another might not.'

"What is the cause, what is the reason, lord, whereby one might and another might not?"

"There is the case, Ānanda, where a monk, having practiced in this way—(thinking) 'It should not be, it should not occur to me; it will not be, it will not occur to me. What is, what has come to be, that I abandon'—obtains equanimity. He relishes that equanimity, welcomes it, remains fastened to it. As he relishes that equanimity, welcomes it, remains fastened to it, his consciousness is dependent on it, is sustained by it [clings to it]. With clinging/sustenance, Ānanda, a monk is not totally unbound."

"Being sustained, lord, where is that monk sustained?"

"The dimension of neither perception nor non-perception."

"Then, indeed, being sustained, he is sustained by the supreme sustenance."

"Being sustained, Ānanda, he *is* sustained by the supreme sustenance; for this—the dimension of neither perception nor non-perception—is the supreme sustenance. There is (however) the case where a monk, having practiced in this way—'It should not be, it should not occur to me; it will not be, it will not occur to me. What is, what has come to be, that I abandon'—obtains equanimity. He does not relish that equanimity, does not welcome it, does not remain fastened to it. As does not relish that equanimity, does not welcome it, does not remain fastened to it, his consciousness is not dependent on it, is not sustained by it [does not cling to it]. Without clinging/sustenance, Ānanda, a monk is totally unbound."

"It's amazing, lord. It's astounding. For truly, the Blessed One has declared to us the way to cross over the flood by going from one support to the next. But what is the noble liberation?"

"There is the case, Ānanda, where a disciple of the noble ones considers this: 'Sensuality here & now; sensuality in lives to come; sensual perceptions here & now; sensual perceptions in lives to come; forms here & now; forms in lives to come; form-perceptions here & now; form-perceptions in lives to come; perceptions of the imperturbable; perceptions of the dimension of nothingness; perceptions of the dimension of neither perception nor non-perception: That is an identity, to the extent that there is an identity. This is deathless: the liberation of the mind through lack of clinging/sustenance.'

"Now, Ānanda, I have taught the practice conducive to the imperturbable. I have taught the practice conducive to the dimension of nothingness. I have taught the practice conducive to the dimension of neither perception nor non-perception. I have taught the way to cross over the flood by going from one support to the next, the noble liberation. Whatever a teacher should do—seeking the welfare of his disciples, out of sympathy for them—that have I done for you. Over there are the roots of trees; over there, empty dwellings. Practice jhāna, Ānanda. Don't be heedless. Don't later fall into remorse. That is our message to you all."

That is what the Blessed One said. Gratified, Ven. Ānanda delighted in the Blessed One's words.

NOTE: 1. According to the commentaries, "imperturbable" denotes the fourth jhāna and the four formless attainments. MN 66 provides partial support for this interpretation, saying that the first three jhānas are perturbable while the fourth is not, but this sutta does not include the dimension of nothingness under the term—or, apparently, any of the formless attainments higher than that.

See also: MN 66; MN 102; MN 121; MN 140; SN 22:55; Ud 3:3; Sn 5:14

108 Moggallāna the Guardsman

Gopaka Moggallāna Sutta

This discourse presents a picture of life in the early Buddhist community shortly after the Buddha's passing away. On the one hand, it shows the relationship between the monastic community and the political powers that be: the monks are polite and courteous to political functionaries, but the existence of this discourse shows that they had no qualms about depicting those functionaries as a little dense. On the other hand, it shows that early Buddhist practice had no room for many practices that later developed in Buddhist traditions, such as appointed lineage holders, elected ecclesiastical heads, or the use of mental defilements as a basis for concentration practice.

* * *

I have heard that on one occasion Ven. Ānanda was staying near Rājagaha in the Bamboo Grove, the Squirrels' Sanctuary, not long after the Blessed One's total unbinding.

Now at that time King Ajātasattu Vedehiputta of Magadha, suspicious of King Pajjota, was having Rājagaha fortified.

Then in the early morning, Ven. Ānanda, having adjusted his under robe and carrying his bowl & outer robe, went into Rājagaha for alms. The thought occurred to him, "It's too early to go for alms in Rājagaha. What if I were to go to the brahman Moggallāna the Guardsman at his construction site?" So he went to Moggallāna the Guardsman at his construction site. Moggallāna the Guardsman saw him coming from afar, and on seeing him said to him, "Come, Master Ānanda. Welcome, Master Ānanda. It has been a long time since Master Ānanda has found the time to come here. Sit down, Master Ānanda. Here is a seat made ready for you."

So Ven. Ānanda sat down on the seat made ready. Moggallāna the Guardsman, taking a lower seat, sat to one side.

As he was sitting there, he said to Ven. Ānanda: "Master Ānanda, is there any one monk endowed in each & every way with the qualities with which Master Gotama—worthy & rightly self-awakened—was endowed?"

"No, brahman, there isn't any one monk endowed in each & every way with the qualities with which the Blessed One—worthy & rightly self-awakened—was endowed. For the Blessed One was the arouser of the unarisen path, the begetter of the unbegotten path, the expounder of the unexpounded path, the knower of the path, the expert with regard to the path, adept at the path. And now his disciples follow the path and become endowed with it after him."

And then Ven. Ānanda's discussion with Moggallāna the Guardsman was interrupted in mid-course, for the brahman Vassakāra, the Magadhan administrator, on an inspection tour of the construction sites in Rājagaha, went to Ven. Ānanda at Moggallāna the Guardsman's construction site. On arrival, he exchanged courteous greetings with Ven. Ānanda. After an exchange of friendly greetings & courtesies, he sat to one side. As he was sitting there, he said to Ven. Ānanda, "Just now, for what discussion were you sitting together when you were interrupted in mid-course?"

"Just now, brahman, Moggallāna the Guardsman said to me, 'Master Ānanda, is there any one monk endowed in each & every way with the qualities with which Master Gotama—worthy & rightly self-awakened—was endowed?' And when this was said, I said to him, 'No, brahman, there isn't any one monk endowed in each & every way with the qualities with which the Blessed One—worthy & rightly self-awakened—was endowed. For the Blessed One was the arouser of the unarisen path, the begetter of the unbegotten path, the expounder of the unexpounded path, the knower of the path, the expert with regard to the path, adept at the path. And now his disciples follow the path and become endowed with it after him.' This was my discussion with the brahman Moggallāna the Guardsman that was interrupted in mid-course when you arrived."

"Master Ānanda, is there any one monk appointed by Master Gotama (with the words), 'He will be your arbitrator after I am gone,' to whom you now turn?"

"No, brahman. There isn't any one monk appointed by the Blessed One—the one who knows, the one who sees, worthy & rightly self-awakened—(with the words), 'He will be your arbitrator after I am gone,' to whom we now turn."

"Then is there any one monk authorized by the Saṅgha and appointed by a large body of elder monks (with the words), 'He will be our arbitrator after the Blessed One is gone,' to whom you now turn?"

"No, brahman. There isn't any one monk authorized by the Saṅgha and appointed by a large body of elder monks (with the words), 'He will be our arbitrator after the Blessed One is gone,' to whom we now turn."

"Being thus without an arbitrator, Master Ānanda, what is the reason for your concord?"

"It's not the case, brahman, that we're without an arbitrator. We have an arbitrator. The Dhamma is our arbitrator."

"When asked, 'Master Ānanda, is there any one monk appointed by Master Gotama (with the words), "He will be your arbitrator after I am gone," to whom you now turn?' you said, 'No, brahman. There isn't any one monk appointed by the Blessed One... to whom we now turn.'

"When asked, 'Then is there any one monk authorized by the Saṅgha... to whom you now turn?' you said, 'No, brahman. There isn't any one monk authorized by the Saṅgha... to whom we now turn.'

"When asked, 'Being thus without an arbitrator, Master Ānanda, what is the reason for your concord?' you said, 'It's not the case, brahman, that we're without an arbitrator. We have an arbitrator. The Dhamma is our arbitrator.' Now how is the meaning of what you have said to be understood?"

"Brahman, there is a training rule laid down by the Blessed One—the one who knows, the one who sees, worthy & rightly self-awakened—a Pāṭimokkha that has been codified. On the uposatha day, all of us who live dependent on a single township gather together in one place. Having gathered together, we invite the one to whom it falls (to recite the Pāṭimokkha). If, while he is reciting, a monk remembers an offense or transgression, we deal with him in accordance with the Dhamma, in accordance with what has been instructed. *We're* not the ones who deal with that venerable one. Rather, the Dhamma is what deals with us."

"Is there, Master Ānanda, any one monk you now honor, respect, revere, & venerate, on whom—honoring & respecting—you live in dependence?"

"Yes, brahman, there is a monk we now honor, respect, revere, & venerate, on whom—honoring & respecting—we live in dependence."

"When asked, 'Master Ānanda, is there any one monk appointed by Master Gotama (with the words), "He will be your arbitrator after I am gone," to whom you now turn?' you said, 'No, brahman. There isn't any one monk appointed by the Blessed One... to whom we now turn.'

"When asked, 'Then is there any one monk authorized by the Saṅgha... to whom you now turn?' you said, 'No, brahman.

There isn't any one monk authorized by the Saṅgha... to whom we now turn.'

"When asked, 'Is there, Master Ānanda, any one monk you now honor, respect, revere, & venerate, on whom—honoring & respecting—you live in dependence?' you said, 'Yes, brahman, there is a monk we now honor, respect, revere, & venerate, on whom—honoring & respecting—we live in dependence.' Now how is the meaning of what you have said to be understood?"

"Brahman, there are ten inspiring qualities expounded by the Blessed One—the one who knows, the one who sees, worthy & rightly self-awakened. In whoever among us those ten qualities are found, we now honor, respect, revere, & venerate him; honoring & respecting him, we live in dependence on him. Which ten?

"[1] There is the case where a monk is virtuous. He dwells restrained in accordance with the Pāṭimokkha, consummate in his behavior & sphere of activity. He trains himself, having undertaken the training rules, seeing danger in the slightest faults.

"[2] He has heard much, has retained what he has heard, has stored what he has heard. Whatever teachings are admirable in the beginning, admirable in the middle, admirable in the end, that—in their meaning & expression—proclaim the holy life entirely perfect & pure: those he has listened to often, retained, discussed, accumulated, examined with his mind, and well-penetrated in terms of his views.

"[3] He is content with robes, alms food, lodgings, & medicinal requisites for curing the sick.

"[4] He attains—whenever he wants, without strain, without difficulty—the four jhānas that are heightened mental states, pleasant abidings in the here-&-now.

"[5] He experiences manifold supranormal powers. Having been one he becomes many; having been many he becomes one. He appears. He vanishes. He goes unimpeded through walls, ramparts, & mountains as if through space. He dives in & out of the earth as if it were water. He walks on water without sinking as if it were dry land. Sitting crosslegged he flies through the air like a winged bird. With his hand he touches & strokes even the sun & moon, so mighty & powerful. He exercises influence with his body even as far as the Brahmā worlds.

"[6] He hears—by means of the divine ear-element, purified & surpassing the human—both kinds of sounds: divine & human, whether near or far.

"[7] He knows the awareness of other beings, other individuals, having encompassed it with his own awareness. He discerns a mind with passion as 'a mind with passion,' and a mind without passion as 'a mind without passion.' He discerns a mind with aversion as 'a mind with aversion,' and a mind without aversion as 'a mind without aversion.' He discerns a mind with delusion as 'a mind with delusion,' and a mind without delusion as 'a mind without delusion.' He discerns a restricted mind as 'a restricted mind,' and a scattered mind as 'a scattered mind.' He discerns an enlarged mind as 'an enlarged mind,' and an unenlarged mind as 'an unenlarged mind.' He discerns a surpassed mind [one that is not at the most excellent level] as 'a surpassed mind,' and an unsurpassed mind as 'an unsurpassed mind.' He discerns a concentrated mind as 'a concentrated mind,' and an unconcentrated mind as 'an unconcentrated mind.' He discerns a released mind as 'a released mind,' and an unreleased mind as 'an unreleased mind.'

"[8] He recollects his manifold past lives [lit: previous homes], i.e., one birth, two births, three births, four, five, ten, twenty, thirty, forty, fifty, one hundred, one thousand, one hundred thousand, many eons of cosmic contraction, many eons of cosmic expansion, many eons of cosmic contraction & expansion, (recollecting,) 'There I had such a name, belonged to such a clan, had such an appearance. Such was my food, such my experience of pleasure & pain, such the end of my life. Passing away from that state, I re-arose there. There too I had such a name, belonged to such a clan, had such an appearance. Such was my food, such my experience of pleasure & pain, such the end of my life. Passing away from that state, I re-arose here.' Thus he remembers his manifold past lives in their modes & details.

"[9] He sees—by means of the divine eye, purified & surpassing the human—beings passing away and re-appearing, and he discerns how they are inferior & superior, beautiful & ugly, fortunate & unfortunate in accordance with their kamma: 'These beings—who were endowed with bad conduct of body, speech, & mind, who reviled the noble ones, held wrong views and undertook actions under the influence of wrong views—with the break-up of the body, after death, have re-appeared in a plane of deprivation, a bad destination, a lower realm, hell. But these beings—who were endowed with good conduct of body, speech, & mind, who did not revile the noble ones, who held right views and undertook actions under the influence of right views—with the break-up of the body, after death, have re-appeared in a good destination, a heavenly world.' Thus—by means of the divine eye, purified & surpassing the human—he sees beings passing away and re-appearing, and he discerns how they are inferior & superior, beautiful & ugly, fortunate & unfortunate in accordance with their kamma.

"[10] Through the ending of effluents, he remains in the effluent-free awareness-release & discernment-release, having known & realized them for himself right in the here & now.

"These, brahman, are the ten inspiring qualities expounded by the Blessed One—the one who knows, the one who sees, worthy & rightly self-awakened. In whoever among us these ten qualities are found, we now honor, respect, revere, & venerate him; honoring & respecting him, we live in dependence on him."

When this was said, the brahman Vassakāra, the Magadhan administrator, turned to General Upananda and said, "What do you think, general? Do these venerable ones honor what should be honored, respect what should be respected, revere what should be revered, venerate what should be venerated? Of course they honor what should be honored, respect what should be respected, revere what should be revered, venerate what should be venerated. For if they did not honor, respect, revere, or venerate a person like this, then what sort of person would they honor, respect, revere, & venerate; on what sort of person, honor & respecting, would they live in dependence?"

Then the brahman Vassakāra, the Magadhan administrator, said to Ven. Ānanda, "But where are you staying now, Master Ānanda?"

"I am now staying at the Bamboo Grove, brahman."

"I trust, Master Ānanda, that the Bamboo Grove is delightful, with few noises or sounds of voices, with an air of isolation, private from human beings, and appropriate for seclusion."

"Certainly, brahman, the Bamboo Grove is delightful, with few noises or sounds of voices, with an air of isolation, private from human beings, and appropriate for seclusion because of guardians & protectors like yourself."

"Certainly, Master Ānanda, the Bamboo Grove is delightful, with few noises or sounds of voices, with an air of isolation, private from human beings, and appropriate for seclusion because of venerable ones who are endowed with mental absorption *[jhāna]*, who make mental absorption their habit. You venerable ones are both endowed with mental absorption & make mental absorption your habit.

"Once, Ven. Ānanda, Master Gotama was staying near Vesālī in the Peaked Roofed Pavilion in the Great Wood. I went to him at the Peaked Roofed Pavilion in the Great Wood, and there he spoke in a variety of ways on mental absorption. Master Gotama was both endowed with mental absorption & made mental absorption his habit. In fact, he praised mental absorption of every sort."

"It wasn't the case, brahman, that the Blessed One praised mental absorption of every sort, nor did he criticize mental absorption of every sort. And what sort of mental absorption did he not praise? There is the case where a certain person dwells with his awareness overcome by sensual passion, seized with sensual passion. He does not discern the escape, as it has come to be, from sensual passion once it has arisen. Making that sensual passion the focal point, he absorbs himself with it, besorbs, resorbs, & supersorbs himself with it.

"He dwells with his awareness overcome by ill will....

"He dwells with his awareness overcome by sloth & drowsiness....

"He dwells with his awareness overcome by restlessness & anxiety....

"He dwells with his awareness overcome by uncertainty, seized with uncertainty. He does not discern the escape, as it has come to be, from uncertainty once it has arisen. Making that uncertainty the focal point, he absorbs himself with it, besorbs, resorbs, & supersorbs himself with it. This is the sort of mental absorption that the Blessed One did not praise.

"And what sort of mental absorption did he praise? There is the case where a monk—quite secluded from sensuality, secluded from unskillful qualities—enters & remains in the first jhāna: rapture & pleasure born of seclusion, accompanied by directed thought & evaluation. With the stilling of directed thoughts & evaluations, he enters & remains in the second jhāna: rapture & pleasure born of concentration, unification of awareness free from directed thought & evaluation—internal assurance. With the fading of rapture, he remains equanimous, mindful, & alert, and senses pleasure with the body. He enters & remains in the third jhāna, of which the noble ones declare, 'Equanimous & mindful, he has a pleasant abiding.' With the abandoning of pleasure & pain—as with the earlier disappearance of elation & distress—he enters & remains in the fourth jhāna: purity of equanimity & mindfulness, neither pleasure nor pain. This is the sort of mental absorption that the Blessed One praised.

"It would seem, Ven. Ānanda, that Master Gotama criticized the mental absorption that deserves criticism, and praised that which deserves praise.

"Well, now, Master Ānanda, I must be going. Many are my duties, many the things I must do."

"Then do, brahman, what you think it is now time to do."

So the brahman Vassakāra, the Magadhan administrator, delighting & rejoicing in what Ven. Ānanda had said, got up from his seat & left.

Then, not long after he had left, Moggallāna the Guardsman said to Ven. Ānanda, "Master Ānanda, you still haven't answered what I asked you."

"Didn't I just tell you, brahman? There isn't any one monk endowed in each & every way with the qualities with which the Blessed One—worthy & rightly self-awakened—was endowed. For the Blessed One was the arouser of the unarisen path, the begetter of the unbegotten path, the expounder of the unexpounded path, the knower of the path, the expert with regard to the path, adept at the path. And now his disciples follow the path and become endowed with it after him."

See also: SN 22:90; AN 6:12; AN 7:21; AN 11:10

109 *The Great Full-Moon Night Discourse*

Mahā Puṇṇama Sutta

This sutta provides a thorough discussion of issues related to the five aggregates. Toward the end of the discussion, a monk thinks that he has found a loophole in the teaching. The way the Buddha handles this incident shows the proper use of the teachings on the aggregates: not as a metaphysical theory, but as a tool for questioning clinging and so gaining release.

* * *

I have heard that on one occasion the Blessed One was staying near Sāvatthī in the Eastern Monastery, the palace of Migāra's mother. And on that occasion—the uposatha of the fifteenth, the night of a very full moon—he was sitting out in the open with the Saṅgha of monks.

Then a certain monk, rising from his seat, arranging his robe over one shoulder, and placing his hands palm-to-palm over the heart, said to the Blessed One: "Venerable sir, there is an area where, if the Blessed One would give me leave, I would like the answer to a question."

"Very well, then, monk. Sit back down in your seat and ask whatever you want."

Responding to the Blessed One, "Yes, lord," the monk sat back down in his seat and said to the Blessed One, "Aren't these the five clinging-aggregates, i.e., the form clinging-aggregate, the feeling clinging-aggregate, the perception clinging-aggregate, the fabrications clinging-aggregate, the consciousness clinging-aggregate."

"Monk, these are the five clinging-aggregates, i.e., the form clinging-aggregate, the feeling clinging-aggregate, the perception clinging-aggregate, the fabrications clinging-aggregate, the consciousness clinging-aggregate."

Saying, "Very good, lord," the monk delighted & approved of the Blessed One's words and then asked him a further question: "But in what, lord, are these five clinging-aggregates rooted?"

"Monk, these five clinging-aggregates are rooted in desire."[1]

Saying, "Very good, lord," the monk… asked him a further question: "Is clinging the same thing as the five clinging-aggregates, or is clinging separate from the five clinging-aggregates?"

"Monk, clinging is neither the same thing as the five clinging-aggregates, nor is it separate from the five clinging-aggregates. Just that whatever passion & delight is there, that's the clinging there."

Saying, "Very good, lord," the monk… asked him a further question: "Might there be diversity in the desire & passion for the five clinging-aggregates?"

"There might, monk. There is the case where the thought occurs to someone, 'May I be one with such a form in the future. May I be one with such a feeling… perception… fabrications… such a consciousness in the future. This is how there would be diversity in the desire & passion for the five clinging-aggregates."

Saying, "Very good, lord," the monk… asked him a further question: "To what extent does the designation 'aggregate' apply to the aggregates?"

"Monk, whatever form is past, future, or present; internal or external; blatant or subtle; common or sublime; far or near: That is called the form aggregate. Whatever feeling is past, future, or present; internal or external; blatant or subtle; common or sublime; far or near: That is called the feeling aggregate. Whatever perception is past, future, or present; internal or external; blatant or subtle; common or sublime; far or near: That is called the perception aggregate. Whatever fabrications are past, future, or present; internal or external; blatant or subtle; common or sublime; far or near: Those are called the fabrications aggregate. Whatever consciousness is past, future, or present; internal or external; blatant or subtle; common or sublime; far or near: That is called the consciousness aggregate.[2] This is the extent to which the term 'aggregate' applies to the aggregates."

Saying, "Very good, lord," the monk… asked him a further question: "Lord, what is the cause, what the condition, for the delineation[3] of the form aggregate? What is the cause, what the condition, for the delineation of the feeling aggregate… the perception aggregate… the fabrications aggregate… the consciousness aggregate?"

"Monk, the four great existents [earth, water, fire, & wind] are the cause, the four great existents the condition, for the delineation of the form aggregate. Contact is the cause, contact the condition, for the delineation of the feeling aggregate. Contact is the cause, contact the condition, for the delineation of the perception aggregate. Contact is the cause, contact the condition, for the delineation of the fabrications aggregate. Name-&-form is the cause, name-&-form the condition, for the delineation of the consciousness aggregate."

Saying, "Very good, lord," the monk... asked him a further question: "Lord, how does self-identification view come about?"

"There is the case, monk, where an uninstructed run-of-the-mill person—who has no regard for noble ones, is not well-versed or disciplined in their Dhamma; who has no regard for people of integrity, is not well-versed or disciplined in their Dhamma—assumes form to be the self, or the self as possessing form, or form as in the self, or the self as in form.

"He assumes feeling to be the self, or the self as possessing feeling, or feeling as in the self, or the self as in feeling. He assumes perception to be the self, or the self as possessing perception, or perception as in the self, or the self as in perception. He assumes fabrications to be the self, or the self as possessing fabrications, or fabrications as in the self, or the self as in fabrications. He assumes consciousness to be the self, or the self as possessing consciousness, or consciousness as in the self, or the self as in consciousness.

"This, monk, is how self-identification view comes about."

Saying, "Very good, lord," the monk... asked him a further question: "Lord, how does self-identification view no longer come about?"

"There is the case, monk, where a well-instructed disciple of the noble ones—who has regard for noble ones, is well-versed & disciplined in their Dhamma; who has regard for people of integrity, is well-versed & disciplined in their Dhamma—doesn't assume form to be the self, or the self as possessing form, or form as in the self, or the self as in form. He doesn't assume feeling to be the self.... doesn't assume perception to be the self.... doesn't assume fabrications to be the self.... He doesn't assume consciousness to be the self, or the self as possessing consciousness, or consciousness as in the self, or the self as in consciousness.

"This, monk, is how self-identification view no longer comes about."

Saying, "Very good, lord," the monk... asked him a further question: "What, lord, is the allure of form? What is its drawback? What is the escape from it? What is the allure of feeling... perception... fabrications... consciousness? What is its drawback? What is the escape from it?"

"Monk, whatever pleasure & joy arises dependent on form: That is the allure of form. The fact that form is inconstant, stressful, subject to change: That is the drawback of form. The subduing of desire & passion, the abandoning of desire & passion for form: That is the escape from form.

"Whatever pleasure & joy arises dependent on feeling: That is the allure of feeling....

"Whatever pleasure & joy arises dependent on perception: That is the allure of perception....

"Whatever pleasure & joy arises dependent on fabrications: That is the allure of fabrications....

"Whatever pleasure & joy arises dependent on consciousness: That is the allure of consciousness. The fact that consciousness is inconstant, stressful, subject to change: That is the drawback of consciousness. The subduing of desire & passion, the abandoning of desire & passion for consciousness: That is the escape from consciousness."

Saying, "Very good, lord," the monk... asked him a further question: "Knowing in what way, seeing in what way, is there—with regard to this body endowed with consciousness, and with regard to all external signs—no longer any I-making, or my-making, or obsession with conceit?"

"Monk, one sees any form whatsoever—past, future, or present; internal or external; blatant or subtle; common or sublime; far or near—every form, as it has come to be with right discernment: 'This is not mine. This is not my self. This is not what I am.'

"One sees any feeling whatsoever... any perception whatsoever... any fabrications whatsoever...

"One sees any consciousness whatsoever—past, future, or present; internal or external; blatant or subtle; common or sublime; far or near—every consciousness—as it has come to be with right discernment: 'This is not mine. This is not my self. This is not what I am.'"

"Monk, knowing in this way, seeing in this way is there—with regard to this body endowed with consciousness, and with regard to all external signs—no longer any I-making, or my-making, or obsession with conceit."

Now at that moment this line of thinking appeared in the awareness of a certain monk: "So—form is not-self, feeling is not-self, perception is not-self, fabrications are not-self, consciousness is not-self. Then what self will be touched by the actions done by what is not-self?"

Then the Blessed One, realizing with his awareness the line of thinking in that monk's awareness, addressed the monks: "It's possible that a senseless person—immersed in ignorance, overcome with craving—might think that he could outsmart the Teacher's message in this way: 'So—form is not-self, feeling is not-self, perception is not-self, fabrications are not-self, consciousness is not-self.

Then what self will be touched by the actions done by what is not-self?' Now, monks, haven't I trained you in counter-questioning with regard to this & that topic here & there? What do you think? Is form constant or inconstant?"—"Inconstant, lord."—"And is that which is inconstant easeful or stressful?"—"Stressful, lord."—"And is it fitting to regard what is inconstant, stressful, subject to change as: 'This is mine. This is my self. This is what I am'?"

"No, lord."

"... Is feeling constant or inconstant?"—"Inconstant, lord." ...

"... Is perception constant or inconstant?"—"Inconstant, lord." ...

"... Are fabrications constant or inconstant?"—"Inconstant, lord." ...

"What do you think, monks? Is consciousness constant or inconstant?"—"Inconstant, lord."—"And is that which is inconstant easeful or stressful?"—"Stressful, lord."—"And is it fitting to regard what is inconstant, stressful, subject to change as: 'This is mine. This is my self. This is what I am'?"

"No, lord."

"Thus, monks, any form whatsoever that is past, future, or present; internal or external; blatant or subtle; common or sublime; far or near: Every form is to be seen as it has come to be with right discernment as: 'This is not mine. This is not my self. This is not what I am.'

"Any feeling whatsoever...

"Any perception whatsoever...

"Any fabrications whatsoever...

"Any consciousness whatsoever that is past, future, or present; internal or external; blatant or subtle; common or sublime; far or near: Every consciousness is to be seen as it has come to be with right discernment as: 'This is not mine. This is not my self. This is not what I am.'

"Seeing thus, the instructed disciple of the noble ones grows disenchanted with form, disenchanted with feeling, disenchanted with perception, disenchanted with fabrications, disenchanted with consciousness. Disenchanted, he becomes dispassionate. Through dispassion, he is released. With release, there is the knowledge, 'Released.' He discerns that 'Birth is ended, the holy life fulfilled, the task done. There is nothing further for this world.'"

That is what the Blessed One said. Gratified, the monks delighted in the Blessed One's words. And while this explanation was being given, the minds of sixty monks, through lack of clinging/sustenance, were released from effluents.

NOTES

1. As AN 10:58 notes, all phenomena *(dhamma)* are rooted in desire.

2. One form of consciousness apparently does not come under the aggregate of consciousness. This is termed *viññāṇaṁ anidassanaṁ*—consciousness without a surface, or consciousness without feature. MN 49 says specifically that this consciousness is not experienced through the "allness of the all," the "all" being conterminous with the six sense media and the five aggregates (SN 35:23). DN 11 states that in this consciousness name and form—which are also conterminous with the five aggregates—are not found. Because the aggregate of consciousness cannot arise apart from the other aggregates (SN 22:53–54), *viññāṇaṁ anidassanaṁ* would not fit under the aggregate of consciousness.

Furthermore, the standard definition of the aggregate of consciousness states that this aggregate includes all consciousness, "past, present, or future… near or far." However, because *viññāṇaṁ anidassanaṁ* stands outside of space and time it would not be covered by these terms. Similarly, where SN 22:97 says that no consciousness is eternal, "eternal" is a concept that applies only within the dimension of time, and thus would not apply to this form of consciousness.

3. Delineation *(paññāpana)* literally means, "making discernible." This apparently refers to the intentional aspect of perception, which takes the objective side of experience and fabricates it into discernible objects. In the case of the aggregates, the four great existents, contact, and name-&-form provide the objective basis for discerning them, while the process of fabrication takes the raw material provided by the objective basis and turns it into discernible instances of the aggregates. This process is described in slightly different terms in SN 22:79.

See also: MN 28; MN 122; SN 1:25; SN 22

110 *The Shorter Full-Moon Night Discourse*

Cūḷa Puṇṇama Sutta

I have heard that on one occasion the Blessed One was staying near Sāvatthī in the Eastern Monastery, the palace of Migāra's mother. And on that occasion—the uposatha of the fifteenth, the night of a very full moon—he was sitting out in the open with the Saṅgha of monks. Then, having surveyed the silent Saṅgha of monks, he addressed them: "Monks, could a person of no integrity know of a person of no integrity: 'This is a person of no integrity'?"

"No, lord."

"Good, monks. It's impossible, there's no way, that a person of no integrity would know of a person of no integrity: 'This is a person of no integrity.'

"Could a person of no integrity know of a person of integrity: 'This is a person of integrity'?"

"No, lord."

"Good, monks. It's impossible, there's no way, that a person of no integrity would know of a person of integrity: 'This is a person of integrity.'

"A person of no integrity is endowed with qualities of no integrity; he is a person of no integrity in his friendship, in the way he wills, the way he gives advice, the way he speaks, the way he acts, the views he holds, & the way he gives a gift.

"And how is a person of no integrity endowed with qualities of no integrity? There is the case where a person of no integrity is lacking in conviction, lacking in shame, lacking in compunction; he is unlearned, lazy, of muddled mindfulness, & poor discernment. This is how a person of no integrity is endowed with qualities of no integrity."

"And how is a person of no integrity a person of no integrity in his friendship? There is the case where a person of no integrity has, as his friends & companions, those contemplatives & brahmans who are lacking in conviction, lacking in shame, lacking in compunction, unlearned, lazy, of muddled mindfulness, & poor discernment. This is how a person of no integrity is a person of no integrity in his friendship.

"And how is a person of no integrity a person of no integrity in the way he wills? There is the case where a person of no integrity wills for his own affliction, or for the affliction of others, or for the affliction of both. This is how a person of no integrity is a person of no integrity in the way he wills.

"And how is a person of no integrity a person of no integrity in the way he gives advice? There is the case where a person of no integrity gives advice for his own affliction, or for the affliction of others, or for the affliction of both. This is how a person of no integrity is a person of no integrity in the way he gives advice.

"And how is a person of no integrity a person of no integrity in the way he speaks? There is the case where a person of no integrity is one who tells lies, engages in divisive tale-bearing, engages in harsh speech, engages in idle chatter. This is how a person of no integrity is a person of no integrity in the way he speaks.

"And how is a person of no integrity a person of no integrity in the way he acts? There is the case where a person of no integrity is one who takes life, steals, engages in illicit sex. This is how a person of no integrity is a person of no integrity in the way he acts.

"And how is a person of no integrity a person of no integrity in the views he holds? There is the case where a person of no integrity is one who holds a view like this: 'There is nothing given, nothing offered, nothing sacrificed. There is no fruit or result of good or bad actions. There is no this world, no next world, no mother, no father, no spontaneously reborn beings; no contemplatives or brahmans who, faring rightly & practicing rightly, proclaim this world & the next after having directly known & realized it for themselves.' This is how a person of no integrity is a person of no integrity in the views he holds.

"And how is a person of no integrity a person of no integrity in the way he gives a gift? There is the case where a person of no integrity gives a gift inattentively, not with his own hand, disrespectfully, as if throwing it away, with the view that nothing will come of it. This is how a person of no integrity is a person of no integrity in the way he gives a gift.

"This person of no integrity—thus endowed with qualities of no integrity; a person of no integrity in his friendship, in the way he wills, the way he gives advice, the way he speaks, the way he acts, the views he holds, & the way he gives a gift—on the break-up of the body, after death, reappears in the destination of people of no integrity. And what is the destination of people of no integrity? Hell or the animal womb.

"Now, monks, could a person of integrity know of a person of no integrity: 'This is a person of no integrity'?"

"Yes, lord."

"Good, monks. It is possible that a person of integrity would know of a person of no integrity: 'This is a person of no integrity.'

"Could a person of integrity know of a person of integrity: 'This is a person of integrity'?"

"Yes, lord."

"Good, monks. It is possible that a person of integrity would know of a person of integrity: 'This is a person of integrity.'

"A person of integrity is endowed with qualities of integrity; he is a person of integrity in his friendship, in the way he wills, the way he gives advice, the way he speaks, the way he acts, the views he holds, & the way he gives a gift.

"And how is a person of integrity endowed with qualities of integrity? There is the case where a person of integrity is endowed with conviction, shame, compunction; he is learned, with aroused persistence, unmuddled mindfulness, & good discernment. This is how a person of integrity is endowed with qualities of integrity."

"And how is a person of integrity a person of integrity in his friendship? There is the case where a person of integrity has, as his friends & companions, those contemplatives & brahmans who are endowed with conviction, shame, compunction; who are learned, with aroused persistence, unmuddled mindfulness, & good discernment. This is how a person of integrity is a person of integrity in his friendship.

"And how is a person of integrity a person of integrity in the way he wills? There is the case where a person of integrity wills neither for his own affliction, nor for the affliction of others, nor for the affliction of both. This is how a person of integrity is a person of integrity in the way he wills.

"And how is a person of integrity a person of integrity in the way he gives advice? There is the case where a person of integrity gives advice neither for his own affliction, nor for the affliction of others, nor for the affliction of both. This is how a person of integrity is a person of integrity in the way he gives advice.

"And how is a person of integrity a person of integrity in the way he speaks? There is the case where a person of integrity is one who refrains from lies, refrains from divisive tale-bearing, refrains from harsh speech, refrains from idle chatter. This is how a person of integrity is a person of integrity in the way he speaks.

"And how is a person of integrity a person of integrity in the way he acts? There is the case where a person of integrity is one who refrains from taking life, refrains from stealing, refrains from illicit sex. This is how a person of integrity is a person of integrity in the way he acts.

"And how is a person of integrity a person of integrity in the views he holds? There is the case where a person of integrity is one who holds a view like this: 'There is what is given, what is offered, what is sacrificed. There are fruits & results of good & bad actions. There is this world & the next world. There is mother & father. There are spontaneously reborn beings; there are contemplatives & brahmans who, faring rightly & practicing rightly, proclaim this world & the next after having directly known & realized it for themselves.' This is how a person of integrity is a person of integrity in the views he holds.

"And how is a person of integrity a person of integrity in the way he gives a gift? There is the case where a person of integrity gives a gift attentively, with his own hand, respectfully, not as if throwing it away, with the view that something will come of it. This is how a person of integrity is a person of integrity in the way he gives a gift.

"This person of integrity—thus endowed with qualities of integrity; a person of integrity in his friendship, in the way he wills, the way he gives advice, the way he speaks, the way he acts, the views he holds, & the way he gives a gift—on the break-up of the body, after death, reappears in the destination of people of integrity. And what is the destination of people of integrity? Greatness among devas or among human beings."

That is what the Blessed One said. Gratified, the monks delighted in the Blessed One's words.

See also: MN 113; SN 55:5; AN 2:31–32; AN 4:73; AN 4:192; AN 5:148; AN 8:54; Iti 17

111 *One After Another*

Anupada Sutta

I have heard that on one occasion the Blessed One was staying near Sāvatthī in Jeta's Grove, Anāthapiṇḍika's monastery. There he addressed the monks, saying, "Monks!"

"Yes, lord," the monks responded to him.

The Blessed One said, "Monks, Sāriputta is wise, of great discernment, deep discernment, wide... joyous... rapid... quick... penetrating discernment. For half a month, Sāriputta clearly saw insight[1] into mental qualities one after another. This is what occurred to Sāriputta through insight into mental qualities one after another:

"There was the case where Sāriputta—quite secluded from sensuality, secluded from unskillful qualities—entered & remained in the first jhāna: rapture & pleasure born of seclusion, accompanied by directed thought & evaluation. Whatever qualities there are in the first jhāna—directed thought, evaluation, rapture, pleasure, singleness of mind, contact, feeling, perception, intention, consciousness,[2] desire, decision, persistence, mindfulness, equanimity, & attention—he ferreted them out one after another. Known to him they arose, known to him they became established, known to him they subsided. He discerned, 'So this is how these qualities, not having been, come into play. Having been, they vanish.' He remained unattracted & unrepelled with regard to those qualities, independent, detached, released, dissociated, with an awareness rid of barriers. He discerned that 'There is a further escape,' and pursuing it, he confirmed that 'There is.'

"And further, with the stilling of directed thoughts & evaluations, Sāriputta entered & remained in the second jhāna: rapture & pleasure born of concentration, unification of awareness free from directed thought & evaluation—internal assurance. Whatever qualities there are in the second jhāna—internal assurance, rapture, pleasure, singleness of mind, contact, feeling, perception, intention, consciousness, desire, decision, persistence, mindfulness, equanimity, & attention—he ferreted them out one after another. Known to him they arose, known to him they became established, known to him they subsided. He discerned, 'So this is how these qualities, not having been, come into play. Having been, they vanish.' He remained unattracted & unrepelled with regard to those qualities, independent, detached, released, dissociated, with an awareness rid of barriers. He discerned that 'There is a further escape,' and pursuing it, he confirmed that 'There is.'

"And further, with the fading of rapture, Sāriputta—remaining equanimous, mindful, & alert, and sensing pleasure with the body—entered & remained in the third jhāna, of which the noble ones declare, 'Equanimous & mindful, he has a pleasant abiding.' Whatever qualities there are in the third jhāna—equanimity, pleasure, mindfulness, alertness, singleness of mind, contact, feeling, perception, intention, consciousness, desire, decision, persistence, mindfulness, equanimity, & attention—he ferreted them out one after another. Known to him they arose, known to him they became established, known to him they subsided. He discerned, 'So this is how these qualities, not having been, come into play. Having been, they vanish.' He remained unattracted & unrepelled with regard to those qualities, independent, detached, released, dissociated, with an awareness rid of barriers. He discerned that 'There is a further escape,' and pursuing it, he confirmed that 'There is.'

"And further, with the abandoning of pleasure & pain—as with the earlier disappearance of joys & distresses—Sāriputta entered & remained in the fourth jhāna: purity of equanimity & mindfulness, neither-pleasure-nor-pain. Whatever qualities there are in the fourth jhāna—a feeling of equanimity, neither pleasure nor pain; an unconcern due to calmness[3] of awareness; singleness of mind, contact, feeling, perception, intention, consciousness, desire, decision, persistence, mindfulness, equanimity, & attention—he ferreted them out one after another. Known to him they arose, known to him they became established, known to him they subsided. He discerned, 'So this is how these qualities, not having been, come into play. Having been, they vanish.' He remained unattracted & unrepelled with regard to those qualities, independent, detached, released, dissociated, with an awareness rid of barriers. He discerned that 'There is a further escape,' and pursuing it, he confirmed that 'There is.'

"And further, with the complete transcending of perceptions of (physical) form, with the disappearance of perceptions of resistance, and not attending to perceptions of multiplicity, (perceiving,) 'Infinite space,' Sāriputta entered & remained in the dimension of the infinitude of space. Whatever qualities there are in the dimension of the infinitude of space—the perception of the dimension of the infinitude of space, singleness of mind, contact, feeling, perception, intention, consciousness, desire, decision, persistence, mindfulness, equanimity, & attention—he ferreted them out one after another. Known to him they arose, known to him they became established, known to him they subsided. He discerned, 'So this is how these qualities, not having been, come into play. Having been, they vanish.' He remained unattracted & unrepelled with regard to those qualities, independent, detached, released, dissociated, with an awareness rid of barriers. He discerned that 'There is a further escape,' and pursuing it, he confirmed that 'There is.'

"And further, with the complete transcending of the dimension of the infinitude of space, (perceiving,) 'Infinite consciousness,' Sāriputta entered & remained in the dimension of the infinitude of consciousness. Whatever qualities there are in the dimension of the infinitude of consciousness—the perception of the dimension of the infinitude of consciousness, singleness of mind, contact, feeling, perception, intention, consciousness, desire, decision, persistence, mindfulness, equanimity, & attention—he ferreted them out one after another. Known to him they arose, known to him they became established, known to him they subsided. He discerned, 'So this is how these qualities, not having been, come into play. Having been, they vanish.' He remained unattracted & unrepelled with regard to those qualities, independent, detached, released, dissociated, with an awareness rid of barriers. He discerned that 'There is a further escape,' and pursuing it, he confirmed that 'There is.'

"And further, with the complete transcending of the dimension of the infinitude of consciousness, (perceiving,) 'There is nothing,' Sāriputta entered & remained in the dimension of nothingness. Whatever qualities there are in the dimension of nothingness—the perception of the dimension of nothingness, singleness of mind, contact, feeling, perception, intention, consciousness, desire, decision, persistence, mindfulness, equanimity, & attention—he ferreted them out one after another. Known to him they arose, known to him they became established, known to him they subsided. He discerned, 'So this is how these qualities, not having been, come into play. Having been, they vanish.' He remained unattracted & unrepelled with regard to those qualities, independent, detached, released, dissociated, with an awareness rid of barriers. He discerned that 'There is a further escape,' and pursuing it, he confirmed that 'There is.'

"And further, with the complete transcending of the dimension of nothingness, Sāriputta entered & remained in the dimension of neither perception nor non-perception. He emerged mindfully from that attainment. On emerging mindfully from that attainment, he regarded the past qualities that had ceased & changed: 'So this is how these qualities, not having been, come into play. Having been, they vanish.' He remained unattracted & unrepelled with regard to those qualities, independent, detached, released, dissociated, with an awareness rid of barriers. He discerned that 'There is a further escape,' and pursuing it, he confirmed that 'There is.'[4]

"And further, with the complete transcending of the dimension of neither perception nor non-perception, Sāriputta entered & remained in the cessation of perception & feeling. And when he saw with discernment, his effluents were totally ended. He emerged mindfully from that attainment. On emerging mindfully from that attainment, he regarded the past qualities that had ceased & changed: 'So this is how these qualities, not having been, come into play. Having been, they vanish.'[5] He remained unattracted & unrepelled with regard to those qualities, independent, detached, released, dissociated, with an awareness rid of barriers. He discerned that 'There is no further escape,' and pursuing it, he confirmed that 'There isn't.'

"If a person, rightly saying it of anyone, were to say, 'He has attained mastery & perfection in noble virtue... noble concentration... noble discernment... noble release,' he would be rightly saying it of Sāriputta if he were to say: 'He has attained mastery & perfection in noble virtue... noble concentration... noble discernment... noble release.'

"If a person, rightly saying it of anyone, were to say, 'He is the Blessed One's son, his offspring—born of his mouth, born of the Dhamma, created by the Dhamma, his heir in the Dhamma, not his heir in material things,' he would be rightly saying it of Sāriputta if he were to say: 'He is the Blessed One's son, his offspring—born of his mouth, born of the Dhamma, created by the Dhamma, his heir in the Dhamma, not his heir in material things.' Sāriputta, monks, takes the unexcelled wheel of Dhamma set rolling by the Tathāgata, and keeps it rolling rightly."

That is what the Blessed One said. Gratified, the monks delighted in the Blessed One's words.

NOTES

1. "Clearly saw insight": In Pali, this is *vipassanaṁ vipassi,* which could be translated literally as "clearly saw clear seeing" or "insighted insight." The Commentary states that the half-month mentioned here refers to the half month between Ven. Sāriputta's ordination and his attainment of arahantship, described in MN 74. These two suttas treat Sāriputta's attainment from two different perspectives. This sutta

shows it from the standpoint of his mastery of the four jhānas and the formless attainments based on the fourth jhāna. That sutta shows it as occurring when he starts reflecting on a point while listening to a discourse that the Buddha is giving to his nephew. To put the two suttas together, we can infer that prior to the discourse given in MN 74, Sāriputta had mastered the dimension of neither perception nor non-perception. While listening to the discourse, he reflected on the point that the Buddha recommended abandoning all mental qualities through direct knowledge. This would have led him to the cessation of perception and feeling (during which he would not be listening to the discourse) and so to awakening.

2. Reading *viññāṇaṁ* with the Thai edition of the Canon. The Burmese and PTS editions read *cittaṁ,* which could mean "mind" or "intent" (as in the four bases of success).

3. Reading *passaddhattā* with the Burmese edition. The Thai edition reads, *parisuddhatā,* "through purity." The Sinhalese edition reads *pasiddhatā,* which would mean "empowerment" (?—this term is not listed in the PTS Dictionary). The PTS edition reads *passi vedanā,* which is unintelligible.

4. Notice that, with each of the previous levels of attainment, Sāriputta was able to ferret out the various mental qualities arising there while he was still in the attainment. With this attainment and the following one, however, he was not able to analyze the mental qualities present and absent there until after he had left the attainment. The difference here is related to the point made in AN 9:36 that all the attainments up through the dimension of nothingness are "perception-attainments." And that, "As far as the perception-attainments go, that is as far as gnosis-penetration goes. As for these two dimensions—the attainment of the dimension of neither perception nor non-perception & the attainment of the cessation of perception & feeling—I tell you that they are to be rightly explained by those monks who are meditators, skilled at attainment, skilled in attainment-emergence, who have attained & emerged in dependence on them."

For a discussion of how insight can be developed in the context of jhāna, see *The Wings to Awakening, IIIF.*

5. For a more detailed description of what a meditator experiences on emerging from the cessation of perception and feeling, see MN 44.

See also: MN 43; MN 52; MN 140; AN 5:28; AN 9:36

113 *A Person of Integrity*

Sappurisa Sutta

I have heard that on one occasion the Blessed One was staying near Sāvatthī in Jeta's Grove, Anāthapiṇḍika's monastery. There he addressed the monks: "Monks!"

"Yes, lord," the monks responded to him.

The Blessed One said, "Monks, I will teach you the quality of a person of integrity and the quality of a person of no integrity. Listen, and pay close attention. I will speak."

"Yes, lord," the monks responded to him.

The Blessed One said: "And which is the quality of a person of no integrity?

"There is the case where a person of no integrity goes forth from a high-ranking family. He notices, 'I have gone forth from a high-ranking family, but these other monks have not gone forth from a high-ranking family.' He exalts himself for having a high-ranking family and disparages others. This is the quality of a person of no integrity.

"But a person of integrity notices, 'It's not through having a high-ranking family that the quality of greed goes to its end; it's not through having a high-ranking family that the quality of aversion… the quality of delusion goes to its end. Even though one has not gone forth from a high-ranking family, if—practicing the Dhamma in line with the Dhamma, practicing masterfully—he is one who follows the Dhamma, he is to be honored for that, praised for that.' So, giving priority just to the practice, he neither exalts himself for having a high-ranking family nor disparages others. This is the quality of a person of integrity.

"And further, a person of no integrity goes forth from a great family… a family of great wealth… a family of extensive wealth. He notices, 'I have gone forth from a family of extensive wealth, but these other monks have not gone forth from a family of extensive wealth.' He exalts himself for having a family of extensive wealth and disparages others. This is the quality of a person of no integrity.

"But a person of integrity notices, 'It's not through having a family of extensive wealth that the quality of greed goes to its end; it's not through having a family of extensive wealth that the quality of aversion… the quality of delusion goes to its end. Even though one has not gone forth from a family of extensive wealth, if—practicing the Dhamma in line with the Dhamma, practicing masterfully—he is one who follows the Dhamma, he is to be honored for that, praised for that.' So, giving priority just to the practice, he neither exalts himself for having a family of extensive wealth nor disparages others. This is the quality of a person of integrity.

"And further, a person of no integrity is well-known & highly regarded. He notices, 'I am well-known & highly regarded, but these other monks are hardly known & have hardly any influence.' He exalts himself for being well-known & highly regarded and disparages others. This is the quality of a person of no integrity.

"But a person of integrity notices, 'It's not through being well-known & highly regarded that the quality of greed goes to its end; it's not through being well-known & highly regarded that the quality of aversion… the quality of delusion goes to its end. Even though one is not well-known & highly regarded, if—practicing the Dhamma in line with the Dhamma, practicing masterfully—he is one who follows the Dhamma, he is to be honored for that, praised for that.' So, giving priority just to the practice, he neither exalts himself for being well-known nor disparages others. This is the quality of a person of integrity.

"And further, a person of no integrity is one who gains robe-cloth, alms-food, lodgings, & medicinal requisites for the sick. He notices, 'I am one who gains robe-cloth, alms-food, lodgings, & medicinal requisites for the sick, but these other monks are not ones who gain robe-cloth, alms-food, lodgings, & medicinal requisites for the sick. He exalts himself for being one who gains robe-cloth, alms-food, lodgings, & medicinal requisites for the sick and disparages others. This is the quality of a person of no integrity.

"But a person of integrity notices, 'It's not through gains that the quality of greed goes to its end; it's not through gains that the quality of aversion… the quality of delusion goes to its end. Even though one is not one who gains robe-cloth, alms-food, lodgings, & medicinal requisites for the sick, if—practicing the Dhamma in line with the Dhamma, practicing masterfully—he is one who follows the Dhamma, he is to be honored for that, praised for that.' So, giving priority just to the practice, he neither exalts himself for his gains nor disparages others. This is the quality of a person of integrity.

"And further, a person of no integrity is learned… a master of the Vinaya… a Dhamma-speaker. He notices, 'I am a Dhamma-speaker, but these other monks are not Dhamma-speakers. He exalts himself for being a Dhamma-speaker and disparages others. This is the quality of a person of no integrity.

"But a person of integrity notices, 'It's not through being a Dhamma-speaker that the quality of greed goes to its end; it's not through being a Dhamma-speaker that the quality of aversion... the quality of delusion goes to its end. Even though one is not a Dhamma-speaker, if—practicing the Dhamma in line with the Dhamma, practicing masterfully—he is one who follows the Dhamma, he is to be honored for that, praised for that.' So, giving priority just to the practice, he neither exalts himself for being a Dhamma-speaker nor disparages others. This is the quality of a person of integrity.

"And further, a person of no integrity is a wilderness dweller.[1] He notices, 'I am a wilderness dweller, but these other monks are not wilderness dwellers.' He exalts himself for being a wilderness dweller and disparages others. This is the quality of a person of no integrity.

"But a person of integrity notices, 'It's not through being a wilderness dweller that the quality of greed goes to its end; it's not through being a wilderness dweller that the quality of aversion... the quality of delusion goes to its end. Even though one is not a wilderness dweller, if—practicing the Dhamma in line with the Dhamma, practicing masterfully—he is one who follows the Dhamma, he is to be honored for that, praised for that.' So, giving priority just to the practice, he neither exalts himself for being a wilderness dweller nor disparages others. This is the quality of a person of integrity.

"And further, a person of no integrity is one who wears robes of thrown-away rags... an alms-goer... one who dwells at the root of a tree... a cemetery dweller... one who lives in the open air... one who doesn't lie down... one who is content with whatever dwelling is assigned to him... one who eats only one meal a day. He notices, 'I am one who eats only one meal a day, but these other monks do not eat only one meal a day.' He exalts himself for being one who eats only one meal a day and disparages others. This is the quality of a person of no integrity.

"But a person of integrity notices, 'It's not through being one who eats only one meal a day that the quality of greed goes to its end; it's not through being one who eats only one meal a day that the quality of aversion... the quality of delusion goes to its end. Even though one is not one who eats only one meal a day, if—practicing the Dhamma in line with the Dhamma, practicing masterfully—he is one who follows the Dhamma, he is to be honored for that, praised for that.' So, giving priority just to the practice, he neither exalts himself for being one who eats only one meal a day nor disparages others. This is the quality of a person of integrity.

"And further, a person of no integrity—secluded from sensuality, secluded from unskillful qualities, enters & remains in the first jhāna: rapture & pleasure born of seclusion, accompanied by directed thought & evaluation. He notices, 'I have gained the attainment of the first jhāna, but these other monks have not gained the attainment of the first jhāna.' He exalts himself for the attainment of the first jhāna and disparages others. This is the quality of a person of no integrity.

"But a person of integrity notices, 'The Blessed One has spoken of non-fashioning[2] even with regard to the attainment of the first jhāna, for by whatever means they suppose it, it becomes otherwise from that.'[3] So, giving priority to non-fashioning, he neither exalts himself for the attainment of the first jhāna nor disparages others. This is the quality of a person of integrity.

"And further, a person of no integrity… enters & remains in the second jhāna… the third jhāna… the fourth jhāna… the dimension of the infinitude of space… the dimension of the infinitude of consciousness… the dimension of nothingness… the dimension of neither perception nor non-perception. He notices, 'I have gained the attainment of the dimension of neither perception nor non-perception, but these other monks have not gained the attainment of the dimension of neither perception nor non-perception.' He exalts himself for the attainment of the dimension of neither perception nor non-perception and disparages others. This is the quality of a person of no integrity.

"A person of integrity notices, 'The Blessed One has spoken of non-fashioning even with regard to the attainment of the dimension of neither perception nor non-perception, for by whatever means they suppose it, it becomes otherwise from that.' So, giving priority to non-fashioning, he neither exalts himself for the attainment of the dimension of neither perception nor non-perception nor disparages others. This is the quality of a person of integrity.

"A person of integrity, completely transcending the dimension of neither perception nor non-perception, enters & remains in the cessation of perception & feeling. When he sees with discernment, his effluents are ended. This is a monk who does not suppose anything, does not suppose anywhere, does not suppose in any way."

That is what the Blessed One said. Gratified, the monks delighted in the Blessed One's words.

NOTES

1. The nine practices mentioned here—being a wilderness dweller, one who wears robes of thrown-away rags, an alms-goer, one who dwells at the root of a tree, a cemetery dweller, one who lives in the open air, one who doesn't lie down, one who is content with whatever dwelling is assigned to him, or one who eats only one meal a day—are among the thirteen optional ascetic *(dhutaṅga)* practices that monks may undertake. The other four are: possessing only one set of the triple robe, bypassing no donors on one's almsround, eating only from one's bowl, and not accepting food brought after one's almsround. All thirteen practices are listed in Thag 16:7.

2. *Atammayatā.* For discussions of the role of non-fashioning in the practice, see *The Wings to Awakening,* II/B and III/G, and *The Paradox of Becoming,* Chapter 6.

3. In other words, whatever the condition of the ground on which one might base a state of becoming—a sense of one's self or the world one inhabits—by the time that state of becoming has taken shape, the ground has already changed. In this case, if one tries to shape a sense of self around one's attainment of jhāna, the attainment itself has already changed.

See also: MN 110; SN 55:5; AN 2:31–32; AN 4:73; AN 4:192; AN 5:148; AN 8:54; Iti 17

117 The Great Forty

Mahā Cattārīsaka Sutta

I have heard that on one occasion the Blessed One was staying near Sāvatthī in Jeta's Grove, Anāthapiṇḍika's monastery. There he addressed the monks: "Monks!"

"Yes, lord," the monks responded to him.

The Blessed One said, "Monks, I will teach you noble right concentration with its supports & requisite conditions. Listen, and pay close attention. I will speak."

"Yes, lord," the monks responded to him.

The Blessed One said: "Now what, monks, is noble right concentration with its supports & requisite conditions? Any singleness of mind equipped with these seven factors—right view, right resolve, right speech, right action, right livelihood, right effort, & right mindfulness—is called noble right concentration with its supports & requisite conditions.[1]

"[1] Of those, right view is the forerunner. And how is right view the forerunner? One discerns wrong view as wrong view, and right view as right view. This is one's right view. And what is wrong view? 'There is nothing given, nothing offered, nothing sacrificed. There is no fruit or result of good or bad actions. There is no this world, no next world, no mother, no father, no spontaneously reborn beings; no contemplatives or brahmans who, faring rightly & practicing rightly, proclaim this world & the next after having directly known & realized it for themselves.' This is wrong view.

"And what is right view? Right view, I tell you, is of two sorts: There is right view with effluents, siding with merit, resulting in acquisitions [of becoming]; there is right view that is noble, without effluents, transcendent, a factor of the path.

"And what is the right view with effluents, siding with merit, resulting in acquisitions? 'There is what is given, what is offered, what is sacrificed. There are fruits & results of good & bad actions. There is this world & the next world. There is mother & father. There are spontaneously reborn beings; there are contemplatives & brahmans who, faring rightly & practicing rightly, proclaim this world & the next after having directly known & realized it for themselves.' This is the right view with effluents, siding with merit, resulting in acquisitions.[2]

"And what is the right view that is noble, without effluents, transcendent, a factor of the path? The discernment, the faculty of discernment, the strength of discernment, analysis of qualities as a factor for awakening, the path factor of right view[3] in one developing the noble path whose mind is noble, whose mind is without effluents, who is fully possessed of the noble path. This is the right view that is noble, without effluents, transcendent, a factor of the path.

"One makes an effort for the abandoning of wrong view & for entering into right view: This is one's right effort. One is mindful to abandon wrong view & to enter & remain in right view: This is one's right mindfulness.[4] Thus these three qualities—right view, right effort, & right mindfulness—run & circle around right view.

"[2] Of those, right view is the forerunner. And how is right view the forerunner? One discerns wrong resolve as wrong resolve, and right resolve as right resolve. This is one's right view. And what is wrong resolve? Being resolved on sensuality, on ill will, on harmfulness. This is wrong resolve.

"And what is right resolve? Right resolve, I tell you, is of two sorts: There is right resolve with effluents, siding with merit, resulting in acquisitions; there is right resolve that is noble, without effluents, transcendent, a factor of the path.

"And what is the right resolve with effluents, siding with merit, resulting in acquisitions? Resolve for renunciation, resolve for freedom from ill will, resolve for harmlessness. This is the right resolve with effluents, siding with merit, resulting in acquisitions.

"And what is the right resolve that is noble, without effluents, transcendent, a factor of the path? The thinking, directed thinking, resolve, mental fixity, mental transfixion, focused awareness, & verbal fabrications[5] in one developing the noble path whose mind is noble, whose mind is without effluents, who is fully possessed of the noble path. This is the right resolve that is noble, without effluents, transcendent, a factor of the path."

"One makes an effort for the abandoning of wrong resolve & for entering right resolve: This is one's right effort. One is mindful to abandon wrong resolve & to enter & remain in right resolve: This is one's right mindfulness. Thus these three qualities—right view, right effort, & right mindfulness—run & circle around right resolve.

"[3] Of those, right view is the forerunner. And how is right view the forerunner? One discerns wrong speech as wrong speech, and right speech as right speech. This is one's right view. And what is wrong speech? Lying, divisive tale-bearing, abusive speech, & idle chatter. This is wrong speech.

"And what is right speech? Right speech, I tell you, is of two sorts: There is right speech with effluents, siding with merit, resulting in acquisitions; there is right speech that is noble, without effluents, transcendent, a factor of the path.

"And what is the right speech with effluents, siding with merit, resulting in acquisitions? Abstaining from lying, from divisive tale-bearing, from abusive speech, & from idle chatter. This is the right speech with effluents, siding with merit, resulting in acquisitions.

"And what is the right speech that is noble, without effluents, transcendent, a factor of the path? The abstaining, desisting, abstinence, avoidance of the four forms of verbal misconduct in one developing the noble path whose mind is noble, whose mind is without effluents, who is fully possessed of the noble path. This is the right speech that is noble, without effluents, transcendent, a factor of the path.

"One makes an effort for the abandoning of wrong speech & for entering right speech: This is one's right effort. One is mindful to abandon wrong speech & to enter & remain in right speech: This is one's right mindfulness. Thus these three qualities—right view, right effort, & right mindfulness—run & circle around right speech.

"[4] Of those, right view is the forerunner. And how is right view the forerunner? One discerns wrong action as wrong action, and right action as right action. This is one's right view. And what is wrong action? Killing, taking what is not given, illicit sex. This is wrong action.

"And what is right action? Right action, I tell you, is of two sorts: There is right action with effluents, siding with merit, resulting in acquisitions; there is right action that is noble, without effluents, transcendent, a factor of the path.

"And what is the right action with effluents, siding with merit, resulting in acquisitions? Abstaining from killing, from taking what is not given, & from illicit sex.[6] This is the right action with effluents, siding with merit, resulting in acquisitions.

"And what is the right action that is noble, without effluents, transcendent, a factor of the path? The abstaining, desisting, abstinence, avoidance of the three forms of bodily misconduct in one developing the noble path whose mind is noble, whose mind is without effluents, who is fully possessed of the noble path. This is the right action that is noble, without effluents, transcendent, a factor of the path.

"One makes an effort for the abandoning of wrong action & for entering into right action: This is one's right effort. One is mindful to abandon wrong action & to enter & remain in right action: This is one's right mindfulness. Thus these three qualities—right view, right effort, & right mindfulness—run & circle around right action.

"[5] Of those, right view is the forerunner. And how is right view the forerunner? One discerns wrong livelihood as wrong livelihood, and right livelihood as right livelihood. This is one's right view. And what is wrong livelihood? Scheming, persuading, hinting, belittling, & pursuing gain with gain.[7] This is wrong livelihood.

"And what is right livelihood? Right livelihood, I tell you, is of two sorts: There is right livelihood with effluents, siding with merit, resulting in acquisitions; there is right livelihood that is noble, without effluents, transcendent, a factor of the path.

"And what is the right livelihood with effluents, siding with merit, resulting in acquisitions? There is the case where a disciple of the noble ones abandons wrong livelihood and maintains his life with right livelihood. This is the right livelihood with effluents, siding with merit, resulting in acquisitions.

"And what is the right livelihood that is noble, without effluents, transcendent, a factor of the path? The abstaining, desisting, abstinence, avoidance of wrong livelihood in one developing the noble path whose mind is noble, whose mind is without effluents, who is fully possessed of the noble path. This is the right livelihood that is noble, without effluents, transcendent, a factor of the path.

"One tries to abandon wrong livelihood & to enter into right livelihood: This is one's right effort. One is mindful to abandon wrong livelihood & to enter & remain in right livelihood: This is one's right mindfulness. Thus these three qualities—right view, right effort, & right mindfulness—run & circle around right livelihood.

"Of those, right view is the forerunner. And how is right view the forerunner? In one of right view, right resolve comes into being. In one of right resolve, right speech comes into being. In one of right speech, right action.... In one of right action, right livelihood.... In one of right livelihood, right effort.... In one of right effort, right mindfulness.... In one of right mindfulness, right concentration.... In one of right concentration, right knowledge.... In one of right knowledge, right release comes into being.[8] Thus the learner is endowed with eight factors, and the arahant with ten.

"Of those, right view is the forerunner. And how is right view the forerunner? In one of right view, wrong view is abolished. The many evil, unskillful qualities that come into play with wrong view as their condition are also abolished, while the many skillful qualities that have right view as their condition go to the culmination of their development. In one of right resolve, wrong resolve is abolished.... In one of right speech, wrong speech is abolished.... In one of right action, wrong action is abolished.... In one of right livelihood, wrong livelihood is abolished.... In one of right effort, wrong effort is abolished.... In one of right mindfulness, wrong mindfulness is abolished.... In one of right concentration, wrong concentration is abolished.... In one of right knowledge, wrong knowledge is abolished.... In one of right release, wrong release is abolished. The many evil, unskillful qualities that come into play with wrong release as their condition are also abolished, while the many skillful qualities that have right release as their condition go to the culmination of their development.

"Thus, monks, there are twenty factors siding with skillfulness, and twenty with unskillfulness.

"This Dhamma discourse on the Great Forty has been set rolling and cannot be stopped by any contemplative or brahman or deva or Māra and Brahmā or anyone at all in the world.

"If any contemplative or brahman might think that this Great Forty Dhamma discourse should be censured & rejected, there are ten legitimate implications of his statement that would form grounds for censuring him here & now. If he censures right view, then he would honor any contemplatives & brahmans who are of wrong view; he would praise them. If he censures right resolve... right speech... right action... right livelihood... right effort... right mindfulness... right concentration... right knowledge.... If he censures right release, then he would honor any contemplatives & brahmans who are of wrong release; he would praise them. If any contemplative or brahman might think that this Great Forty Dhamma discourse should be censured & rejected, there are these ten legitimate implications of his statement that would form grounds for censuring him here & now.

"Even Vassa & Bhañña—those teachers from Ukkala who were proponents of no-causality, no-action, & no-existence—would not think that this Dhamma discourse on the Great Forty should be censured & rejected. Why is that? For fear of criticism, opposition, & reproach."

That is what the Blessed One said. Gratified, the monks delighted in the Blessed One's words.

NOTES

1. It has been argued that this definition of right concentration differs from the standard definition that equates right concentration with the four jhānas. This argument, however, misses two points. The first is that this definition differs in no way from the opening part of the

definition of the first jhāna: "There is the case where a monk—quite secluded from sensuality, secluded from unskillful qualities—enters & remains in the first jhāna." The "unskillful qualities" in this passage are identified by SN 45:22 as "wrong view, wrong resolve, wrong speech, wrong action, wrong livelihood, wrong effort, wrong mindfulness, wrong concentration." And of course, sensuality is renounced through mundane right resolve. In fact, MN 78 indicates a direct connection between right resolve and jhāna, stating that the first jhāna is where all unskillful resolves cease without trace. This means that any concentration truly endowed with right resolve would have to be at least the first jhāna.

The second point is that this sutta defines noble right resolve as the resolves present in the first jhāna. See note 5, below.

So there is nothing to indicate that this definition of right concentration refers to anything but jhāna.

2. See MN 41, note 5.

3. These various factors are all equivalent to knowledge in terms of the four noble truths. The relationship between these four truths and the issue of skillful and unskillful action is shown in SN 46:51, which notes that analysis of qualities as a factor for awakening is fed by paying appropriate attention to qualities as to whether they are skillful or unskillful. See also MN 9.

4. Notice that mindfulness plays an active role here and with all the path factors. It is not simply a receptive acceptance of wrong and right views. Instead—in its canonical sense of keeping something in mind—it keeps remembering to abandon the factors of the wrong path, and to enter and remain in the factors of the right path. For more on the active role of mindfulness in the practice of abandoning unskillful qualities and developing skillful ones, see AN 4:245 and AN 7:63.

5. According to MN 44, verbal fabrications are directed thought and evaluation. The definition of noble right resolve here appears to refer to the resolves present in the first jhāna (see MN 78), thus connecting noble right resolve with right concentration.

6. SN 45:8 defines right action as abstaining from killing, abstaining from taking what is not given, & abstaining from uncelibacy.

7. This definition appears to refer to wrong livelihood for monks and nuns.

8. SN 48:46 equates noble release with the faculty of concentration (see also SN 48:10).

See also: SN 12:15; SN 45:1; SN 45:8; SN 48:46; AN 5:25; AN 5:28

118 Mindfulness of Breathing

Ānāpānasati Sutta

I have heard that on one occasion the Blessed One was staying near Sāvatthī in the Eastern Monastery, the palace of Migāra's mother, together with many well-known elder disciples—Ven. Sāriputta, Ven. Mahā Moggallāna, Ven. Mahā Kassapa, Ven. Mahā Kaccāna, Ven. Mahā Koṭṭhita, Ven. Mahā Kappina, Ven. Mahā Cunda, Ven. Revata, Ven. Ānanda, and other well-known elder disciples. On that occasion the elder monks were teaching & instructing. Some elder monks were teaching & instructing ten monks, some were teaching & instructing twenty monks, some were teaching & instructing thirty monks, some were teaching & instructing forty monks. The new monks, being taught & instructed by the elder monks, were discerning grand, successive distinctions.

Now on that occasion—the uposatha day of the fifteenth, the full-moon night of the Pavāraṇā ceremony—the Blessed One was seated in the open air surrounded by the Saṅgha of monks. Surveying the silent Saṅgha of monks, he addressed them:

"Monks, I am content with this practice. I am content at heart with this practice. So arouse even more intense persistence for the attaining of the as-yet-unattained, the reaching of the as-yet-unreached, the realization of the as-yet-unrealized. I will remain right here at Sāvatthī (for another month) through the 'White Water-lily' Month, the fourth month of the rains."

The monks in the countryside heard, "The Blessed One, they say, will remain right there at Sāvatthī through the White Water-lily Month, the fourth month of the rains." So they left for Sāvatthī to see the Blessed One.

Then the elder monks taught & instructed the new monks even more intensely. Some elder monks were teaching & instructing ten monks, some were teaching & instructing twenty monks, some were teaching & instructing thirty monks, some were teaching & instructing forty monks. The new monks, being taught & instructed by the elder monks, were discerning grand, successive distinctions.

Now on that occasion—the uposatha day of the fifteenth, the full-moon night of the White Water-lily Month, the fourth month of the rains—the Blessed One was seated in the open air surrounded by the Saṅgha of monks. Surveying the silent Saṅgha of monks, he addressed them:

"Monks, this assembly is free from idle chatter, devoid of idle chatter, and is established on pure heartwood: Such is this Saṅgha of monks, such is this assembly. The sort of assembly that is worthy of gifts, worthy of hospitality, worthy of offerings, worthy of respect, an incomparable field of merit for the world: Such is this Saṅgha of monks, such is this assembly. The sort of assembly to which a small gift, when given, becomes great, and a great gift greater: Such is this Saṅgha of monks, such is this assembly. The sort of assembly that is rare to see in the world: Such is this Saṅgha of monks, such is this assembly—the sort of assembly that it would be worth traveling for leagues, taking along provisions, in order to see.

"In this Saṅgha of monks there are monks who are arahants, whose effluents are ended, who have reached fulfillment, done the task, laid down the burden, attained the true goal, laid to waste the fetter of becoming, and who are released through right gnosis: Such are the monks in this Saṅgha of monks.

"In this Saṅgha of monks there are monks who, with the wasting away of the five lower fetters, are due to arise spontaneously (in the Pure Abodes), there to be totally unbound, destined never again to return from that world: Such are the monks in this Saṅgha of monks.

"In this Saṅgha of monks there are monks who, with the wasting away of (the first) three fetters, and with the attenuation of passion, aversion, & delusion, are once-returners, who—on returning only once more to this world—will make an ending to stress: Such are the monks in this Saṅgha of monks.

"In this Saṅgha of monks there are monks who, with the wasting away of (the first) three fetters, are stream-enterers, certain, never again destined for the lower realms, headed for self-awakening: Such are the monks in this Saṅgha of monks.

"In this Saṅgha of monks there are monks who remain devoted to the development of the four establishings of mindfulness... the four right exertions... the four bases of power... the five faculties... the five strengths... the seven factors for awakening... the noble eightfold path: Such are the monks in this Saṅgha of monks.

"In this Saṅgha of monks there are monks who remain devoted to the development of good will... compassion... empathetic joy... equanimity... (the perception of the) unattractiveness (of the body)... the perception of inconstancy: Such are the monks in this Saṅgha of monks.

"In this Saṅgha of monks there are monks who remain devoted to mindfulness of in-&-out breathing.

"Mindfulness of in-&-out breathing, when developed & pursued, is of great fruit, of great benefit. Mindfulness of in-&-out breathing, when developed & pursued, brings the four establishings of mindfulness to their culmination. The four establishings of mindfulness, when developed & pursued, bring the seven factors for awakening to their culmination. The seven factors for awakening, when developed & pursued, bring clear knowing & release to their culmination.

MINDFULNESS OF IN-&-OUT BREATHING

"Now how is mindfulness of in-&-out breathing developed & pursued so as to be of great fruit, of great benefit?

"There is the case where a monk, having gone to the wilderness, to the shade of a tree, or to an empty building, sits down folding his legs crosswise, holding his body erect, and establishing mindfulness to the fore.[1] Always mindful, he breathes in; mindful he breathes out.

"[1] Breathing in long, he discerns, 'I am breathing in long'; or breathing out long, he discerns, 'I am breathing out long.' [2] Or breathing in short, he discerns, 'I am breathing in short'; or breathing out short, he discerns, 'I am breathing out short.' [3] He trains himself, 'I will breathe in sensitive to the entire body.'[2] He trains himself, 'I will breathe out sensitive to the entire body.' [4] He trains himself, 'I will breathe in calming bodily fabrication.'[3] He trains himself, 'I will breathe out calming bodily fabrication.'

"[5] He trains himself, 'I will breathe in sensitive to rapture.' He trains himself, 'I will breathe out sensitive to rapture.' [6] He trains himself, 'I will breathe in sensitive to pleasure.' He trains himself, 'I will breathe out sensitive to pleasure.' [7] He trains himself, 'I will breathe in sensitive to mental fabrication.'[4] He trains himself, 'I will breathe out sensitive to mental fabrication.' [8] He trains himself, 'I will breathe in calming mental fabrication.' He trains himself, 'I will breathe out calming mental fabrication.'

"[9] He trains himself, 'I will breathe in sensitive to the mind.' He trains himself, 'I will breathe out sensitive to the mind.' [10] He trains himself, 'I will breathe in gladdening the mind.' He trains himself, 'I will breathe out gladdening the mind.' [11] He trains himself, 'I will breathe in steadying the mind.' He trains himself, 'I will breathe out steadying the mind.' [12] He trains himself, 'I will breathe in releasing the mind.'[5] He trains himself, 'I will breathe out releasing the mind.'

"[13] He trains himself, 'I will breathe in focusing on inconstancy.' He trains himself, 'I will breathe out focusing on inconstancy.'

[14] He trains himself, 'I will breathe in focusing on dispassion [or: fading].' He trains himself, 'I will breathe out focusing on dispassion.' [15] He trains himself, 'I will breathe in focusing on cessation.' He trains himself, 'I will breathe out focusing on cessation.' [16] He trains himself, 'I will breathe in focusing on relinquishing.' He trains himself, 'I will breathe out focusing on relinquishing.'

"This is how mindfulness of in-&-out breathing is developed & pursued so as to be of great fruit, of great benefit.

THE FOUR ESTABLISHINGS OF MINDFULNESS

"And how is mindfulness of in-&-out breathing developed & pursued so as to bring the four establishings of mindfulness to their culmination?

"[1] On whatever occasion a monk breathing in long discerns, 'I am breathing in long'; or breathing out long, discerns, 'I am breathing out long'; or breathing in short, discerns, 'I am breathing in short'; or breathing out short, discerns, 'I am breathing out short'; trains himself, 'I will breathe in…&… out sensitive to the entire body'; trains himself, 'I will breathe in…&…out calming bodily fabrication': On that occasion the monk remains focused on the *body* in & of itself—ardent, alert, & mindful—subduing greed & distress with reference to the world. I tell you, monks, that this—the in-&-out breath—is classed as a body among bodies, which is why the monk on that occasion remains focused on the body in & of itself—ardent, alert, & mindful—subduing greed & distress with reference to the world.

"[2] On whatever occasion a monk trains himself, 'I will breathe in…&…out sensitive to rapture'; trains himself, 'I will breathe in…&…out sensitive to pleasure'; trains himself, 'I will breathe in…&…out sensitive to mental fabrication'; trains himself, 'I will breathe in…&…out calming mental fabrication': On that occasion the monk remains focused on *feelings* in & of themselves—ardent, alert, & mindful—subduing greed & distress with reference to the world. I tell you, monks, that this—careful attention to in-&-out breaths—is classed as a feeling among feelings,[6] which is why the monk on that occasion remains focused on feelings in & of themselves—ardent, alert, & mindful—subduing greed & distress with reference to the world.

"[3] On whatever occasion a monk trains himself, 'I will breathe in…&…out sensitive to the mind'; trains himself, 'I will breathe in…&…out gladdening the mind'; trains himself, 'I will breathe in…&…out steadying the mind'; trains himself, 'I will breathe in…&…out releasing the mind': On that occasion the monk remains focused on the *mind* in & of itself—ardent, alert, & mindful—subduing greed & distress with reference to the world. I don't say that there is mindfulness of in-&-out breathing in one of lapsed mindfulness and no alertness, which is why the monk on that occasion remains focused on the mind in & of itself—ardent, alert, & mindful—subduing greed & distress with reference to the world.

"[4] On whatever occasion a monk trains himself, 'I will breathe in…&…out focusing on inconstancy'; trains himself, 'I will breathe in…&…out focusing on dispassion'; trains himself, 'I will breathe in…&…out focusing on cessation'; trains himself, 'I will breathe in…&…out focusing on relinquishing': On that occasion the monk remains focused on *mental qualities* in & of themselves—ardent, alert, & mindful—subduing greed & distress with reference to the world. He who sees with discernment the abandoning of greed & distress is one who watches carefully with equanimity, which is why the monk on that occasion remains focused on mental qualities in & of themselves—ardent, alert, & mindful—subduing greed & distress with reference to the world.

"This is how mindfulness of in-&-out breathing is developed & pursued so as to bring the four establishings of mindfulness to their culmination.

THE SEVEN FACTORS FOR AWAKENING

"And how are the four establishings of mindfulness developed & pursued so as to bring the seven factors for awakening to their culmination?

"[1] On whatever occasion the monk remains focused on the *body* in & of itself—ardent, alert, & mindful—subduing greed & distress with reference to the world, on that occasion his mindfulness is steady & without lapse. When his mindfulness is steady & without lapse, then *mindfulness* as a factor for awakening becomes aroused. He develops it, and for him it goes to the culmination of its development.

"[2] Remaining mindful in this way, he examines, analyzes, & comes to a comprehension of that quality with discernment. When he remains mindful in this way, examining, analyzing, & coming to a comprehension of that quality with discernment, then *analysis of qualities* as a factor for awakening becomes aroused. He develops it, and for him it goes to the culmination of its development.

"[3] In one who examines, analyzes, & comes to a comprehension of that quality with discernment, persistence is aroused unflaggingly. When persistence is aroused unflaggingly in one who examines, analyzes, & comes to a comprehension of that quality with discernment, then *persistence* as a factor for awakening becomes aroused. He develops it, and for him it goes to the culmination of its development.

"[4] In one whose persistence is aroused, a rapture not of the flesh arises. When a rapture not of the flesh arises in one whose persistence is aroused, then *rapture* as a factor for awakening becomes aroused. He develops it, and for him it goes to the culmination of its development.

"[5] For one enraptured at heart, the body grows calm and the mind grows calm. When the body & mind of a monk enraptured at heart grow calm, then *calm* as a factor for awakening becomes aroused. He develops it, and for him it goes to the culmination of its development.

"[6] For one who is at ease—his body calmed—the mind becomes concentrated. When the mind of one who is at ease—his body calmed—becomes concentrated, then *concentration* as a factor for awakening becomes aroused. He develops it, and for him it goes to the culmination of its development.

"[7] He carefully watches the mind thus concentrated with equanimity. When he carefully watches the mind thus concentrated with equanimity, *equanimity* as a factor for awakening becomes aroused. He develops it, and for him it goes to the culmination of its development.

[Similarly with the other three establishings of mindfulness: feelings, mind, & mental qualities.]

"This is how the four establishings of mindfulness are developed & pursued so as to bring the seven factors for awakening to their culmination.

CLEAR KNOWING & RELEASE

"And how are the seven factors for awakening developed & pursued so as to bring clear knowing & release to their culmination? There is the case where a monk develops *mindfulness* as a factor for awakening dependent on seclusion, dependent on dispassion, dependent on cessation, resulting in relinquishment. He develops *analysis of qualities... persistence... rapture... calm... concentration... equanimity* as a factor for awakening dependent on seclusion, dependent on dispassion, dependent on cessation, resulting in relinquishment.

"This is how the seven factors for awakening are developed & pursued so as to bring clear knowing & release to their culmination."

That is what the Blessed One said. Gratified, the monks delighted in the Blessed One's words.

NOTES

1. To the fore *(parimukhaṁ):* An Abhidhamma text, Vibhaṅga 12:1, defines this term as meaning "the tip of the nose or the sign of the mouth." However, the term appears as part of a stock phrase describing a person engaged in meditation, even for themes that have nothing to do with the body at all, such as sublime-attitude *(brahma-vihāra)* meditation (AN 3:64). Thus it seems more likely that the term is used in an idiomatic sense, which is how I have translated it here.

2. The commentaries insist that "body" here means the full length of the breath, but this is unlikely in this context, for two reasons: (a) The first two steps already require being aware of the entire length of the breath. Otherwise, the meditator wouldn't know if a breath was short or long. (b) As AN 10:20 indicates, the fourth step refers to bringing the mind to the fourth jhāna, a state in which in-and-out breathing grows still (SN 36:11; AN 10:72) and the body is filled with pure, bright awareness (after awareness has been extended to be sensitive to the entire body beginning with the first jhāna (DN 2; MN 119)). Because the fourth step focuses on the stilling of the breath, there has to be a step in which the awareness is extended to fill the entire body. That would be this step.

3. "In-&-out breaths are bodily; these are things tied up with the body. That's why in-&-out breaths are bodily fabrications." — MN 44

"And how is a monk calmed in his bodily fabrication? There is the case where a monk, with the abandoning of pleasure & pain—as with the earlier disappearance of elation & distress—enters & remains in the fourth jhāna: purity of equanimity & mindfulness, neither pleasure nor pain." — AN 10:20

"When one has attained the fourth jhāna, in-and-out breaths have ceased." — SN 36:11 & AN 9:31

4. "Perceptions & feelings are mental; these are things tied up with the mind. That's why perceptions & feelings are mental fabrications." — MN 44

5. AN 9:34 shows how the mind, step by step, is temporarily released from burdensome mental states of greater and greater refinement as it advances through the stages of jhāna. MN 111 shows how a meditator, using discernment, can be released from the factors of a jhāna attainment while still in that attainment.

6. As this shows, a meditator focusing on feelings in themselves as a frame of reference should not abandon the breath as the basis for his/her concentration.

For a full discussion of this sutta, see *Right Mindfulness.*

See also: MN 62; SN 54:6; SN 54:8; AN 3:103; AN 5:96–98

119 *Mindfulness Immersed in the Body*

Kāyagatā-sati Sutta

I have heard that on one occasion the Blessed One was staying near Sāvatthī in Jeta's Grove, Anāthapiṇḍika's monastery. Now at that time a large number of monks, after the meal, on returning from their alms round, had gathered at the meeting hall when this discussion arose: "Isn't it amazing, friends! Isn't it astounding!—the extent to which mindfulness immersed in the body, when developed & pursued, is said by the Blessed One who knows, who sees—the worthy one, rightly self-awakened—to be of great fruit & great benefit." And this discussion came to no conclusion.

Then the Blessed One, emerging from his seclusion in the late afternoon, went to the meeting hall and, on arrival, sat down on a seat made ready. As he was sitting there, he addressed the monks: "For what topic are you gathered together here? And what was the discussion that came to no conclusion?"

"Just now, lord, after the meal, on returning from our alms round, we gathered at the meeting hall when this discussion arose: 'Isn't it amazing, friends! Isn't it astounding!—the extent to which mindfulness immersed in the body, when developed & pursued, is said by the Blessed One who knows, who sees—worthy & rightly self-awakened—to be of great fruit & great benefit.' This was the discussion that had come to no conclusion when the Blessed One arrived."

(The Blessed One said:) "And how is mindfulness immersed in the body developed, how is it pursued, so as to be of great fruit & great benefit?

"There is the case where a monk—having gone to the wilderness, to the shade of a tree, or to an empty building—sits down folding his legs crosswise, holding his body erect and establishing mindfulness to the fore. Always mindful, he breathes in; mindful he breathes out.[1]

Breathing in long, he discerns, 'I am breathing in long'; or breathing out long, he discerns, 'I am breathing out long.' Or breathing in short, he discerns, 'I am breathing in short'; or breathing out short, he discerns, 'I am breathing out short.' He trains himself, 'I will breathe in sensitive to the entire body.' He trains himself, 'I will breathe out sensitive to the entire body.' He trains himself, 'I will breathe in calming bodily fabrication.' He trains himself, 'I will breathe out calming bodily fabrication.' And as he remains thus heedful, ardent, & resolute, any memories & resolves related to the household life are abandoned, and with their abandoning his mind gathers & settles inwardly, grows unified & concentrated. This is how a monk develops mindfulness immersed in the body.

"And further, when walking, the monk discerns, 'I am walking.' When standing, he discerns, 'I am standing.' When sitting, he discerns, 'I am sitting.' When lying down, he discerns, 'I am lying down.' Or however his body is disposed, that is how he discerns it. And as he remains thus heedful, ardent, & resolute, any memories & resolves related to the household life are abandoned, and with their abandoning his mind gathers & settles inwardly, grows unified & concentrated. This is how a monk develops mindfulness immersed in the body.

"And further, when going forward & returning, he makes himself fully alert; when looking toward & looking away... when bending & extending his limbs... when carrying his outer cloak, his upper robe, & his bowl... when eating, drinking, chewing, & savoring... when urinating & defecating... when walking, standing, sitting, falling asleep, waking up, talking, & remaining silent, he makes himself fully alert. And as he remains thus heedful, ardent, & resolute, any memories & resolves related to the household life are abandoned, and with their abandoning his mind gathers & settles inwardly, grows unified & concentrated. This is how a monk develops mindfulness immersed in the body.

"And further, the monk reflects on this very body from the soles of the feet on up, from the crown of the head on down, surrounded by skin and full of various kinds of unclean things: 'In this body there are head hairs, body hairs, nails, teeth, skin, flesh, tendons, bones, bone marrow, kidneys, heart, liver, pleura, spleen, lungs, large intestines, small intestines, gorge, feces, bile, phlegm, pus, blood, sweat, fat, tears, skin-oil, saliva, mucus, fluid in the joints, urine.' Just as if a sack with openings at both ends were full of various kinds of grain—wheat, rice, mung beans, kidney beans, sesame seeds, husked rice—and a man with good eyesight, pouring it out, were to reflect, 'This is wheat. This is rice. These are mung beans. These are kidney beans. These are sesame seeds. This is husked rice'; in the same way, the monk reflects on this very body from the soles of the feet on up, from the crown of the head on down, surrounded by skin and full of various kinds of unclean things: 'In this body there are head hairs, body hairs, nails, teeth, skin, flesh, tendons, bones, bone marrow, kidneys, heart, liver, pleura, spleen, lungs, large intestines, small intestines, gorge, feces, bile, phlegm, pus, blood, sweat, fat, tears, skin-oil, saliva, mucus, fluid in the joints, urine.' And as he remains thus heedful, ardent, & resolute, any memories & resolves related to the household life are abandoned, and with their abandoning his mind gathers & settles inwardly, grows unified & concentrated. This is how a monk develops mindfulness immersed in the body.

"And further, the monk contemplates this very body—however it stands, however it is disposed—in terms of properties: 'In this body there is the earth property, the liquid property, the fire property, & the wind property.' Just as a dexterous butcher or his apprentice, having killed a cow, would sit at a crossroads cutting it up into pieces, the monk contemplates this very body—however it stands, however it is disposed—in terms of properties: 'In this body there is the earth property, the liquid property, the fire property, & the wind property.' And as he remains thus heedful, ardent, & resolute, any memories & resolves related to the household life are abandoned, and with their abandoning his mind gathers & settles inwardly, grows unified & concentrated. This is how a monk develops mindfulness immersed in the body.

"And further, as if he were to see a corpse cast away in a charnel ground—one day, two days, three days dead—bloated, livid, & festering, he applies it to this very body, 'This body, too: Such is its nature, such is its future, such its unavoidable fate'...

"Or again, as if he were to see a corpse cast away in a charnel ground, picked at by crows, vultures, & hawks, by dogs, hyenas, & various other creatures... a skeleton smeared with flesh & blood, connected with tendons... a fleshless skeleton smeared with blood, connected with tendons... a skeleton without flesh or blood, connected with tendons... bones detached from their tendons, scattered in all directions—here a hand bone, there a foot bone, here a shin bone, there a thigh bone, here a hip bone, there a back bone, here a rib, there a chest bone, here a shoulder bone, there a neck bone, here a jaw bone, there a tooth, here a skull... the bones whitened, somewhat like the color of shells... piled up, more than a year old... decomposed into a powder: He applies it to this very body, 'This body, too: Such is its nature, such is its future, such its unavoidable fate.'

"And as he remains thus heedful, ardent, & resolute, any memories & resolves related to the household life are abandoned, and with their abandoning his mind gathers & settles inwardly, grows unified & concentrated. This is how a monk develops mindfulness immersed in the body.

THE FOUR JHĀNAS

"And further, quite secluded from sensuality, secluded from unskillful qualities, he enters & remains in the first jhāna: rapture & pleasure born of seclusion, accompanied by directed thought & evaluation. He permeates & pervades, suffuses & fills this very body[2] with the rapture & pleasure born of seclusion. Just as if a dexterous bathman or bathman's apprentice would pour bath powder into a brass basin and knead it together, sprinkling it again & again with water, so that his ball of bath powder—saturated, moisture-laden, permeated within & without—would nevertheless not drip; even so, the monk permeates... this very body with the rapture & pleasure born of seclusion. There is nothing of his entire body unpervaded by rapture & pleasure born of seclusion. And as he remains thus heedful, ardent, & resolute, any memories & resolves related to the household life are abandoned, and with their abandoning his mind gathers & settles inwardly, grows unified & concentrated. This is how a monk develops mindfulness immersed in the body.

"Then, with the stilling of directed thoughts & evaluations, he enters & remains in the second jhāna: rapture & pleasure born of concentration, unification of awareness free from directed thought & evaluation—internal assurance. He permeates & pervades, suffuses & fills this very body with the rapture & pleasure born of concentration. Just like a lake with spring-water welling up from within, having no inflow from the east, west, north, or south, and with the skies supplying abundant showers time & again,[3] so that the cool fount of water welling up from within the lake would permeate & pervade, suffuse & fill it with cool waters, there being no part of the lake unpervaded by the cool waters; even so, the monk permeates... this very body with the rapture & pleasure born of concentration. There is nothing of his entire body unpervaded by rapture & pleasure born of concentration. And as he remains thus heedful, ardent, & resolute, any memories & resolves related to the household life are abandoned, and with their abandoning his mind gathers & settles inwardly, grows unified & concentrated. This is how a monk develops mindfulness immersed in the body.

"Then, with the fading of rapture, he remains equanimous, mindful, & alert, and senses pleasure with the body. He enters & remains in the third jhāna, of which the noble ones declare, 'Equanimous & mindful, he has a pleasant abiding.' He permeates & pervades, suffuses & fills this very body with the pleasure divested of rapture. Just as in a lotus pond, some of the lotuses, born & growing in the water, stay immersed in the water and flourish without standing up out of the water, so that they are permeated & pervaded, suffused & filled with cool water from their roots to their tips, and nothing of those lotuses would be unpervaded with cool water; even so, the monk permeates... this very body with the pleasure divested of rapture. There is nothing of his entire body unpervaded with pleasure divested of rapture. And as he remains thus heedful, ardent, & resolute, any memories & resolves related to the household life are abandoned, and with their abandoning his mind gathers & settles inwardly, grows unified & concentrated. This is how a monk develops mindfulness immersed in the body.

"Then, with the abandoning of pleasure & pain—as with the earlier disappearance of joys & distresses—he enters & remains in the fourth jhāna: purity of equanimity & mindfulness, neither-pleasure-nor-pain. He sits, permeating the body with a pure, bright awareness. Just as if a man were sitting covered from head to foot with a white cloth so that there would be no part of his body to which the white cloth did not extend; even so, the monk sits, permeating the body with a pure, bright awareness. There is nothing of his entire body unpervaded by pure, bright awareness. And as he remains thus heedful, ardent, & resolute, any memories & resolves related to the household life are abandoned, and with their abandoning his mind gathers & settles inwardly, grows unified & concentrated. This is how a monk develops mindfulness immersed in the body.

FULLNESS OF MIND

"Monks, whoever develops & pursues mindfulness immersed in the body encompasses whatever skillful qualities are on the side of clear knowing. Just as whoever pervades the great ocean with his awareness encompasses whatever rivulets flow down into the ocean, in the same way, whoever develops & pursues mindfulness immersed in the body encompasses whatever skillful qualities are on the side of clear knowing.

"In whomever mindfulness immersed in the body is not developed, not pursued, Māra gains entry, Māra gains a foothold.

"Suppose that a man were to throw a heavy stone ball into a pile of wet clay. What do you think, monks? Would the heavy stone ball gain entry into the pile of wet clay?"

"Yes, lord."

"In the same way, in whomever mindfulness immersed in the body is not developed, not pursued, Māra gains entry, Māra gains a foothold.

"Now, suppose that there were a dry, sapless piece of timber, and a man were to come along with an upper fire-stick, thinking, 'I'll light a fire. I'll produce heat.' What do you think? Would he be able to light a fire and produce heat by rubbing the upper fire-stick in the dry, sapless piece of timber?"

"Yes, lord."

"In the same way, in whomever mindfulness immersed in the body is not developed, not pursued, Māra gains entry, Māra gains a foothold.

"Now, suppose that there were an empty, hollow water-pot set on a stand, and a man were to come along carrying a load of water. What do you think—would he get a place to put his water?"

"Yes, lord."

"In the same way, in whomever mindfulness immersed in the body is not developed, not pursued, Māra gains entry, Māra gains a foothold.

"Now, in whomever mindfulness immersed in the body is developed, is pursued, Māra gains no entry, Māra gains no foothold. Suppose that a man were to throw a ball of string against a door panel made entirely of heartwood. What do you think? Would that light ball of string gain entry into that door panel made entirely of heartwood?"

"No, lord."

"In the same way, in whomever mindfulness immersed in the body is developed, is pursued, Māra gains no entry, Māra gains no foothold.

"Now, suppose that there were a wet, sappy piece of timber, and a man were to come along with an upper fire-stick, thinking, 'I'll light a fire. I'll produce heat.' What do you think? Would he be able to light a fire and produce heat by rubbing the upper fire-stick in the wet, sappy piece of timber?"

"No, lord."

"In the same way, in whomever mindfulness immersed in the body is developed, is pursued, Māra gains no entry, Māra gains no foothold.

"Now, suppose that there were a water-pot set on a stand, full of water up to the brim so that crows could drink out of it, and a man were to come along carrying a load of water. What do you think? Would he get a place to put his water?"

"No, lord."

"In the same way, in whomever mindfulness immersed in the body is developed, is pursued, Māra gains no entry, Māra gains no foothold.

AN OPENING TO THE HIGHER KNOWLEDGES

"When anyone has developed & pursued mindfulness immersed in the body, then whichever of the six higher knowledges he turns his mind to know & realize, he can witness them for himself whenever there is an opening.

"Suppose that there were a water jar, set on a stand, brimful of water so that a crow could drink from it. If a strong man were to tip it in any way at all, would water spill out?"

"Yes, lord."

"In the same way, when anyone has developed & pursued mindfulness immersed in the body, then whichever of the six higher knowledges he turns his mind to know & realize, he can witness them for himself whenever there is an opening.

"Suppose there were a rectangular water tank—set on level ground, bounded by dikes—brimful of water so that a crow could drink from it. If a strong man were to loosen the dikes anywhere at all, would water spill out?"

"Yes, lord."

"In the same way, when anyone has developed & pursued mindfulness immersed in the body, then whichever of the six higher knowledges he turns his mind to know & realize, he can witness them for himself whenever there is an opening.

"Suppose there were a chariot on level ground at four crossroads, harnessed to thoroughbreds, waiting with whips lying ready, so that a dexterous driver, a trainer of tamable horses, might mount and—taking the reins with his left hand and the whip with his right—drive out & back, to whatever place & by whichever road he liked; in the same way, when anyone has developed & pursued mindfulness immersed in the body, then whichever of the six higher knowledges he turns his mind to know & realize, he can witness them for himself whenever there is an opening.

TEN BENEFITS

"Monks, for one in whom mindfulness immersed in the body is cultivated, developed, pursued, given a means of transport, given a grounding, steadied, consolidated, & well-undertaken, ten benefits can be expected. Which ten?

"[1] He conquers displeasure & delight, and displeasure does not conquer him. He remains victorious over any displeasure that has arisen.

"[2] He conquers fear & dread, and fear & dread do not conquer him. He remains victorious over any fear & dread that have arisen.

"[3] He is resistant to cold, heat, hunger, thirst, the touch of gadflies & mosquitoes, wind & sun & creeping things; to abusive, hurtful language; he is the sort that can endure bodily feelings that, when they arise, are painful, sharp, stabbing, fierce, distasteful, disagreeable, deadly.

"[4] He can attain at will, without trouble or difficulty, the four jhānas—heightened mental states providing a pleasant abiding in the here & now.

"[5] He wields manifold supranormal powers. Having been one he becomes many; having been many he becomes one. He appears. He vanishes. He goes unimpeded through walls, ramparts, & mountains as if through space. He dives in & out of the earth as if it were water. He walks on water without sinking as if it were dry land. Sitting cross-legged he flies through the air like a winged bird. With his hand he touches & strokes even the sun & moon, so mighty & powerful. He exercises influence with his body even as far as the Brahmā worlds.

"[6] He hears—by means of the divine ear-element, purified & surpassing the human—both kinds of sounds: divine & human, whether near or far.

"[7] He knows the awareness of other beings, other individuals, having encompassed it with his own awareness. He discerns a mind with passion as 'a mind with passion,' and a mind without passion as 'a mind without passion.' He discerns a mind with aversion as 'a mind with aversion,' and a mind without aversion as 'a mind without aversion.' He discerns a mind with delusion as 'a mind with delusion,' and a mind without delusion as 'a mind without delusion.' He discerns a restricted mind as 'a restricted mind,' and a scattered mind as 'a scattered mind.' He discerns an enlarged mind as 'an enlarged mind,' and an unenlarged mind as 'an unenlarged mind.' He discerns a surpassed mind [one that is not at the most excellent level] as 'a surpassed mind,' and an unsurpassed mind as 'an unsurpassed mind.' He discerns a concentrated mind as 'a concentrated mind,' and an unconcentrated mind as 'an unconcentrated mind.' He discerns a released mind as 'a released mind,' and an unreleased mind as 'an unreleased mind.'

"[8] He recollects his manifold past lives [lit: previous homes], i.e., one birth, two births, three births, four, five, ten, twenty, thirty, forty, fifty, one hundred, one thousand, one hundred thousand, many eons of cosmic contraction, many eons of cosmic expansion, many eons of cosmic contraction & expansion, (recollecting,) 'There I had such a name, belonged to such a clan, had such an appearance. Such was my food, such my experience of pleasure & pain, such the end of my life. Passing away from that state, I re-arose there. There too I had such a name, belonged to such a clan, had such an appearance. Such was my food, such my experience of pleasure & pain, such the end of my life. Passing away from that state, I re-arose here.' Thus he remembers his manifold past lives in their modes & details.

"[9] He sees—by means of the divine eye, purified & surpassing the human—beings passing away & re-appearing, and he discerns how they are inferior & superior, beautiful & ugly, fortunate & unfortunate in accordance with their kamma: 'These beings—who were endowed with bad conduct of body, speech, & mind, who reviled the noble ones, held wrong views and undertook actions under the influence of wrong views—with the break-up of the body, after death, have re-appeared in a plane of deprivation, a bad destination, a lower realm, hell. But these beings—who were endowed with good conduct of body, speech, & mind, who did not revile the noble ones, who held right views and undertook actions under the influence a right views—with the break-up of the body, after death, have re-appeared in the good destination, a heavenly world.' Thus—by means of the divine eye, purified & surpassing the human—he sees beings passing away & re-appearing, and he discerns how they are inferior & superior, beautiful & ugly, fortunate & unfortunate in accordance with their kamma.

"[10] Through the ending of effluents, he remains in the effluent-free awareness-release & discernment-release, having known and realized them for himself right in the here & now.

"Monks, for one in whom mindfulness immersed in the body is cultivated, developed, pursued, given a means of transport, given a grounding, steadied, consolidated, & well-undertaken, these ten benefits can be expected."

That is what the Blessed One said. Gratified, the monks delighted in the Blessed One's words.

NOTES

1. For notes on these four steps of breath meditation, see notes 1–3 under MN 118.

2. The fact that the discussion goes straight from the mindfulness immersed in the body to the four jhānas without a redefinition of terms shows that "body" has the same meaning in both contexts: i.e., the physical body.

3. Reading, *Devo ca kālena kālaṁ sammādhāraṁ anuppaveccheyya,* with the Thai edition.

See also: SN 35:206; SN 47:20; AN 4:159; AN 4:184; AN 7:48; Sn 1:11; Sn 5:16; Thag 1:104; Thag 2:16; Thag 5:1; Thag 10:5; Thig 5:4; Thig 14

121 *The Shorter Discourse on Emptiness*

Cūḷa Suññata Sutta

I have heard that on one occasion the Blessed One was staying near Sāvatthī in the Eastern Monastery, the palace of Migāra's mother. Then Ven. Ānanda, emerging from his seclusion in the late afternoon, went to the Blessed One and, on arrival, having bowed down, sat to one side. As he was sitting there, he said to the Blessed One: "On one occasion, when the Blessed One was staying among the Sakyans in a Sakyan town named Nagaraka, there—face-to-face with the Blessed One—I heard this, face-to-face I learned this: 'I now remain fully in a dwelling of emptiness.' Did I hear that correctly, learn it correctly, attend to it correctly, remember it correctly?"

[The Buddha:] "Yes, Ānanda, you heard that correctly, learned it correctly, attended to it correctly, remembered it correctly. Now, as well as before, I remain fully in a dwelling of emptiness. Just as this palace of Migāra's mother is empty of elephants, cattle, & mares, empty of gold & silver, empty of assemblies of women & men, and there is only this non-emptiness—the singleness based on the Saṅgha of monks; even so, Ānanda, a monk—not attending to the perception [mental note] of village, not attending to the perception of human being—attends to the singleness based on the perception of wilderness. His mind takes pleasure, finds satisfaction, settles, & indulges in its perception of wilderness.

"He discerns that 'Whatever disturbances that would exist based on the perception of village are not present. Whatever disturbances that would exist based on the perception of human being are not present. There is only this modicum of disturbance: the singleness based on the perception of wilderness.' He discerns that 'This mode of perception is empty of the perception of village. This mode of perception is empty of the perception of human being. There is only this non-emptiness: the singleness based on the perception of wilderness.' Thus he regards it as empty of whatever is not there. Whatever remains, he discerns as present: 'There is this.' And so this, his entry into emptiness, accords with actuality, is undistorted in meaning, & pure.

THE PERCEPTION OF EARTH

"Further, Ānanda, the monk—not attending to the perception of human being, not attending to the perception of wilderness—attends to the singleness based on the perception of earth. His mind takes pleasure, finds satisfaction, settles, & indulges in its perception of earth. Just as a bull's hide is stretched free from wrinkles with a hundred stakes, even so—without attending to all the ridges & hollows, the river ravines, the tracts of stumps & thorns, the craggy irregularities of this earth—he attends to the singleness based on the perception of earth. His mind takes pleasure, finds satisfaction, settles, & indulges in its perception of earth.

"He discerns that 'Whatever disturbances that would exist based on the perception of human being are not present. Whatever disturbances that would exist based on the perception of wilderness are not present. There is only this modicum of disturbance: the singleness based on the perception of earth.' He discerns that 'This mode of perception is empty of the perception of human being. This mode of perception is empty of the perception of wilderness. There is only this non-emptiness: the singleness based on the perception of earth.' Thus he regards it as empty of whatever is not there. Whatever remains, he discerns as present: 'There is this.' And so this, his entry into emptiness, accords with actuality, is undistorted in meaning, & pure.

THE INFINITUDE OF SPACE

"Further, Ānanda, the monk—not attending to the perception of wilderness, not attending to the perception of earth—attends to the singleness based on the perception of the dimension of the infinitude of space. His mind takes pleasure, finds satisfaction, settles, & indulges in its perception of the dimension of the infinitude of space.

"He discerns that 'Whatever disturbances that would exist based on the perception of wilderness are not present. Whatever disturbances that would exist based on the perception of earth are not present. There is only this modicum of disturbance: the singleness based on the perception of the dimension of the infinitude of space.' He discerns that 'This mode of perception is empty of the perception of wilderness. This mode of perception is empty of the perception of earth. There is only this non-emptiness: the singleness based on the perception of the dimension of the infinitude of space.' Thus he regards it as empty of whatever is not there. Whatever remains, he discerns as present: 'There is this.' And so this, his entry into emptiness, accords with actuality, is undistorted in meaning, & pure.

THE INFINITUDE OF CONSCIOUSNESS

"Further, Ānanda, the monk—not attending to the perception of earth, not attending to the perception of the dimension of the infinitude of space—attends to the singleness based on the perception of the dimension of the infinitude of consciousness. His mind takes pleasure, finds satisfaction, settles, & indulges in its perception of the dimension of the infinitude of consciousness.

"He discerns that 'Whatever disturbances that would exist based on the perception of earth are not present. Whatever disturbances that would exist based on the perception of the dimension of the infinitude of space are not present. There is only this modicum of disturbance: the singleness based on the perception of the dimension of the infinitude of consciousness.' He discerns that 'This mode of perception is empty of the perception of earth. This mode of perception is empty of the perception of the dimension of the infinitude of space. There is only this non-emptiness: the singleness based on the perception of the dimension of the infinitude of consciousness.' Thus he regards it as empty of whatever is not there. Whatever remains, he discerns as present: 'There is this.' And so this, his entry into emptiness, accords with actuality, is undistorted in meaning, & pure.

NOTHINGNESS

"Further, Ānanda, the monk—not attending to the perception of the dimension of the infinitude of space, not attending to the perception of the dimension of the infinitude of consciousness—attends to the singleness based on the perception of the dimension of nothingness. His mind takes pleasure, finds satisfaction, settles, & indulges in its perception of the dimension of nothingness.

"He discerns that 'Whatever disturbances that would exist based on the perception of the dimension of the infinitude of space are not present. Whatever disturbances that would exist based on the perception of the dimension of the infinitude of consciousness are not present. There is only this modicum of disturbance: the singleness based on the perception of the dimension of nothingness.' He discerns that 'This mode of perception is empty of the perception of the dimension of the infinitude of space. This mode of perception is empty of the perception of the dimension of the infinitude of consciousness. There is only this non-emptiness: the singleness based on the perception of the dimension of nothingness.' Thus he regards it as empty of whatever is not there. Whatever remains, he discerns as present: 'There is this.' And so this, his entry into emptiness, accords with actuality, is undistorted in meaning, & pure.

NEITHER PERCEPTION NOR NON-PERCEPTION

"Further, Ānanda, the monk—not attending to the perception of the dimension of the infinitude of consciousness, not attending to the perception of the dimension of nothingness—attends to the singleness based on the dimension of neither perception nor non-perception. His mind takes pleasure, finds satisfaction, settles, & indulges in the dimension of neither perception nor non-perception.

"He discerns that 'Whatever disturbances that would exist based on the perception of the dimension of the infinitude of consciousness are not present. Whatever disturbances that would exist based on the perception of the dimension of nothingness are not present. There is only this modicum of disturbance: the singleness based on the dimension of neither perception nor non-perception.' He discerns that 'This mode of perception is empty of the perception of the dimension of the infinitude of consciousness. This mode of perception is empty of the perception of the dimension of nothingness. There is only this non-emptiness: the singleness based on the dimension of neither perception nor non-perception.' Thus he regards it as empty of whatever is not there. Whatever remains, he discerns as present: 'There is this.' And so this, his entry into emptiness, accords with actuality, is undistorted in meaning, & pure.

THEME-LESS CONCENTRATION

"Further, Ānanda, the monk—not attending to the perception of the dimension of nothingness, not attending to the perception of the dimension of neither perception nor non-perception—attends to the singleness based on the theme-less concentration of awareness. His mind takes pleasure, finds satisfaction, settles, & indulges in its theme-less concentration of awareness.

"He discerns that 'Whatever disturbances that would exist based on the perception of the dimension of nothingness are not present. Whatever disturbances that would exist based on the perception of the dimension of neither perception nor non-perception, are not present. And there is only this modicum of disturbance: that connected with the six sensory spheres, dependent on this very body with life as its condition.' He discerns that 'This mode of perception is empty of the perception of the dimension of nothingness. This mode of perception is empty of the perception of the dimension of neither perception nor non-perception. There is only this non-emptiness: that connected with the six sensory spheres, dependent on this very body with life as its condition.' Thus he regards it as empty of whatever is not there. Whatever remains, he discerns as present: 'There is this.' And so this, his entry into emptiness, accords with actuality, is undistorted in meaning, & pure.

RELEASE

"Further, Ānanda, the monk—not attending to the perception of the dimension of nothingness, not attending to the perception of the dimension of neither perception nor non-perception—attends to the singleness based on the theme-less concentration of awareness. His mind takes pleasure, finds satisfaction, settles, & indulges in its theme-less concentration of awareness.

"He discerns that 'This theme-less concentration of awareness is fabricated & mentally fashioned.' And he discerns that 'Whatever is fabricated & mentally fashioned is inconstant & subject to cessation.' Thus knowing, thus seeing, his heart is released from the effluent of sensuality, released from the effluent of becoming, released from the effluent of ignorance. With release, there is the knowledge, 'Released.' He discerns that 'Birth is ended, the holy life fulfilled, the task done. There is nothing further for this world.'

"He discerns that 'Whatever disturbances would exist based on the effluent of sensuality...the effluent of becoming...the effluent of ignorance, are not present. And there is only this modicum of disturbance: that connected with the six sensory spheres, dependent on this very body with life as its condition.' He discerns that 'This mode of perception is empty of the effluent of sensuality...becoming...ignorance. And there is just this non-emptiness: that connected with the six sensory spheres, dependent on this very body with life as its condition.' Thus he regards it as empty of whatever is not there. Whatever remains, he discerns as present: 'There is this.' And so this, his entry into emptiness, accords with actuality, is undistorted in meaning, pure—superior & unsurpassed.

"Ānanda, whatever contemplatives and brahmans who in the past entered & remained in an emptiness that was pure, superior, & unsurpassed, they all entered & remained in this very same emptiness that is pure, superior, & unsurpassed. Whatever contemplatives and brahmans who in the future will enter & remain in an emptiness that will be pure, superior, & unsurpassed, they all will enter & remain in this very same emptiness that is pure, superior, & unsurpassed. Whatever contemplatives and brahmans who at present enter & remain in an emptiness that is pure, superior, & unsurpassed, they all enter & remain in this very same emptiness that is pure, superior, & unsurpassed.

"Therefore, Ānanda, you should train yourselves: 'We will enter & remain in the emptiness that is pure, superior, & unsurpassed.'"

That is what the Blessed One said. Gratified, Ven. Ānanda delighted in the Blessed One's words.

See also: DN 22; MN 43; MN 61; MN 106; MN 122; MN 140; SN 5:10; SN 12:15; SN 35:85; Ud 1:10; Sn 5:15

122 The Greater Discourse on Emptiness

Mahā Suññata Sutta

INTRODUCTION

This sutta gives many valuable lessons on practical issues surrounding the attempt to develop an internal meditative dwelling of emptiness, to maintain it, and to see it through to awakening. Some of these issues include the need for seclusion as a conducive setting for the practice, types of conversation and thinking that are beneficial and harmful for the practice, the dangers of being distracted by visitors, and the proper attitude to have toward one's teacher. However, for an explanation of emptiness in and of itself, it's necessary to look elsewhere in the Canon.

There you find emptiness approached from three perspectives, treating it (1) as a meditative dwelling, (2) as an attribute of objects, and (3) as a type of awareness-release. The first approach is obviously the most immediately relevant to the discussion in this sutta, but in fact all three approaches play a role here.

Emptiness as a meditative dwelling is most fully discussed in MN 121. Essentially, it boils down to the ability to center the mind in a particular mode of perception, to maintain it there, and then to notice the absence and presence of disturbance within that mode. The process starts with perceptions of one's external surroundings—village, wilderness, the earth property—and then moves internally to the four formless states, the "themeless concentration of awareness," and finally to release from all effluents. Each step is compared to the one preceding it to see how its more refined perception engenders less disturbance. For instance, if you move from a perception of the wilderness to a perception of earth, the first step is to settle and "indulge" in that perception. Then you notice what types of disturbance have been abandoned in the move from the perception of wilderness to the perception of earth—for example, all thought of the dangers of wilderness are gone—and then to see what disturbances remain based on the latter perception. Then you abandon the perception causing those disturbances and move on to a more refined level of perception. This process is pursued until it arrives at the "themeless concentration of awareness." When noting that even this refined level of concentration is fabricated, inconstant, and subject to cessation, one gains total release from all mental effluents and the disturbances that would arise based on them. This is the level of emptiness that is "superior and unsurpassed," and is apparently what the Buddha is referring to in this sutta when he says that by "not attending to any themes, he enters & remains in internal emptiness."

Notice that in every step along the way of this process, the emptiness is the lack of disturbance experienced in a particular mind state. This means that the mind state is to be perceived simply as an example of the presence and absence of stress. In other words, emptiness in this sense relates directly to the second of the three characteristics—stress or suffering. The pursuit of this emptiness relates to the four noble truths, as it looks for the causes of stress and uses tranquility together with insight to abandon those causes in a quest to put a total end to suffering.

Emptiness in its second meaning, as an attribute of objects, is most fully discussed in SN 35:85. That sutta describes emptiness as meaning the lack of self or anything pertaining to a self in the internal and external sense media. Whatever sense of self that may surround these objects is not inherent in them, and is instead simply the result of one's own penchant for "I-making" and "my-making." Seeing the artificiality of "I-making" and "my-making" in this way helps lead to a sense of disenchantment with these "makings," thus helping to abandon any clinging associated with them.

Thus emptiness in this sense relates directly to the third of the three characteristics: not-self. However, just as the three characteristics are not radically separate from one another—everything stressful is for that reason not-self—the practical application of this sense of emptiness is not radically different from the first. As SN 12:15 points out, when one no longer latches onto any idea of "my self," one sees phenomena within and without simply as examples of stress arising and passing away. To practice meditation from this perspective—seeing each state of concentration as an example of stress arising and passing away—is to develop emptiness as a meditative dwelling.

Emptiness in its third meaning, as a type of awareness-release, is an application of emptiness in its second meaning. MN 43 describes this state of concentration as follows: "There is the case where a monk—having gone into the wilderness, to the root of a tree, or into an empty dwelling—considers this: 'This is empty of self or of anything pertaining to self.'" It adds that this awareness-release is different from the awareness-release that results when one doesn't attend to any themes. Thus this state of concentration cannot be entirely equated with the emptiness as a meditative dwelling mentioned in this sutta. MN 106 further adds that if one frequently abides in the emptiness awareness-release, one may either attain the dimension of nothingness—one of the formless states—or be committed to the discernment that will lead to Awakening. The first of these two alternatives is another way in which emptiness as an awareness-release differs from emptiness as a meditative dwelling as defined in MN 121. However, because the standard definition of discernment is seeing phenomena in terms of the four noble truths, the second alternative—being committed to discernment—would apparently follow the same pattern suggested by SN 12:15, above. In other words, as one no longer perceives phenomena in terms of self, one tends to view them simply as examples of stress arising and passing away. So, again, this third meaning of emptiness, like the second, eventually leads in practice back to the first. As MN 43 notes, when one attains full awakening, the themeless awareness-release and the emptiness awareness-release come to differ only in name, and not in actuality.

In reading the following sutta, you will notice that the various meanings of emptiness will fit some contexts better than others. Still, it is important to remember that in the course of practice, all three meanings are related and all will inevitably play a role in awakening.

* * *

I have heard that on one occasion the Blessed One was staying among the Sakyans at Kapilavatthu in the Banyan Park. Then in the early morning, the Blessed One, having adjusted his under robe and carrying his bowl & outer robe, went into Kapilavatthu for alms. Having gone for alms in Kapilavatthu, after the meal, returning from his alms round, he went to the dwelling of Kāḷa-khemaka the Sakyan for the day's abiding. Now at that time many resting places had been prepared in Kāḷa-khemaka the Sakyan's dwelling. The Blessed One saw the many resting places prepared there and, on seeing them, the thought occurred to him, "There are many resting places prepared here. Do many monks live here?"

Now at that time Ven. Ānanda, together with many other monks, was making robes at the dwelling of Ghāṭā the Sakyan. Then the Blessed One, emerging from his from seclusion in the late afternoon, went to the dwelling of Ghāṭā the Sakyan. On arrival, he sat down on a seat made ready. Having sat down, he asked Ven. Ānanda, "There are many resting places prepared in Kāḷa-khemaka the Sakyan's dwelling. Do many monks live there?"

"Yes, lord, there are many resting places prepared in Kāḷa-khemaka the Sakyan's dwelling. Many monks live there. Our time for making robes has come around."

"Ānanda, a monk does not shine if he delights in company, enjoys company, is committed to delighting in company; if he delights in a group, enjoys a group, rejoices in a group. Indeed, Ānanda, it is impossible that a monk who delights in company, enjoys company, is committed to delighting in company; who delights in a group, enjoys a group, rejoices in a group, will obtain at will—without difficulty, without trouble—the pleasure of renunciation, the pleasure of seclusion, the pleasure of peace, the pleasure of self-awakening. But it is possible that a monk who lives alone, withdrawn from the group, can expect to obtain at will—without difficulty, without trouble—the pleasure of renunciation, the pleasure of seclusion, the pleasure of peace, the pleasure of self-awakening.

"Indeed, Ānanda, it is impossible that a monk who delights in company, enjoys company, is committed to delighting in company; who delights in a group, enjoys a group, rejoices in a group, will enter & remain in the awareness-release that is temporary and pleasing, or in the awareness-release that is not-temporary and beyond provocation. But it is possible that a monk who lives alone, withdrawn from the group, can expect to enter & remain in the awareness-release that is temporary and pleasing, or in the awareness-release that is not-temporary and beyond provocation.

"Ānanda, I do not envision even a single form whose change & alteration would not give rise to sorrow, lamentation, pain, distress, & despair in one who is passionate for it and takes delight in it.

"But there is this (mental) dwelling discovered by the Tathāgata where, not attending to any themes, he enters & remains in internal emptiness. If, while he is dwelling there by means of this dwelling, he is visited by monks, nuns, lay men, lay women, kings, royal ministers, sectarians & their disciples, then—with his mind bent on seclusion, tending toward seclusion, inclined toward seclusion, aiming at seclusion, relishing renunciation, having destroyed those qualities that are the basis for effluents—he converses with them only as much is necessary for them to take their leave.[1]

"So, Ānanda, if a monk should wish, 'May I enter & remain in internal emptiness,' then he should get the mind steadied right within, settled, unified, & concentrated. And how does the monk get the mind steadied right within, settled, unified, & concentrated? There is the case where a monk—quite secluded from sensuality, secluded from unskillful qualities—enters & remains in the first jhāna... the second jhāna... the third jhāna... the fourth jhāna: purity of equanimity & mindfulness, neither-pleasure-nor-pain. That is how a monk gets the mind steadied right within, settled, unified, & concentrated.

"He attends to internal emptiness. While he is attending to internal emptiness, his mind does not take pleasure, find satisfaction, grow steady, or indulge in internal emptiness. When this is the case, he discerns, 'While I am attending to internal emptiness, my mind does not take pleasure, find satisfaction, grow steady, or indulge in internal emptiness.' In this way he is alert there.

"He attends to external emptiness....[2]

"He attends to internal & external emptiness....

"He attends to the imperturbable.[3] While he is attending to the imperturbable, his mind does not take pleasure, find satisfaction, grow steady, or indulge in the imperturbable. When this is the case, he discerns, 'While I am attending to the imperturbable, my mind does not take pleasure, find satisfaction, grow steady, or indulge in the imperturbable.' In this way he is alert there.

"When that is the case, he should get the mind steadied right within, settled, unified, & concentrated in his first theme of concentration.

"He then attends to internal emptiness. While he is attending to internal emptiness, his mind takes pleasure, finds satisfaction, grows steady, & indulges in internal emptiness. When this is the case, he discerns, 'While I am attending to internal emptiness, my mind takes pleasure, finds satisfaction, grows steady, & indulges in internal emptiness.' In this way he is alert there.

"He attends to external emptiness....

"He attends to internal & external emptiness....

"He attends to the imperturbable. While he is attending to the imperturbable, his mind takes pleasure, finds satisfaction, grows steady, & indulges in the imperturbable. When this is the case, he discerns, 'While I am attending to the imperturbable, my mind takes pleasure, finds satisfaction, grows steady, & indulges in the imperturbable.' In this way he is alert there.

"If, while the monk is dwelling by means of this dwelling, his mind inclines to walking back & forth, he walks back & forth (thinking,) 'While I am walking thus, no covetousness or sadness, no evil, unskillful qualities will take possession of me.' In this way he is alert there.

"If, while he is dwelling by means of this dwelling, his mind inclines to standing... to sitting... to lying down, he lies down, (thinking,) 'While I am lying down thus, no covetousness or sadness, no evil, unskillful qualities will take possession of me.' In this way he is alert there.

"If, while he is dwelling by means of this dwelling, his mind inclines to speaking, he resolves that 'I will not engage in talk that is base, vulgar, common, ignoble, unbeneficial, that does not lead to disenchantment, dispassion, cessation, calm, direct knowledge, self-awakening, or unbinding—i.e., talk about kings, robbers, &

ministers of state; armies, alarms, & battles; food & drink; clothing, furniture, garlands, & scents; relatives; vehicles; villages, towns, cities, the countryside; women & heroes; the gossip of the street & the well; tales of the dead; tales of diversity, the creation of the world & of the sea; talk of whether things exist or not.' In this way he is alert there.

"'But,' (he resolves,) 'I will engage in talk that is scrupulous, conducive to awareness-release, and leads exclusively to disenchantment, dispassion, cessation, calm, direct knowledge, self-awakening, & unbinding—i.e., talk on modesty, contentment, seclusion, non-entanglement, arousing persistence, virtue, concentration, discernment, release, and the knowledge & vision of release.' In this way he is alert there.

"If, while he is dwelling by means of this dwelling, his mind inclines to thinking, he resolves that 'I will not think thoughts that are base, vulgar, common, ignoble, unbeneficial, that do not lead to disenchantment, dispassion, cessation, calm, direct knowledge, self-awakening, or unbinding—i.e., thoughts of sensuality, thoughts of ill will, thoughts of harmfulness.' In this way he is alert there.

"'But,' (he resolves,) 'I will think thoughts that are noble, onward-leading, that lead to the right ending of stress for the person who acts on them—i.e., thoughts of renunciation, thoughts of no ill will, thoughts of harmlessness.' In this way he is alert there.

"Ānanda, there are these five strings of sensuality. Which five? Forms cognizable via the eye—agreeable, pleasing, charming, endearing, enticing, linked with sensual desire. Sounds cognizable via the ear… Aromas cognizable via the nose… Flavors cognizable via the tongue… Tactile sensations cognizable via the body—agreeable, pleasing, charming, endearing, enticing, linked with sensual desire. These are the five strings of sensuality where a monk should reflect on his mind repeatedly: 'Is there within me, in any circumstance or another, any engagement of awareness that arises with regard to these five strings of sensuality?' If, on reflection, the monk discerns, 'There is within me, in one circumstance or another, an engagement of awareness that arises with regard to these five strings of sensuality,' then—this being the case—he discerns that 'Desire-passion for the five strings of sensuality has not been abandoned by me.' But if, on reflection, he discerns, 'There is not within me, in any circumstance or another, any engagement of awareness that arises with regard to these five strings of sensuality,' then—this being the case—he discerns that 'Desire-passion for the five strings of sensuality has been abandoned by me.' In this way he is alert there.

"There are these five clinging-aggregates where a monk should stay, keeping track of arising & passing away (thus): 'Such is form, such its origination, such its disappearance. Such is feeling... Such is perception... Such are fabrications... Such is consciousness, such its origination, such its disappearance.' As he stays keeping track of arising & passing away with regard to these five clinging-aggregates, he abandons any conceit that 'I am' with regard to these five clinging-aggregates. This being the case, he discerns, 'I have abandoned any conceit that "I am" with regard to these five clinging-aggregates.' In this way he is alert there.

"These qualities, Ānanda, are exclusively skillful in their grounding, noble, transcendent, inaccessible to the Evil One.

"What do you think, Ānanda? When envisioning what aim is it proper for a disciple to follow after the Teacher even when being rebuked?"

"For us, lord, the teachings have the Blessed One as their root, their guide, & their arbitrator. It would be good if the Blessed One himself would explicate the meaning of this statement. Having heard it from the Blessed One, the monks will remember it."

"Ānanda, it's not proper for a disciple to follow after the Teacher to hear discourses, verses, or catechisms. Why is that? For a long time, Ānanda, have you listened to the teachings, retained them, discussed them, accumulated them, examined them with your mind, and penetrated them well in terms of your views. But as for talk that is scrupulous, conducive to release of awareness, and leads exclusively to disenchantment, dispassion, cessation, calm, direct knowledge, self-awakening, & unbinding—i.e., talk on modesty, contentment, seclusion, non-entanglement, arousing persistence, virtue, concentration, discernment, release, and the knowledge & vision of release: It's for the sake of hearing talk of this sort that it is proper for a disciple to follow after the Teacher as if yoked to him.

"This being the case, there is the teacher's undoing, there is the student's undoing, there is the undoing of one who leads the holy life.

"And how is there the teacher's undoing? There is the case where a certain (non-Buddhist) teacher resorts to a secluded dwelling: a wilderness, the shade of a tree, a mountain, a glen, a hillside cave, a charnel ground, a forest grove, the open air, a heap of straw. While he is living thus secluded, brahmans & householders from town & countryside visit him. When they visit him, he gets smitten with things that infatuate, falls into greed, and reverts to luxury. This is called a teacher undone with a teacher's undoing. He has been struck down by evil, unskillful qualities that defile, that lead to further becoming, are troublesome, ripen in pain, and lead to future birth, aging, & death. Such is the teacher's undoing.[4]

"And how is there the student's undoing? A student of that teacher, imitating his teacher's seclusion, resorts to a secluded dwelling: a wilderness, the shade of a tree… a heap of straw. While he is living thus secluded, brahmans & householders from town & countryside visit him. When they visit him, he gets smitten with things that infatuate, falls into greed, and reverts to luxury. This is called a student undone with a student's undoing. He has been struck down by evil, unskillful qualities that defile, that lead to further becoming, are troublesome, ripen in pain, and lead to future birth, aging, & death. Such is the student's undoing.

"And how is there the undoing of one who leads the holy life? There is the case where a Tathāgata arises in the world, worthy & rightly self-awakened, consummate in clear-knowing & conduct, well-gone, an expert with regard to the cosmos, unexcelled trainer of people fit to be tamed, teacher of devas & human beings, awakened, blessed. He resorts to a secluded dwelling: a wilderness, the shade of a tree, a mountain, a glen, a hillside cave, a charnel ground, a forest grove, the open air, a heap of straw. While he is living thus secluded, brahmans & householders from town & countryside visit him. When they visit him, he doesn't get smitten with things that infatuate, doesn't fall into greed, doesn't revert to luxury. A student of that teacher, imitating his teacher's seclusion, resorts to a secluded dwelling: a wilderness, the shade of a tree… a heap of straw. While he is living thus secluded, brahmans & householders from town & countryside visit him. When they visit him, he gets smitten with things that infatuate, falls into greed, and reverts to luxury. This is called one following the holy life who is undone with the undoing of one who leads the holy life. He has been struck down by evil, unskillful qualities that defile, that lead to further becoming, are troublesome, ripen in pain, and lead to future birth, aging, & death. Such is the undoing of one who leads the holy life.

"And in this regard, Ānanda, the undoing of one who leads the holy life ripens in more pain, more bitterness, than the teacher's undoing or the student's undoing. It leads even to the states of deprivation.

"Therefore, Ānanda, engage with me in friendliness and not in opposition. That will be for your long-term well-being & happiness.

"And how do students engage with the teacher in opposition and not in friendliness? There is the case where a teacher teaches the Dhamma to his students sympathetically, seeking their well-being, out of sympathy: 'This is for your well-being; this is for your happiness.' His disciples do not listen or lend ear or apply their minds to gnosis. Turning aside, they stray from the Teacher's message. This is how students engage with the teacher in opposition and not in friendliness.[5]

"And how do students engage with the teacher in friendliness and not in opposition? There is the case where a teacher teaches the Dhamma to his students sympathetically, seeking their well-being, out of sympathy: 'This is for your well-being; this is for your happiness.' His disciples listen, lend ear, & apply their minds to gnosis. Not turning aside, they don't stray from the Teacher's message. This is how students engage with the Teacher in friendliness and not in opposition.

"Therefore, Ānanda, engage with me in friendliness and not in opposition. That will be for your long-term well-being & happiness.

"I won't hover over you the way a potter hovers over damp, unbaked clay goods. Scolding again & again, I will speak. Encouraging again & again, I will speak. Whatever is of essential worth will remain."

That is what the Blessed One said. Gratified, Ven. Ānanda delighted in the Blessed One's words.

NOTES

1. See AN 8:103.

2. Because all three types of emptiness apply both internally and externally, it would seem that when the Buddha mentions external emptiness here, he could be referring to the way any of the three types of emptiness applies to external phenomena. Similarly, when he mentions internal emptiness, he could be referring to the way any of them applies within.

3. See MN 106.

4. See Iti 109

5. See MN 137

See also: DN 12; MN 121; SN 35:85; AN 5:30; AN 6:42; AN 8:30; AN 8:103; AN 10:72; Ud 3:3; Sn 1:3; Sn 5:15

126 To Bhūmija

Bhūmija Sutta

I have heard that on one occasion the Blessed One was staying near Rājagaha in the Bamboo Grove, the Squirrels' Sanctuary.

Then, early in the morning, Ven. Bhūmija—having adjusted his under robe and carrying his bowl & outer robe—went to Prince Jayasena's residence.[1] On arrival, he sat down on a seat made ready. Prince Jayasena went to Ven. Bhūmija and, on arrival, exchanged courteous greetings with him. After an exchange of friendly greetings & courtesies, he sat to one side. As he was sitting there he said to Ven. Bhūmija, "Master Bhūmija, there are some contemplatives & brahmans who espouse this teaching, espouse this view: 'If one follows the holy life, even when having made a wish (for results), one is incapable of obtaining results. If one follows the holy life even when having made no wish, one is incapable of obtaining results. If one follows the holy life even when both having made a wish and having made no wish, one is incapable of obtaining results. If one follows the holy life even when neither having made a wish nor having made no wish, one is incapable of obtaining results.'[2] With regard to that, what does Master Bhūmija's teacher say, what is his view, what does he declare?"

"I haven't heard this face to face with the Blessed One, prince, I haven't received this face to face with the Blessed One, but there is the possibility that the Blessed One would answer in this way: 'If one follows the holy life inappropriately, even when having made a wish (for results), one is incapable of obtaining results. If one follows the holy life inappropriately, even when having made no wish… both having made a wish and having made no wish… neither having made a wish nor having made no wish, one is incapable of obtaining results. (But) if one follows the holy life appropriately, even when having made a wish, one is capable of obtaining results. If one follows the holy life appropriately, even when having made no wish… both having made a wish and having made no wish… neither having made a wish nor having made no wish, one is capable of obtaining results.' I haven't heard this face to face with the Blessed One, I haven't received this face to face with the Blessed

One, but there is the possibility that the Blessed One would answer in this way."

"If that is what Master Bhūmija's teacher says, if that is his view, if that is what he declares, then yes, Master Bhūmija's teacher stands, as it were, having struck all of those many contemplatives & brahmans down by the head."

Prince Jayasena then served Ven. Bhūmija from his own dish of milk rice.

Then Ven. Bhūmija, after his meal, returning from his almsround, went to the Blessed One. On arrival, having bowed down to the Blessed One, he sat to one side. As he was sitting there he said to the Blessed One: "Just now, lord, early in the morning—having adjusted my under robe and carrying my bowl & outer robe—I went to Prince Jayasena's residence. On arrival, I sat down on a seat made ready. Then Prince Jayasena went to me and, on arrival, exchanged courteous greetings with me. After an exchange of friendly greetings & courtesies, he sat to one side. As he was sitting there he said to me, 'Master Bhūmija, there are some contemplatives & brahmans who espouse this teaching, espouse this view: "If one follows the holy life even when having made a wish (for results)... having made no wish... both having made a wish and having made no wish... neither having made a wish nor having made no wish, one is incapable of obtaining results." With regard to that, what does Master Bhūmija's teacher say, what is his view, what does he declare?'

"When this was said, I replied to Prince Jayasena, 'I haven't heard this face to face with the Blessed One, prince, I haven't received this face to face with the Blessed One, but there is the possibility that the Blessed One would answer in this way: "If one follows the holy life inappropriately, even when having made a wish (for results)... having made no wish... both having made a wish and having made no wish... neither having made a wish nor having made no wish, one is incapable of obtaining results. (But) if one follows the holy life appropriately, even when having made a wish... having made no wish... both having made a wish and having made no wish... neither having made a wish nor having made no wish, one is capable of obtaining results." I haven't heard this face to face with the Blessed One, I haven't received this face to face with the Blessed One, but there is the possibility that the Blessed One would answer in this way.'

"'If that is what Master Bhūmija's teacher says, if that is his view, if that is what he declares, then yes, Master Bhūmija's teacher stands, as it were, having struck all of those many contemplatives & brahmans down by the head.'

"Answering in this way when thus asked, lord, am I speaking in line with what the Blessed One has said, am I not misrepresenting the Blessed One with what is unfactual, am I answering in line with the Dhamma so that no one whose thinking is in line with the Dhamma will have grounds for criticizing me?"

"Certainly, Bhūmija, in answering in this way when thus asked, you are speaking in line with what I have said, you are not misrepresenting me with what is unfactual, and you are answering in line with the Dhamma so that no one whose thinking is in line with the Dhamma will have grounds for criticizing you. For any contemplatives or brahmans endowed with wrong view, wrong resolve, wrong speech, wrong action, wrong livelihood, wrong effort, wrong mindfulness, & wrong concentration: If they follow the holy life even when having made a wish (for results), they are incapable of obtaining results. If they follow the holy life even when having made no wish, they are incapable of obtaining results. If they follow the holy life even when both having made a wish and having made no wish, they are incapable of obtaining results. If they follow the holy life even when neither having made a wish nor having made no wish, they are incapable of obtaining results. Why is that? Because it is an inappropriate way of obtaining results.

"Suppose a man in need of oil, looking for oil, wandering in search of oil, would pile gravel in a tub and press it, sprinkling it again & again with water. If he were to pile gravel in a tub and press it, sprinkling it again & again with water even when having made a wish (for results)... having made no wish... both having made a wish and having made no wish... neither having made a wish nor having made no wish, he would be incapable of obtaining results. Why is that? Because it is an inappropriate way of obtaining results.

"In the same way, any contemplatives or brahmans endowed with wrong view, wrong resolve, wrong speech, wrong action, wrong livelihood, wrong effort, wrong mindfulness, & wrong concentration: If they follow the holy life even when having made a wish (for results)... having made no wish... both having made a wish and having made no wish... neither having made a wish nor having made no wish, they are incapable of obtaining results. Why is that? Because it is an inappropriate way of obtaining results.

"Suppose a man in need of milk, looking for milk, wandering in search of milk, would twist the horn of a newly-calved cow. If he were to twist the horn of a newly-calved cow even when having made a wish (for results)... having made no wish... both having made a wish and having made no wish... neither having made a wish nor having made no wish, he would be incapable of obtaining results. Why is that? Because it is an inappropriate way of obtaining results.

"In the same way, any contemplatives or brahmans endowed with wrong view, wrong resolve, wrong speech, wrong action, wrong livelihood, wrong effort, wrong mindfulness, & wrong concentration: If they follow the holy life even when having made a wish (for results)... having made no wish... both having made a wish and having made no wish... neither having made a wish nor having made no wish, they are incapable of obtaining results. Why is that? Because it is an inappropriate way of obtaining results.

"Suppose a man in need of butter, looking for butter, wandering in search of butter, would sprinkle water on water in a crock and twirl it with a churn-stick. If he were to sprinkle water on water in a crock and twirl it with a churn-stick even when having made a wish (for results)... having made no wish... both having made a wish and having made no wish... neither having made a wish nor having made no wish, he would be incapable of obtaining results. Why is that? Because it is an inappropriate way of obtaining results.

"In the same way, any contemplatives or brahmans endowed with wrong view, wrong resolve, wrong speech, wrong action, wrong livelihood, wrong effort, wrong mindfulness, & wrong concentration: If they follow the holy life even when having made a wish (for results)... having made no wish... both having made a wish and having made no wish... neither having made a wish nor having made no wish, they are incapable of obtaining results. Why is that? Because it is an inappropriate way of obtaining results.

"Suppose a man in need of fire, looking for fire, wandering in search of fire, would take a fire stick and rub it into a wet, sappy piece of wood. If he were to take a fire stick and rub it into a wet, sappy piece of wood even when having made a wish (for results)... having made no wish... both having made a wish and having made no wish... neither having made a wish nor having made no wish, he would be incapable of obtaining results. Why is that? Because it is an inappropriate way of obtaining results.

"In the same way, any contemplatives or brahmans endowed with wrong view, wrong resolve, wrong speech, wrong action, wrong livelihood, wrong effort, wrong mindfulness, & wrong concentration: If they follow the holy life even when having made a wish (for results)... having made no wish... both having made a wish and having made no wish... neither having made a wish nor having made no wish, they are incapable of obtaining results. Why is that? Because it is an inappropriate way of obtaining results.

"But as for any contemplatives or brahmans endowed with right view, right resolve, right speech, right action, right livelihood, right effort, right mindfulness, & right concentration: If they follow the holy life even when having made a wish, they are capable of obtaining results. If they follow the holy life even when having made no wish, they are capable of obtaining results. If they follow the holy life even when both having made a wish and having made no wish, they are capable of obtaining results. If they follow the holy life even when neither having made a wish nor having made no wish, they are capable of obtaining results. Why is that? Because it is an appropriate way of obtaining results.

"Suppose a man in need of oil, looking for oil, wandering in search of oil, would pile sesame seeds in a tub and press them, sprinkling them again & again with water. If he were to pile sesame seeds in a tub and press them, sprinkling them again & again with water, even when having made a wish (for results)... having made no wish... both having made a wish and having made no wish... neither having made a wish nor having made no wish, he would be capable of obtaining results. Why is that? Because it is an appropriate way of obtaining results.

"In the same way, any contemplatives or brahmans endowed with right view, right resolve, right speech, right action, right livelihood, right effort, right mindfulness, & right concentration: If they follow the holy life even when having made a wish (for results)... having made no wish... both having made a wish and having made no wish... neither having made a wish nor having made no wish, they are capable of obtaining results. Why is that? Because it is an appropriate way of obtaining results.

"Suppose a man in need of milk, looking for milk, wandering in search of milk, would pull the teat of a newly-calved cow. If he were to pull the teat of a newly-calved cow even when having made a wish (for results)... having made no wish... both having made a wish and having made no wish... neither having made a wish nor having made no wish, he would be capable of obtaining results. Why is that? Because it is an appropriate way of obtaining results.

"In the same way, any contemplatives or brahmans endowed with right view, right resolve, right speech, right action, right livelihood, right effort, right mindfulness, & right concentration: If they follow the holy life even when having made a wish (for results)... having made no wish... both having made a wish and having made no wish... neither having made a wish nor having made no wish, they are capable of obtaining results. Why is that? Because it is an appropriate way of obtaining results.

"Suppose a man in need of butter, looking for butter, wandering in search of butter, would sprinkle water on curds in a crock and twirl them with a churn-stick.[3] If he were to sprinkle water on curds in a crock and twirl them with a churn-stick even when having made a wish (for results)... having made no wish... both having made a wish and having made no wish... neither having made a wish nor having made no wish, he would be capable of obtaining results. Why is that? Because it is an appropriate way of obtaining results.

"In the same way, any contemplatives or brahmans endowed with right view, right resolve, right speech, right action, right livelihood, right effort, right mindfulness, & right concentration: If they follow the holy life even when having made a wish (for results)... having made no wish... both having made a wish and having made no wish... neither having made a wish nor having made no wish, they are capable of obtaining results. Why is that? Because it is an appropriate way of obtaining results.

"Suppose a man in need of fire, looking for fire, wandering in search of fire, would take a fire stick and rub it into a dry, sapless piece of wood. If he were to take a fire stick and rub it into a dry, sapless piece of wood even when having made a wish (for results)... having made no wish... both having made a wish and having made no wish... neither having made a wish nor having made no wish, he would be capable of obtaining results. Why is that? Because it is an appropriate way of obtaining results.

"In the same way, any contemplatives or brahmans endowed with right view, right resolve, right speech, right action, right livelihood, right effort, right mindfulness, & right concentration: If they follow the holy life even when having made a wish (for results), they are capable of obtaining results. If they follow the holy life even when having made no wish, they are capable of obtaining results. If they follow the holy life even when both having made a wish and having made no wish, they are capable of obtaining results. If they follow the holy life even when neither having made a wish nor having made no wish, they are capable of obtaining results. Why is that? Because it is an appropriate way of obtaining results.

"Bhūmija, if these four similes had occurred to you in the presence of Prince Jayasena, he would have naturally felt confidence in you and—feeling confidence—would have shown his confidence in you."

"But, lord, how could these four similes have occurred to me in the presence of Prince Jayasena, as they are natural to the Blessed One and have never before been heard from him?"

That is what the Blessed One said. Gratified, Ven. Bhūmija delighted in the Blessed One's words.

NOTES

1. According to the Commentary, Ven. Bhūmija was Prince Jayasena's uncle.

2. These contemplatives & brahmans are probably the proponents of non-action, annihilation, and non-relatedness as presented in DN 2.

3. To this day, this is the way butter is obtained in rural north India. The churn-stick is a small stick that has attached to its end blocks of wood resembling an orange with alternate sections removed. This is twirled in the curds. The water sprinkled on the curds dilutes the buttermilk, which helps separate it from the milk fat left on the blocks of the churn-stick.

See also: MN 117; SN 22:101; SN 42:6; SN 45:8; AN 5:43; Thig 12

130 *The Deva Messengers*

Devadūta Sutta

I have heard that on one occasion the Blessed One was staying near Sāvatthī in Jeta's Grove, Anāthapiṇḍika's monastery. There he addressed the monks, "Monks!"

"Yes, lord," the monks responded to him.

The Blessed One said, "Monks, it's as if there were two households with doors, and a man of good eyesight, standing there between them, would see people entering & leaving a house, wandering out & about. In the same way, I—by means of the divine eye, purified & surpassing the human—see beings passing away & re-appearing, and I discern how they are inferior & superior, beautiful & ugly, fortunate & unfortunate in accordance with their actions: 'O, how these beings—who were endowed with good conduct of body, speech, & mind, who did not revile noble ones, who held right views and undertook actions under the influence of right views—with the break-up of the body, after death, have re-appeared in a good destination, a heavenly world. Or how these beings—who were endowed with bad conduct of body, speech & mind, who reviled noble ones, held wrong views and undertook actions under the influence of wrong views—with the break-up of the body, after death, have re-appeared in the realm of the hungry ghosts. Or how these beings—who were endowed with bad conduct of body, speech & mind, who reviled noble ones, held wrong views and undertook actions under the influence of wrong views—with the break-up of the body, after death, have re-appeared in the animal womb. Or how these beings—who were endowed with bad conduct of body, speech & mind, who reviled noble ones, held wrong views and undertook actions under the influence of wrong views—with the break-up of the body, after death, have re-appeared in a plane of deprivation, a bad destination, a lower realm, hell.'

"Then the hell-wardens, seizing (such a being) by the arms, present him to King Yama: 'This is a man, your majesty, with no respect for mother, no respect for father,[1] no reverence for contemplatives, no reverence for brahmans, no honor for the leaders of his clan. Let your majesty decree his punishment.'

"Then King Yama interrogates & interpellates & castigates the man regarding the first deva messenger: 'My good man, didn't you see the first deva messenger that has appeared among human beings?'

"'I didn't, lord,' he says.

Then King Yama says, 'My good man, didn't you see among human beings a tender baby boy lying prone in its own urine & excrement?'

"'I did, lord,' he says.

Then King Yama says, 'My good man, didn't the thought occur to you—observant & mature: "I, too, am subject to birth, have not gone beyond birth. I'd better do good with body, speech, & mind"?'

"'I couldn't, lord. I was heedless, lord.'

Then King Yama says, 'My good man, through heedlessness you did not do what is good with body, speech, & mind. And of course, my good man, they will deal with you in accordance with your heedlessness. For that evil kamma[2] of yours was neither done by your mother, nor done by your father, nor done by your brother, nor done by your sister, nor done by your friends & companions, nor done by your kinsmen & relatives, nor done by the devas. That evil kamma was done by you yourself, and you yourself will experience its result.'

"Then, having interrogated & interpellated & castigated the man regarding the first deva messenger, King Yama interrogates & interpellates & castigates him regarding the second: 'My good man, didn't you see the second deva messenger that has appeared among human beings?'

"'I didn't, lord,' he says.

"Then King Yama says, 'My good man, didn't you see among human beings a woman or man eighty, ninety, one hundred years old: aged, roof-rafter crooked, bent-over, supported by a cane, palsied, miserable, broken-toothed, gray-haired, scanty-haired, bald, wrinkled, with limbs all blotchy?'

"'I did, lord,' he says.

"Then King Yama says, 'My good man, didn't the thought occur to you—observant & mature: "I, too, am subject to aging, have not gone beyond aging. I'd better do good with body, speech, & mind"?'

"'I couldn't, lord. I was heedless, lord.'

"Then King Yama says, 'My good man, through heedlessness you did not do what is good with body, speech, & mind. And of course, my good man, they will deal with you in accordance with your heedlessness. For that evil kamma of yours was neither done by your mother, nor done by your father, nor done by your brother, nor done by your sister, nor done by your friends & companions, nor done by your kinsmen & relatives, nor done by the devas. That evil kamma was done by you yourself, and you yourself will experience its result.'

"Then, having interrogated & interpellated & castigated the man regarding the second deva messenger, King Yama interrogates & interpellates & castigates him regarding the third: 'My good man, didn't you see the third deva messenger that has appeared among human beings?'

"'I didn't, lord,' he says.

"Then King Yama says, 'My good man, didn't you see among human beings a woman or man diseased, in pain, severely ill, lying in her/his own urine & excrement, lifted up by others, laid down by others?'

"'I did, lord,' he says.

"Then King Yama says, 'My good man, didn't the thought occur to you—observant & mature: "I, too, am subject to illness, have not gone beyond illness. I'd better do good with body, speech, & mind"?'

"'I couldn't, lord. I was heedless, lord.'

"Then King Yama says, 'My good man, through heedlessness you did not do what is good with body, speech, & mind. And of course, my good man, they will deal with you in accordance with your heedlessness. For that evil kamma of yours was neither done by your mother, nor done by your father, nor done by your brother, nor done by your sister, nor done by your friends & companions, nor done by your kinsmen & relatives, nor done by the devas. That evil kamma was done by you yourself, and you yourself will experience its result.'

"Then, having interrogated & interpellated & castigated the man regarding the third deva messenger, King Yama interrogates & interpellates & castigates him regarding the fourth: 'My good man, didn't you see the fourth deva messenger that has appeared among human beings?'

"'I didn't, lord,' he says.

"Then King Yama says, 'My good man, didn't you see among human beings kings—catching a thief, a criminal—having him tortured in many ways: flogging him with whips, beating him with canes, beating him with clubs; cutting off his hands, cutting off his feet, cut off his hands & feet; cutting off his ears, cutting off his nose, cutting off his ears & nose; subjecting him to the 'porridge pot,' the 'polished-shell shave,' the 'Rāhu's mouth,' the 'flaming garland,' the 'blazing hand,' the 'grass-duty (ascetic),' the 'bark-dress (ascetic),' the 'burning antelope,' the 'meat hooks,' the 'coin-gouging,' the 'lye pickling,' the 'pivot on a stake,' the 'rolled-up bed'; having him splashed with boiling oil, devoured by dogs, impaled alive on a stake; cutting off his head with a sword?'

"'I did, lord,' he says.

"Then King Yama says, 'My good man, didn't the thought occur to you—observant & mature: "It seems that those who do evil actions are tortured in these many ways in the here-&-now. And how much more in the hereafter? I'd better do good with body, speech, & mind"?'

"'I couldn't, lord. I was heedless, lord.'

"Then King Yama says, 'My good man, through heedlessness you did not do what is good with body, speech, & mind. And of course, my good man, they will deal with you in accordance with your heedlessness. For that evil kamma of yours was neither done by your mother, nor done by your father, nor done by your brother, nor done by your sister, nor done by your friends & companions, nor done by your kinsmen & relatives, nor done by the devas. That evil kamma was done by you yourself, and you yourself will experience its result.'

"Then, having interrogated & interpellated & castigated the man regarding the fourth deva messenger, King Yama interrogates & interpellates & castigates him regarding the fifth: 'My good man, didn't you see the fifth deva messenger that has appeared among human beings?'

"'I didn't, lord,' he says.

"Then King Yama says, 'My good man, didn't you see among human beings a woman or man, one day, two days, or three days dead: bloated, livid, oozing with lymph?'

"'I did, lord,' he says.

"Then King Yama says, 'My good man, didn't the thought occur to you—observant & mature: "I, too, am subject to death, have not gone beyond death. I'd better do good with body, speech, & mind"?'

"'I couldn't, lord. I was heedless, lord.'

"Then King Yama says, 'My good man, through heedlessness you did not do what is good with body, speech, & mind. And of course, my good man, they will deal with you in accordance with your heedlessness. For that evil kamma of yours was neither done by your mother, nor done by your father, nor done by your brother, nor done by your sister, nor done by your friends & companions, nor done by your kinsmen & relatives, nor done by the devas. That evil kamma was done by you yourself, and you yourself will experience its result.'

"Then, having interrogated & interpellated & castigated the man regarding the fifth deva messenger, King Yama falls silent.[3]

"Then the hell-wardens torture (the evil-doer) with what's called a five-fold imprisonment. They drive a red-hot iron stake through one hand, they drive a red-hot iron stake through the other hand, they drive a red-hot iron stake through one foot, they drive a red-hot iron stake through the other foot, they drive a red-hot iron stake through the middle of his chest. There he feels painful, racking, piercing feelings, yet he does not die as long as his evil kamma is not exhausted.

"Then the hell-wardens lay him down and slice him with axes. Then they hold him feet up & head down and slice him with adzes. Then they harness him to a chariot and drive him back & forth over ground that is burning, blazing, & glowing. Then they make him climb up & down a vast mountain of embers that is burning, blazing, & glowing. Then they hold him feet up & head down and plunge him into a red-hot copper cauldron that is burning, blazing, & glowing. There he boils with bubbles foaming. And as he is boiling there with bubbles foaming, he goes now up, he goes now down, he goes now around. There he feels painful, racking, piercing feelings, yet he does not die as long as his evil kamma is not exhausted.[4]

"Then the hell-wardens throw him into the Great Hell. And as to the Great Hell, monks:

> It's four-cornered & has four gates
> set in the middle of each side.
> It's surrounded by an iron fortress wall
> and roofed with iron.
> Its floor is made of red-hot iron,
> heated, fully blazing.
> It stands always, spreading 100 leagues all around.

"The flame that leaps from the eastern wall of the Great Hell strikes the western wall. The flame that leaps from the western wall strikes the eastern wall. The flame that leaps from the northern wall strikes the southern wall. The flame that leaps from the southern wall strikes the northern wall. The flame that leaps from the bottom strikes the top. The flame that leaps from the top strikes the bottom. There he feels painful, racking, piercing feelings, yet he does not die as long as his evil kamma is not exhausted.

"There comes a time when, ultimately, with the passing of a long stretch of time, the eastern gate of the Great Hell opens. He runs there, rushing quickly. As he runs there, rushing quickly, his outer skin burns, his inner skin burns, his flesh burns, his tendons burn, even his bones turn to smoke. When (his foot) is lifted, he is just the same.[5] But when he finally arrives, the door slams shut. There he feels painful, racking, piercing feelings, yet he does not die as long as his evil kamma is not exhausted.

"There comes a time when, ultimately, with the passing of a long stretch of time, the western gate of the Great Hell opens… the northern gate… the southern gate of the Great Hell opens. He runs there, rushing quickly. As he runs there, rushing quickly, his outer skin burns, his inner skin burns, his flesh burns, his tendons burn, even his bones turn to smoke. When (his foot) is lifted, he is the just same. But when he finally arrives, the door slams shut. There he feels painful, racking, piercing feelings, yet he does not die as long as his evil kamma is not exhausted.

"There comes a time when, ultimately, with the passing of a long stretch of time, the eastern gate of the Great Hell opens. He runs there, rushing quickly. As he runs there, rushing quickly, his outer skin burns, his inner skin burns, his flesh burns, his tendons burn, even his bones turn to smoke. When (his foot) is lifted, he is the just same. He gets out through the gate. But right next to the Great Hell is a vast Excrement Hell. He falls into that. And in that Excrement Hell needle-mouth beings bore into his outer skin. Having bored into his outer skin, they bore into his inner skin… his flesh… his tendons… the bone. Having bored into the bone, they feed on the marrow. There he feels painful, racking, piercing feelings, yet he does not die as long as his evil kamma is not exhausted.

"Right next to the Excrement Hell is the vast Hot Ashes Hell. He falls into that. There he feels painful, racking, piercing feelings, yet he does not die as long as his evil kamma is not exhausted.

"Right next to the Hot Ashes Hell is the vast Simbali Forest, (with trees) reaching up a league, covered with thorns sixteen fingerbreadths long—burning, blazing, & glowing. He enters that and is made to climb up & down them. There he feels painful, racking, piercing feelings, yet he does not die as long as his evil kamma is not exhausted.

"Right next to the Simbali Forest is the vast Sword-leaf Forest. He enters that. There the leaves, stirred by the wind, cut off his hand, cut off his foot, cut off his hand & foot, cut off his ear, cut off his nose, cut off his ear & nose. There he feels painful, racking, piercing feelings, yet he does not die as long as his evil kamma is not exhausted.

"Right next to the Sword-leaf Forest is the vast Lye-water River. He falls into that. There he is swept downstream, he is swept upstream, he is swept downstream & upstream. There he feels painful, racking, piercing feelings, yet he does not die as long as his evil kamma is not exhausted.

"Then the hell-wardens pull him out with a hook and, placing him on the ground, say to him, 'Well, good man, what do you want?' He replies, 'I'm hungry, venerable sirs.' So the hell-wardens pry open his mouth with red-hot iron tongs—burning, blazing, & glowing—and throw into it a copper ball, burning, blazing, & glowing. It burns his lips, it burns his mouth, it burns his stomach and comes out the lower side, carrying along his bowels & intestines. There he feels painful, racking, piercing feelings, yet he does not die as long as his evil kamma is not exhausted.

"Then the hell-wardens say to him, 'Well, good man, what do you want?' He replies, 'I'm thirsty, venerable sirs.' So the hell-wardens pry open his mouth with red-hot iron tongs—burning, blazing, & glowing—and pour into it molten copper, burning, blazing, & glowing. It burns his lips, it burns his mouth, it burns his stomach and comes out the lower side, carrying along his bowels & intestines. There he feels painful, racking, piercing feelings, yet he does not die as long as his evil kamma is not exhausted.

"Then the hell-wardens throw him back into the Great Hell once more.[6]

"Once, monks, the thought occurred to King Yama: 'Those who did evil actions in the world are tortured in these many ways. O that I might gain the human state! And that a Tathāgata—worthy & rightly self-awakened—might arise in the world! And that I might attend to that Tathāgata! And that he might teach me the Dhamma! And that I might understand his Dhamma!'

"I tell you this, monks, not from having heard it from another contemplative or brahman. On the contrary, I tell you this just as I have known for myself, seen for myself, understood for myself."

That is what the Blessed One said. Having said that, the One Well-Gone, the Teacher, said further:

> Warned by the deva messengers,
> those youths who are heedless
> grieve for a long, long time—
> people entering a lower state.

But those here who are good,
    people of integrity,
when warned by the deva messengers
    aren't heedless
    of the noble Dhamma—ever.
Seeing danger in clinging,
    in the coming-into-play
    of birth & death,
they are released from lack of clinging,
    in the ending
    of birth & death.
They, happy, arriving at safety,
fully unbound in the here-&-now,
having gone beyond
    all animosity & danger
have escaped
    all suffering & stress.

NOTES

1. The word "no respect for father" *(apetteyyo)* does not appear in the Thai edition, but does appear in the Sri Lankan, Burmese, and PTS editions.

2. The Pali uses the word "kamma" in the singular here, as if it were an uncountable noun (like "water" or "information"). In other words, though singular in form, it could mean any number of actions. Because English does not have an equivalent uncountable noun for action, I have—in the translation of this discourse—kept the word "kamma" when it is in the singular in the Pali, and have used the word "actions" when "kamma" is in the plural or part of a compound where it could be either singular or plural.

3. In Asian Buddhist kingdoms, there was a custom that when a king was sentencing a criminal to death or to be tortured, he would not actually express the sentence, but would simply fall silent. The Commentary counsels that if a student asks not to hear the description of hell (which follows from this point), a teacher should teach the student meditation and then wait until the student has reached stream-entry before returning to the description of hell.

4. In the Sri Lankan, Burmese, and PTS editions, the sentence, "There he feels painful, racking, piercing feelings, yet he does not die as long as his evil kamma is not exhausted," appears after each of the

punishments listed in this paragraph. In the Thai edition, which I have chosen to follow here, it appears only at the end of the paragraph.

5. The Commentary does not explain the meaning of this ambiguous sentence. It could mean that when the hell-being's foot is lifted from the hot, burning floor, either (1) his skin, etc., continues burning or (2) his body returns to its original form. Either arrangement would be gruesome.

6. The Commentary notes that not everyone who falls into hell is tortured with all of these punishments: Some of the tortures are skipped; in some cases the hell-being's kamma is exhausted before the full round of tortures is completed, so that he dies and is reborn elsewhere; and not everyone undergoes repeated rounds. Also, we should note that punishment in hell is not for an eternity. As the discourse implies, when the hell-being's bad kamma is exhausted, he dies and is reborn elsewhere, in accordance with his remaining kamma.

See also: MN 45; MN 97; MN 135; MN 136; SN 3:20; SN 35:135; SN 42:8; AN 3:101

131 *An Auspicious Day*

Bhaddekaratta Sutta

I have heard that on one occasion the Blessed One was staying near Sāvatthī in Jeta's Grove, Anāthapiṇḍika's monastery. There he addressed the monks: "Monks!"

"Yes, lord," the monks responded to him.

The Blessed One said: "Monks, I will teach you the summary & exposition of one who has had an auspicious day. Listen & pay close attention. I will speak."

"As you say, lord," the monks responded to him.

The Blessed One said:

You shouldn't chase after the past
or place expectations on the future.
What is past
    is left behind.
The future
    is as yet unreached.
Whatever quality is present
you clearly see   right there,
            right there.
        Not taken in,
        unshaken,
that's how you develop the heart.

Ardently doing
what should be done   today,
for—who knows?—   tomorrow
    death.
There is no bargaining
with Mortality & his mighty horde.

Whoever lives thus ardently,
    relentlessly
    both day & night,
has truly had an auspicious day:[1]
        So says the Peaceful Sage.

"And how, monks, does one chase after the past? One gets carried away with the delight of 'In the past I had such a form' ... 'In the past I had such a feeling' ... 'In the past I had such a perception' ... 'In the past I had such a fabrication" ... 'In the past I had such a consciousness.' This is called chasing after the past.

"And how does one not chase after the past? One does not get carried away with the delight of 'In the past I had such a form' ... 'In the past I had such a feeling' ... 'In the past I had such a perception' ... 'In the past I had such a fabrication" ... 'In the past I had such a consciousness.' This is called not chasing after the past.

"And how does one place expectations on the future? One gets carried away with the delight of 'In the future I might have such a form' ... 'In the future I might have such a feeling' ... 'In the future I might have such a perception' ... 'In the future I might have such a fabrication" ... 'In the future I might have such a consciousness.' This is called placing expectations on the future.

"And how does one not place expectations on the future? One does not get carried away with the delight of 'In the future I might have such a form' ... 'In the future I might have such a feeling' ... 'In the future I might have such a perception' ... 'In the future I might have such a fabrication" ... 'In the future I might have such a consciousness.' This is called not placing expectations on the future.

"And how is one taken in with regard to present qualities? There is the case where an uninstructed run-of-the-mill person who has not seen the noble ones, is not versed in the teachings of the noble ones, is not trained in the teachings of the noble ones, sees form as self, or self as possessing form, or form as in self, or self as in form.

"He/she sees feeling as self, or self as possessing feeling, or feeling as in self, or self as in feeling.

"He/she sees perception as self, or self as possessing perception, or perception as in self, or self as in perception.

"He/she sees fabrications as self, or self as possessing fabrications, or fabrications as in self, or self as in fabrications.

"He/she sees consciousness as self, or self as possessing consciousness, or consciousness as in self, or self as in consciousness. This is called being taken in with regard to present qualities.

"And how is one not taken in with regard to present qualities? There is the case where a disciple of the noble ones who has seen the noble ones, is versed in the teachings of the noble ones, is well-trained in the teachings of the noble ones, does not see form as self, or self as possessing form, or form as in self, or self as in form.

"He/she does not see feeling as self, or self as possessing feeling, or feeling as in self, or self as in feeling.

"He/she does not see perception as self, or self as possessing perception, or perception as in self, or self as in perception.

"He/she does not see fabrications as self, or self as possessing fabrications, or fabrications as in self, or self as in fabrications.

"He/she does not see consciousness as self, or self as possessing consciousness, or consciousness as in self, or self as in consciousness. This is called not being taken in with regard to present qualities.

You shouldn't chase after the past
or place expectations on the future.
What is past
    is left behind.
The future
    is as yet unreached.
Whatever quality is present
you clearly see   right there,
        right there.
    Not taken in,
    unshaken,
that's how you develop the heart.

Ardently doing
what should be done   today,
for—who knows?—   tomorrow
    death.
There is no bargaining
with Mortality & his mighty horde.

Whoever lives thus ardently,
    relentlessly
    both day & night,
has truly had an auspicious day:
    So says the Peaceful Sage.

"'Monks, I will teach you the summary & exposition of one who has had an auspicious day': Thus it was said, and in reference to this was it said."

That is what the Blessed One said. Gratified, the monks delighted in the Blessed One's words.

NOTE: 1. The Pali literally says, "an auspicious night," but this should be interpreted in light of the custom—common in cultures that follow the lunar calendar—of calling a 24-hour period of day-and-night a "night."

See also: SN 21:10; SN: 22:1; AN 6:19–20; AN 10:51; Ud 1:10

135 *The Shorter Analysis of Action*

Cūḷa Kamma-vibhaṅga Sutta

I have heard that on one occasion the Blessed One was staying near Sāvatthī in Jeta's Grove, Anāthapiṇḍika's monastery. Then Subha the student, Todeyya's son, went to the Blessed One and, on arrival, exchanged courteous greetings with him. After an exchange of friendly greetings & courtesies, he sat to one side. As he was sitting there, he said to the Blessed One: "Master Gotama, what is the reason, what is the cause, why baseness & excellence are seen among human beings, among the human race? For short-lived & long-lived people are to be seen, sickly & healthy, ugly & beautiful, uninfluential & influential, poor & rich, low-born & high-born, stupid & discerning people are to be seen. So what is the reason, what is the cause, why baseness & excellence are seen among human beings, among the human race?"

"Student, beings are owners of their actions, heirs of their actions, born of their actions, related through their actions, and have their actions as their arbitrator. Action is what differentiates beings in terms of baseness & excellence."

"I don't understand the detailed meaning of Master Gotama's statement spoken in brief without explaining the detailed meaning. It would be good if Master Gotama taught me the Dhamma so that I might understand the detailed meaning of his brief statement."

"In that case, student, listen & pay close attention. I will speak."

"As you say, Master Gotama," Subha the student responded to the Blessed One.

The Blessed One said: "There is the case, student, where a woman or man is a killer of living beings, brutal, bloody-handed, given to killing & slaying, showing no mercy to living beings. Through having adopted & carried out such actions, on the break-up of the body, after death, he/she reappears in a plane of deprivation, a bad destination, a lower realm, hell. If, on the break-up of the body, after death—instead of reappearing in a plane of deprivation, a bad destination, a lower realm, hell—he/she comes to the human state, then he/she is short-lived wherever reborn. This is the way leading to a short life: to be a killer of living beings, brutal, bloody-handed, given to killing & slaying, showing no mercy to living beings.

"But then there is the case where a woman or man, having abandoned the killing of living beings, abstains from killing living beings, and dwells with the rod laid down, the knife laid down, scrupulous, merciful, & sympathetic for the welfare of all living beings. Through having adopted & carried out such actions, on the break-up of the body, after death, he/she reappears in a good destination, a heavenly world. If, on the break-up of the body, after death—instead of reappearing in a good destination, a heavenly world—he/she comes to the human state, then he/she is long-lived wherever reborn. This is the way leading to a long life: to have abandoned the killing of living beings, to abstain from killing living beings, to dwell with one's rod laid down, one's knife laid down, scrupulous, merciful, & sympathetic for the welfare of all living beings.

"There is the case where a woman or man is one who harms beings with his/her fists, with clods, with sticks, or with knives. Through having adopted & carried out such actions, on the break-up of the body, after death, he/she reappears in a plane of deprivation... If instead he/she comes to the human state, then he/she is sickly wherever reborn. This is the way leading to sickliness: to be one who harms beings with one's fists, with clods, with sticks, or with knives.

"But then there is the case where a woman or man is not one who harms beings with his/her fists, with clods, with sticks, or with knives. Through having adopted & carried out such actions, on the break-up of the body, after death, he/she reappears in a good destination... If instead he/she comes to the human state, then he/she is healthy wherever reborn. This is the way leading to health: not to be one who harms beings with one's fists, with clods, with sticks, or with knives.

"There is the case, where a woman or man is ill-tempered & easily upset; even when lightly criticized, he/she grows offended, provoked, malicious, & resentful; shows annoyance, aversion, & bitterness. Through having adopted & carried out such actions, on the break-up of the body, after death, he/she reappears in a plane of deprivation... If instead he/she comes to the human state, then he/she is ugly wherever reborn. This is the way leading to ugliness: to be ill-tempered & easily upset; even when lightly criticized, to grow offended, provoked, malicious, & resentful; to show annoyance, aversion, & bitterness.

"But then there is the case where a woman or man is not ill-tempered or easily upset; even when heavily criticized, he/she doesn't grow offended, provoked, malicious, or resentful; doesn't show annoyance, aversion, or bitterness. Through having adopted & carried out such actions, on the break-up of the body, after death, he/she reappears in a good destination… If instead he/she comes to the human state, then he/she is beautiful wherever reborn. This is the way leading to beauty: not to be ill-tempered or easily upset; even when heavily criticized, not to be offended, provoked, malicious, or resentful; nor to show annoyance, aversion, & bitterness.

"There is the case where a woman or man is envious. He/she envies, begrudges, & broods about others' gains, honor, respect, reverence, salutations, & veneration. Through having adopted & carried out such actions, on the break-up of the body, after death, he/she reappears in a plane of deprivation… If instead he/she comes to the human state, then he/she is not influential wherever reborn. This is the way leading to being uninfluential: to be envious, to envy, begrudge, & brood about others' gains, honor, respect, reverence, salutations, & veneration.

"But then there is the case where a woman or man is not envious. He/she does not envy, begrudge, or brood about others' gains, honor, respect, reverence, salutations, or veneration. Through having adopted & carried out such actions, on the break-up of the body, after death, he/she reappears in a good destination… If instead he/she comes to the human state, he/she is influential wherever reborn. This is the way leading to being influential: not to be envious; not to envy, begrudge, or brood about others' gains, honor, respect, reverence, salutations, or veneration.

"There is the case where a woman or man is not a giver of food, drink, cloth, sandals, garlands, scents, ointments, beds, dwellings, or lighting to contemplatives or brahmans. Through having adopted & carried out such actions, on the break-up of the body, after death he/she reappears in a plane of deprivation… If instead he/she comes to the human state, he/she is poor wherever reborn. This is the way leading to poverty: not to be a giver of food, drink, cloth, sandals, garlands, scents, ointments, beds, dwellings, or lighting to contemplatives or brahmans.

"But then there is the case where a woman or man is a giver of food, drink, cloth, sandals, scents, ointments, beds, dwellings, & lighting to contemplatives & brahmans. Through having adopted & carried out such actions, on the break-up of the body, after death, he/she reappears in a good destination… If instead he/she comes to the human state, then he/she is wealthy wherever reborn. This is the way leading to great wealth: to be a giver of food, drink, cloth, sandals, garlands, scents, ointments, beds, dwellings, & lighting to contemplatives & brahmans.

"There is the case where a woman or man is obstinate & arrogant. He/she does not pay homage to those who deserve homage, rise up for those for whom one should rise up, give a seat to those to whom one should give a seat, make way for those for whom one should make way, worship those who should be worshipped, respect those who should be respected, revere those who should be revered, or honor those who should be honored. Through having adopted & carried out such actions, on the break-up of the body, after death, he/she reappears in a plane of deprivation... If instead he/she comes to the human state, then he/she is low-born wherever reborn. This is the way leading to a low birth: to be obstinate & arrogant, not to pay homage to those who deserve homage, nor rise up for... nor give a seat to... nor make way for... nor worship... nor respect... nor revere... nor honor those who should be honored.

"But then there is the case where a woman or man is not obstinate or arrogant; he/she pays homage to those who deserve homage, rises up... gives a seat... makes way... worships... respects... reveres... honors those who should be honored. Through having adopted & carried out such actions, on the break-up of the body, after death, he/she reappears in a good destination... If instead he/she comes to the human state, then he/she is highborn wherever reborn. This is the way leading to a high birth: not to be obstinate or arrogant; to pay homage to those who deserve homage, to rise up... give a seat... make way... worship... respect... revere... honor those who should be honored.

"There is the case where a woman or man when visiting a contemplative or brahman, does not ask: 'What is skillful, venerable sir? What is unskillful? What is blameworthy? What is blameless? What should be cultivated? What should not be cultivated? What, having been done by me, will be for my long-term harm & suffering? Or what, having been done by me, will be for my long-term welfare & happiness?' Through having adopted & carried out such actions, Through having adopted & carried out such actions, on the break-up of the body, after death, he/she reappears in a plane of deprivation, a bad destination, a lower realm, hell. If, on the break-up of the body, after death—instead of reappearing in a plane of deprivation, a bad destination, a lower realm, hell—he/she comes to the human state, then he/she will be stupid wherever reborn. This is the way leading to stupidity: when visiting a contemplative or brahman, not to ask: 'What is skillful? ... Or what, having been done by me, will be for my long-term welfare & happiness?'

"But then there is the case where a woman or man when visiting a contemplative or brahman, asks: 'What is skillful, venerable sir? What is unskillful? What is blameworthy? What is blameless? What should be cultivated? What should not be cultivated? What, having been done by me, will be for my long-term harm & suffering? Or what, having been done by me, will be for my long-term welfare & happiness?' Through having adopted & carried out such actions, on the break-up of the body, after death, he/she reappears in a good destination, a heavenly world. If, on the break-up of the body, after death—instead of reappearing in a good destination, a heavenly world—he/she comes to the human state, then he/she is discerning wherever reborn. This is the way leading to discernment: when visiting a contemplative or brahman, to ask: 'What is skillful?... Or what, having been done by me, will be for my long-term welfare & happiness?'

"So, student, the way leading to short life makes people short-lived, the way leading to long life makes people long-lived. The way leading to sickliness makes people sickly, the way leading to health makes people healthy. The way leading to ugliness makes people ugly, the way leading to beauty makes people beautiful. The way leading to lack of influence makes people uninfluential, the way leading to influence makes people influential. The way leading to poverty makes people poor, the way leading to wealth makes people wealthy. The way leading to low birth makes people low-born, the way leading to high birth makes people highborn. The way leading to stupidity makes people stupid, the way leading to discernment makes people discerning.

"Beings are owners of their actions, heirs of their actions, born of their actions, related through their actions, and have their actions as their arbitrator. Action is what differentiates beings in terms of baseness & excellence."

When this was said, Subha the student, Todeyya's son, said to the Blessed One: "Magnificent, Master Gotama! Magnificent! Just as if he were to place upright what was overturned, to reveal what was hidden, to show the way to one who was lost, or to carry a lamp into the dark so that those with eyes could see forms, in the same way has Master Gotama—through many lines of reasoning—made the Dhamma clear. I go to Master Gotama for refuge, to the Dhamma, and to the Saṅgha of monks. May Master Gotama remember me as a lay follower who has gone to him for refuge, from this day forward, for life."

See also: MN 41; SN 12:46; SN 42:6; SN 42:8; SN 42: 13; AN 3:101; AN 4:85; AN 4:237; AN 5:57; AN 6:63; AN 8:39–40; AN 8:54; AN 10:165

136 The Greater Analysis of Action

Mahā Kamma-vibhaṅga Sutta

I have heard that on one occasion the Blessed One was staying near Rājagaha at the Bamboo Grove in the Squirrels' Sanctuary. And on that occasion Ven. Samiddhi was staying in a wilderness hut. Then Potaliputta the wanderer, while walking & wandering around to exercise his legs, went to Ven. Samiddhi and exchanged courteous greetings with him. After an exchange of friendly greetings & courtesies, he sat to one side. As he was sitting there, he said to Ven. Samiddhi, "Face to face with Gotama the contemplative have I heard this, face to face have I learned this: 'Bodily action is barren, verbal action is barren, only mental action is true. And there is an attainment in which, on being attained, nothing is felt.'"

"Don't say that, friend. Don't slander the Blessed One. For it's not good to slander the Blessed One; the Blessed One would not say that: 'Bodily action is barren, verbal action is barren, only mental action is true.' But there is, friend, an attainment in which, on being attained, nothing is felt."[1]

"How long has it been, friend Samiddhi, since you went forth (into homelessness)?"

"Not long, friend. Three years."

"Then what now should I say about the elder monks, when a junior monk would suppose that his Teacher is to be defended in this way? Having intentionally done an action with body, with speech, or with mind, what does one experience?"

"Having intentionally done an action with body, with speech, or with mind, one experiences stress."

Then Potaliputta the wanderer neither delighted in nor scorned Ven. Samiddhi's words. Neither delighting nor scorning, he got up from his seat and left.

Then, not long after Potaliputta the wanderer had left, Ven. Samiddhi went to Ven. Ānanda and, on arrival, exchanged courteous greetings with him. After an exchange of friendly greetings & courtesies, he sat to one side. As he was sitting there, he reported to Ven. Ānanda the Elder[2] the entirety of his discussion with Potaliputta the wanderer. When this was said, Ven. Ānanda said to him, "Friend Samiddhi, there is warrant here for seeing the Blessed One.

Let's go to the Blessed One and, on arrival, report this matter to him. However he explains it to us, that's how we should bear it in mind."

"As you say, friend, Ven. Samiddhi responded to Ven. Ānanda.

So Ven. Samiddhi and Ven. Ānanda went to the Blessed One and, on arrival, having bowed down to him, sat to one side. As they were sitting there, Ven. Ānanda reported to the Blessed One the entirety of the discussion between Ven. Samiddhi and Potaliputta the wanderer.

When this was said, the Blessed One said, "I do not recall even having seen Potaliputta the wanderer, much less having that sort of discussion. And his question, which deserved an analytical answer, has been given a categorical answer by this worthless man, Samiddhi."

When this was said, Ven. Udāyin said to the Blessed One, "But what if Ven. Samiddhi was speaking in reference to this: 'Whatever is felt comes under stress'?"

When this was said, the Blessed One said to Ven. Ānanda, "Look, Ānanda, at how this worthless Udāyin interrupts. I knew just now that he would interrupt in an inappropriate way. From the very beginning, Potaliputta the wanderer was asking about the three kinds of feeling. When this worthless Samiddhi was asked by him in this way, he should have answered, 'Having intentionally done—with body, with speech, or with mind—an action that is to be felt as pleasure, one experiences pleasure. Having intentionally done—with body, with speech, or with mind—an action that is to be felt as pain, one experiences pain. Having intentionally done—with body, with speech, or with mind—an action that is to be felt as neither-pleasure-nor-pain, one experiences neither-pleasure-nor-pain.' Answering this way, this worthless Samiddhi would have rightly answered Potaliputta the wanderer. But then who[3] are these wanderers of other sects, foolish & inexperienced? And who would understand the Tathāgata's greater analysis of action—if you were to listen, Ānanda, to the Tathāgata analyzing the greater analysis of action?"

"This is the time, O Blessed One. This is the time, O One Well-Gone, for the Blessed One to analyze the greater analysis of action. Having heard the Blessed One, the monks will bear it in mind."

"In that case, Ānanda, listen and pay close attention. I will speak."

"As you say, lord," Ven. Ānanda responded to the Blessed One.

The Blessed One said, "Ānanda, there are four kinds of person to be found in the world. Which four? There is the case where a certain person is one who takes life, takes what is not given [steals], engages in illicit sex, lies, speaks divisively, speaks abusively, engages in idle chatter; is covetous, malevolent, & holds wrong view. With the breakup of the body, after death, he reappears in a plane of deprivation, a bad destination, a lower realm, hell.

"But there is also the case where a certain person is one who takes life, takes what is not given, engages in illicit sex, lies, speaks divisively, speaks abusively, engages in idle chatter; is covetous, malevolent, & holds wrong view, (yet) with the breakup of the body, after death, he reappears in a good destination, a heavenly world.

"And there is the case where a certain person is one who abstains from taking life, abstains from taking what is not given, abstains from illicit sex, abstains from lying, abstains from speaking divisively, abstains from speaking abusively, abstains from idle chatter, is not covetous, not malevolent, & holds right view. With the breakup of the body, after death, he reappears in a good destination, a heavenly world.

"But there is also the case where a certain person is one who abstains from taking life, abstains from taking what is not given, abstains from illicit sex, abstains from lying, abstains from speaking divisively, abstains from speaking abusively, abstains from idle chatter, is not covetous, not malevolent, & holds right view, (yet) with the breakup of the body, after death, he reappears in a plane of deprivation, a bad destination, a lower realm, hell.

"There is the case, Ānanda, where a certain contemplative or brahman—through ardency, exertion, commitment, heedfulness, & right attention—touches the sort of concentration of awareness that, when his mind is thus concentrated, he sees with the divine eye, pure and surpassing the human, that person—the case where one who takes life, takes what is not given, engages in illicit sex, lies, speaks divisively, speaks abusively, engages in idle chatter, is covetous, malevolent, & holds wrong view, with the breakup of the body, after death, has reappeared in a plane of deprivation, a bad destination, a lower realm, hell.

"He says, 'So there really are evil actions, there really is the result of misconduct. For I saw the case where a person who took life… & held wrong view, with the breakup of the body, after death, has reappeared in a plane of deprivation, a bad destination, a lower realm, hell.' He says, 'Anyone who takes life… & holds wrong view: They all, on the breakup of the body, after death, reappear in a plane of deprivation, a bad destination, a lower realm, hell. Whoever knows this, knows rightly. Whoever knows otherwise, their knowledge is wrong.' Insisting through obstinacy &

grasping right there on what was seen by himself, known by himself, understood by himself, he states: 'Only this is true. Everything otherwise is worthless.'

"Then there is the case, Ānanda, where a certain contemplative or brahman—through ardency, exertion, commitment, heedfulness, & right attention—touches the sort of concentration of awareness that, when his mind is thus concentrated, he sees with the divine eye, pure and surpassing the human, that person—the case where one who takes life, takes what is not given, engages in illicit sex, lies, speaks divisively, speaks abusively, engages in idle chatter, is covetous, malevolent, & holds wrong view, with the breakup of the body, after death, has reappeared in a good destination, a heavenly world.

"He says, 'So there really are no evil actions, there really is no result of misconduct. For I saw the case where a person who took life… & held wrong view, with the breakup of the body, after death, has reappeared in a good destination, a heavenly world.' He says, 'Anyone who takes life… & holds wrong view: They all, on the breakup of the body, after death, reappear in a good destination, a heavenly world. Whoever knows this, knows rightly. Whoever knows otherwise, their knowledge is wrong.' Insisting through obstinacy & grasping right there on what was seen by himself, known by himself, understood by himself, he states: 'Only this is true. Everything otherwise is worthless.'

"Then there is the case, Ānanda, where a certain contemplative or brahman—through ardency, exertion, commitment, heedfulness, & right attention—touches the sort of concentration of awareness that, when his mind is thus concentrated, he sees with the divine eye, pure and surpassing the human, that person—the case where one who abstains from taking life, abstains from taking what is not given, abstains from illicit sex, abstains from lying, abstains from speaking divisively, abstains from speaking abusively, abstains from idle chatter, is not covetous, not malevolent, & holds right view, with the breakup of the body, after death, reappears in a good destination, a heavenly world.

"He says, 'So there really are fine actions, there really is the result of good conduct. For I saw the case where a person who abstained from taking life… & held right view, with the breakup of the body, after death, has reappeared in a good destination, a heavenly world.' He says, 'Anyone who abstains from taking life… & holds right view: They all, on the breakup of the body, after death, reappear in a good destination, a heavenly world. Whoever knows this, knows rightly. Whoever knows otherwise, their knowledge is wrong.' Insisting through obstinacy & grasping right there on what was seen by himself, known by himself, understood by himself, he states: 'Only this is true. Everything otherwise is worthless.'

"Then there is the case, Ānanda, where a certain contemplative or brahman—through ardency, exertion, commitment, heedfulness, & right attention—touches the sort of concentration of awareness that, when his mind is thus concentrated, he sees with the divine eye, pure and surpassing the human, that person—the case where one who abstains from taking life, abstains from taking what is not given, abstains from illicit sex, abstains from lying, abstains from speaking divisively, abstains from speaking abusively, abstains from idle chatter, is not covetous, not malevolent, & holds right view, with the breakup of the body, after death, reappears in a plane of deprivation, a bad destination, a lower realm, hell.

"He says, 'So there really are no fine actions, there really is no result of good conduct. For I saw the case where a person who abstained from taking life… & held right view, with the breakup of the body, after death, has reappeared in a plane of deprivation, a bad destination, a lower realm, hell.' He says, 'Anyone who abstains from taking life… & holds right view: They all, on the breakup of the body, after death, reappear in a plane of deprivation, a bad destination, a lower realm, hell. Whoever knows this, knows rightly. Whoever knows otherwise, their knowledge is wrong.' Insisting through obstinacy & grasping right there on what was seen by himself, known by himself, understood by himself, he states: 'Only this is true. Everything otherwise is worthless.'

"Now, Ānanda, in the case where the contemplative or brahman says, 'So there really are evil actions, there really is the result of misconduct,' I allow him that. When he says, 'For I saw the case where a person who took life… & held wrong view, with the breakup of the body, after death, has reappeared in a plane of deprivation, a bad destination, a lower realm, hell,' I allow him that, too. But when he says, 'Anyone who takes life… & holds wrong view: They all, on the breakup of the body, after death, reappear in a plane of deprivation, a bad destination, a lower realm, hell,' I don't allow him that. And when he says, 'Whoever knows this, knows rightly; whoever knows otherwise, their knowledge is wrong,' I don't allow him that. When, insisting through obstinacy & grasping right there on what was seen by himself, known by himself, understood by himself, he states: 'Only this is true. Everything otherwise is worthless,' I don't allow him that, either. Why is that? Because the Tathāgata's knowledge with regard to the greater analysis of action is otherwise.

"Now, Ānanda, in the case where the contemplative or brahman says, 'So there really are no evil actions, there really is no result of misconduct,' I don't allow him that. But when he says, 'For I saw the case where a person who took life... & held wrong view, with the breakup of the body, after death, has reappeared in a good destination, a heavenly world,' I do allow him that. But when he says, 'Anyone who takes life... & holds wrong view: They all, on the breakup of the body, after death, reappear in a good destination, a heavenly world,' I don't allow him that. And when he says, 'Whoever knows this, knows rightly. Whoever knows otherwise, their knowledge is wrong,' I don't allow him that. When, insisting through obstinacy & grasping right there on what was seen by himself, known by himself, understood by himself, he states: 'Only this is true. Everything otherwise is worthless,' I don't allow him that, either. Why is that? Because the Tathāgata's knowledge with regard to the greater analysis of action is otherwise.

"Now, Ānanda, in the case where the contemplative or brahman says, 'So there really are fine actions, there really is the result of good conduct,' I allow him that. And when he says, 'For I saw the case where a person who abstained from taking life... & held right view, with the breakup of the body, after death, has reappeared in a good destination, a heavenly world,' I allow him that, too. But when he says, 'Anyone who abstains from taking life... & holds right view: They all, on the breakup of the body, after death, reappear in a good destination, a heavenly world,' I don't allow him that. And when he says, 'Whoever knows this, knows rightly. Whoever knows otherwise, their knowledge is wrong,' I don't allow him that. When, insisting through obstinacy & grasping right there on what was seen by himself, known by himself, understood by himself, he states: 'Only this is true. Everything otherwise is worthless,' I don't allow him that, either. Why is that? Because the Tathāgata's knowledge with regard to the greater analysis of action is otherwise.

"Now, Ānanda, in the case where the contemplative or brahman says, 'So there really are no fine actions, there really is no result of good conduct,' I don't allow him that. But when he says, 'For I saw the case where a person who abstained from taking life... & held right view, with the breakup of the body, after death, has reappeared in a plane of deprivation, a bad destination, a lower realm, hell,' I do allow him that. But when he says, 'Anyone who abstains from taking life... & holds right view: They all, on the breakup of the body, after death, reappear in a plane of deprivation, a bad destination, a lower realm, hell,' I don't allow him that. And when he says, 'Whoever knows this, knows rightly. Whoever knows otherwise, their knowledge is wrong,' I don't allow him that. When, insisting through obstinacy & grasping right there on what was seen by himself, known by himself, understood by himself, he states: 'Only this is true. Everything otherwise is worthless,' I don't allow him that, either. Why is that? Because the Tathāgata's knowledge with regard to the greater analysis of action is otherwise.

"Now, Ānanda, in the case of the person who takes life... & holds wrong view and, with the breakup of the body, after death, reappears in a plane of deprivation, a bad destination, a lower realm, hell: Either earlier he performed evil action that is to be felt as painful, or later he performed evil action that is to be felt as painful, or at the time of death he adopted & carried out wrong view. Because of that, with the breakup of the body, after death, he reappears in a plane of deprivation, a bad destination, a lower realm, hell. And as for the results of taking life... holding wrong view, he will feel them either right here & now, or in the next (lifetime), or following that.

"In the case of the person who takes life... & holds wrong view (yet), with the breakup of the body, after death, reappears in a good destination, a heavenly world: Either earlier he performed fine action that is to be felt as pleasant, or later he performed fine action that is to be felt as pleasant, or at the time of death he adopted & carried out right view. Because of that, with the breakup of the body, after death, he reappears in a good destination, a heavenly world. But as for the results of taking life... holding wrong view, he will feel them either right here & now, or in the next (lifetime), or following that.

"In the case of the person who abstains from taking life... & holds right view and, with the breakup of the body, after death, reappears in a good destination, a heavenly world: either earlier he performed fine action that is to be felt as pleasant, or later he performed fine action that is to be felt as pleasant, or at the time of death he adopted & carried out right view. Because of that, with the breakup of the body, after death, he reappears in a good destination, a heavenly world. And as for the results of abstaining from taking life... holding right view, he will feel them either right here & now, or in the next (lifetime), or following that."

"In the case of the person who abstains from taking life... & holds right view (yet) with the breakup of the body, after death, reappears in a plane of deprivation, a bad destination, a lower realm, hell: Either earlier he performed evil action that is to be felt as painful, or later he performed evil action that is to be felt as painful, or at the time of death he adopted & carried out wrong view. Because of that, with the breakup of the body, after death, he reappears in a plane of deprivation, a bad destination, a lower realm, hell. But as for the results of abstaining from taking life… holding right view, he will feel them either right here & now, or in the next (lifetime), or following that.

"Thus, Ānanda, there is action that is ineffectual and apparently ineffectual. There is action that is ineffectual but apparently effectual. There is action that is both effectual and apparently effectual. There is action that is effectual but apparently ineffectual."

That is what the Blessed One said. Gratified, Ven. Ānanda delighted in the Blessed One's words.

NOTES

1. See AN 9:34. The Buddha, when later criticizing Ven. Samiddhi's answer, does not criticize this part of it.

2. This is the one place in this discourse where Ven. Ānanda is called Ānanda the Elder.

3. Reading *ke ca* with the Burmese and PTS editions of the Canon. The Sri Lankan edition here reads *keci;* the Thai edition, *te.*

For a discussion of this discourse as an example of an analytical answer to a question, see *Skill in Questions,* chapter four.

See also: MN 41; MN 135; SN 42:13; AN 3:61; AN 4:77; AN 6:63; AN 8:40

137 *An Analysis of the Six Sense-Media*

Saḷāyatana-vibhaṅga Sutta

INTRODUCTION

Despite the abstract format of this discourse, it deals with an emotional topic: the source of emotions, the use of the emotions in the course of the practice, and the ideal emotional state of a person who has completed the path and is fit to teach others. In particular, this discourse counters a common misperception: that the distress that comes from having an unachieved goal is an obstacle in the practice, and that the antidote for that distress is to renounce any sense of goals. In actuality, that distress—termed "renunciation-based distress"—has an important role in the practice: to overcome the distress that comes with a sense of loss over sensual pleasures that have not been attained, or those that have been attained in the past but now no longer exist. Renunciation-based distress serves as a reminder that the loss of sensual pleasures is not a serious matter. As for renunciation-based distress, it is overcome, not by abandoning any sense of goal, but by following the path and realizing the joy that comes when the goal is reached.

This discourse counters another misperception as well: that equanimity is the goal of the practice. In actuality, renunciation-based equanimity serves a function as part of the path of practice—as a tool for letting go of renunciation-based joy—and then it, too, is transcended by the state called "non-fashioning" (atammayatā), *in which there is no act of intention, not even the intention underlying equanimity, at all.*

* * *

I have heard that on one occasion the Blessed One was staying near Sāvatthī in Jeta's Grove, Anāthapiṇḍika's monastery. There he addressed the monks, "Monks!"

"Yes, lord," the monks responded to him.

The Blessed One said: "Monks, I will teach you the analysis of the six sense media. Listen, and pay close attention. I will speak."

"Yes, lord," the monks responded to him.

The Blessed One said: "The six internal sense-media should be known. The six external sense-media should be known. The six classes of consciousness should be known. The six classes of contact should be known. The eighteen explorations for the intellect should be known. The thirty-six emotions to which beings are attached[1] should be known. With regard to them, depending on this, abandon that. There are three establishings of mindfulness that a noble one cultivates, cultivating which he is a teacher fit to instruct a group. Among master trainers, he is said to be the unexcelled trainer of people fit to be tamed. This is the summary of the analysis of the six sense-media.

"'The six internal sense-media should be known': Thus was it said. And in reference to what was it said? The eye-medium, the ear-medium, the nose-medium, the tongue-medium, the body-medium, the intellect-medium. 'The six internal sense-media should be known': Thus was it said. And in reference to this was it said.

"'The six external sense-media should be known': Thus was it said. And in reference to what was it said? The form-medium, the sound-medium, the aroma-medium, the flavor-medium, the tactile-sensation-medium, the idea-medium. 'The six external sense-media should be known': Thus was it said. And in reference to this was it said.

"'The six classes of consciousness should be known': Thus was it said. And in reference to what was it said? Eye-consciousness, ear-consciousness, nose-consciousness, tongue-consciousness, body-consciousness, intellect-consciousness. 'The six classes of consciousness should be known': Thus was it said. And in reference to this was it said.

"'The six classes of contact should be known': Thus was it said. And in reference to what was it said? Eye-contact, ear-contact, nose-contact, tongue-contact, body-contact, intellect-contact. 'The six classes of contact should be known': Thus was it said. And in reference to this was it said.

"'The eighteen explorations for the intellect should be known': Thus was it said. And in reference to what was it said? Seeing a form via the eye, one explores a form that can act as the basis for happiness, one explores a form that can act as the basis for unhappiness, one explores a form that can act as the basis for equanimity. Hearing a sound via the ear... Smelling an aroma via the nose... Tasting a flavor via the tongue... Touching a tactile sensation via the body... Cognizing an idea via the intellect, one explores an idea that can act as the basis for happiness, one explores an idea that can act as the basis for unhappiness, one explores an idea that can act as the basis for equanimity. The eighteen explorations for the intellect should be known': Thus was it said. And in reference to this was it said.

"'The thirty-six emotions to which beings are attached should be known': Thus was it said. And in reference to what was it said? Six kinds of house-based happiness & six kinds of renunciation-based happiness; six kinds of house-based distress & six kinds of renunciation-based distress; six kinds of house-based equanimity & six kinds of renunciation-based equanimity.

"And what are the six kinds of house-based happiness? The happiness that arises when one regards as an acquisition the acquisition of forms cognizable by the eye—agreeable, pleasing, charming, endearing, connected with worldly baits—or when one recalls the previous acquisition of such forms after they have passed, ceased, & changed: That is called house-based happiness. [Similarly with sounds, smells, tastes, tactile sensations, & ideas.]

"And what are the six kinds of renunciation-based happiness? The happiness that arises when—experiencing the inconstancy of those very forms, their change, fading, & cessation—one sees with right discernment as it has come to be that all forms, both before and now, are inconstant, stressful, subject to change: That is called renunciation-based happiness. [Similarly with sounds, smells, tastes, tactile sensations, & ideas.]

"And what are the six kinds of house-based distress? The distress that arises when one regards as a non-acquisition the non-acquisition of forms cognizable by the eye—agreeable, pleasing, charming, endearing, connected with worldly baits—or when one recalls the previous non-acquisition of such forms after they have passed, ceased, & changed: That is called house-based distress. [Similarly with sounds, smells, tastes, tactile sensations, & ideas.]

"And what are the six kinds of renunciation-based distress? The distress coming from the longing that arises in one who is filled with longing for the unexcelled liberations when—experiencing the inconstancy of those very forms, their change, fading, & cessation—he sees with right discernment as it has come to be that all forms, both before and now, are inconstant, stressful, subject to change and he is filled with this longing: 'O when will I enter & remain in the dimension[2] that the noble ones now enter & remain in?' This is called renunciation-based distress. [Similarly with sounds, smells, tastes, tactile sensations, & ideas.]

"And what are the six kinds of house-based equanimity? The equanimity that arises when a foolish, deluded person—a run-of-the-mill, untaught person who has not conquered his limitations or the results of action[3] & who is blind to danger[4]—sees a form with the eye. Such equanimity does not go beyond the form, which is why it is called house-based equanimity. [Similarly with sounds, smells, tastes, tactile sensations, & ideas.]

"And what are the six kinds of renunciation-based equanimity? The equanimity that arises when—experiencing the inconstancy of those very forms, their change, fading, & cessation—one sees with right discernment as it has come to be that all forms, both before and now, are inconstant, stressful, subject to change: This equanimity goes beyond form, which is why it is called renunciation-based equanimity. [Similarly with sounds, smells, tastes, tactile sensations, & ideas.]

"'The thirty-six emotions to which beings are attached should be known': Thus was it said. And in reference to this was it said.

"'With regard to them, depending on this, abandon that': Thus was it said. And in reference to what was it said?

"Here, by depending & relying on the six kinds of renunciation-based happiness, abandon & transcend the six kinds of house-based happiness. Such is their abandoning, such is their transcending. By depending & relying on the six kinds of renunciation-based distress, abandon & transcend the six kinds of house-based distress. Such is their abandoning, such is their transcending. By depending & relying on the six kinds of renunciation-based equanimity, abandon & transcend the six kinds of house-based equanimity. Such is their abandoning, such their transcending.

"By depending & relying on the six kinds of renunciation-based happiness, abandon & transcend the six kinds of renunciation-based distress. Such is their abandoning, such is their transcending. By depending & relying on the six kinds of renunciation-based equanimity, abandon & transcend the six kinds of renunciation-based happiness. Such is their abandoning, such their transcending.

"There is equanimity coming from multiplicity, dependent on multiplicity; and there is equanimity coming from singleness, dependent on singleness.

"And what is equanimity coming from multiplicity, dependent on multiplicity? There is equanimity with regard to forms, equanimity with regard to sounds... smells... tastes... tactile sensations [& ideas: this word appears in one of the recensions]. This is equanimity coming from multiplicity, dependent on multiplicity.

"And what is equanimity coming from singleness, dependent on singleness? There is equanimity dependent on the dimension of the infinitude of space, equanimity dependent on the dimension of the infinitude of consciousness... dependent on the dimension of nothingness... dependent on the dimension of neither perception nor non-perception. This is equanimity coming from singleness, dependent on singleness.

"By depending & relying on equanimity coming from singleness, dependent on singleness, abandon & transcend equanimity coming from multiplicity, dependent on multiplicity. Such is its abandoning, such its transcending.

"By depending & relying on non-fashioning,[5] abandon & transcend the equanimity coming from singleness, dependent on singleness. Such is its abandoning, such its transcending.

"'Depending on this, abandon that': Thus was it said. And in reference to this was it said.

"'There are three establishings of mindfulness that a noble one cultivates, cultivating which he is a teacher fit to instruct a group': Thus was it said. And in reference to what was it said?

"There is the case where the Teacher—out of sympathy, seeking their well-being—teaches the Dhamma to his disciples: 'This is for your well-being, this is for your happiness.' His disciples do not listen or lend ear or apply their minds to gnosis. Turning aside, they stray from the Teacher's message. In this case the Tathāgata is not satisfied nor is he sensitive to satisfaction, yet he remains untroubled, mindful, & alert. This is the first establishing of mindfulness that a noble one cultivates, cultivating which he is a teacher fit to instruct a group.

"And further, there is the case where the Teacher—out of sympathy, seeking their well-being—teaches the Dhamma to his disciples: 'This is for your well-being, this is for your happiness.' Some of his disciples do not listen or lend ear or apply their minds to gnosis. Turning aside, they stray from the Teacher's message. But some of his disciples listen, lend ear, & apply their minds to gnosis. They do not turn aside or stray from the Teacher's message. In this case the Tathāgata is not satisfied nor is he sensitive to satisfaction; at the same time he is not dissatisfied nor is he sensitive to dissatisfaction. Free from both satisfaction & dissatisfaction, he remains equanimous, mindful, & alert. This is the second establishing of mindfulness....

"And further, there is the case where the Teacher—out of sympathy, seeking their well-being—teaches the Dhamma to his disciples: 'This is for your well-being, this is for your happiness.' His disciples listen, lend ear, & apply their minds to gnosis. They do not turn aside or stray from the Teacher's message. In this case the Tathāgata is satisfied and is sensitive to satisfaction, yet he remains untroubled, mindful, & alert. This is the third establishing of mindfulness that a noble one cultivates, cultivating which he is a teacher fit to instruct a group.

"'There are three establishings of mindfulness that a noble one cultivates, cultivating which he is a teacher fit to instruct a group': Thus was it said. And in reference to this was it said.

"'Among master trainers, he is said to be the unexcelled trainer of people fit to be tamed': Thus was it said. And in reference to what was it said?

"Steered by the elephant trainer, the elephant to be tamed runs in only one direction: east, west, north, or south. Steered by the horse trainer, the horse to be tamed runs in only one direction: east, west, north, or south. Steered by the ox trainer, the ox to be tamed runs in only one direction: east, west, north, or south.

"But steered by the Tathāgata—worthy & rightly self-awakened—the person to be tamed fans out in eight directions.

"Possessed of form, he/she sees forms. This is the first direction.

"Not percipient of form internally, he/she sees forms externally. This is the second direction.

"He/she is intent only on the beautiful. This is the third direction.

"With the complete transcending of perceptions of (physical) form, with the disappearance of perceptions of resistance, and not attending to perceptions of multiplicity, (perceiving,) 'Infinite space,' he/she enters and remains in the dimension of the infinitude of space. This is the fourth direction.

"With the complete transcending of the dimension of the infinitude of space, (perceiving,) 'Infinite consciousness,' he/she enters and remains in the dimension of the infinitude of consciousness. This is the fifth direction.

"With the complete transcending of the dimension of the infinitude of consciousness, (perceiving,) 'There is nothing,' he/she enters and remains in the dimension of nothingness. This is the sixth direction.

"With the complete transcending of the dimension of nothingness, he/she enters and remains in the dimension of neither perception nor non-perception. This is the seventh direction.

"With the complete transcending of the dimension of neither perception nor non-perception, he/she enters and remains in the cessation of perception and feeling. This is the eighth direction.

"Steered by the Tathāgata—worthy & rightly self-awakened—the person to be tamed fans out in eight directions.

"'Among master trainers, he [the Tathāgata] is said to be the unexcelled trainer of people fit to be tamed': Thus was it said. And in reference to this was it said."

That is what the Blessed One said. Gratified, the monks delighted in the Blessed One's words.

NOTES

1. *Satta-pada.* The question in translating this compound is whether *satta* means "living being" or "attached to." In this translation, I have opted for both.

2. See SN 4:19, SN 35:117, and Ud 8:1.

3. A person who "has not conquered his limitations or the results of action": this passage seems related to the passage in AN 3:99, which defines a person of limited mind, prey to the results of past bad actions, as one who is "undeveloped in contemplating the body, undeveloped in virtue, undeveloped in concentration, and undeveloped in discernment; restricted, small-hearted, dwelling with suffering." As AN 3:99 points out, such a person suffers more intensely from the results of past unskillful actions than does one whose awareness is unrestricted. SN 42:8 recommends the practice of the four sublime attitudes as a way of developing an unrestricted awareness that weakens the results of past unskillful actions.

4. A person who is "blind to danger" is one who does not see the drawbacks of sensual pleasure or attachment to the body. For such a person, moments of equanimity are usually a dull spot in the midst of the quest for sensual pleasure. This is why such moments do not go beyond the sensory stimulus that generated them.

5. *Atammayatā.* Literally, "not-made-of-that-ness." See the introductions to sections II/B and III/G in *The Wings to Awakening.*

See also: DN 12; SN 35:204; SN 42:7; SN 56:11; AN 3:61; AN 4:94; AN 4:111; AN 4:113; AN 4:159; AN 4:170; AN 9:41; AN 10:71

138 An Analysis of the Statement

Uddesa-vibhaṅga Sutta

I have heard that on one occasion the Blessed One was staying near Sāvatthī in Jeta's Grove, Anāthapiṇḍika's monastery. There he addressed the monks: "Monks!"

"Yes, lord," the monks responded to him.

The Blessed One said: "Monks, I will teach you a statement & its analysis. Listen & pay close attention. I will speak."

"As you say, lord," the monks responded to him.

The Blessed One said, "A monk should investigate in such a way that, his consciousness neither externally scattered & diffused, nor internally positioned, he would from lack of clinging/sustenance be unagitated. When—his consciousness neither externally scattered & diffused, nor internally positioned—from lack of clinging/sustenance he would be unagitated, there is no seed for the conditions of future birth, aging, death, or stress."

That is what the Blessed One said. Having said it, he—the One Well-Gone—got up from his seat and went into his dwelling.

Then, not long after the Blessed One had left, this thought occurred to the monks: "This brief statement the Blessed One made, after which he went into his dwelling without analyzing the detailed meaning—i.e., 'A monk should investigate in such a way that, his consciousness neither externally scattered & diffused, nor internally positioned, he would from lack of clinging/sustenance be unagitated. When—his consciousness neither externally scattered & diffused, nor internally positioned—from lack of clinging/sustenance he would be unagitated, there is no seed for the conditions of future birth, aging, death, or stress': Now who might analyze the unanalyzed detailed meaning of this brief statement?" Then the thought occurred to them, "Ven. Mahā Kaccāna is praised by the Teacher and esteemed by his observant companions in the holy life. He is capable of analyzing the unanalyzed detailed meaning of this brief statement. Suppose we were to go to him and, on arrival, cross-question him about this matter."

So the monks went to Ven. Mahā Kaccāna and, on arrival exchanged courteous greetings with him. After an exchange of friendly greetings & courtesies, they sat to one side. As they were standing there, they [told him what had happened, and added,] "Analyze the meaning, Ven. Mahā Kaccāna!"

(He replied:) "Friends, it's as if a man needing heartwood, looking for heartwood, wandering in search of heartwood—passing over the root & trunk of a standing tree possessing heartwood—were to imagine that heartwood should be sought among its branches & leaves. So it is with you, who—having bypassed the Blessed One when you were face to face with him, the Teacher—imagine that I should be asked about this matter. For knowing, the Blessed One knows; seeing, he sees. He is the Eye, he is Knowledge, he is Dhamma, he is Brahmā. He is the speaker, the proclaimer, the elucidator of meaning, the giver of the deathless, the lord of the Dhamma, the Tathāgata. That was the time when you should have cross-questioned him about this matter. However he answered, that was how you should have remembered it."

"Yes, friend Kaccāna: Knowing, the Blessed One knows; seeing, he sees. He is the Eye, he is Knowledge, he is Dhamma, he is Brahmā. He is the speaker, the proclaimer, the elucidator of meaning, the giver of the deathless, the lord of the Dhamma, the Tathāgata. That was the time when we should have cross-questioned him about this matter. However he answered, that was how we should have remembered it. But you are praised by the Teacher and esteemed by your observant companions in the holy life. You are capable of analyzing the unanalyzed detailed meaning of this brief statement. Analyze the meaning, Ven. Mahā Kaccāna, without making it difficult!"

"In that case, my friends, listen & pay close attention. I will speak."

"As you say, friend," the monks responded to him.

Ven. Mahā Kaccāna said this: "Concerning the brief statement the Blessed One made, after which he entered his dwelling without analyzing the detailed meaning—i.e., 'A monk should investigate in such a way that, his consciousness neither externally scattered & diffused, nor internally positioned, he would from lack of clinging/sustenance be unagitated. When—his consciousness neither externally scattered & diffused, nor internally positioned—from lack of clinging/sustenance he would be unagitated, there is no seed for the conditions of future birth, aging, death, or stress'—I understand the detailed meaning to be this:

"How is consciousness said to be scattered & diffused? There is the case where, having seen a form with the eye, consciousness follows the drift of [lit: flows after] the theme of the form, is tied to the attraction of the theme of the form, is chained to the attraction of the theme of the form, is fettered & joined to the attraction of the theme of the form: Consciousness is said to be externally scattered & diffused.

"There is the case where, having heard a sound with the ear... having smelled an aroma with the nose... having tasted a flavor with the tongue... having touched a tactile sensation with the body... having cognized an idea with the intellect, consciousness follows the drift of the theme of the idea, is tied to the attraction of the theme of the idea, is chained to the attraction of the theme of the idea, is fettered & joined to the attraction of the theme of the idea: Consciousness is said to be externally scattered & diffused.

"And how is consciousness said not to be externally scattered & diffused? There is the case where, having seen a form with the eye, consciousness does not follow the drift of the theme of the form, is not tied to... chained to... fettered, or joined to the attraction of the theme of the form: Consciousness is said not to be externally scattered & diffused.

"There is the case where, having heard a sound with the ear... having smelled an aroma with the nose... having tasted a flavor with the tongue... having touched a tactile sensation with the body... having cognized an idea with the intellect, consciousness does not follow the drift of the theme of the idea, is not tied to... chained to... fettered, or joined to the attraction of the theme of the idea: Consciousness is said not to be externally scattered & diffused.

"And how is the mind said to be internally positioned? There is the case where a monk, quite secluded from sensuality, secluded from unskillful qualities, enters & remains in the first jhāna: rapture & pleasure born of seclusion, accompanied by directed thought & evaluation. His consciousness follows the drift of the rapture & pleasure born of seclusion, is tied to... chained... fettered, & joined to the attraction of the rapture & pleasure born of seclusion. Or further, with the stilling of directed thoughts & evaluations, he enters & remains in the second jhāna: rapture & pleasure born of concentration, unification of awareness free from directed thought & evaluation—internal assurance. His consciousness follows the drift of the rapture & pleasure born of composure, is tied to... chained... fettered, & joined to the attraction of the rapture & pleasure born of concentration. Or further, with the fading of rapture, he remains equanimous, mindful, &

alert, and senses pleasure with the body. He enters & remains in the third jhāna, of which the noble ones declare, 'Equanimous & mindful, he has a pleasant abiding.' His consciousness follows the drift of the equanimity & pleasure, is tied to… chained… fettered, & joined to the attraction of the equanimity & pleasure. Or further, with the abandoning of pleasure & pain—as with the earlier disappearance of elation & distress—he enters & remains in the fourth jhāna: purity of equanimity & mindfulness, neither pleasure nor pain. His consciousness follows the drift of the neither pleasure nor pain, is tied to… chained to… fettered, & joined to the attraction of the neither pleasure nor pain: The mind is said to be internally positioned.

"And how is the mind said not to be internally positioned? There is the case where a monk, quite secluded from sensuality, secluded from unskillful qualities, enters & remains in the first jhāna: rapture & pleasure born of seclusion, accompanied by directed thought & evaluation. His consciousness does not follow the drift of the rapture & pleasure born of seclusion, is not tied to… chained to… fettered, or joined to the attraction of the rapture & pleasure born of seclusion. Or further, with the stilling of directed thoughts & evaluations, he enters & remains in the second jhāna: rapture & pleasure born of concentration, unification of awareness free from directed thought & evaluation—internal assurance. His consciousness does not follow the drift of the rapture & pleasure born of concentration, is not tied to… chained… fettered, or joined to the attraction of the rapture & pleasure born of concentration. Or further, with the fading of rapture, he remains equanimous, mindful, & alert, and senses pleasure with the body. He enters & remains in the third jhāna, of which the noble ones declare, 'Equanimous & mindful, he has a pleasant abiding.' His consciousness does not follow the drift of the equanimity & pleasure, is not tied to… chained… fettered, or joined to the attraction of the equanimity & pleasure. Or further, with the abandoning of pleasure & pain—as with the earlier disappearance of elation & distress—he enters & remains in the fourth jhāna: purity of equanimity & mindfulness, neither pleasure nor pain. His consciousness does not follow the drift of the neither pleasure nor pain, is not tied to… chained to… fettered, or joined to the attraction of the neither pleasure nor pain: The mind is said to be not internally positioned.

"And how is agitation caused by clinging/sustenance? There is the case where an uninstructed run-of-the-mill person—who has no regard for noble ones, is not well-versed or disciplined in their Dhamma; who has no regard for people of integrity, is not well-versed or disciplined in their Dhamma—assumes form to be the self, or the self as possessing form, or form as in the self, or the self as in form. His form changes & is unstable. Because of the change & instability of form, his consciousness alters in accordance with the change in form. With the agitation born from the alteration in accordance with the change in form and coming from the co-arising of (unskillful mental) qualities, his mind stays consumed. And because of the consumption of awareness, he feels fearful, threatened, & solicitous.

"He assumes feeling to be the self....

"He assumes perception to be the self....

"He assumes fabrications to be the self....

"He assumes consciousness to be the self, of the self as possessing consciousness, or consciousness as in the self, or the self as in consciousness. His consciousness changes & is unstable. Because of the change & instability of consciousness, his consciousness alters in accordance with the change in consciousness. With the agitation born from the alteration in accordance with the change in consciousness and coming from the co-arising of (unskillful mental) qualities, his mind stays consumed. And because of the consumption of awareness, he feels fearful, threatened, & solicitous.

"This, friends, is how agitation is caused by clinging/sustenance.

"And how is non-agitation caused by lack of clinging/sustenance? There is the case where an instructed disciple of the noble ones—who has regard for noble ones, is well-versed & disciplined in their Dhamma; who has regard for people of integrity, is well-versed & disciplined in their Dhamma—doesn't assume form to be the self, or the self as possessing form, or form as in the self, or the self as in form. His form changes & is unstable, but his consciousness doesn't—because of the change & instability of form—alter in accordance with the change in form. His mind is not consumed with any agitation born from an alteration in accordance with the change in form or coming from the co-arising of (unskillful mental) qualities. And because his awareness is not consumed, he feels neither fearful, threatened, nor solicitous.

"He doesn't assume feeling to be the self....

"He doesn't assume perception to be the self....

"He doesn't assume fabrications to be the self....

"He doesn't assume consciousness to be the self, or the self as possessing consciousness, or consciousness as in the self, or the self as in consciousness. His consciousness changes & is unstable, but his consciousness doesn't—because of the change & instability of consciousness—alter in accordance with the change in consciousness.

His mind is not consumed with any agitation born from an alteration in accordance with the change in consciousness or coming from the co-arising of (unskillful mental) qualities. And because his awareness is not consumed, he feels neither fearful, threatened, nor solicitous.

"This, friends, is how non-agitation is caused by lack of clinging/ sustenance.

"So, concerning the brief statement the Blessed One made, after which he entered his dwelling without analyzing the detailed meaning—i.e., 'A monk should investigate in such a way that, his consciousness neither externally scattered & diffused, nor internally positioned, he would from lack of clinging/sustenance be unagitated. When—his consciousness neither externally scattered & diffused, nor internally positioned—from lack of clinging/ sustenance he would be unagitated, there is no seed for the conditions of future birth, aging, death, or stress'—this is how I understand the detailed meaning. Now, friends, if you wish, having gone to the Blessed One, cross-question him about this matter. However he answers is how you should remember it."

Then the monks, delighting in & approving of Ven. Mahā Kaccāna's words, rose from their seats and went to the Blessed One. On arrival, having bowed down to him, they sat to one side. As they were sitting there, they [told him what had happened after he had gone into his dwelling, and ended by saying,] "Then Ven. Mahā Kaccāna analyzed the meaning using these words, these statements, these phrases."

"Mahā Kaccāna is wise, monks. He is a person of great discernment. If you had asked me about this matter, I too would have answered in the same way he did. That is its meaning, and that is how you should remember it."

That is what the Blessed One said. Gratified, the monks delighted in the Blessed One's words.

See also: MN 18; AN 4:178; AN 4:192; AN 7:64; AN 8:54; Ud 6:2

140 *An Analysis of the Properties*

Dhātu-vibhaṅga Sutta

I have heard that on one occasion, as the Blessed One was wandering among the Magadhans, he entered Rājagaha, went to the potter Bhaggava, and on arrival said to him, "If it is no inconvenience for you, Bhaggava, I will stay for one night in your shed."

"It's no inconvenience for me, lord, but there is a wanderer who has already taken up residence there. If he gives his permission, you may stay there as you like."

Now at that time a clansman named Pukkusāti had left home and gone forth into homelessness through faith, out of dedication to the Blessed One. He was the one who had already taken up residence in the potter's shed. So the Blessed One approached Ven. Pukkusāti and, on arrival, said to him, "If it is no inconvenience for you, monk, I will stay one night in the shed."

"The shed is roomy, my friend. Stay as you like."

So the Blessed One, entering the potter's shed and setting out a spread of grass to one side, sat down folding his legs crosswise, holding his body erect, and setting mindfulness to the fore. He spent most of the night sitting (in meditation). Ven. Pukkusāti also spent most of the night sitting (in meditation). The thought occurred to the Blessed One, "How inspiring is the way this clansman behaves! What if I were to question him?" So he said to Ven. Pukkusāti, "Out of dedication to whom, monk, have you gone forth? Who is your teacher? Of whose Dhamma do you approve?"

"There is, my friend, Gotama the contemplative, a son of the Sakyans, gone forth from a Sakyan clan. Now, this excellent report about Master Gotama has been spread about: 'Indeed, the Blessed One is worthy & rightly self-awakened, consummate in clear-knowing & conduct, well-gone, an expert with regard to the cosmos, unexcelled trainer of people fit to be tamed, teacher of devas & human beings, awakened, blessed.' I have gone forth out of dedication to that Blessed One. That Blessed One is my teacher. It is of that Blessed One's Dhamma that I approve."

"But where, monk, is that Blessed One—worthy & rightly self-awakened—staying now?"

"There is, my friend, a city in the northern lands named Sāvatthī. That is where the Blessed One—worthy & rightly self-awakened—is staying now."

"Have you ever seen that Blessed One before? On seeing him, would you recognize him?"

"No, my friend, I have never seen the Blessed One before, nor on seeing him would I recognize him."

Then the thought occurred to the Blessed One: "It's out of dedication to me that this clansman has gone forth. What if I were to teach him the Dhamma?" So he said to Ven. Pukkusāti, "I will teach you the Dhamma, monk. Listen & pay close attention. I will speak."

"As you say, friend," Ven. Pukkusāti responded to the Blessed One.

The Blessed One said: "A person has six properties, six media of sensory contact, eighteen considerations, & four determinations. He has been stilled where the currents of supposition do not flow. And when the currents of supposition do not flow, he is said to be a sage at peace. One should not be negligent of discernment, should guard the truth, be devoted to relinquishment, and train only for calm. This is the summary of the analysis of the six properties.

"'A person has six properties.' Thus it was said. In reference to what was it said? These are the six properties: the earth property, the liquid property, the fire property, the wind property, the space property, the consciousness property. 'A person has six properties.' Thus it was said, and in reference to this was it said.

"'A person has six media of sensory contact.' Thus it was said. In reference to what was it said? These are the six media of sensory contact: the eye as a medium of sensory contact, the ear... the nose... the tongue... the body... the intellect as a medium of sensory contact. 'A person has six media of sensory contact.' Thus it was said, and in reference to this was it said.

"'A person has eighteen considerations.' Thus it was said. In reference to what was it said? These are the eighteen considerations: On seeing a form with the eye, one considers a form that can act as a basis for joy, a form that can act as a basis for sadness, or a form that can act as a basis for equanimity. On hearing a sound with the ear.... On smelling an aroma with the nose.... On tasting a flavor with the tongue.... On touching a tactile sensation with the body.... On cognizing an idea with the intellect, one considers an idea that can act as a basis for joy, an idea that can act as a basis for sadness, or an idea that can act as a basis for equanimity. Thus there are six considerations conducive to joy, six conducive to sadness, & six conducive to equanimity. 'A person has eighteen considerations.' Thus it was said, and in reference to this was it said.

"'A person has four determinations.' Thus it was said. In reference to what was it said? These are the four determinations: the determination for discernment, the determination for truth, the determination for relinquishment, the determination for calm. 'A person has four determinations.' Thus it was said, and in reference to this was it said.

"'One should not be negligent of discernment, should guard the truth, be devoted to relinquishment, and train only for calm.' Thus it was said. In reference to what was it said? And how is one not negligent of discernment? These are the six properties: the earth property, the liquid property, the fire property, the wind property, the space property, the consciousness property.

"And what is the earth property? The earth property can be either internal or external. What is the internal earth property? Anything internal, within oneself, that's hard, solid, & sustained (by craving): head hairs, body hairs, nails, teeth, skin, flesh, tendons, bones, bone marrow, kidneys, heart, liver, membranes, spleen, lungs, large intestines, small intestines, contents of the stomach, feces, or anything else internal, within oneself, that's hard, solid, and sustained: This is called the internal earth property. Now both the internal earth property & the external earth property are simply earth property. And that should be seen as it has come to be with right discernment: 'This is not mine, this is not me, this is not my self.' When one sees it thus as it has come to be with right discernment, one becomes disenchanted with the earth property and makes the earth property fade from the mind.

"And what is the liquid property? The liquid property may be either internal or external. What is the internal liquid property? Anything internal, belonging to oneself, that's liquid, watery, & sustained: bile, phlegm, pus, blood, sweat, fat, tears, oil, saliva, mucus, oil-of-the-joints, urine, or anything else internal, within oneself, that's liquid, watery, & sustained: This is called the internal liquid property. Now both the internal liquid property & the external liquid property are simply liquid property. And that should be seen as it has come to be with right discernment: 'This is not mine, this is not me, this is not my self.' When one sees it thus as it has come to be with right discernment, one becomes disenchanted with the liquid property and makes the liquid property fade from the mind.

"And what is the fire property? The fire property may be either internal or external. What is the internal fire property? Anything internal, belonging to oneself, that's fire, fiery, & sustained: that by which (the body) is warmed, aged, & consumed with fever; and that by which what is eaten, drunk, chewed, & savored gets properly digested; or anything else internal, within oneself, that's fire, fiery, & sustained: This is called the internal fire property. Now both the internal fire property & the external fire property are simply fire property. And that should be seen as it has come to be with right discernment: 'This is not mine, this is not me, this is not my self.' When one sees it thus as it has come to be with right discernment, one becomes disenchanted with the fire property and makes the fire property fade from the mind.

"And what is the wind property? The wind property may be either internal or external. What is the internal wind property? Anything internal, belonging to oneself, that's wind, windy, & sustained: up-going winds, down-going winds, winds in the stomach, winds in the intestines, winds that course through the body, in-and-out breathing, or anything else internal, within oneself, that's wind, windy, & sustained: This is called the internal wind property. Now both the internal wind property & the external wind property are simply wind property. And that should be seen as it has come to be with right discernment: 'This is not mine, this is not me, this is not my self.' When one sees it thus as it has come to be with right discernment, one becomes disenchanted with the wind property and makes the wind property fade from the mind.

"And what is the space property? The space property may be either internal or external. What is the internal space property? Anything internal, belonging to oneself, that's space, spatial, & sustained: the holes of the ears, the nostrils, the mouth, the (passage) whereby what is eaten, drunk, consumed, & tasted gets swallowed, and where it collects, and whereby it is excreted from below, or anything else internal, within oneself, that's space, spatial, & sustained: This is called the internal space property. Now both the internal space property & the external space property are simply space property. And that should be seen as it has come to be with right discernment: 'This is not mine, this is not me, this is not my self.' When one sees it thus as it has come to be with right discernment, one becomes disenchanted with the space property and makes the space property fade from the mind.

"There remains only consciousness: pure & bright. What does one cognize with that consciousness? One cognizes 'pleasure.' One cognizes 'pain.' One cognizes 'neither pleasure nor pain.' In dependence on a sensory contact that is to be felt as pleasure, there arises a feeling of pleasure. When sensing a feeling of pleasure, one discerns that 'I am sensing a feeling of pleasure.' One discerns that

'With the cessation of that very sensory contact that is to be felt as pleasure, the concomitant feeling—the feeling of pleasure that has arisen in dependence on the sensory contact that is to be felt as pleasure—ceases, is stilled.' In dependence on a sensory contact that is to be felt as pain.... In dependence on a sensory contact that is to be felt as neither pleasure nor pain, there arises a feeling of neither pleasure nor pain. When sensing a feeling of neither pleasure nor pain, one discerns that 'I am sensing a feeling of neither pleasure nor pain.' One discerns that 'With the cessation of that very sensory contact that is to be felt as neither pleasure nor pain, the concomitant feeling—the feeling of neither pleasure nor pain that has arisen in dependence on the sensory contact that is to be felt as neither pleasure nor pain—ceases, is stilled.'

"Just as when, from the friction & conjunction of two fire sticks, heat is born and fire appears, and from the separation & disjunction of those very same fire sticks, the concomitant heat ceases, is stilled; in the same way, in dependence on a sensory contact that is to be felt as pleasure, there arises a feeling of pleasure.... In dependence on a sensory contact that is to be felt as pain.... In dependence on a sensory contact that is to be felt as neither pleasure nor pain, there arises a feeling of neither pleasure nor pain.... One discerns that 'With the cessation of that very sensory contact that is to be felt as neither pleasure nor pain, the concomitant feeling... ceases, is stilled.'

"There remains only equanimity: pure & bright, pliant, malleable, & luminous. Just as if a dexterous goldsmith or goldsmith's apprentice were to prepare a furnace, heat up a crucible, and, taking gold with a pair of tongs, place it in the crucible: He would blow on it time & again, sprinkle water on it time & again, examine it time & again, so that the gold would become refined, well-refined, thoroughly refined, flawless, free from dross, pliant, malleable, & luminous. Then whatever sort of ornament he had in mind—whether a belt, an earring, a necklace, or a gold chain—it would serve his purpose. In the same way, there remains only equanimity: pure & bright, pliant, malleable, & luminous. One discerns that 'If I were to direct equanimity as pure & bright as this toward the dimension of the infinitude of space, I would develop the mind along those lines, and thus this equanimity of mine—thus supported, thus sustained—would last for a long time. One discerns that 'If I were to direct equanimity as pure and bright as this toward the dimension of the infinitude of consciousness... the dimension of nothingness... the dimension of neither perception nor non-perception, I would develop the mind along those lines, and thus this equanimity of mine—thus supported, thus sustained—would last for a long time.'

"One discerns that 'If I were to direct equanimity as pure & bright as this toward the dimension of the infinitude of space and to develop the mind along those lines, that would be fabricated. One discerns that 'If I were to direct equanimity as pure and bright as this toward the dimension of the infinitude of consciousness... the dimension of nothingness... the dimension of neither perception nor non-perception and to develop the mind along those lines, that would be fabricated.' One neither fabricates nor mentally fashions for the sake of becoming or un-becoming. This being the case, one is not sustained by anything [doesn't cling to anything] in the world. Unsustained, one is not agitated. Unagitated, one is totally unbound right within. One discerns that 'Birth is ended, the holy life fulfilled, the task done. There is nothing further for this world.'

"If sensing a feeling of pleasure, one discerns it as 'inconstant.' One discerns it as 'not grasped at.' One discerns it as 'not relished.' If sensing a feeling of pain, one discerns it as 'inconstant.' One discerns it as 'not grasped at.' One discerns it as 'not relished.' If sensing a feeling of neither pleasure nor pain, one discerns it as 'inconstant.' One discerns it as 'not grasped at.' One discerns it as 'not relished.'

"If sensing a feeling of pleasure, one senses it disjoined from it. If sensing a feeling of pain, one senses it disjoined from it. If sensing a feeling of neither pleasure nor pain, one senses it disjoined from it. When sensing a feeling limited to the body, one discerns, 'I am sensing a feeling limited to the body.' When sensing a feeling limited to life, one discerns, 'I am sensing a feeling limited to life.' One discerns, 'With the break-up of the body, after the termination of life, all that is experienced, not being relished, will grow cold right here.'

"Just as an oil lamp would burn in dependence on oil & wick and, from the termination of the oil & wick, it would go out unnourished; in the same way, when sensing a feeling limited to the body, one discerns, 'I am sensing a feeling limited to the body.' When sensing a feeling limited to life, one discerns, 'I am sensing a feeling limited to life.' One discerns, 'With the break-up of the body, after the termination of life, all that is experienced, not being relished, will grow cold right here.'

"Thus a monk so endowed is endowed with the highest determination for discernment, for this—the knowledge of the passing away of all suffering & stress—is the highest noble discernment.

"His release, being founded on truth, does not fluctuate, for whatever is deceptive is false; unbinding—the undeceptive—is true. Thus a monk so endowed is endowed with the highest determination for truth, for this—unbinding, the undeceptive—is the highest noble truth.

"Whereas formerly he foolishly had taken on mental acquisitions and brought them to completion, he has now abandoned them, their root destroyed, made like a palmyra stump, deprived of the conditions of development, not destined for future arising. Thus a monk so endowed is endowed with the highest determination for relinquishment, for this—the renunciation of all mental acquisitions—is the highest noble relinquishment.

"Whereas formerly he foolishly had greed—as well as desire & infatuation—he has now abandoned them, their root destroyed, made like a palmyra stump, deprived of the conditions of development, not destined for future arising. Whereas formerly he foolishly had malice—as well as ill-will & hatred—he has now abandoned them.... Whereas formerly he foolishly had ignorance—as well as delusion & confusion—he has now abandoned them, their root destroyed, made like a palmyra stump, deprived of the conditions of development, not destined for future arising. Thus a monk so endowed is endowed with the highest determination for calm, for this—the calming of passions, aversions, & delusions—is the highest noble calm. 'One should not be negligent of discernment, should guard the truth, be devoted to relinquishment, and train only for calm.' Thus it was said, and in reference to this was it said.

"'He has been stilled where the currents of supposition do not flow. And when the currents of supposition do not flow, he is said to be a sage at peace.' Thus it was said. With reference to what was it said? 'I am' is a supposition. 'I am this' is a supposition. 'I shall be' is a supposition. 'I shall not be' ... 'I shall be possessed of form' ... 'I shall not be possessed of form' ... 'I shall be percipient' ... 'I shall not be percipient' ... 'I shall be neither percipient nor non-percipient' is a supposition. Supposition is a disease, supposition is a cancer, supposition is an arrow. By going beyond all supposition, he is called a sage at peace.

"And further, a sage at peace is not born, does not age, does not die, is unagitated, and is free from longing. He has nothing whereby he would be born. Not being born, will he age? Not aging, will he die? Not dying, will he be agitated? Not being agitated, for what will he long? It was in reference to this that it was said, 'He has been stilled where the currents of supposition do not flow. And when the currents of supposition do not flow, he is said to be a sage at peace.' Now, monk, you should remember this, my brief analysis of the six properties."

Then the thought occurred to Ven. Pukkusāti: "Surely, the Teacher has come to me! Surely, the One Well-Gone has come to me! Surely, the Rightly Self-awakened One has come to me!" Getting up from his seat, arranging his upper robe over one shoulder, and bowing down with his head at the Blessed One's feet, he said, "A transgression has overcome me, lord, in that I was so foolish, so muddle-headed, and so unskilled as to assume that it was proper to address the Blessed One as 'friend.' May the Blessed One please accept this confession of my transgression as such, so that I may restrain myself in the future."

"Yes, monk, a transgression overcame you in that you were so foolish, so muddle-headed, and so unskilled as to assume that it was proper to address me as 'friend.' But because you see your transgression as such and make amends in accordance with the Dhamma, we accept your confession. For it is a cause of growth in the discipline of the noble ones when, seeing a transgression as such, one makes amends in accordance with the Dhamma and exercises restraint in the future."

"Lord, may I receive full acceptance [ordination as a monk] from the Blessed One?"

"And are your robes & bowl complete?"

"No, lord, my robes & bowl are not complete."

"Tathāgatas do not give full acceptance to one whose robes & bowl are incomplete."

Then Ven. Pukkusāti, delighting & rejoicing in the Blessed One's words, got up from his seat, bowed down to the Blessed One and, keeping him on his right, left in search of robes & a bowl. And while he was searching for robes & a bowl, a runaway cow killed him.

Then a large number of monks approached the Blessed One and, on arrival, having bowed down to him, sat to one side. As they were sitting there, they said to the Blessed One, "Lord, the clansman Pukkusāti, whom the Blessed One instructed with a brief instruction, has died. What is his destination? What is his future state?"

"Monks, the clansman Pukkusāti was wise. He practiced the Dhamma in accordance with the Dhamma and did not pester me with issues related to the Dhamma. With the destruction of the five lower fetters, he has arisen spontaneously (in the Pure Abodes), there to be totally unbound, never again to return from that world."

That is what the Blessed One said. Gratified, the monks delighted in the Blessed One's words.

See also: MN 28; MN 106; SN 35:207; SN 36:7; AN 9:36; Ud 1:10

141 *An Analysis of the Truths*

Sacca-vibhaṅga Sutta

I have heard that on one occasion the Blessed One was staying near Vārāṇasī in the Deer Park at Isipatana. There he addressed the monks: "Monks!"

"Yes, lord," the monks responded to him.

The Blessed One said, "Monks, near Vārāṇasī, in the Deer Park at Isipatana, the Tathāgata—worthy & rightly self-awakened—set in motion the unexcelled Wheel of Dhamma that cannot be stopped by contemplative or brahman, deva, Māra, or Brahmā or anyone at all in the cosmos: in other words, the declaration, teaching, description, setting-forth, revelation, explanation, and making-plain of the four noble truths. Of which four? The declaration, teaching, description, setting-forth, revelation, explanation, and making-plain of the noble truth of stress. The declaration, teaching, description, setting forth, revelation, explanation, and making-plain of the noble truth of the origination of stress... the noble truth of the cessation of stress... the noble truth of the path of practice leading to the cessation of stress. Near Vārāṇasī, in the Deer Park at Isipatana, the Tathāgata—worthy & rightly self-awakened—set in motion the unexcelled Wheel of Dhamma that cannot be stopped by contemplative or brahman, deva, Māra, or Brahmā or anyone at all in the cosmos: in other words, the declaration, teaching, description, setting-forth, revelation, explanation, and making-plain of these four noble truths.

"Monks, associate with Sāriputta & Moggallāna. Consort with Sāriputta & Moggallāna. Sāriputta & Moggallāna are wise & sympathetic toward the monks who are their companions in the holy life. Like the mother giving birth: That's Sāriputta. Like the nurse raising a child after it's born: That's Moggallāna. Sāriputta trains (others) to the fruit of stream-entry; Moggallāna, to the highest goal.[1] Sāriputta is capable of declaring, teaching, describing, setting forth, revealing, explaining, and making plain the four noble truths in detail."

That is what the Blessed One said. Having said it, he—the One Well-Gone—rose from his seat and entered his dwelling.

Then Ven. Sāriputta, not long after the Blessed One had left, addressed the monks, "Friends!"

"Yes, friend," the monks responded to him.

Ven. Sāriputta said, "Friends, near Vārāṇasī, in the Deer Park at Isipatana, the Tathāgata—worthy & rightly self-awakened—set in motion the unexcelled Wheel of Dhamma that cannot be stopped by contemplative or brahman, deva, Māra, or Brahmā or anyone at all in the cosmos: in other words, the declaration, teaching, description, setting-forth, revelation, explanation, and making-plain of the four noble truths. Of which four? The declaration, teaching, description, setting-forth, revelation, explanation, and making-plain of the noble truth of stress... the noble truth of the origination of stress... the noble truth of the cessation of stress... the noble truth of the path of practice leading to the cessation of stress. Near Vārāṇasī, in the Deer Park at Isipatana, the Tathāgata—the worthy & rightly self-awakened—set in motion the unexcelled Wheel of Dhamma that cannot be stopped by contemplative or brahman, deva, Māra, or Brahmā or anyone at all in the cosmos: in other words, the declaration, teaching, description, setting-forth, revelation, explanation, and making-plain of these four noble truths.

"Now what, friends, is the noble truth of stress? Birth is stressful, aging is stressful, death is stressful; sorrow, lamentation, pain, distress, & despair are stressful; not getting what is wanted is stressful.[2] In short, the five clinging-aggregates are stressful.

"And what is *birth?* Whatever birth, taking birth, descent, coming-to-be, coming-forth, appearance of aggregates, & acquisition of (sense) spheres of the various beings in this or that group of beings, that is called birth.

"And what is *aging?* Whatever aging, decrepitude, brokenness, graying, wrinkling, decline of life-force, weakening of the faculties of the various beings in this or that group of beings, that is called aging.

"And what is *death?* Whatever deceasing, passing away, breaking up, disappearance, dying, death, completion of time, break-up of the aggregates, casting off of the body, interruption in the life faculty of the various beings in this or that group of beings, that is called death.

"And what is *sorrow?* Whatever sorrow, sorrowing, sadness, inward sorrow, inward sadness of anyone suffering from misfortune, touched by a painful thing, that is called sorrow.

"And what is *lamentation?* Whatever crying, grieving, lamenting, weeping, wailing, lamentation of anyone suffering from misfortune, touched by a painful thing, that is called lamentation.

"And what is *pain?* Whatever is experienced as bodily pain, bodily discomfort, pain or discomfort born of bodily contact, that is called pain.

"And what is *distress?* Whatever is experienced as mental pain, mental discomfort, pain or discomfort born of mental contact, that is called distress.

"And what is *despair?* Whatever despair, despondency, desperation of anyone suffering from misfortune, touched by a painful thing, that is called despair.

"And what is the stress of *not getting what is wanted?* In beings subject to birth, the wish arises, 'O, may we not be subject to birth, and may birth not come to us.' But this is not to be achieved by wishing. This is the stress of not getting what is wanted. In beings subject to aging... illness... death... sorrow, lamentation, pain, distress, & despair, the wish arises, 'O, may we not be subject to aging... illness... death... sorrow, lamentation, pain, distress, & despair, and may aging... illness... death... sorrow, lamentation, pain, distress, & despair not come to us.' But this is not to be achieved by wishing. This is the stress of not getting what is wanted.

"And what are the *five clinging-aggregates* that, in short, are stressful? The form clinging-aggregate, the feeling clinging-aggregate, the perception clinging-aggregate, the fabrication clinging-aggregate, the consciousness clinging-aggregate: These are called the five clinging-aggregates that, in short, are stressful.

"This, friends, is called the noble truth of stress.

"And what, friends, is the noble truth of the origination of stress? The craving that makes for further becoming—accompanied by passion & delight, relishing now here & now there—i.e., craving for sensuality, craving for becoming, craving for non-becoming.

"This is called the noble truth of the origination of stress.

"And what, friends, is the noble truth of the cessation of stress? The remainderless fading & cessation, renunciation, relinquishment, release, & letting go of that very craving.

"This is called the noble truth of the cessation of stress.

"And what, friends, is the noble truth of the path of practice leading to the cessation of stress? Just this very noble eightfold path: right view, right resolve, right speech, right action, right livelihood, right effort, right mindfulness, right concentration.

"And what is right view? Knowledge in terms of stress, knowledge in terms of the origination of stress, knowledge in terms of the cessation of stress, knowledge in terms of the way of practice leading to the cessation of stress: This is called right view.

"And what is right resolve? The resolve for renunciation, for freedom from ill will, for harmlessness: This is called right resolve.

"And what is right speech? Abstaining from lying, from divisive speech, from abusive speech, & from idle chatter: This is called right speech.

"And what is right action? Abstaining from taking life, from stealing, & from sexual misconduct: This is called right action.

"And what is right livelihood? There is the case where a disciple of the noble ones, having abandoned dishonest livelihood, keeps his life going with right livelihood: This is called right livelihood.

"And what is right effort? There is the case where a monk generates desire, endeavors, arouses persistence, upholds & exerts his intent for the sake of the non-arising of evil, unskillful qualities that have not yet arisen... for the sake of the abandoning of evil, unskillful qualities that have arisen... for the sake of the arising of skillful qualities that have not yet arisen... (and) for the maintenance, non-confusion, increase, plenitude, development, & culmination of skillful qualities that have arisen: This is called right effort.

"And what is right mindfulness? There is the case where a monk remains focused on the body in & of itself—ardent, alert, & mindful—putting aside greed & distress with reference to the world. He remains focused on feelings in & of themselves... the mind in & of itself... mental qualities in & of themselves—ardent, alert, & mindful—putting aside greed & distress with reference to the world. This is called right mindfulness.

"And what is right concentration? There is the case where a monk—quite secluded from sensuality, secluded from unskillful qualities—enters & remains in the first jhāna: rapture & pleasure born of seclusion, accompanied by directed thought & evaluation. With the stilling of directed thoughts & evaluations, he enters & remains in the second jhāna: rapture & pleasure born of concentration, unification of awareness free from directed thought & evaluation—internal assurance. With the fading of rapture he remains equanimous, mindful, & alert, and senses pleasure with the body. He enters & remains in the third jhāna, of which the noble ones declare, 'Equanimous & mindful, he has a pleasant abiding.' With the abandoning of pleasure & pain—as with the earlier disappearance of elation & distress—he enters & remains in the fourth jhāna: purity of equanimity & mindfulness, neither pleasure nor pain. This is called right concentration.

"This is called the noble truth of the path of practice leading to the cessation of stress.

"Friends, near Vārāṇasī, in the Deer Park at Isipatana, the Tathāgata—the worthy & rightly self-awakened—set in motion the unexcelled Wheel of Dhamma that cannot be stopped by contemplative or brahman, deva, Māra, or Brahmā or anyone at all in the cosmos: in other words, the declaration, teaching, description, setting-forth, revelation, explanation, and making-plain of these four noble truths."

That is what Ven. Sāriputta said. Gratified, the monks delighted in Ven. Sāriputta's words.

NOTES

1. The Buddha declared Sāriputta to be foremost among his disciples in terms of discernment; Moggallāna, foremost in terms of psychic powers. It might seem strange, then, that Sāriputta takes on what seems to be a lower job, but as many Buddhist teachers have commented, it's much harder to train an ordinary person to enter the stream than it is to train a stream-winner to reach the highest goal.

2. In passages where the Buddha defines stress, (e.g., SN 56:11, DN 22), he includes the statements, "association with the unbeloved is stressful; separation from the loved is stressful," prior to "not getting what one wants is stressful." For some reason, in passages where Ven. Sāriputta defines stress (here and at MN 9 and MN 28), he drops these statements from the definition.

See also: DN 22; SN 12:20; SN 56:11; AN 3:137

143 *The Exhortation to Anāthapiṇḍika*

Anāthapiṇḍikovāda Sutta

I have heard that on one occasion the Blessed One was staying near Sāvatthī in Jeta's Grove, Anāthapiṇḍika's monastery. And on that occasion Anāthapiṇḍika the householder was diseased, in pain, severely ill. Then Anāthapiṇḍika the householder said to one of his men, "Come, my good man. Go to the Blessed One and, on arrival, pay homage to his feet with your head in my name and say 'Lord, Anāthapiṇḍika the householder is diseased, in pain, severely ill. He pays homage with his head to the Blessed One's feet.' Then go to Ven. Sāriputta and, on arrival, pay homage to his feet with your head in my name and say 'Venerable sir, Anāthapiṇḍika the householder is diseased, in pain, severely ill. He pays homage with his head to your feet.' Then say: 'It would be good if Ven. Sāriputta would visit Anāthapiṇḍika's home, out of sympathy for him.'"

Responding, "As you say, lord," to Anāthapiṇḍika the householder, the man went to the Blessed One and, on arrival, having bowed down to him, sat to one side. As he was sitting there he said, "Lord, Anāthapiṇḍika the householder is diseased, in pain, severely ill. He pays homage with his head to the Blessed One's feet." Then he went to Ven. Sāriputta and, on arrival, having bowed down to him, sat to one side. As he was sitting there he said, 'Venerable sir, Anāthapiṇḍika the householder is diseased, in pain, severely ill. He pays homage with his head to your feet." Then he said, "It would be good if Ven. Sāriputta would visit Anāthapiṇḍika's home, out of sympathy for him."

Then Ven. Sāriputta—having adjusted his under robe and carrying his bowl & outer robe—went to the home of Anāthapiṇḍika the householder with Ven. Ānanda as his attendant. On arrival, he sat down on a seat made ready and said to Anāthapiṇḍika the householder: "I hope you are getting better, householder. I hope you are comfortable. I hope that your pains are lessening and not increasing. I hope that there are signs of their lessening, and not of their increasing."

[Anāthapiṇḍika:] "I am not getting better, venerable sir. I am not comfortable. My extreme pains are increasing, not lessening. There are signs of their increasing, and not of their lessening.

Extreme forces slice through my head, just as if a strong man were slicing my head open with a sharp sword.... Extreme pains have arisen in my head, just as if a strong man were tightening a turban made of tough leather straps around my head.... Extreme forces carve up my stomach cavity, just as if a butcher or his apprentice were to carve up the stomach cavity of an ox.... There is an extreme burning in my body, just as if two strong men, grabbing a weaker man by the arms, were to roast and broil him over a pit of hot embers. I am not getting better, venerable sir. I am not comfortable. My extreme pains are increasing, not lessening. There are signs of their increasing, and not of their lessening."

[Ven. Sāriputta:] "Then, householder, you should train yourself in this way: 'I won't cling to the eye; my consciousness will not be dependent on the eye.' That's how you should train yourself. 'I won't cling to the ear... nose... tongue... body; my consciousness will not be dependent on the body.' ... 'I won't cling to the intellect; my consciousness will not be dependent on the intellect.' That's how you should train yourself.

"Then, householder, you should train yourself in this way: 'I won't cling to forms... sounds... smells... tastes... tactile sensations; my consciousness will not be dependent on tactile sensations.' ... 'I won't cling to ideas; my consciousness will not be dependent on ideas.' That's how you should train yourself.

"Then, householder, you should train yourself in this way: 'I won't cling to eye-consciousness... ear-consciousness... nose-consciousness... tongue-consciousness... body-consciousness; my consciousness will not be dependent on body-consciousness.' ... 'I won't cling to intellect-consciousness; my consciousness will not be dependent on intellect-consciousness.' That's how you should train yourself.

"Then, householder, you should train yourself in this way: 'I won't cling to contact at the eye... contact at the ear... contact at the nose... contact at the tongue... contact at the body; my consciousness will not be dependent on contact at the body.' ... 'I won't cling to contact at the intellect; my consciousness will not be dependent on contact at the intellect.' That's how you should train yourself.

"Then, householder, you should train yourself in this way: 'I won't cling to feeling born of contact at the eye... feeling born of contact at the ear... feeling born of contact at the nose... feeling born of contact at the tongue... feeling born of contact at the body; my consciousness will not be dependent on feeling born of contact at the body.' ... 'I won't cling to feeling born of contact at the intellect; my consciousness will not be dependent on feeling born of contact at the intellect.' That's how you should train yourself.

"Then, householder, you should train yourself in this way: 'I won't cling to the earth property... liquid property... fire property... wind property... space property; my consciousness will not be dependent on the space property.' ... 'I won't cling to the consciousness property; my consciousness will not be dependent on the consciousness property.' That's how you should train yourself.

"Then, householder, you should train yourself in this way: 'I won't cling to form... feeling... perception... fabrications; my consciousness will not be dependent on fabrications.' ... 'I won't cling to consciousness; my consciousness will not be dependent on consciousness.' That's how you should train yourself.

"Then, householder, you should train yourself in this way: 'I won't cling to the dimension of the infinitude of space... the dimension of the infinitude of consciousness... the dimension of nothingness; my consciousness will not be dependent on the dimension of nothingness.' ... 'I won't cling to the dimension of neither perception nor non-perception; my consciousness will not be dependent on the dimension of neither perception nor non-perception.' That's how you should train yourself.

"Then, householder, you should train yourself in this way: 'I won't cling to this world; my consciousness will not be dependent on this world... I won't cling to the world beyond; my consciousness will not be dependent on the world beyond.' That's how you should train yourself.

"Then, householder, you should train yourself in this way: 'I won't cling to what is seen, heard, sensed, cognized, attained, sought after, pondered by the intellect; my consciousness will not be dependent on that.' That's how you should train yourself."

When this was said, Anāthapiṇḍika the householder wept and shed tears. Ven. Ānanda said to him, "Are you sinking, householder? Are you foundering?"

"No, venerable sir. I'm not sinking, nor am I foundering. It's just that for a long time I have attended to the Teacher, and to the monks who inspire my heart, but never before have I heard a talk on the Dhamma like this."

"This sort of talk on the Dhamma, householder, is not given to lay people clad in white. This sort of talk on the Dhamma is given to those gone forth."

"In that case, Ven. Sāriputta, please let this sort of talk on the Dhamma be given to lay people clad in white. There are clansmen with little dust in their eyes who are wasting away through not hearing (this) Dhamma. There will be those who will understand it."

Then Ven. Sāriputta and Ven. Ānanda, having given this instruction to Anāthapiṇḍika the householder, got up from their seats and left. Then, not long after they left, Anāthapiṇḍika the householder died and reappeared in the Tusita heaven. Then Anāthapiṇḍika the deva's son, in the far extreme of the night, his extreme radiance lighting up the entirety of Jeta's Grove, went to the Blessed One and, on arrival, having bowed down to him, stood to one side. As he was standing there, he addressed the Blessed One with this verse:

> This blessed Jeta's Grove,
> home to the community of seers,
> where there dwells the Dhamma King:
> the source of rapture for me.
>
> Action, clear-knowing, & mental qualities,[1]
> virtue, the highest (way of) life:
> Through this are mortals purified,
> not through clan or wealth.
>
> Thus the wise,
> seeing their own benefit,
> investigating the Dhamma appropriately,
> should purify themselves right there.
>
> As for Sāriputta:
> Any monk who has gone beyond,
> at best can only equal him
> in discernment, virtue, & calm.

That is what Anāthapiṇḍika the deva's son said. The Teacher approved. Then Anāthapiṇḍika the deva's son, (knowing,) "The Teacher has approved of me," bowed down to him, circled him three times, keeping him to his right, and then disappeared right there.

Then when the night had past, The Blessed One addressed the monks: "Last night, monks, a certain deva's son in the far extreme of the night, his extreme radiance lighting up the entirety of Jeta's Grove, came to me and, on arrival, having bowed down to me, stood to one side. As he was standing there, he addressed me with this verse:

This blessed Jeta's Grove,
home to the community of seers,
where there dwells the Dhamma King:
    the source of rapture for me.

Action, clear-knowing, & mental qualities,
virtue, the highest (way of) life:
    Through this are mortals purified,
    not through clan or wealth.

Thus the wise,
seeing their own benefit,
investigating the Dhamma appropriately,
should purify themselves right there.

As for Sāriputta:
    Any monk who has gone beyond,
    at best can only equal him
    in discernment, virtue, & calm.

"That is what the deva's son said. And (thinking,) 'The Teacher has approved of me,' he bowed down to me, circled me three times, and then disappeared right there."

When this was said, Ven. Ānanda said to the Blessed One, "Lord, that must have been Anāthapiṇḍika the deva's son. Anāthapiṇḍika the householder had supreme confidence in Ven. Sāriputta."

"Very good, Ānanda. Very good, to the extent that you have deduced what can be arrived at through logic. That *was* Anāthapiṇḍika the deva's son, and no one else."

That is what the Blessed One said. Gratified, Ven. Ānanda delighted in the Blessed One's words.

NOTE: 1. The Thai edition, which I have followed here, reads *dhammā:* mental qualities. Other editions read *dhammo:* the Dhamma. The Commentary maintains that this refers to the mental qualities conducive to concentration.

See also: MN 97; MN 138; SN 2:19; SN 10:8; SN 12:38; SN 12:64; SN 22:54; SN 41:10; SN 55:54; AN 4:184; AN 6:16; AN 7:58; AN 11:10; Ud 8:1; Sn 5:4

146 Nandaka's Exhortation

Nandakovāda Sutta

I have heard that on one occasion the Blessed One was staying near Sāvatthī in Jeta's Grove, Anāthapiṇḍika's monastery. Then Mahāpajāpati Gotamī, together with about 500 other nuns, went to the Blessed One and, on arrival, having bowed down to him, stood to one side. As she was standing there she said to him, "Lord, may the Blessed One exhort the nuns. Lord, may the Blessed One instruct the nuns. Lord, may the Blessed One give the nuns a talk on Dhamma."

Now at that time the elder monks were taking turns in exhorting the nuns, but Ven. Nandaka didn't want to exhort the nuns when his turn came. So the Blessed One addressed Ven. Ānanda: "Ānanda, whose turn is it to exhort the nuns today?"

"Lord, everyone has taken his turn[1] in exhorting the nuns, except for Ven. Nandaka, here, who doesn't want to exhort the nuns when his turn comes."

Then the Blessed One addressed Ven. Nandaka: "Exhort the nuns, Nandaka. Instruct the nuns, Nandaka. Give the nuns a talk on Dhamma, you brahman!"

"As you say, lord," Ven. Nandaka responded to the Blessed One. Then, early in the morning—having adjusted his under robe and carrying his bowl & outer robe—he went into Sāvatthī for alms. After his meal, on returning from his alms round, he went with a companion to Rājaka Park. The nuns saw him coming from afar and, on seeing him, arranged a seat and set out water for his feet. Ven. Nandaka sat down on the arranged seat and washed his feet. The nuns, having bowed down to him, sat to one side.

As they were sitting there, Ven. Nandaka said to them: "This will be a question-response talk, sisters. Where you understand, you should say, 'We understand.' Where you don't, you should say, 'We don't understand.' Where you are doubtful or perplexed, you should question me in response: 'How is this, venerable sir? What is the meaning of this?'"

"Venerable sir, we are gratified & delighted that you invite us in this way."

"So then, sisters, what do you think? Is the eye constant or inconstant?"

"Inconstant, venerable sir."

"And is that which is inconstant easeful or stressful?"

"Stressful, venerable sir."

"And is it fitting to regard what is inconstant, stressful, subject to change as: 'This is mine. This is my self. This is what I am'?"

"No, venerable sir."

"... Is the ear constant or inconstant?"

"Inconstant, venerable sir." ...

"... Is the nose constant or inconstant?"

"Inconstant, venerable sir." ...

"... Is the tongue constant or inconstant?"

"Inconstant, venerable sir." ...

"... Is the body constant or inconstant?"

"Inconstant, venerable sir." ...

"What do you think, sisters? Is the intellect constant or inconstant?"

"Inconstant, venerable sir."

"And is that which is inconstant easeful or stressful?"

"Stressful, venerable sir."

"And is it fitting to regard what is inconstant, stressful, subject to change as: 'This is mine. This is my self. This is what I am'?"

"No, venerable sir. Why is that? Because we have already seen it well as it has come to be, with right discernment, that these six internal media are inconstant."

"Good, good, sisters. That's how it is for a disciple of the noble ones who has seen it as it has come to be with right discernment.

"Now what do you think, sisters? Are forms constant or inconstant?" "Inconstant, venerable sir." "And is that which is inconstant easeful or stressful?" "Stressful, venerable sir." "And is it fitting to regard what is inconstant, stressful, subject to change as: 'This is mine. This is my self. This is what I am'?"

"No, venerable sir."

"... Are sounds constant or inconstant?"

"Inconstant, venerable sir." ...

"... Are aromas constant or inconstant?"

"Inconstant, venerable sir." ...

"... Are flavors constant or inconstant?"

"Inconstant, venerable sir." ...

"... Are tactile sensations constant or inconstant?"

"Inconstant, venerable sir." ...

"What do you think, sisters? Are ideas constant or inconstant?"

"Inconstant, venerable sir."

"And is that which is inconstant easeful or stressful?"

"Stressful, venerable sir."

"And is it fitting to regard what is inconstant, stressful, subject to change as: 'This is mine. This is my self. This is what I am'?"

"No, venerable sir. Why is that? Because we have already seen it well as it has come to be, with right discernment, that these six external media are also inconstant."

"Good, good, sisters. That's how it is for a disciple of the noble ones who has seen it as it has come to be with right discernment.

"Now what do you think, sisters? Is eye-consciousness constant or inconstant?"

"Inconstant, venerable sir."

"And is that which is inconstant easeful or stressful?"

"Stressful, venerable sir."

"And is it fitting to regard what is inconstant, stressful, subject to change as: 'This is mine. This is my self. This is what I am'?"

"No, venerable sir."

"... Is ear-consciousness constant or inconstant?"

"Inconstant, venerable sir." ...

"... Is nose-consciousness constant or inconstant?"

"Inconstant, venerable sir." ...

"... Is tongue-consciousness constant or inconstant?"

"Inconstant, venerable sir." ...

"... Is body-consciousness constant or inconstant?"

"Inconstant, venerable sir." ...

"What do you think, sisters? Is intellect-consciousness constant or inconstant?"

"Inconstant, venerable sir."

"And is that which is inconstant easeful or stressful?"

"Stressful, venerable sir." "And is it fitting to regard what is inconstant, stressful, subject to change as: 'This is mine. This is my self. This is what I am'?"

"No, venerable sir. Why is that? Because we have already seen it well as it has come to be, with right discernment, that these six consciousness-groups, too, are inconstant."

"Good, good, sisters. That's how it is for a disciple of the noble ones who has seen it as it has come to be with right discernment.

"Just as when the oil in a burning oil lamp is inconstant & subject to change, its wick is inconstant & subject to change, its flame is inconstant & subject to change, its light is inconstant & subject to change. If someone were to say, 'The oil in that burning oil lamp is inconstant & subject to change, its wick is inconstant & subject to change, its flame is inconstant & subject to change, but as for its light, that is constant, everlasting, eternal, & not subject to change': Would he be speaking rightly?"

"No, venerable sir. Why is that? Because the oil in that burning oil lamp is inconstant & subject to change, its wick is inconstant &

subject to change, its flame is inconstant & subject to change, so how much more should its light be inconstant & subject to change."

"In the same way, sisters, if someone were to say, 'My six internal media are inconstant, but what I experience based on the six internal media—pleasure, pain, or neither pleasure nor pain—that is constant, everlasting, eternal, & not subject to change': Would he be speaking rightly?"

"No, venerable sir. Why is that? Because each feeling arises dependent on its corresponding condition. With the cessation of its corresponding condition, it ceases."

"Good, good, sisters. That's how it is for a disciple of the noble ones who has seen it as it has come to be with right discernment.

"Just as when the root of a great, standing tree—possessed of heartwood—is inconstant & subject to change, its trunk is inconstant & subject to change, its branches & foliage are inconstant & subject to change, its shadow is inconstant & subject to change. If someone were to say, 'The root of that great, standing tree—possessed of heartwood—is inconstant & subject to change, its trunk is inconstant & subject to change, its branches & foliage are inconstant & subject to change, but as for its shadow, that is constant, everlasting, eternal, & not subject to change': Would he be speaking rightly?"

"No, venerable sir. Why is that? Because the root of that great, standing tree—possessed of heartwood—is inconstant & subject to change, its trunk is inconstant & subject to change, its branches & foliage are inconstant & subject to change, so how much more should its shadow be inconstant & subject to change."

"In the same way, sisters, if someone were to say, 'My six external media are inconstant, but what I experience based on the six external media—pleasure, pain, or neither pleasure nor pain—that is constant, everlasting, eternal, & not subject to change': Would he be speaking rightly?"

"No, venerable sir. Why is that? Because each feeling arises dependent on its corresponding condition. With the cessation of its corresponding condition, it ceases."

"Good, good, sisters. That's how it is for a disciple of the noble ones who has seen it as it has come to be with right discernment.

"Just as if a dexterous butcher or butcher's apprentice, having killed a cow, were to carve it up with a sharp carving knife so that—without damaging the substance of the inner flesh, without damaging the substance of the outer hide—he would cut, sever, & detach only the skin muscles, connective tissues, & attachments in between. Having cut, severed, & detached the outer skin, and then covering the cow again with that very skin, if he were to say that the cow was joined to the skin just as it had been: Would he be speaking rightly?"

"No, venerable sir. Why is that? Because if the dexterous butcher or butcher's apprentice, having killed a cow, were to… cut, sever, & detach only the skin muscles, connective tissues, & attachments in between; and… having covered the cow again with that very skin, then no matter how much he might say that the cow was joined to the skin just as it had been, the cow would still be disjoined from the skin."

"This simile, sisters, I have given to convey a message. The message is this: The substance of the inner flesh stands for the six internal media; the substance of the outer hide, for the six external media. The skin muscles, connective tissues, & attachments in between stand for passion & delight. And the sharp knife stands for noble discernment—the noble discernment that cuts, severs, & detaches the defilements, fetters, & bonds in between.[2]

"Sisters, there are these seven factors for awakening[3] through whose development & pursuit a monk enters & remains in the effluent-free awareness-release & discernment-release,[4] having directly known & realized them for himself right in the here & now. Which seven? There is the case where a monk develops *mindfulness* as a factor for awakening dependent on seclusion, dependent on dispassion, dependent on cessation, resulting in relinquishment. He develops *analysis of qualities* as a factor for awakening… *persistence* as a factor for awakening… *rapture* as a factor for awakening… *calm* as a factor for awakening… *concentration* as a factor for awakening… *equanimity* as a factor for awakening dependent on seclusion, dependent on dispassion, dependent on cessation, resulting in relinquishment. These are the seven factors for awakening through whose development & pursuit a monk enters & remains in the effluent-free awareness-release & discernment-release, having directly known & realized them for himself right in the here & now."

Then, having exhorted the nuns with this exhortation, Ven. Nandaka dismissed them, saying, "Go, sisters. The time has come." The nuns, delighting in and approving of Ven. Nandaka's exhortation, got up from their seats, bowed down to him, circumambulated him—keeping him to the right—and went to the Blessed One. On arrival, having bowed down to the Blessed One, they stood to one side. As they were standing there, the Blessed One said to them, "Go, nuns. The time has come." So the nuns, having bowed down to the Blessed One, circumambulated him—keeping him to the right—and departed.

Then not long after the nuns' departure the Blessed One addressed the monks: "Monks, just as on the uposatha day of the fourteenth, people at large are not doubtful or perplexed as to whether the moon is lacking or full, for it is clearly lacking[5]; in the same way, even though the nuns are gratified with Nandaka's Dhamma-teaching, their resolves have not yet been fulfilled." So he addressed Ven. Nandaka: "In that case, Nandaka, exhort the nuns again tomorrow with the exact same exhortation."

"As you say, lord," Ven. Nandaka replied. Then, after the night had passed, early in the morning—having adjusted his under robe and carrying his bowl & outer robe—he went into Sāvatthī for alms... [as before, up to:]

Then not long after the nuns' departure the Blessed One addressed the monks: "Monks, just as on the uposatha day of the fifteenth, people at large are not doubtful or perplexed as to whether the moon is lacking or full, for it is clearly full; in the same way, the nuns are gratified with Nandaka's Dhamma-teaching, and their resolves have been fulfilled. Of these 500 nuns, the most backward is a stream-winner, not destined for the planes of deprivation, headed to self-awakening for sure."

That is what the Blessed One said. Gratified, the monks delighted in the Blessed One's words.

NOTES

1. This phrase is not in the PTS edition.

2. This simile also illustrates the point that the arahant, after awakening, is still aware of contact via the six sense media, but senses it "disjoined from it." See MN 140.

3. The commentary explains that Ven. Nandaka introduces the topic of the seven factors of awakening here to indicate where the nuns have more work to do in their practice. From the questions and answers, it is obvious that they have developed the second factor of awakening—analysis of qualities (or dhammas)—which is the factor associated with insight and discernment. However, for their resolves to be fulfilled, they need to focus on developing the factors associated with tranquility and concentration.

4. On awareness-release and discernment-release, see MN 43, AN 3:30, and AN 9:44. Discernment-release is always transcendent; awareness-release, only when effluent-free.

5. Apparently, in the Buddha's time, the 29-day lunar month was divided so that the half ending in the new moon uposatha had fourteen days, and the half ending in the full moon uposatha, fifteen. How they compensated for the fact that the lunar month is not exactly 29 days is not known.

See also: SN 35:93; SN 35:101; SN 35:193; SN 36:7; SN 46:51; AN 4:94

147 The Shorter Exhortation to Rāhula

Cūḷa Rāhulovāda Sutta

I have heard that on one occasion the Blessed One was staying near Sāvatthī in Jeta's Grove, Anāthapiṇḍika's Monastery. Then, as he was alone in seclusion, this line of thinking arose in the Blessed One's awareness: "The mental qualities that ripen in release have ripened in Rāhula. What if I were to lead Rāhula further to the ending of the effluents?"

Then the Blessed One, early in the morning—having adjusted his under robe and carrying his bowl & outer robe—went into Sāvatthī for alms. Having gone for alms in Sāvatthī, after the meal, returning from his alms round, he said to Ven. Rāhula, "Fetch your sitting cloth, Rāhula. We will go to the Grove of the Blind to spend the day."

Responding, "As you say, lord," to the Blessed One, Ven. Rāhula, carrying his sitting cloth, followed behind the Blessed One. Now at that time, many thousands of devas were following behind the Blessed One, (thinking,) "Today the Blessed One will lead Ven. Rāhula further to the ending of the effluents."

Then the Blessed One, having plunged into the Grove of the Blind, sat down on a seat made ready at the foot of a tree. Ven. Rāhula, having bowed down to the Blessed One, sat to one side.

As he was sitting there, the Blessed One said to him, "What do you think, Rāhula? Is the eye constant or inconstant?"

"Inconstant, lord."

"And is that which is inconstant easeful or stressful?"

"Stressful, lord."

"And is it fitting to regard what is inconstant, stressful, subject to change as: 'This is mine. This is my self. This is what I am'?"

"No, lord."

"What do you think? Are forms constant or inconstant?"

"Inconstant, lord."

"And is that which is inconstant easeful or stressful?"

"Stressful, lord."

"And is it fitting to regard what is inconstant, stressful, subject to change as: 'This is mine. This is my self. This is what I am'?"

"No, lord."

"What do you think? Is consciousness at the eye constant or inconstant?"

"Inconstant, lord."

"And is that which is inconstant easeful or stressful?"

"Stressful, lord."

"And is it fitting to regard what is inconstant, stressful, subject to change as: 'This is mine. This is my self. This is what I am'?"

"No, lord."

"What do you think? Is contact at the eye constant or inconstant?"

"Inconstant, lord."

"And is that which is inconstant easeful or stressful?"

"Stressful, lord."

"And is it fitting to regard what is inconstant, stressful, subject to change as: 'This is mine. This is my self. This is what I am'?"

"No, lord."

"What do you think? Whatever there is that arises in dependence on contact at the eye as a mode of feeling, a mode of perception, a mode of fabrication, or a mode of consciousness:[1] Is it constant or inconstant?"

"Inconstant, lord."

"And is that which is inconstant easeful or stressful?"

"Stressful, lord."

"And is it fitting to regard what is inconstant, stressful, subject to change as: 'This is mine. This is my self. This is what I am'?"

"No, lord."

"What do you think, Rāhula? Is the ear constant or inconstant?"

"Inconstant, lord" …

"What do you think, Rāhula? Is the nose constant or inconstant?"

"Inconstant, lord" …

"What do you think, Rāhula? Is the tongue constant or inconstant?"

"Inconstant, lord" …

"What do you think, Rāhula? Is the body constant or inconstant?"

"Inconstant, lord" …

"What do you think, Rāhula? Is the intellect constant or inconstant?"

"Inconstant, lord."

"And is that which is inconstant easeful or stressful?"

"Stressful, lord."

"And is it fitting to regard what is inconstant, stressful, subject to change as: 'This is mine. This is my self. This is what I am'?"

"No, lord."

"What do you think? Are ideas constant or inconstant?"

"Inconstant, lord."

"And is that which is inconstant easeful or stressful?"

"Stressful, lord."

"And is it fitting to regard what is inconstant, stressful, subject to change as: 'This is mine. This is my self. This is what I am'?"

"No, lord."

"What do you think? Is consciousness at the intellect constant or inconstant?"

"Inconstant, lord."

"And is that which is inconstant easeful or stressful?"

"Stressful, lord."

"And is it fitting to regard what is inconstant, stressful, subject to change as: 'This is mine. This is my self. This is what I am'?"

"No, lord."

"What do you think? Is contact at the intellect constant or inconstant?"

"Inconstant, lord."

"And is that which is inconstant easeful or stressful?"

"Stressful, lord."

"And is it fitting to regard what is inconstant, stressful, subject to change as: 'This is mine. This is my self. This is what I am'?"

"No, lord."

"What do you think? Whatever there is that arises in dependence on contact at the intellect as a mode of feeling, a mode of perception, a mode of fabrication, or a mode of consciousness: Is it constant or inconstant?"

"Inconstant, lord."

"And is that which is inconstant easeful or stressful?"

"Stressful, lord."

"And is it fitting to regard what is inconstant, stressful, subject to change as: 'This is mine. This is my self. This is what I am'?"

"No, lord."

"Seeing thus, Rāhula, the instructed disciple of the noble ones grows disenchanted with the eye, disenchanted with forms, disenchanted with consciousness at the eye, disenchanted with contact at the eye. And whatever there is that arises in dependence on contact at the eye as a mode of feeling, a mode of perception, a mode of fabrication, or a mode of consciousness: With that, too, he grows disenchanted.

"He grows disenchanted with the ear. . . .

"He grows disenchanted with the nose. . . .

"He grows disenchanted with the tongue. . . .

"He grows disenchanted with the body. . . .

"He grows disenchanted with the intellect, disenchanted with ideas, disenchanted with consciousness at the intellect, disenchanted with contact at the intellect. And whatever there is that arises in dependence on contact at the intellect as a mode of feeling, a mode of perception, a mode of fabrication, or a mode of consciousness: With that, too, he grows disenchanted. Disenchanted, he becomes dispassionate. Through dispassion, he is released. With release, there is the knowledge, 'Released.' He discerns that 'Birth is ended, the holy life fulfilled, the task done. There is nothing further for this world.'"

That is what the Blessed One said. Gratified, Ven. Rāhula delighted in the Blessed One's words. And while this explanation was being given, Ven. Rāhula's mind, through lack of clinging/sustenance, was released from effluents. And to those many thousands of devas there arose the dustless, stainless Dhamma eye: "Whatever is subject to origination is all subject to cessation."

NOTE: 1. The Buddha's basic approach in this discourse is to take a line of questioning that he usually applies to the five aggregates (see SN 22:59) and to apply it to the framework of the six sense media as given in SN 35:28. This phrase, however, is the one point where this sutta deviates from that framework. The corresponding phrase in SN 35:28 focuses exclusively on feelings. The passage here—*vedanāgataṁ, saññāgataṁ, saṅkhārāgataṁ, viññāṇagataṁ*—focuses on all four mental aggregates. For another example of translating *–gataṁ* as "mode," see the phrase "mode of perception" *(saññāgataṁ)* in MN 121. For another example of a teaching that combines the two frameworks of five aggregates and six sense media, see MN 28.

See also: MN 61; MN 62; Thag 4:8

148 The Six Sextets

Chachakka Sutta

I have heard that on one occasion the Blessed One was staying near Sāvatthī in Jeta's Grove, Anāthapiṇḍika's Monastery. There he addressed the monks: "Monks!"

"Yes, lord," the monks responded to him.

"Monks, I will teach you the Dhamma admirable in the beginning, admirable in the middle, admirable in the end; I will expound the holy life both in its particulars & in its essence, entirely complete, surpassingly pure—in other words, the six sextets. Listen & pay close attention. I will speak."

"As you say, lord," the monks responded to him.

The Blessed One said: "The six internal media should be known. The six external media should be known. The six classes of consciousness should be known. The six classes of contact should be known. The six classes of feeling should be known. The six classes of craving should be known.

"'The six internal media should be known.' Thus it was said. In reference to what was it said? The eye-medium, the ear-medium, the nose-medium, the tongue-medium, the body-medium, the intellect-medium. 'The six internal media should be known.' Thus it was said. And in reference to this was it said. This is the first sextet.

"'The six external media should be known.' Thus it was said. In reference to what was it said? The form-medium, the sound-medium, the aroma-medium, the flavor-medium, the tactile sensation-medium, the idea-medium. 'The six external media should be known.' Thus it was said. And in reference to this was it said. This is the second sextet.

"'The six classes of consciousness should be known.' Thus it was said. In reference to what was it said? Dependent on the eye & forms there arises consciousness at the eye. Dependent on the ear & sounds there arises consciousness at the ear. Dependent on the nose & aromas there arises consciousness at the nose. Dependent on the tongue & flavors there arises consciousness at the tongue. Dependent on the body & tactile sensations there arises consciousness at the body. Dependent on the intellect & ideas there arises consciousness at the intellect. 'The six classes of consciousness should be known.' Thus it was said. And in reference to this was it said. This is the third sextet.

"'The six classes of contact should be known.' Thus it was said. In reference to what was it said? Dependent on the eye & forms there arises consciousness at the eye. The meeting of the three is contact. Dependent on the ear & sounds there arises consciousness at the ear. The meeting of the three is contact. Dependent on the nose & aromas there arises consciousness at the nose. The meeting of the three is contact. Dependent on the tongue & flavors there arises consciousness at the tongue. The meeting of the three is contact. Dependent on the body & tactile sensations there arises consciousness at the body. The meeting of the three is contact. Dependent on the intellect & ideas there arises consciousness at the intellect. The meeting of the three is contact. 'The six classes of contact should be known.' Thus it was said. And in reference to this was it said. This is the fourth sextet.

"'The six classes of feeling should be known.' Thus it was said. In reference to what was it said? Dependent on the eye & forms there arises consciousness at the eye. The meeting of the three is contact. With contact as a requisite condition there is feeling. Dependent on the ear & sounds there arises consciousness at the ear. The meeting of the three is contact. With contact as a requisite condition there is feeling. Dependent on the nose & aromas there arises consciousness at the nose. The meeting of the three is contact. With contact as a requisite condition there is feeling. Dependent on the tongue & flavors there arises consciousness at the tongue. The meeting of the three is contact. With contact as a requisite condition there is feeling. Dependent on the body & tactile sensations there arises consciousness at the body. The meeting of the three is contact. With contact as a requisite condition there is feeling. Dependent on the intellect & ideas there arises consciousness at the intellect. The meeting of the three is contact. With contact as a requisite condition there is feeling. 'The six classes of feeling should be known.' Thus it was said. And in reference to this was it said. This is the fifth sextet.

"'The six classes of craving should be known.' Thus it was said. In reference to what was it said? Dependent on the eye & forms there arises consciousness at the eye. The meeting of the three is contact. With contact as a requisite condition there is feeling. With feeling as a requisite condition there is craving. Dependent on the ear & sounds there arises consciousness at the ear. The meeting of the three is contact. With contact as a requisite condition there is feeling. With feeling as a requisite condition there is craving. Dependent on the nose & aromas there arises consciousness at the nose. The meeting of the three is contact. With contact as a requisite condition there is feeling. With feeling as a requisite condition there is craving. Dependent on the tongue & flavors there arises consciousness at the tongue. The meeting of the three is contact. With contact as a requisite condition there is feeling. With feeling as a requisite condition there is craving. Dependent on the body & tactile sensations there arises consciousness at the body. The meeting of the three is contact. With contact as a requisite condition there is feeling. With feeling as a requisite condition there is craving. Dependent on the intellect & ideas there arises consciousness at the intellect. The meeting of the three is contact. With contact as a requisite condition there is feeling. With feeling as a requisite condition there is craving. 'The six classes of craving should be known.' Thus it was said. And in reference to this was it said. This is the sixth sextet.

"If anyone were to say, 'The eye is the self,' that wouldn't be tenable. The arising & falling away of the eye are discerned. And when its arising & falling away are discerned, it would follow that 'My self arises & falls away.' That's why it wouldn't be tenable if anyone were to say, 'The eye is the self.' So the eye is not-self.[1] If anyone were to say, 'Forms are the self,' that wouldn't be tenable.... Thus the eye is not-self and forms are not-self. If anyone were to say, 'Consciousness at the eye is the self,' that wouldn't be tenable.... Thus the eye is not-self, forms are not-self, consciousness at the eye is not-self. If anyone were to say, 'Contact at the eye is the self,' that wouldn't be tenable.... Thus the eye is not-self, forms are not-self, consciousness at the eye is not-self, contact at the eye is not-self. If anyone were to say, 'Feeling is the self,' that wouldn't be tenable.... Thus the eye is not-self, forms are not-self, consciousness at the eye is not-self, contact at the eye is not-self, feeling is not self. If anyone were to say, 'Craving is the self,' that wouldn't be tenable. The arising & falling away of craving are discerned. And when its arising & falling away are discerned, it would follow that 'My self arises & falls away.' That's why it wouldn't be tenable if anyone were to say, 'Craving is the self.' Thus the eye is not-self, forms are not-self, consciousness at the eye is not-self, contact at the eye is not-self, feeling is not self, craving is not-self.

"If anyone were to say, 'The ear is the self,' that wouldn't be tenable....

"If anyone were to say, 'The nose is the self,' that wouldn't be tenable...."

"If anyone were to say, 'The tongue is the self,' that wouldn't be tenable....

"If anyone were to say, 'The body is the self,' that wouldn't be tenable....

"If anyone were to say, 'The intellect is the self,' that wouldn't be tenable. The arising & falling away of the intellect are discerned. And when its arising & falling away are discerned, it would follow that 'My self arises & falls away.' That's why it wouldn't be tenable if anyone were to say, 'The intellect is the self.' So the intellect is not-self. If anyone were to say, 'Ideas are the self,' that wouldn't be tenable.... Thus the intellect is not-self and ideas are not-self. If anyone were to say, 'Consciousness at the intellect is the self,' that wouldn't be tenable.... Thus the intellect is not-self, ideas are not-self, consciousness at the intellect is not-self. If anyone were to say, 'Contact at the intellect is the self,' that wouldn't be tenable.... Thus the intellect is not-self, ideas are not-self, consciousness at the intellect is not-self, contact at the intellect is not-self. If anyone were to say, 'Feeling is the self,' that wouldn't be tenable.... Thus the intellect is not-self, ideas are not-self, consciousness at the intellect is not-self, contact at the intellect is not-self, feeling is not self. If anyone were to say, 'Craving is the self,' that wouldn't be tenable. The arising & falling away of craving are discerned. And when its arising & falling away are discerned, it would follow that 'My self arises & falls away.' That's why it wouldn't be tenable if anyone were to say, 'Craving is the self.' Thus the intellect is not-self, ideas are not-self, consciousness at the intellect is not-self, contact at the intellect is not-self, feeling is not self, craving is not-self.

"This, monks, is the path of practice leading to self-identification. One assumes about the eye that 'This is me, this is my self, this is what I am.' One assumes about forms.... One assumes about consciousness at the eye.... One assumes about contact at the eye.... One assumes about feeling.... One assumes about craving that 'This is me, this is my self, this is what I am.'

"One assumes about the ear....

"One assumes about the nose....

"One assumes about the tongue....

"One assumes about the body....

"One assumes about the intellect that 'This is me, this is my self, this is what I am.' One assumes about ideas.... One assumes about consciousness at the intellect.... One assumes about contact at the intellect.... One assumes about feeling.... One assumes about craving that 'This is me, this is my self, this is what I am.'

"Now, this is the path of practice leading to the cessation of self-identification. One assumes about the eye that 'This is not me, this is not my self, this is not what I am.' One assumes about forms.... One assumes about consciousness at the eye.... One assumes about contact at the eye.... One assumes about feeling.... One assumes about craving that 'This is not me, this is not my self, this is not what I am.'

"One assumes about the ear....

"One assumes about the nose....

"One assumes about the tongue....

"One assumes about the body....

"One assumes about the intellect that 'This is not me, this is not my self, this is not what I am.' One assumes about ideas.... One assumes about consciousness at the intellect.... One assumes about contact at the intellect.... One assumes about feeling.... One assumes about craving that 'This is not me, this is not my self, this is not what I am.'

"Dependent on the eye & forms there arises consciousness at the eye. The meeting of the three is contact. With contact as a requisite condition, there arises what is felt either as pleasure, pain, or neither pleasure nor pain. If, when touched by a feeling of pleasure, one relishes it, welcomes it, or remains fastened to it, then one's passion-obsession gets obsessed. If, when touched by a feeling of pain, one sorrows, grieves, & laments, beats one's breast, becomes distraught, then one's resistance-obsession gets obsessed. If, when touched by a feeling of neither pleasure nor pain, one does not discern, as it has come to be, the origination, passing away, allure, drawback, or escape from that feeling, then one's ignorance-obsession gets obsessed. That a person—without abandoning passion-obsession with regard to a feeling of pleasure, without abolishing resistance-obsession with regard to a feeling of pain, without uprooting ignorance-obsession with regard to a feeling of neither pleasure nor pain, without abandoning ignorance and giving rise to clear knowing—would put an end to suffering & stress in the here & now: Such a thing isn't possible.

"Dependent on the ear & sounds....

"Dependent on the nose & aromas....

"Dependent on the tongue & flavors....

"Dependent on the body & tactile sensations....

"Dependent on the intellect & ideas there arises consciousness at the intellect. The meeting of the three is contact. With contact as a requisite condition, there arises what is felt either as pleasure, pain, or neither pleasure nor pain. If, when touched by a feeling of pleasure, one relishes it, welcomes it, or remains fastened to it, then one's passion-obsession gets obsessed. If, when touched by a feeling of pain, one sorrows, grieves, & laments, beats one's breast, becomes distraught, then one's resistance-obsession gets obsessed. If, when touched by a feeling of neither pleasure nor pain, one does not discern, as it has come to be, the origination, passing away, allure, drawback, or escape from that feeling, then one's ignorance-obsession gets obsessed. That a person—without abandoning passion-obsession with regard to a feeling of pleasure, without abolishing resistance-obsession with regard to a feeling of pain, without uprooting ignorance-obsession with regard to a feeling of neither pleasure nor pain, without abandoning ignorance and giving rise to clear knowing—would put an end to suffering & stress in the here & now: Such a thing isn't possible.

"Dependent on the eye & forms there arises consciousness at the eye. The meeting of the three is contact. With contact as a requisite condition, there arises what is felt either as pleasure, pain, or neither pleasure nor pain. If, when touched by a feeling of pleasure, one does not relish it, welcome it, or remain fastened to it, then one's passion-obsession doesn't get obsessed. If, when touched by a feeling of pain, one does not sorrow, grieve, or lament, beat one's breast or become distraught, then one's resistance-obsession doesn't get obsessed. If, when touched by a feeling of neither pleasure nor pain, one discerns, as it has come to be, the origination, passing away, allure, drawback, & escape from that feeling, then one's ignorance-obsession doesn't get obsessed. That a person—through abandoning passion-obsession with regard to a feeling of pleasure, through abolishing resistance-obsession with regard to a feeling of pain, through uprooting ignorance-obsession with regard to a feeling of neither pleasure nor pain, through abandoning ignorance and giving rise to clear knowing—would put an end to suffering & stress in the here & now: Such a thing is possible.

"Dependent on the ear & sounds....

"Dependent on the nose & aromas....

"Dependent on the tongue & flavors....

"Dependent on the body & tactile sensations....

"Dependent on the intellect & ideas there arises consciousness at the intellect. The meeting of the three is contact. With contact as a requisite condition, there arises what is felt either as pleasure, pain, or neither pleasure nor pain. If, when touched by a feeling of pleasure, one does not relish it, welcome it, or remain fastened to it, then one's passion-obsession does not get obsessed. If, when touched by a feeling of pain, one does not sorrow, grieve, or lament, beat one's breast or become distraught, then one's resistance-obsession does not get obsessed. If, when touched by a feeling of neither pleasure nor pain, one discerns, as it has come to be, the origination, passing away, allure, drawback, & escape from that feeling, then one's ignorance-obsession does not get obsessed. That a person—through abandoning passion-obsession with regard to a feeling of pleasure, through abolishing resistance-obsession with regard to a feeling of pain, through uprooting ignorance-obsession with regard to a feeling of neither pleasure nor pain, through abandoning ignorance and giving rise to clear knowing—would put an end to suffering & stress in the here & now: Such a thing is possible.

"Seeing thus, the instructed disciple of the noble ones grows disenchanted with the eye, disenchanted with forms, disenchanted with consciousness at the eye, disenchanted with contact at the eye, disenchanted with feeling, disenchanted with craving.

"He grows disenchanted with the ear…

"He grows disenchanted with the nose…

"He grows disenchanted with the tongue…

"He grows disenchanted with the body…

"He grows disenchanted with the intellect, disenchanted with ideas, disenchanted with consciousness at the intellect, disenchanted with contact at the intellect, disenchanted with feeling, disenchanted with craving. Disenchanted, he becomes dispassionate. Through dispassion, he is released. With release, there is the knowledge, 'Released.' He discerns that 'Birth is ended, the holy life fulfilled, the task done. There is nothing further for this world.'"

That is what the Blessed One said. Gratified, the monks delighted at his words. And while this explanation was being given, the hearts of sixty monks, through lack of clinging/sustenance, were released from effluents.

NOTE: 1. The reasoning here appears to be that nothing can discern itself arising and passing away, so if one can discern x arising and passing away, one cannot be identical with x. So x cannot be one's self.

See also: DN 15; MN 18; MN 44; SN 22:56; SN 35:23; SN 35:191

149 The Great Six Sense-Media Discourse

Mahā Saḷāyatanika Sutta

I have heard that on one occasion the Blessed One was staying near Sāvatthī in Jeta's Grove, Anāthapiṇḍika's Monastery. There he addressed the monks: "Monks!"

"Yes, lord," the monks responded to him.

"Monks, I will teach you the great six sense-media (discourse). Listen & pay close attention. I will speak."

"As you say, lord," the monks responded to him.

The Blessed One said: "Not knowing, not seeing the eye as it has come to be; not knowing, not seeing forms… consciousness at the eye… contact at the eye as they have come to be; not knowing, not seeing whatever arises conditioned through contact at the eye—experienced as pleasure, pain, or neither-pleasure-nor-pain—as it has come to be, one is infatuated with the eye… forms… consciousness at the eye… contact at the eye… whatever arises conditioned by contact at the eye and is experienced as pleasure, pain, or neither-pleasure-nor-pain.

"For him—infatuated, attached, confused, not remaining focused on their drawbacks—the five clinging-aggregates head toward future accumulation. The craving that makes for further becoming—accompanied by passion & delight, relishing now here & now here—grows within him. His bodily disturbances & mental disturbances grow. His bodily torments & mental torments grow. His bodily distresses & mental distresses grow. He is sensitive both to bodily stress & mental stress.

"Not knowing, not seeing the ear.... Not knowing, not seeing the nose.... Not knowing, not seeing the tongue.... Not knowing, not seeing the body....

"Not knowing, not seeing the intellect as it has come to be; not knowing, not seeing ideas… consciousness at the intellect… contact at the intellect as they have come to be; not knowing, not seeing whatever arises conditioned through intellect-contact—experienced as pleasure, pain, or neither-pleasure-nor-pain—as it has come to be, one is infatuated with the intellect… ideas… consciousness at the intellect… contact at the intellect… whatever arises conditioned by contact at the intellect and is experienced as pleasure, pain, or neither-pleasure-nor-pain.

"For him—infatuated, attached, confused, not remaining focused on their drawbacks—the five clinging-aggregates head toward future accumulation. The craving that makes for further becoming—accompanied by passion & delight, relishing now here & now there—grows within him. His bodily disturbances & mental disturbances grow. His bodily torments & mental torments grow. His bodily distresses & mental distresses grow. He is sensitive both to bodily stress & mental stress.

"However, knowing & seeing the eye as it has come to be, knowing & seeing forms... consciousness at the eye... contact at the eye as they have come to be, knowing & seeing whatever arises conditioned through contact at the eye—experienced as pleasure, pain, or neither-pleasure-nor-pain—as it has come to be, one is not infatuated with the eye... forms... consciousness at the eye... contact at the eye... whatever arises conditioned by contact at the eye and is experienced as pleasure, pain, or neither-pleasure-nor-pain.

"For him—uninfatuated, unattached, unconfused, remaining focused on their drawbacks—the five clinging-aggregates head toward future diminution. The craving that makes for further becoming—accompanied by passion & delight, relishing now here & now there—is abandoned by him. His bodily disturbances & mental disturbances are abandoned. His bodily torments & mental torments are abandoned. His bodily distresses & mental distresses are abandoned. He is sensitive both to ease of body & ease of awareness.

"Any view belonging to one who has come to be like this is his right view. Any resolve, his right resolve. Any effort, his right effort. Any mindfulness, his right mindfulness. Any concentration, his right concentration: just as earlier his actions, speech, & livelihood were already well-purified. Thus for him, having thus developed the noble eightfold path, the four establishings of mindfulness go to the culmination of their development. The four right exertions... the four bases of power... the five faculties... the five strengths... the seven factors for awakening go to the culmination of their development.[1] (And) for him these two qualities occur in tandem: tranquility & insight.

"He comprehends through direct knowledge whatever qualities are to be comprehended through direct knowledge, abandons through direct knowledge whatever qualities are to be abandoned through direct knowledge, develops through direct knowledge whatever qualities are to be developed through direct knowledge, and realizes through direct knowledge whatever qualities are to be realized through direct knowledge.

"And which qualities are to be comprehended through direct knowledge? 'The five clinging-aggregates,' should be the reply. Which five? The form clinging-aggregate, the feeling clinging-aggregate, the perception clinging-aggregate, the fabrications clinging-aggregate, the consciousness clinging-aggregate: These are the qualities that are to be comprehended through direct knowledge.

"And which qualities are to be abandoned through direct knowledge? Ignorance & craving for becoming: These are the qualities that are to be abandoned through direct knowledge.

"And which qualities are to be developed through direct knowledge? Tranquility & insight: these are the qualities that are to be developed through direct knowledge.

"And which qualities are to be realized through direct knowledge? Clear knowing & release: These are the qualities that are to be realized through direct knowledge.[2]

"Knowing & seeing the ear....

"Knowing & seeing the nose....

"Knowing & seeing the tongue....

"Knowing & seeing the body....

"Knowing & seeing the intellect as it has come to be, knowing & seeing ideas... consciousness at the intellect... contact at the intellect as they have come to be, knowing & seeing whatever arises conditioned through contact at the intellect—experienced as pleasure, pain, or neither-pleasure-nor-pain—as it has come to be, one is not infatuated with the intellect... ideas... consciousness at the intellect... contact at the intellect... whatever arises conditioned by contact at the intellect and is experienced as pleasure, pain, or neither-pleasure-nor-pain.

"For him—uninfatuated, unattached, unconfused, remaining focused on their drawbacks—the five clinging-aggregates head toward future diminution. The craving that makes for further becoming—accompanied by passion & delight, relishing now here & now there—is abandoned by him. His bodily disturbances & mental disturbances are abandoned. His bodily torments & mental torments are abandoned. His bodily distresses & mental distresses are abandoned. He is sensitive both to ease of body & ease of awareness.

"Any view belonging to one who has come to be like this is his right view. Any resolve, his right resolve. Any effort, his right effort. Any mindfulness, his right mindfulness. Any concentration, his right concentration: just as earlier his actions, speech, & livelihood were already well-purified. Thus for him, having thus developed the noble eightfold path, the four establishings of mindfulness go to the culmination of their development. The four right exertions... the four bases of power... the five faculties... the five strengths... the seven factors for awakening go to the culmination of their development. (And) for him these two qualities occur in tandem: tranquility & insight.

"He comprehends through direct knowledge whatever qualities are to be comprehended through direct knowledge, abandons through direct knowledge whatever qualities are to be abandoned through direct knowledge, develops through direct knowledge whatever qualities are to be developed through direct knowledge, and realizes through direct knowledge whatever qualities are to be realized through direct knowledge.

"And which qualities are to be comprehended through direct knowledge? 'The five clinging-aggregates,' should be the reply. Which five? The form clinging-aggregate, the feeling clinging-aggregate, the perception clinging-aggregate, the fabrications clinging-aggregate, the consciousness clinging-aggregate: These are the qualities that are to be comprehended through direct knowledge.

"And which qualities are to be abandoned through direct knowledge? Ignorance & craving for becoming: These are the qualities that are to be abandoned through direct knowledge.

"And which qualities are to be developed through direct knowledge? Tranquility & insight: these are the qualities that are to be developed through direct knowledge.

"And which qualities are to be realized through direct knowledge? Clear knowing & release: these are the qualities that are to be realized through direct knowledge."

That is what the Blessed One said. Gratified, the monks delighted in the Blessed One's words.

NOTES

1. The four establishings of mindfulness, the four right exertions, the four bases of power, the five faculties, the five strengths, the seven factors for awakening, and the noble eightfold path are termed the Wings to Awakening *(bodhi-pakkhiya-dhamma).* DN 16 reports that toward the end of his life, the Buddha recommended these qualities as the essence of his teaching. See *The Wings to Awakening* for more details.

2. The duties outlined in this section parallel the duties appropriate to the four noble truths, as outlined in the "wheel" of the Buddha's first sermon. See SN 56:11.

See also: SN 22:23; SN 35:204; SN 38:14; AN 2:29; AN 4:94; AN 4:170

152 *The Development of the Faculties*

Indriya-bhāvanā Sutta

I have heard that on one occasion the Blessed One was staying among the Kajjaṅgalas in the Bamboo Grove. Then the young brahman Uttara, a student of Pārāsiri [Pārāsivi] went to the Blessed One and, on arrival, exchanged friendly greetings & courtesies. After this exchange of courteous greetings he sat to one side.

As he was sitting there, the Blessed One said to him: "Uttara, does the brahman Pārāsiri teach his followers the development of the faculties?"

"Yes, master Gotama, he does."

"And how does he teach his followers the development of the faculties?"

"There is the case where one does not see forms with the eye, or hear sounds with the ear [in a trance of non-perception]. That's how the brahman Pārāsiri teaches his followers the development of the faculties."

"That being the case, Uttara, then a blind person will have developed faculties, and a deaf person will have developed faculties, according to the words of the brahman Pārāsiri. For a blind person does not see forms with the eye, and a deaf person does not hear sounds with the ear."

When this was said, the young brahman Uttara sat silent & abashed, his shoulders slumped, his head down, brooding, at a loss for words. The Blessed One—noticing that Uttara was sitting silent & abashed, his shoulders slumped, his head down, brooding, at a loss for words—said to Ven. Ānanda, "Ānanda, the development of the faculties that the brahman Pārāsiri teaches his followers is one thing, but the unexcelled development of the faculties in the discipline of a noble one is something else entirely."

"Now is the time, O Blessed One. Now is the time, O One Well-Gone, for the Blessed One to teach the unexcelled development of the faculties in the discipline of the noble one. Having heard the Blessed One, the monks will remember it."

"In that case, Ānanda, listen & pay close attention. I will speak."

"As you say, lord," Ven. Ānanda responded to the Blessed One.

The Blessed One said: "Now how, Ānanda, in the discipline of a noble one is there the unexcelled development of the faculties? There is the case where, when seeing a form with the eye, there arises in a monk an agreeable (reaction), a disagreeable (reaction), an agreeable & disagreeable (reaction). He discerns that 'This agreeable (reaction) has arisen in me, this disagreeable (reaction)... this agreeable & disagreeable (reaction) has arisen in me. And that is fabricated, gross, dependently co-arisen. But this is peaceful, this is exquisite, i.e., equanimity.' With that, the arisen agreeable... disagreeable... agreeable & disagreeable (reaction) ceases, and equanimity takes a stance. Just as a man with good eyes, having closed them, might open them; or having opened them, might close them, that is how quickly, how rapidly, how easily, no matter what it refers to, the arisen agreeable... disagreeable... agreeable & disagreeable (reaction) ceases, and equanimity takes a stance. In the discipline of a noble one, this is called the unexcelled development of the faculties with regard to forms cognizable by the eye.

"And further, when hearing a sound with the ear, there arises in a monk an agreeable (reaction), a disagreeable (reaction), an agreeable & disagreeable (reaction). He discerns that 'This agreeable (reaction) has arisen in me, this disagreeable (reaction)... this agreeable & disagreeable (reaction) has arisen in me. And that is fabricated, gross, dependently co-arisen. But this is peaceful, this is exquisite, i.e., equanimity.' With that, the arisen agreeable... disagreeable... agreeable & disagreeable (reaction) ceases, and equanimity takes a stance. Just as a strong man might easily snap his fingers, that is how quickly, how rapidly, how easily, no matter what it refers to, the arisen agreeable... disagreeable... agreeable & disagreeable (reaction) ceases, and equanimity takes a stance. In the discipline of a noble one, this is called the unexcelled development of the faculties with regard to sounds cognizable by the ear.

"And further, when smelling an aroma with the nose, there arises in a monk an agreeable (reaction), a disagreeable (reaction), an agreeable & disagreeable (reaction). He discerns that 'This agreeable (reaction) has arisen in me, this disagreeable (reaction)... this agreeable & disagreeable (reaction) has arisen in me. And that is fabricated, gross, dependently co-arisen. But this is peaceful, this is exquisite, i.e., equanimity.' With that, the arisen agreeable... disagreeable... agreeable & disagreeable (reaction) ceases, and equanimity takes a stance. Just as drops of water roll off a gently sloping lotus leaf & do not remain there, that is how quickly, how rapidly, how easily, no matter what it refers to, the arisen agreeable... disagreeable... agreeable & disagreeable (reaction) ceases, and equanimity takes a stance. In the discipline of a noble one, this is called the unexcelled development of the faculties with regard to aromas cognizable by the nose.

"And further, when tasting a flavor with the tongue, there arises in a monk an agreeable (reaction), a disagreeable (reaction), an agreeable & disagreeable (reaction). He discerns that 'This agreeable (reaction) has arisen in me, this disagreeable (reaction)... this agreeable & disagreeable (reaction) has arisen in me. And that is fabricated, gross, dependently co-arisen. But this is peaceful, this is exquisite, i.e., equanimity.' With that, the arisen agreeable... disagreeable... agreeable & disagreeable (reaction) ceases, and equanimity takes a stance. Just as a strong man might easily spit out a ball of saliva gathered on the tip of his tongue, that is how quickly, how rapidly, how easily, no matter what it refers to, the arisen agreeable... disagreeable... agreeable & disagreeable (reaction) ceases, and equanimity takes a stance. In the discipline of a noble one, this is called the unexcelled development of the faculties with regard to flavors cognizable by the tongue.

"And further, when touching a tactile sensation with the body, there arises in a monk an agreeable (reaction), a disagreeable (reaction), an agreeable & disagreeable (reaction). He discerns that 'This agreeable (reaction) has arisen in me, this disagreeable (reaction)... this agreeable & disagreeable (reaction) has arisen in me. And that is fabricated, gross, dependently co-arisen. But this is peaceful, this is exquisite, i.e., equanimity.' With that, the arisen agreeable... disagreeable... agreeable & disagreeable (reaction) ceases, and equanimity takes a stance. Just as a strong man might easily extend his flexed arm or flex his extended arm, that is how quickly, how rapidly, how easily, no matter what it refers to, the arisen agreeable... disagreeable... agreeable & disagreeable (reaction) ceases, and equanimity takes a stance. In the discipline of a noble one, this is called the unexcelled development of the faculties with regard to tactile sensations cognizable by the body.

"And further, when cognizing an idea with the intellect, there arises in a monk an agreeable (reaction), a disagreeable (reaction), an agreeable & disagreeable (reaction). He discerns that 'This agreeable (reaction) has arisen in me, this disagreeable (reaction)... this agreeable & disagreeable (reaction) has arisen in me. And that is fabricated, gross, dependently co-arisen. But this is peaceful, this is exquisite, i.e., equanimity.' With that, the arisen agreeable... disagreeable... agreeable & disagreeable (reaction) ceases, and equanimity takes a stance. Just as a strong man might let two or three drops of water fall onto an iron pan heated all day:

Slow would the falling of the drops of water, but they quickly would vanish & disappear. That is how quickly, how rapidly, how easily, no matter what it refers to, the arisen agreeable... disagreeable... agreeable & disagreeable (reaction) ceases, and equanimity takes a stance. In the discipline of a noble one, this is called the unexcelled development of the faculties with regard to ideas cognizable by the intellect.

"And how is one a person in training, someone following the way? There is the case where, when seeing a form with the eye, there arises in a monk an agreeable (reaction), a disagreeable (reaction), an agreeable & disagreeable (reaction). He feels horrified, humiliated, & disgusted with the arisen agreeable... disagreeable... agreeable & disagreeable (reaction).

"When hearing a sound with the ear.... When smelling an aroma with the nose.... When tasting a flavor with the tongue.... When touching a tactile sensation with the body.... When cognizing an idea with the intellect, there arises in a monk an agreeable (reaction), a disagreeable (reaction), an agreeable & disagreeable (reaction). He feels horrified, humiliated, & disgusted with the arisen agreeable... disagreeable... agreeable & disagreeable (reaction).

"This is how one is a person in training, someone following the way.

"And how is one a noble one with developed faculties? There is the case where, when seeing a form with the eye, there arises in a monk an agreeable (reaction), a disagreeable (reaction), an agreeable & disagreeable (reaction). If he wants, he remains percipient of loathsomeness in the presence of what is not loathsome. If he wants, he remains percipient of unloathsomeness in the presence of what is loathsome. If he wants, he remains percipient of loathsomeness in the presence of what is not loathsome & what is. If he wants, he remains percipient of unloathsomeness in the presence of what is loathsome & what is not. If he wants—in the presence of what is loathsome & what is not—cutting himself off from both, he remains equanimous, alert, & mindful.

"When hearing a sound with the ear.... When smelling an aroma with the nose.... When tasting a flavor with the tongue.... When touching a tactile sensation with the body.... When cognizing an idea with the intellect, there arises in a monk an agreeable (reaction), a disagreeable (reaction), an agreeable & disagreeable (reaction). If he wants, he remains percipient of loathsomeness in the presence of what is not loathsome. If he wants, he remains percipient of unloathsomeness in the presence of what is loathsome. If he wants, he remains percipient of loathsomeness in the presence of what is not loathsome & what is. If he wants, he remains percipient of unloathsomeness in the presence of what is loathsome & what is not. If he wants—in the presence of what is loathsome & what is not—cutting himself off from both, he remains equanimous, alert, & mindful.

"This is how one is a noble one with developed faculties.

"So, Ānanda, I have taught you the unexcelled development of the faculties in the discipline of a noble one; I have taught you how one is a person in training, someone following the way; I have taught you how one is a noble one with developed faculties. Whatever a teacher should do—seeking the welfare of his disciples, out of sympathy for them—that have I done for you. Over there are the roots of trees; over there, empty dwellings. Practice jhāna, Ānanda. Don't be heedless. Don't later fall into remorse. That is our message to you all."

That is what the Blessed One said. Gratified, Ven. Ānanda delighted in the Blessed One's words.

See also: MN 78; SN 35:153; SN 46:54; AN 6:55; AN 9:37; Ud 3:4; Ud 4:4

Glossary

PALI - ENGLISH

Abhidhamma: (1) In the discourses of the Pali Canon, this term simply means "higher Dhamma," and a systematic attempt to define the Buddha's teachings and understand their interrelationships. (2) A later collection of treatises collating lists of categories drawn from the teachings in the discourses, added to the Canon several centuries after the Buddha's life.

Arahant: A "worthy one" or "pure one"; a person whose mind is free of defilement and thus is not destined for further rebirth. A title for the Buddha and the highest level of his noble disciples.

Āsava: Effluent; fermentation. Four qualities—sensuality, views, becoming, and ignorance—that "flow out" of the mind and create the flood of the round of death and rebirth.

Asura: A member of a race of beings who, like the Titans in Greek mythology, battled the devas for sovereignty in heaven and lost.

Bodhisatta: "A being (striving) for awakening;" the term used to describe the Buddha before he actually became Buddha, from his first aspiration to Buddhahood until the time of his full awakening. Sanskrit form: *Bodhisattva.*

Brahman: In common usage, a brahman is a member of the priestly caste, which claimed to be the highest caste in India, based on birth. In a specifically Buddhist usage, "brahman" can also mean an arahant, conveying the point that excellence is based, not on birth or race, but on the qualities attained in the mind.

Brahmā: A deva inhabiting the realms of form or formlessness.

Deva: Literally, "shining one." An inhabitant of the terrestrial and celestial realms higher than the human.

Dhamma: (1) Event; action; (2) a phenomenon in and of itself; (3) mental quality; (4) doctrine, teaching; (5) *nibbāna* (although there are passages describing nibbāna as the abandoning of all dhammas). Sanskrit form: *Dharma.*

Jhāna: Mental absorption. A state of strong concentration focused on a single sensation or mental notion. This term is derived from the verb *jhāyati,* which means to burn with a steady, still flame.

Kamma: Intentional act. Sanskrit form: *Karma.*

Māra: The personification of temptation and all forces, within and without, that create obstacles to release from *saṁsāra.*

Nāga: A magical serpent, technically classed as a common animal, but possessing many of the powers of a deva, including the ability to take on human shape. Sometimes this term is used metaphorically, in the sense of "Great One," to indicate an arahant.

Nibbāna: Literally, the "unbinding" of the mind from passion, aversion, and delusion, and from the entire round of death and rebirth. As this term also denotes the extinguishing of a fire, it carries connotations of stilling, cooling, and peace. "Total nibbāna" in some contexts denotes the experience of awakening; in others, the final passing away of an arahant. Sanskrit form: *Nirvāṇa.*

Paṭicca-samuppāda: Dependent co-arising; dependent origination. A map showing the way ignorance and craving interact with the aggregates *(khandha)* and sense media *(āyatana)* to bring about stress and suffering. As the interactions are complex, there are several different versions of *paṭicca samuppāda* given in the suttas. In the most common one, the map starts with ignorance. In another common one (given in DN 15), the map starts with the interrelation between name *(nāma)* and form *(rūpa)* on the one hand, and sensory consciousness on the other.

Pāṭimokkha: Basic code of monastic discipline, composed of 227 rules for monks and 311 for nuns.

Samaṇa: Contemplative. Literally, a person who abandons the conventional obligations of social life in order to find a way of life more "in tune" *(sama)* with the ways of nature.

Saṁsāra: Transmigration; the process of wandering through repeated states of becoming, with their attendant death and rebirth.

Saṁvega: A sense of dismay over the meaninglessness and futility of life as it is ordinarily lived, combined with a strong sense of urgency in looking for a way out.

Saṅgha: On the conventional *(sammati)* level, this term denotes the communities of Buddhist monks and nuns. On the ideal *(ariya)* level, it denotes those followers of the Buddha, lay or ordained, who have attained at least stream-entry.

Tādin: "Such," an adjective to describe one who has attained the goal. It indicates that the person's state is indefinable but not subject to change or influences of any sort.

Tathāgata: Literally, "one who has become authentic *(tatha-āgata)*" or "one who is truly gone *(tathā-gata)*": an epithet used in ancient India for a person who has attained the highest religious goal. In Buddhism, it usually denotes the Buddha, although occasionally it also denotes any of his arahant disciples.

Uposatha: Observance day, coinciding with the full moon, new moon, and half moons. Lay Buddhists often observe the eight precepts on this day. Monks recite the Pāṭimokkha on the full moon and new moon uposathas.

Vinaya: The monastic discipline, whose rules and traditions comprise six volumes in printed text.

Yakkha: Spirit; a lower level of deva—sometimes friendly to human beings, sometimes not—often dwelling in trees or other wild places.

ENGLISH - PALI

Although I have tried to be as consistent as possible in rendering Pali terms into English, there are a few cases where a single English term will not do justice to all the meanings of a Pali term. Although the rule of one English equivalent per one Pali word makes for consistency, any truly bilingual person will know that such a rule can create ludicrous distortions in translation. Thus, while I have not consciously used one English term to translate two different Pali terms, there are cases where I have found it necessary to render single Pali terms with two or more English terms, depending on context. *Citta* in some cases is rendered as mind, in others as intent. Similarly, *loka* is rendered either as cosmos or world, *manas* as intellect or heart, *āyatana* as medium or dimension, *upādāna* as clinging or sustenance, and *dhamma* as phenomenon, quality, or principle.

Also, for some of the Pali terms playing a central role in the teaching, I have chosen equivalents that do not follow general usage. In the following list I have marked these equivalents with asterisks. Explanations for these choices are provided at the end of the list.

acceptance — *upasampadā*
acquisition — *upadhi*
aggregate — *khandha*
alertness — *sampajañña*
appropriate attention — *yoniso manasikāra*
awakening — *bodhi*
awareness — *cetas*
awareness-release — *cetovimutti*
becoming — *bhava*
clear knowing — *vijjā*
clinging* — *upādāna*
compunction — *ottappa*
contemplative — *samaṇa*
conviction — *saddhā*
cosmos — *loka*
craving — *taṇhā*
dependent co-arising — *paṭicca samuppāda*
desire — *chanda*
dimension — *āyatana*
directed thought — *vitakka*
discern — *pajānāti*
discernment — *paññā*
discernment-release — *paññāvimutti*
discrimination — *vimaṁsā*
disenchantment — *nibbidā*
dispassion — *virāga*
effluent* — *āsava*
emptiness — *suññatā*
enlightened one* — *dhīra*
establishing of mindfulness — *satipaṭṭhāna*
evaluation — *vicāra*
fabricated — *saṅkhata*
fabrication — *saṅkhāra*
fetter — *saṅyojana*
gnosis — *añña*
goodwill — *mettā*
habit — *sīla*
heart — *manas; citta*
identity — *sakkāya*
inconstant* — *anicca*
insight — *vipassanā*
intellect — *manas*
intent — *citta*

intention — *cetanā*
medium — *āyatana*
mind — *citta*
not-self — *anattā*
objectification* — *papañca*
obsession* — *anusaya*
origination — *samudaya*
perception — *saññā*
persistence — *viriya*
phenomenon — *dhamma*
property — *dhātu*
quality — *dhamma*
release — *vimutti*
resolve — *saṅkappa*
self-awakening — *sambodhi*
self-identification — *sakkāya*
sensuality — *kāma*
shame — *hiri*
skillful — *kusala*
stream-entry — *sotāpatti*
stress* — *dukkha*
supposition — *maññita*
sustenance* — *upādāna*
theme — *nimitta*
tranquility — *samatha*
transcendent — *lokuttara*
unbinding* — *nibbāna*
unfabricated — *asaṅkhata*
virtue — *sīla*
world — *loka*

Acquisition: *Upadhi* literally means "belongings," "baggage," "paraphernalia." In the suttas, it means mental baggage. The Cūḷaniddesa, a late canonical work, lists ten types of upadhi: craving, views, defilement, action, misconduct, nutriment (physical and mental), irritation, the four physical properties sustained in the body (earth, water, wind, and fire), the six external sense media, and the six forms of corresponding sensory consciousness. The state without upadhi or acquisitions is unbinding.

Aggregate: Any of the five types of phenomena that serve as objects of clinging and as bases for a sense of self: form, feeling, perception, mental fabrications, and consciousness.

Becoming: a sense of identity within a particular world of experience—a process that begins within the mind and that allows for physical or mental birth on any of three levels: the level of sensuality, the level of form, and the level of formlessness.

Clinging/sustenance: The Pali term *upādāna,* which is used both on the physical and psychological levels, carries a double meaning on both levels. On the physical level, it denotes both the fuel of a fire and to the fire's act of clinging to its fuel. On the psychological level, it denotes both the sustenance for becoming that the mind clings to, and to the act of clinging to its sustenance. To capture these double meanings, I have sometimes rendered *upādāna* as clinging, sometimes as sustenance, and sometimes as both.

Enlightened one: Throughout these volumes I have rendered *buddha* as "awakened," and *dhīra* as "enlightened." As Jan Gonda points out in his book, *The Vision of the Vedic Poets,* the word *dhīra* was used in Vedic and Buddhist poetry to mean a person who has the heightened powers of mental vision needed to perceive the "light" of the underlying principles of the cosmos, together with the expertise to implement those principles in the affairs of life and to reveal them to others. A person enlightened in this sense may also be awakened in the formal Buddhist sense, but is not necessarily so. As for *buddha,* SN 1:7 clearly contrasts this term with being asleep, indicating that it is best rendered as "awakened" or "awake."

Fabrication: *Saṅkhāra* literally means "putting together," and carries connotations of jerry-rigged artificiality. It is applied to physical and to mental processes, as well as to the products of those processes. Various English words and phrases have been suggested as renderings for *saṅkhāra,* such as "formation," "determination," "force," and "constructive activity." However, "fabrication," in both of its senses, as the process of fabrication and the fabricated things that result, seems the best equivalent for capturing the connotations as well as the denotations of the term.

Inconstant: The usual rendering for *anicca* is "impermanent." However, the antonym of the term, *nicca,* carries connotations of constancy and reliability; and as *anicca* is used to emphasize the point that conditioned phenomena are unreliable as a basis for true happiness, this seems a useful rendering for conveying this point.

Objectification: The term *papañca* has entered popular usage in Buddhist circles to indicate obsessive, runaway thoughts that harass the mind. But in the suttas, the term is used to indicate, not the *amount* of thinking that harasses the mind, but the *categories* used in a particular type of thinking that harasses the mind and extends outward to create conflict with others. Sn 4:14 states that the root of the categories of *papañca* is the perception, "I am the thinker." From this self-objectifying thought, in which one takes on the identity of a being, a number of categories can be derived: being/not-being, me/not-me, mine/not-mine, doer/done-to, feeder/food. This last pair of categories comes from the fact that, as a being, one has to lay claim to food, both physical and mental, to maintain that being (Khp 4). Thinking in terms of these categories inevitably leads to conflict, as different beings fight over their food. Because this harassment and conflict come from a self-objectifying thought that leads to the objectification of others as well, *objectification* seems to be the best English equivalent for *papañca.*

Obsession: *Anusaya* is usually translated as "underlying tendency" or "latent tendency." These translations are based on the etymology of the term, which literally means, "to lie down with." However, in actual usage, the related verb *(anuseti)* means to be obsessed with something, for one's thoughts to return and "lie down with it" (or, in our idiom, to "dwell on it") over and over again.

Stress: The Pali term *dukkha,* which is traditionally translated in the commentaries as, "that which is hard to bear," is notorious for having no truly adequate equivalent in English, but stress—in its basic sense as a strain on body or mind—seems as close as English can get. In the Canon, *dukkha* applies both to physical and to mental phenomena, ranging from the intense stress of acute anguish or pain to the innate burdensomeness of even the most subtle mental or physical fabrications.

Unbinding: Because *nibbāna* is used to denote not only the Buddhist goal but also the extinguishing of a fire, it is usually rendered as "extinguishing" or, even worse, "extinction." However, a close look at ancient Indian views of the workings of fire (see *The Mind Like Fire Unbound)* shows that people of the Buddha's time felt that a fire, in going out, did not go out of existence but was simply freed from its agitation and attachment to its fuel. Thus, when applied to the Buddhist goal, the primary connotation of *nibbāna* is one of release and liberation. According to the commentaries, the literal meaning of the word *nibbāna* is "unbinding," and as this is a rare case where the literal and contextual meanings of a term coincide, this seems to be the ideal English equivalent.

Index

SUBJECTS

stress and, 165-166
torture of, 293, 304 *et seq.*, 311
Self-awakening
alone, living and, 511
Buddha's, 115-116, 120, 125 *et seq.*, 172, 178-179, 182, 219, 261, 270, 452 *et seq.*
capability for, 176
company, living in and, 510-511
Dhamma not leading to, 108 *et seq.*
pleasure of, 333, 510-511
Self-control, 297-298
Self-identification, 10, 237 *et seq.*, 262 n.7, 462, 594
Sense restraint, 124, 202, 210 *et seq.*, 269 *et seq.*, 308, 428, 447
Sensual pleasures
in general, 80, 83 *et seq.*, 237, 244 *et seq.*, 350, 374
abandoning of, 232
arising of, 286
covetousness for, effect of, 14
craving for, 33, 237, 351
fear of, 332
indulging in, 95 n.4, 351
jhāna and, *see* Hindrances
loss of, 549
quest for, 189
sensuality and, 286
Sensuality
in general, 45-46, 48, 52, 176, 448 *et seq.*, 513
clinging, as type of, 37
conduct based on, 147 n.2, 220, 222
desire for, 147 n.2, 176, 513
discernment and, 275 *et seq.*
drawback of, 45 *et seq.*, 52-54, 275 *et seq.*
dukkha and, 275 *et seq.*
five strands of, 46, 52, 116-117, 199, 286, 332, 442, 513
monks and, 156-157, 159, 250-251
perception and, 147 n.2, 448 *et seq.*
pleasure having nothing to do with, 179
release from effluent of, 128, 217, 311, 430, 506
resolve for, 147 n.2, 359
stress and, 46, 51 *et seq.*
thinking imbued with, 66 *et seq.*
yoke of, 274 n.4
Sensuality-perception, 359
Seven factors of awakening, *see* Factors of awakening
Sexual intercourse, 80, 95 n.4, 220
Sexual misconduct
defined, 220, 222
integrity and, 467, 469
kamma and, 542 *et seq.*
wrong action, as, 482
Shame, 209 *et seq.*, 270, 312 *et seq.*, 466 *et seq.*
Shrines, 15
Signless, 240, 243 n.2
Singleness
direct knowing of, 4 *et seq.*
perception, based on, 502, *et seq.*
perception of, 3, 7 n.5, 433 *et seq.*, 439 n.1
Six higher knowledges, 499
Six sense media, 60, 438
analysis of, 549 *et seq.*, 563 *et seq.*
cessation of, 60, 197-198
contact and, 39, 195 *et seq.*, 549, 550, 563, 590 *et seq.*
dependent co-arising and, 195 *et seq.*
external, 581 *et seq.*, 590 *et seq.*
infatuation with, 597 *et seq.*
intellect-faculty, *see* Intellect-faculty
internal, 549-550, 581 *et seq.*, 590 *et seq.*
knowing of, 549 *et seq.*, 590 *et seq.*, 597 *et seq.*
non-emptiness of, 506
right view and, 39-40
Skillful, noble search for, 108
Slander, 226 n.2
Slaves, 107
Sloth & drowsiness
abandoning of, 125, 203, 213, 232, 309, 428
absorption in, 458
mind of, effect of, 14
jhāna and, *see* Hindrances
monks and, 250
Smells
development of faculties and, 602-603
equanimity, 279 n.1, 550-552, 563
exploration of with intellect, 550
inconstancy of, 551, 581
infatuation with, 200, 204
unsuitable, pursuit of, 444 *et seq.*
Sophists, 161, 169 n.1, 170
Sorrow
in general, 107-108, 111, 116
cessation of, 197-198
dear, as born from one who is, 384-388
definition of, 571
dependent co-arising and, 195 *et seq.*

PROPER NAMES

SIMILES